Lecture Notes in Computer Science 2609

Edited by G. Goos, J. Hartmanis, and J. van Leeuwen

Springer
Berlin
Heidelberg
New York
Hong Kong
London
Milan
Paris
Tokyo

Mitsuhiro Okada   Benjamin Pierce
Andre Scedrov   Hideyuki Tokuda
Akinori Yonezawa (Eds.)

Software Security – Theories and Systems

Mext-NSF-JSPS International Symposium, ISSS 2002
Tokyo, Japan, November 8-10, 2002
Revised Papers

Springer

Series Editors

Gerhard Goos, Karlsruhe University, Germany
Juris Hartmanis, Cornell University, NY, USA
Jan van Leeuwen, Utrecht University, The Netherlands

Volume Editors

Mitsuhiro Okada
Keio University, 2-15-45 Mita, Minatoku, Tokyo, 108-8345, Japan
E-mail: mitsu@abelard.flet.keio.ac.jp

Benjamin C. Pierce
University of Pennsylvania, 200 South 33rd St., Philadelphia, PA 19104, USA
Andre Scedrov
University of Pennsylvania, 209 South 33rd St., Philadelphia, PA 19104-6395, USA
E-mail: {bcpierce/scedrov}@cis.upenn.edu

Hideyuki Tokuda
Keio University, 5322 Endoh, Fujisawa 252-8520, Japan
E-mail: hxt@sfc.keio.ac.jp

Akinori Yonezawa
University of Tokyo, 7-3-1 Hongo, Bunkyo-ku, Tokyo 113, Japan
E-mail: yonezawa@is.s.u-tokyo.ac.jp

Cataloging-in-Publication Data applied for

A catalog record for this book is available from the Library of Congress.

Bibliographic information published by Die Deutsche Bibliothek
Die Deutsche Bibliothek lists this publication in the Deutsche Nationalbibliografie;
detailed bibliographic data is available in the Internet at <http://dnb.ddb.de>.

CR Subject Classification (1998): C.2.0, D.4.6, E.3, D.3, F.3, K.6.5

ISSN 0302-9743
ISBN 3-540-00708-3 Springer-Verlag Berlin Heidelberg New York

Springer-Verlag Berlin Heidelberg New York
a member of BertelsmannSpringer Science+Business Media GmbH

http://www.springer.de

© Springer-Verlag Berlin Heidelberg 2003
Printed in Germany

Typesetting: Camera-ready by author, data conversion by PTP-Berlin, Stefan Sossna e. K.
Printed on acid-free paper   SPIN: 10872823   06/3142   5 4 3 2 1 0

Preface

As networked computer systems of all scales have come to constitute an integral and indispensable part of social infrastructures, the security and reliability of their software systems are now a major social concern. For more than the last three decades, the security of software systems has been an important area of computer science, yet it is a rather recent general recognition that technologies for software security are highly needed. This recognition was formed, of course, as a result of the social losses caused by recurring attacks against various server systems and the software failures of personal computers due to computer viruses. Many such attacks and failures could have been prevented with currently available techniques. Even in the immediate future, however, computers will be much more pervasive and will be operated by more complex software systems. The chances of creating security holes in their software construction will ever increase. Also, the attack methods and mechanisms will be much more sophisticated. Although we face such a grave reality, our technology for software security is still in its infancy. More intensive and wider ranging research is critical for making software social infrastructures secure and dependable.

The International Symposium on Software Security 2002, held in Keio University, Tokyo, November 8–10, 2002, aimed to provide a forum for research discussions and exchanges among world-leading scientists in the fields of both theoretical and system aspects of security in software construction. The program of the symposium was a combination of invited talks and selected presentations of research works. It included the most recent visions and research of the invited speakers, as well as 12 contributions of the research funded by a MEXT grant-in-aid for scientific research on the priority area "Implementation Scheme for Secure Computing."

This volume is composed of revised versions of the papers read at the symposium. It covers recently developed topics such as the security of pervasive computing, P2P systems and autonomous distributed agents, secure software circulation, compilers for fail-safe C language, the construction of secure mail systems, type systems and multiset rewriting systems for security protocols, and privacy issues.

As the collected papers are strong, the editing process of this volume was smooth and enjoyable. But successfully holding the symposium itself required a lot of work, which was heavily dependent on staffs and graduate students of Keio University, the Tokyo University of Science, and the University of Tokyo. I would very much to thank them, especially for their enthusiasm. Finally, on behalf of the program committee, I would like to express our sincere thanks to the external reviewers whose names are listed on a separate page. Their comments significantly strengthened the papers.

December 2002   Akinori Yonezawa

Organization

Program Committee

Mitsuhiro Okada	Keio University
Benjamin Pierce	University of Pennsylvania
Andre Scedrov (Co-chair)	University of Pennsylvania
Hideyuki Tokuda	Keio University
Akinori Yonezawa (Co-chair)	University of Tokyo

Organizing Committee

Kokichi Futatsugi	JAIST
Fumio Mizoguchi	Tokyo University of Science
Mitsuhiro Okada	Keio University
Benjamin Pierce	University of Pennsylvania
Andre Scedrov	University of Pennsylvania
Hideyuki Tokuda	Keio University
Akinori Yonezawa (Chair)	University of Tokyo

Sponsors

Japanese Ministry of Education, Science and Culture (MEXT)
National Science Foundation (NSF)
Japanese Society for the Promotion of Science (JSPS)
Keio University (G-Sec and Oogata Kenkyu Josei)

External Reviewers

Roy Campbell
Iliano Cervesato
Kokichi Futatsugi
Masami Hagiya
Kazuhiko Kato
Naoki Kobayashi
Catherine Meadows
Dale Miller
John Mitchell
George Necula
Kazuhiro Ogata
Robert Schneck
Tatsuro Sekiguchi
Etsuya Shibayama
Vitaly Shmatikov
Frank Stajano
Doug Tygar
Naoki Yonezaki
Dan Wallach

Table of Contents

Part 10: Multiset Rewriting for Protocol Analysis

Part 11: Verification Methods and Tools

Towards Security and Privacy for Pervasive Computing*

Roy Campbell, Jalal Al-Muhtadi, Prasad Naldurg, Geetanjali Sampemane,
and M. Dennis Mickunas

Department of Computer Science, University of Illinois at Urbana Champaign,
1304 W. Springfield Ave., Urbana, IL 61801.
{rhc, almuhtad, naldurg, geta, mickunas}@cs.uiuc.edu

Abstract. Pervasive computing environments with their interconnected devices
and services promise seamless integration of digital infrastructure into our
everyday lives. While the focus of current research is on how to connect new
devices and build useful applications to improve functionality, the security and
privacy issues in such environments have not been explored in any depth. While
traditional distributed computing research attempts to abstract away physical
location of users and resources, pervasive computing applications often exploit
physical location and other context information about users and resources to
enhance the user experience. The need to share resources and collaborate
introduces new types of interaction among users as well as between the virtual
and physical worlds. In this context, it becomes difficult to separate physical
security from digital security. Existing policies and mechanisms may not
provide adequate guarantees to deal with new exposures and vulnerabilities
introduced by the pervasive computing paradigm. In this paper we explore the
challenges for building security and privacy into pervasive computing
environments, describe our prototype implementation that addresses some of
these issues, and propose some directions for future work.

1 Introduction

We are witnessing the birth of a revolutionary computing paradigm that promises to
have a profound effect on the way we interact with computers, devices, physical
spaces, and other people. This new technology envisions a world where embedded
processors, computers, sensors, and digital communications are inexpensive
commodities that are available everywhere. This eliminates time and place barriers by
making services available to users anytime and anywhere.

Pervasive computing will surround users with a comfortable and convenient
information environment that merges physical and computational infrastructures into
an integrated habitat. This habitat will feature a proliferation of hundreds or thousands
of computing devices and sensors that will provide new functionality, offer
specialized services, and boost productivity and interaction. Context-awareness will
allow this habitat to take on the responsibility of serving users, by tailoring itself to

---

* This research is supported by a grant from the National Science Foundation, NSF CCR 0086094 ITR
and NSF 99-72884 EQ.

M. Okada et al. (Eds.): ISSS 2002, LNCS 2609, pp. 1–15, 2003.

their preferences as well as performing tasks and group activities according to the nature of the physical space. We term this dynamic, information-rich habitat an "active space." Within this space, individuals may interact with flexible applications that may follow the user, define and control the function of the space, or collaborate with remote users and applications.

The realization of this computing paradigm is not far fetched. An average person today already owns vast numbers of consumer devices, electronic gadgets, and gizmos that already have processors, microcontrollers, and memory chips embedded into them, like VCRs, TVs, washers and dryers. The vehicles we use on daily basis already have a large number of embedded computers handling different subsystems of the vehicle, like ABS (Anti-lock Braking System) and ESP (Electronic Stability Program). Technologies like Bluetooth [1] and Wi-Fi [2] make it possible to embed networking capabilities into any small devices without hassle. In effect, these technologies help make networking much more general and achievable even on elementary devices, like toasters and paperclips.

1.1 Pervasive Computing Abstractions

To have a better understanding of the challenges associated with securing pervasive computing environments, it is important to list the salient features of pervasive computing. These include the following.

Extending Computing Boundaries. While traditional computing encompassed hardware and software entities, pervasive computing extends the boundaries of computing to include physical spaces, building infrastructures, and the devices contained within. This aims to transform dull spaces into interactive, dynamic, and programmable spaces that are coordinated through a software infrastructure and populated with a large number of mobile users and devices.

Invisibility and non-intrusiveness. In current computing models, computers are still the focus of attention. In effect, people have to change some of their behavior and the way they perform tasks so that these tasks can be computerized. To boost productivity, it is important that computing machinery disappear and leave the spotlight. Computers should blend in the background allowing people to perform their duties without having machines at the center of their focus.

Creating smart and sentient spaces. A dust of invisible embedded devices and sensors are incorporated to turn physical spaces into active, smart surroundings that can sense, "see," and "hear," effectively, making the space sentient and adaptable. Ultimately, the space should become intelligent enough to understand users' intent and become an integral part of users' everyday life.

Context awareness. A pervasive computing environment should be able to capture the different context and situational information and integrate them with users and devices. This allows the active space to take on the responsibility of serving users and automatically tailoring itself to meet their expectations and preferences.

Mobility and adaptability. To be truly omnipresent, the pervasive computing environment should be as mobile as its users. It should be able to adapt itself to environments with scarce resources, while being able to evolve and extend once more resources become available.

1.2   The Problem

Current research in pervasive computing focuses on building infrastructures for managing active spaces, connecting new devices, or building useful applications to improve functionality. Security and privacy issues in such environments, however, have not been explored in depth. Indeed, several researchers and practitioners have admitted that security and privacy in this new computing paradigm are real problems. Langheinrich [3, 4] warns us about the possibility of an Orwellian nightmare in which current pervasive computing research continues on without considering privacy in the system. Stajano [5] notices that while researchers are busy thinking about the killer applications for pervasive computing, cyber-criminals and computer villains are already considering new, ingenious attacks that are not possible in traditional computing environments. Kagal et al. [6, 7] admit that securing pervasive computing environments presents challenges at many levels.

The very same features that make pervasive computing environments convenient and powerful make them vulnerable to new security and privacy threats. Traditional security mechanisms and policies may not provide adequate guarantees to deal with the new exposures and vulnerabilities.

In this paper we address some of these issues as follows. In Section 2 we explore the challenges for building security and privacy into pervasive computing environments. In Section 3 we describe our prototype implementation that addresses some of these issues. In Section 4 we propose some directions for future work and conclude.

2   Security Challenges and Requirements

In this section, we talk about the major challenges and requirements for securing pervasive computing environments.

2.1   Challenges

As mentioned before, the additional features and the extended functionality that pervasive computing offers make it prone to additional vulnerabilities and exposures. Below, we mention these features that add extra burden to the security subsystem.

2.1.1.   The Extended Computing Boundary

Traditional computing is confined to the virtual computing world where data and programs reside. Current distributed computing research tends to abstract away physical locations of users and resources. Pervasive computing, however, extends its reach beyond the computational infrastructure and attempts to encompass the surrounding physical spaces as well. Pervasive computing applications often exploit physical location and other context information about users and resources to enhance the user experience. Under such scenarios, information and physical security become interdependent. As a result, such environments become prone to more severe security threats that can threaten people and equipment in the physical world as much as they can threaten their data and programs in the virtual world. Therefore, traditional mechanisms that focus merely on digital security become inadequate.

2.1.2.   Privacy Issues

The physical outreach of pervasive computing makes preserving users' privacy a much more difficult task. Augmenting active spaces with active sensors and actuators enables the construction of more intelligent spaces and computing capabilities that are truly omnipresent. Through various sensors and embedded devices, active spaces can automatically be tailored to users' preferences and can capture and utilize context information fully. Unfortunately, this very feature could threaten the privacy of users severely. For instance, this capability can be exploited by intruders, malicious insiders, or even curious system administrators to track or electronically stalk particular users. The entire system now becomes a distributed surveillance system that can capture too much information about users. In some environments, like homes and clinics, there is usually an abundance of sensitive and personal information that must be secured. Moreover, there are certain situations when people do not want to be tracked.

2.1.3.   User Interaction Issues

One of the main characteristics of pervasive applications is a richer user-interface for interaction between users and the space. A variety of multimedia mechanisms are used for input and output, and to control the physical aspects of the space. At any point of time, the set of users in the space affects the security properties of the space. Because of the nature of these interactions, users in the space cannot easily be prevented from seeing and hearing things happening in it, so this has to be taken into account while designing access control mechanisms. We believe that the access control mechanisms should allow groups of users and devices to use the space in a manner that facilitates collaboration, while enforcing the appropriate access control policies and preventing unauthorized use. Thus the physical and "virtual" aspects of access control for such spaces have to be considered together.

2.1.4.   Security Policies

It is important in pervasive computing to have a flexible and convenient method for defining and managing security policies in a dynamic and flexible fashion. Policy Management tools provide administrators the ability to specify, implement, and enforce rules to exercise greater control over the behavior of entities in their systems. Currently, most network policies are implemented by systems administrators using tools based on scripting applications [8, 9] that iterate through lists of low-level interfaces and change values of entity-specific system variables. The policy management software maintains an exhaustive database of corresponding device and resource interfaces. With the proliferation of heterogeneous device-specific and vendor-specific interfaces, these tools may need to be updated frequently to accommodate new hardware or software, and the system typically becomes difficult to manage. As a result, general purpose low-level management tools are limited in their functionality, and are forced to implement only generic or coarse-grained policies [10].

Since most policy management tools deal with these low-level interfaces, administrators may not have a clear picture of the ramifications of their policy management actions. Dependencies among objects can lead to unexpected side effects and undesirable behavior [11]. Further, the disclosure of security policies may be a breach of security. For example, knowing whether the system is on the lookout for an intruder could actually be a secret. Thus, unauthorized personnel should not be able to know what the security policy might become under a certain circumstance.

2.1.5. Info Ops

There is a great deal of concern over new types of threats, namely, Information Operations (info ops) and cyber-terrorism, which are natural consequences of the increasing importance of electronic information and the heavy reliance on digital communication networks in most civilian and military activities. Info ops, which can be defined as "actions taken that affect adversary information and information systems while defending one's own information and information systems," [12] is a serious concern in today's networks. In such a scenario, cyber-terrorists and other techno-villains can exploit computer networks, inject misleading information, steal electronic assets, or disrupt critical services. Pervasive computing gives extreme leverage and adds much more capabilities to the arsenal of info warriors, making info ops a much more severe threat.

2.2   Security Requirements

To deal with the new vulnerabilities introduced by pervasive computing, security and privacy guarantees in pervasive computing environments should be specified and drafted early into the design process rather than being considered as add-ons or afterthoughts. Previous efforts in retrofitting security and anonymity into existing systems have proved to be inefficient and ineffective. The Internet and Wi-Fi are two such examples both of which still suffer from inadequate security. In this section, we briefly mention the important requirements needed for a security subsystem for pervasive computing environments.

2.2.1.   Transparency and Unobtrusiveness

The focal point of pervasive computing is to transform users into first class entities, who no longer need to exert much of their attention to computing machinery. Therefore, even the security subsystem should be transparent to some level, blending into the background without distracting users too much.

2.2.2.   Multilevel

When it comes to security, one size does not fit all. Hence, the security architecture deployed should be able to provide different levels of security services based on system policy, context information, environmental situations, temporal circumstances, available resources, etc. In some instances, this may go against the previous point. Scenarios which require a higher-level of assurance or greater security may require users to interact with the security subsystem explicitly by, say, authenticating themselves using a variety of means to boost system's confidence.

2.2.3.   Context-Awareness

Often, traditional security is somewhat static and context insensitive. Pervasive computing integrates context and situational information, transforming the computing environment into a sentient space. The security aspects of it are no exceptions. Security services should make extensive use of context information available. For example, access control decisions may depend on time or special circumstances. Context data can provide valuable information for intrusion detection mechanisms. The principal of "need to know" should be applied on temporal and situational basis. For instance, security policies should be able to change dynamically to limit the permissions to the times or situations when they are needed. However, viewing what the security policy might become in a particular time or under a particular situation should not be possible. In addition, there is a need to verify the authenticity and integrity of the context information acquired. This is sometimes necessary in order to thwart false context information obtained from rogue or malfunctioning sensors.

2.2.4.   Flexibility and Customizability

The security subsystem should be flexible, adaptable, and customizable. It must be able to adapt to environments with extreme conditions and scarce resources, yet, it is able to evolve and provide additional functionality when more resources become available. Tools for defining and managing policies should be as dynamic as the environment itself.

2.2.5.   Interoperability

With many different security technologies surfacing and being deployed, the assumption that a particular security mechanism will eventually prevail is flawed. For that reason, it is necessary to support multiple security mechanisms and negotiate security requirements.

2.2.6.   Extended Boundaries

While traditional security was restricted to the virtual world, security now should incorporate some aspects of the physical world, e.g. preventing intruders from accessing physical spaces. In essence, virtual and physical security become interdependent.

2.2.7.   Scalability

Pervasive computing environments can host hundreds or thousands of diverse devices. The security services should be able to scale to the "dust" of mobile and embedded devices available at some particular instance of time. In addition, the security services need to be able to support huge numbers of users with different roles and privileges, under different situational information.

In the following section, we suggest solutions that address some of the issues mentioned above.

3   Case Study: Gaia OS Security

Gaia [13–15] is a component-based, middleware operating system that provides a generic infrastructure for constructing pervasive computing environments. Gaia provides the necessary core services to support and manage active spaces and the pervasive applications that run within these spaces. By using Gaia, it is possible to construct a multipurpose, prototype active space. This active space contains state-of-the-art equipment, including a surround audio system, four touch plasma panels with HDTV support, HDTV video wall, X10 devices, electronic white boards, IR beacons, Wi-Fi and Bluetooth access points, video cameras, and flat panel desktop displays. Currently, this active space is used for group meetings, seminars, presentations, demos, and for entertainment purposes (like listening to music and watching movies). The different uses of this active space translate into different contexts. In this active space, we deployed several security mechanisms that addresses some of the issues mentioned in this paper.

3.1   Gaia Authentication

Authentication mechanisms in pervasive computing environments should strike a balance between authentication strength and non-intrusiveness. A smart badge that broadcasts short range radio signals, for instance, is a good non-intrusive authentication mechanism; however, it only provides weak authentication. A challenge-response mechanism provides stronger authentication, but often at the expense of additional interactions on behalf of the user. We let context decide how strong the authentication needs to be. This allows the authentication process to enable principals to authenticate themselves to the system using a variety of means. These include the use of wearable devices, face recognition, smart badges, fingerprint identification, retinal scans, etc. To enable this, we differentiate between different strengths of authentication by associating *confidence values* to each authentication process. This confidence value represents how "confident" the authentication system is about the identity of the principal. We represent this by a number between 0 and 1. This confidence value is based on the authentication device and the authentication protocol used. Principals can employ multiple authentication methods in order to increase the confidence values associated with them. Access control decisions can now become more flexible by utilizing confidence information. Several reasoning techniques can be used to combine confidence values and calculate a net confidence value for a particular principal. The techniques we have considered so far include simple probabilities, Bayesian probability, and fuzzy logic [16]. The authentication service is managed by authentication-related policies. These policies are expressed as rules in first order predicate logic. The logic used includes temporal and fuzzy operators that allow the policies to capture context or temporal information, like revocation of authentication credentials under certain circumstances and so on.

Since there are a large number of diverse devices that can be deployed for identification and authentication purposes, and as technology advances, we expect many new authentication devices to become available. This makes it necessary to have dynamic means for adding new authentication devices and associating them with different capabilities and protocols. Naturally, some means of authentication are more reliable and secure than others. For example, it is easy for smart badges to be misplaced or stolen. On the other hand, the use of biometrics, retinal scans for instance, is a fairly good means of authentication that is difficult to forge. Because of the various authentication methods and their different strengths, it is sensible to accommodate different levels of confidence and incorporate context and sensor information to infer more information or buildup additional confidence in a principal's identity. Further, the same techniques can assist in detecting intruders and unauthorized accesses and assessing their threat level.

The various means of authenticating principals and the notion of different confidence levels associated with authenticated principals constitute additional information that can enrich the context awareness of smart spaces. In a later section, we illustrate how such information is inferred and exchanged with other Gaia core services.

To meet the stated requirements we propose a federated authentication service that is based on distributed, pluggable authentication modules. Fig. 1 provides a sketch of the authentication architecture that incorporates the objectives mentioned above. PAM (Pluggable Authentication Module) [17] provides an authentication method that allows the separation of applications from the actual authentication mechanisms and devices. Dynamically pluggable modules allow the authentication subsystem to incorporate additional authentication mechanisms on the fly as they become available. The Gaia PAM (GPAM) is wrapped by two APIs. One interface is made available for applications, services, and other Gaia components, to request authentication of entities or inquire about authenticated principals. Since the authentication service can be running anywhere in the space (possibly federated) we use CORBA facilities to allow the discovery and remote invocation of the authentication services that serve a particular smart space. The authentication modules themselves are divided into two types: Gaia Authentication Mechanisms Modules (AMM), which implement general authentication mechanisms or protocols that are independent of the actual device being used for authentication. These modules include a Kerberos authentication module, a SESAME [18] authentication module, the traditional username/password-based module, a challenge-response through a shared secret module, etc. The other type of modules is the Authentication Device Modules (ADM). These modules are independent of the actual authentication protocol; instead, they are dependent on the particular authentication device.

This decoupling enables greater flexibility. When a new authentication protocol is devised, an AMM module can be written and plugged in to support that particular protocol. Devices that can capture the information required for completing the protocol can use the new authentication module with minimal changes to their device drivers. When a new authentication device is incorporated to the system, a new ADM module is implemented in order to incorporate the device into the active space. However, the device can use existing security mechanisms by using CORBA facilities to discover and invoke authentication mechanisms that are compatible with its capabilities. In effect, this creates an architecture similar to PAM and is also federated through the use of CORBA. Many CORBA implementations are heavyweight and require significant resources. To overcome this hurdle, we used the Universally Interoperable Core (UIC), which provides a lightweight, high-performance implementation of basic CORBA services [19].

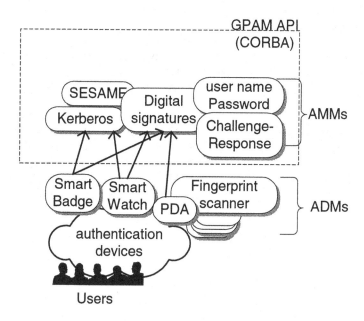

Fig. 1. Gaia Authentication Service

3.2 Mist – Privacy Communication

To address the privacy problems in pervasive computing, we introduce Mist [20, 21] a general communication infrastructure that preserves privacy in pervasive computing environments. Mist facilitates the separation of location from identity. This allows authorized entities to access services while protecting their location privacy. Here, we just give a brief overview of how Mist works. Mist consists of a privacy-preserving hierarchy of *Mist Routers* that form an overlay network, as illustrated in Fig. 2. This overlay network facilitates private communication by routing packets using a *hop-by-hop, handle-based routing* protocol. We employ public key cryptography in the initial setup of these handles. These techniques make communication infeasible to trace by eavesdroppers and untrusted third parties.

A handle is an identifier that is unique per Mist Router. Every incoming packet has an "incoming handle" that is used by the Mist Router to identify the next hop to which to forward the packet. The incoming handle is replaced by an outgoing handle before the packet is transmitted to the next hop. This hop-by-hop routing protocol allows a Mist Router to forward the packet to the next hop, while hiding the original source and final destination. In effect, this process creates "virtual circuits" over which data can flow securely and privately.

Mist introduces *Portals* that are installed at various locations in the pervasive computing environment. These Portals are devices capable of detecting the presence of people and objects through the use of base stations or sensors. However, they are incapable of positively identifying the users. To effectively hide a user's location, we introduce a special Mist Router referred to as a *Lighthouse*. A user registers with this Lighthouse, which allows packets to be routed to and from the user. The Lighthouse of a user exists at a "higher level" in the hierarchy, high enough not to be able to deduce the actual physical location of the user. However, the Lighthouse is kept in the dark about the actual physical location of the user (thanks to the hop-by-hop routing protocol).

To illustrate, in Fig. 2 Alice, who is in active space 3, is detected by the Portal in that space. The Portal only detects Alice's badge ID (or other information embedded into other devices that Alice is carrying or wearing) however, this information alone is insufficient to indicate that this is actually Alice. The campus Mist Router is designated as Alice's Lighthouse. A secure channel between Alice's devices and her Lighthouse is established, going through the Portal, node 1, node 2, node 3, and

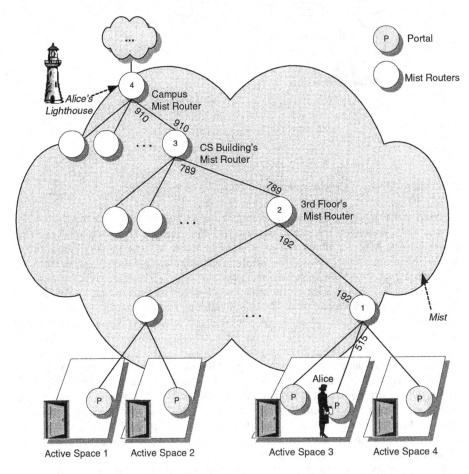

Fig. 2. The Mist communication protocol.

finally node 4. To prevent private information from leaking, encryption is employed. The numbers over the links shown in the figure represents the handles. As depicted, the handles are valid only over a single hop. The intermediate nodes translate an incoming handle to an outgoing one (e.g. Mist Router 1 in the figure translates the incoming handle 515 to outgoing handle 192). Thus, intermediate Mist Routers can only route to the next hop correctly, but do not know the actual destination or source. Mist distributes the trust to better preserve the privacy. Only if enough intermediate Mist Routers collude, can the true location of Alice be found. Note that in the example, Alice's Lighthouse can only infer that Alice is located somewhere within the campus. Mist provides a customizable level of privacy. A user can enjoy better location privacy if he or she chooses a Lighthouse that is higher in the hierarchy, e.g. choosing the campus Lighthouse as opposed to the CS building Lighthouse. Since users can register anonymously with Portals, their anonymity is preserved.

3.3   Dynamic Security Policies

To address the new challenges in defining and managing security policies in pervasive computing environments, we propose a new class of policies called dynamic policies [22–24] that are designed with explicit knowledge of system behavior, focusing on the interactions between various system objects. We develop behavioral descriptions of programs that can be sent across networks to change a system's software state, while preserving certain security and privacy properties. These program modules correspond to the dynamic policy implementation, and can be enforced by executing them in a suitable software context.

We explore the nature of security guarantees that can be made about the system state before, during, and after the execution of dynamic policies. We believe that security concerns need to be integrated into models of system behavior, and security policies have to form an integral part of system specifications. This research is crucial in the context of active spaces and in other dynamic environments where operational parameters are constantly changing. Dynamic policies enable the creation of customizable programs that can be deployed on-the-fly, to enforce and implement strong security policies that can adapt to a changing software environment. In [24] we present a powerful set of formal methods and mechanisms that can be used to create policies with strong security guarantees, eliminating guesswork in the design and deployment of reactive security systems.

To illustrate this procedure, we present the policy development life-cycle for dynamic access control policies. We construct dynamic access control policies by building a formal behavioral model of an access control system. The state of the system in our formal specification includes all entities that participate in an access control decision. This includes sets of all subjects, objects, and corresponding permissions. The specification of the system encompasses the dynamic behavior of the state variables. This is specified by state transitions that correspond to all methods in our implementation that change the list of subjects, objects and their corresponding permissions.

The set of access rights triples (subject, object, permissions) forms a conceptual access control matrix. Given the behavioral specification of our access control system, we define what security properties we want to preserve when the system state changes dynamically. An access control model is secure if and only if, starting from an empty (or safe) access control matrix, the state transitions in the model add only authorized access rights to the matrix. In other words, an access control model is secure if all access rights are authorized. This property has to be preserved by the access control system even when the state of the system changes dynamically, due to users and devices entering and leaving an active space. The definition of authorized access right depends on the type of access control policy. For example in MAC (Mandatory access control) system, only an administrator is authorized to add a new access right to the system. In DAC (Discretionary Access Control) object owners can add access rights.

In order to enforce the access control safety property, we annotate the specification we built earlier with authorization proofs. These proofs are subroutines that use credentials to attest the ownership of an object by a subject (for DAC) or the type of subject (for MAC). The credentials are cryptographically protected by digital signatures and/or encryption. All state transitions in the access control specification are rewritten as guarded commands. The guards verify access control safety condition, by validating authorization proofs. The commands (that correspond to methods that change state variables) are executed only if the guard can be validated. This annotation (the guard) to each dynamic state transition automatically guarantees the safety properties even when the access matrix is allowed to change dynamically, preserving the security of the system at all times.

Similar to access control safety, we have developed dynamic policies for some information flow and availability properties. These security properties are a combination of safety and liveness properties and include temporal quantifiers. At a more fundamental level, we argue that dynamic environments require dynamic security solutions. Dynamic policies enable administrators to react to vulnerabilities detected by IDS and risk analyzers with greater confidence. By including temporal properties in our design of security policies, we can change our system implementations in a controlled manner, and turn on restrictive attack resilient policies at will, without sacrificing security guarantees. This dynamism also allows us to change back to default policies after the attack has been mitigated, allowing us to implement minimal security solutions on a need to protect basis, and amortize performance penalties.

3.4   Access Control

Smart rooms are typically shared by different groups of users for different activities at different points in time. Each activity-specific incarnation of an active space (such as a "classroom" or a "meeting") is called a "Virtual Space". Access control policies and mechanisms are necessary to ensure that users only use the resources (both hardware and software) in an active space in authorized ways, and to allow shared use of the space. These different virtual spaces have varying access control requirements, and the access control policies and mechanisms should allow seamless transitions between virtual spaces, without sacrificing security properties. In addition, the policies should be easy to configure, enforce, and administer.

We are in the process of developing an access control system [25] for Gaia. Our access control system supports customizable access control policies, and integrates physical and virtual aspects of the environment into the access control decision mechanisms. It can reconfigure an active space dynamically to support different access control policies for different virtual spaces, depending on the set of users and the activity being undertaken in the space. We also provide dynamic support for explicit cooperation between different users, groups of users, and devices.

Our system uses the RBAC model [26] for policy configuration, and implements both discretionary and mandatory access controls, providing flexibility and expressiveness. We define three types of roles viz., system, space, and application roles. Each role can be managed by a different administrator, thus allowing for decentralized administration.

Within each active space, access control policies are expressed in terms of *space roles*. The space administrator sets access control policies for resources within a particular space. These policies are in the form of access lists for resources within the space, expressed in terms of space roles and permissions. When users enter a space, their system role is mapped into an appropriate space role automatically.

We also build an explicit notion of cooperation into our access control model using the concept of the *space mode*. We define four distinct modes of collaboration in our model: individual, shared, supervised-use and collaborative, corresponding to different levels of cooperation between users in the space who do not necessarily trust each other. The mode of the space depends on the users within the space and the activity being performed.

This model of access control is useful in developing access control policies that are appropriate for collaborative applications that are common in such environments.

4 Conclusion and Future Directions

The shift to the pervasive computing paradigm brings forth new challenges to security and privacy, which cannot be addressed by mere adaptation of existing security and privacy mechanisms. Unless security concerns are accommodated early in the design phase, pervasive computing environments will be rife with vulnerabilities and exposures. In this paper we talked about some of these challenges. We also presented some solutions in our prototype implementation.

The construction of complete, integrated pervasive environments and their real-life deployment are still things of the future. Security in pervasive computing is expected to be an integral part of the whole system, which is not realized yet. It should be noted, however, that there is no single "magical" protocol or mechanism that can address all the security issues and meet the requirements and expectations of secure pervasive computing. Moreover, security itself consists of a variety of different and broad aspects each of which requires detailed research and customized solutions. For these reasons, our prototype implementations are not meant to be a solution for all problems. Instead, they represent milestones towards the construction of a full-fledged security subsystem.

Promising future directions include the development of formal specifications of desirable behavior in the form of security and privacy properties in pervasive computing. Access control, information flow, availability, and secure protocols for authentication, non-repudiation, confidentiality and integrity can be specified in terms of system properties such as safety and liveness. It is also promising to incorporate intelligence and automated reasoning into the security architecture. This "intelligent" security system would be able to make judgments and give assistance in securing the environment without too much intervention by users or administrators. Therefore, we are exploring the possibility of incorporating automated reasoning and learning into the active spaces security architecture, enabling it to perform intelligent inferences under different contexts despite the uncertainties that arise as a result of bridging the physical and virtual worlds.

We are also looking into the development of several middleware reflective object-oriented patterns that can support the different aspects of security, including authentication, access control, anonymity, and policy management, as well as how to instantiate them with diverse mechanisms. Finally, because it is difficult to develop security models that involve people and physical spaces, more studies on integrating virtual and physical security need to be considered.

References

[1]   "Bluetooth." http://www.bluetooth.com/.
[2]   "Reference number ISO/IEC 8802-11:1999(E) IEEE Std 802.11, 1999 edition. International Standard [for] Information Technology-Telecommunications and information exchange between systems-Local and metropolitan area networks-Specific Requirements-Part 11: Wireless LAN Medium Access Control (MAC) and Physical Layer (PHY) specifications," *IEEE*, 1999.
[3]   M. Langheinrich, "Privacy by Design – Principles of Privacy-Aware Ubiquitous Systems," presented at ACM UbiComp 2001, Atlanta, GA, 2001.
[4]   M. Langheinrich, "A Privacy Awareness System for Ubiquitous Computing Environments," presented at 4th International Conference on Ubiquitous Computing, 2002.
[5]   F. Stajano, *Security for Ubiquitous Computing*: Halsted Press, 2002.
[6]   L. Kagal, T. Finin, and A. Joshi, "Trust-Based Security in Pervasive Computing Environments," *IEEE Computer*, 2001.
[7]   L. Kagal, J. Undercoffer, F. Perich, A. Joshi, and T. Finin, "Vigil: Enforcing Security in Ubiquitous Environments," in *Grace Hopper Celebration of Women in Computing 2002*, 2002.
[8]   J. Boyle and e. al, "The COPS Protocol." Internet Draft, Feb. 24, 1999.
[9]   R. Mundy, D. Partain, and B. Stewart, "Introduction to SNMPv3." RFC 2570, April 1999.
[10] M. Stevens and e. al, "Policy Framework." IETF draft, September 1999.
[11] P. Loscocco and S. Smalley, "Integrating Flexible Support for Security Policies into the Linux Operating System," presented at Proceedings of the FREENIX Track of the 2001 USENIX, 2001.
[12] E. A. M. Luiijf, "Information Assurance and the Information Society," presented at EICAR Best Paper Proceedings, 1999.
[13] M. Román, C. K. Hess, R. Cerqueira, A. Ranganat, R. H. Campbell, and K. Nahrstedt, "Gaia: A Middleware Infrastructure to Enable Active Spaces," *IEEE Pervasive Computing (accepted)*, 2002.
[14] M. Roman and R. Campbell, "GAIA: Enabling Active Spaces," presented at 9th ACM SIGOPS European Workshop, Kolding, Denmark, 2000.
[15] M. Roman, C. Hess, A. Ranganathan, P. Madhavarapu, B. Borthakur, P. Viswanathan, R. Cerqueira, R. Campbell, and M. D. Mickunas, "GaiaOS: An Infrastructure for Active Spaces," University of Illinois at Urbana-Champaign Technical Report UIUCDCS-R-2001-2224 UILU-ENG-2001-1731, 2001.

[16] L. Zadeh, "Fuzzy sets as basis for a theory of possibility," *Fuzzy Sets and Systems*, vol. 1, pp. 3–28, 1978.

[17] V. Samar and R. Schemers, "Unified Login with Pluggable Authentication Modules (PAM)," RFC 86.0, 1995.

[18] P. Kaijser, T. Parker, and D. Pinkas, "SESAME: The Solution to Security for Open Distributed Systems," *Computer Communications*, vol. 17, pp. 501–518, 1994.

[19] M. Roman, F. Kon, and R. H. Campbell, "Reflective Middleware: From Your Desk to Your Hand," *IEEE Distributed Systems Online Journal, Special Issue on Reflective Middleware*, 2001.

[20] J. Al-Muhtadi, R. Campbell, A. Kapadia, D. Mickunas, and S. Yi, "Routing Through the Mist: Privacy Preserving Communication in Ubiquitous Computing Environments," presented at International Conference of Distributed Computing Systems (ICDCS 2002), Vienna, Austria, 2002.

[21] J. Al-Muhtadi, R. Campbell, A. Kapadia, D. Mickunas, and S. Yi, "Routing through the Mist: Design and Implementation," UIUCDCS-R-2002-2267, March 2002.

[22] Z. Liu, P. Naldurg, S. Yi, R. H. Campbell, and M. D. Mickunas, "An Agent Based Architecture for Supporting Application Level Security," presented at DARPA Information Survivability Conference (DISCEX 2000), Hilton Head Island, South Carolina, 2000.

[23] P. Naldurg and R. Campbell, "Dynamic Access Control Policies in Seraphim," Department of Computer Science, University of Illinois at Urbana-Champaign UIUCDCS-R-2002-2260, 2002.

[24] P. Naldurg, R. Campbell, and M. D. Mickunas, "Developing Dynamic Security Policies," presented at Proceedings of the 2002 DARPA Active Networks Conference and Exposition (DANCE 2002), San Francisco, CA, USA, 2002.

[25] G. Sampemane, P. Naldurg, and R. Campbell, "Access Control for Active Spaces," presented at the Annual Computer Security Applications Conference (ACSAC), Las Vegas, NV, 2002.

[26] R. Sandhu, E. Coyne, H. Fienstein, and C. Youman, "Role Based Access Control Models," in *IEEE Computer*, vol. 29, 1996.

Security for Whom?
The Shifting Security Assumptions of Pervasive Computing

Frank Stajano

University of Cambridge
http://www-lce.eng.cam.ac.uk/~fms27/

Abstract. Pervasive computing will introduce hundreds of computing devices per user. This change is of such magnitude that it is qualitative as well as quantitative. Old solutions may not scale when the size of the problem grows by such a factor—passwords, for example, will no longer be a suitable user authentication method.

In this paper we examine new security issues for pervasive computing including authentication, biometrics and digital rights management. But the potential impact of pervasive computing on society is such that we have a responsibility to look further than just the technical issues.

1 Introduction

The Weiser vision [1] of computers becoming ubiquitous and invisible is now turning into reality: most of us own, and daily interact with, dozens of processor-driven devices. Today watches, telephones, home video systems, cameras, cars, musical instruments, washing machines and even toilet seats often embed one or more microprocessors. Computers migrate into everyday objects and break away from the cliché of keyboard-and-monitor boxes. There was a time in the recent past in which being able to afford one computer per person—as opposed to one per department or, going further back, one per country—was considered as the ultimate luxury. Tomorrow, hundreds of invisible computers per person (a situation indicated as *ubiquitous* or *pervasive* computing, or *ubicomp* for short) will be normal and unremarkable.

Superficially, this transition may appear as nothing more than a quantitative change: the ratio of computers per person, formerly a small fraction below unity, now becomes a two-digit integer. Reality, however, is more complex, and quantitative changes of several orders of magnitude often also imply *qualitative* changes. When the size of the problem grows by a hundred times, there is no guarantee that the old solution will scale in the same way. Think for example about user authentication to a computer, traditionally solved by asking the user to remember and utter on demand a hard-to-guess password; then imagine how practical it would be to have to do the same with hundreds of different ones. Multiplying the old solution by the same growth factor as that of the problem may make it completely impractical. To put things into their correct perspective

M. Okada et al. (Eds.): ISSS 2002, LNCS 2609, pp. 16–27, 2003.
© Springer-Verlag Berlin Heidelberg 2003

it is therefore appropriate to look at pervasive and ubiquitous computing not as an incremental change, but rather as a paradigm shift—something as significant and revolutionary as the World Wide Web.

As an example, witness how many current PC applications expect, if not demand, to be run maximized, monopolizing all the available screen space and impeding any other concurrent activity. They constrain their users with obsolete usage patterns from the 1970s, when personal computers were strictly single-task machines and all screens had the same size. This widespread and contagious mistake (witness the many web pages that demand a full screen to be usable) is not the product of backwards compatibility obligations: it is just the consequence of blindly reusing a surpassed paradigm (a more comfortable choice for the lazy programmer) without noticing that the computing context has evolved.

Failing to recognize that pervasive computing is a substantive qualitative change will cause us to apply surpassed computing paradigms to many other situations. However, in the security domain, applying obsolete paradigms when assumptions have changed is a guaranteed recipe for expensive mistakes.

2   Authentication and Usability

The three fundamental security properties of confidentiality (preventing unauthorized reads), integrity (preventing unauthorized writes) and availability (ensuring authorized users are not denied service) all rest firmly on a distinction between authorized and unauthorized users. This in turn depends on being able to discriminate between these two classes, often in the Turing-test-like context in which all the available evidence consists of bits supplied by the user being verified. The archetypal example is the familiar twofold interrogation of "Userid? Password?", consisting of a trivial *identification* phase ("Who do you claim to be?") followed by the crucial *authentication* phase ("Prove it."). After successful authentication, *authorization* ("I'll grant you these rights.") may follow, depending on the verified identity of the claimant.

As we said above, it is obvious that passwords are no longer a viable solution to the problem of authentication when each user interacts daily with hundreds of computers. But is authentication always necessary?

The very first computers, of ENIAC and EDSAC vintage, didn't have any authentication procedures. An operator would just walk up to the machine, input a program, let it run and collect the result. The very notion of user accounts was not needed until the time when shared resources (in particular online storage) became available and the need arose for allocating ownership of and controlling access to such resources.

Three decades later, the first personal computers also didn't require any authentication—precisely because they were *personal* and therefore each one of them was completely dedicated to one user who had complete control over it. The login interrogation was only re-introduced once these personal computers were connected together to form a LAN.

Nowadays it still is uncommon for personal computers in the home to ask for a password, except perhaps if they're owned by nerds; but a password is usually needed to log in to the ISP that offers network connectivity.

The Big Stick principle [2, section 4.2.8], a very high level security policy model [3], identifies a class of cases in which authentication is superfluous:

Big Stick principle: Whoever has physical access to the device is allowed to take it over.

This is the way in which most of our everyday devices behave: from fridges and lawnmowers to CD players and calculators, if you can touch them, you can operate them. One of the reasons why the Big Stick principle is better than so many other policies is because it is cynically realistic: when someone has unsupervised physical access to the device, she can usually do anything she wants to it [4,5]. Consequently, most of the policies that go against the Big Stick principle are very difficult to enforce and therefore of little practical use.

Of course there are cases for which the Big Stick principle is definitely an inappropriate model—think of a vending machine, or a safe. Besides, Big-Stick-compliant devices have no protection against loss or theft. To offer stronger protection, authentication is usually adopted (although it will often be defeatable unless coupled with an adequate amount of tamper resistance).

From the point of view of the pervasive computing scenario, some interesting questions arise:

1. How often do we really need a stronger protection than that afforded by the Big Stick principle?
2. When Big Stick is no longer enough, do we always need *user* authentication?
3. In cases where user authentication is required, can't we adopt a more friendly mechanism than passwords?

To answer the first question, let's ask two more:

1a. Do we consider today's fridges, lawnmowers etc. to be insecure?
1b. If we find them acceptable as they are, will the situation change once we move into pervasive computing?

The extremely paranoid might label yesterday's fridge as too insecure, in so far as Alice can take out and eat the ice cream bought by Bob. Most regular humans, though, will dismiss this threat as unworthy of countermeasures, particularly in the common case in which the two characters are sister and brother. The Big Stick principle seems appropriate for a fridge: if you can open the door (i.e. if you are in the house), you are authorized to eat the ice cream—even if it was actually bought by your brother. Non-home environments may be border-line cases ("Other unknown students drank the beers I left in my college fridge!" was one of the comments to the above scenario) but on the whole the most appropriate protection seems to be social and territorial ("if we allow you to be in here, surely we also allow you to drink what's in the fridge—within reason").

In other words, the social convention implicitly recognizes that the guest, once inside, could do much worse damage than drinking all the beers in the fridge, and that he is trusted to behave correctly or he wouldn't have been allowed in. We don't *expect* him to drink all the beers, but we don't go to any trouble to ensure that he won't be able to.

As for sub-question 1b, the major changes I see in the move to pervasive computing are *storage of private data* inside the devices and *spontaneous wireless connectivity*. Let's see if they introduce any security requirements not satisfied by the Big Stick principle.

Let's imagine a **digital media jukebox** for the home—the natural evolution of the hi-fi in the pervasive computing era: a multi-terabyte repository with all the movies, camcorder clips, still images and music that members of the household have acquired or generated. Particularly for user-generated material I feel that, while sharing should obviously be allowed wherever desired, individual family members should also have the option of keeping some data items private. This will require some form of access control and consequently user authentication.

Similarly, if bathroom scales, heart monitor and fridge all cooperate to monitor our health, it seems courteous to keep the results private unless the subject explicitly wishes to divulge them to other family members. This, again, requires user authentication. Besides, at least user *identification*, if not authentication, is absolutely necessary in order for the individual measurements to be meaningfully correlated—it would otherwise make no sense to check whether Alice's heart rate matches Bob's weight, or to warn Alice that today she is 22 kg lighter if yesterday's measurement was actually Bob's.

The spontaneous wireless connectivity, on the other hand, an essential element of the ubicomp vision, corresponds to invisible hands plugging and unplugging invisible cables into the devices, and sucking and blowing data and commands at will. Since the invisible cables might even terminate outside the household, the territorial model breaks down: even someone without physical access to the device is able to manipulate it. If we want to be able to prevent this, some form of access control (though not necessarily authentication) is clearly necessary.

Coming back specifically to question 2 on page 18, regulating access to private data such as weight measurements certainly requires user authentication; however, as far as securing wireless connections goes, it is possible (using encryption) to reproduce the level of security afforded by cables without for that having to identify the user. In this case, though, before deciding on a scheme, some thought must go to the situation in which one of the devices is stolen. Does this just cause the loss of that device (reasonable) or does it also imply a compromise of all the other entities that were happy to connect to that device (much less desirable)?

There are also cases in which neither Big Stick nor user authentication is sufficient: a vending machine, for example, which as we already remarked needs to be governed by a stronger policy than Big Stick[1], is still subject to denial of service attacks of the glue-in-the-coin-slot variety, which a hypothetical user authentication mechanism for buyers would do nothing to prevent.

The third question on our list, about alternatives to passwords for user authentication, is probably the most important. The well-known (but not necessarily exhaustive) taxonomy of authentication methods refers to "something you know, something you have or something you are", suggesting in the first instance tokens and biometrics as candidate replacements for passwords.

Tokens are familiar and time-honoured authentication devices for home users: the front door, the car, the bike chain and the desk drawer are all unlocked with a cleverly shaped metal token. The main inherent vulnerability of a token-based system is the one arising from loss or theft of the token and consequent impersonation of the owner by another party. On the other hand, the ability to delegate access rights simply by lending the token may in some cases be a great advantage, as may the plausible deniability [6] (i.e. the fact that it's impossible to disprove your claim that someone else was using your key instead of you). We shall discuss related ideas in section 4.

In the pervasive computing context, tokens in the shape of metal keys would probably not be practical, but contactless tokens that could perform the authentication wirelessly within a radius of half a meter or so might be an interesting choice and would blend in well with the ideal of "do-nothing technology" [2, section 2.5]. Issues to be carefully evaluated include replay attacks, man in the middle and just spontaneously authenticating to a malicious device without the consent or knowledge of the token holder.

Biometrics [7, chapter 13] such as fingerprints or iris recognition have not gained widespread use as yet, but they offer the advantage of providing an authenticator that can't be inadvertently left at home (unlike a token) or forgotten (unlike a PIN). The absolute performance of such systems depends on the usual tradeoff between false positives (mistakenly accepting an impersonator) and false negatives (denying access to a legitimate user).

One inherent problem of such systems is the difficulty of revocation: what can I do when a crook makes a plastic clone of my index finger from the prints I left on that drink glass?

Another one is the potential for discrimination: the rich Westerners, for whom the iris and fingerprint recognition systems would work without problems, would be placing other races (dark-eyed Africans or Asians) and social classes (manual workers with damaged or missing fingers) at a disadvantage by inflicting usability problems on them.

Finally, looking at the whole system as opposed to the authentication subsystem in isolation, there may be scenarios in which biometrics prevent one kind of crime but trigger a worse one: if your expensive motorbike won't start unless the ignition button senses your thumbprint, the bad guys will be forced to chop off your finger rather than just stealing your keyring. But this is not the main problem, and it may be argued that a better technology would be able to tell

---

[1] Note how this translates directly into a tamper resistance requirement.

the difference between a live and a dead finger (although recent studies [8] indicate that we are not quite there yet). For the ubicomp context of hundreds of authentications per day, the issues of usability and intrusiveness are much more relevant.

Combinations of the above technologies may offer benefits not available from any single one. For example I like the idea of two wireless tokens, one in my pocket and one in my watch, that spontaneously authenticate me to the ubicomp gadgets I walk past; the tokens would be initially activated by me typing a PIN, and they would deactivate automatically when out of range of each other—so losing one would not be as bad as losing my keys, while losing both at the same time would be unlikely. Of course, man-in-the-middle and related issues still need a solution as in the case of the single token.

I also think that the importance and relevance of the Big Stick principle to ubicomp is underestimated. While do-nothing solutions (in which everything happens spontaneously through a wireless link) have clear usability benefits, security might be enhanced if the device had a way to distinguish remote commands from those issued by a local user. A physical button on the device may still be a useful discriminator in such cases.

Talking of usability and security we cannot fail to mention the problem of administration and maintenance. The problem is already hard enough for single desktop computers in the hands of non-expert users, so it ought to be clear that the standard approach (hole discovered, fix developed, security bulletin issued, patch applied by diligent administrator) will never scale to the ubicomp scenario of hundreds of machines per user. Even professional system administrators fail to keep up with all the fixes that manufacturers issue, so we cannot rely on ordinary mortals applying all the required security patches. Ubicomp systems must be designed for resilience, with the reasonable expectation that some of the devices I own will at some point be compromised. Interaction protocols must be designed in such a way that this kind of failure will not contaminate all of my other devices. In other words we must account for the possibility of insider fraud, as opposed to partitioning the world into the trusted "us" and the untrusted "them".

Finally, while we have so far insisted on the assumptions of the developers, the assumptions of the *users* are equally important. In the ubicomp scenario, computers hide inside everyday objects and disappear from view. Users will therefore expect certain behaviours of these objects, based on a mental model that does not involve computers. In people's experience, real world objects such as furniture and clothes don't randomly "break"—so the unexpected failures of the programs running on the invisible computers inside those objects will always be shocking. In the words of my colleague Jon Crowcroft, "Have you ever seen someone having to reboot a car? It does happen, but it sure confuses people!".

3   Security for Whom?

As we have seen, the three traditional security properties of confidentiality, integrity and availability rely entirely on authentication—on a method, that is, to distinguish authorized users from unauthorized ones. But there is a more fundamental question that is rarely asked: authorized by whom? For whose benefit? This question is directly relevant to pervasive computing and has recently been made topical by the surge of interest [9,10] around what has been euphemistically[2] called *Digital Rights Management* (DRM).

Until recently, if the question was seldom asked, it was perhaps because the answer was obvious: the owner (or at any rate the principal in charge) of the system, the one who demands and pays for the security countermeasures to be installed, is the one who sets the security policy and decides who is and who is not authorized. But things aren't that simple any more. When my minidisc player prevents me from backing up my own recordings of my own university lectures [2, section 2.6.12], for whom is it providing security? Who is the bad guy being kept out?

Secure software needs a Trusted Computing Base to bootstrap. But trusted by whom? Could there be a conflict of interests between owner (buyer) and maker? If so, how can the owner believe (or check) that her rights are being honoured? And what should these rights be in the first place? What rights is it fair for the owner to claim? We should first form clear ideas on this, then state our requirements for the security architecture. Allowing deployed technology to dictate "this is what you can do, so these are your rights" is to exchange cause and effect.

The technical requirements of Hollywood (a standard nickname for the big-name content producers, regardless of whether their products are movies, music, books or whatever else) are straightforward to understand: assuming that the ability to duplicate digital material without loss of quality is a disincentive to the purchase of the material, they seek to be able to sell (or, better, license) digital bits that will be useless to anyone other than the principal who paid the appropriate fee. In order to do this they need complete control of the playback devices, which must refuse to play content unless *they* (not the owner of the player, of course) authorize it. So, for Digital Rights Management to work, every media player must be part of Hollywood's Trusted Computing Base. A player that were not Hollywood-compliant could otherwise save a plaintext copy of the content after having made it playable. This is a system-level observation that stands regardless of the particular DRM implementation.

Such restrictions, however, almost invariably clash with some perfectly legitimate uses of the devices. I mentioned above the case of my digital minidisc recorder that doesn't allow me to take a bit-by-bit backup of my discs—even

---

[2] Stallman [11], with characteristic sarcasm, redefines the DRM acronym as "Digital Restrictions Management". He also renames "Trusted Computing" as "Treacherous Computing", correctly remarking that the allegedly "trusted" computer will actually disobey its owner.

when all the content has been generated and is copyrighted by me. Another situation is that of the digital media jukebox introduced above in section 2 on page 19. Such a jukebox will either offer or not offer the capability of backing up its content and restoring it to another jukebox. If it will, then it will be possible to duplicate movies without authorization. If it won't (which appears more likely given Hollywood's clearly expressed desiderata) then, if the jukebox breaks down or is stolen, all its content will be lost.

The point being made here is that Hollywood's explanation for the legitimacy of their requests ("we produced this content so we should have the technical means to disallow its unauthorized duplication") glosses over the equally legitimate requests of honest users. If the movies I buy are only delivered to me as bits over the wire, and they disappear if my jukebox breaks because I can't back them up, then shouldn't Hollywood be liable for the loss of my entire software collection (probably one or two orders of magnitude more expensive than the hardware of the jukebox) because it prevented me from protecting it?

The alternative technical solution of checking licences online, which both Microsoft and Apple have adopted for their latest operating system products, is easily subject to abuse and privacy invasion: do you really wish Hollywood to know which disc you're playing every time you do? Microsoft, for example, is not new to using the backchannel provided by the licence checking system (or by their update-via-web service) to acquire and log detailed information on the hardware and software configuration of your machine.

4   Ethics

Security for pervasive computing will require many new technical solutions to address new technical problems. But it would be a mistake to focus only on these. When computers pervade our environment, the impact on society is going to be significant. Before delving into the technical questions it will be worth investigating basic issues of policy. Not "how do we protect it?" but "*what* should we protect?", and why, and for whose benefit?

Without exaggeration, with ubicomp we are building a new world. We must foresee the consequences of this act. In particular, as architects of the new world, we have a moral duty to protect the technically illiterate for whom this new wave of invisible and pervasive technology will be an inescapable and unsolicited imposition. These people are the ones who won't understand the risks and who won't be able to defend themselves: it is our responsibility to make this new world fair towards them as well.

As for biometrics, for example, we saw above that it is not clear whether they provide a suitable technical answer to the authentication problem in ubicomp. Assuming they did, though, it would still be unwise to adopt them without a critical assessment not just of their security (in the narrowly technical sense) but also of their side effects. A hypothetically perfect biometric authentication method, non-intrusive and with negligible false positives and false negatives, would always yield the unforgeable identity of the user at each attempted access.

But a side effect of user authentication is a proof that the authenticated individual was accessing the service at that time and, at least in most cases involving biometrics, that the user was physically there at that time. This side effect may not be intended, but it is inescapable. It becomes dangerous if, perhaps owing to auditing requirements, that information is not thrown away immediately. The pervasiveness of devices requiring authentication would then cause users to leave around very explicit and detailed trails of their whereabouts and activities.

Concerns about this kind of issue are often dismissed with superficial comments to the effect that "only dishonest users have anything to hide" and that honest ones will never worry about disclosing where they have been. Such a comment is arrogant and short-sighted. The fact that you were not doing anything illegal should not automatically mean that you have no reason to retain your right to decide who gets to know precisely what you did over the past month on a minute-by-minute basis. Giving up this right, and welcoming complete observability, is akin to welcoming thought police—after all, by the same argument, why would an honest individual worry about thought police?

A comment I always found inspiring was offered in 1996 by Phil Zimmermann [12], creator of PGP. It was originally about Clipper (the infamous "key escrow" mechanism by which the government would have been able to wiretap encrypted communications), but applies equally well to the subject discussed above:

> When making public policy decisions about new technologies for the government, I think one should ask oneself which technologies would best strengthen the hand of a police state. Then, do not allow the government to deploy those technologies. This is simply a matter of good civic hygiene.

It would be irresponsible for us to build a pervasive computing world that could easily be misused as surveillance infrastructure. As Zimmermann himself remarks elsewhere in the same piece, this would also remove the feedback mechanism by which a healthy society can get rid of bad laws, or of bad lawmakers. The simple-minded comment that "if you don't do anything illegal you have nothing to hide" actually depends on the definition of "illegal", which may change much more rapidly and dramatically than a deployed information infrastructure. Think of what counts as "illegal" not just in your country today, but in a dictatorship. Protecting privacy and anonymity is also a system-level safeguard to protect free speech from the censors.

It would be evil if pervasive surveillance were built into ubicomp on purpose, but it would be tragically idiotic if this just happened by negligence—simply because thinking of appropriate safeguards was too hard and therefore too expensive.

It is also irresponsible for technologists to assume that, if nobody complains, there is no problem. Often the public does not complain because it lacks the technical astuteness even to *see* the problem—but it would complain if only it understood what is at stake. I have been in the privileged position of spending a decade in a research environment equipped with a system to track the location of personnel in real time [2, section 2.5]; this gives me a unique perspective on the relevant privacy issues based on actual *experience*, as opposed to speculation and conjecture. From this point of view it is interesting to note that many visitors to our laboratory, when first introduced to our Active Badge [13] and Active Bat [14] systems, used to voice concerns about the privacy implications of divulging one's location information; but none of them had any second thoughts about voluntarily carrying that global location-tracking device known as the *mobile phone*! So mobile phones might easily raise concerns of location privacy, if only users realized that the devices continuously report their geographical location[3]. One of the great merits of the Badge and Bat projects in this context was to make the issue visible and explicit.

Beresford and I [15] are currently studying location privacy, based on the experimental setup of the Active Bat but keeping in mind applicability to other location systems including those based on mobile phones. We have been working both on protection techniques and on measurement techniques to assess the actual strength of the protection that can be provided.

For another example of the necessity to think about a fair policy before attempting implementation, let's go back to the digital recordings of my lectures (see section 2 on page 22). The risk that a DRM infrastructure such as TCPA might be abused [10, question 11]) is so great that it is probably unwise to accept its deployment in the first place. But even if, as a society, we decided to grant Hollywood the right to control the distribution of the content it produces, then why shouldn't individuals be granted the same right for *their* own creations? In other words, why shouldn't you be able to control, with similar mechanisms, who gets access to the songs you compose, the novels you write, the photographs you take? (And of course you should be free to choose whether to charge for such access or not; your policy wouldn't have to be the same as Hollywood's.) Why should this right only be granted to you if you accept the intermediation (and taxation, and potential censorship) of a Hollywood member? Think back to the Web and to the unquestionable libertarian[4] revolution it triggered by giving everyone the option to become a publisher. If we built a world in which access to digital content were ubiquitously governed by DRM systems, then giving Hollywood the *exclusive* licence to publish would mean a return to the digital Middle Ages. Giving the same digital authorship rights to all individuals, instead, would restore some of the freedom that the Web originally introduced.

---

[3] Awareness of this fact is slightly higher now, as a consequence of the published requirement of being able to trace emergency calls from mobiles. But, in the mid-1990s, very few members of the general public understood that they could be located through their cellular phone.

[4] To avoid potential misunderstandings: I use this word in the etymological sense of "in favour of liberty", without any of the right-wing overtones it might suggest to some US readers.

5 Conclusions

Pervasive computing is happening. Computers already pervade our society and our lifestyles. More computers will integrate into more everyday objects. We are inevitably making ourselves more dependent on the machines. But there is no reason to see this as a bad thing, so long as we choose the rules and foresee the consequences.

I invite the reader to rethink about security for pervasive computing by challenging any implicit assumptions. What needs protection, and why, and from what threat, and for whose benefit? An awareness of the big picture is necessary to allow us to build a pervasive computing world that is empowering and liberating, rather than irritating and oppressive.

By being professionally active now in this field, we are blessed with a unique chance to create a new world. This brings along exciting opportunities, but also great responsibilities. Let's think about policy before burying our brains in the details of implementation, and let's think about fairness towards the future inhabitants of this new world before agreeing to any policy.

Acknowledgements. I am grateful to Alastair Beresford, Richard Clayton, Bruno Crispo, Jon Crowcroft and Stewart Lee for their comments on a previous draft of this paper, as well as to several attendees of the Symposium for resonating with me on these issues.

Going up a level, I am also grateful to all the responsible computer professionals (some of whom appear in the bibliography) who are raising awareness of the security issues of ubicomp. Above all, I especially thank those who are already devoting their skill, expertise and creativity to the development of ethical solutions to these problems.

References

1. Mark Weiser. "The Computer for the Twenty-First Century". *Scientific American*, **265**(3):94–104, Sep 1991.
   http://www.ubiq.com/hypertext/weiser/SciAmDraft3.html.
2. Frank Stajano. *Security for Ubiquitous Computing*. John Wiley and Sons, Feb 2002. ISBN 0-470-84493-0. http://www-lce.eng.cam.ac.uk/~fms27/secubicomp/.
3. Ross Anderson, Frank Stajano and Jong-Hyeon Lee. "Security Policies". In Marvin V. Zelkowitz (ed.), "(untitled)", vol. 55 of *Advances in Computers*, pp. 185–235. Academic Press, 2001. ISBN 0-12-012155-7.
4. Ross Anderson and Markus Kuhn. "Tamper Resistance—A Cautionary Note". In "Proc. 2nd USENIX Workshop on Electronic Commerce", 1996. ISBN 1-880446-83-9. http://www.cl.cam.ac.uk/~mgk25/tamper.pdf.
5. Oliver Kömmerling and Markus G. Kuhn. "Design Principles for Tamper-Resistant Smartcard Processors". In "Proceedings of the USENIX Workshop on Smartcard Technology (Smartcard '99)", pp. 9–20. USENIX Association, Chicago, IL, 10–11 May 1999. ISBN 1-880446-34-0.
   http://www.cl.cam.ac.uk/~mgk25/sc99-tamper.pdf.

6. Michael Roe. *Cryptography and Evidence*. Ph.D. thesis, University of Cambridge, 1997. http://www.research.microsoft.com/users/mroe/THESIS.PDF.
7. Ross Anderson. *Security Engineering—A Guide to Building Dependable Distributed Systems*. John Wiley & Sons, 2001. ISBN 0-471-38922-6.
8. Lisa Thalheim, Jan Krissler and Peter-Michael Ziegler. "Body Check: Biometric Access Protection Devices and their Programs Put to the Test". *c't*, **11**:114ff., 22 May 2002. http://www.heise.de/ct/english/02/11/114/. Originally in German, but translated into English at the URL provided.
9. John Gilmore. "What's Wrong With Copy Protection", 16 Feb 2001. http://www.toad.com/gnu/whatswrong.html. Originally posted to the mailing list cryptography@c2.net on 2001-01-18 in response to an invitation by Ron Rivest.
10. Ross Anderson. "TCPA / Palladium Frequently Asked Questions, Version 1.0", Jul 2002. http://www.cl.cam.ac.uk/users/rja14/tcpa-faq.html.
11. Richard Stallman. "Can you trust your computer?", 21 Oct 2002. http://newsforge.com/newsforge/02/10/21/1449250.shtml?tid=19. Also archived at http://www.gnu.org/philosophy/can-you-trust.html.
12. Philip R. Zimmermann. "Testimony of Philip R. Zimmermann to the Subcommittee on Science, Technology, and Space of the US Senate Committee on Commerce, Science, and Transportation", 26 Jun 1996. http://www.cdt.org/crypto/current_legis/960626_Zimm_test.html.
13. Roy Want, Andy Hopper, Veronica Falcão and Jonathan Gibbons. "The Active Badge Location System". *ACM Transactions on Information Systems*, **10**(1):91–102, Jan 1992. ftp://ftp.uk.research.att.com/pub/docs/att/tr.92.1.pdf. Also available as AT&T Laboratories Cambridge Technical Report 92.1.
14. Andy Ward, Alan Jones and Andy Hopper. "A New Location Technique for the Active Office". *IEEE Personal Communications*, **4**(5):42–47, Oct 1997. ftp://ftp.uk.research.att.com/pub/docs/att/tr.97.10.pdf. Also available as AT&T Laboratories Cambridge Technical Report 97.10.
15. Alastair Beresford and Frank Stajano. "Location Privacy in Pervasive Computing", 2003. Accepted by *IEEE Pervasive Computing*. To appear.

Active Authentication for Pervasive Computing Environments

Kenta Matsumiya, Soko Aoki, Masana Murase, and Hideyuki Tokuda

Graduate School of Media and Governance, Keio University
{kenta, soko, masana, hxt}@ht.sfc.keio.ac.jp

Abstract. We propose a Zero-stop Authentication model, which models the process of actively authenticating users in an environment populated with various mobile and embedded devices. In such an environment, since users are mobile, an authentication mechanism that does not disturb the user movement, and that decreases the user burden is needed. The model determines the timing constraint needed to realize "zero-stop" property from the speed of the users, size of the sensing area, and the overhead of sensing and authentication process. We also present a Zero-stop Authentication system to realize the model, and demonstrate the prototype implementation.

1 Introduction

Computing environment surrounding us are becoming pervasive and ubiquitous [1], populated with mobile devices and various appliances. With the use of these devices, we can access computational resources with increased mobility. In such an environment, users need to authenticate themselves to multiple systems as they move. To sustain mobility of the users, the authentication process needs to complete within a certain pereod of time, and to decrease their burden, it should require only a small amount of input from them. Also, when users carry objects that need to be identified such as merchandises in supermarkets and books in libraries, they need to be correctly recognized as objects belonging to a user. An active authentication mechanism that diminishes the burden of the users is needed. We propose Zero-stop Authentication model, which models the process of actively authenticating users passing through a certain physical point. We call such a point "gate" and assume that an authentication mechanism is embedded in it. By active authentication, we mean that the users are detected using sensors in the environment [2] [3], and that the environment initiates the authentication process to the mobile devices users carry. The model determines the timing constraint of the authentication process from the speed of the users, size of the sensing area, and the overhead of sensing and authentication process. We also propose Zero-stop Authentication system, which is an active authentication system that provides "zero-stop" property. We define "zero-stop" property as a property of an authentication system to not make moving users pause in the course of authentication. To achieve this property, a system needs to meet the following four challenges.

M. Okada et al. (Eds.): ISSS 2002, LNCS 2609, pp. 28–41, 2003.

- Correctly detecting users and objects,
- providing active authentication that requires no input from users,
- providing real time response, and
- presenting feedback.

Some existing systems [4] [5], mainly in the Intelligent Transport System [6] field have properties of an active authentication system, but they lack generality, and does not aim to associate objects with the users.

The rest of this paper is organized as follows. In section 2 we introduce our Zero-stop Authentication model. Section 3 discusses the design of Zero-stop Authentication system, and in section 4 we explain issues in binding objects to users. Section 5 explains our prototype implementation. Finally, we conclude this paper in section 6.

2   Models for Zero-Stop Authentication

We formulate Zero-stop Authentication models in this section. To realize zero-stop operations of authentication, an authentication mechnism embedded in a gate must detect users and objects by cooperating with various sensors, and then authenticates users within a cetain timing constraint.

2.1   Basic Notation and Models

In this section, we introduce four models of zero-stop authentication and their notations. These models can be applied to several secure applications such as library check-out applications and supermarket check-out applications.

Let us assume an environment where a user-detecting sensor, S_{usr} observes N users, and an object-detecting sensor S_{obj} recognizes M_N objects, where M_i is the number of objects carried by user i.

The reason why we assume two types of sensors, S_{usr} and S_{obj} is to make the model practical. It is considered that inexpensive sensors can be used to detect objects, while richer sensors that can perform authentication protocols are needed for users.

In order to specify various Zero-stop Authentication models, we adopt the following notation.

$p/N \times q/M$ **Model**

where p and q describe the number of S_{usr} and S_{obj}, respectively. N and M denotes the number of users and objects in the model. For instance, $2/N \times 2/M$ indicates a model where two user-detecting sensors detect N users and two object-deteting sensors observe M objects concurrently. Increasing numbers of sensors and redundancy of sensor data is useful way to reduce the sensors' error-occurrence and to enhance a successful zero-stop operation.

However, in this paper, we focus on the following four simple models of zero-stop authentication to analyse the feasibility of the authentication mechanisms.

(a) $1/1 \times 1/1$ **model**

In this model, both the user-detecting sensor and the object-detecting sensor sense the only one entity at a time.

(b) $1/1 \times 1/M$ **model**

In this model, the user-detecting sensor detects only one user, while the object-detecting sensor recognizes multiple objects at a time.

(c) $1/N \times 1/1$ **model**

In this model, the user-detecting sensor detects N users, while the object-detecting sensor detects an object per user.

(d) $1/N \times 1/M$ **model**

In this model, a user-detecting sensor observes N users, and one object-detecting sensor recognizes M_N objects per user.

2.2   Models of Environment

Figure 1 illustrates the environment we assume for our models. Although coverage-shapes of all sensors are not circular, many RF sensors with omni-directional antennas such as IEEE-802.11b standardized devices and RF-ID readers can detect objects appeared in a certain circular area. Thus, we model that the coverage areas of the user-detecting sensor and the object-detecting sensor are circles of radius R_{usr} and R_{obj}, respectively. If $R_{usr} \leq R_{obj}$ is satisfied, two sensors and a gate are placed as Figure 1-(a) shows (each sensors are located at the gate). Figure 1-(b) depicts the contrary case i.e., in the case of $R_{usr} > R_{obj}$.

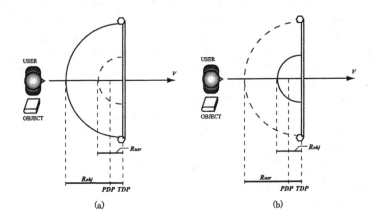

Fig. 1. Environment of The Zero-Stop Authentication System

As for user movement, we assume that a user walks straight along the collinear line of two sensors and the gate at a constant velocity, V. By the time when a user reaches a processing deadline point (PDP), the gate should finish both the authentication and the object processing. Then the server temporarily stores those results in its memory or storage. The gate updates information about the user and objects by the time when the user passes through the gate (transaction deadline point: TDP). Users can obtain the feedback of authentication and object-binding by the gate while they exist between PDP and TDP. The length between PDP and TDP depends on applications, since each application consumes different time required for feedback to users.

2.3   Time Constrained Operations

(a) 1/1 × 1/1 Model. In a single user case, we assume that the user enters the coverage area of the user-detecting sensor or the object-detecting sensor at time $t = 0$. In this condition, the gate should authenticate the user within the following given time:

$$\frac{R_{usr} - l}{V} - \alpha - \beta - AT \geq 0 \tag{1}$$

where l stands for the distance between PDP and TDP, α is the processing time of the user-detecting sensor to discover users, β stands for the time to transfer a user-ID datum from the user-detecting sensor to the gate, and AT is the authentication time.

The velocity of objects can be obtained by approximating user's velocity. This is because objects travel at the same velocity V, since the user carries objects. The gate should process operations for the object within the time:

$$\frac{R_{obj} - l}{V} - \gamma - \delta - OT \geq 0 \tag{2}$$

where the parameter γ is the processing time of the object-detecting sensor, δ is the communication time to transfer an object-ID datum from the object-detecting sensor to the gate, and OT stands for the time taken by the gate to process the operation for the single object.

(b) 1/1 × 1/M Model. The constraint of the authentication is the same inequality as formula 1, since the gate also authenticate a single user in case (b). However, the gate processes operations for M objects. Therefore, it should satisfy the following relationship to realize that the user does not need to stop at the gate:

$$\frac{R_{obj} - l}{V} - \sum_{j=1}^{M} \gamma_j - \sum_{j=1}^{M} \delta_j - \sum_{j=1}^{M} OT_j \geq 0 \tag{3}$$

for $1 \leq j \leq M$, where γ_j is the processing time consumed by the object-detecting sensor to discover object j, γ_j represents the communication time to send the ID of object j from the object-detecting sensor to the gate, and OT_j is the processing time to modify the state of object j. Formula 3 assumes that the object-detecting sensor can not concurrently scan multiple objects. If it is possible, the new formula becomes simpler: $\sum_{j=1}^{M} \gamma_j$ is substituted with γ_{max} which is the greatest value of all γ_j. In addition, the communication time, $\sum_{j=1}^{M} \delta_j$, can be reduced, if object ID data can be transfered by less than M packets.

(c) $1/N \times 1/1$ Model. We consider a more complex case than case (a) and (b): N users pass through a gate carrying a single object for each. In the multiple users case, user i enters into the coverage area of a user-detecting sensor or an object-detecting sensor at time t_i. In this case, the time-constrained computation for authenticating user i is as follows:

$$t_i + \frac{R_{usr} - l}{V_i} - \alpha_i - \beta_i - AT_i \geq t_i \qquad (4)$$

for $1 \leq i \leq N$, where α_i represents the time to detect user i, β_i is the communication time between the user-detecting sensor and the gate, and AT_i is the time taken by the gate to authenticate user i.

If $\forall V_i = \forall V_j$ $(i \neq j)$ is met, or operations for each users are serialized like ATM in a bank, the gate server just authenticates users, following the first-in-first-out (FIFO) discipline; otherwise the gate should reschedule the order of authentication operations to minimize deadline misses. To address this issue, we have two approaches. One is using the earliest-deadline-first algorithm [7] which schedules the user with the closest deadline first. According to this scheduling policy, the gate can determine the priority of each user by calculating D_i in the formula:

$$D_i = ET_i + \frac{R_{usr} - l}{V_i} - \alpha_i - \beta_i - AT_i \qquad (5)$$

where ET_i is the time when user i enters the coverage area of the user-detecting sensor.

The other one is building least-slack-time scheduling [8] into the gate. In this case, the slack time for authenticating user i at time t is $D_i - p_i - t$, where p_i is the processing time to authenticate users.

(d) $1/N \times 1/M$ Model. A model for multiple users carrying multiple objects for each is discussed here. The order to authenticate all N users can be determined by user selection algorithms. To realize Zero-stop operations, the gate should meet the following formula to modify the state of object j:

$$\frac{R_{obj} - l}{V_i} - \sum_{j=1}^{M_i} \gamma_j - \sum_{j=1}^{M_i} \delta_j - \sum_{j=1}^{M_i} OT_j \geq 0 \qquad (6)$$

for $1 \leq i \leq N$ and $1 \leq j \leq M_i$, where M_i is the number of objects that user i carries.

3   Object Binding

In both $1/N \times 1/1$ model and $1/N \times 1/M$ model, the authentication system needs to bind objects to users. Examples of objects are books in libraries, and merchandises in supermarkets. If these objects are appropriately bound to users, applications will be able to register, or charge them to the user. The main challenge is to correctly sense and distinguish objects belonging to a user. While mechanisms to sense an object is maturing, those to distinguish it, and to bind it to an appropriate user is not as thoroughly investigated.

We introduce three ideas in the following that can be used to effectively distinguish between objects belonging to a user from others'. In our assumption, objects are tagged with wireless identification devices, such as RF tags. We will classify these tags into two groups: Read-Only, and Read-Write.

Guidance. The guidance approach is a technique to transform $1/N \times 1/1$ model or $1/N \times 1/M$ model to $1/1 \times 1/1$ model. In this approach, users are physically guided, so only one user is sensed by the system at a time. This method has analogies to traditional object binding methods, such as in supermarkets. However users often queue in supermarkets, so enough gates to realize the zero-stop property is required.

Insulation. We use an insulator to obstruct radio wave to or from the tags attached to the objects. The insulator will likely take the form of specialized containers, such as shopping carts. In this approach, the authentication system detects a user who exists close to the gate, and authenticates him or her. After that, the authorized user opens the container so that the objects are exposed to, or freed to give off radio waves. The identification of the objects recognized at that point is bound to the target of the authentication. Other users must not open their container during this process, because object binding misses occur.

Marking. Objects have writable tags attached, and users use devices to write their IDs to those tags. When objects are sensed, these IDs are also sensed, and reported to the system, allowing it to bind the objects to the user.

Table 1 classifies each binding method by types of tags and required devices.

Table 1. Binding methods

method	tag type	device
guidance	RO	gate
insulation	RO	insulation container
marking	RW	marking device

4   System Architecture

There are six modules as shown in Figure2 in our system. We assume that devices such as sensors, displays, and speakers can be controlled directly over a network, or from a computer that is connected to a network. The system itself runs on a designated computer. *Detection module* manages sensors which detect users and objects, and throws events or data obtained from sensors. *Event process module* processes the raw events or data into a form that is recognizable to the rest of the system. It passes user identifiers to the authentication module, and object identifiers to the binding module. *Authentication module* manages authentication mechanisms and protocols, and conducts user authentication. If the authentication succeeds, *binding module* binds objects with the user. *Feedback process module* processes commands for output devices, from the feedback information passed from applications. *Output module* manages output devices, and dispatches commands to the correct output device based on users' context or requirements. Applications may choose to use the feedback functions of the system, or choose not to do so.

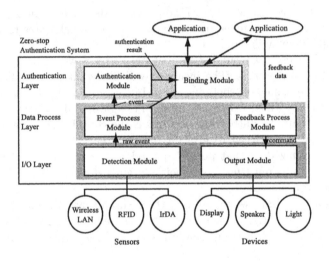

Fig. 2. Architecture

In the rest of this section, we describe in detail about four features which our authentication needs to acquire: Recognition and guidance of users and objects, binding objects to users, maintaining user and object state, and presentation of feedback and error correction.

4.1 Recognition and Guidance

The system needs to physically recognize and guide users and objects. Recognition may be done by existing sensor mechanisms. In order to achieve zero-stop property, users need to be successfully authenticated within a specific period of time. Thus, there are constraints on sensing overhead.

Guidance is an issue related to recognition. Existing examples of physical guidance include gates and doors at building entrances, cash counters in supermarkets, and various toll gates on roadways. Some sensing technologies have problems in sensing multiple objects within same physical area, or objects moving in exceedingly high speed. In order to accomplish the authentication task using such sensing technologies, objects must be physically guided to support the sensors. Objects are guided to pass a particular area, managed into sequential queues, and their speed may be reduced.

In case users carry objects that need to be bound to themselves such as merchandises in supermarkets, the sensors need to distinguish between multiple objects, or between objects belonging to an user from those that belong to others. If the sensors were not able to accomplish this task, objects may need to be bundled or separated accordingly.

4.2   User and Object State

The system need to keep track of user and object state. Their physical context should be mapped accordingly to the internal objects maintained by the system. Figure 3 illustrates the state graph of users and objects.

The system may loose or mix up users and objects due to sensing problems, and incorrect binding may occur. The system need to recover from these errors, and allow users to correct improper transactions.

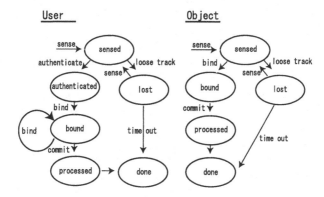

Fig. 3. State graph of users and objects

4.3   Feedback and Error Correction

The objective of the feedback is to allow users to acknowledge the result of the authentication, verify if objects were correctly bound to them, and browse other related information such as a due date of a book or credits withdrawn from their bank accounts.

The presentation of the feedback can be done visually, or through other methods such as audio synthesizing. Simple results that can be expressed in several patterns, may be presented using simple and intuitive presentation methods, such as color pattern of an LCD. We believe that this kind of presentation method will gain more popularity in the forthcoming ubiquitous computing environment as a way to output computational results.

Error correction is another important field for our system to address. Authentication and transaction might generate errors such as authentication failure, miss-binding of objects, and unreasonable withdrawal of credits. The system need to permit users to interact with the system, and correct these errors.

Traditional interaction devices such as keyboards and mice are not an ideal candidate for our interaction methods, since they are immobile and interaction intensive. One way to go around this problem is to construct a user interface which is accessible from voice operation or gesture operation. Their interaction method and physical form may vary between the different applications that adopt them. Another solution may be to construct a software agent that automatically corrects the errors on behalf of the users.

4.4 Security Concerns

Dealing with security issues in the Zero-stop Authentication system is also important to deploy our system. Unlike current authentication systems, our Zero-stop Authentication system does not require users to input their passwords or names. Instead of users' inputs, their portable terminals answer to the gate. Although it realizes the zero-stop property, it makes the system vulnerable. If the client device is stolen, his or her identity is also stolen at the same time. To protect users' portable devices, biometrics is a usable and practical solution. When a user desires to utilize the client device, a finger print recognition system on the client device authenticate the user. Thus, only authorized users can utilize their portable devices.

In addition, communication between client devices and the gate should be protected because attackers can eavesdrop on a series of the authentication process. It is useful to utilize existing secure communication protocols, such as SSL/TSL and IPsec. Since these protocols are able to encrypt data exchanged between the server and the client, authentication can be processed securely. Moreover, SSL prevents the server and client spoofing problem by using trusted third parties' certification messages.

5 Prototype Implementation

We prototyped sensor-based authentication system based on the Zero-stop Authentication model proposed in this paper. Besides the prototype system of Zero-stop Authentication, a library check-out application is also implemented using JDK 1.3.1.

5.1   Authentication System and Application

Figure 4 depicts Smart Furniture which is an experimental platform of a gate. Two types of sensors are equipped with the gate, and they are RF-based sensor devices; a wireless LAN device to detect users and an RFID tag sensor to detect objects. Hardware composition is explained in Figure 5 with its specification in Table 2.

(a)   (b)

Fig. 4. Smart Furniture: (a) a testbed for uqibuitous applications; (b) Zero-stop Authentication system with a library application

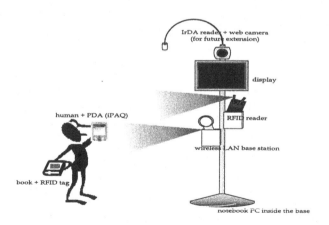

Fig. 5. Hardware Composition

The prototype authentication system is composed of six modules mentioned in Section 6. In our current implementation, the detection module obtains sen-

Table 2. Utilized Computers

item	iPAQ	ThinkPAD
Type	User Terminal (PDA)	Gate (notebook PC)
CPU	StrongARM 206MHz	Intel PentiumIII 850MHz
Memory	64MB	256MB
OS	Familiar Linux v0.5.1	FreeBSD 5.0 CURRENT
Network Interface	802.11b	802.11b (IBSS-Mode)
Others	TFT Display	

sor data from the wireless LAN device and the RFID tag sensor. Therefore, we developed their sensor driver programs for sending sensor data to the detection module. The wireless LAN sensor driver program detects users' portable devices using signal strength, and then provides the IP address of the user's terminal with the highest level of signal strength among others detected by the sensor. To measure signal strength, we utilize IBSS mode of an IEEE 802.11b standardized device. After obtaining the IP address, the authentication module tries to communicate with the host to which the IP address is assigned, and then it starts an authentication process (simple challenge-response protocol). The authentication module authenticates users by searching within a PostgreSQL based data base server where student information (IDs, passwords, names etc.) is stored. In the authentication process, the communication link between users' terminals and the gate is protected by SSL.

After authenticating the user successfully, the RFID tag sensor driver program detects books to which RFID tags are attached. At the same time, the binding module binds the user and books, and provides the authentication module with the binding information. Finally, the output module indicates authentication results on the LCD screen of Smart Furniture for users so as to confirm details. Figure 6-(b) illustrates the screen dump of graphical user interface which appears during the authentication process for the confirmation.

If the authentication fails, the object detection operation above is not processed. In stead of this operation, the feedback module produces error messages, and shows them on the LCD screen of Smart Furniture cooperating with the output module as Figure 6-(c) shows. Furthermore, it also blocks the path of a user by closing the library gate, or setting off an alarm.

5.2   Serialization Scheme

Since we have utilized RFIDs which are not data writable and read only, we have adopted the guidance method described in section 5 for the object binding.

Our library application and authentication system should deal with a concurrency access problem. When several users concurrently access the gate at the same place, the gate can not realize zero-stop property. Some tasks may fail and miss their deadline, because the gate can not provide enough resources. To address this issue, the serialization scheme is introduced in our system as Figure 7 illustrates.

(a) (b) (c)

Fig. 6. Screen dump of authentication results: (a) waiting for authentication; (b) authentication is successfully done; (c) authentication failure occurs

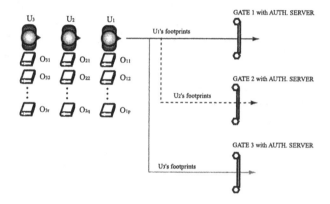

Fig. 7. Serialization Scheme

6 Related Work

The ActiveBadge system [2] and BAT system [3] are sensor management systems for context-aware applications which tracks users and objects. In this tracking system, the users and various objects are tagged with the wireless transmitters, and their location is stored in a database. Therefore, the main goal of the BAT system is detection of users' and objects' accurate location. Since the objective of Zero-stop Authentication system is to build an authentication system on top of a sensor system, the ActiveBadge and the BAT can complement our system.

Intelligent Transport System (ITS) [6], especially, the electronic toll collection (ETC) system [5] allows cars to go through the toll gate without stopping. To realize non-stop payment at the toll gate, automotive vehicles are equipped with devices capable of wireless communication with the toll gate. When these vehicles enter the communication area that a toll gate covers, the toll gate begins to authenticate vehicles, and then withdraws money from banks. In this authentication process, it is necessary to identify automotive vehicles or IDs such as a credit card number or a unique number bound to a credit card number. [4]

proposes the method to identify automotive vehicles by using a retroreflective optical scanner, whereas [9] identifies moving vehicles by smart cards with radio frequency (RF) or infrared (IR) transponders or RF smart tags. However, the ETC model does not address the binding problem since it assumes all the vehicles are serialized. Our model, on the other hand, deals with cases where multiple users bringing multiple objects need to be authenticated at a time.

Zero-Interaction Authentication (ZIA) [10] is an authentication system in which a user wears a small authentication token that communicates with a laptop computer over a short-range wireless link. Whenever the laptop needs decryption authority, the laptop acquires the decryption authority from the token and authority is retained only as long as it's necessary. ZIA is similar to our model in its goal of authenticating the user without stopping them. The main differences between these two models are that our model authenticate both users and objects, and formalizes their mobility by considering the real time aspect.

Recently, there have been several research projects working on authentication in smart environments. In Gaia[11], flexible and convenient methods for authentication is provided[12]. It supports different authentication methods such as identification badges, smart accessories, PDAs, traditional passwords and biometrics. When using wearable devices as authentication methods, the environment actively starts authentication process, and authenticates users for multiple services in the environment with a system similar to Kerberos. It is close to our system in that it uses wearable devices as one of the authentication methods, and that the environment actively authenticates users. However, it does not address how to bind objects to users, and also does not consider real-time response.

7 Conclusion

We presented the Zero-stop Authentication system that reduces users' burden in authentication process. The key contribution of this paper is to model Zero-stop Authentication, the $1/N \times 1/M$ model. In this model, time constrained operations for users and objects are formalized. Additionally, we not only prototyped the library authentication system based on the $1/N \times 1/M$ model, but also verified the system by the feasibility testing. By extending this model to a $P/N \times Q/M$ model, we will be able to realize the fault tolerance of sensors. We are extending the current system to cope with several problems which are not overcome. Two examples of future work are object binding problem and terminal theft problem.

In our prototype implementation, we adopted the guidance method for object binding. Since it can transform complicated models into $1/1 \times 1/1$ model, we were able to keep the system simple. However, in order to provide higher usability by not making users queue up, the system needs to support $1/N \times 1/1$ model or $1/N \times 1/M$ model. To realize these models, we need to implement a more complex system, and at the same time apply other binding methods such as insulation and marking.

We have tried to simplify the current complicated authentication process without diminishing security level by using several security and encryption technologies. However, there is still a threat that a client device or a tag which a user should have would be stolen. For these problems, authentication technology for the device such as biometrics is usable.

References

1. Weiser, M.: The computer for the twenty-century. **265** (1991) 94–104 Scientific American.
2. Want, R., Hopper, A., Falcao, V., Gibbons, J.: The active badge location system. Technical Report 92.1, ORL, 24a Trumpington Street, Cambridge CB2 1QA (1992)
3. Harter, A., Hopper, A., Steggles, P., Ward, A., Webster, P.: The anatomy of a context-aware application. In: International Conference on Mobile Computing and Networking. (1999) 59–68
4. Okabe, H., K.Takemura, Ogata, S., Yamashita, T.: Compact vehicle sensor using a retroreflective optical scanner. In: IEEE Conference of Intelligent Transportation Systems. (1997) 201–205
5. ETTM On The Web: Electoronic toll collection system (2002) http://www.ettm.com/.
6. ITS America: Intelligent transportation system (2002) http://www.itsa.org/standards.
7. Dertouzos, M.L.: Control robotics: The procedural control of physical processes. In: Proceedings of the IFIP Congress. (1974) 807–813
8. Conway, R.W., Maxwell, M.L., Miller, L.W.: Theory of scheduling (1967) Addison-Wesley.
9. ETTM On The Web: Automatic vehicle identification (2002) http://www.ettm.com/avi.htm.
10. Corner, M., Noble, B.: Zero-interaction authentication. In: International Conference on Mobile Computing and Networking. (2002)
11. Cerqueira, R., Hess, C., Roman, M., Campbell, R.: Gaia: A development infrastructure for acctive spaces. In: Workshop on Middleware for Mobile Computing, Atlanta, USA (2001)
12. Al-Muhtadi, J., Ranganathan, A., Campbell, R., Mickunas, M.D.: A flexible, privacy-preserving authentication framework for ubiquitous computing environments. In: International Workshop on Smart Appliances and Wearable Computing (IWSAWC 2002), Vienna, Austria (2002) 771–776

A Survey of Peer-to-Peer Security Issues

Dan S. Wallach

Rice University, Houston, TX 77005, USA
dwallach@cs.rice.edu

Abstract. Peer-to-peer (p2p) networking technologies have gained popularity as a mechanism for users to share files without the need for centralized servers. A p2p network provides a scalable and fault-tolerant mechanism to locate nodes anywhere on a network without maintaining a large amount of routing state. This allows for a variety of applications beyond simple file sharing. Examples include multicast systems, anonymous communications systems, and web caches. We survey security issues that occur in the underlying p2p routing protocols, as well as fairness and trust issues that occur in file sharing and other p2p applications. We discuss how techniques, ranging from cryptography, to random network probing, to economic incentives, can be used to address these problems.

1 Introduction

Peer-to-peer systems, beginning with Napster, Gnutella, and several other related systems, became immensely popular in the past few years, primarily because they offered a way for people to get music without paying for it. However, under the hood, these systems represent a paradigm shift from the usual web client/server model, where there are no "servers;" every system acts as a peer, and by virtue of the huge number of peers, objects can be widely replicated, providing the opportunity for high availability and scalability, despite the lack of centralized infrastructure.

Capitalizing on this trend, researchers have defined structured peer-to-peer (p2p) overlays such as CAN [1], Chord [2], Pastry [3] and Tapestry [4] provide a self-organizing substrate for large-scale p2p applications. Unlike earlier systems, these have been subject to more extensive analysis and more careful design to guarantee scalability and efficiency. Also, rather than being designed specifically for the purpose of sharing unlawful music, these systems provide a powerful platform for the construction of a variety of decentralized services, including network storage, content distribution, web caching, searching and indexing, and application-level multicast. Structured overlays allow applications to locate any object in a probabilistically bounded, small number of network hops, while requiring per-node routing tables with only a small number of entries. Moreover, the systems are scalable, fault-tolerant and provide effective load balancing.

Making these systems "secure" is a significant challenge [5,6]. In general, any system not designed to withstand an adversary is going to be broken easily by one, and p2p systems are no exception. If p2p systems are to be widely deployed on the Internet (at least, for applications beyond sharing "pirate" music files), they must be robust against a conspiracy of some nodes, acting in concert, to attack the remainder of the nodes. A malicious node might give erroneous responses to a request, both at the application

M. Okada et al. (Eds.): ISSS 2002, LNCS 2609, pp. 42–57, 2003.

level (returning false data to a query, perhaps in an attempt to censor the data) or at the network level (returning false routes, perhaps in an attempt to partition the network). Attackers might have a number of other goals, including traffic analysis against systems that try to provide anonymous communication, and censorship against systems that try to provide high availability.

In addition to such "hard" attacks, some users may simply wish to gain more from the network than they give back to it. Such disparities could be expressed in terms of disk space (where an attacker wants to store more data on p2p nodes than is allowed on the attacker's home node), or in terms of bandwidth (where an attacker refuses to use its limited network bandwidth to transmit a file, forcing the requester to use some other replica). While many p2p applications are explicitly designed to spread load across nodes, "hot-spots" can still occur, particularly if one node is responsible for a particularly popular document.

Furthermore, a number of "trust" issues occur in p2p networks. As new p2p applications are designed, the code for them must be deployed. In current p2p systems, the code to implement the p2p system must be trusted to operate correctly; p2p servers typically execute with full privileges to access the network and hard disk. If arbitrary users are to create code to run on p2p systems, an architecture to safely execute untrusted code must be deployed. Likewise, the data being shared, itself, might not be trustworthy. Popularity-based ranking systems will be necessary to help users discover documents that they desire.

Of course, many other issues exist that could be classified as security issues that will not be considered in this paper. For example, one pressing problem with the Kazaa system, often used to share pirated music and movies, is its use of bandwidth [7], which has led many ISPs and universities to either throttle the bandwidth or ban these systems outright. Likewise, this paper only considers security for one high-level p2p application: sharing files. There are numerous other possible applications that can be built using p2p systems (e.g., event notification systems [8,9]), which would have their own security issues.

The remainder of this paper is a survey of research in these areas. Section 3 discusses correctness issues in p2p routing. Section 4 discusses correctness and fairness issues in p2p data storage and file sharing. Section 5 discusses trust issues. Section 6 presents related work and Section 7 has conclusions.

2   Background, Models, and Solution

In this section, we present some background on structured p2p overlay protocols like CAN, Chord, Tapestry and Pastry. Space limitations prevent us from giving a detailed overview of each protocol. Instead, we describe an abstract model of structured p2p overlay networks that we use to keep the discussion independent of any particular protocol. For concreteness, we also give an overview of Pastry and point out relevant differences between it and the other protocols. Next, we describe models and assumptions used later in the paper about how nodes might misbehave. Finally, we define secure routing and outline our solution.

Throughout this paper, most of the analyses and techniques are presented in terms of this model and should apply to other structured overlays except when otherwise noted. However, the security and performance of our techniques was fully evaluated only in the context of Pastry; a full evaluation of the techniques in other protocols is future work.

2.1   Routing Overlay Model

We define an abstract model of a structured p2p routing overlay, designed to capture the key concepts common to overlays such as CAN, Chord, Tapestry and Pastry.

In our model, participating nodes are assigned uniform random identifiers, *nodeIds*, from a large *id space* (e.g., the set of 128-bit unsigned integers). Application-specific objects are assigned unique identifiers, called *keys*, selected from the same id space. Each key is mapped by the overlay to a unique live node, called the key's *root*. The protocol routes messages with a given key to its associated root.

To route messages efficiently, all nodes maintain a *routing table* with the nodeIds of several other nodes and their associated IP addresses. Moreover, each node maintains a *neighbor set*, consisting of some number of nodes with nodeIds nearest itself in the id space. Since nodeId assignment is random, any neighbor set represents a random sample of all participating nodes.

For fault tolerance, application objects are stored at more than one node in the overlay. A *replica function* maps an object's key to a set of *replica keys*, such that the set of *replica roots* associated with the replica keys represents a random sample of participating nodes in the overlay. Each replica root stores a copy of the object.

Next, we discuss existing structured p2p overlay protocols and how they relate to our abstract model.

2.2   Pastry

Pastry nodeIds are assigned randomly with uniform distribution from a circular 128-bit id space. Given a 128-bit key, Pastry routes an associated message toward the live node whose nodeId is numerically closest to the key. Each Pastry node keeps track of its neighbor set and notifies applications of changes in the set.

Node state: For the purpose of routing, nodeIds and keys are thought of as a sequence of digits in base 2^b (b is a configuration parameter with typical value 4). A node's routing table is organized into $128/2^b$ rows and 2^b columns. The 2^b entries in row r of the routing table contain the IP addresses of nodes whose nodeIds share the first r digits with the given node's nodeId; the $r + 1$th nodeId digit of the node in column c of row r equals c. The column in row r that corresponds to the value of the $r + 1$th digit of the local node's nodeId remains empty. A routing table entry is left empty if no node with the appropriate nodeId prefix is known. Figure 1 depicts an example routing table.

Each node also maintains a neighbor set. The neighbor set is the set of l nodes with nodeIds that are numerically closest to a given node's nodeId, with $l/2$ larger and $l/2$ smaller nodeIds than the given node's id. The value of l is constant for all nodes in the overlay, with a typical value of approximately $\lceil 8 * log_{2^b} N \rceil$, where N is the number of expected nodes in the overlay. The leaf set ensures reliable message delivery and is used to store replicas of application objects.

0	1	2	3	4	5	6	7	8	9	a	b	c	d	e	f
0x	1x	2x	3x	4x	5x		7x	8x	9x	ax	bx	cx	dx	ex	fx
60x	61x	62x	63x	64x			67x	68x	69x	6ax	6bx	6cx	6dx	6ex	6fx
650x	651x	652x	653x	654x	655x	656x	657x	658x	659x		65bx	65cx	65dx	65ex	65fx
65a0x		65a2x	65a3x	65a4x	65a5x	65a6x	65a7x	65a8x	65a9x	65aax	65abx	65acx	65adx	65aex	65afx

Fig. 1. Routing table of a Pastry node with nodeId $65a1x$, $b = 4$. Digits are in base 16, x represents an arbitrary suffix.

Message routing: At each routing step, a node seeks to forward the message to a node in the routing table whose nodeId shares with the key a prefix that is at least one digit (or b bits) longer than the prefix that the key shares with the current node's id. If no such node can be found, the message is forwarded to a node whose nodeId shares a prefix with the key as long as the current node, but is numerically closer to the key than the current node's id. If no appropriate node exists in either the routing table or neighbor set, then the current node or its immediate neighbor is the message's final destination.

Figure 2 shows the path of an example message. Analysis shows that the expected number of routing hops is slightly below $log_{2^b} N$, with a distribution that is tight around the mean. Moreover, simulation shows that the routing is highly resilient to crash failures.

To achieve self-organization, Pastry nodes must dynamically maintain their node state, i.e., the routing table and neighbor set, in the presence of node arrivals and node failures. A newly arriving node with the new nodeId X can initialize its state by asking any existing Pastry node A to route a special message using X as the key. The message is routed to the existing node Z with nodeId numerically closest to X. X then obtains the neighbor set from Z and constructs its routing table by copying rows from the routing tables of the nodes it encountered on the original route from A to Z. Finally, X announces its presence to the initial members of its neighbor set, which in turn update their own neighbor sets and routing tables. Similarly, the overlay can adapt to abrupt node failure by exchanging a small number of messages ($O(log_{2^b} N)$) among a small number of nodes.

2.3   CAN, Chord, Tapestry

Next, we briefly describe CAN, Chord and Tapestry, with an emphasis on the differences relative to Pastry.

Tapestry is very similar to Pastry but differs in its approach to mapping keys to nodes and in how it manages replication. In Tapestry, neighboring nodes in the namespace are

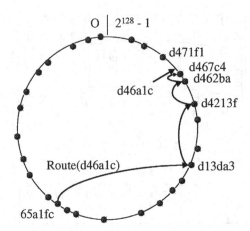

Fig. 2. Routing a message from node $65a1fc$ with key $d46a1c$. The dots depict live nodes in Pastry's circular namespace.

not aware of each other. When a node's routing table does not have an entry for a node that matches a key's nth digit, the message is forwarded to the node with the next higher value in the nth digit, modulo 2^b, found in the routing table. This procedure, called *surrogate routing*, maps keys to a unique live node if the node routing tables are consistent. Tapestry does not have a direct analog to a neighbor set, although one can think of the lowest populated level of the Tapestry routing table as a neighbor set. For fault tolerance, Tapestry's replica function produces a set of random keys, yielding a set of replica roots at random points in the id space. The expected number of routing hops in Tapestry is $log_{2^b} N$.

Chord uses a 160-bit circular id space. Unlike Pastry, Chord forwards messages only in clockwise direction in the circular id space. Instead of the prefix-based routing table in Pastry, Chord nodes maintain a routing table consisting of up to 160 pointers to other live nodes (called a "finger table"). The ith entry in the finger table of node n refers to the live node with the smallest nodeId clockwise from $n + 2^{i-1}$. The first entry points to n's successor, and subsequent entries refer to nodes at repeatedly doubling distances from n. Each node in Chord also maintains pointers to its predecessor and to its n successors in the nodeId space (this successor list represents the neighbor set in our model). Like Pastry, Chord's replica function maps an object's key to the nodeIds in the neighbor set of the key's root, i.e., replicas are stored in the neighbor set of the key's root for fault tolerance. The expected number of routing hops in Chord is $\frac{1}{2} log_2 N$.

CAN routes messages in a d-dimensional space, where each node maintains a routing table with $O(d)$ entries and any node can be reached in $(d/4)(N^{1/d})$ routing hops on average. The entries in a node's routing table refer to its neighbors in the d-dimensional space. CAN's neighbor table duals as both the routing table and the neighbor set in our model. Like Tapestry, CAN's replica function produces random keys for storing replicas at diverse locations. Unlike Pastry, Tapestry and Chord, CAN's routing table does not grow with the network size, but the number of routing hops grows faster than $\log N$ in this case.

Tapestry and Pastry construct their overlay in a Internet topology-aware manner to reduce routing delays and network utilization. In these protocols, routing table entries can be chosen arbitrarily from an entire segment of the nodeId space without increasing the expected number of routing hops. The protocols exploit this by initializing the routing table to refer to nodes that are nearby in the network topology and have the appropriate nodeId prefix. This greatly facilitates proximity routing [3]. However, it also makes these systems vulnerable to attacks where an attacker can exploit his locality to the victim.

The choice of entries in CAN's and Chord's routing tables is tightly constrained. The CAN routing table entries refer to specific neighboring nodes in each dimension, while the Chord finger table entries refer to specific points in the nodeId space. This makes proximity routing harder, but it protects nodes from attacks that exploit attacking nodes' proximity to their victims.

2.4   System Model

The system runs on a set of N nodes that form an overlay using one of the protocols described in the previous section. We assume a bound f $(0 \leq f < 1)$ on the fraction of nodes that may be faulty. Faults are modeled using a constrained-collusion Byzantine failure model, i.e., faulty nodes can behave arbitrarily and they may not all necessarily be operating as a single conspiracy. The set of faulty nodes is partitioned into independent coalitions, which are disjoint sets with size bounded by cN $(1/N \leq c \leq f)$. When $c = f$, all faulty nodes may collude with each other to cause the most damage to the system. We model the case where faulty nodes are grouped into multiple independent coalitions by setting $c < f$. Members of a coalition can work together to corrupt the overlay but are unaware of nodes in other coalitions. We studied the behavior of the system with c ranging from $1/N$ to f to model different failure scenarios.

We assume that every node in the p2p overlay has a static IP address at which it can be contacted. In this paper, we ignore nodes with dynamically assigned IP addresses, as well as nodes behind network address translation boxes or firewalls. While p2p overlays can be extended to address these concerns, this paper focuses on more traditional network hosts.

All nodes communicate over normal Internet connections. We distinguish between two types of communication: *network-level*, where nodes communicate directly without routing through the overlay, and *overlay-level*, where messages are routed through the overlay using one of the protocols discussed in the previous section. We use cryptographic techniques to prevent adversaries from observing or modifying network-level communication between legitimate nodes. An adversary has complete control over network-level communication to and from nodes that it controls. This gives an adversary an opportunity to observe and either discard or misroute traffic through faulty nodes it controls. If the messages are protected by appropriate cryptography, then modifications to them should be detected. Some messages, such as routing updates, may not be easily amenable to the application of cryptographic techniques.

3   Routing in p2p Systems

The routing primitives implemented by current structured p2p overlays provide a best-effort service to deliver a message to a replica root associated with a given key. As discussed above, a malicious overlay node has ample opportunities to corrupt overlay-level communication. Therefore, these primitives are not sufficient to construct secure applications. For example, when inserting an object, an application cannot ensure that the replicas are placed on legitimate, diverse replica roots as opposed to faulty nodes that impersonate replica roots. Even if applications use cryptographic methods to authenticate objects, malicious nodes may still corrupt, delete, deny access to or supply stale copies of all replicas of an object.

To address this problem, we must create a secure routing primitive. *The secure routing primitive ensures that when a non-faulty node sends a message to a key k, the message reaches all non-faulty members in the set of replica roots R_k with very high probability.* R_k is defined as the set of nodes that contains, for each member of the set of replica keys associated with k, a live root node that is responsible for that replica key. In Pastry, for instance, R_k is simply a set of live nodes with nodeIds numerically closest to the key. Secure routing ensures that (1) the message is eventually delivered, despite nodes that may corrupt, drop or misroute the message; and (2) the message is delivered to all legitimate replica roots for the key, despite nodes that may attempt to impersonate a replica root.

Secure routing can be combined with existing security techniques to safely maintain state in a structured p2p overlay. For instance, *self-certifying data* can be stored on the replica roots, or a Byzantine-fault-tolerant replication algorithm [10] can be used to maintain the replicated state. Secure routing guarantees that the replicas are initially placed on legitimate replica roots, and that a lookup message reaches a replica if one exists. Similarly, secure routing can be used to build other secure services, such as maintaining file metadata and user quotas in a distributed storage utility. The details of such services are beyond the scope of this paper.

Implementing the secure routing primitive requires the solution of three problems: securely assigning nodeIds to nodes, securely maintaining the routing tables, and securely forwarding messages. Secure nodeId assignment ensures that an attacker cannot choose the value of nodeIds assigned to the nodes that the attacker controls. Without it, the attacker could arrange to control all replicas of a given object, or to mediate all traffic to and from a victim node.

Secure routing table maintenance ensures that the fraction of faulty nodes that appear in the routing tables of correct nodes does not exceed, on average, the fraction of faulty nodes in the entire overlay. Without it, an attacker could prevent correct message delivery, given only a relatively small number of faulty nodes. Finally, secure message forwarding ensures that at least one copy of a message sent to a key reaches each correct replica root for the key with high probability. These techniques are described in greater detail in Castro et al. [5], but are outlined here.

3.1   Secure nodeId Assignment

In the original design of Pastry, and in many other p2p systems, nodeIds are chosen at random from the space of all identifiers (i.e., for Pastry, a randomly chosen 128-bit number). The problem with such a system is that a node might choose its identifier maliciously. A coalition of malicious nodes that wishes to censor a specific document could easily allocate itself a collection of nodeIds closer to that document's key than any existing nodes in the system. This would allow the coalition to control all the replica roots for that document, giving them the ability to censor the document from the network. Likewise, a coalition could similarly choose nodeIds to maximize its chances of appearing in a victim node's routing tables. If all the outgoing routes from a victim point to nodes controlled by the coalition, then *all* of the victim's access to the overlay network is mediated (and possibly censored) by the coalition. It's necessary, therefore, to guarantee that nodeIds are assigned randomly.

The simplest design to perform secure nodeId assignments is to have a centralized authority that produces cryptographic nodeId certificates, a straightforward extension to standard cryptographic techniques: rather than binding an e-mail address to a public key, these certificates instead bind a nodeId, chosen randomly by the server, to a public key generated by the client machine. The server is only consulted when new nodes join and is otherwise uninvolved in the actions of the p2p system. As such, such a server would have no impact on the scalability or reliability of the p2p overlay.

Regardless, to make such a design work, we must concern ourselves with Sybil attacks [11], wherein a hostile node or coalition of nodes might try to get a large number of nodeIds. Even if those nodeIds are random, a large enough collection of them would still give the attackers disproportionate control over the network. The best solution we currently have to this problem is to moderate the *rate* at which nodeIds are given out. Possible solutions include charging money in return for certificates or requiring some form of external authentication. While it may be possible to use some form of cryptographic puzzles [12], these still allow attackers with large computational resources to get a disproportionate number of nodeIds.

An open problem is assigning random nodeIds without needing a centralized authority. We considered a number of possibilities, including variations on cryptographic puzzles and multi-party bit-commitment schemes. Unfortunately, all such schemes appear to open the possibility that an attacker can rejoin the network, repeatedly, and eventually gain an advantage.

3.2   Robust Routing Primitives

Even with perfect nodeId assignment, when an attacker controls a fraction f of the nodes in the p2p network, we would expect that each entry in every routing table would have a probability of f of pointing to a malicious node. If a desired route consumes h hops, then the odds of a complete route being free of malicious nodes is $(1 - f)^h$. In practice, with Pastry, if 50% of nodes are malicious, then the probability of a route reaching the correct destination ranges between about 50% for overlay networks with 1000 nodes, to about 25% for overlay networks with 1000000 nodes. These odds assume, however, that an adversary cannot increase its probability of being on a given route. However, if the adversary could take advantage of its locality to a given victim node to get more entries in that node's routing table, then the adversary could increase its odds of controlling any given route that uses the victim node.

To prevent locality-based attacks, we introduced a technique called *constrained routing*, which trades off locality vs. performance. Where Pastry normally tries to fill the routing table with "local" nodes (i.e., low latency, high bandwidth) having the necessary nodeIds, a constrained routing table insists on having the closest nodes, in nodeId space, to keys which have the necessary prefix and the same suffix as the node itself.

Next, we would like to increase the odds of a message reaching the desired replica roots beyond the $(1 - f)^h$, described above. To do this, we can attempt multiple, redundant routes from the source to the destination. In Pastry, we do this by sending the message from the source node to all of its neighbors in the p2p overlay. Because nodeIds are random, the neighbors should represent a random, geographically diverse, sampling of the nodes in the p2p overlay. From there, each neighbor node forwards the message toward the target node. If at least one of the neighbors can achieve a successful route, then the message is considered successfully delivered. Based on modeling and corroborated with simulations, we have measured that this operation can be successful with a 99.9% probability, as long as $f \leq 30\%$.

3.3   Ejecting Misbehaving Nodes

Our existing models and simulations show Pastry can route successfully when as many as 30% of the nodes in the p2p overlay network are malicious. However, it would be preferable to have mechanisms to actively *remove* malicious nodes when they are detected. An interesting open problem is how to remove a malicious node from the overlay. While all p2p overlays must have provisions for recovering when a node fails, we would like these mechanisms to be invocable when a node is still alive and functioning. When one node accuses another of cheating, there needs to be some way that it can *prove* its accusation, in order to convince other nodes to eject the malicious node from the network.

While such a proof may be generated at the application layer (see the discussion in Section 4.2), it's not clear how such a proof could be generated at the routing layer. If a node is simply dropping messages with some probability or is pretending that perfectly valid nodes do not exist, such behavior could also be explained by failures in the underlying Internet fabric. Addressing this, in general, is an interesting open problem.

4   Storage

In the following, we describe how applications can securely maintain state while minimizing the use of secure routing for performance reasons. A common approach to reduce reliance on secure routing, when reading an object, is to store *self-certifying data* in the overlay. For example, CFS [13] uses a cryptographic hash of a file's contents as the key during insertion and lookup of the file, and PAST [14] inserts signed content into the overlay. This allows the client to use insecure, more efficient routing to retrieve a copy of a file for reading. When the client receives a copy of the file, it checks its integrity. If the client fails to receive a copy of the file or if the integrity check fails, then the client can use secure routing to retrieve a (hopefully) correct copy or to verify that the file is simply unavailable in the overlay. Of course, it is important to use secure routing for any object insertions because, otherwise, all replicas of the new version may be stored on faulty nodes.

Self-certifying data is a useful solution only when the client knows a hash for the document it's looking for. Even with self-certifying path names [15], or other forms of Merkle hash trees [12] where the user has a secure hash of the document being requested before it is loaded, the user must trust the origin of that secure hash. If the user is using some kind of search engine, cryptographic techniques cannot prevent undesirable documents appearing in the list of search results. And, no amount of cryptographic integrity checking can prevent denial of service attacks.

However, once these problems are considered, the issue of *incentives* emerges as the predominant problem for multiple users sharing their disk space with one another. Why should one computer user allow her disk space and network bandwidth to be used by another user, somewhere else? If possible, she might prefer to contribute nothing for the common good, and consume others' resources without paying them. To prevent such a *tragedy of the commons*, the system must be designed to limit how much remote space one can consume without providing a suitable amount of storage for the use of others.

4.1   Quota Architectures

In the Farsite study [16], the authors noted that hard drives are often relatively empty. As hard drives grow larger and larger, this trend seems likely to continue. If the goal is to create a distributed storage system using this empty space, an interesting fairness issue occurs. A malicious node might choose to claim its storage is full, when it actually has free space. Or, more generally, it might wish to use more storage from remote nodes than it provides for the use of others in the p2p system. Our goal is to create a quota system that guarantees equitable sharing of these resources.

As with nodeId assignment, a simple solution is to require the use of a universally trusted quota authority. However, in the nodeId assignment problem, the nodeId authority need only be consulted when a new node wishes to acquire a nodeId. Otherwise, the nodeId authority need not be involved in the activity of the p2p network. With a centralized quota authority, every request to store a document would require a query to the quota authority. This would create a huge bottleneck as the size of the p2p overlay scaled up.

To distribute this authority, the original design of PAST [14] hypothesized that a smart card would be attached to each node of the network. The smartcards would be responsible for tracking each node's use of remote resources and would issue digitally signed tickets, allowing the local node to prove to a remote node that it was under its quota. Of course, it may not be practical to issue smartcards to millions of nodes. Furthermore, if p2p users can compromise the key material inside their smartcards, they would gain effectively unlimited storage within the p2p overlay.

An alternative architecture would be to ask a node's neighbors to act as *quota managers* on behalf of the node. Collectively, a node's neighbors can act together to endorse a node's request to store a document in the same way as the local smartcard might. The quota information would be distributed and replicated among the neighbors in precisely the same was as any other data in PAST. The main weakness with this scheme is that the quota managers do not have any particular *incentive* to participate in maintaining the quota information. It would be cheaper to track nothing and always endorse a request. Ideally, we would like to create a system where nodes have a natural economic incentive to keep track of each other's disk storage. This is an instance of a problem in distributed algorithm mechanism design [17].

4.2 Distributed Auditing

We can look at disk space as a commodity, and the sharing of disk space in a p2p overlay network as a barter economy of disk space. Nodes trade the use of their local storage for the use of other nodes' remote storage. What mechanisms can be used to implement such an economy? We are currently studying the use of *auditing*. In our system, each node publishes, and digitally signs, two logs: the *local list* of files that the local node is storing on behalf of remote nodes, and the *remote list* of files that other nodes are storing on behalf of the local node. Each entry in the logs contains the name of the remote node responsible and the size of the object being stored. Also, the local list contains the amount of free space available on the local node.

This now creates a nicely balanced system. If a node, A wishes to store a file on B, then B need only read A's logs to make sure that A is using less resources than it is providing.

In general, when B is storing a file on behalf of A, B has an incentive to audit A to make sure that A is "paying" for its storage. If A does not list the file in its remote list, then it's not "paying" anything to B; B should therefore feel free to delete the file. Likewise, A has an incentive to audit B, to make sure that B is actually storing the file, versus quietly dropping the file and perhaps relying on the other replicas to maintain the file. If A queries B for random portions of its file (while first alerting any other replicas that an audit is under way) and B cannot answer, then A can remove B from its remote list; there's no reason for A to pay for service it's not using.

But, what if A wishes to lie to B, feeding it a log that understates its remote storage usage? To address this, we need anonymous communication. Luckily, many architectures are available to do this. In particular, Crowds [18] maps very easily onto a p2p overlay network. So long as audits are timed randomly, where A does not know whether the node checking on it is B or perhaps some other node with which it's done business, then A cannot customize its logs to present itself in a better light to B. Or, if it did, the signed log forms a digital "confession" of its misbehavior when compared with the logs it sends to other nodes.

Of particular interest, once we've created this disk economy, is that we now have mechanisms suitable for applying peer pressure. Fehr and Gachter [19] have shown that people are willing to spend money to eject cheaters from an economy, allowing the economy to quickly reach a stable state, free of cheaters. This auditing system allows for nodes to "spend" disk space simply by increasing the size of the remote list, thereby "paying" for somebody to be ejected. Combining that with any "confessions" from misbehaving nodes, and the system appears to provide strong disincentives to cheaters.

One remaining issue is what we call "cheating chains." It's possible for one node to push its deficits off its own books by conspiring with other nodes. A can claim it is storing a large file on behalf of B. So long as B claims it's storing the file on A, the audit logs check out. If A and B are conspiring together, then no actual files need be stored. Furthermore, imagine that B claims its storing a file on behalf of C, and C claims it's storing a file on behalf of D. Again, when they're all conspiring, nobody need actually store any files, and the only way somebody might detect that A were cheating would be to audit A, then B, then C, and finally D before detecting, perhaps, that D's books were out of balance. The best solution we have to this problem is for all nodes in the p2p overlay to perform *random audits*, choosing a key, at random, and auditing the node with the closest nodeId, comparing that node's logs to the logs of every node with which it claims it's sharing. If every node chooses another node at random, on a regular basis, then every node will be audited with a very high probability. Our current simulations show that the cost of this auditing is quite reasonable, consuming an aggregate bandwidth of only 100-200 bits/second, even in large p2p overlays, although this bandwidth does increase with the size of the logs.

4.3   Other Forms of Fairness

This paper has focused primarily on fair sharing of disk space, but there are many other aspects to fair sharing. In particular, we would like to guarantee fair sharing of network bandwidth. In current p2p networks, nodes can easily find themselves hosting a huge amount of traffic on behalf of other nodes, even while making very little use of the network on their own behalf. With the Kazaa system, in particular, the bandwidth generated by some nodes has been enough to force many universities to use traffic shaping technologies to prevent student machines, running Kazaa, from overwhelming the campus's limited bandwidth to the Internet.

One conceivable solution would require the use of micropayment systems. When a user wishes to query the p2p overlay, that would require spending a token. When the user's machine receives a query, it also receives a token that it can use later. If a given machine has more tokens than it needs, perhaps it would refuse to service any queries. Unfortunately, it's not clear whether any current micropayment schemes scale to support so many nodes making so many small queries of each other. While it might be possible to add these bandwidth tokens onto the audit logs described above, the cost of evaluating whether a token is valid could be significantly greater than simply servicing the request without checking the token's validity.

Another issue, assuming the token scheme can be made to work, would be suitably redesigning file sharing to preserve the availability of data. In effect, we would allow nodes to deliberately fail to service requests because they had no more need for tokens. To compensate for this, data will need to be much more widely replicated than in traditional p2p overlays.

5   Trust in p2p Overlays

P2p systems generally require a remarkable amount of trust from their participants. A node must trust that other nodes implement the same protocols and will respect the goals of the system. In previous sections, we have discussed how mechanisms can be developed to work around a certain percent of the nodes violating the rules, but there are many other aspects where trust issues arise.

Popularity. When documents are requested based on keywords, rather than cryptographically strong hashes, it becomes possible for an adversary to spoof the results. The recording industry, in particular, has apparently been deploying "decoy" music files in p2p networks that have the same name as music files by popular artists. The decoy files have approximately the correct length, but do not contain the desired music. Similar issues have traditionally hurt search engines, where any page with a given search term inside it had an equal chance of appearing highly on the search results. The best solution to the search engine problem, as used by Google's PageRank technology, has been to form a notion of popularity. For Google, pages that are linked from "popular" pages are themselves more popular. An interesting issue is how to add such a notion of popularity into a p2p storage system. It might be possible to extend the audit logs, from Section 4.2, to allow nodes to indicate the value, or lack thereof, of a given file. If users can then rank each others rankings, this could potentially allow the creation of a system comparable to Google's PageRank.

Code. Fundamentally, p2p systems require the user to install a program on their computer that will work with other p2p nodes to implement the system. Since many applications can be built on a generic p2p substrate, an interesting issue becomes how to distribute the code to support these p2p applications. Users should not necessarily trust arbitrary programs, written by third parties, to run on their system. Recently, some commercial p2p systems were discovered to redirect sales commissions from online purchases to the p2p developers [20] and might also sell the use of CPU cycles on a user's computer to third parties, without the user getting any reimbursement [21]. Why should a user arbitrarily grant such privileges to p2p code? In many respects, this same problem occurred with active networks [22], except, in those systems, the computational model could be restricted [23]. For p2p systems, where applications can perform significant computations and consume vast amounts of disk storage, it would appear that a general-purpose mobile code security architecture [24] is necessary.

6   Related Work

P2p systems have been designed in the past to address numerous security concerns, providing anonymous communication, censorship resistance, and other features. Many such systems, including onion routing [25], Crowds [18], Publius [26], and Tangler [27], fundamentally assume a relatively small number of nodes in the network, all well-known to each other. To scale to larger numbers of nodes, where it is not possible to maintain a canonical list of the nodes in the network, additional mechanisms are necessary. Some recent p2p systems have also been developed to support censorship resistance [28] and anonymity [29,30].

Sit and Morris [6] present a framework for performing security analyses of p2p networks. Their adversarial model allows for nodes to generate packets with arbitrary contents, but assumes that nodes cannot intercept arbitrary traffic. They then present a taxonomy of possible attacks. At the routing layer, they identify node lookup, routing table maintenance, and network partitioning / virtualization as security risks. They also discuss issues in higher-level protocols, such as file storage, where nodes may not necessarily maintain the necessary invariants, such as storage replication. Finally, they discuss various classes of denial-of-service attacks, including rapidly joining and leaving the network, or arranging for other nodes to send bulk volumes of data to overload a victim's network connection (i.e., distributed denial of service attacks).

Dingledine *et al.* [31] and Douceur [11] discuss address spoofing attacks. With a large number of potentially malicious nodes in the system and without a trusted central authority to certify node identities, it becomes very difficult to know whether you can trust the claimed identity of somebody with whom you have never before communicated. Dingledine proposes to address this with various schemes, including the use of microcash, that allow nodes to build up *reputations*.

Bellovin [32] identifies a number of issues with Napster and Gnutella. He discusses how difficult it might be to limit Napster and Gnutella use via firewalls, and how they can leak information that users might consider private, such as the search queries they issue to the network. Bellovin also expresses concern over Gnutella's "push" feature, intended to work around firewalls, which might be useful for distributed denial of service attacks. He considers Napster's centralized architecture to be more secure against such attacks, although it requires all users to trust the central server.

7 Conclusions

This paper has surveyed some security issues that occur in peer-to-peer overlay networks, both at the network layer and at the application layer. We have shown how techniques ranging from cryptography through redundant routing to economic methods can be applied to increase the security, fairness, and trust for applications on the p2p network. Because of the diversity of how p2p systems are used, there will be a corresponding diversity of security solutions applied to the problems.

Acknowledgments. This paper draws on conversations, speculations, and joint research with many of my colleagues. I specifically thank Peter Druschel, Antony Rowstron, Ayalvadi Ganesh, and Miguel Castro, with whom I have studied techniques for securing p2p overlay routing, and Tsuen Wan "Johnny" Ngan, with whom I've been working on auditing architectures for p2p file storage. I also thank Tracy Volz for suggestions on this work. This work was supported in part by NSF grant CCR-9985332.

References

1. Ratnasamy, S., Francis, P., Handley, M., Karp, R., Shenker, S.: A scalable content-addressable network. In: Proc. ACM SIGCOMM'01, San Diego, California (2001)
2. Stoica, I., Morris, R., Karger, D., Kaashoek, M.F., Balakrishnan, H.: Chord: A scalable peer-to-peer lookup service for Internet applications. In: Proc. ACM SIGCOMM'01, San Diego, California (2001)

3. Rowstron, A., Druschel, P.: Pastry: Scalable, distributed object location and routing for large-scale peer-to-peer systems. In: Proc. IFIP/ACM Middleware 2001, Heidelberg, Germany (2001)

4. Zhao, B.Y., Kubiatowicz, J.D., Joseph, A.D.: Tapestry: An infrastructure for fault-resilient wide-area location and routing. Technical Report UCB//CSD-01-1141, U. C. Berkeley (2001)

5. Castro, M., Druschel, P., Ganesh, A., Rowstron, A., Wallach, D.S.: Secure routing for structured peer-to-peer overlay networks. In: Proc. OSDI 2002, Boston, Massachusetts (2002) To appear.

6. Sit, E., Morris, R.: Security considerations for peer-to-peer distributed hash tables. In: Proceedings for the 1st International Workshop on Peer-to-Peer Systems (IPTPS '02), Cambridge, Massachusetts (2002)

7. Saroiu, S., Gummadi, K.P., Dunn, R.J., Gribble, S.D., Levy, H.M.: An analysis of internet content delivery systems. In: Proceedings of the 5th Symposium on Operating Systems Design and Implementation (OSDI 2002), Boston, Massachusetts (2002)

8. Rowstron, A., Kermarrec, A.M., Druschel, P., Castro, M.: Scribe: The design of a large-scale event notification infrastructure. In: Proc. NGC'2001, London, UK (2001)

9. Castro, M., Druschel, P., Kermarrec, A.M., Rowstron, A.: SCRIBE: A large-scale and decentralized application-level mul ticast infrastructure. IEEE JSAC **20** (2002)

10. Castro, M., Liskov, B.: Practical byzantine fault tolerance. In: Proceedings of the Third Symposium on Operating Systems Design and Implementation (OSDI'99), New Orleans, Louisiana (1999)

11. Douceur, J.R.: The Sybil attack. In: Proceedings for the 1st International Workshop on Peer-to-Peer Systems (IPTPS '02), Cambridge, Massachusetts (2002)

12. Merkle, R.C.: Secure communications over insecure channels. Communications of the ACM **21** (1978) 294–299

13. Dabek, F., Kaashoek, M.F., Karger, D., Morris, R., Stoica, I.: Wide-area cooperative storage with CFS. In: Proc. ACM SOSP'01, Banff, Canada (2001)

14. Rowstron, A., Druschel, P.: Storage management and caching in PAST, a large-scale, persistent peer-to-peer storage utility. In: Proc. ACM SOSP'01, Banff, Canada (2001)

15. Mazières, D., Kaminsky, M., Kaashoek, M.F., Witchel, E.: Separating key management from file system security. In: Proc. SOSP'99, Kiawah Island, South Carolina (1999)

16. Bolosky, W.J., Douceur, J.R., Ely, D., Theimer, M.: Feasibility of a serverless distributed file system deployed on an existing set of desktop PCs. In: Proc. SIGMETRICS'2000, Santa Clara, California (2000)

17. Feigenbaum, J., Shenker, S.: Distributed algorithmic mechanism design: Recent results and future directions. In: Proceedings of the 6th International Workshop on Discrete Algorithms and Methods for Mobile Computing and Communications (DIAL-M 2002), Atlanta, Georgia (2002) 1–13

18. Reiter, M.K., Rubin, A.D.: Anonymous Web transactions with Crowds. Communications of the ACM **42** (1999) 32–48

19. Fehr, E., Gachter, S.: Altruistic punishment in humans. Nature (2002) 137–140

20. Schwartz, J., Tedeschi, B.: New software quietly diverts sales commissions. New York Times (2002) http://www.nytimes.com/2002/09/27/technology/27FREE.html.

21. Spring, T.: KaZaA sneakware stirs inside PCs. PC World (2002) http://www.cnn.com/2002/TECH/internet/05/07/kazaa.software.idg/index.html.

22. Weatherall, D.: Active network vision and reality: lessons from a capsule-based system. In: Proceedings of the Seventeenth ACM Symposium on Operating System Principles, Kiawah Island, SC (1999) 64–79

23. Hicks, M., Kakkar, P., Moore, J.T., Gunter, C.A., Nettles, S.: PLAN: A Packet Language for Active Networks. In: Proceedings of the Third ACM SIGPLAN International Conference on Functional Programming Languages, ACM (1998) 86–93

24. Wallach, D.S., Balfanz, D., Dean, D., Felten, E.W.: Extensible security architectures for Java. In: Proceedings of the Sixteenth ACM Symposium on Operating System Principles, Saint-Malo, France (1997) 116–128
25. Reed, M.G., Syverson, P.F., Goldschlag, D.M.: Anonymous connections and onion routing. IEEE Journal on Selected Areas in Communication: Special Issue on Copyright and Privacy Protection **16** (1998)
26. Waldman, M., Rubin, A.D., Cranor, L.F.: Publius: A robust, tamper-evident, censorship-resistant, web publishing system. In: Proc. 9th USENIX Security Symposium, Denver, Colorado (2000) 59–72
27. Waldman, M., Mazires, D.: Tangler: A censorship resistant publishing system based on document entanglements. In: 8th ACM Conference on Computer and Communcation Security (CCS-8), Philadelphia, Pennsylvania (2001)
28. Hazel, S., Wiley, B.: Achord: A variant of the Chord lookup service for use in censorship resistant peer-to-peer. In: Proceedings for the 1st International Workshop on Peer-to-Peer Systems (IPTPS '02), Cambridge, Massachusetts (2002)
29. Serjantov, A.: Anonymizing censorship resistant systems. In: Proceedings for the 1st International Workshop on Peer-to-Peer Systems (IPTPS '02), Cambridge, Massachusetts (2002)
30. Freedman, M.J., Sit, E., Cates, J., Morris, R.: Tarzan: A peer-to-peer anonymizing network layer. In: Proceedings for the 1st International Workshop on Peer-to-Peer Systems (IPTPS '02), Cambridge, Massachusetts (2002)
31. Dingledine, R., Freedman, M.J., Molnar, D.: Accountability measures for peer-to-peer systems. In: Peer-to-Peer: Harnessing the Power of Disruptive Technologies, O'Reilly and Associates (2000)
32. Bellovin, S.: Security aspects of Napster and Gnutella. In: 2001 Usenix Annual Technical Conference, Boston, Massachusetts (2001) Invited talk.

Autonomous Nodes and Distributed Mechanisms*

John C. Mitchell and Vanessa Teague

Stanford University, Stanford CA 94305, USA,
{mitchell,vteague}@cs.stanford.edu

Abstract. We extend distributed algorithmic mechanism design by considering a new model that allows autonomous nodes executing a distributed mechanism to strategically deviate from the prescribed protocol. Our goal is to motivate agents to contribute to a global objective and resist disruption by a limited number of malicious irrational agents, augmenting market incentives with cryptographic primitives to make certain forms of behavior computationally infeasible. Several techniques for distributing market computation among autonomous agents are illustrated using a marginal cost mechanism for multicast cost sharing from [3].

1 Introduction

Standard distributed algorithmic mechanism design [1,2,3] uses a model that separates the computational entities implementing the algorithm from the strategic entities that provide its inputs. In the standard model, there may be several strategic agents who reside at each computational node in the network. The agents provide some input to the node, possibly lying, and the node then faithfully executes the algorithmic mechanism. This model reflects the most important characteristics of market situations, such as satellite television with tamper-resistant receivers in customer homes, in which the mechanism designer has complete control over the hardware and software used to implement the mechanism. However, the standard model omits an important aspect of user behavior in systems such as network routing in which autonomously administered routers may be configured in complex ways to serve the business objectives of their owners. In Internet routing, a system administrator may choose to modify router software if this improves local performance, regardless of whether the modification deviates from published Internet routing standards. Further, malicious or careless administrators may do so in ways that are not even beneficial to themselves (by standard measures). In this paper, we consider the consequences of employing hardware or software that is controlled by strategic agents. We assume that strategic agents control the computation at each local node that implements part

---

* This work was supported by the DoD University Research Initiative (URI) program administered by the Office of Naval Research under Grant N00014-01-1-0795 and also ONR MURI grant N00014-97-1-0505, Semantic Consistency in Information Exchange.

M. Okada et al. (Eds.): ISSS 2002, LNCS 2609, pp. 58–83, 2003.

of a distributed algorithmic mechanism. For simplicity, and to aid comparison between our "autonomous nodes " model and standard distributed algorithmic mechanism design, we investigate multicast cost sharing, a traditional problem with known "tamper-proof nodes " distributed solutions [3].

We use a network model that includes mostly selfish agents with some completely honest and a few malicious ones. We consider this a reasonable model for many Internet applications, possibly closer to reality than either the trusting distributed algorithmic mechanism design view or the security view that emphasizes worst-case scenarios. The vast majority of nodes on the Internet today are corporations that make rational decisions designed to maximize their profits. There are a few benevolent nodes (such as universities or government-subsidized sites) and a small number of actively malicious ones.

We focus on the example of the marginal cost mechanism for multicast cost sharing described by Feigenbaum et al. [3]. This mechanism shares the cost of a multicast transmission, such as a movie, among a tree of participating nodes. We may think of their distributed algorithm as being run by tamper-proof routers or set-top boxes. We will refer to this protocol as "the FPS protocol."

If the FPS protocol is implemented naively in the new model where the nodes can implement the algorithm of their choice, then selfish agents can benefit from cheats that are not possible in the model where the nodes must execute the algorithm correctly. They can improve their welfare by telling different lies at different steps in the protocol, lying about what they have received from others or paying the incorrect amount at the end.

The multicast model includes a content provider that initiates the transmission and receives payments from each agent. This provides a convenient central point for providing further economic motivations to the agents. One method we use adds extra authentication to the protocol to allow each agent to "prove" that it behaved honestly. The content provider audits every agent with some probability and fines those who cannot produce a "proof". The content provider's computational burden and communication cost can be made constant by increasing the size of the fines with the size of the network. It must do a small number of local checks of one agent at a time. In other applications, where payments may not all reach a central point, we expect the same idea to apply in a more distributed fashion. We present two slightly different authenticated protocols, each with different messages and incentives. The first one is a lighter protocol whose main property is that honesty is an equilibrium – no agent is motivated to deviate from it if it believes that all the others will execute it correctly. Furthermore, as long as agents are selfish and keep to the protocol when there isn't a strictly better option, all agents execute the protocol correctly. The second protocol contains an additional signed message and is much stronger: we show that keeping to it is strictly more profitable than any alternative.

We examine security by introducing a malicious agent into the system and considering how much it can cause the mechanism to fall below the social optimum. We are also interested in how much such attacks cost, but do not expect the malicious agent to be rational. We show that the FPS scheme in its original model is quite secure against attack by a single agent, but that an unauthenticated implementation is not at all secure in the model where nodes can deviate from the protocol at will. We then show that our strongest authenticated scheme is almost as secure as forbidding the agents to deviate from the protocol, and that the presence of malicious nodes does not cause selfish ones to wish to deviate from the protocol. The only requirement is that all the malicious node's neighbors are honest.

In the next section we describe related work, then give some brief game theory background and an overview of the distributed algorithmic mechanism of [3]. In section 3.1 we describe our model which dispenses with the assumption that the nodes executing the protocol can be trusted to do so correctly. In the following section we give some examples that show that the new model allows new cheating opportunities that can be exploited if we implement the mechanism naively. In section 4 we present and analyze the two authenticated versions of the protocol. In the final section we investigate the security properties of these schemes.

2   Background and Related Work

Algorithmic mechanism design was introduced by Nisan and Ronen in [8]. This involves applying ideas from Game Theory (specifically, mechanism design) to solve algorithmic and network problems. They assume a central mechanism administrator that can communicate freely with the nodes.

A different computational implementation of mechanism design, based on secure function evaluation, is presented in [7]. The mechanism is administered by two agents who are assumed not to collude.

Distributed algorithmic mechanisms are described in [1], [2] and [3]. The mechanism is administered by the network nodes themselves. Several agents inhabit each network node, and may lie to the node, but the network nodes always implement their part of the distributed algorithm correctly. We aim to extend their ideas to the case where the nodes are strategic (aiming to maximize their resident user's profit) and may implement any computationally feasible algorithm.

Feigenbaum et al. ([3]) provide and analyze two distributed mechanisms for multicast cost sharing. We will concentrate on the Marginal Cost Pricing mechanism, first presented in [6]. It is one of a class of mechanisms known as VCG mechanisms that have many desirable properties, including that an agent maximizes its welfare by telling the truth. We first review some standard definitions and results from game theory, then describe the centralized algorithm and distributed scheme from [3].

2.1   Game Theory Background

Briefly, an agent has a *dominant strategy* if it has one strategy that is a best response to all possible behaviors of others. A mechanism is *strategyproof* if it is a dominant strategy to tell the truth. More detailed background is contained in [8] and [9].

2.2 Feigenbaum et al.'s Scheme

This section gives a much-simplified description of the distributed mechanism of [3], in the special case that will be relevant for the rest of this paper.

We are interested in distributing a multicast transmission from a source node to the agents on a network. The network is a tree consisting of a set of nodes and a set of links, in which one agent resides at each node. Each link has a cost known to the nodes at each end. For any set of receivers define the *multicast tree* as the minimal subtree required to reach all those receivers. The cost of sending the transmission to a set of receivers is the sum of the costs of the links in the multicast tree.

Each agent derives some utility from receiving the transmission. The global benefit gained is the sum of the utilities of the receiving agents. We define the *net worth* to be the difference between global benefit and incurred link cost. This is the net benefit of sending the transmission along the multicast tree.

A *mechanism* takes as input a description of the network (including link costs) and a stated utility from each agent. The mechanism's outcome is a set of recipients and a payment vector stating how much each agent should pay the content provider. We assume that each agent may lie to the mechanism about its utility and that each agent seeks to maximize its utility minus its payment.

The mechanism design problem is to find a mechanism with the following two properties:

- Every agent's dominant strategy is to report its true utility to the mechanism (*i.e.* it maximizes its true utility minus payment by doing so).
- The recipient set selected by the mechanism maximizes net worth.

The Marginal Cost Pricing Mechanism is a mechanism for solving this problem. The centralized scheme for implementing it is described below. The distributed scheme (described afterwards) is a distributed algorithm for implementing the centralized scheme.

The centralized scheme. The centralized scheme consists of the following steps:

1. Each agent reports its utility to the mechanism.
2. The mechanism computes which agents receive the transmission.
3. The mechanism computes a payment for each agent.

Call a recipient set *efficient* if it maximizes net worth. In step 2, the mechanism selects the largest efficient set, based on stated utilities, and sends the transmission to those agents. The largest efficient set exists because the union of any two efficient sets is itself an efficient set.

To compute payments in step 3, the mechanism first computes for each subtree how much the total agent utility derived exceeds the link cost incurred. This quantity is called the welfare of the subtree. Let u^i be agent i's utility and c^i be the cost of the link joining the node where i resides to its parent in the tree.

Definition 1. *The* welfare W^i *of the subtree rooted at the node where i resides is:*

$$W^i = u^i + \left(\sum_{\substack{j \text{ resides at a} \\ \text{child of } i\text{'s node} \\ \text{and } W^j \geq 0}} W^j \right) - c^i \tag{1}$$

Let the minimum welfare on any path between i's node and the root (inclusive) be A^i. If $A^i < 0$ then agent i does not receive the transmission. Otherwise, it receives it and pays:

$$pay^i = \max(0, u^i - A^i) \tag{2}$$

It is proved in [3] that agent i's net benefit is exactly the marginal contribution to the overall welfare provided by its having a nonzero valuation for the transmission. For a proof that the mechanism is strategyproof, see [6].

The distributed scheme. In [3], there is a distributed algorithm for implementing the mechanism described above. First, each agent reports its utility to its node. The nodes then execute a two-pass algorithm at the end of which every node knows whether its resident agent receives the transmission and how much the agent has to pay for it. The payments and recipient set are the same as in the centralized scheme.

The first pass computes all of the W^i bottom-up. Every node sends its welfare to its parent. The parent calculates its welfare using its children's welfares and equation 1.

The second pass is for computing, for each node, the minimum welfare between that node and the root. This can easily be computed top-down: suppose a node has resident agent i and it knows the minimum welfare $A^{\text{parent}(i)}$ of any node between its parent and the root. Then the minimum welfare on any path between i's node and the root is given by:

$$A^i = \min(A^{\text{parent}(i)}, W^i) \tag{3}$$

Payment is a function of A^i and utility u^i, given by equation 2.

This is an efficient solution when the nodes are honest. In the next section we allow the nodes themselves to be strategic, their interests aligned with those of their resident agent. Our proofs of correctness rely on checking equations 1, 2 and 3.

3   Cheating in a Different Network Model

3.1   The Network Model

In many settings where distributed algorithms are run, the strategic agents have control over the computers that are implementing the algorithm. Television viewers may try to modify the set-top boxes in their homes, or the administrators of autonomous computers on a network may alter the networking software for their own ends. Then it is no longer reasonable to assume that each agent reports its utility to its node which then runs the correct algorithm—an agent might alter its node's behavior to improve its own welfare beyond what it could achieve by simply reporting a utility to it.

For the rest of this paper we will identify the game-theoretic agents with their nodes. That is, each node is an agent that has complete control over the messages it sends and receives. It can elect to implement the algorithm as it is instructed by the mechanism designer, or it can implement any other computationally feasible algorithm and send whatever messages it chooses. We need to design an algorithm so that each strategic node's best strategy is to implement the algorithm as instructed.

We will refer to the centralized game-theoretic model used in the first part of section 2.2 as the game theory model, the distributed model where nodes always implement the specified algorithm as the tamper-proof nodes model (this is the model employed in [3] and the second part of section 2.2), and our new model of selfish nodes as the autonomous nodes model.

In this paper we consider just the example of multicast cost sharing presented in [3]. Each node derives some utility from receiving the transmission, which it has to pay for, and its aim is to maximize utility minus price. We will show that in this model a naive implementation of the FPS protocol is susceptible to cheating, and propose authenticated versions that produce the right outcome among selfish agents.

The content provider is also the administrator of the mechanism. This entity receives payments and provides the transmission. It also enforces some of the incentives of the mechanism, including levying fines and providing rewards. Our aim is to design a scheme with minimal communication between the content provider and the nodes.

The next section contains one scenario in which a user can benefit by lying under the autonomous nodes model. This does not contradict the result in [3] that their distributed game is strategyproof. It is based on the observation that the autonomous nodes model allows new ways of cheating that are not possible the tamper-proof nodes model. Two other examples are contained in Appendix A.

3.2   Some Examples of Agents Behaving Badly

In this example an agent sends one welfare value to its parent node, then sends a *different* value to its child node. It succeeds in paying one unit less than it should for the transmission and tricking its child into paying one extra.

In order for a deception to be successful, every other agent in the tree must receive a consistent set of messages. For the cheating example shown, we also provide the honest agents' perspective, showing that in each case for each honest agent there is a set of utilities that produces exactly the set of messages received by that agent during the cheat.

3.3   Wrongfully Getting the Transmission while Others Pay Extra

The true state of the network is shown in Figure 1. Node 0 is the root of the distribution tree and we don't consider its payments in this example. If all agents behave truthfully, then all agents receive the transmission, agent 1 pays 1 and agent 2 pays 6 (see equation 2).

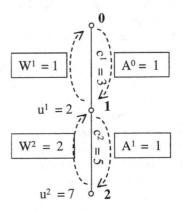

Fig. 1. The truth. $pay^1 = 1$ and $pay^2 = 6$.

Figure 2 shows a successful cheat by agent 1, which effectively lies to node 0 about its child's utility. Again both agents receive the transmission, but now honest agent 2 pays 7 (believing that this is what it owes) while agent 1 pays nothing. We assume that agent 2 does not communicate directly with node 0, and that agent 2 does not see how much agent 1 pays. The cheat succeeds because each of the honest agents has a consistent view of the network, shown in figures 3 (node 0's view) and 4 (node 2's view).

This attack is possible because agent 1 can lie to the source node about both its utility and the utility of agent 2. In the centralized game, it could lie about its own utility but not about another's.

This examples shows that if agents are not forced to implement the FPS algorithm then it is not a dominant strategy for them to do so faithfully with their true utility as input. A rational agent can sometimes gain a greater payoff by some other strategy not based on the FPS algorithm at all. The main ways

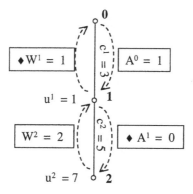

Fig. 2. The cheat. Agent 1 pays 0 and agent 2 pays 7.

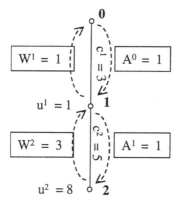

Fig. 3. View of agent 0. $pay^1 = 0$ and $pay^2 = 7$

to cheat are to send inconsistent messages up and down the tree and to pay an incorrect amount.

Appendix A contains two other examples of cheating. In the first, an agent receives the transmission for free even though its subtree's welfare is negative. In the second, an agent pays less than it ought to. These examples demonstrate that in order to check that an agent isn't cheating, it is necessary to check at least the agent's received messages, the welfare it sent and its payment.

Proposition 1. *In order to check whether a given agent has paid the correct amount, it is necessary to check the consistency of that agent's payment, the welfare value that it sent to its parent, and all the messages that it received from its children and parent.*

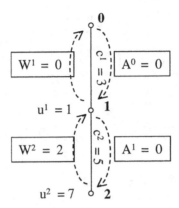

Fig. 4. View of agent 2. $pay^1 = 1$ and $pay^2 = 7$.

4   Improvements

We introduce the threat of auditing by the content provider to motivate rational agents to execute the protocol. In both the protocols described below, each agent collects enough signed messages during the protocol to "prove" that it didn't cheat (in the second protocol, some of this "proof" is stored at the agent's children). Proposition 1 shows the minimum that the content provider must check for each agent. At the end of the protocol, the content provider audits every agent with some probability which was common knowledge from the beginning. It imposes a large fine on those who can't prove that they were honest. We make the fine large enough that even a small probability of incurring it motivates risk-neutral rational agents to execute the algorithm correctly, including carrying out some checks on others' messages.

The first protocol (protocol A) is designed for agents that would deviate from the protocol only if it strictly benefitted them. We prove that honesty is an equilibrium, *i.e.* that if each agent assumes that all the others will be honest, it maximizes its welfare by implementing the protocol correctly. We then show the stronger result that if each agent assumes that all the others only deviate from the protocol in ways that strictly improve their welfare, it maximizes its welfare by implementing the protocol correctly. We also prove that an agent is only fined if it has actually cheated, so honest agents never pay more than their utility.

The second protocol (protocol B) adds an extra message and some extra incentives to the first one. This protocol works correctly for any welfare-maximizing agents, because following it is strictly better than diverging from it in any computationally feasible way.

Both protocols have the property that when all the agents are rational there should be no cheating. In both cases an agent may cause the protocol to abort if it detects another cheating, in which case no transmission is sent and the net worth is zero. This may seem to be an unduly harsh response, but we assume that the protocol could be restarted, possibly after excluding the (irrational) node that had caused the problem. However, all the following analysis is for one run of the protocol. A session number or timestamp would be needed for multiple runs.

The issue of how to guarantee that the transmission actually goes to the correct set of recipients is also beyond the scope of our discussion. We also don't consider collusion among agents, because the underlying Marginal Cost Pricing mechanism does not prevent collusion. See [1] for more on the issue of collusion.

4.1   Model of the Agents and Authentication

We model four different types of agents. Reporting of other agents' cheats is considered part of executing the protocol. The agents are:

honest: Always follows the protocol correctly.

selfish-but-agreeable: Maximizes its own welfare. Deviates from the protocol only if it strictly improves its welfare.

selfish-and-annoying: Maximizes its own welfare. Has no preference for following the protocol unless that is the only action that maximizes its welfare.

malicious: May deviate arbitrarily from the protocol. Isn't deterred by fines.

Selfish-but-agreeable is a reasonable model for many applications, because most users of a device (or software) that implemented the desired algorithm would bother meddling with the device only if doing so was beneficial.

In this section we will include only honest and selfish agents. We consider security issues in section 5 by adding malicious agents.

We assume an idealized version of digital authentication. Informally, we assume a public key infrastructure in which the content provider knows everyone's public key and everyone knows their children's, parent's and grandparent's public keys. The idealized signatures have the following properties (based on those in [5])

- Signed messages sent by an honest agent to a parent, child or grandchild cannot be altered or manufactured by others.
- Any receiver can identify the agent that originated a signed message, provided the originator is honest and is a parent, child or grandparent of the recipient.
- Signed messages sent by an honest agent to the content provider cannot be altered or manufactured by others.
- The content provider can identify the agent that originated a signed message, provided the originator is honest.

The assumptions about agents are expressed only in terms of honest agents' properties because a non-honest agent could release its private signing key to others. We will show that both types of selfish agent will keep their keys secret given our incentives, so the two conditions stated above will apply to their signatures also.

We write $sig_i(m)$ to mean the message m signed with the private key of agent i, and $sig_i((m_1, m_2))$ to mean the messages m_1 and m_2 concatenated and signed by i.

The content provider knows the network topology, all the network costs and what payments were received from what nodes. It has the authority to impose large fines on the participants and enough money to offer them significant rewards. More specifically, we assume there is a value C greater than the amount an agent can gain by cheating. This could be any amount greater than the maximum utility that any agent derives from receiving the transmission. The provider has some way to charge this amount, or multiples of this amount, as a fine. For example it could insist that every participant deposits some multiple of C as a bond before joining the network (as in [4]).

4.2   An Authenticated Protocol (Protocol A)

Protocol Description. Assume every node knows its parent, all of its children and the costs of the network links adjacent to itself. We have already assumed that each node can recognize the signatures of its children, parent and grandparent. If some child fails to respond it will notice. All other information must be gained by receiving messages.

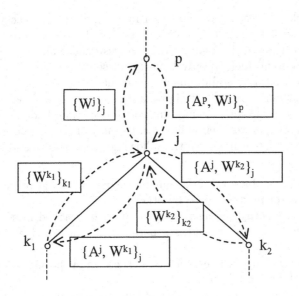

Fig. 5. Protocol A, messages to and from j

See Figure 5 for a diagram of protocol A. The idea is that at the end of this protocol each agent should be able to "prove" to the content provider that it paid the correct amount. The bottom-up pass is identical to the one in section 2.2, except that agents sign the welfare that they send up. In the top down pass, each agent j sends to each child k:

$$sig_j(A^j, W^k)$$

The first part of this signed message is just the message sent in the top-down pass of the protocol in 2.2. The second part provides k with a verification of the welfare value that k itself sent up the tree in the first pass.

At the end of the first pass each node checks that it has received a correctly signed message of the correct form from all of its children. In the second pass, it similarly checks its parent's message. If any agent detects a protocol violation by another, such as a signature that doesn't verify or a failure to send a message of the correct form, it immediately notifies the content provider and the protocol is stopped.

Recall that C is a quantity greater than the amount an agent could gain by cheating. If an agent can provide two conflicting messages both signed by another (such as two different signed welfares) and it reports this, then the reporting agent receives a reward C and the agent that signed two conflicting messages receives a penalty C. If an agent releases its private signing key (which is a protocol violation) then an honest agent is allowed to use that key to sign two conflicting messages, claim the reward and cause the agent that released its key to be fined.

At the end of this protocol each agent has a "proof" that it paid the correct amount, consisting of the messages it received during the protocol (see Definition 2). The content provider may audit each proof with some probability q (which is common knowledge) at the end of the protocol and if an agent fails to produce the appropriate proof that agent is fined C/q.

Definition 2. *A   proof of paying $Proof_j$ for node j with parent p is a pair consisting of the signed messages that j received during the protocol.*

$$Proof_j = \langle sig_p(A^p, W^j), \{sig_{k_1}(W^{k_1}), \dots, sig_{k_l}(W^{k_l})\}\rangle$$

where $k_1, \dots, k_l$ are all j's children.

A proof of paying $Proof_j$ determines what j should pay, because it allows the content provider to compute j's utility u^j and contains a record of the minimum welfare on the path from j to the root. Hence it makes sense to check whether j did actually pay the amount computed from the proof. A proof of paying is correct if the agent chose a valid welfare (one that corresponded to a non-negative utility) and it actually paid the amount it should have paid.

Definition 3. *The utility derived from a proof of paying $Proof_j$ is $u^j = c^j + W^j - \sum_{h=1}^{l} W^{k_h}$. The proof $Proof_j$ is correct if $u^j \geq 0$ and j paid*

$$pay^j = \begin{cases} 0 & \text{if } \min(W^j, A^p) < 0 \\ \max(0, u^j - \min(W^j, A^p)) & \text{otherwise} \end{cases}$$

This corresponds to satisfying equations 1 and 2.

Our content provider is not like the game-theoretic central authority that inputs everyone's utility and computes the outcome. Each audit of each agent uses only local information from one agent's proof of paying. If the content provider is able to impose large fines then it can set its probability of auditing very low, meaning that it has to audit very few if any agents in each run of the protocol. Hence there can be very little communication between the content provider and the agents.

Why selfish agents' signatures are reliable. An agent's expected welfare decreases if it releases its private signing key, since another agent might use the key to sign conflicting messages, then report these conflicting messages to the content distributor, collect the reward C and cause the agent that released its private signing key to be fined C. Since receiving a reward C is greater than any benefit gained by cheating, any agent that learnt another's signing key would report it, and the agent whose key was revealed would lose more than it could gain by cheating.

Why honesty is an equilibrium. We will show that if every other agent is honest, a single selfish agent maximizes its welfare by executing the protocol correctly also.

Suppose initially that the content provider's checking probability is 1, *i.e.* all nodes must always send in their proof of paying at the end of the protocol. In this case it is easy to show by case analysis that a node with honest ancestors and children cannot gain by cheating.

Lemma 1. *Let j be a node with parent p and children $k_1, \ldots, k_l$. Suppose all nodes other than j are honest. Assume that the content provider checks every node with probability 1 and that its fines are more than j could gain by cheating. Then j's welfare is maximized by implementing the protocol correctly with its true utility.*

Proof. Since j's neighbors are honest we can assume that j will not receive any contradictory signed messages, forged signatures, or other protocol violations that it would be obliged to report to the content provider. It cannot benefit by falsely reporting anyone to the content provider because it cannot fabricate a pair of contradictory signed messages and any other kind of violation stops the protocol and gives j a welfare of zero. If j sends two contradictory signed messages to a neighbor, then the neighbor will report it and j will receive a fine greater than the money it could have made by cheating. If it fails to send any message for some part of the protocol, the protocol will time out or fail to terminate and j will receive a welfare of zero. Hence j maximizes its payoff by sending exactly one message for each of the three classes of message it is supposed to send in the protocol, namely W^j to its parent and $W^{k_1}, \ldots, W^{k_l}$ and A^j to its children. It also chooses a payment pay^j at the end of the communication steps. We consider each of these messages in turn and show that j cannot benefit by lying about them.

A^j: This message is sent down the tree and no other message is received from j's children afterwards. It consequently doesn't affect $Proof_j$ or whether j receives the transmission, so j does not benefit by lying about it.

$W^{k_1}, \ldots, W^{k_l}$: By the same argument, j has no motive to lie about these either.

W^j and pay^j: Choosing a value of W^j fixes j's utility given its children's welfares and its uplink cost (by the formula in definition 3). Since all the other agents in the tree are honest, the value of A that j receives from its parent is the same as the value it would have received in a correct execution of the protocol in which it sent the same value of W^j. Likewise, since j's parent is honest, $Proof_j$ contains exactly the value of W^j that j sent. The content provider will ensure that $Proof_j$ is correct, namely that the signed values in it are consistent with j's payment. Therefore j's payment is fixed by $Proof_j$ (via the formula in definition 3) to be exactly the amount it would have paid in a correct execution of the protocol with utility as given in definition 3.

This shows that j maximizes its welfare by executing the protocol correctly with some utility. Since truth-telling is a dominant strategy when the protocol is executed correctly by everyone, j maximizes its welfare by using its true utility.
$\Diamond$

Lemma 2. *Let j be a node with parent p and children $k_1, \ldots, k_l$. Suppose all nodes other than j are honest. Assume that the content provider checks every node with probability q and that its fines are more than $1/q$ times what j could gain by cheating. Then j's expected welfare is maximized by implementing the protocol correctly with its true utility.*

Proof. By an argument similar to the proof of lemma 1, if j has a correct proof of checking $Proof_j$ at the end of the protocol then its welfare is no greater than it would have been by correctly executing the protocol with its true utility. If it doesn't have a correct proof of checking at the end then its expected welfare is negative because the auditor's fine is so high. Hence its best strategy is to execute the protocol correctly and ensure a correct proof of checking. By the strategyproofness of the underlying mechanism, it should choose its true utility.
$\Diamond$

Equilibrium is an important and often-studied concept in game theory. However, we would like show the stronger condition that truth telling is still a dominant strategy. This is not quite the case, but if it is common knowledge that all agents are restricted to being selfish-but-lazy then it is a best strategy to follow the protocol truthfully.

Why agents follow the protocol if others are only selfishly dishonest.
We show that an agent maximizes its payoff by being truthful, assuming that all the others are honest or selfish-but-agreeable.

The protocol is designed so that if some agent deviates from the protocol then any other agent that detects this will be motivated to report it, either to receive the reward or to avoid being fined for the lack of a correct proof of paying. Every cheat not detectable by others risks a fine from the content provider. Hence no agent is motivated to deviate from the protocol.

We will show first that honest agents do not incur fines, so the protocol still satisfies the voluntary participation constraint.

Lemma 3. *If an agent j has a chance of being fined at the end of the protocol, then j failed to follow the protocol.*

Proof. The agent is fined either for not having a correct proof of paying or because another agent a could produce two contradictory messages signed by j. In the first case, j has clearly not followed the protocol since it was supposed to report any incorrect signatures or missing or badly formed messages as soon as it received them. If it received a complete set of well-formed, correctly signed messages, then this always constitutes a correct proof of paying for some payment pay^j given by definition 3. In the second case, j either signed two contradictory messages or released its private key (which are certainly protocol violations), or another agent succeeded in forging j's signature, which we assume is impossible. $\Diamond$

Corollary 1. *An agent cannot gain a reward when no other agent cheated.*

Lemma 4. *If the protocol completes without any agent reporting a failure, then for each agent j there is exactly one correct proof of paying that j can produce.*

Proof. An agent with no correct proof risks being fined, so as long as the expected value of the fine is greater than the maximum profit it could make by cheating, the node will ensure that it has at least one correct proof.

An agent with two or more different proofs all consistent with its payment must have at least two contradictory signatures from some other agent. Therefore, as long as the reward for reporting contradictory signed messages is greater than the maximum profit it could make by cheating, the agent will report it and take the reward rather than continuing with the protocol. $\Diamond$

Lemma 5. *Agents are not motivated to send false messages down the tree.*

Proof. The messages that an agent sends down the tree to not affect its proof of paying and consequently don't alter how much it has to pay. Nor do they affect whether the agent gets the transmission, since no information from these messages is transmitted back to the source. $\Diamond$

An agent also has no motive for sending the correct values down the tree, which is why we allow only selfish-but-agreeable agents.

Lemma 6. *If the other agents deviate are selfish-but-agreeable, and if the protocol completes without any agent reporting a failure, then an agent j with one correct proof of checking $Proof_j$ has the same welfare at the end of the protocol as it would have had if it had executed the protocol honestly with utility u^j as derived from $Proof_j$.*

Proof. By lemma 5 (and induction down the tree) we can assume that the signed values of A and W^j that j receives are the true ones that were correctly calculated from the welfares sent up the tree. By lemma 4 and the definition of correctness, each welfare value sent up the tree must have been consistent with some valid (*i.e.* non-negative) utility. Therefore the value that the auditor computes for j to pay based on *Proof$_j$* is exactly what it would have paid had it been honest, given the utilities of the agents above and below it as derived from their proofs.
$\diamondsuit$

Theorem 1. *Assuming it is common knowledge that all agents are honest or selfish-but-agreeable, each agent implements Protocol A correctly with its true utility.*

Proof. If the protocol does not complete, all agents who have not reported another's cheating receive a welfare of zero. Reporting another agent for cheating is always more profitable than cheating, but only if the report is true (by Corollary 1). Hence agents truthfully report a protocol failure. By lemma 4, if there is no protocol failure then each agent has only one proof of checking and by lemma 6, each agent has the same welfare as it would have if it had executed the protocol honestly with whatever utility the proof implies. Since it's a best strategy to use the true utility in the underlying mechanism, it is a best strategy to use the true utility in this scheme also. $\diamondsuit$

This result would not be true if we included malicious or selfish-and-annoying nodes. If an agent cheats without benefiting itself, such as by sending the wrong messages down the tree, then another agent (even a selfish-but-agreeable one) can still profit by lying.

4.3   A Stronger Authenticated Protocol (Protocol B)

In the previous section we had to make the assumption that agents would deviate from the protocol only if it strictly benefited them to do so. In this section we add an extra message and an extra check to the protocol to ensure that implementing it correctly (with some utility) is strictly better than any kind of cheating. This means the protocol can withstand selfish-but-annoying agents. The main difference is that the protocol ensures that agents send the correct messages down the tree, rather than relying on the fact that an agent's downward messages don't affect its own welfare.

Protocol Description. Figure 6 shows a diagram of protocol B. This protocol is very similar to protocol A, except that the top-down pass has one additional message: each node j with parent p sends to each child k not only $sig_j(A^j, W^k)$ but also $sig_p(A^p, W^j)$, which is the message that it would have received from its parent in protocol A. This is enough to "prove" to j's child (and to the auditor) that j computed A^j correctly (satisfying equation 3). We will call this pair of

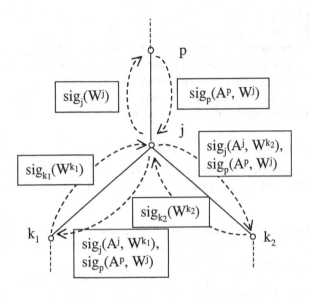

Fig. 6. Protocol B, messages to and from j

messages k's *proof of parent* and denote it by $ParentProof_k$. Child node k checks the signatures on this proof and checks that the values satisfy equation 3.

We retain the same checking, fines and rewards as for protocol A (including the fine for signing contradictory messages) and add one: when the content provider checks $Proof_j$ it also chooses one of j's children k at random and requests $ParentProof_k$. It checks that the signatures and value of A^j are correct and that the value of W^k is the same as that in $Proof_j$. If all of these checks succeed, j receives a bonus of 1. If not, k is fined an amount Cl/q, where l is the number of children.

Why Rational Agents Follow the Protocol

Lemma 7. *If an agent j has a chance of being fined at the end of the protocol, then j failed to follow the protocol.*

Proof. Same as Lemma 3   ◇

Corollary 2. *No agent can gain a reward when no other agent has cheated.*

Lemma 8. *For each step of the protocol, each agent sends at most one message.*

Proof. Direct from the fine for signing contradictory messages and the reward for the agent who reports it.   ◇

Lemma 9. *If the protocol completes without any agent reporting a failure, then for each agent i there is exactly one correct proof of paying and exactly one correct proof of parent that i can produce.*

Proof. Similar to Lemma 4. $\Diamond$

Lemma 10. *Sending the correct messages down the tree is strictly more profitable than sending incorrect ones.*

"Correct" means consistent with the values received from the agent's parent and children.

Proof. Consider agent j with child k and parent p. By lemma 9 either the protocol will be interrupted by someone reporting cheating, or k will receive a correct proof of parent. If the protocol is interrupted by someone other than j then j gets a welfare of at most zero. So suppose k receives a correct proof of parent. By lemma 8, j sent each part of this proof at most once. It is impossible for j or k to alter the message received from p, hence j must have calculated A^j correctly. By lemma 8 again, k sent only one welfare value up the tree. Since j cannot forge k's signature, and since the definition of correctness for proofs of parent includes consistency with the parent's proof of paying, j must have sent the correct value of W^k down the tree. In this case j has positive expected welfare because there is some chance that it will be audited and receive the small bonus for having given its child a correct proof of parent. Hence it is strictly better for j to send the correct messages down the tree than any incorrect ones. $\Diamond$

Lemma 11. *Suppose the protocol completes without any agent reporting a failure and that agent j with child k has one correct proof of checking $Proof_j$ which implies a utility of u^j. Then j has the same welfare at the end of the protocol as it would have had if it had executed the protocol honestly with utility u^j, except possibly for the extra bonus for having provided a correct proof of parent to k, which is independent of u^j.*

Proof. Similar to lemma 6, using lemma 10. $\Diamond$

Theorem 2. *Assuming it is common knowledge that all agents are honest, selfish-but-agreeable or selfish-and-annoying, each agent implements Protocol B correctly with its true utility.*

Proof. Similar to Theorem 1. $\Diamond$

5 Security Perspective

We are interested in designing systems which assume that most agents are selfish but are still robust against occasional malicious nodes. Useful properties to consider include reducing the extent to which the malicious node(s) can reduce the group welfare, increasing the cost of being malicious and making sure that other nodes continue to behave correctly in the presence of malicious ones.

In this section we consider what can be achieved by an adversary trying to reduce the group welfare while unconcerned about its own. In a traditional security model we would assume that this adversary could compromise several nodes at once, but since this scheme is susceptible to collusion anyway that seems to be too strong a model. Hence for this section we consider one adversary that controls only one node.

We consider first the security of the original FPS scheme in the tamper-proof nodes model as a basis for comparison. We then consider the unauthenticated scheme in the autonomous nodes model. Finally we compare these to the behavior of protocol B and find that, except for denial of service attacks, its security is almost as good as that in the tamper-proof nodes model, as long as all malicious nodes have honest neighbors. The only shortcoming is that protocol B does not prevent a malicious node from stating a negative utility, then executing the protocol correctly. We show that this possibility does not encourage selfish nodes to change their behavior. Such a malicious node would eventually be audited by the content provider and its cheating would be detected.

When evaluating the success of the adversary, we consider the difference between the net worth if it had behaved truthfully and the net worth after it cheated. We exclude the utility of the compromised node from the calculation. We will also consider the cost incurred by the adversary.

5.1   Security in the Tamper-Proof Nodes Model

The tamper-proof nodes model is susceptible to collusion among nodes (see [1]) but is quite secure against single malicious nodes. The security in this model is our basis for comparison of protocol B's security. We show that a single adversary can significantly reduce the group welfare but only by incurring a large cost to itself.

Lemma 12. *Let the adversary be node i. Suppose it wasn't going to receive the transmission by bidding zero. Then it cannot reduce the group welfare by more than it pays.*

Proof. Let A_0^i be the minimum welfare of any node from i to the root (inclusive) when i bids 0. Since i does not receive the transmission, A_0^i must be negative. If i bids less than $-A_0^i$ then it does not receive the transmission and the set of receivers is the same as if it had bid zero. Hence the group welfare is also unchanged. If it bids $u^i \geq -A_0^i$ then the minimum welfare A^i of any node from i to the root is $u^i + A_0^i$ so the agent pays $pay^i = u^i - A^i = -A_0^i$ (See equation 2). The difference in group welfares between bidding zero and bidding u^i, excluding the welfare of agent i, is the cost of including the subtree tree whose true welfare is $-A_0^i$. This is exactly what i pays. $\Diamond$

Lemma 13. *Let the adversary be i. Suppose it was going to receive the transmission by bidding zero. Then it cannot reduce the group welfare.*

Proof. Overbidding does not alter where the transmission is sent and consequently doesn't affect the group welfare. Underbidding is impossible.   ◇

5.2   Security of the Original Protocol in the Autonomous Nodes Model

A naive implementation of the FPS protocol in the autonomous nodes model is not secure. The method of attack and the amount of damage an agent can do depends on whether it would have received the transmission by truthfully bidding zero or not.

If adversary i would have received the transmission by executing the protocol correctly with a utility of zero, then it cannot reduce the group welfare by more than W^i. It can easily prevent its descendants from receiving the transmission. Its interference in other parts of the tree is achieved only by altering the value of W^i that it sends up. In the worst case it can set this to zero, causing a tree of total welfare at most W^i not to receive the transmission. This attack costs i zero.

If a would not have received the transmission by executing the protocol correctly with a utility of zero, then it can reduce the group welfare by a large amount (minus the lowest node welfare on its path to the root) by overbidding. Furthermore, it can avoid paying anything by transferring the cost of its overbidding to its descendants.

5.3   Security of Protocol B

We will show that, even if an agent doesn't care about maximizing its welfare, it can't undetectably harm the system much more than it could in the tamper-proof nodes model, as long as all its neighbors are all honest. It can still pretend it has a negative utility in some cases by declaring that the welfare of its node is 0, but we will show that this possibility doesn't change the behavior of the selfish nodes in the tree and can eventually be detected by the content provider.

A malicious node can perform denial of service attacks by not sending messages when it is its turn, or by falsely reporting that another agent has cheated. Cheating in a detectable fashion could also be regarded as a denial of service attack since it stops the protocol. It could also release its private key to other (selfish) agents, allowing them to print contradictory messages that appear to have been signed by the malicious node and collect the reward for reporting this. This would be expensive for the malicious node. We assume that if the protocol is aborted in this way then it is restarted, with some clever way of ensuring that messages from different protocol runs can't be confused. Hence a denial-of-service attack could be annoying but is unlikely to last very long because the content provider could eventually exclude the malicious node from the network.

We will show that apart from these denial-of-service attacks, a malicious node that isn't reported for cheating must have executed the protocol correctly with some utility, which may be negative.

Lemma 14. *Let j be a malicious agent with children $k_1, \ldots, k_l$ and parent p. If $k_1, \ldots, k_l$ and p are honest and the transmission is sent then j must have sent consistent messages.*

Proof. There is always some utility consistent with the welfare j sent, according to equation 1. The honest children check that the values of A^j sent down were consistent with that welfare, *i.e.* satisfying equation 3. $\diamond$

Note that j needn't have paid the correct amount, relying on the chance of not being checked. It also may have sent messages consistent only with a negative utility. We show next that the possibility of negative utilities doesn't cause the selfish agents to change their (honest) behavior.

Lemma 15. *Assume the game theory model with exactly one agent at each node, but let there be some (malicious) agents that are allowed to state negative utilities. Then it is still a dominant strategy for the other agents to state their true utility.*

Proof. Without loss of generality consider the strategy of agent 1 and suppose that agents $2 \ldots m$, with uplink costs $c^2, \ldots, c^m$ respectively, make negative bids $u^2, \ldots, u^m$ respectively (and there are no other negative bids). Then the welfares of each subtree and the value of A^1 are the same as they would be in the tree where the uplink costs of agents $2 \ldots m$ were $c^2 + u^2, \ldots, c^m + u^m$ and they stated utilities of zero. Therefore how much agent 1 pays and whether it receives the transmission is the same as in that case, so its best strategy is the same, *i.e.* to state its true utility. $\diamond$

Lemma 16. *If there may be honest, selfish and malicious agents in the tree, and all malicious ones have only honest neighbors, then every selfish agent's best strategy is to follow the protocol correctly.*

Proof. Similar argument to lemma 11. $\diamond$

Theorem 3. *If there may be honest, selfish and malicious agents in the tree, and all malicious ones have only honest neighbors, then every selfish agent's best strategy is to follow the protocol correctly with its true utility.*

Proof. Direct from lemmas 15 and 16. $\diamond$

A malicious agent can still reduce the group welfare significantly without being detected, but only by executing the protocol correctly (with a possibly false and/or negative utility). Even the negative utilities are detectable by the auditor if it happens to audit the malicious node, so that node could eventually be caught and excluded from the network. The important point is that the possible presence of some malicious nodes doesn't cause the rest of the nodes to deviate from their honest strategy.

6   Conclusions and Further Work

We illustrate some general techniques by transforming a distributed mechanism from one that assumes all nodes faithfully implement a specified algorithm into one that assumes nodes are strategic in all of their actions. The transformation involves some cryptography and some extra economic incentives. Our two authenticated protocols are designed for two slightly different agent models. Protocol A works correctly if we assume that it is common knowledge that agents deviate from the protocol only if it strictly improves their welfare. Protocol B is appropriate for agents that are selfish but will not follow the protocol unless they have some reason to do so. We prove that it is strictly better to implement the correct algorithm than to try to cheat.

We also evaluate the robustness of protocol B when malicious agents with honest neighbors are present, showing that these malicious agents can only reduce global welfare within limits and cannot give other agents an incentive to deviate from the protocol. We compare the security of protocol B to that of the FPS protocol in the tamper-proof nodes model and show that it is almost as strong, as long as malicious nodes have all honest neighbors. This is a significant improvement over a naive implementation of the tamper-proof nodes algorithm in the autonomous nodes model.

We hope to extend our ideas to other Internet applications such as BGP ([2]) by distributing the auditing functions. A node expecting to be paid by another could probabilistically demand a proof that it is being paid correctly. The challenge is to try to distribute the punishment and reward ideas without giving agents too many new ways to cheat the system. If misbehaving nodes are punished by excluding them from the network and routing around them, then this not only provides an incentive for rational agents but also quarantines malicious nodes and limits their impact on the global system.

Acknowledgements. We thank Joan Feigenbaum, Amir Ronen, Rahul Sami, and Andre Scedrov for helpful discussions about this work.

References

1. J. Feigenbaum, A. Krishnamurthy, R. Sami, and S. Shenker. Approximation and collusion in multicast cost sharing. In *Proceedings of the 3rd Conference on Electronic Commerce*, pages 253–255, New York, 2001. ACM Press.
2. J. Feigenbaum, C. Papadimitriou, R. Sami, and S. Shenker. A bgp-based mechanism for lowest-cost routing. In *Proceedings of the 21st Symposium on Principles of Distributed Computing*, pages 173–182, New York, 2002. ACM Press.
3. J. Feigenbaum, C. Papadimitriou, and S. Shenker. Sharing the cost of multicast transmissions. *Journal of Computer and System Sciences*, 63:21–41, 2001. Special issue on Internet Algorithms.
4. P. Golle, K. Leyton-Brown, and I. Mironov. Incentives for sharing in peer-to-peer networks. In *Proceedings of the ACM Conference on Electronic Commerce*, 2001.

5. L. Gong, P. Lincoln, and J. Rushby. Byzantine agreement with authentication: Observations and applications in tolerating hybrid and link faults. In R. K. Iyer, M. Morganti, W. K. Fuchs, and V. Gligor, editors, *Dependable Computing for Critical Applications—5*, volume 10 of *Dependable Computing and Fault Tolerant Systems*, pages 139–157, Champaign, IL, sep 1995. IEEE Computer Society.
6. H. Moulin and S. Shenker. Strategyproof sharing of submodular costs:budget balance versus efficiency. *Economic Theory*, 18(3):511–533, 2001.
7. M. Naor, B. Pinkas, and R. Sumner. Privacy preserving auctions and mechanism design. In *Proceedings of the 1st ACM conf. on Electronic Commerce*, 1999.
8. N. Nisan and A. Ronen. Algorithmic mechanism design. *Games and Economic Behavior*, 35:166–196, 2001.
9. M. J. Osborne and A. Rubinstein. *A course in game theory*. MIT Press, Cambridge, Mass., 1994.

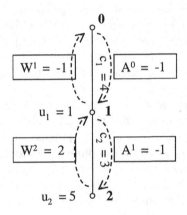

Fig. 7. 2nd cheat: The truth. No transmission is sent.

A   Other Cheating Examples

A.1   Second Cheat: Getting the Transmission for Less while Others Pay Extra

This attack relies on agents' confusion about the costs of links they are not adjacent to.

We assume:

- agent 2 does not communicate directly with agent 0 (it does communicate indirectly via node 1),
- each agent knows the link costs of only those edges it is adjacent to.

We dispense with the assumption that payments are secret — this attack succeeds even if every agent can see every other's payment.

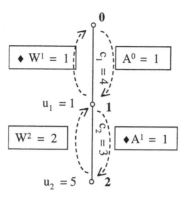

Fig. 8. 2nd Cheat: The cheat. Agent 1 pays 0, agent 2 pays 4.

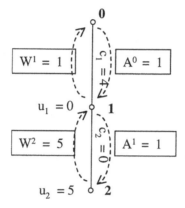

Fig. 9. 2nd Cheat: View of agent 0. $pay^1 = 0, pay^2 = 4$.

The true state of the network is shown in Figure 7. Here the tree's net welfare is negative, so no transmission is sent. Figure 8 shows the attack, where Agent 1 lies so as to receive the transmission for free, while making agent 2 pay for it and causing the content provider to lose revenue. Agent 1 gains by one unit because it receives for free a transmission it values at one.

Figures 9 and 10 demonstrate that each of the honest agents receives a consistent view of the network. Agents 0 and 2 could not detect the cheat even if they could communicate about their supposed values for u^1 and u^2 (but not if they could compare link costs). Figure 10 shows that agent 2 can be allowed to observe that agent 1 doesn't pay. In that network, $A^1 = A^2 = 1$ but $u^1 = 0 < A^1$ so agent 1 pays nothing. Also, agent 1 lies consistently in the sense that the W^1 it sends up the tree is equal to the value of A^1 that it sends down. That is,

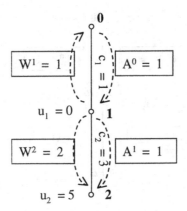

Fig. 10. 2nd Cheat: View of agent 2. $pay^1 = 0, pay^2 = 4$.

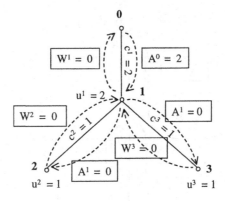

Fig. 11. 3rd Cheat: The truth. $pay^1 = 2, pay^2 = pay^3 = 1$.

watching agent 1's incoming and outgoing messages to check for consistency would also not reveal that it was cheating.

A.2   Third Cheat: Short Changing the Content Provider

In this example a cheater succeeds in paying less than it ought to for a transmission. It first lies consistently about its utility, then pays an amount inconsistent with that lie. This is interpreted by the other agents as implying that one of the children of the cheater had a higher utility than it really did.

The cheat works even if we assume all of the following:

1. link costs are not secret,
2. payments are not secret,
3. each agent i is magically forced to lie consistently, *i.e.* to send down a value for A^i that is truly $\min\{A^{\mathrm{parent}(i)}, W^i\}$ where W^i was the welfare it sent.

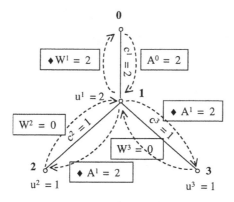

Fig. 12. 3rd Cheat: The cheat. Agent 1 pays 0, agents 2 and 3 pay 1.

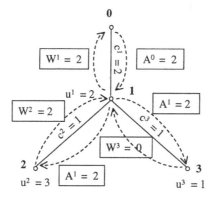

Fig. 13. 3rd Cheat: view of agents 3 and 0. $pay^1 = 0, pay^2 = pay^3 = 1$.

The point here is that the node can cheat just by paying a wrong amount, so any solution must include scrutiny of each node's inputs, welfare and payment.

Figure 11 shows the true state of the network. Every agent receives the transmission, the two leaf agents pay 1 each and agent 1 pays 2. Figure 12 shows a successful cheat by agent 1: it first lies consistently about its utility, effectively inflating it by two, so every other agent in the tree believes the total welfare to be two greater than it really is. It then pays zero, leading every other agent to believe that one of the leaf agents bid two more than it truly did. The network states assumed by agent 3 (and possibly agent 0) are shown in Figure 13. The perspective of agent 2 is like Figure 13 with the roles of agents 2 and 3 reversed.

Privacy in Sensor Webs and Distributed Information Systems

J.D. Tygar

EECS and SIMS
University of California, Berkeley
USA
tygar@cs.berkeley.edu

Abstract. We are seeing rapid development of sensor webs that collect information and distributed information aggregation systems – and these trends are present both in industry and government. This paper outlines a research agenda for address privacy questions raised by sensors webs and distributed information systems.

1 The Role of Privacy

Privacy has taken on new importance after the tragic events of September 11, 2001. In response to terrorist attacks, governments are preparing systems that

- Anticipate potential threats; and
- Respond to actual threats.

The first item often includes improved intelligence systems; the second item includes systems that accurately report on the results of terrorist attacks. For example, in the US, the Defense Advanced Research Projects Agency has created two new offices: the Information Awareness Office and the Information Exploitation Office [9], to deal with these two phases respectively. The Information Awareness Office is developing a major new system called Total Information Awareness [5,8] to address issues of anticipation. Work going on in several places on wireless sensor webs [4] is partially motivated by issues of response. These systems have much potential in providing increased intelligence and emergency response capabilities, but at the same time, provide the capability for sophisticated and universal surveillance, to a degree previously not seen.

But the contemporary computer security community is ill-prepared to address questions of privacy. Indeed, privacy is usually treated as the poor step-child of computer security. Although a leading IEEE conference in our field is called *The Symposium on Security and Privacy*, even a casual glance through any recent proceedings will reveal that privacy usually receives little attention – and when it does, it is ancillary to a much larger and more important point about computer security. Other leading

M. Okada et al. (Eds.): ISSS 2002, LNCS 2609, pp. 84–95, 2003.

conferences, run by the ACM, USENIX, or the Internet Society don't mention privacy at all in their titles, and privacy papers in those conferences are no more likely than in our IEEE conference.

It is more than a little surprising that privacy receives so little attention[1]. Such systems are ubiquitous in the private sphere (consider, for example, the stunning amount of personal data collected by the private firm Acxiom.) But although the most serious privacy questions exist in private systems, concerns are also raised in government systems – both existing and proposed. In the United States, for example, a large number of government agencies, ranging from the Internal Revenue Service to the Federal Bureau of Investigation to the Social Security Administration to the Immigration and Nationalization Service today collect large amounts of personal information.

A number of continuing trends (such as the spread of the Internet, the increase in electronic payment methods, near-universal use of cellular phone communications, ubiquitous computation, sensor webs, etc.) mean that private organizations will have increased ability to build detailed profiles of individual Americans. And on the government side, there have been widespread calls in the media in the wake of the September 11, 2001 terrorist attacks for government organizations to share information and "connect the dots."

Privacy poses significant, challenging problems. These are not merely hypothetical problems: commercial use of data means that these problems are present, important, and pressing today.

This paper presents some preliminary results on the problem of privacy, but its primary focus is to set forth proposals for a research agenda in privacy. Now the problems associated with privacy are well-understood to be difficult. But this paper presents concerns in a true spirit of research – merely stating that a problem is difficult is no reason to avoid studying it. Indeed, in the face of nearly certain increased private commercial and governmental surveillance, the problems of privacy demand attention, regardless of their inherent difficulty.

Privacy is an issue that includes both technical and policy elements, and a full consideration of privacy must necessarily touch on policy issues. However, for this paper, my focus is entirely on the technical aspects of privacy.

If we can make progress on the privacy problem, we will benefit from many powerful spin-off technologies. Better privacy means better handling of sensitive information, which can directly lead to better computer security. If we can deny attackers access to sensitive information, we raise the bar on the ability of attackers to successfully attack systems. This point lies behind much of the concerns raised by the President's Critical Infrastructure Protection Board's September 18, 2002 *Draft National Strategy to Secure Cyberspace* [6].

In addition, we can also hope that this technology will see use in the commercial sphere, as mentioned above.

Finally, in the wake of the terrorist attacks of September 11, 2001, intelligence handling by several United States government agencies, including the Federal Bureau

---

[1] The excellent paper on *Negotiated Privacy* by Jarecki, Lincoln, and Shmatikov in this anthology is a happy exception to this general rule.

of Investigation, the Immigration and Naturalization Service, and the National Security Agency were widely criticized in the media. Part of this poor handling came from awkward handling of "private" information (that is, information that was about private individuals – if we had better privacy controls, we could hope that critical information could reach the right people while protecting irrelevant personal information from being disclosed, yielding improved intelligence.

2 Privacy Challenge: Distributed Information Systems

In November 2002, numerous newspaper articles in the United States pointed to one example of a proposed distributed information system, the Total Information Awareness (TIA) system proposed by the United States Defense Advanced Research Projects Agency. In many ways, the focus on TIA is unfair: TIA is actually behind what is going on in the commercial sphere. Neither is the debate on the role of government databases unique to the United States. In Canada, Europe, and Japan, similar concerns have arisen – for example, just consider the concern of Japan's computerized citizen information system *Zyuumin Kihon Daityou.*

But perhaps TIA stands out since privacy has been a central goal of the program since the beginning, and since it has the support of the United States Defense Advanced Research Projects Agency (DARPA), an organization famous for solving apparently unsolvable problems. So let us begin by considering TIA. (To be clear, this paper is not a review of TIA, and does not mean to endorse or criticize TIA. However, the reality is that commercial firms such as Acxiom have substantial data aggregation and surveillance capabilities today. A government system such as TIA is likely – perhaps less ambitious, perhaps more ambitious, perhaps with different sorts of data. But it simply defies political imagination to assume that government will not play a role in using data aggregation techniques that are now ubiquitous in industry. The question raised by this paper is: *Given the contemporary, real development of sensor webs and distributed information systems, what can researchers do to help find ways to protect privacy?*) Doug Dyer of DARPA describes the rationale behind Genisys, a significant component of TIA, as follows [1]:

> "In 1995, Aum Shinri Kyo attacked the Tokyo subway system using sarin gas, killing 11 and sending hundreds to the hospital. This attack is a prototypical, perhaps extreme example of predictive precursor events. Prior to the 1995 attack, Aum Shinri Kyo cultists led by Shoko Asahara had tried to buy US and Russian chemical munitions. When that failed, they engaged in a substantial weapons development program aimed at mass effects. They created elaborate development facilities for producing sarin, purchased expensive equipment, and accumulated huge chemical stockpiles. Following several malicious attempts with ineffective agents, they created a test facility in Australia and tested sarin by killing sheep whose remains were later discov-

ered. Noxious chemical leaks were reported by neighbors near their development facility in Japan, but police still made no arrests. Asahara broadcast his intentions clearly via radio. And months before the subway attack, cultists used sarin in an overt attempt to kill three judges in the city of Matsumoto. In this example, just as in the case of 9/11, fragments of information, known by different parties in different organizations, contained a predictive pattern that could have been identified had the information been shared and properly analyzed."

Among the types of information anticipated to be collected in TIA is transactional information including communication records, financial records, education records, travel records, records of country entry, place or event entry, medical records, veterinary records, transportation records, housing records, transportation records, housing records, critical resource records, and government records. These records may be gathered from private sources or governmental sources. [5]

What techniques can we use to address privacy concerns in distributed information systems? We can clearly leverage from recent technical advances including:

- Powerful strong audit systems, that maintain tamper-resistance audits (for example, see [2]).
- The ability to search on encrypted data without revealing information about the query itself or its response. For example Dawn Song, Adrian Perrig, and David Wagner present powerful techniques that allow information to be searched in data repositories, without revealing the nature of the of the queries or the results either to eavesdroppers or the data repositories itself (see Figure 1). [7] This work, which has since been built on by a number of researchers, offers a surprising result – we can build databases that are secure, both in a conventional sense but in a new stronger distributed sense. This suggests that a number of extensions may be possible: (a) government agencies may be able to use data from private organizations such as Acxiom without revealing the nature of inquires or searches to Acxiom. Since private commercial organizations often have appalling security (example: the widely reported recent "identity theft" of highly sensitive private information using poor security at private credit agencies and their clients), protecting the nature of queries is a central concern for effective government use of private information. (b) To the extent that privacy handling rules can be expressed in computer readable format, it may be possible to enforce privacy restrictions within the framework of an automated processing system. Now, I do not mean to imply that this technology is ready to use "off the shelf" – it does not fully support the functionality listed above and has efficiency issues. But the theoretical success of the Song/Perrig/Wagner approach suggests that we will be able to make real progress on an ideal system that will be efficient and support the above goals.

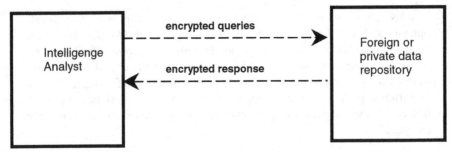

Fig. 1. A schematic representation of the Song/Perrig/Wagner secure query system

- Improved techniques in program analysis, including advances such as Peter Lee and George Necula's Proof Carrying Code to prove that mobile code has certain properties, static analysis of programs, and projects such as UC Berkeley's Athena system for automatically synthesizing cryptographic protocols with given properties.
- Stunning advances in dynamic coalitions that can allow diverse, constantly changing sets of parties to cooperate and work together.

2.1   An Outline of Privacy Research Goals for Distributed Information Systems

Here are three techniques that show strong promise for protecting distributed information systems:

- **Selective revelation**. Rather than revealing all data to queries, data can be distributed in discrete chunks that require positive approval to advance. The goal is to minimize revelation of personal data while supporting analysis. The approach revolves around partial, incremental revelation of personal data. Initial revelation is handled by statistics and categories; subsequent revelations occur as justified by earlier results. Such a system is powerful – it can support both *standing queries* ("tell me all of the foreigners from watchlist countries who are enrolled in flight school") as well as specific real-time queries ("tell me the where the money involved in Transaction X may have come from"). Selective revelation is a method for minimizing exposure of individual information while supporting continuous analysis of all data. The challenge in doing this is that much of the data is private information about people which cannot necessarily be revealed to a person. Even data that is derived via an analysis algorithm may be private, depending on the status of the data from which it was derived, and on the nature of the algorithm.

    The idea of selective revelation is that initially we reveal information to the analyst only in sanitized form, that is, in terms of statistics and categories that do not reveal (directly or indirectly) anyone's private information. If the analyst sees reason for concern he or she can follow up by seeking permission to get more precise information. This permission would be granted if the initial information provides sufficient cause to allow the revelation of more information, under appropriate legal and policy guidelines.

For example, an analyst might issue a query asking whether there is any individual who has recently bought unusual quantities of certain chemicals, and has rented a large truck. The algorithm could respond by saying yes or no, rather than revealing the identity of an individual. The analyst might then take that information to a judge or other appropriate body, seeking permission to learn the individual's name, or other information about the individual. By revealing information iteratively, we prevent the disclosure of private information except when a sufficient showing has been made to justify that revelation.

Selective revelation works by putting a security barrier between the private data and the analyst, and controlling what information can flow across that barrier to the analyst. The analyst injects a query that uses the private data to determine a result, which is a high-level sanitized description of the query result. That result must not leak any private information to the analyst.

Selective revelation must accommodate multiple data sources, all of which lie behind the (conceptual) security barrier. Private information is not made available directly to the analyst, but only through the security barrier.

A key technology challenge is making data relationships successively refinable, and thus selectively revealable. One way to address this challenge is to develop data ontologies that provide structured and logical ways for the analyst to make appropriate queries.

But of course, as the careful reader will have already noted, this creates an architectural problem. It is easiest to to think of a protective privacy/security barrier as existing outside a single monolithic repository. However, for the applications listed above, the single monolithic repository will not exist. In the sort of systems necessary to support detailed analysis, information must be collected and aggregated from multiple repositories. In this sort of system, there can be no central privacy/security barrier – each repository must have its own barriers, and those barriers must be coordinated to support privacy restrictions of the system as a whole and of the individual repositories.

- **Strong audit.** Perhaps the strongest protection against abuse of information systems is strong audit mechanisms. We need to "watch the watchers." These audit systems must be tamper-evident or tamper-resistant, and since repositories span different organizations, must themselves span different organizations. If such audit mechanisms exist, we will realize substantial advantages. (For example, a strong audit mechanism would have been likely to identify a spy such as Aldrich Ames or Jonathan Pollard very early on.) However, these audit systems themselves pose a substantial challenge. Audit data will be voluminous and highly sensitive (certainly, foreign intelligence agents would be very interested in finding out what sorts of queries are run through a government's commercial or governmental information systems.) How can we find instances of inappropriate queries? In many ways, this is a recursive instance of the general intelligence data mining problem, and should probably be considered in conjunction with that problem. This hall of mirrors presents a number of technical challenges, and would benefit from the research community's attention.

- **Better rule proceeding technologies.** Distributed information systems combine data from diverse sources. Their privacy systems must support privacy constraints: both systemic privacy constraints and privacy constraints specific to a particular set of information repositories. (For example, information derived from a foreign source, such as country X's information repositories, may come with specific privacy concerns attached.) Since computers in general can not understand the underlying representation of private information, it is necessary to label data with information that will allow it to be properly processed, both with respect to privacy constraints but also with respect to general constraints. Information varies tremendously in quality as well. For example, substantial anecdotal evidence supports the claim that a significant data appearing in commercial credit bureau sources is not always accurate. Information from foreign sources may be tampered with. Government agencies vary in the degree of scrutiny they apply to keep data accurate. All of this poses issues for accurate labeling. Further concerns arise because even a new information system will likely build on substantial amounts of (unlabeled or inaccurately labeled) previously existing *legacy data*. And problems continue to increase in complexity: what happens when data is combined to produced *derived data*. How should the derived data be labeled? A conservative approach would suggest labeling the derived data with the most conservative labels possible. However, in many cases, this will be inappropriate – derived data is often sanitized and poses less privacy restrictions than the original source data used. On the other hand, in some cases derived data may actually be more sensitive than the original source data.

  Data labeling is actually an old idea – it dates back to the some of the earliest discussions in the security community. And yet, labeling enjoys at best a checkered reputation: for example, as this author has elsewhere argued, data labeling was a spectacular failure in the attempts to define standards such as the US Department of Defense's Trusted Computer Systems Evaluation Criteria (the "Orange Book.") But there is reason for optimism: when labeling is used to support advisory functions or review functions, one would expect considerably better performance than in the classic mandatory security systems that formed the heart of higher levels of the Orange Book. Indeed, labeling is going through something of a renaissance at present: consider its use in a variety of digital rights management systems (DRMs) (although, of course, these DRM systems are now widely recognized to have only partial effectiveness.)

  If labeling can take place, substantial advantages can be realized. For example, consider the complexity of privacy law in the United States. Different laws apply to protecting video rentals and airline tickets, audio recordings and video recordings, information from foreign sources and domestic sources, information concerning US persons and foreigners, etc.

  This poses risks in multiple directions. On the one hand, there is the risk that current complexity of US privacy laws and rules may result in inappropriate disclosure of information. But perhaps, as some former US Justice Department members have argued, in many cases, intelligence analysts and law enforcement personnel miss the opportunity to use essential intelligence information: in their desire to comply with privacy rules, the government officials fail to use material that they are legally entitled to use. In other words, the haze of privacy law makes officials go beyond legislative and regulatory privacy restrictions and means that the government misses the chance to "connect the dots."

Clearly, we have a significant challenge in allowing users of databases (whether employees of companies such as Acxiom or law enforcement officials or intelligence analysts) reasonably understand what the real privacy restrictions are. Here is a place where technology can help – if we can develop a "privacy toolbar" that helps inform users of privacy restrictions, we can help eliminate mistakes caused by human misunderstanding of the United State's currently complex privacy law. This especially applies when rules interact. If a privacy restriction is reached, such a system can help explain the procedures necessary to legally access data.

Moving towards more advanced and speculative research, we envision a system which can simulate different information handling policies. Such a system would use synthetic data and run queries against them. By comparing different privacy policies, we aspire to find examples that will help illustrate respective advantages and disadvantages of a variety of privacy policies. This could help inform debate by policy makers as they consider different privacy policies. (This stands in marked contrast to contemporary approaches to privacy policy making, which is often marked by political rhetoric and vague sociological characterizations.) However such a simulator faces substantial challenges: we need to design the simulator itself, we must find a way to generate meaningful synthetic data, and we must find ways to verify or validate the accuracy of reports from the simulator. These are all hard problems, and their solution is far from obvious. This is an example of "high-risk" (the challenges are real), "high-payoff" (even partial solutions can help shed considerable light on policy making) research.

But within the framework outlined here, considerable questions remain. Consider the problem of adaptation. As people realize that certain data is subject to surveillance or response, they change their behavior. Here is an example familiar to any frequent flier in the United States: prior to the terrorist attacks of September 11, 2001, many experienced airline passengers angled to be among the very first in line to board commercial airplanes – in that way, the passengers could place their carry-on luggage and settle in before the rest of passengers boarded. In the wake of the September 11, 2001 terrorist attacks, authorities instituted thorough searches of some passengers (and their carry-on luggage) boarding flights. While these checks are ostensibly random, they in fact tend to select more highly from the first people to board a flight. Now, experienced travelers angle to be the tenth in line instead of the first in line.

In the same way, information systems designed to identify certain groups of people are likely to result in different behavior from both the people they are intended to track as well as innocent people who for personal reasons desire to evade surveillance (for example, observe the "arms race" in the United States between telephone caller-ID systems, those who desire to make anonymous calls, those who desire to reject anonymous calls, etc.) Failure to correctly anticipate this sort of adaptation is likely to lead to unexpected and (often undesirable) results. In the worst case, this pattern of adaptation could lead to widespread evasion of surveillance, followed by a counter-move of analysts who need to dig deeper into private data, leading to a spiral resulting in markedly decreased privacy in practice. To some degree, simulation as mentioned above may help prevent this. But beyond that, it makes sense to attempt to user large scale real-user experiments. One way to accomplish this may be to adapt commercial multiplayer games (along the lines of *Everquest* or *Baldur's Gate*) to see how real users (albeit, a highly self-selected group) adapt to specific policies.

3 Privacy Challenge: Sensor Webs

Sensor webs use small, independent sensors that communicate wirelessly over microcells to collect and share a wide variety of information about their environments, including people in the environment. As part of the CITRIS project at Berkeley, the author and his colleagues at Berkeley have been developing and deploying such sensors Among the explicit purposes of such devices are to report on people in the building and the status of the building in case of a disaster such as an earthquake, fire, or terrorist attack on a building. These reports are explicitly designed to report on the position and status of people in a building. This raises obvious privacy concerns.

Today, the sensors used are obvious – while small, they are still visible to the naked eye. However, with successful further development, some aspire to develop truly dust-sized sensors that can even be mixed in a paint can painted onto the wall. Using ambient power sources (such as temperature differentials or small movements), these dust-sized sensors could function indefinitely. Forming an ad hoc network on the fly, these sensors could pass along a variety of information, eventually linking that information up with a base station.

In [4], the author of this paper and Adrian Perrig describe how to arrange sensors into a secure network. We describe the configuration that we used for our actual system:

"By design, these sensors are inexpensive, low-power devices. As a result, they have limited computational and communication resources. The sensors form a self-organizing wireless network and form a multihop routing topology. Typical applications may periodically transmit sensor readings for processing. Our current prototype consists of nodes, small battery powered devices, that communicate with a more powerful base station, which in turn is connected to an outside network. . . . At 4MHz, they are slow and underpowered (the CPU has good support for bit and byte level I/O operations, but lacks support for many arithmetic and some logic operations). They are only 8-bit processors (note that . . . 80% of all microprocessors shipped in 2000 were 4 bit or 8 bit devices. Communication is slow at 10 kilobits per second. The operating system is particularly interesting for these devices. . . . [TinyOS, a] small, event-driven operating system sonsumes almost half of the 8K bytes of instruction flas memory, leaving just 4500 bytes for security and the application. Significantly more powerful devices would also consume significantly more power. The energy source on our devices is a small battery, so we are stuck with relatively limited computational devices. Wireless communication is the most energy-consuming function performed by these devices, so we need to minimize communications overhead. The limited energy supplies creat tensions for security: on the one hand, security needs to limit its consumption of processor power; on the other hand, limited power supply limits the lifetime of keys (battery replacement is designed to reinitialize devices and zero out keys.)"

Given the severe limitations of such an environment, the technical reader is likely to doubt that security is even possible. However, in the book, we go on to describe in great detail a set of algorithms which do secure these systems, and we go on to describe an actual implementation of those algorithms on these very sensors.

3.1 An Outline of Privacy Architecture for Sensor Webs

Privacy on sensor webs can be considered in three levels:

- **Fundamental security primitives:** Examples include low level encryption, authentication, secure broadcast, and synchronization protocols. These are challenging because of the limited computational power of sensor webs, but as outlined in [4], substantial progress has been made on these topics, and this particular level seems particularly tractable.

- **Privacy policies[2]:** We need a way to specify what information is recorded, made available and distributed: to whom and under what conditions. A large variety of privacy policies can be considered – here are some examples: "location information of individuals is not recorded or made available except in case of an emergency; and such an emergency must be accompanied by a loud alarm", "users can specify whether they want their location information revealed or not", "location information is made available, but the identities of the persons are anonymized." Not only must these policies be specified, but we must provide a formal, machine understandable language to interpret these policies.

- **Human interfaces:** Humans interact with sensor webs in at least two ways: as subjects who are potentially under surveillance by the sensor web and as users who may need to access information collected or synthesized by the sensor web. In both cases, we need good ways to provide user interfaces. For subjects, we have the questions of how they receive notice ("you are under surveillance in the following ways") and how they specify preferences ("please allow people in my work group to know my location except when I am on my lunch break.") For users of sensor web, we need good ways to specify queries, to receive easily understandable answers to queries, and to specify and monitor policies.

---

[2] Note that here we are using policy in its technical sense as a set of rules, rather than in its more general sense as an instance of "public policy".

Once these techniques are in place, we can conduct a variety of important experiments and analyses:

- **Experimentation on Policies:** In addition to examining our human interfaces to determine their clarity and effectiveness, we can use this system as a sociological testbed to see individual's comfort with different types of monitoring policies. Do people gradually acclimate to monitoring policies? Or do monitoring policies have an observable change on behavior and work habits? Is notice effective? Do people understand what is being collected, and what consequences it has?
- **Security Analyses:** To what extent are privacy safeguards designed into the sensor web vulnerable to attack? Are there single points of failure which if breached present a serious risk of large scale release of private information?
- **Masking Strategies:** How effective in practice are anonymizing masking strategies such as adding noise to data or presenting data in a purely statistical form?
- **Legal Analyses:** What is effectively done with technology, and what gaps remain? Where do we need additional regulation to protect individual privacy? What sort of legal regulation is well supported by technology and what laws are not? Are there laws which are effectively unenforceable because technology can not support those laws?

A fully completed analysis along these lines could yield a substantially deeper understanding of privacy issues in sensor webs.

Acknowledgements. I began thinking about this material as I chaired the US Department of Defense Information Science and Technology Study Group on Security with Privacy. While the members of that study chose to remain anonymous, the author is deeply grateful to them for many detailed discussions. Portions of section 2.1 of this paper was adapted from my commentary to that study. I would also like to thank the staff of DARPA, and the Information Awareness Office, for answering many questions with openness.

Material in Section 3 grew out of discussions I have had with Tom Kalil, Yutaka Miyake, Deirdre Mulligan, Adrian Perrig, and Paul Wright.

My thinking about this subject was stimulated by my students in my Fall 2002 Graduate Computer Science Seminar on Privacy.

I was supported during the writing of this study from grants from the United States National Science Foundation and the United States Postal Service.

The Tokuda Lab at Keio University, the Institute for International Policy Studies, and the National Science Council of Taiwan (through the International Computer Symposium) helped provide partial travel support to present this material in Japan and Taiwan. I am particularly grateful to Mr. Isao Hiroki, Professor Shiuhpyng Shieh, and Professor Hide Tokuda, and for facilitating this Asian support.

While I benefited from a broad variety of advice, input and financial support for this study, the opinions in the report are my own. They do not necessarily reflect the opinions of any person or organization mentioned above, any funding agency, or of the US Government or any of its agencies.

References

1. D. Dyer. *Genisys*. In [8]
2. S. Haber and W. Stornetta. "How to Timestamp a Digital Document." *Journal of Cryptology*, Vol. 3, No. 2, pp. 99–111, 1991
3. G. Mack, B. Bebee, I. Shafti, G. Wenzel, B. Mediary, E. Yuan. *Total Information Awareness Program (TIA) System Description Document (SDD), Version 1.1.* July 19, 2002. In [8].
4. A. Perrig and J. D. Tygar, *Secure Broadcast Communication: in Wired and Wireless Communications*, Kluwer, 2002.
5. J. Poindexter. *DARPA's Initiative on Countering Terrorism: Total Information Awareness.* In [8].
6. President's National Critical Infrastructure Boad. *Draft National Strategy to Secure Cyberspace: Draft for Comment.* September 18, 2002. http://www.whitehouse.gov/pcipb/
7. D. Song, D. Wagner, and A. Perrig. "Practical Techniques for Search on Encrypted Data." In *Proceedings 2000 IEEE Symposium on Security and Privacy.*
8. *Total Information Awareness* (CD-ROM) distributed at DARPATech 2002, July 2002.
9. See URLs http://www.darpa.mil/iao and http://www.darpa.mil/ixo.

Negotiated Privacy

(Extended Abstract)

Stanisław Jarecki[1], Patrick Lincoln[2], and Vitaly Shmatikov[2*]

[1] Computer Science Department, Stanford University, Stanford, CA 94305 U.S.A.
stasio@theory.stanford.edu
[2] SRI International, 333 Ravenswood Avenue, Menlo Park, CA 94025 U.S.A.
{lincoln,shmat}@csl.sri.com

Abstract. Exponential growth in digital information gathering, storage, and processing capabilities inexorably leads to conflict between well-intentioned government or commercial datamining, and fundamental privacy interests of individuals and organizations. This paper proposes a mechanism that provides cryptographic fetters on the mining of personal data, enabling efficient mining of previously-negotiated properties, but preventing any other uses of the protected personal data. Our approach does not rely on complete trust in the analysts to use the data appropriately, nor does it rely on incorruptible escrow agents. Instead, we propose conditional data escrow where the data generators, not the analysts, hold the keys to the data, but analysts can verify that the pre-negotiated queries are enabled. Our solution relies on verifiable, anonymous, and deterministic commitments which play the role of tags that mark encrypted entries in the analyst's database. The database owner cannot learn anything from the encrypted entries, or even verify his guess of the plaintext on which these entries are based. On the other hand, the verifiable and deterministic property ensures that the entries are marked with consistent tags, so that the database manager learns when the number of entries required to enable some query reaches the pre-negotiated threshold.

1 Introduction

Striking the right balance between security and privacy is a challenging task. Massive collection of personal data and ubiquitous monitoring of individuals and organizations is increasingly seen as a necessary step to thwart crime, fraud, and terrorism, ensure early detection of epidemics, monitor compliance with financial regulations, etc. Once the data are gathered, privacy laws and codes of conduct restrict how they can be mined and/or what queries may be performed on them. Searching patient records to find the source of an infectious disease is acceptable. Rifling through a neighbor's medical history is not. Development of

---

* Partially supported by ONR Grants N00014-02-1-0109 and N00014-01-1-0837, DARPA contract 9N66001-00-C-8015 and NSF grant INT98-15731.

a practical mechanism to ensure that the usage of collected data complies with the privacy policy is thus of paramount importance.

Simply declaring any form of personal data collection illegal is not a realistic option. In many situations—national security, law enforcement, financial supervision—massive monitoring is inevitable. Moreover, consumer incentive schemes such as grocery discount cards and frequent flyer programs have motivated many people to complain if detailed records are *not* kept of all their activities. It is, however, imperative to ensure that the monitoring process cannot be abused. The conventional approach places trust in the individuals and organizations who access the data. IRS workers are trusted not to take voyeuristic forays into famous actors' or their acquaintances' private tax information. Department of Motor Vehicles (DMV) workers are trusted not to provide unauthorized access to databases containing private address and other information. Such a system of trust is only as strong as its weakest link, which is often -a low-level clerk.

Negotiated Privacy is a technical solution to this problem which is based on the concept of *personal data escrow*. The proposed approach relies on *self-reporting* of *self-encrypted* data by the subjects of monitoring. The data are reported in an encrypted escrowed form, which is verifiable, yet preserves privacy. This ensures both i) *accuracy*, *i.e.*, the subjects are prevented from cheating or lying about their activities, and ii) *privacy*, *i.e.*, the collectors of data are able to perform only authorized queries on the collected data. The properties of personal data escrow make all unauthorized queries on the collected data computationally infeasible. The most important feature of the proposed approach is that it does not require any trust to be placed either in the subjects of monitoring, or the collectors of data.

We assume that, before the monitoring system is initialized, the set of permitted queries is pre-negotiated between all stakeholders: legislators, monitoring agencies, privacy advocates, etc. This approach balances the need of the individuals to protect the privacy of their personal data, and that of the data collectors, such as law enforcement agencies, to obtain accurate information. In the simplest version of the scheme, the set of permitted queries is known to everybody involved. We believe that transparency is extremely important when collecting massive amounts of data about individuals and organizations. We expect that public and legislative support for any data collection scheme will be preceded by a consensus about the queries that the data collectors are permitted to evaluate.

2   Applications of Negotiated Privacy

Negotiated Privacy based on personal data escrow can be used in any context where the goal of data collection is to detect and reveal an "exceptional" combination of events, while keeping routine events completely private.

For example, consider a hypothetical Biological Warning and Communication System (BWACS) monitoring infrastructure for infectious diseases maintained by Centers for Disease Control and Prevention (CDC) Such a system is particularly important for rare infectious diseases, whose initial symptoms may be almost consistent with a common illness and thus often be misdiagnosed by the primary care physician, resulting in continuing spread of the epidemic unless detected early. To ensure early detection, the CDC may automatically collect all medical records from primary care facilities around the nation. Each record is escrowed so that no CDC staffer, even someone with unrestricted access to the BWACS database, can look up the details of a particular record at her whim. At the same time, certain queries, *e.g.*, "If there are 5 or more patients with a particular combination of symptoms treated in the same metropolitan area within 24 hours of each other, reveal some more information from records related to those patients," must be efficiently computable, without leaking *any* information about the patients who had different symptoms, or any information whatsoever if there were fewer than 5 patients that fit the specified pattern.

In another example, Food and Drug Administration (FDA) may analyze the progress of a new drug study by requiring that a record describing every patient's reaction be submitted in an escrowed form. The records cannot be viewed, unless there is a patient with more than 3 adverse reactions, in which case all records *pertaining to that patient* should be disclosed. Moreover, agents responsible for populating the monitoring database (*e.g.*, pharmaceutical companies conducting the drug trial) should not be able to conceal some of the records, or prevent the FDA from learning that the database contains an over-the-threshold number of records pertaining to the same patient and documenting adverse reactions.

In the national security arena, intelligence officials may be interested in learning "Has anyone flown to an airport within 100 miles of Kandahar 3 times in the last year?," but any information about individuals who flew fewer than 3 times, or flew elsewhere, should not be revealed. Another example is banking and finance, where fraud investigators may wish to look for specific repeated patterns of transactions, but individuals and organizations want to preserve the proprietary transaction details. Certain steps of auditing and even shareholder review of corporate finances could be enabled by personal data escrow, while preserving the privacy of transaction details.

As a last motivating example, consider the partially adversarial interests of a digital media user and a digital media platform provider. A user may wish to employ various digital artifacts such as computer software, music, video, etc. A provider of such valuable content may wish to restrict the use of that content. Peripherals or network devices such as video display boards, web services, and audio output devices play an essential role in the transactions of interest. A digital rights management system has the difficult task of providing some controls over the potential abuses of digital content (ie copying), while not providing the content provider intrusive access into the users entire system context and history. Negotiated privacy may allow a user to purchase the rights to use a piece of content or web service a limited number of times, and enable a analyst to determine if the limit has been exceeded.

3   What Negotiated Privacy Is NOT

Private information retrieval. The setting and the goals of negotiated privacy are different from those of private information retrieval (PIR) schemes [CGKS98] or symmetric PIR schemes [GIKM98]. In the PIR setting, the database manager is trusted to populate the database with correct entries, but he may be curious to learn which entries the client chooses to retrieve. Negotiated Privacy offers a means to privately *populate* databases while PIR offers a means to privately *retrieve* data from a database. However, techniques for oblivious polynomial evaluation [NP98,KY01] can be useful in the Negotiated Privacy setting for constructing an efficient threshold escrow protocol or for keeping the privacy disclosure conditions secret from the user.

Searching on encrypted data. There has been significant recent work on the problem of searching on encrypted data [SWP00,BO02]. Unlike general computation on encrypted data [AF88], the search problem has received efficient solutions for the case of symmetric [SWP00] and asymmetric [BO02] encryption schemes. In this scenario, the user gives to the server a database of ciphertexts, and then the user is able to efficiently search over this database for records containing specific plaintexts, or the user can enable the server itself to perform some restricted searches on this database. The encrypted data search problem does not have *verifiability* and *conditional secret release* properties needed in the Negotiated Privacy system. The encrypted search problem does not protect against a dishonest user, while in the Negotiated Privacy system the analyst needs to *verify* that the user's entries are formed from a correctly computed commitment and a ciphertext. Moreover, whereas in the work of [SWP00,BO02] the client could give a trapdoor to the database server which allows the server to identify some fields in the database, in the Negotiated Privacy scenario we need to support a conditional release of the plaintext of database fields to the server.

Digital cash. Digital cash schemes [CFN88] hold the promise of enabling transfer of value over digital media, and have been the subject of intense academic and commercial interest. Some digital cash schemes enable disclosure of information once a certain threshold is exceeded. For example, the user can remain anonymous as long as he spends each digital coin no more than once, but an attempt to double-spend results in disclosure of his identity. However, such schemes are insufficient for Negotiated Privacy because we also need to enforce that the user always uses the same coin when he escrows activities that are subject to the same privacy disclosure condition.

Privacy preserving datamining. Privacy preserving datamining focuses on deducing certain associations in a large database without revealing private information contained in the database. Two approaches to this problem include sanitizing the data prior to mining it [ERAG02] and splitting the data among multiple organizations while ensuring that no organization obtains private information about the other's data [LP00]. These problems are very different from the focus of this research. Negotiated Privacy is about controlling the conditions under which private information is exposed (*e.g.*, a passenger's ID is revealed after three trips to Kandahar). There is no datamining taking place since the type of information revealed is negotiated ahead of time.

Other related work. Extensions to the basic Negotiated Privacy scheme, such as threshold escrows with automatic disclosure, can employ (verifiable) secret sharing techniques [Sha79,Fel87]. General multi-party computation [Yao82,GMW87] and research on practical fault-tolerant distributed computation of various cryptographic functions [DF89] can also be instrumental in building efficient scalable solutions. Key escrow schemes [Mic92,KL95,YY98], blind signatures, anonymous credentials, and anonymous (or "key-private") public-key encryption are also closely related to Negotiated Privacy, but do not provide all the required properties [Cha82,KP98,Bra00,CL01,AR02,BBDP01].

4   Security Model

We describe the basic research problem underlying Negotiated Privacy, explain our model of privacy disclosure policies, the roles of the entities involved in the system, and the threat model. The *only* entity that must be trusted in order for Negotiated Privacy to work is the public-key infrastructure. The proposed approach is secure against threats presented by any other participant.

4.1   Basic Problem of Personal Data Escrow

Conditional data escrow. Consider for a moment just two parties, a *user* who performs some activities, and an *analyst* who wants to record all of the user's activities in his database. To balance the analyst's need to monitor all activities and the user's right to privacy, the records should be encoded in such a way that the analyst learns something useful from them if and only if the user's activities match some pre-specified suspicious pattern or *disclosure condition*. We call this conditional release of information *personal data escrow* because, by default, the owner of the database cannot decrypt the records,

A data escrow protocol is an example of a secure two-party computation. While, in principle, there are polynomial-time protocols for secure computation of any functionality that can be encoded as a polynomial-time algorithm [Yao82], including personal data escrow, their complexity depends at least linearly on the size of the logic circuit that implements this functionality, rendering them utterly impractical. Therefore, we propose techniques that *efficiently* solve the particular case of two-party computation needed for Negotiated Privacy: the personal data escrow problem.

Why "Negotiated Privacy"? We foresee a political or commercial process of *negotiation* aimed to balance the objective of protecting people's privacy against the objective to gather information, *e.g.*, for national security purposes. Negotiation would lead to the establishment of an acceptable trade-off, specifying exceptional patterns of activities that should trigger disclosure of personal records. For example, an acceptable disclosure policy, arrived at as a result of negotiation between all stakeholders, might specify that the only time individual medical records are disclosed to CDC is when more than 100 people in the same zip code exhibit certain disease symptoms. Similarly, commercial negotiation might lead to a policy specifying that the only time personal data of a software user are revealed to the software manufacturer is when the user installs the same copy of software on three or more different computers. Our research project, however, does not deal with the political, legal, organizational, or commercial aspects of this negotiation process. Instead, assuming that such negotiation will lead to the establishment of binding privacy disclosure conditions for some class of activities, we propose to investigate the technical means of implementing a monitoring system which ensures, based on strong cryptographic assumptions, that the established privacy disclosure conditions are adhered to.

4.2   Disclosure Policies: Predicates and Privacy Thresholds

Negotiated Privacy can support any disclosure policy that consists of setting a numerical *privacy threshold* for a certain class of events. The database of escrowed entries should satisfy the following property: the database owner only learns the plaintext of the entries that correspond to events which (1) belong to the same class, and (2) their number is no less than the pre-negotiated privacy threshold for this event class. Each permitted query must be of the following form: "if the database contains at least k entries, each of which satisfies a particular predicate P, reveal all entries satisfying P." A privacy disclosure condition is thus fully specified by the $\langle P, k \rangle$ pair. All of the examples outlined above can be implemented with threshold disclosure conditions. For example, an intelligence agency might establish the privacy threshold of 3 for events in the "itineraries with destination within 100 miles of Kandahar" class.

The disclosure predicate P may evaluate the user's activity at different levels of granularity. A patient's medical record might contain information relevant to a given query, such as blood pressure readings, but also irrelevant information, such as the social security number, marital status, etc. A passenger itinerary may include relevant fields, such as destination, and irrelevant fields, such as the name of the airline. Whether a particular field of the user's entry is relevant or not depends on the disclosure predicate. We will refer to the smallest subset of the user's entry that determines the value of the disclosure predicate as the *core* of that entry. Formally, given two entries t and t' and a predicate P, if $\mathsf{core}(t) = \mathsf{core}(t')$, then $P(t) = P(t')$.

4.3   Principals

Analyst. We use the term *analyst* for the owner of the database in which information about individuals, organizations, and their activities is collected. The role of the analyst can be played, for example, by a law enforcement or medical agency, government regulator, etc. The analyst issues a digitally signed credential or *receipt* for each escrowed datum he receives. The data escrow protocol must ensure that the analyst outputs a valid credential on a datum if and only if he receives a valid escrow of that datum. Secondly, the analyst should be able to efficiently evaluate on his database only the queries allowed by the pre-negotiated privacy disclosure policies.

User. A *user* is an individual or organization whose information is being collected in the analyst's database. We use the term *activity* to refer to the information that is of potential interest to the analyst. We assume that each activity is performed on the user's behalf by some service provider.

Service provider. A *service provider* is an agent who performs activities on users' behalf. For example, a commercial airline (service provider) transports a passenger (user) who has to report an escrow of his itinerary (activity) to an Office of Homeland Security database (analyst). Each service provider performs the requested service only if it is accompanied by a valid receipt issued by the analyst. An honest service provider should consider the receipt valid only if the user has previously submitted a correctly formed escrow to the analyst. We assume that the service provider knows the user's identity and the requested activity, but the user can choose which service provider he wants to receive services from. If the user wishes to protect his privacy, he is free to pick a provider he trusts not to reveal his activities to other parties. We consider the threats presented by malicious service providers below.

PKI/Magistrate. The magistrate is an independent official, trusted by all principals involved in Negotiated Privacy. The magistrate plays the role of a Public-Key Infrastructure (PKI), and can be replaced by a conventional PKI if one is available. The magistrate is employed only when the system is initialized and, in some variants of Negotiated Privacy, for dispute resolution.

4.4 Threat Model

Since no assumptions are made about the trustworthiness of any of the principals except PKI, the Negotiated Privacy system must be secure against malicious misbehavior of any of the principals.

Malicious analyst. A malicious analyst should not be able to extract any information from the escrowed entries unless they satisfy one of the pre-negotiated disclosure conditions. Even then, the analyst should not learn the plaintext of the escrows that do not satisfy any such condition. If the analyst guesses the value of the plaintext on which the escrow is based, he should not be able to verify whether his guess is correct or not. Given two escrows, the analyst should not be able to determine whether they originate from the same user, or are based on the same plaintext.

Malicious user. A malicious user should not be able to obtain a valid receipt without submitting to the analyst a properly formed escrow. He also should not be able to prevent the analyst from efficiently recognizing that a subset of escrows accumulated in the analyst's database satisfies some disclosure condition, and can thus be feasibly opened.

Malicious service provider. If the service provider cooperates with the analyst against the user, no privacy can be guaranteed for the data that pass through that provider since the latter learns their contents in their entirety (*e.g.*, a passenger's itinerary cannot be hidden from the airline that transports this passenger). The analyst should be prevented, however, from learning the contents of *other* escrows, including those created by the same user and based on the same core plaintext (see lemma 4).

No data collection or monitoring scheme is feasible if the service provider cooperates with the *user* against the analyst and simply performs the requested activity without verifying whether the user has received a valid receipt from the analyst. If an airline is willing to transport passengers without any checks, then it is impossible to collect any reliable information about passenger itineraries. Therefore, our proposed scheme does not address this threat.

5   Cryptographic Toolkit

The Negotiated Privacy solution we propose is based on the assumption that computing so-called Decisional Diffie-Hellman (DDH) problem is intractable. Even though this assumption is not equivalent to the assumption of hardness of discrete logarithm computation, the two assumptions are related, and so far the only known way to compute DDH is to compute discrete logarithms. (See [Bon98] for a review of the literature on the hardness of computing DDH and on the use of this assumption in cryptographic literature.) The DDH problem is as follows. Let p and q be large primes and g be a generator of a subgroup $G_q = \{g^0, \dots, g^{q-1}\}$ of order q of the multiplicative group $Z_p^* = \{1, \dots, p-1\}$. In the DDH problem one is asked to distinguish between tuples of form $\{g, g^a, g^b, g^{ab}\}$ where a, b are distributed uniformly in Z_q, from tuples $\{g, g^a, g^b, g^c\}$ where a, b, c are distributed uniformly in Z_q. The DDH assumption is that the task of distinguishing between such tuples is intractable.

In our solution we assume the discrete-log setting given by the tuple (p, q, g) as above. We furthermore assume a hash function hash : $\{0,1\}^* \to G_q$, which can be implemented with SHA-1 or MD5. In our analysis we will treat this hash function as an ideal hash function (see, *e.g.*, [BR93]). We also assume an a semantically secure symmetric encryption and a chosen-message-attack secure signature scheme.

5.1   First Tool: Anonymous Commitment and Encryption

Each user U has a private/public key pair (x, y). Suppose that plaintext t describes U's planned reportable activity (*e.g.*, airline travel). If $P(t)$ evaluates to true, then the user must submit a personal data escrow $\lceil t \rceil_x$ to the analyst's database.

The escrow must satisfy several requirements. First, it must contain a tag which is a *commitment* to i) the user's identity, and ii) the core plaintext core(t), *i.e.*, the part that determines the value of the disclosure predicate P. The user should not be able to open this commitment with t' which has a different disclosure predicate, *i.e.*, such that core(t') $\neq$ core(t), or with x' that is different from the private key x that corresponds to the user's public key certificate issued by the magistrate. Moreover, this commitment must be *deterministic*, *i.e.*, the value of the commitment must be the same each time the user computes it for the given values of core(t) and x. The reason for this is that the analyst must be able to determine when the threshold number of escrows based on the same core(t) and x has been reached, in order to effect disclosure. Third, this commitment must be verifiable without the user revealing his private key x. Instead, the service provider must be able to verify that the commitment is computed correctly only knowing the user's public key y. Fourth, this commitment must protect anonymity of the user. Namely, given $\lceil t \rceil_x$, the analyst should not be able to determine if this escrow corresponds to some user U with public key y and/or some reportable activity t. The analyst should also not be able to determine if some escrows $\lceil t_i \rceil_{x_i}$ correspond to the same or different users or to the same reportable activities.

In addition to the tag which is a commitment to x and core(t), the escrow $\lceil t \rceil_x$ must also contain an encryption of the value t itself. When the required privacy threshold for events that meet some disclosure condition is reached, the analyst will ask the user to open the escrows whose tag matches this disclosure condition. Because this encryption must also be verifiable by the service provider, and it must protect the anonymity of the user, we implement both functionalities with the same tool of an anonymous one-way function which is unpredictable on random inputs.

Let hash be an ideal hash function and Enc a semantically secure symmetric encryption. Assuming the hardness of the DDH problem, the function we will use is $f_x(m) = m^x (\mathrm{mod}\, p)$. The encryption part of an escrow $\lceil t \rceil_x$ is a pair $s^x (\mathrm{mod}\, p)$, $Enc_s\{t\}$, where s is a randomly chosen element in G_q, and Enc is a semantically secure symmetric encryption scheme. Under DDH this is a semantically secure encryption scheme. The tag part of the $\lceil t \rceil_x$ escrow is a commitment to x and core(t) computed using the same function as $tag = h^x (\mathrm{mod}\, p)$, where $h = $ hash(core(t)). Under DDH, both functionalities are *anonymous* in the sense that they cannot be matched to a public key $y = g^x (\mathrm{mod}\, p)$.

5.2   Second Tool: Verifiability via Zero-Knowledge

The encryption and commitment functions (hash(core(t)))^x and s^x, $Enc_s\{t\}$ protect user's anonymity, but we need to provide, *e.g.*, to the service provider, the ability to verify that these functions were correctly computed without the user having to reveal his secret key x. Note that to prove that the value

$z = h^x$ has been correctly computed, the user has to prove that the discrete logarithm $DL_h(z) = DL_h(h^x) = x$ is equal to the discrete logarithm $DL_g(y) = DL_g(g^x) = x$. To do that, we use the non-interactive zero-knowledge proof of equality of discrete logarithms based on standard honest-verifier zero-knowledge proof due to Schnorr [Sch91]. (See Appendix A.)

Using this proof, the user who reveals t, s, and his public key $y = g^x$ to the service provider can prove that the tag part of $\lceil t \rceil_x$ is indeed equal to h^x, where $h = \mathsf{hash}(\mathsf{core}(t))$ can be computed by the service provider himself, and that the ciphertext part of $\lceil t \rceil_x$ is indeed a pair $(s^x, Enc_s\{t\})$.

6   Negotiated Privacy Database System

We describe the procedures for managing the Negotiated Privacy database for a single disclosure condition $\langle P, k \rangle$. The procedure can be easily generalized to multiple disclosure conditions by executing the steps described in section 6.2 with a separate key for each condition whenever a new escrow is added to the database.

Let U be the user, A the analyst and S the service provider. We assume that the disclosure conditions are publicly known, and therefore both U, A, S can derive the disclosure predicate P, the projection core, and the disclosure threshold k, for any activity t. We assume that the values of projection $\mathsf{core}(\cdot)$ are unique for every predicate P, i.e., that for $P \neq P'$, for every t, t' such that $P(t)$ and $P'(t')$ are both true, $\mathsf{core}_P(t) \neq \mathsf{core}_{P'}(t')$. This can be easily achieved by appending a description $\langle P \rangle$ to $\mathsf{core}(t)$.

With Negotiated Privacy, the user encrypts the plaintext record t describing his activities, but does not reveal the record to the analyst unless the disclosure condition is satisfied. We assume that each t includes some verifiably fresh information that can be traced to the user, for example, the user's signature on the current time.

Although the analyst cannot verify that the record accurately describes the user's activity, he issues a digitally signed receipt for the user-submitted escrow. The service provider will require the user to open the analyst-signed encryption and verify that the record is indeed accurate and that the analyst's signature is fresh and valid.

In our solution, the analyst simply accumulates the encryptions and, once the disclosure threshold is reached, refuses to issue further receipts unless the user decrypts all of his previous encryptions together with the current one (and proves that he decrypted them correctly). From then on, this user will get the analyst's signature only if he reports his activity to the analyst in the clear.

6.1   Initialization

During initialization, the user creates a key pair $\langle x, y = g^x \rangle$, where g is some suitable base, x is the private key and the pair g^x, g is the public key. The user then approaches the magistrate, who, given g and $y = g^x$, verifies that the user

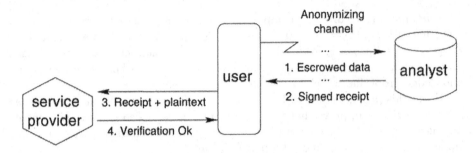

Fig. 1. Submitting and verifying a new escrow

indeed knows x (using, *e.g.*, Schnorr's authentication protocol [Sch91]) and issues a digitally signed certificate for the user's public key, binding the user's identity to the user's public key: $sig_{K_M}(U,y)$. It is important that no more than one certificate is issued to each user. The user will need to present this certificate to service providers so that they can verify compliance as described in section 6.3 before performing a reportable activity.

The private key x and the corresponding public key certificate are the only values that the user has to remember to participate in Negotiated Privacy. The user-side software can, therefore, be implemented in constant memory and stored, for example, on a "trusted traveller" smartcard. Our scheme imposes fairly modest computational requirements on the user. In particular, the user does not need to obtain a special token from the magistrate for each activity.

6.2   Submitting a New Escrow

The user generates the escrow $[t]_x = (tag, c, Enc_s\{t\}, k)$ consisting of the following parts:

1. $tag = h^x$ where $h = \mathsf{hash}(\mathsf{core}(t))$
2. $c = s^x$ where s is a fresh random element in G_q
3. $Enc_s\{t\}$, which is t encrypted using a symmetric cipher under a key derived by hashing s into the key space of the cipher
4. k, the anonymity threshold value

The user then sends this escrow to the analyst A. We assume that the user and the analyst communicate via an anonymizing channel (*e.g.*, an onion routing network [GRS99] or simply a public online bulletin board) that prevents the analyst from deducing the submitter's identity.

A keeps a database indexed by tag fields. After receiving the above escrow $[t]_x = (tag, c, Enc_s\{t\}, k)$, A checks that this escrow has not been submitted before. If it is fresh, the analyst checks whether the number of escrows in its database indexed with the same tag index is under $k - 1$. If it is larger, A requests that U open his escrow (see section 6.4). If it is equal to $k - 1$, A

furthermore requests that U decrypts all of his previous ciphertexts of the other $k-1$ escrows indexed by the same tag field. If the user complies or if there are fewer than $k-1$ escrows with this tag field in A's database, A issues the receipt by signing the entire received escrow. The procedure for submitting and verifying a new escrow is summarized in fig. 1.

6.3   Compliance Checking

We rely on the service provider S to perform all the checks necessary to ensure that the escrow submitted by the user was is correctly formed and based on accurate information. We furthermore assume that the activity description t contains enough specific and timely details to guarantee that the same description cannot be used twice. While this approach requires that service providers be trusted to perform the checks, this is inevitable as discussed in section 4.4.

Before the service provider S provides a service or performs an activity on behalf of user U, S requests the record t describing the details of the activity from U and evaluates the disclosure predicate P. If $P(t)$ is true, then U should have submitted an escrow $\lceil t \rceil_x$ based on t to the analyst. S requests the following:

- $\mathsf{sig}_{K_A}(tag, c, Enc_s\{t\}, k)$, the digitally signed receipt from the analyst containing the entire escrow submitted by U;
- $\mathsf{sig}_{K_M}(U, y)$, the digitally signed certificate from the magistrate binding U's identity to U's public key y;
- the one-time key material s;
- a non-interactive zero-knowledge proof that $tag = h^x$, $c = s^x$, and $y = g^x$.

After receiving these items, S performs the following checks:

- Verify the magistrate's digital signature on the certificate $\mathsf{sig}_{K_M}(U, y)$ and the analyst's signature on $\mathsf{sig}_{K_A}(tag, c, Enc_s\{t\}, k)$.
- Compute the activity description t by decrypting the $Enc_s\{t\}$ ciphertext with a key derived by hashing the one-time key material s.
- Verify that the user's identity is indeed U, that the activity performed is adequately described by t (including the user's signature on a plausible time value), and that the anonymity threshold for this activity is indeed k.
- Given t, compute $h = \mathsf{hash}(\mathsf{core}(t))$, and verify the non-interactive zero-knowledge proof that $tag = h^x$, $c = s^x$, and $y = g^x$ (see section 5.2).

6.4   Disclosure

If the database contains $k-1$ escrows with the same index $tag = \mathsf{hash}(\mathsf{core}(t))^x$, the analyst refuses to issue a receipt for any user-submitted escrow with that index unless the user decrypts all his escrows associated with the index. Since an analyst-signed receipt is necessary to perform a reportable activity, this ensures proper disclosure. The user does not need to remember his old escrows. The analyst simply presents the list of escrows stored under the tag index back to the user and asks him to open them.

To open any escrow $\lceil t \rceil_x = (tag, c, Enc_s\{t\}, k)$, the user uses his private key x to compute $s = (c)^{\frac{1}{x}}$, computes t by decrypting $Enc_s\{t\}$ with the key derived from s, computes $h = \mathsf{hash}(\mathsf{core}(t))$, and sends to the analyst values h, s, his certificate $\mathsf{sig}_{K_M}(U, y)$, and a non-interactive zero-knowledge proof that $tag = h^x$, $c = s^x$, and $y = g^x$.

The analyst checks these values similarly to the verification procedure of the service provider described in section 6.3. In this process, the analyst learns the activity description t and the user's identity U.

6.5   Security Properties of Negotiated Privacy

Assuming the hardness of the DDH problem, the following properties follow immediately in the random oracle model:

Lemma 1. *Given t and $h = \mathsf{hash}(\mathsf{core}(t))$ and the user's public key y, the adversary cannot distinguish $tag = h^x$ from a random element in G_q.*

Therefore, the analyst who guesses the value of t and the user's identity U, y, cannot verify this guess.

Lemma 2. *Given t, t' and $h = \mathsf{hash}(\mathsf{core}(t))$, $h' = \mathsf{hash}(\mathsf{core}'(t'))$ s.t. $h \neq h'$, the adversary cannot distinguish between pairs $h^x, (h')^x$ and pairs $h^x, (h')^{x'}$ for any pair of public keys $y = g^x, y' = g^{x'}$.*

Therefore, given two encrypted values, the analyst cannot determine whether they were generated by the same user or by two different users.

Lemma 3. *Given t, t' and $h = \mathsf{hash}(\mathsf{core}(t))$, $h' = \mathsf{hash}(\mathsf{core}'(t'))$ s.t. $h \neq h'$, the adversary cannot distinguish between pairs $h^x, h^{x'}$ and pairs $h^x, (h')^{x'}$ for any pair of public keys $y = g^x, y' = g^{x'}$ (including pairs s.t. $y = y'$).*

Therefore, given two encrypted values, the analyst cannot determine whether they encrypt the same or different plaintext, *i.e.*, the analyst cannot tell whether they were generated because of the same predicate or two different predicates.

Moreover, we can show the following:

Lemma 4. *If the service provider is cooperating with the analyst, the analyst learns nothing except*

- *Values t and U for all escrows verified by that provider.*
- *Associations between values tag and values U and $t^* = \mathsf{core}(t)$. This allows the analyst to tell how many reportable activities of type t^* are performed by user U. It does not leak, however, any more specific information about these activities.*

7   Conclusions

We presented a simple technique that provides an efficient and, assuming the Decisional Diffie-Hellman problem is intractable, provably secure way for a subject of monitoring to escrow his or her personal data in a Negotiated Privacy database and be assured that the database owner cannot extract any information from it. At the same time, the database owner is assured that the collected escrows accurately describe the monitored activities and, if one of the pre-negotiated disclosure conditions is satisfied, he will be able to open the relevant escrows and learn the details of the disclosed activities. In the future, we envision extending this approach to enable automatic opening of escrows once the privacy threshold is reached and to ensure privacy for subjects of monitoring even when corrupt service providers are cooperating with the analyst.

References

[AF88]   M. Abadi and J. Feigenbaum. A simple protocol for secure circuit evaluation. In *Proc. STACS '88*, pages 264–272, 1988.

[AR02]   M. Abadi and P. Rogaway. Reconciling two views of cryptography (the computational soundness of formal encryption). *J. Cryptology*, 15(2):103–127, 2002.

[BBDP01]   M. Bellare, A. Boldyreva, A. Desai, and D. Pointcheval. Key-privacy in public-key encryption. In *Proc. ASIACRYPT '01*, pages 566–582, 2001.

[BO02]   D. Boneh and R. Ostrovsky. Search on encrypted data, 2002.

[Bon98]   D. Boneh. The decisional Diffie-Hellman problem. In *Proc. 3rd Algorithmic Number Theory Symposium*, volume 1423 of *LNCS*, pages 48–63. Springer-Verlag, 1998.

[BR93]   M. Bellare and P. Rogaway. Random oracles are practical: a paradigm for designing efficient protocols. In *Proc. ACM Conference on Computer and Communications Security*, pages 62–73, 1993.

[Bra00]   S. Brands. *Rethinking Public Key Infrastructure and Digital Certificates – Building in Privacy*. MIT Press, Cambridge, MA, 2000.

[CFN88]   D. Chaum, A. Fiat, and M. Naor. Untraceable electronic cash. In *Proc. CRYPTO '88*, volume 403 of *LNCS*, pages 319–327. Springer-Verlag, 1988.

[CGKS98]   B. Chor, O. Goldreich, E. Kushilevitz, and M. Sudan. Private information retrieval. *J. ACM*, 45(6):965–981, 1998.

[Cha82]   D. Chaum. Blind signatures for untracable payments. In *Proc. CRYPTO '82*, pages 199–203, 1982.

[CL01]   J. Camenisch and A. Lysyanskaya. An efficient system for non-transferable anonymous credentials with optional anonymity revocation. In *Proc. EUROCRYPT '01*, volume 2045 of *LNCS*, pages 93–118. Springer-Verlag, 2001.

[CP92]   D. Chaum and T. Pedersen. Wallet databases with observers. In *Proc. CRYPTO '92*, volume 740 of *LNCS*, pages 89–105. Springer-Verlag, 1992.

[DF89]   Y. Desmedt and Y. Frankel. Threshold cryptosystems. In *Proc. CRYPTO '89*, volume 435 of *LNCS*, pages 307–315. Springer-Verlag, 1989.

[ERAG02]   A. Evfimievski, R.Srikant, R. Agrawal, and J. Gehrke. Privacy preserving mining of association rules. In *Proc. 8th ACM SIGKDD Int'l Conference on Knowledge Discovery in Databases and Data Mining*, 2002.

[Fel87]   P. Feldman. A practical scheme for non-interactive verifiable secret sharing. In *Proc. 28th IEEE Symposium on Foundations of Comp. Science*, pages 427–438, 1987.

[GIKM98]   Y. Gertner, Y. Ishai, E. Kushilevitz, and T. Malkin. Protecting data privacy in private inforamtion retrieval schemes. In *Proc. 31th Annual ACM Symposium on Theory of Computing*, pages 151–160, 1998.

[GMW87]   O. Goldreich, S. Micali, and A. Wigderson. How to play any mental game or a completeness theorem for protocols with and honest majority. In *Proc. 19th Annual ACM Symposium on Theory of Computing*, pages 218–229, 1987.

[GRS99]   D. Goldschlag, M. Reed, and P. Syverson. Onion routing for anonymous and private Internet connections. *Communications of the ACM*, 42(2):39–41, 1999.

[KL95]   J. Kilian and F.T. Leighton. Fair cryptosystems, revisited. In *Proc. EUROCRYPT '95*, volume 963 of *LNCS*, pages 208–220. Springer-Verlag, 1995.

[KP98]   J. Kilian and E. Petrank. Identity escrow. In *Proc. CRYPTO '98*, volume 1462 of *LNCS*, pages 169–185. Springer-Verlag, 1998.

[KY01]   A. Kiayias and M. Yung. Secure games with polynomial expressions. In *ICALP '01*, pages 939–950, 2001.

[LP00]   Y. Lindell and B. Pinkas. Privacy preserving data mining. In *Proc. CRYPTO '00*, volume 1880 of *LNCS*, pages 36–47. Springer-Verlag, 2000.

[Mic92]   S. Micali. Fair public-key cryptosystems. In *Proc. CRYPTO '92*, volume 740 of *LNCS*, pages 113–138. Springer-Verlag, 1992.

[NP98]   M. Naor and B. Pinkas. Oblivious transfer and polynomial evaluation. In *Proc. 31th Annual ACM Symposium on Theory of Computing*, pages 245–254, 1998.

[Sch91]   C.P. Schnorr. Efficient signature generation by smart cards. *J. Cryptology*, 4(3):161–174, 1991.

[Sha79]   A. Shamir. How to share a secret. *Communications of the ACM*, 22(11):612–613, 1979.

[SWP00]   D.X. Song, D. Wagner, and A. Perrig. Practical techniques for searches on encrypted data. In *Proc. IEEE Symposium on Security and Privacy*, pages 44–55, 2000.

[Yao82]   A.C. Yao. Protocols for secure computations. In *Proc. 23rd IEEE Symposium on Foundations of Comp. Science*, pages 160–164, 1982.

[YY98]   A. Young and M. Yung. Auto-recoverable and auto-certifiable cryptosystems. In *Proc. EUROCRYPT '98*, volume 1043 of *LNCS*, pages 17–31. Springer-Verlag, 1998.

A   Zero-Knowledge Proof of Equality of Discrete Logs

To prove the equality of discrete logarithms, namely to prove that $DL_h(z) = DL_g(y)$, we use the following zero-knowledge proof due to Chaum and Pedersen [CP92]:

The prover's (user) secret input is x, a number in Z_q, and the verifier's (service provider) inputs are g, h, y, z, two numbers in G_q. To prove that $y = g^x$ and $z = h^x$, the prover picks a random number k in Z_q and sends $u = g^k$ and $v = h^k$ to the verifier. The verifier picks a random challenge e in Z_q and sends it to the prover. The prover sends back a response $f = k + ex$. The verifier accepts the interactive proof if $u = g^f/y^e$ and $v = h^f/z^e$. This protocol is zero-knowledge only for honest-verifiers, but in the random oracle model it can be converted to a non-interactive zero-knowledge proof by setting the challenge $e = H(g, h, y, z, u, v)$. In other words, the user generates the values k, u, v as above, computes $e = H(g, h, y, z, u, v)$ and $f = k + ex$, and sends to the service provider the pair (e, f) as the proof of discrete logarithms equality. To check this proof, the service provider computes $u = g^f/y^e$ and $v = h^f/z^e$ as above, and accepts if $e = H(g, h, y, z, u, v)$.

We note that this protocol can easily be extended to prove equality of three (or more) discrete logarithms. Moreover, it can be used as a way to authenticate the user by requiring that the challenge e is computed by hashing also a random authentication challenge sent to the user by the verifier, or by including in this hash the current time value.

SoftwarePot: An Encapsulated Transferable File System for Secure Software Circulation

Kazuhiko Kato[1,2] and Yoshihiro Oyama[2]

[1] Institute of Information Sciences and Electronics
University of Tsukuba
Tennoudai 1-1-1, Tsukuba, Ibaraki 305-8573, Japan
[2] Japan Science and Technology Corporation
{kato,yosh}@osss.is.tsukuba.ac.jp
http://www.osss.is.tsukuba.ac.jp/~kato/ and /~yosh/

Abstract. We have developed a general approach to enable secure circulation of software in an open network environment such as the Internet. By software circulation, we mean a generalized conventional software distribution concept in which software can be transferred even in an iterative manner such as through redistribution or using mobile agents. To clarify the problem that arises when software is circulated in an open network environment, we first considered a simple model for unsecure software circulation and then developed a model for secure software circulation (SSC). In the SSC model, we extended the sandbox concept to include its own file system and to have the ability to be transferred via a network. In this sense, our approach is characterized by an encapsulated, transferable file system. We describe how the SoftwarePot system was designed to implement the SSC model, and discuss the implications of experimental results that we obtained during the implementation.

1 Introduction

One of the most notable features of the Internet is that it is a truly open environment. Not only is it being constantly extended worldwide, no one can fully control or determine who the users are, or what software and content are exchanged through it. These features are in stark contrast to traditional, closed computing environments such as batch, TSS, LAN, or personal systems. Throughout the history of computing systems, the computing environment has almost always been closed, so designers of system software have implicitly assumed a closed environment was the norm. The worldwide spread of the Internet occurred within a relatively short portion of the history of computing system development, so there was little time for designers of system software to fully anticipate the issues that would arise when closed environments became open. Though the environment has drastically opened up, we still use system software whose basic design is based on an assumption of a closed environment. Thus, current computer systems can often be characterized as *putting new wine in old bottles*.

If a network environment is closed and users cannot access an open network environment such as the Internet, malicious users and the files created by such

M. Okada et al. (Eds.): ISSS 2002, LNCS 2609, pp. 112–132, 2003.

users are far less likely to exist. Unfortunately, in the Internet environment, we *cannot* assume this. Thus, obtaining files, particularly software that includes executable or interpreted code, from the Internet can be a risky activity. One approach now being used to lessen the risk is to use a code-signing technique, such as Microsoft's Authenticode. Being able to obtain information about a distributor's identity is useful, but users still face a non-technical problem as to whether they can trust the distributor. A promising technical approach to solve this problem is to create a "sandbox" and encapsulate risky effects in a limited, controllable environment separate from the users' ordinary environment. This approach has been adopted in many systems, such as Java, SFI [18], Janus [5], MAPbox [1], and SubDomain [4].

In this paper, we discuss a general approach that we have developed to allow secure software circulation in the Internet environment. By software circulation, we mean conventional software distribution, even where software is transferred in an iterative manner such as through redistribution or by mobile agents. To clearly define the problem that arises when software is circulated in an open network environment, we first consider a simple model for *unsecure* software circulation, then propose a model for *secure* software circulation. In the secure software circulation model, we extend the sandbox concept to include its own file system and network transferability. In this sense, our approach is characterized by an encapsulated, transferable file system. We designed the system named *SoftwarePot* based on the approach [11]. In the SoftwarePot system, all circulated files are encapsulated into a transferable file system called *pot*. We say that a pot is closed if it is perfectly self-contained and does not need to input or output files other than those contained in the pot. The execution of codes included in a closed pot is guaranteed to not affect the user's file system outside of the pot. Sometimes, though, it is necessary to affect the user's file system in a securely controlled way. For this purpose, SoftwarePot provides a mechanism to map between the files in a pot and those in the user's file system. By associating the mapping requirement of a pot, the user of the pot can know which files need to be accessed before execution. This helps to develop security policies for the executing sites. Furthermore, SoftwarePot incorporates a lazy file transfer mechanism, by which we mean that only references to files are stored in a pot, instead of the file entities themselves, and each file entity is automatically transferred only when requested during execution. These mechanisms allow use of the SoftwarePot system as a general tool to circulate software in the Internet environment.

The rest of the paper is organized as follows. Section 2 describes the models for *unsecure* and *secure* software circulation. It also shows that many useful software transfer patterns can be naturally modeled by combining the basic operations of the models. Section 3 explains how the SoftwarePot system is designed to implement the secure software circulation model. Section 4 shows some of our experimental results obtained during the system implementation. Section 5 discusses related work. Finally, Section 6 concludes the paper.

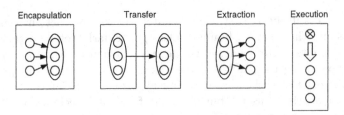

Fig. 1. The four basic operations of the unsecure software circulation model.

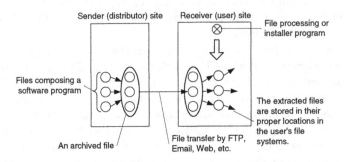

Fig. 2. Software distribution.

2   Software Circulation Models

To clarify the concept of secure software circulation, we first present a model for *unsecure* software circulation, which is a generalization of software distribution as conventionally performed. We then present a model for *secure* software circulation and explain how it can be used.

2.1   A Model for Unsecure Software Circulation

Software circulation is the term we use to refer to a generalization of the "software distribution" concept. Software distribution usually means unidirectional, one-time, one-to-many distribution of a software package. By relaxing these properties, that is, by making software distribution multidirectional, multi-time, many-to-many, we obtain the concept of software circulation. Software circulation is composed of four basic operations: encapsulation, transfer, extraction, and execution. For each operation, we use a graphic representation as shown in Fig. 1.

- The encapsulation operation is applied to one or more files and creates an archive file that encapsulate those files.
- The transfer operation moves an encapsulated file from a source site to a destination site.
- The extraction operation is the inverse of the encapsulation operation: one or more files are extracted from an archive file. Extracted files are stored somewhere in the file system of the site where the operation is performed.

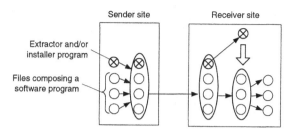

Extractor and/or
installer program

Files composing a
software program

Fig. 3. Transfer of a self-extraction file.

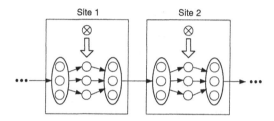

Fig. 4. Workflow.

File allocation, naming, and access-control setting are performed at that
time.

- In the execution operation, an executable program (shown as the circle containing a cross in Fig. 1) is executed. During the execution, files (the circles
  without a cross) may be inputted, outputted, or modified.

By combining these operations, we can represent typical software circulation
scenarios. Figure 2 illustrates software distribution. At the sender site (e.g., a
distributor of a software package), the files of a package are encapsulated into
a archive file by using an archiving program. The archived file is transferred
from the distributor's site to a receiver (user) site. At the user's site, the archive
file is extracted and stored in the user's file system. Figure 3 shows a variation;
an extraction and/or installation program are included within the archive file.
This is flexible and convenient, since the distributor can do anything during the
installation by describing it in the installation program, even if the user does
not have an extraction or installation program. Figures 4 and 5 show iterative
styles of software circulation. In the former, a program is applied to circulated
files and this models a workflow system. In the latter, a program included in the
circulated file is executed and this models a mobile agent system.

The presented model is unsecure in the following aspects:

- In the encapsulation operation, a malicious person may lay traps in the
  archive file; for example, by including files that perform malicious things
  when executed or that overwrite existing files for malicious purposes when
  extracted.

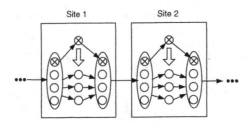

Fig. 5. Mobile agent.

- During the transfer operation, files may be maliciously interrupted, intercepted, modified, or fabricated [15].
- During the extraction operation, extracted files are stored in the user's file system, and their file storage is allocated and named and their access control is set at that time. These operations are critical for the management of the user's file system, and are quite dangerous if they are not done according to the user's management policy.
- The execution operation, needless to say, involves a potential lack of security. All effects of the execution on the computer resources should be controlled in accordance with the user's security policy.

For these reasons, we call this model the *unsecure software circulation* (USC) model.

2.2   A Model for Secure Software Circulation

Now, we consider a model for *secure software circulation* (the SSC model). To start with, we should explain what we mean here by "secure." First, it is generally accepted that an absolutely "secure" system is virtually impossible to design. This model and our implemented system based on this model (described in the next section) is simply more secure than the USC model regarding security-related issues that are more easily handled in a systematic way. Second, the unsecure aspects of the *transfer* operation are not limited to software circulation; they are also issues of concern in general information transfer. However, we will not discuss these issues any further in this paper.

The central idea of the SSC model is that we distinguish the *inner* and the *outer* parts of circulated software during both the execution and the encapsulation. To enable this, we introduced two concepts into the model. First, we do not extract files from archives; instead, we extend the concept of using archive files as a file system. Second, we enable program execution *within* a distinct virtual address space associated with the archive space. The SSC model integrates the two spaces—the virtual address space and the file system—into one to create a sandbox called a *pot*. Each pot has its own, distinct view for both a virtual address space and a virtual file space.

We define the basic operation of the SSC model as follows (see Fig. 6 for a graphical representation).

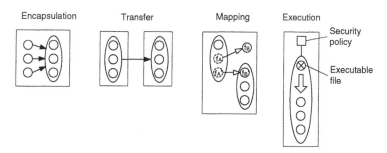

Fig. 6. The four basic operations of the secure software circulation model.

- The encapsulation operation is applied to one or more files and stores them in a pot. During storing, each file is given a unique pathname compatible with the Unix file system, and the attribute-information, such as time of last modification and executability, is recorded.
- The transfer operation moves an encapsulated file from a source site to a destination site.
- The mapping operation in the SSC model is a substitute for the extraction operation of the USC model. In Fig. 6, the mapping operations are represented by arrows with unshaded heads. The mapping from file f_A in a pot to file f_B in a pot or local file means that every access to f_A during execution within the pot is redirected to f_B.
- In the execution operation, a program is not executed in a virtual address space that shares a file system of the executing site. A pot is instead associated with a virtual process space just like its own file system, and a program in the pot is executed within that environment; no files other than those appearing in the pot can be seen. When execution is initiated, a security policy specification is associated with the execution. It specifies a mapping scheme and the resources allowed to be used.

As described above, a pot has two states depending on whether a process is associated with the pot. To distinguish between the two states, we use the terminology *pot-file* when a process is not associated with the pot, and *pot-process* when it is associated.

Figure 7 illustrates a typical use of the SSC model combining the four basic operations. In the sender site, one executable file (a circle containing a cross) and one data file (a solid circle with no cross) processed by the executable file are encapsulated. The remaining two files (broken circles) do not exist physically in the pot at the sender site and their file entities are mapped in the receiver site at the execution time. The archived file is transferred from the sender site to the receiver site via any transfer method such as FTP, WWW, or e-mail. At the receiver site, the user prepares a security policy description that specifies the mapping schemes between the file in the pot and a local file and between the file in the pot and a file in another pot. During the execution, no other files in the local file system of the receiver site can be seen. The security policy file can also

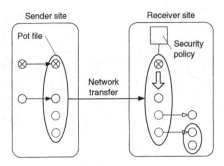

Fig. 7. Typical use of the secure software circulation model.

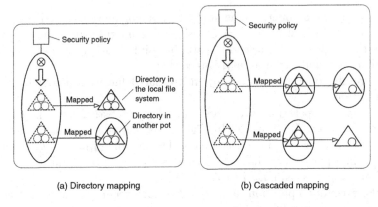

(a) Directory mapping   (b) Cascaded mapping

Fig. 8. Mapping directories in SoftwarePot.

specify system calls of the OS kernel allowed to be issued in the execution. Thus, the pot constitutes a sandbox distinct from the ordinary execution environment in user processes.

Last, we want to point out two slight extensions to the mapping operation. We permit the mapping of a directory in a pot to a directory in another pot or in a local ordinary file system as shown in Fig. 8(a). Furthermore, we permit cascading of the mapping as shown in Fig. 8(b). The informal operational semantics of the cascaded mapping is as follows. The cascaded mapping operation results in a totally ordered relationship between multiple directories in pots and/or an ordinary file system. When the pathname of a file is retrieved, the totally ordered directories are retrieved in the total order, and the first one found is the result. These extensions are useful in that they facilitate and simplify the description of security policies, and also make the computing of transferred pots more flexible.

2.3   Utilization of the SSC Model

Now we show how we can apply the SSC model to represent typical computation requiring secure software transfer in an open network environment.

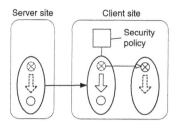

Fig. 9. Secure interpretation of downloaded code.

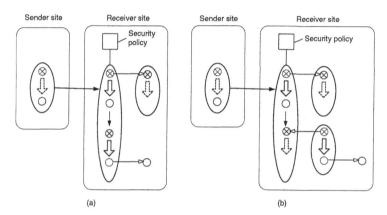

Fig. 10. Secure execution of dynamically generated native code. The code generation and the execution of the generated code are done in a single pot in Fig. 10(a), and in different pots in Fig. 10(b)

Secure interpretation of downloaded code. A typical use of SSC is the secure interpretation of downloaded code. This form of computation has been made popular by the widespread use of Java and its applet system. SSC can be used to provide a general framework that enables secure interpretation of downloaded code (Fig. 9). The server site stores a pot that includes code which will be interpreted by an interpreter stored at a client site. In the figure, the interpreter is also assumed to be stored in a pot. Through the mapping operation, the interpreter entity appears in the pot sent from the sender and interprets the code under the control of the associated security policy. Note that this framework for the secure interpretation of downloaded code does not limit which programming language system or virtual machine instruction set can be used.

Secure execution of dynamically generated native code. Next, we will describe a more advanced form of downloaded code execution (Fig. 10). In this, the code downloaded from server to client is compiled into native code for the client's CPU architecture then the generated native code is executed at the client site. This form of computation is usually called execution by *just-in-time compilation.* As shown in the figure, such computation is represented by simply combining

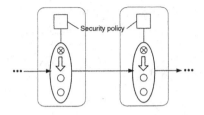

Fig. 11. Secure execution of mobile agents.

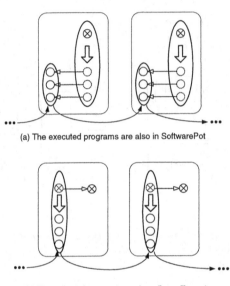

(a) The executed programs are also in SoftwarePot

(b) The executed programs are in ordinary file system

Fig. 12. Secure workflow computing.

the basic operations. Thus, we expect a system implementing the SSC model to be able to realize such relatively complicated computation in a systematic way.

Secure execution of mobile agents. Mobile agent systems represent one of the most sophisticated forms of distributed computation. Interestingly, this form of computation can be represented in a straightforward way, in principle, by using the SSC model (Fig. 11). At the receiver site, after receiving a pot, the program stored in the pot is executed within the pot environment under the control of the specified security policy. This figure illustrates only the principle of mobile agent computation. More complicated settings will be required in real situations. For instance, files of a local file system at the receiver site might be mapped to the pot, the executed code might be interpreted as shown in Fig. 9, or the code might be executed using a JIT-compiler as shown in Fig. 10.

```
static:
  /data/pic1.jpg   /home/user1/picture/picA.jpg
  /data/pic2.jpg   /home/user1/picture/picB.jpg
  /mybin/viewer    /usr/local/bin/viewer
  /mybin/runner    /home/user1/bin/runner
dynamic:
  /mybin/viewer_plugin1   http://www.foo.com/viewer_plugin1
  /mybin/viewer_plugin2   /home/user1/bin/viewer_plugin2
required:
  /var
  /extern_world
saved:
  /log
entry:
  /mybin/runner
```

Fig. 13. Example specification for encapsulation.

Secure workflow computing. A representation for secure workflow computation can be obtained by slightly modifying that for the secure mobile agent computation. The difference is that the program code is included in the transferred pot in mobile agent computation, while each executed program code is usually locally prepared at each computing site in workflow computation. Typical settings are shown in Fig. 12.

3   SoftwarePot: An Implementation of the SSC Model

The SSC model described in Section 2 can be implemented in several ways. This section describes a portable approach that does not modify the OS kernel. Instead, it uses functionalities extensively to intercept and manipulate issued system calls. Such functionalities are provided in many modern operating systems such as Solaris, Linux, and FreeBSD. The system designed based on this approach is called *SoftwarePot*. It supports the four basic operations of the SSC model described in Section 2.2. One of these operations, the transfer operation, can be implemented by any common network transfer method, such as FTP, Web, or e-mail. In the rest of this section, we will explain our implementation scheme for the three remaining operations.

3.1   Encapsulation Operation

The encapsulation operation is implemented by collecting files specified as encapsulated and storing these files in a pot-file. Figure 13 shows an example of encapsulation specification. The lines preceded by the keyword static: specify that the file of the local file system specified in the second column is stored in the pot-file with the pathname specified in the first column. For example, the second

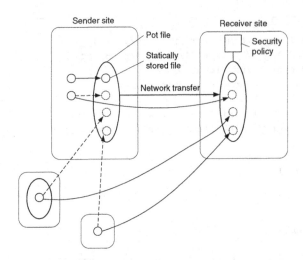

Fig. 14. Dynamic file transfer.

line in the figure specifies that the local file /home/user1/picture/picA.jpg is stored in the pot-file with the pathname /data/pic1.jpg.

In addition to the basic function to store a file in a pot-file statically, the SoftwarePot system has a function used to store only the original location of the files to be stored, and the contents of the files are dynamically transferred when required (Fig. 14). This is specified in the dynamic: section in an encapsulation specification. In the example in Fig. 13, the file of pathname /mybin/viewer_plugin1 should be obtained from the location specified by the URL http://www.foo.com/viewer_plugin1, and the file /mybin/viewer_plugin2 should be obtained from the location /home/user1/bin/viewer_plugin2 at the site where the pot-file is created. The static method is useful for storing absolutely necessary files, while the dynamic method is useful for storing optionally necessary files and for reducing the size of a pot-file.

The section preceded by required: specifies which files or directories must be mapped at the execution time. In Fig. 13, the example specification specifies that directories /var and /extern_world must be mapped at the execution time. The saved: section specifies that the modification of files in the listed directories should be permanently reflected in the pot-file system; the modification of other files is only temporarily reflected within the execution session and is thrown away after the session. The entry: section specifies the default program file that is first to be executed.

The entities of the files are stored in the area named *file store*. We adopted a modular structure to store files in the file store; currently the *tar*, *tar+gzip*, or *zip* formats can be used. The selection of storing format is completely transparent to the programs executed in a pot-process owing to the mechanism described in the next subsection.

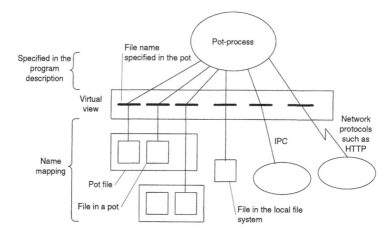

Fig. 15. Implementation scheme.

3.2   Mapping and Execution Operations

The implementation of the mapping and execution operations is integrated in the SoftwarePot system, thus we will describe them together.

The essence of both operations is name translation; that is, every primitive operation to manipulate files (such as open, read, write, lseek, close system-calls) is redirected to the mapped destination file. Figure 15 illustrates this name translation scheme. All the file accesses in the pot—whether to mapped files or to unmapped files—can be treated uniformly through the mapping since we extract the files stored statically in a pot-file into the local file system by the time they are accessed. For the extraction, we provide two modes: the *eager* one and the *lazy* one. In the eager extraction mode, all the files statically stored in a pot-file are extracted at once when the execution operation is initiated. In the lazy extraction mode, on the other hand, each file is extracted only when it needs to be accessed.

In the middle of the initial setting of a pot-process, the name translation scheme is prepared according to a *mapping and security policy description*. The file-system space viewed from a pot-process is a virtual one created by the name translation specification, and a pot-process can never directly see the "real" file system of the executing operating system. We will explain how we can describe a specification for name mapping and security policy in SoftwarePot using the example shown in Fig. 16.

– The map: section specifies that each file or directory in the pot-file specified in the first column is mapped to the existing files or directories specified in the second column. In the example, the line /etc/termcap /lib/tools.pot:/etc/termcap specifies that the /etc/termcap file accessed in the pot-process is redirected to the file having the same name in the pot-file named /lib/tools.pot. The line /alpha /beta,/gamma,/delta

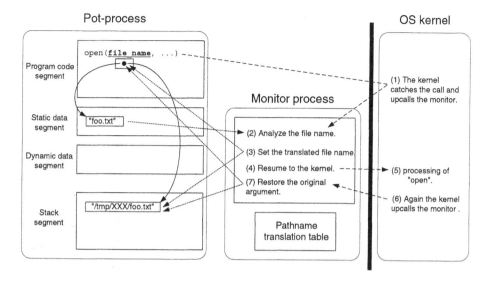

Fig. 17. Implementation trick for name translation.

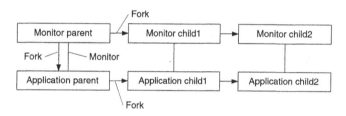

Fig. 18. Implementation of fork.

at the execution time. Most modern operating systems support functions to intercept system calls just before and after the execution of the calls in the OS kernel, and for user-level code to be executed upon each interception. Also, modern OSs allow a user process to examine and modify the contents of another user process in a controlled manner. By combining these functions, we implemented the required name mapping mechanism transparently[1] without modifying the OS kernels. In the following explanation, each number in parentheses corresponds to that in Fig. 17. As the initial setting, a *monitor process* (monitor for short) is initiated and associated to a pot-process to monitor the execution. In the initial setting, the monitor process reads a mapping and security-policy description and records the information in its internal tables. The setting for name mapping is recorded in the *pathname translation table* in Fig. 17.

(1) When a pot-process issues an **open** system call, the kernel catches the call and calls up the monitor.

---

[1] The programs executed in a pot-process cannot detect such name translation and cannot modify or avoid the name translation.

Table 1. Summary of the implementation scheme.

Operation	Implementation method	Current implementation
Encapsulation	Data archiving/storing format	Modular
Transfer	Data transfer method	Static (transferred before execution)
		Dynamic (transferred within execution time)
Map	Name mapping method	System-call interception
	File extraction method	Eager (extracted before execution)
		Lazy (extracted within execution)

(2) The monitor looks into the contents of the pot-process and obtains the path-name of the file being opened. By referring to the pathname translation table, the monitor decides to which actual file the open system call should be applied. If the lazy file extraction mode is specified, the file is extracted from the file-store of the pot-file; if cascaded mapping is specified, file-retrieving is done according to the specified totally-ordered directory list; if dynamic file transfer is specified in the mapping specification, the appropriate file is obtained via the network; if the indirect: option is specified, the specified process is initiated and interprocess communication between the pot-process and the initiated process is established.

(3) The monitor process writes the translated pathname to the unused area in the pot-process, and rewrites the register storing pointer to the pathname so as to reference the translated filename. Just before rewriting the register, the monitor process saves its content to be restored later.

(4) The monitor then tells the kernel to perform the actual processing of open.

(5) The kernel performs the processing for open.

(6) The kernel again calls up the monitor.

(7) The monitor restores the content of the register and erases the translated pathname written in (3). Finally, the monitor tells the kernel that the execution of the pot-process should be resumed.

During the execution, the pot-process may issue fork system calls and spawn other pot-processes. At that time, provided that a fork system call is allowed by the security policy description, the monitor will also fork and the child monitor process will monitor the child pot-process (Fig. 18).

All other system calls, apart from those explicitly specified as allowed in the security policy description, are intercepted by the monitor with the help of the kernel. Such calls are then examined and judged according to the security policy. When a violation is detected, the monitor takes a predetermined action, such as aborting the pot-process.

We have summarized the current implementation of SoftwarePot in Table 1.

4   Experiments

We implemented the SoftwarePot system on top of the Solaris 5.6 operating system based on the implementation scheme described in Section 3. About 5,000 lines of C program code were required to implement. This section describes the experimental results we obtained from the implementation. The hardware platform was a Sun Ultra 60 workstation (CPU: UltraSPARC II, 4MB cache memory, 512 MB main memory, 36GB hard disk).

4.1 Application Benchmark

We executed some real applications with SoftwarePot to determine its execution overhead. These applications are described below:

Emacs Lisp We used a pot-file that contained a shell script and 216 Emacs Lisp files (.el files). The script invoked emacs in the batch mode. The invoked program then byte-compiled all the .el files into .elc files. After the compilation, the script copied the .elc files to the directory specified by the user.

LaTeX We used a pot-file that contained a shell script, a LaTeXsource file, three LaTeXstyle files, and 17 encapsulated PostScript files. The script first compiled the LaTeXsource file into a DVI file by invoking latex. Then it created a PostScript (PS) file from the DVI file by invoking dvi2ps. Finally, it copied the PS file to the directory specified by the user. The size of the PS file was 1.6 megabytes, which was equivalent to a PS file containing a 15-page paper written in English.

make & gcc We used a pot-file that contained a shell script and a source tree of the grep utility. The script first compiled source files by invoking make and gcc. Then the script verified the behavior of the newly-made grep binary with the test suite contained in the source tree. Finally, it installed the binary to the directory specified by the user.

catman We used a pot-file that contained a shell script and 189 nroff input files (which made up the second section of an online manual). The script invoked catman and created preformatted versions of the manual and the windex database from the input files. Then it copied the windex database to the directory specified by the user.

The pot-files used in the applications did not necessarily contain all the files required by the program binaries (e.g., dynamic libraries); the required files in a real file system are mapped to their counterparts in the virtual file system. We used the eager extraction mode throughout this experiment.

Figure 19 shows the normalized execution time of the applications with and without SoftwarePot, including the time needed for file extraction. The performance degradation of Emacs Lisp caused by SoftwarePot was fairly small (a 21% slowdown), probably because of the long computation time in the Emacs Lisp interpreter. The interpreter is so slow that overheads added to file accesses become proportionately less conspicuous. SoftwarePot will have little performance impact on this kind of CPU-intensive applications. On the other hand, the slowdown in the execution of LaTeX, make, and catman exceeded 50%. We think the overheads in these three applications, which are not negligible, were due to the

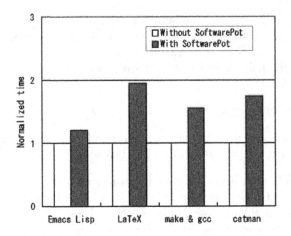

Fig. 19. The application results.

frequent file accesses required to complete the applications. Since this preliminary implementation of SoftwarePot significantly increased overheads, we are
now working on reducing these overheads by optimizing the SoftwarePot code.

5   Related Work

Chroot-based Systems. Many systems use the chroot facility to run untrusted
programs in a confined file tree [10,14,16]. These systems put application programs and the files they will access (e.g., data files, shared libraries, and configuration files below /etc) into a directory and then chroot it. The systems can
thus prevent the application programs from accessing files outside the chrooted
directory. Sbox [16] is a system for Web servers which confines CGI scripts to a
chrooted directory. The File Monitoring and Access Control (FMAC) tool [14]
provides extensive support for setting up a chrooted directory. Some Linux dis-
tributions use the chroot facility aggressively to enhance their security. For example, Kaladix Linux [10] confines nearly all daemons including Apache and
BIND to a chrooted environment.

Those who use these systems must themselves set up a chrooted file tree. It
is the users' responsibility to identify the set of files required to execute their
software. SoftwarePot users do not have to do that because circulated pot-files
contain their private file tree. Another advantage of SoftwarePot is its flexibility.
Specifically, it can map "external" files to "internal" ones using the granularity
of the files. The chroot-based systems either forbid access to external files, or
else allow only mappings realized through special mechanisms such as NFS or
samba. Note that the granularity of the mappings is a directory and that the
control of NFS demands the root privilege.

Installation Tools. RPM [6] is a tool for managing software packages. Packages created by RPM (RPM packages) contain file archives and scripts needed for their installation. Unlike SoftwarePot, RPM pays little attention to security concerns: RPM executes installation scripts with no security check. Scripts in RPM packages run at the user's privilege and the user is sometimes `root`. Hence malicious RPM packages can seriously damage a system (e.g., can maliciously modify `~/.cshrc` or `/etc/passwd`).

Executable installers, including self-extracting archives, have the same problem. Most installers do not take security into account; those who execute installers are faced with a threat of executing malicious code (e.g., Trojan horses) with their privilege.

SoftwarePot addresses this problem by running programs in a confined file tree. Malicious code can read and update the files inside the tree, but it cannot access files residing outside.

Virtual OS. VMware [17] lets one operating system (a guest OS) run on top of another (the host OS). VMware is useful for executing untrusted software because software running in the guest OS cannot directly access files in the host OS. However, VMware is not intended for use in software circulation.

The world OS server [8] also allows users to create an execution environment that has its own virtual file system. This server helps execute untrusted software securely: damage caused by the software is confined to the virtual file system. The latest version of the server is based on system call interception and runs at the user level. Unlike SoftwarePot, though, the server provides no support for circulating software.

Secure Mobile Code. FlexxGuard [9] is also a framework for secure software circulation. SoftwarePot shares many ideas with FlexxGuard. The differences between SoftwarePot and FlexxGuard include their target languages and the mechanisms for security enforcement. FlexxGuard is targeted towards Java, and the custom class loader controls the protection domain of downloaded applets. SoftwarePot is targeted towards general software, and enforces security by virtually constructing a private file tree.

Java's permission mechanism can restrict a set of resources that can be accessed and a set of operations that can be performed to access the resources. It is similar to SoftwarePot's access control facility. A difference between SoftwarePot and Java is that SoftwarePot can virtualize resources, in particular, file spaces. Resource virtualization brings great convenience to users. For example, users can protect their password file by creating a fake `/etc/passwd` file in a pot. They can also construct distributed file spaces by mapping virtual files to processes.

Developers of ActiveX software can attach digital signatures to their code, and users decide whether to execute given code by examining the signature attached to it. A large problem with this approach is that users can only choose whether to trust the principal who wrote the code. Hence, there are only two levels of execution control: giving all privileges or abandoning its execution. Running ActiveX software requires complete trust to its developer. On the other hand, SoftwarePot provides more fine-grained control on software execution and consequently enables secure execution of software written by untrusted principals.

Sandboxing Tools. Janus [5], MAPbox [1], and SubDomain [4] are confinement systems that intercept system calls and kills an application if the system call invoked is determined to be malicious. Safe-Tcl [13] achieves a similar effect in the context of scripting languages by intercepting library commands. Users of these systems describe a policy file that dictates a set of allowed operations. These systems can be used for secure software circulation in a way very similar to that of SoftwarePot: software distributors bundle policy files with their software and the users execute the software on top of the systems to which they give the policy files.

Software Fault Isolation (SFI) [18] is a technique that modifies memory access instructions in a given program to prevent the processes executing the program from accessing addresses outside their address space. SoftwarePot realizes a similar effect in the context of files: an invocation of a pathname-related system call that tries to access a file outside the virtual file system is transformed into another invocation that tries to access a file inside the virtual file system. The relationship between SoftwarePot and SFI is similar to the relationship between chroot and process-based memory protection. SoftwarePot and chroot protect files, whereas the others protect memory. SoftwarePot and SFI are user-level services, whereas chroot and process-based memory protection are kernel-level ones.

File System Extension. The cascaded mapping mechanism of SoftwarePot relates to the viewpath mechanism supported in some distributed file systems such as the translucent file system [7] or the 3D file system [12]. Ufo [2] is a file system that allows users to treat remote files exactly as if they were local. Ufo is built on top of the system call interception facility provided by the /proc file system. Like SoftwarePot, Ufo works completely at the user level. The low-level mechanism used in Ufo is almost the same as the one used in SoftwarePot. While SoftwarePot focuses on confining untrusted applications and circulating software, Ufo focuses on providing a global file system.

6   Conclusion

We have introduced the concept of software circulation. With this concept, a category of useful software-transfer usage, including software distribution, workflow, and mobile agent approaches, was modeled by combining four basic operations. In an open network environment, such as the Internet, we cannot assume that every user or software application is trustworthy. To enable secure software circulation in such an environment, we reevaluated and redesigned the four basic operations. We designed the SecurePot system to support the redesigned four basic operations. The system supports an encapsulated, transferable file system. The system also supports additional advanced functions such as cascade directory mapping, temporary file mapping, file-process mapping, and dynamic file transfer. Our portable implementation of SoftwarePot did not modify existing operating system kernels. Experiments to evaluate the implemented system showed that the overhead depended on how many issued system calls were watched and intercepted during the runtime of the SoftwarePot system. If there were many intercepted system calls, the overhead became a significant problem. However, for the ordinary practical setting of realistic applications, we believe the overhead is reasonable and within an acceptable range for practical use.

Several interesting items for future work remain. First, we should develop implementation techniques that lower the runtime overhead. One obvious way is to implement the system at the level of OS kernels. Fortunately, most recent operating systems provide *kernel modules* that allow dynamic loading into OS kernels without requiring reconfiguration or recompilation of the kernels. Thus, we are now developing a Linux kernel module to implement the SoftwarePot functions. Second, we plan to use the SoftwarePot system to implement practical software tools that contribute to secure software circulation. We are developing a tool for software distribution that, like RedHat's RPM system [6], does not require "installation" into the user's local file system in the conventional sense. We are also developing a mobile agent system that can use existing scripting language systems such as Perl, Python, or Lisp. Third, we hope to develop a theoretical foundation for secure software circulation and the SoftwarePot system. A possible starting point will be to apply and extend the framework of *mobile ambients* proposed by Cardelli [3].

Information of the SoftwarePot system is available in
`http://www.osss.is.tsukuba.ac.jp/pot/` .

Acknowledgements. We thank Katsunori Kanda and Hirotake Abe for his helpful discussions concerning the design and implementation of the SoftwarePot system. We also thank Hiroshi Ohkubo for developing a Perl-based mobile agent system with SoftwarePot.

References

1. A. Acharya and M. Raje. MAPbox: Using Parameterized Behavior Classes to Confine Untrusted Applications. In *Proceedings of the 9th USENIX Security Symposium*, Denver, August 2000.
2. A. Alexandrov, M. Ibel, K. E. Schauser, and C. J. Scheiman. UFO: A Personal Global File System Based on User-Level Extensions to the Operating System. *ACM Transactions on Computer Systems*, 16(3):207–233, August 1998.
3. L. Cardelli and A. D. Gordon. Mobile ambients. *Theoretical Computer Science*, 204/1, Jul. 2000. Special issue on Coordination.

4. C. Cowan, S. Beattie, G. K.-Hartman, C. Pu, P. Wagle, and V. Gligor. SubDomain: Parsimonious Server Security. In *Proceedings of the 14th Systems Administration Conference (LISA 2000)*, New Orleans, December 2000.

5. I. Goldberg, D. Wagner, R. Thomas, and E. A. Brewer. A Secure Environment for Untrusted Helper Applications: Confining the Wily Hacker. In *Proceedings of the 6th USENIX Security Symposium*, San Jose, July 1996.

6. Red Hat. RPM. http://www.rpm.org/.

7. D. Hendricks. A filesystem for software development. In *USENIX-Summer'90*, pages 333–340, Jun. 1990.

8. K. Ishii, Y. Shinjo, K. Nishio, J. Sun, and K. Itano. The Implementation of an Operating System Based on the Parallel World Model by Tracing System Calls. In *Proceedings of the IEICE/IPSJ CPSY OS '99*, Okinawa, May 1999. In Japanese.

9. N. Islam, R. Anand, T. Jaeger, and J. R. Rao. A Flexible Security System for Using Internet Content. *IEEE Software*, 14(5):52–59, 1997.

10. Kaladix linux. http://www.kaladix.org/.

11. K. Kato and Y. Oyama. Softwarepot: An encapsulated transferable file system for secure software circulation. Technical Report ISE-TR-02-185, Institute of Information Sciences and Electronics, University of Tsukuba, Jan. 2002.

12. D. G. Korn and E. Krell. A New Dimension for the Unix File System. *Software – Practice and Experience*, 20(S1):19–34, 1990.

13. J. Y. Levy, L. Demailly, J. K. Ousterhout, and B. B. Welch. The Safe-Tcl Security Model. In *Proceedings of the USENIX Annual Technical Conference (NO 98)*, New Orleans, June 1998.

14. V. Prevelakis and D. Spinellis. Sandboxing Applications. In *Proceedings of 2001 USENIX Annual Technical Conference, FREENIX Track*, Boston, June 2001.

15. William Stallings. *Cryptography and Network Security – Principles and Practice*. Prentice-Hall, 2nd edition, 1999.

16. L. D. Stein. SBOX: Put CGI Scripts in a Box. In *Proceedings of the USENIX Annual Technical Conference*, Monterey, June 1999.

17. VMware. VMware. http://www.vmware.com/.

18. R. Wahbe, S. Lucco, T. E. Anderson, and S. L. Graham. Efficient Software-Based Fault Isolation. In *Proceedings of the 14th ACM Symposium on Operating System Principles (SOSP '93)*, pages 203–216, Asheville, December 1993.

Fail-Safe ANSI-C Compiler: An Approach to Making C Programs Secure
Progress Report

Yutaka Oiwa[1], Tatsurou Sekiguchi[1,2], Eijiro Sumii[1], and Akinori Yonezawa[1]

[1] University of Tokyo, 7–3–1 Hongo, Bunkyo-ku, Tokyo 113-0033 JAPAN
[2] PRESTO, Japan Science and Technology Corporation

Abstract. It is well known that programs written in C are apt to suffer from nasty errors due to dangling pointers and/or buffer overflow. In particular, such errors in Internet servers are often exploited by malicious attackers to "crack" an entire system, which becomes even social problems nowadays. Nevertheless, it is yet unrealistic to throw away the C language at once because of legacy programs and legacy *programmers*. To alleviate this dilemma, many approaches to safe implementations of the C language—such as Safe C and CCured—have been proposed and implemented. To our knowledge, however, none of them support all the features of the ANSI C standard *and* prevent all unsafe operations. (By unsafe operations, we mean any operation that leads to "undefined behavior", such as array boundary overrun and dereference of a pointer in a wrong type.)

This paper describes a memory-safe implementation of the *full* ANSI C language. Our implementation detects and disallows all unsafe operations, yet conforming to the full ANSI C standard (including casts and unions) and even supporting many "dirty tricks" common in programs beyond ANSI C. This is achieved using sophisticated representations of pointers (and integers) that contain dynamic type and size information. We also devise several techniques—both compile-time and runtime—to reduce the overhead of runtime checks.

1 Introduction

The C language, which was originally designed for writing early Unix systems, allows a programmer to code flexible memory operations for high runtime performance. Especially, the C language provides flexible pointer arithmetic and type casting of pointers, which can be used for direct access to raw memory. Thus it can be used as an easy-to-use replacement for assembly languages to write many low-level system programs such as operating systems, device drivers and runtime systems of programming languages.

Today, the C language is still one of the major languages for writing application programs including various Internet servers. As requirements for applications become complex, programs written in the C language have come to

M. Okada et al. (Eds.): ISSS 2002, LNCS 2609, pp. 133–153, 2003.
© Springer-Verlag Berlin Heidelberg 2003

perform complex pointer manipulations very frequently, which tends to cause serious security bugs. In particular, destroying on-memory data structures by array buffer overflows or dangling pointers makes the behavior of a running program completely different from its text. In addition, by forging specially formed input data, malicious attackers can sometimes take over the behavior of such buggy programs. Most of recently reported security holes are due to such misbehavior.

To resolve the current situation, we propose a method for safe execution which can accept all programs written in conformity with the ANSI C specification. The notion of safety can be stated basically in terms of "well-definedness" in ANSI C. The phrase *behavior undefined* in the specification implies that any behavior including memory corruption or program crashes conforms to the specification. In other words, all unsafe behavior of existing programs corresponds to the undefined behavior in the specification. So, if the runtime system detects all operations whose behavior is undefined, we can achieve safe execution of programs. Our compiler inserts check code into the program to prevent operations which destroy memory structures or execution states. If a buggy program attempts to access a data structure in a way which leads to memory corruption, the inserted code reports the error and then terminates the execution. By using our compiler system instead of usual C compilers, existing C programs can be executed safely without change.

2   Basic Approach

This section explains our basic approach to preventing memory failure, using a simple model.

In a safe programming language with dynamic typing such as Scheme and Lisp, memory safety is usually assured by a tag assigned to each memory block as well as by runtime type checking. This idea can also be applied to the C language. (Actually, some interpreter implementations of the C language take this approach.) Each contiguous memory region has a tag which keeps type information about that region. Accordingly, a source program is transformed into an equivalent program with runtime checking inserted. (Currently, the target language is also C.) Every memory access is in principle type-checked at runtime, although most of such runtime checking is actually omitted without losing safety, thanks to our representations of integers and pointers described later.

2.1   Integer and Pointer Representations

We use a kind of smart pointers called *fat pointers*. A pointer is represented by a triple and every pointer operation in a source program is translated into operations on the triple. The representations of integers and pointers in our execution model can be described as follows:

$$v ::= \mathrm{num}(n) \mid \mathrm{ptr}(b, o, f)$$

An integer is denoted by num(n) where n is the value of the integer, while a pointer is denoted by ptr(b, o, f) where b is the base address of some contiguous memory region, o is an offset in the memory region, and f is a *cast flag*. The NULL value is represented by num(0). When the cast flag of a pointer is set, it indicates that the pointer *may* refer to a value of a type different from its static type.

$e ::=$		(typed expression)
	$v : t$	(constant)
	$x : t$	(variable)
	$* e : t$	(dereference)
	$* e = e : t$	(update)
	$(t)e : t$	(cast)
	$e + e : t$	(addition)
	new$\langle t \rangle (e) : t$	(new)
	let $x : t = e$ in $e : t$	(let binding)

Fig. 1. Typed expressions

2.2 Expressions and Heaps

A simple language with a type system and an operational semantics is introduced to illustrate how pointers and integers are handled in our implementation. Expressions of the language are defined in Fig. 1. *Every* expression in the language is typed. This reflects the fact that the semantics of C is defined according to the type of an expression. For example, when a pointer p points to some element in an array, p + 1 have the address of the next element, while (int)p + 1 evaluates to the address of the next byte. A type is either the integer type or a pointer type:

$$t ::= \text{int} \mid t \text{ pointer}$$

A heap H is a partial mapping from base addresses to finite vectors of values. Pointer ptr(b, o, f) refers to the o-th element of a vector associated with b in a heap. Each element of a heap has its type, which is defined by a heap typing HT. A heap typing is a partial mapping from base addresses to vectors of types.

We always force heaps and heap typings to keep the invariant condition that each element in a heap is either:

1. int(v),
2. ptr($b, o, 0$) of a correct type (i.e., the heap type of the region containing the value is $HT(b)$ pointer), or
3. ptr($b, o, 1$) of any type.

The runtime system manipulates the cast flags so that the type of a pointer whose cast flag is off is always trustworthy, that is, the static type of such a pointer is correct. It only checks the type of the pointers whose cast flags are set.

We do not have a condition that an offset of a pointer is within a valid region since the ANSI C Standard allows a pointer which exceeds its limit by one when the control exits out of a for- or while-statement. Such an invalid pointer *per se* does not bring about undefined behavior unless it is dereferenced. We therefore postpone the boundary check until the pointer is dereferenced.

2.3   Pointer Operations

The relation $H, HT; e : t \rightsquigarrow H', HT'; e' : t$ means that the expression $e : t$ reduces to $e' : t$ in one step under the heap H and the heap typing HT, and the heap and the heap typing are updated to H' and HT' respectively. In addition, $H, HT; e : t \rightsquigarrow$ fail means that the evaluation of $e : t$ causes handled error under H and HT. The part "$H, HT;$" may be omitted if the operations do not modify or depend on heap states.

Cast. The cast operation is defined as follows:

$$H, HT; (t) (\mathrm{num}(n)) : t \rightsquigarrow H, HT; \mathrm{num}(n) : t$$

$$\frac{HT(b) = t}{H, HT; (t \text{ pointer}) (\mathrm{ptr}(b, o, f)) : t \text{ pointer} \rightsquigarrow H, HT; \mathrm{ptr}(b, o, 0) : t \text{ pointer}}$$

$$\frac{HT(b) \neq t}{H, HT; (t \text{ pointer}) (\mathrm{ptr}(b, o, f)) : t \text{ pointer} \rightsquigarrow H, HT; \mathrm{ptr}(b, o, 1) : t \text{ pointer}}$$

$$H, HT; (int) (\mathrm{ptr}(b, o, f)) : int \rightsquigarrow H, HT; \mathrm{ptr}(b, o, 1) : int$$

In conventional compilers, cast operations over pointers are usually an identity function. In Fail-Safe C, however, cast operations become more complex because our invariant conditions on pointer values refer to the static types of pointers. A cast operator checks the dynamic type of the region pointed to by a pointer, and if the pointer refers to a value of a wrong type, the cast flag of the pointer is set.[1]

Note that when a pointer value is cast to an integer, its result is still of the form $\mathrm{ptr}(b, o, 1)$, called a *fat integer*, so that it can be cast back to a pointer. This is due to an ANSI C requirement: if an integer variable has enough width (i.e. if `sizeof(int)` $\geq$ `sizeof(void*)`), then the variable must be able to hold pointer values which may be cast back to pointer types later.

---

[1] Alternatively, we can set the cast flag without runtime type checking. In this case, type check is performed on each memory access. We think this algorithm will have worse performance than that shown in the main text, because cast pointers are often used more than once, but rarely discarded without being used.

Dereference. A pointer in C may refer to a location outside of a valid region. So our compiler always inserts boundary checking code unless an optimizer recognizes the pointer to be inside a valid region [2,15,16]. It is impossible to make a pointer referring to a memory region from a pointer referring to another memory region in the ANSI-C. Consequently a pointer whose offset is outside of its referred region is always invalid. That is, when two pointers which refer to different memory regions are subtracted, the result is defined to be "undefined".

$$H, HT; *(\text{num}(n)) : t \rightsquigarrow \text{fail}$$

$$\frac{o \text{ outside } H(b)}{H, HT; *(\text{ptr}(b, o, f)) : t \rightsquigarrow \text{fail}}$$

If the cast flag of a pointer is unset (i.e., $f = 0$), the value read via the pointer is guaranteed to have the correct type by the invariant stated above. Therefore, no type checking is needed when such a pointer is dereferenced.

$$\frac{o \text{ inside } H(b) \qquad HT(b) = t}{H, HT; *(\text{ptr}(b, o, 0)) : t \rightsquigarrow H, HT; v : t} \qquad \text{where } v \text{ is the } o\text{-th element of } H(b)$$

On the other hand, a value read using a pointer with $f = 1$ may have an incorrect type. Therefore, the type of the value to be read is checked. The cast operator (t) shown in the rule below represents this runtime type check.

$$\frac{o \text{ inside } H(b)}{H, HT; *(\text{ptr}(b, o, 1)) : t \rightsquigarrow H, HT; (t)v : t} \qquad \text{where } v \text{ is the } o\text{-th element of } H(b)$$

Update. Memory writing operation $*e : t = v$ is defined as follows: If the pointer operand is actually an integer, the program execution is terminated.

$$H, HT; *(\text{num}(n)) = v \rightsquigarrow \text{fail}$$

When the cast flag of the pointer is not set, the runtime system checks whether the offset is inside the boundary. If the check succeeds, the value of the second operand is stored.

$$\frac{o \text{ inside } H(B)}{H, HT; *(\text{ptr}(b, o, 0)) = v \rightsquigarrow H[(b, o) := v], HT; v}$$

$$\frac{o \text{ outside } H(B)}{H, HT; *(\text{ptr}(b, o, 0)) = v \rightsquigarrow \text{fail}}$$

However, if the cast flag of the pointer operand is set, the second operand is converted as if it is cast into the element type of the first operand.

$$\frac{o \text{ outside } H(B)}{H, HT;\ *(\mathrm{ptr}(b, o, 1)) = v \rightsquigarrow \text{fail}}$$

$$\frac{o \text{ inside } H(B)}{H, HT;\ *(\mathrm{ptr}(b, o, 1)) = \mathrm{num}(n) \rightsquigarrow H[(b, o) := \mathrm{num}(n)], HT;\ v}$$

$$\frac{o \text{ inside } H(B) \qquad HT(b') \text{ pointer} = HT(b)}{H, HT;\ *(\mathrm{ptr}(b, o, 1)) = \mathrm{ptr}(b', o', f') \rightsquigarrow H[(b, o) := \mathrm{ptr}(b', o', 0)], HT;\ v}$$

$$\frac{o \text{ inside } H(B) \qquad HT(b') \text{ pointer} \neq HT(b)}{H, HT;\ *(\mathrm{ptr}(b, o, 1)) = \mathrm{ptr}(b', o', f') \rightsquigarrow H[(b, o) := \mathrm{ptr}(b', o', 1)], HT;\ v}$$

2.4   Integer and Pointer Arithmetic

Addition is defined as follows:

Adding two integers:

$$\mathrm{num}(n_1) : \mathrm{int} + \mathrm{num}(n_2) : \mathrm{int} \rightsquigarrow \mathrm{num}(n_1 + n_2) : \mathrm{int}$$
$$\mathrm{ptr}(b_1, o_1, f_1) : \mathrm{int} + \mathrm{num}(n_2) : \mathrm{int} \rightsquigarrow \mathrm{num}(b_1 + o_1 + n_2) : \mathrm{int}$$
$$\mathrm{num}(n_1) : \mathrm{int} + \mathrm{ptr}(b_2, o_2, f_2) : \mathrm{int} \rightsquigarrow \mathrm{num}(n_1 + b_2 + o_2) : \mathrm{int}$$
$$\mathrm{ptr}(b_1, o_1, f_1) : \mathrm{int} + \mathrm{ptr}(b_2, o_2, f_2) : \mathrm{int} \rightsquigarrow \mathrm{num}(b_1 + o_1 + b_2 + o_2) : \mathrm{int}$$

When two integers are added, the arguments must be treated as numbers. We define the *integer interpretation* of the value $\mathrm{ptr}(b, o, f)$ to be $(b + o)$, which equals the usual representation of pointer values in conventional compilers.[2] Both arguments are converted to their integer interpretations and then added. The result will not be a pointer.[3]

---

[2] We take care of this equivalence, because this is the easiest way to retain the property that any different pointers have the different integer values, which many programs rely on (although this is not guaranteed by ANSI-C). See Section 6.2 for some discussion.

[3] Alternatively, we can keep the base value of one operand when the other operand is statically known to be non-pointer (e.g., a constant value). By this trick our compiler can support some non-ANSI-C hacks, e.g., (int *)((int)p & ~3) to get aligned pointers. In this paper, however, we does not take this into account because we cannot define the semantic consistently, e.g., it is unclear which of two base values should be kept when two pointer values are added. We will consider such tricks in our future version of compiler as a kind of "dirty" compatibility features.

Adding a pointer and an integer:

$$\mathrm{ptr}(b_1, o_1, f_1) : t \text{ pointer} + \mathrm{num}(n_2) : \mathrm{int} \rightsquigarrow \mathrm{ptr}(b_1, o_1 + n_2, f_1) : t \text{ pointer}$$
$$\mathrm{ptr}(b_1, o_1, f_1) : t \text{ pointer} + \mathrm{ptr}(b_2, o_2, f_2) : \mathrm{int} \rightsquigarrow \mathrm{ptr}(b_1, o_1 + b_2 + o_2, f_1) : t \text{ pointer}$$
$$\mathrm{num}(n_1) : t \text{ pointer} + \mathrm{num}(n_2) : \mathrm{int} \rightsquigarrow \mathrm{num}(n_1 + n_2) : t \text{ pointer}$$
$$\mathrm{num}(n_1) : t \text{ pointer} + \mathrm{ptr}(b_2, o_2, f_2) : \mathrm{int} \rightsquigarrow \mathrm{num}(n_1 + b_2 + o_2) : t \text{ pointer}$$

When an integer is added to a pointer, the base (b_1) and the flag (f_1) of the pointer operand are kept in the result. A pointer of the integer type loses its pointer information. All the rules of the operational semantics are listed in the Appendix.

3   Implementation

3.1   Encoded Pointers and Integers

As described in the previous section, pointers and integers in Fail-Safe C contain more information than those in usual implementations. Both pointers and integers are represented by two machine words. We use one word for the base (b) and another for the offset (o), and borrow the least significant bit from the base word for the cast flag (f), assuming that base values are at least 2-byte aligned (i.e., its least significant bit is always zero). Non-pointer values (num) are stored in offset fields and the base fields are kept to be zero which means null (invalid) base.

If the base of a pointer is non-zero, the value of the base must point to the top of a valid memory block. In addition, if the cast flag of a pointer is unset, it indicates that 1) the pointer refers to the region of a correct type, and that 2) the offset of the pointer is correctly aligned according to the static type of the pointer.

Figure 2 illustrates those representations. In each case, the value (base + offset) in a fat pointer is equal to its integer interpretation. Those representations are first proposed in our earlier papers [12,13]. In our present scheme, however, we refine them by requiring the pointer whose cast flag is off to be aligned so that alignment checks can also be eliminated.

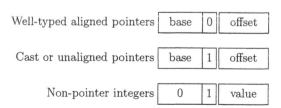

Fig. 2. Representations of fat pointers

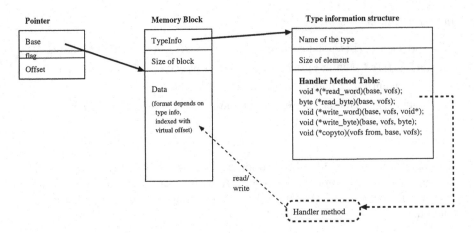

Size of block: Byte count of the data block (= max. virtual offset + 1)

Fig. 3. Structure of memory header and type information

The optimizer may reduce a fat integer to a simple, conventional representation unless doing so changes the semantics of a program. For example, the results of arithmetic operations are always non-pointers, and if a value is used only as an operand to integer arithmetics, it does not need to be a fat integer. In addition, the cast flag can often be proved to be a constant and thus can be omitted. For example, the flags of fat integers are always set and thus can be omitted, because there is no object which may be pointed to by integers without casting. Those properties can be used for optimization to reduce the runtime overhead of our implementation scheme.

3.2   Memory Blocks

Every memory access operation in Fail-Safe C must ensure that the offset and the type of a pointer are valid. To check this property at runtime, the system must know the boundary and the type of the contents of the referred regions. The runtime of Fail-Safe C keeps track of them by using custom memory management routines.

A *memory block* is the atomic unit of memory management and boundary detection. Each block consists of a *block header* and a *data block*. A block header contains information on its size and its dynamic type, which we call *data representation type*. Figure 3 illustrates a pointer and a memory block it refers to.

The actual layout and representation of the data stored in a block may depend on its data representation type. For example, we use a simple array structure identical to those of usual compilers for data of type double, and a packed array of two-word encoded pointers for data of pointer types (e.g. char *).

Virtual Offset. Although the actual representation of data in a memory block is different from that of conventional compilers, the difference should be hidden from user programs. (If a program can access the base field of a pointer by tweaking the offset of a cast pointer, the safety invariants on which the whole runtime system relies may not hold.) For this purpose, we introduce a notion of *virtual offset* to handle all memory accesses by user programs. Virtual offsets are the offsets visible to user programs. More specifically, the virtual offset of an element *e* in a memory block *B* is the difference of *e*'s address from *B*'s base address *in conventional compilers*. For example, the virtual offset of the second element of a pointer array should be *four* in 32 bit architectures, even if it is actually stored at the 8–15th bytes of the memory block.

Type Information and Cast Operation. The TypeInfo field of a memory block is used to support cast operations. The field points to a type information structure, which is generated one per each type appeared in the programs. Whenever a pointer is cast to another type, the runtime compares the typeinfo of the region referred to by the pointer, with the target type of the cast operation. If the types do not match, the runtime set the cast flag of the resulting pointer.

The TypeInfo is also utilized when a cast pointer is used. Although the ANSI-C standard does not support memory accesses via cast pointers, an ill-typed memory access is sometimes safe, e.g., when reading the first byte of a pointer. Actually, a usual C programmer is very skillful in using it and likes to use it. We have decided to allow ill-typed memory access as far as possible unless it collapses runtime memory structures since it appears frequently in usual application programs.

However, it is not always safe to allow arbitrary updates to memory regions. For example, neither overwriting the first byte of an array of pointers by an integer, nor overwriting any byte of the regions pointed to by function pointers is safe. Furthermore, actual operations needed for memory accesses depend on the data representation type of memory regions. This implies that the type check code must know the actual layout of the memory regions and must change its behavior according to the type. We solve this problem by a method quite similar to the so-called virtual function table in C++ implementations.

Every type information structure has a handler method table that contains function pointers to access handler methods for read and write operations. Handler methods have interfaces which are independent of actual data representations in memory blocks. If a pointer with its cast flag set is dereferenced, the read handler method associated with the referred region is called. The method converts the referred contents of the region to a generic fat value and returns it. If a value is written through a cast pointer, the handler checks the runtime type to set the cast flag appropriately. Thus using so-called "method indirections", we can safely allow programs to access the memory via ill-typed pointers (e.g., reading four **chars** through a pointer of type **int** *), even if we adopt different representations for various types as a means of optimization.

Deallocation. Liveness of memory blocks is maintained by garbage collection to prevent the creation of dangling pointers. The library function `free()` does not actually release any memory block, but marks the memory block as "already released" by changing its size field to zero. This disallows further access to that block, yet preventing dangling pointers from capturing another objects allocated at the same location.

3.3   Memory Operations

Dereference of a pointer is not trivial. We need to know if the pointer refers to a valid region and if the type of the target value is correct. The Fail-Safe C compiler translates it to the following sequence of operations.

1. Check if the pointer is NULL (i.e., base = 0). If so, signal a runtime error.
2. If the cast flag is not set, compare the offset with the size of the memory region referred to. If it is inside the boundary, read the content in the memory. Otherwise, signal a runtime error.
3. If the cast flag is set, get the pointer to the handler method from the type information block of the referred region, and invoke it with the pointer as an argument. The value returned from the handler method is converted to the expected result type.

If a pointer is non-null, our invariants on the pointer value shown in Section 2.2 ensures that the value in the base field always points to a correct memory block. Therefore, the data representation type and the size of the referred block is always accessible even if the pointer has been cast.

In step 2, if the cast flag of a non-NULL pointer is not set, the invariants ensures that the referred region has the data representation type expected by the static type of the pointer. Thus exactly one storage format can be assumed. However, if the cast flag is set, the actual representation of the referred block may differ from statically expected one. In this case, the code sequence delegates the actual memory read operation to the handler method associated to the referred block.

Store operations to the memory are performed in almost the same sequence. If a pointer has ever been cast, its handler method performs appropriate cast operations to keep the invariant conditions on its stored value.

3.4   `Malloc()` and Other Allocation Functions

Our guarantee of type safety heavily relies on the type information associated with each memory block. However, the interface of the `malloc()` function in the standard C library does not take any type information. Thus, we have to recover the missing information. Our approach is to "guess" the intended type by analyzing a cast expression whose operand is the return value of the `malloc()` function, and we use an additional argument for the function to pass the type information. If the compiler fails to guess the type, the `malloc()` library function prepares a "large-enough" region, and marks that region as "type undecided". The type information is post-filled upon the first write access to that region, using the write handler method mechanism described before.

We apply this approach not only to the malloc() function but to a more general set of functions. We assume that each function returning void * need a hint about its return type. For each, we add a hidden type parameter to its interface. If such a "polymorphic" function returns a value which is returned from another polymorphic function, we pass the received type hint to the subsidiary function (see Fig. 4 for example). In this way, various malloc()-wrappers can be supported naturally without rewriting source code.

```
void *xalloc(size_t size) {
  void *p = malloc(size);
  if (p) return p;
  abort();        /* allocation failure */
}
```

(a) original source.

```
fat_pointer *xalloc(typeinfo_t __rettype, size_t size) {
  fat_pointer *p = malloc(__rettype, size);
  if (p) return p;
  abort();
}
```

(b) translated program (example).

Fig. 4. An example of type hint passing

3.5   Structures and Unions

When a structure or an array of structures appears in a program, the compiler unfolds the nested structures, and lay each element of the structure continually (except required padding for alignments) on memory. Only one header is added for each array of structures (see Fig. 5). The virtual offset is counted on the basis of the virtual size of each member. The general invariants on pointers to scalar also apply to pointers to structures: a pointer to the inside of an array of structures has the cast flag off only if its type is a pointer to that structure type and its offset is the multiple of the size of the structure.

In this approach, pointers to members of the structures will have the cast flag on. Therefore, taking the address of an internal member (e.g., &(a->elem)) may have some performance penalties. We are currently implementing a pointer range analysis which can reduce this performance penalty. Direct member accesses (e.g., a.elem) and member accesses through pointers to structures (e.g., a->elem) have no additional performance penalties compared with scalar accesses.

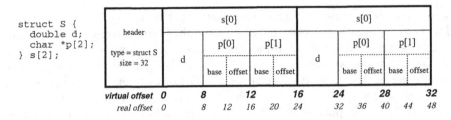

```
struct S {
    double d;
    char *p[2];
} s[2];
```

(We assume the field d never holds any pointer value.)

Fig. 5. An example of the representation of structures

Unions are decomposed to the types of the members, and operations are converted as if there is an explicit cast operation between those types. If a region of union type is initialized (i.e., written for the first time), the TypeInfo field of the region is set to the type of the referenced member of union. Thus the pointer to the union type always has cast flag on. If the value of a pointer to a member of a union is created, the creation is treated as a cast operation: the cast flag is cleared if the referenced member (type) matches the firstly written member (type). If the type does not match, the handler methods associated with the region absorb the difference between structure representations.

For more rigorous and clearer presentation, we plan to formalize the above treatment of structures and unions.

3.6   Function Pointers and Varargs

Pointers to functions are often cast to other types and then called. For example, programmers usually write comparator functions used in qsort as functions taking two pointers to elements, and cast them to type int (*)(void *, void *). The qsort function calls such a function with two void * arguments, and the arguments are implicitly cast to the expected type. Fail-Safe C supports idiomatic operations of this kind.

Functions whose addresses are taken by the & operator are represented by small constant memory blocks. Two entry points are generated by the compiler for each function whose address is taken, and their addresses are stored in the block. The first entry has a normal interface, and used in all cases except for calls through cast pointers. The second entry has an interface which is common to all functions: all arguments are packed into one array of fat values, and results are also encoded to fat values. If a function is invoked through a cast pointer ($f = 1$), the callee converts all arguments to the universal representation (fat integers), calls the second entry, and converts the result back into the expected type. Variable-number arguments (varargs) can also be supported using this scheme. All optional arguments are passed as uniform argument arrays.

3.7   Local Variables

Taking the address of a local variable could be dangerous, as it may result in a dangling pointer if the pointer escapes from the scope of the function. Therefore, if the address of a local variable is taken, that variable should be allocated in a heap rather than on the stack. Appropriate allocation code is inserted by our compiler. Alternatively, an optimizer can perform escape analysis to allocate some of those object blocks on stack. A local variable whose address is not taken can be treated in the standard way: they can be stored either on the stack or in a register.

3.8   External Libraries

Since system calls and lots of C libraries do not respect our representations of pointers and integers, those functions are implemented via wrapper interfaces. A common sequence for such wrappers are:

1. convert scalar arguments,
2. check the boundary of array arguments with predefined constraints,
3. copy the contents of array arguments to a temporally allocated array,
4. call the original function,
5. write back any modification to the array arguments,
6. convert the return value and return it to the caller.

Steps 3. and 5. can be omitted if the internal representation of data is the same as those of a native implementation (e.g., if the dynamic type of an argument is double[]). Since the C-level types of library functions do not have enough information to generate those wrappers, some manual intervention is needed.

Some functions are too complex to be implemented in the above common way. For example, the meaning and type of the third argument of the Unix system call ioctl() depends on the first and second arguments. So the wrapper must parse those arguments to check the correctness of the third argument. The well-known printf() function is another example of such a function. In addition, functions like gets() or scanf() have possibly unlimited side effects—it may write even over the whole memory if the input does not contain the expected delimiter character. In those functions, boundary checks can be performed only during the operations. Functions such as strcat() and strchr() are other examples where wrappers cannot perform boundary checks in advance. We provide hand-written custom wrappers for those functions—or, alternatively, we can just compile them from their source code by using our Fail-Safe C compiler.

4   Preliminary Experiments

4.1   Preliminary Implementation

We implemented a preliminary compiler system of Fail-safe C. To estimate the performance of our system, we conducted small-scale experiments. The compiler

Table 1. Result of experiments

Pentium III 1 GHz	Program	Native	Safe version	Ratio
	Fib	0.648	0.736	1.14
	Int qsort	0.310	1.243	4.01
	Poly qsort	0.821	3.422	4.17

UltraSPARC II 400 MHz	Program	Native	Safe version	Ratio
	Fib	1.301	1.314	1.01
	Int qsort	0.467	2.075	4.44
	Poly qsort	1.993	16.278	8.17

[unit: s (except for ratios)]

consists of a C-to-C source code translator, implemented in Objective Caml, and runtime libraries implemented in the native C language. The translator reads a program, converts representations of pointers or integers, and inserts appropriate check code, most of which are inlined. The converted code is then passed to a native C compiler and compiled into a machine language. In this experiment, garbage collector is not implemented yet.

The translator removes "useless" conversion of integers between native and two-word representations, that is, when the two round-trip conversions appear in sequence in the resulting program. No other optimizations are performed at the source-to-source translation stage, intended to know the *worst-case* estimation of the runtime overhead of our scheme.

4.2   Test Programs

We chose the following three micro-benchmarks as test programs, since these programs represent typical kinds of operations in usual C programs. For each test, we compared the execution time of the translated program to that of the program compiled directly by gcc (version 2.95.2 with -06).

In the first test, we want to measure overheads due to fat integers (arithmetic operations, and increase in function arguments and return values). The second, called int-qsort, sorts an array filled with one-million random integers in ascending order using the quick sort algorithm. This shows the overhead of fat pointer operations, such as boundary and cast flag checks. The last, called poly-qsort, is a polymorphic version of the above quick sort test. It takes a comparator function, a data swap function, and the element size of a target array as additional parameters, thus being able to sort an array of any element type. We use the same input data in int-qsort.

All tests were performed on two different platforms: one is an x86 PC system with a 1 GHz Pentium-III CPU, and the other is Sun's Ultra Enterprise 4500 with 400 MHz UltraSPARC II CPUs.

4.3 Analysis of the Results

The results are shown in Table 1. The overhead of "fib" was between 1% and 14%. In this test, the argument and the return value of the fib function are increased to two words, and before each addition which originally appears in the source code, two word integers are coerced to one word by adding base and offset. Thus, the one step calculation of fib performs three additions and two invocation of function with a two-word argument, which were originally one addition and two invocations with an one-word argument. It seems that the overhead of arithmetic and function invocations introduced by two-word integer representation is relatively small.

In int-qsort, the overhead of safe pointer operations makes the program execution 3–3.5 times slower (including integer overhead). This result is not quite satisfactory, but we believe that the overhead can be considered as a trade-off of efficiency for security in certain application domains. Moreover, we expect that implementing optimizations such as common subexpression elimination([9], for example) and redundant boundary check elimination in our compiler system will reduce this overhead.

Finally, the execution time of poly-qsort in Fail-Safe C is around 4–8 times as large as the original. This is caused by 1) the additional overhead of runtime type checking, and 2) our current poor implementation of function pointers.

We are aware that the programs used in this experiments are very small. We will perform more extensive tests with larger programs as soon as the full implementation is completed.

5 Related Work

There are many related research activities. They can be roughly classified into two categories.

The focus of the first category is to detect various error states at runtime which are common to many programs. For example, Purify [5] and Sabar-C (CodeCenter) [8] dynamically detect memory access errors caused by array boundary overflow. In addition, StackGuard [3] and many other recent implementations focus on preventing well-known security holes such as stack buffer overflow used by many recent security attacks. However, all of them detect only some common patterns of memory misuse, so complete safety is not guaranteed. Loginov et. al. [10] proposes a method to keep pointer safety by adding a 4-bit tag to every octet in the working memory. Backward-compatible bounds checking by Jones and Kelly [7] have modified gcc compiler to insert bounds checking code which uses a table of live objects. By their approach, it is impossible to access a memory which is exterior of any objects (e.g., function return addresses in the stack), but it can still reads and modifies any data in the memory by forging pointer offsets. Jones and Kelly claims their method detects pointer offset forging, but it does not seem to work when on-memory pointers are overwritten by integers.

Safe-C [1] can detect all error caused by early deallocation of memory regions. However, their paper does not mention about cast operations and, as far as we know, supporting unlimited cast operations with Safe-C seems non-trivial, for the same reason as that of Jones and Kelly's work. Patil and Fischer [14] proposed an interesting method to detect memory misuses. Their work perform boundary checking in a separate guard process and use program slice techniques to reduce runtime overhead. However, it has some limitation on the source and destination types of cast operations.

Another category works on safe imperative languages that *resemble* to the C language. The major examples of such languages are CCured and Cyclone. To conform common C programs to Cyclone [4,6], it is reported to require rewriting about 10% of program code (which we consider not so small). Extremely speaking, Java and (the type-safe portion of) C# can also be considered to be examples of such languages, but of course porting C programs to those languages is more burdensome.

CCured [11] supports cast over pointer types. The approach of CCured is to analyze a whole program to split the program into two parts: one is the "type-safe part" which does not use cast operations, and the other is the "type-unsafe part" which can be poisoned by cast operations. However, to our knowledge, they do not focus on source-level compatibility to existing programs, and in fact it supports only a subset of ANSI-C semantics. We are focusing on complete compatibility with the ANSI-C specification, and on the highest compatibility with existing programs. The main technical difference between CCured and our work is that our system allows to use optimized representation for data even if it is pointed from unsafe pointers. Because "wild pointers" in CCured have only a base field and an offset field, the representation of a wild pointer's target must be unique, and thus they cannot point to data in the "safe part" of a program. This means that all objects which can be traced transitively from one single wild pointer must adopt slow and fat representation. We suppose that such a kind of data structures can not be neglected for many programs in the real world, although this supposition must be verified by detailed analysis of existing programs.

6   Current Status and Future Work

6.1   Current Status

We are currently implementing a complete version of the Fail-Safe C compiler. We have already implemented type analysis and program flow analysis, and are currently working on data flow analysis for removing redundant use of fat pointers as much as possible. We will formalize the whole execution model of Fail-Safe C and finish the implementation soon. Then, we are planning to analyze various existing server programs to evaluate the source-level compatibility of our compiler with conventional compilers, and also plan to measure the overhead of our scheme as well as the possibility for further optimization.

6.2   Future Work: Beyond ANSI-C

In this paper, we focus on how to support all the ANSI-C features safely by using runtime checks. We are aware, however, that ANSI-C specification is too restrictive and only few of existing programs are fully ANSI-C compliant. The compiler which only supports fully ANSI-C compatible programs may not be useful for general purposes. For example, ANSI C does not define the behavior of a program which casts a pointer to an integer and take the hash index of it. In addition, the interface of well-known Unix system calls such as `getsockaddr` relies on pointer casting undefined in ANSI-C specification.

For these reasons, our Fail-Safe C system actually accepts some superset of ANSI C language, which is still sufficient to prevent serious misbehavior of programs. The implementation techniques we have described in this paper, especially those of memory block representations and handler methods, are carefully designed to allow extensions beyond the ANSI-C specification which accept many idioms common in existing Unix/C programs. For example, although the result of integer overflow is undefined in ANSI C, our system allows it because it does not cause any unsafe situation by itself.[4] For another example, reading an array of floats via an integer pointer, which our compiler supports by emulation using handler methods, is "safe" in terms of security. Supporting those operations increase the compatibility between Fail-Safe C and conventional implementations of C.

However, our current support for such "beyond ANSI-C" programs is not yet enough to accept many existing programs. For example, using the least significant bits of pointers for the purpose of tagging, which is common in interpreters of dynamically-typed languages, cannot be supported in our current schema, because setting the least significant bits by using integer arithmetic loses the base addresses of pointers.

Thus, we plan to examine existing programs and implement various compatibility features, some of which might be ad-hoc, to our system, provided that they do not affect base-line safety requirements. Of course, not all C programs can be supported on our system. Programs which really depend on the exact structure of memory and hardware, for example operating system kernels, and programs which generate execution code dynamically (e.g., A language runtime with just-in-time compilers) can not be supported at all and are out of the scope of our research. Also, as for programs which allocate memory as a bulk and perform their own memory management inside (e.g., the Apache web server), the protection of such memory regions would be weak (because the allocated bulk memory would become one memory region in our implementation, but execution code injection attack is still impossible) and severe performance penalty

---

[4] We think that defining the behavior of integer overflow in terms of the modulus of 2^{32} or 2^{64} is a reasonable choice for C language implementations. Recently reported security holes related to integer overflow are actually not caused directly by the overflow itself but caused by wrongly implemented array boundary check which goes wrong by integer overflow. As our system performs its own boundary check in a safe way, this does not affect security in Fail-Safe C.

would be caused (because almost all pointers would have cast flag set). One solution for those programs is to remove such custom memory allocators and use the allocator which our runtime provides, but it requires rewriting part of the programs.

At the same time, we may as well give a second, more careful thought to the support of those extended features from the viewpoint of debugging and "further safety". Although some programs really need such "beyond ANSI-C" features as above, those weird operations are simply a bug in many cases. It may sometimes (e.g., for debugging) make more sense to stop the program execution *as soon as* those suspicious operations are performed *before* it reaches to critically dangerous situations such as overrunning buffer boundaries or accessing forged pointers. We also plan to consider the balance between compatibility and strength of error-detection, and provide various options for programmers.

7   Conclusion

We proposed a method for fail-safe implementation of the ANSI C language, and estimated its performance overhead via preliminary experiments. Even without optimizations, the execution time is limited within 1–8 times of the original. We are still developing a complete version of the compiler which can be used as a drop-in replacement for conventional unsafe compilers.

Acknowledgements. We are very grateful to Prof. George Necula and Prof. Benjamin Pierce for their discussions and comments on an early version of the paper. We are also thankful to the members of Yonezawa group, especially Prof. Kenjiro Taura, for many valuable suggestions.

References

1. Todd M. Austin, Scott E. Breach, and Gurindar S. Sohi. Efficient detection of all pointer and array access errors. In *Proc. '94 Conference on Programming Language Design and Implementation (PLDI)*, pages 290–301, 1994.
2. Rastislav Bodik, Rajiv Gupta, and Vivek Sarkar. ABCD: Eliminating Array Bounds Checks on Demand. In *Proceedings of the SIGPLAN '00 Conference on Program Language Design and Implementation*, June 2000.
3. Crispan Cowan, Calton Pu, Dave Maier, Jonathan Walpole, Peat Bakke, Steve Beattie, Aaron Grier, Perry Wagle, Qian Zhang, and Heather Hinton. StackGuard: Automatic adaptive detection and prevention of buffer-overflow attacks. In *Proc. 7th USENIX Security Conference*, pages 63–78, San Antonio, Texas, January 1998.
4. Dan Grossman, Greg Morrisett, Trevor Jim, Michael Hicks, Yanling Wang, and James Cheney. Region-based memory management in Cyclone. In *Proc. ACM Conference on Programming Language Design and Implementation (PLDI)*, pages 282–293, June 2002.
5. Reed Hastings and Bob Joyce. Purify: Fast detection of memory leaks and access errors. In *Proc. 1992 Winter USENIX Conference*, pages 125–136, 1992.

6. Trevor Jim, Greg Morrisett, Dan Grossman, Michael Hicks, James Cheney, and Yanling Wang. Cyclone: A safe dialect of C. In *USENIX Annual Technical Conference*, June 2002.

7. Richard W. M. Jones and Paul H. J. Kelly. Backwards-compatible bounds checking for arrays and pointers in C programs. In *Automated and Algorithmic Debugging*, pages 13–26, 1997.

8. Stephen Kaufer, Russell Lopez, and Sasha Pratap. Saber-C: an interpreter-based programming environment for the C language. In *Proc. 1998 Summer USENIX Conference*, pages 161–171, 1988.

9. Jens Knoop, Oliver Rüthing, and Bernhard Steffen. Lazy Code Motion. In *Proceedings of the 5th ACM SIGPLAN Conference on Programming Language Design and Implementation*, pages 224–234, June 1992.

10. Alexey Loginov, Suan Hsi Yong, Susan Horwitz, and Thomas Reps. Debugging via run-time type checking. *Lecture Notes in Computer Science*, 2029:217–, 2001.

11. George Necula, Scott McPeak, and Westley Weimer. CCured: Type-safe retrofitting of legacy code. In *Proc. The 29th Annual ACM SIGPLAN–SIGACT Symposium on Principles of Programming Languages (POPL2002)*, pages 128–139, January 2002.

12. Yutaka Oiwa, Eijiro Sumii, and Akinori Yonezawa. Implementing a fail-safe ANSI-C compiler. In *JSST 2001*, Hakodate, Japan, 18 September 2001. Japan Society for Software Science and Technology. In Japanese.

13. Yutaka Oiwa, Eijiro Sumii, and Akinori Yonezawa. Implementing a fail-safe ANSI-C compiler. *Computer Software*, 19(3):39–44, May 2002. In Japanese.

14. Harish Patil and Charles Fischer. Low-cost, concurrent checking of pointer and array accesses in C programs. *Software—Practice and Experience*, 27(1):87–110, January 1997.

15. Radu Rugina and Martin Rinard. Symbolic bounds analysis of pointers, array indices, and accessed memory regions. In *Proc. '00 Conference on Programming Language Design and Implementation (PLDI)*, pages 182–195, 2000.

16. David Wagner, Jeffrey S. Foster, Eric A. Brewer, and Alexander Aiken. A first step towards automated detection of buffer overrun vulnerabilities. In *Network and Distributed System Security Symposium*, February 2000.

A   The Semantic Rules

Notations

The meta-functions and judgments used in the rules of dynamic semantics have the following meanings:

- $\Gamma \vdash e : t$

  The expression e is typed to t under environment Γ.

- $H, HT; \ e : t \rightsquigarrow H', HT'; \ e' : t$

  The expression $e : t$ reduces to $e' : t$ in one step under the heap H and the heap typing HT, and the heap and heap typing are updated to H' and HT' after reduction respectively.

  The static type t does not change during evaluation, and is omitted when it is unimportant.

- $H, HT; e : t \rightsquigarrow$ fail
  The reduction of the expression $e : t$ causes a detected runtime error under the heap H and the heap typing HT.
- $H[(b, o) := v]$
  The heap H with the o-th element of $H(b)$ updated to v.
- $H[b := l]$
  The heap H with a new element l added as $H(b)$.
- $HT[b := t]$
  The heap typing HT with a new element t added as $HT(b)$.
- $e[v/x]$
  The expression e with all free occurrences of the variable x substituted with the value v.
- $v \times s$
  A vector of length s with all elements initialized by v.

Static Semantics

We allow both integers and pointers to have *fat pointer* values.[5]

$$\overline{\Gamma \vdash \mathrm{num}(n) : t} \qquad \overline{\Gamma \vdash \mathrm{ptr}(b, o, f) : t}$$

Typing rules for memory operations are as follows:

$$\frac{\Gamma \vdash e : t \text{ pointer}}{\Gamma \vdash *e : t} \qquad \frac{\Gamma \vdash e_1 : t \text{ pointer} \quad \Gamma \vdash e_2 : t}{\Gamma \vdash *e_1 = e_2 : t}$$

We allow cast operations between arbitrary types.

$$\frac{\Gamma \vdash e : t'}{\Gamma \vdash (t)\, e : t}$$

The second operand of an addition must be an integer. The first operand may be either a pointer or integer, and the return value has the same type as the first operand.[6]

$$\frac{\Gamma \vdash e_1 : \mathrm{int} \quad \Gamma \vdash e_2 : \mathrm{int}}{\Gamma \vdash e_1 + e_2 : \mathrm{int}} \qquad \frac{\Gamma \vdash e_1 : t \text{ pointer} \quad \Gamma \vdash e_2 : \mathrm{int}}{\Gamma \vdash e_1 + e_2 : t \text{ pointer}}$$

The typing rules for the other expressions are obvious.

$$\frac{\Gamma \vdash e : \mathrm{int}}{\Gamma \vdash \mathrm{new}\langle t \rangle(e) : t \text{ pointer}}$$

$$\frac{\Gamma \vdash e_1 : t_1 \qquad \Gamma, x : t_1 \vdash e_2 : t_2}{\Gamma \vdash \mathrm{let}\ x : t_1 = e_1\ \mathrm{in}\ e_2 : t_2}$$

$$\frac{\Gamma(x) = t}{\Gamma \vdash x : t}$$

---

[5] Constants which appear in a source program will never have a pointer value, but our typing rule allows them because the transition rules cause such terms during evaluation.

[6] ANSI C allows expressions of the form "integer + pointer", but it can be obviously canonicalized to this form by commutativity.

One-Step Reduction of Innermost Expressions

The rules for dereference, update, cast and additions are already shown in Section 2.

Let

$$H, HT; \text{ let } x : t' = v : t' \text{ in } e : t \rightsquigarrow H, HT; \ e[v/x] : t$$

Allocation. The `new` expression allocates a new block in the heap, and updates H and HT. The complex part of the side condition in the following rule assures the "freshness" of the address of the allocated block, that is, if two different pointers point to two valid locations in the heap, the integer interpretation of the pointers must also differ. The size of the allocation is converted to a simple integer, and the allocation fails if the requested size is not positive.

$$\frac{\forall b' \in H. \ \forall o' \text{ inside } H(b'). \ (b' + o') \notin [b, b + s - 1] \qquad s > 0}{H, HT; \ \text{new}\langle t \rangle(\text{num}(s)) \rightsquigarrow H[b := \text{num}(0) \times s], HT[b := t]; \ \text{ptr}(b, 0, 0) : t \text{ pointer}}$$

$$\frac{s \leq 0}{H, HT; \ \text{new}\langle t \rangle(\text{num}(s)) \rightsquigarrow \text{fail}}$$

$$H, HT; \ \text{new}\langle t \rangle(\text{ptr}(b, o, f)) \rightsquigarrow H, HT; \ \text{new}\langle t \rangle(\text{num}(b + o))$$

One-Step Reduction of Expressions

An evaluation context C determines the order of reductions.

$$C ::= [] \mid * C \mid (t)C \mid C + e \mid v + C \mid * C = e \mid * v = C$$
$$\mid \text{ let } x = C \text{ in } e \mid \text{ let } x = v \text{ in } C \mid \text{new}\langle t \rangle(C)$$

A one-step reduction $\longrightarrow$ is defined by using innermost reductions $\rightsquigarrow$ and the evaluation context. The meaning of H, HT is the same as those of innermost reductions.

$$\frac{H, HT; \ e \rightsquigarrow H', HT'; \ e'}{H, HT; \ C[e] \longrightarrow H', HT'; \ C[e']} \qquad \frac{H, HT; \ e \rightsquigarrow \text{fail}}{H, HT; \ C[e] \longrightarrow \text{fail}}$$

Types and Effects for Non-interfering Program Monitors*

Lujo Bauer, Jarred Ligatti, and David Walker

Department of Computer Science
Princeton University
Princeton, NJ 08544

Abstract. A run-time monitor is a program that runs in parallel with an untrusted application and examines actions from the application's instruction stream. If the sequence of program actions deviates from a specified security policy, the monitor transforms the sequence or terminates the program. We present the design and formal specification of a language for defining the policies enforced by program monitors.

Our language provides a number of facilities for composing complex policies from simpler ones. We allow policies to be parameterized by values or other policies, and we define operators for forming the conjunction and disjunction of policies. Since the computations that implement these policies modify program behavior, naive composition of computations does not necessarily produce the conjunction (or disjunction) of the policies that the computations implement separately. We use a type and effect system to ensure that computations do not interfere with one another when they are composed.

1 Introduction

Any system designed to execute and interoperate with potentially malicious code should implement at least two different sorts of security mechanisms:

1. A safe language and sound type checker to statically rule out simple bugs.
2. A run-time environment that will detect, document, prevent and recover from those errors that cannot be detected beforehand.

Strong type systems such as the ones in the Java Virtual Machine [16] and Common Language Runtime [10,11,17] are the most efficient and most widely deployed mechanisms for ruling out a wide variety of potential security holes ranging from buffer overruns to misuse of system interfaces.

To complement static checking, secure run-time environments normally use auxiliary mechanisms to check properties that cannot be decided at compile time or link time. One of the ways to implement such run-time checks is with program monitors, which examine a sequence of program actions before they are

---

* This research was supported in part by a gift from Microsoft Research, Redmond; DARPA award F30602-99-1-0519; and NSF Trusted Computing grant CCR-0208601.

M. Okada et al. (Eds.): ISSS 2002, LNCS 2609, pp. 154–171, 2003.

executed. If the sequence deviates from a specified policy, the program monitor transforms the sequence or terminates the program.

In this paper, we describe a new general-purpose language called Polymer that can help designers of secure systems detect, prevent and recover from errors in untrusted code at runtime. System architects can use Polymer to write program monitors that run in parallel with an untrusted application. Whenever the untrusted application is about to call a security-sensitive method, control jumps to the Polymer program which determines which of the following will occur:

- the application runs the method and continues with its computation,
- the application is terminated by the monitor,
- the application is not allowed to invoke the given method, but otherwise may continue with its computation, or
- the monitor performs some computation on behalf of the application before or after proceeding with any of the first three options (Figure 1).

This basic architecture has been used in the past to implement secure systems [6,8,9,12,19]. Previous work has shown that the framework effectively subsumes a variety of less general mechanisms such as access-control lists and stack inspection. Unfortunately, there has been a nearly universal lack of concern for precise semantics for these languages, which we seek to remedy in this paper.

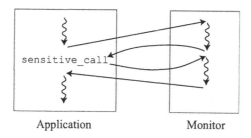

Application   Monitor

Fig. 1. Sample interaction between application and monitor: monitor allows application to make a sensitive call.

We improve upon previous work in a number of ways.

- We present a new, general-purpose language for designing run-time security policies. Policies are able to prevent actions from being executed, execute their own actions, and terminate the offending program. In our language, policies are first-class objects and can be parameterized by other policies or ordinary values. We provide several interesting combinators that allow complex policies to be built from simpler ones.

- We have defined a formal operational semantics for our language, which turns out to be a variant of the computational lambda calculus [18]. To our knowledge, this is the first such semantics for a general-purpose security monitoring language. It provides a tool that system architects can use to reason precisely about their security policies.

- We provide a type system, which we have proved sound with respect to our operational semantics. The type system includes a novel effect system that ensures that composed policies do not interfere with one another.

2   A Calculus for Composing Security Policies

In this section, we provide an informal introduction to our security policy language.

2.1   Simple Policies

Our monitoring language is derived from Moggi's computational lambda calculus [18]; consequently, the language constructs are divided into two groups: pure terms M and computations E. A computation runs in parallel with a *target program* and may have effects on the target's behavior. We call a suspended computation paired with an action set ($\{\texttt{actions} : A; \texttt{policy} : E\}$) a *policy*. A policy is a term that, when its suspended computation E is run, will intercept and manipulate *target actions* in the set A. We call this set of actions the *regulated set*. For the purposes of this paper, a target action is a function or method call that the target application wishes to execute. However, it is easy to imagine a variety of other sorts of target program actions, such as primitive operations like assignment, dereference, iteration, the act of raising particular exceptions, etc., that might also be considered actions that are regulated by a security policy. It should also be noted that the level of abstraction of program actions depends on the language and system interface of the target application (e.g., C system calls versus Java Core API method calls); these concerns, however, are orthogonal to the design of our calculus.

A First Example. Consider the following policy, which enforces a limit on the amount of memory that an application can allocate for itself.

```
fun mpol(q:int).
{
  actions:  malloc();
  policy:
    next →
      case * of
        malloc(n) →
          if ((q-n) > 0) then
            ok; run (mpol (q-n))
          else
            halt
        end
      done → ()
}
```

A recursive policy, like the one above, is a recursive function (a term) with a policy as its body. The recursive function argument q is a memory quota that the application must not exceed. The only action manipulated by this policy is the malloc action. The computation defining the policy begins with the (next → E_1 | done → E_2) computation, which suspends the monitor until the target is about to execute the next action in the regulated set (i.e., the next malloc operation). At this point, the monitor executes E_1. If the program terminates before before executing another regulated action, E_2 will be executed to perform any sort of bookkeeping or application cleanup that is necessary. In this example, we assume no bookkeeping is necessary so the monitor simply returns () to indicate it is done.

The ok statement signals that the current action should be accepted, and halt is the terminal computation, which halts the target program.

A recursive call to a policy involves two steps. The first step is a function application (mpol (q-n)), which returns a policy (a suspended computation). To *run* the suspended computation, we use the run statement (run (mpol (q-n))). Sometimes, computations return interesting values (not just unit) in which case we write let {x} = pol in E. This is the monadic let, which executes its primary argument pol, binds the resulting value to x and continues the computation with E. We also use an ordinary let where convenient: let x = M in E.

Now that we have defined our recursive memory-limit policy, we can initialize it with a quota (q0) simply by applying our recursive function.

```
memLimit = mpol q0
```

The type of any policy is $\mathcal{M}(\tau)$ where τ is the type of the value that the underlying computation returns. Hence, the type of memLimit is $\mathcal{M}(\text{unit})$.

A Second Example. In this example, we restrict access to files by controlling the actions fopen and fclose. For simplicity, we assume that fclose takes a string argument rather than a file descriptor. The first argument to the policy is a function (acl) that returns true if the target is allowed access to the given file in the given mode. The second argument is a list of files that the application has opened so far. The code below uses a number of list processing functions including cons (::), membership test (`member`), and element delete (`delete`).

```
fun fpol(acl:string->mode->bool, files:file list).
{
  actions:  fopen(), fclose();
  policy:
    let fcloses fs = {... fclose f ...} in
    next →
      case * of
        fopen(s,m) →
          if (acl s m) then
            ok; run (fpol acl (s::files))
          else
            run (fcloses files); halt
        fclose(s) →
          if (member files s) then
            ok; run (fpol acl (delete files s))
          else
            sup; run (fpol acl files)
      end
    done →
      run (fcloses files)
}
```

The main additional statement of interest in this policy is the sup statement. We view an attempt to close a file that that has not been opened by the application a benign error. In this case, we do not terminate the application, we simply *suppress* the action and allow the application to continue (if it is able to do so). In practice, the sup expression also throws a security exception that may be caught by the target.

A second point of interest is the fact that our file-system policy is written so that if the target terminates, it will close any files the target has left open. It uses an auxiliary computation `fcloses` to close all the files in the list.

Once again, we must initialize our policy with appropriate arguments.

```
fileAccess = fpol (acl0,[]).
```

2.2 Composing Policies

One of the main novelties of our language is that policies are first-class values. As a result, functions can abstract over policies and policies may be nested inside other policies. Moreover, we provide a variety of combinators that allow programmers to synthesize complex policies from simpler ones.

Parallel Conjunctive Policies. A resource-management policy might want to enforce policies on a variety of different sorts of resources, all defined independently of one another. We use the conjunctive combinator $M_1 \wedge M_2$ to create such a policy. For example, the following policy controls both file access and limits memory consumption.

```
RM = fileAccess ∧ memLimit
```

When this policy is run, target actions are streamed to both `fileAccess` and `memLimit`. Actions such as `malloc`, which are not relevant to the `fileAccess` policy, are ignored by it and automatically deemed OK. The same is true of actions that are not relevant to `memLimit`. The two computations may be seen as running in parallel and if either policy decides to halt the target then the target will be stopped.

The result of a parallel conjunctive policy is a pair of values, one value being returned from each of the two computations. Hence, our resource manager has type $\mathcal{M}(\text{unit} \times \text{unit})$.

Closely related to the parallel conjunctive policy is the trivial policy $\top$, which immediately returns (). The trivial policy is the identity for the parallel conjunctive policy. In other words, $M \wedge \top$ accepts exactly the same sequences of program actions as M.

Higher-order Policies. Since policies are ordinary values, we can parameterize policies by other policies. For example, rather than fix a particular resource management policy once and for all, a system designer might prefer to design a generic resource manager that is composed of a file-access policy and a memory limit policy.

```
genericRM = λfa:M(unit).λml:M(unit).{let {x} = fa ∧ ml in ()}
```

The generic resource manager above abstracts two policies and returns another policy that runs the two policies in conjunction, discards their results and returns unit. We can apply the generic resource manager to the two policies we created above.

```
strictRM = genericRM fileAccess memLimit
```

However, we might need a different policy for a different application. For instance, for a more trusted application, we might choose not to limit memory, but still control file access. In this case, we use the trivial policy instead of `memLimit`.

```
laxRM = genericRM fileAccess ⊤
```

Parallel Disjunctive Policies. A parallel disjunctive policy $M_1 \vee_\tau M_2$ accepts a sequence of operations and returns a result as soon as either M_1 or M_2 would accept the sequence of operations and return. Both policies must agree to halt the target in order to stop it. As in the conjunctive policy, target actions that are not in the regulated set of one of the policies are simply passed over by that policy and implicitly accepted. A disjunctive policy $M_1 \vee_\tau M_2$ has type $\mathcal{M}(\tau)$ when $\tau = \tau_1 + \tau_2$, M_1 has type $\mathcal{M}(\tau_1)$ and M_2 has type $\mathcal{M}(\tau_2)$.

There are several uses for disjunctive policies. At the most basic level, a disjunctive policy can serve to widen an existing policy. For example, suppose we have already implemented a policy for controlling arbitrary, untrusted applications (untrustedPol). Later, we might wish to develop a second policy for more trusted applications that authenticate themselves first (authenticatedPol). By using disjunction we allow applications either to authenticate themselves and gain further privileges or to use the untrusted policy.

```
widenedPol = untrustedPol ∨τ authenticatedPol
```

It is likely possible to rewrite untrustedPol so that it grants extra privileges when a user authenticates himself. However, modular design principles suggest we should leave the code of the initial policy alone and create a separate module (policy) to handle the details of authentication and the extended privileges.

Disjunctive policies also provide a convenient way to create *Chinese wall policies* [5]. A Chinese wall policy allows the target to choose from one of many possible policies. However, when one policy is chosen the others become unavailable. For example, when designing a browser policy, we might expect two different sorts of applets. One sort of applet acts like a proxy for a database or service situated across the net. This kind of applet needs few host system resources other than network access. It takes requests from a user and communicates back to the online database. In particular, it has no use for the file system. Another sort of applet performs tasks for the host system and requires access to host data. In order to allow both sorts of applets to run on the host and yet to protect the privacy of host data, we can create a Chinese wall policy which allows either file-system access or network access but not both.

In the code below, we implement this policy. The patterns File.* and Network.* match all functions in the interface File and Network respectively. We assume the policies filePolicy and networkPolicy have been defined earlier.

```
fileNotNetwork =
{
  actions:  File.*, Network.*;
  policy:
    next →
      case ⋆ of
        File.* → run (filePolicy)
        Network.* → halt
      end
    done → ()
}
```

```
networkNotFile =
{
  actions:  File.*, Network.*;
  policy:
    next →
      case ⋆ of
        File.* → halt
        Network.* → run (networkPolicy)
      end
    done → ()
}
ChineseWall = fileNotNetwork ∨_τ networkNotFile
```

Like conjunction, disjunction has an identity: $\bot$ is the unsatisfiable policy, which halts immediately regardless of any program actions. The policy $M \vee_\tau \bot$ accepts the same sequences of actions as M.

2.3   Interfering Policies

Composition of policies can sometimes lead to policies that are ill-defined or simply wrong. For example, consider the conjunction of two file-system policies, `liberalFilePolicy` and `stricterFilePolicy`. The first policy okays each file-system action while the second policy suppresses some of the file-system actions. What should the result be when one policy suppresses an action and another concurrently allows (and potentially requires) it to occur?

A similar problem would occur if we attempted to compose our original file-system policy `fileAccess` with a logging policy `logPolicy` that stores the sequence of all actions that occur in a system in order to detect suspicious access patterns and to uncover mistakes in a policy. Our original `fileAccess` itself performs certain actions on behalf of the target, including closing target files. If the logging policy operates concurrently with the file-access policy, it cannot detect and log the actions performed by `fileAccess`.

We propose a twofold solution to such problems. First, we use a type and effect system to forbid ill-defined or interfering policies such as the ones considered above. Second, we provide an alternative set of combinators that allow programmers to explicitly sequence policies rather than having them execute in parallel. This gives programmers necessary flexibility in defining policies.

Types and Effects. Our type and effect system gives policies refined types with the form $\mathcal{M}_{A_e}^{A_r}(\tau)$. The set of actions A_r includes all the actions regulated by the policy. The second set A_e specifies the effect of the policy. In other words, it specifies the actions that may be suppressed or initiated on behalf of the program.

These refined types give rise to a new typing rule for parallel conjunctive policies. In the following rule, the context Γ maps variables to their types in the usual way.

$$\frac{\Gamma \vdash M_1 : \mathcal{M}_{A_2}^{A_1}(\tau_1) \qquad \Gamma \vdash M_2 : \mathcal{M}_{A_4}^{A_3}(\tau_2)}{A_1 \cap A_4 = A_2 \cap A_3 = \emptyset}{\Gamma \vdash M_1 \wedge M_2 : \mathcal{M}_{A_2 \cup A_4}^{A_1 \cup A_3}(\tau_1 \times \tau_2)}$$

The constraint in the rule specifies that the effects of one of the policies must not overlap with the set of actions regulated by the other policy. A similar rule constrains the policies that may be composed using parallel disjunction.

$$\frac{\Gamma \vdash M_1 : \mathcal{M}_{A_2}^{A_1}(\tau_1) \qquad \Gamma \vdash M_2 : \mathcal{M}_{A_4}^{A_3}(\tau_2)}{A_1 \cap A_4 = A_2 \cap A_3 = \emptyset}{\Gamma \vdash M_1 \vee_{\tau_1 + \tau_2} M_2 : \mathcal{M}_{A_3 \cup A_4}^{A_1 \cup A_2}(\tau_1 + \tau_2)}$$

Rules for typing other terms and rules for typing computations are explained in Section 3.

Sequential Combinators. Sequential combinators allow programmers to explicitly order the execution of effectful policies that apply to the same set of target actions. The sequential conjunctive policy $M_1 \triangle M_2$ operates as follows. The policy M_1 operates on the target action stream, creating an output stream that may contain new actions that M_1 has injected into the stream and may be missing actions that M_1 has suppressed. The policy M_2 acts as it normally would on the output of M_1. Since this is a conjunctive policy, if either policy decides to terminate the application then the application will be terminated. The sequential disjunctive policy $M_1 \triangledown_\tau M_2$ is similar: M_2 operates on the output of M_1. In this case, however, both M_1 and M_2 must decide to terminate the target in order for the target to be stopped. If one policy signals halt, the disjunction continues to operate as if that policy has no effect on the target.

The typing rules for sequential combinators (shown below) are much more liberal then the typing rules for parallel combinators. By explicit sequencing of operations, the programmer determines how the conflicting decisions should be resolved.

$$\frac{\Gamma \vdash M_1 : \mathcal{M}_{A_2}^{A_1}(\tau_1) \qquad \Gamma \vdash M_2 : \mathcal{M}_{A_4}^{A_3}(\tau_2)}{\Gamma \vdash M_1 \triangle M_2 : \mathcal{M}_{A_2 \cup A_4}^{A_1 \cup A_3}(\tau_1 \times \tau_2)}$$

$$\frac{\Gamma \vdash M_1 : \mathcal{M}_{A_2}^{A_1}(\tau_1) \qquad \Gamma \vdash M_2 : \mathcal{M}_{A_4}^{A_3}(\tau_2)}{\Gamma \vdash M_1 \triangledown_{\tau_1 + \tau_2} M_2 : \mathcal{M}_{A_2 \cup A_4}^{A_1 \cup A_3}(\tau_1 + \tau_2)}$$

Because sequential operators accept a wider range of policies than parallel ones, they can be used to implement any policy that can be implemented with parallel combinators. Parallel combinators, however, ensure the often-desirable property that the two policies being composed do not interfere with each other.

3   Formal Semantics

This section describes the syntax and formal semantics of our calculus.

3.1   Syntax

The syntax of our formal language differs slightly from the syntax used in the previous section. First, we use the metavariable a to range over actions and consider them to be atomic symbols rather than decomposable into class name, method name and arguments. Second, we write the regulated set for a policy using superscript notation: $\{E\}^A$ is the simple policy with the regulated set A and computation E.

There are also a number of differences in the computations. Our `acase` instruction chooses a control flow path based upon whether the current action belongs to an arbitrary subset A of the current possible actions. If we want to store or manipulate the current action, we use the primitive $x \to E$ to bind the current action to the variable x, which may be used in E (intuitively, this takes the place of pattern matching). To invoke one of the atomic program actions, we explicitly write $\mathsf{ins}(a)$. Finally, for each of the policy combinators discussed in the previous section, we add a corresponding computation. Each of these computations is superscripted with the regulated sets for their subcomputations. Figure 2 presents a formal syntax for our language.

3.2   Static Semantics

We specify the static semantics for the language using three main judgments.

Subtyping: $\vdash \tau_1 \leq \tau_2$ The rules for subtyping are mostly standard. Unit, pairs, sums and function types have their usual subtyping rules. We say the type of actions $\mathsf{act}(A)$ is covariant in A since $\mathsf{act}(A)$ is a subtype of $\mathsf{act}(A')$ when $A \subseteq A'$. Policy types are covariant in their return type and effect set but invariant in their regulated set. In other words, it is safe for policies to appear to have a larger effect than they actually do, but they must regulate the set that they claim to regulate.

$$\frac{A \subseteq A'}{\vdash \mathsf{act}(A) \leq \mathsf{act}(A')} \qquad\qquad (\text{Sub-Act})$$

$$\frac{A_2 \subseteq A_2' \quad \vdash \tau \leq \tau'}{\vdash \mathcal{M}_{A_2}^{A_r}(\tau) \leq \mathcal{M}_{A_2}^{A_r}(\tau')} \qquad\qquad (\text{Sub-Monad})$$

Term Typing: $\Gamma \vdash M : \tau$ The term typing rules contain the ordinary introduction and elimination rules for functions, unit, pairs and sums. The treatment of variables is also standard. The basic rule for actions gives an action a the singleton type $\mathsf{act}(\{a\})$. When this rule is used in conjunction with the subsumption rule, an action may be given any type $\mathsf{act}(A)$ such that $a \in A$. The non-standard typing rules for terms are given below.

$$\frac{}{\Gamma \vdash a : \mathsf{act}(\{a\})} \qquad\qquad (\text{S-Act})$$

(Types)	τ	$::=$	$\mathsf{act}(A) \mid \tau_1 \to \tau_2 \mid \mathsf{unit}$	
			$\mid \tau_1 \times \tau_2 \mid \tau_1 + \tau_2 \mid \mathcal{M}_{A_2}^{A_1}(\tau)$	
(Behaviors)	β	$::=$	$\cdot \mid \mathsf{ins}(a) \mid \mathsf{sup}(a) \mid \mathsf{acc}(a)$	
(Terms)	M	$::=$	x	(variable)
		$\mid$	a	(action)
		$\mid$	$\mathsf{fun}\ f{:}\tau\ (x).M$	(recursive function)
		$\mid$	$M_1\ M_2$	(application)
		$\mid$	$()$	(unit)
		$\mid$	$\langle M_1, M_2 \rangle$	(pairing)
		$\mid$	$\pi_1\ M \mid \pi_2\ M$	(first/second projections)
		$\mid$	$\mathsf{inl}_\tau(M_1) \mid \mathsf{inr}_\tau(M_2)$	(left/right injections)
		$\mid$	$\mathsf{case}\ M_1\ (x \to M_2 \mid x \to M_3)$	(case)
		$\mid$	$\{E\}^A$	(simple policy)
		$\mid$	$\top$	(trivially satisfiable policy)
		$\mid$	$M_1 \wedge M_2$	(parallel-conjunctive policy)
		$\mid$	$M_1 \bigtriangleup M_2$	(sequential-conjunctive policy)
		$\mid$	$\bot$	(unsatisfiable policy)
		$\mid$	$M_1 \vee_\tau M_2$	(parallel-disjunctive policy)
		$\mid$	$M_1 \bigtriangledown_\tau M_2$	(sequential-disjunctive policy)
(Values)	v	$::=$	$x \mid a \mid \mathsf{fun}\ f{:}\tau\ (x).M \mid ()$	
		$\mid$	$\langle v_1, v_2 \rangle \mid \mathsf{inl}_\tau(v_1)$	
		$\mid$	$\mathsf{inr}_\tau(v_2) \mid \{E\}^A$	
(Computations)	E	$::=$	M	(return)
		$\mid$	$\mathsf{let}\ \{x\} = M\ \mathsf{in}\ E$	(let)
		$\mid$	$\mathsf{ok};\ E$	(accept action)
		$\mid$	$\mathsf{sup};\ E$	(suppress action)
		$\mid$	$\mathsf{ins}(M);\ E$	(call action)
		$\mid$	$(\mathsf{next} \to E_1 \mid \mathsf{done} \to E_2)$	(next action)
		$\mid$	$x \to E$	(bind action)
		$\mid$	$\mathsf{acase}\ (\star \subseteq A)\ (E_1 \mid E_2)$	(action case)
		$\mid$	$\mathsf{case}\ M\ (x \to E_1 \mid x \to E_2)$	(case)
		$\mid$	any	(trivial computation)
		$\mid$	$E_1 \wedge^{A_1,A_2} E_2$	(parallel-conjunctive computation)
		$\mid$	$E_1 \bigtriangleup^{A_1,A_2} E_2$	(sequential-conjunctive computation)
		$\mid$	halt	(terminal computation)
		$\mid$	$E_1 \vee_\tau^{A_1,A_2} E_2$	(parallel-disjunctive computation)
		$\mid$	$E_1 \bigtriangledown_\tau^{A_1,A_2} E_2$	(sequential-disjunctive computation)

Fig. 2. Syntax

$$\frac{\Gamma;\diamond \vdash^{A_r} E : \tau, A_e}{\Gamma \vdash \{E\}^{A_r} : \mathcal{M}_{A_e}^{A_r}(\tau)} \qquad \text{(S-Sus)}$$

$$\frac{}{\Gamma \vdash \top : \mathcal{M}_\emptyset^\emptyset(\mathsf{unit})} \qquad \text{(S-Top)}$$

$$\frac{\Gamma \vdash M_1 : \mathcal{M}_{A_2}^{A_1}(\tau_1) \quad \Gamma \vdash M_2 : \mathcal{M}_{A_4}^{A_3}(\tau_2) \quad A_1 \cap A_4 = A_2 \cap A_3 = \emptyset}{\Gamma \vdash M_1 \wedge M_2 : \mathcal{M}_{A_2 \cup A_4}^{A_1 \cup A_3}(\tau_1 \times \tau_2)} \qquad \text{(S-ParCon)}$$

$$\frac{\Gamma \vdash M_1 : \mathcal{M}_{A_2}^{A_1}(\tau_1) \quad \Gamma \vdash M_2 : \mathcal{M}_{A_4}^{A_3}(\tau_2)}{\Gamma \vdash M_1 \bigtriangleup M_2 : \mathcal{M}_{A_2 \cup A_4}^{A_1 \cup A_3}(\tau_1 \times \tau_2)} \qquad \text{(S-SeqCon)}$$

$$\overline{\Gamma \vdash \bot : \mathcal{M}_\emptyset^\emptyset(\tau)} \qquad\qquad \text{(S-Bot)}$$

$$\frac{\Gamma \vdash M_1 : \mathcal{M}_{A_2}^{A_1}(\tau_1) \quad \Gamma \vdash M_2 : \mathcal{M}_{A_4}^{A_3}(\tau_2) \quad A_1 \cap A_4 = A_2 \cap A_3 = \emptyset}{\Gamma \vdash M_1 \vee_{\tau_1+\tau_2} M_2 : \mathcal{M}_{A_3 \cup A_4}^{A_1 \cup A_2}(\tau_1 + \tau_2)} \qquad \text{(S-ParDis)}$$

$$\frac{\Gamma \vdash M_1 : \mathcal{M}_{A_2}^{A_1}(\tau_1) \quad \Gamma \vdash M_2 : \mathcal{M}_{A_4}^{A_3}(\tau_2)}{\Gamma \vdash M_1 \bigtriangledown_{\tau_1+\tau_2} M_2 : \mathcal{M}_{A_2 \cup A_4}^{A_1 \cup A_3}(\tau_1 + \tau_2)} \qquad \text{(S-SeqDis)}$$

Elementary policies (rule (S-Sus)) are given the type $\mathcal{M}_{A_e}^{A_r}(\tau)$ when the suspended computation regulates the actions in A_r, has effect A_e and produces a value of type τ. The trivial policy (rule (S-Top)) makes its decisions based upon no regulated actions, has no effect and simply returns unit. The terminal policy (rule (S-Bot)) also makes its decision based upon no regulated actions, has no effect, but instead of returning a value, it immediately calls for termination of the target. Since the terminal policy never returns, we allow its return type to be any type τ.

Rules (S-ParCon) and (S-SeqCon) give types to the two conjunctive policies. In each case, the type of the resulting computation involves taking the union of the regulated sets and the union of the effects since a conjunctive policy makes its decisions based on the regulated actions of both policies and potentially has the effects of either policy. These combinators return a pair of values, which is reflected in the type of the conjunctive combinator. The parallel conjunction is constrained so that the regulated set of one conjunct is disjoint from the effect of the other and vice versa. This constraint prevents one conjunct from inserting or suppressing actions that should be regulated by the other conjunct. Typing for the sequential conjunction is more liberal. It allows one policy to supersede another regardless of the effects of either policy. The rules for the disjunctive combinators ((S-ParDis) and (S-SeqDis)) are analogous to their conjunctive counterparts except that disjunctions return sums rather than pairs.

Computation Typing: $\Gamma; B \vdash^{A_r} E : \tau, A_e$ The basic judgment for typing computations may be read "Computation E produces a value with type τ and has effect A_e in Γ when run against a target whose next action is in B." B ranges over non-empty sets A or the symbol $\diamond$, which represents no knowledge about the next action. The next action might not even exist, as is the case when the target has terminated. We maintain this set of possible next actions so that we know what actions to consider as possible effects of a suppress statement and what actions may be bound to a variable in a bind statement. We do not consider computation judgments to be valid unless either $B \subseteq A_r$ or $B = \diamond$. We define $B \sqcup A_r$ to be B if $B \subseteq A_r$ and $\diamond$ otherwise. Finally, set intersect and set minus operators $\cap_\diamond$ and $\backslash_\diamond$ act like standard set operators, except that instead of returning $\emptyset$ they return $\diamond$.

The computation typing rules are given below.

$$\frac{\Gamma \vdash M : \tau}{\Gamma; B \vdash^{A_r} M : \tau, \emptyset} \qquad \text{(SE-Ret)}$$

$$\frac{\Gamma \vdash M : \mathcal{M}_{A_2}^{A_r'}(\tau') \quad \Gamma, x{:}\tau'; \diamond \vdash^{A_r} E : \tau, A \quad A_r' \subseteq A_r}{\Gamma; B \vdash^{A_r} \text{let } \{x\} = M \text{ in } E : \tau, A \cup A_2} \qquad \text{(SE-Let1)}$$

$$\frac{\Gamma; \diamond \vdash^{A_r} E : \tau, A \quad B \neq \diamond}{\Gamma; B \vdash^{A_r} \text{ok}; E : \tau, A} \qquad \text{(SE-Acc)}$$

$$\frac{\Gamma; \diamond \vdash^{A_r} E : \tau, A \quad B \neq \diamond}{\Gamma; B \vdash^{A_r} \text{sup}; E : \tau, A \cup B} \qquad \text{(SE-Sup)}$$

$$\frac{\Gamma \vdash M : \text{act}(A') \quad \Gamma; B \vdash^{A_r} E : \tau, A}{\Gamma; B \vdash^{A_r} \text{ins}(M); E : \tau, A \cup A'} \qquad \text{(SE-Ins)}$$

$$\frac{\Gamma; A_r \vdash^{A_r} E_1 : \tau, A \quad \Gamma; \diamond \vdash^{A_r} E_2 : \tau, A}{\Gamma; B \vdash^{A_r} (\text{next} \to E_1 \mid \text{done} \to E_2) : \tau, A} \qquad \text{(SE-Next)}$$

$$\frac{\Gamma, x{:}\text{act}(B); B \vdash^{A_r} E : \tau, A \quad B \neq \diamond}{\Gamma; B \vdash^{A_r} x \to E : \tau, A} \qquad \text{(SE-Bind)}$$

$$\frac{\Gamma; B \cap_\diamond A' \vdash^{A_r} E_1 : \tau, A \quad \Gamma; B \setminus_\diamond A' \vdash^{A_r} E_2 : \tau, A}{A' \subseteq A_r \quad B \neq \diamond}{\Gamma; B \vdash^{A_r} \text{acase } (\star \subseteq A') \, (E_1 \mid E_2) : \tau, A} \qquad \text{(SE-Acase)}$$

$$\frac{\Gamma \vdash M : \tau_1 + \tau_2}{\Gamma, x{:}\tau_1; B \vdash^{A_r} E_1 : \tau, A \quad \Gamma, x{:}\tau_2; B \vdash^{A_r} E_2 : \tau, A}{\Gamma; B \vdash^{A_r} \text{case } M \, (x \to E_1 \mid x \to E_2) : \tau, A} \qquad \text{(SE-Case)}$$

$$\frac{}{\Gamma; B \vdash^{A_r} \text{any} : \text{unit}, \emptyset} \qquad \text{(SE-Any)}$$

$$\frac{\Gamma; B \sqcup A_1 \vdash^{A_1} E_1 : \tau_1, A_3 \quad \Gamma; B \sqcup A_2 \vdash^{A_2} E_2 : \tau_2, A_4}{A_1 \cap A_4 = A_2 \cap A_3 = \emptyset \quad A_1 \cup A_2 = A_r}{\Gamma; B \vdash^{A_r} E_1 \wedge^{A_1, A_2} E_2 : \tau_1 \times \tau_2, A_3 \cup A_4} \qquad \text{(SE-ParCon)}$$

$$\frac{\Gamma; B \sqcup A_1 \vdash^{A_1} E_1 : \tau_1, A_3 \quad \Gamma; \diamond \vdash^{A_2} E_2 : \tau_2, A_4 \quad A_1 \cup A_2 = A_r}{\Gamma; B \vdash^{A_r} E_1 \bigtriangleup^{A_1, A_2} E_2 : \tau_1 \times \tau_2, A_3 \cup A_4} \qquad \text{(SE-SeqCon1)}$$

$$\frac{}{\Gamma; B \vdash^{A_r} \text{halt} : \tau, \emptyset} \qquad \text{(SE-Halt)}$$

$$\frac{\Gamma; B \sqcup A_1 \vdash^{A_1} E_1 : \tau_1, A_3 \quad \Gamma; B \sqcup A_2 \vdash^{A_2} E_2 : \tau_2, A_4}{A_1 \cap A_4 = A_2 \cap A_3 = \emptyset \quad A_1 \cup A_2 = A_r}{\Gamma; B \vdash^{A_r} E_1 \vee_{\tau_1 + \tau_2}^{A_1, A_2} E_2 : \tau_1 + \tau_2, A_3 \cup A_4} \qquad \text{(SE-ParDis)}$$

$$\frac{\Gamma; B \sqcup A_1 \vdash^{A_1} E_1 : \tau_1, A_3 \quad \Gamma; \diamond \vdash^{A_2} E_2 : \tau_2, A_4 \quad A_1 \cup A_2 = A_r}{\Gamma; B \vdash^{A_r} E_1 \triangledown^{A_1, A_2}_{\tau_1 + \tau_2} E_2 : \tau_1 + \tau_2, A_3 \cup A_4} \quad \text{(SE-SEQDIS1)}$$

$$\frac{\Gamma; B' \vdash^{A_r} E : \tau', A' \quad (B' = \diamond \text{ or } B \subseteq B') \quad \vdash \tau' \leq \tau \quad A' \subseteq A}{\Gamma; B \vdash^{A_r} E : \tau, A} \quad \text{(SE-SUB)}$$

Terms have no effects, so they are well typed with respect to any next action (SE-Ret).

The let rule (SE-Let1) requires M to be a policy with a regulated set that is a subset of the current computation's regulated set. When this policy returns, we will have no information regarding the next action because the suspended policy may have accepted or suppressed an arbitrary number of actions. As a result, we check E in a context involving $\diamond$.

Rules (SE-Acc) and (SE-Sup) have similar structure. In both cases, we must be sure that the target has produced some action to be accepted or suppressed (i.e., $B \neq \diamond$). The main difference between the two rules is that we record the effect of the suppression, whereas acceptance has no effect. The rule for invoking actions (SE-Ins) adds A' to the effect of the computation when the action called belongs to the set A' (in other words, when the action has type $\text{act}(A')$).

The next/done construct adds A_r to the context for checking E_1 and $\diamond$ for checking E_2 since we only take the first branch when we see an action in the regulated set and we take the second branch when there are no more actions (rule (SE-Next)). Rule (SE-Acase) takes the first or second branch depending upon whether the current action is in the set A_1. We refine the context in each branch to reflect the information that we have about the current action.

Rule (SE-ParCon) places several constraints on parallel conjunction of computations. Since the next action could be in the regulated set of the conjunction but not in the regulated sets of both E_1 and E_2, E_1 and E_2 must both be well typed either with respect to a subset of their regulated sets or with respect to $\diamond$. This is ensured by typing the subcomputations with respect to $B \sqcup A_1$ and $B \sqcup A_2$. In addition, there is not allowed to be a conflict between the regulated actions of one subcomputation and the effects of the other. Finally, the regulated set of the conjunction must be the union of the regulated sets of the subcomputations.

The first rule for sequential conjunction (SE-SeqCon1) is similar, with two exceptions. First, there is no constraint on the regulated and effect sets of the subcomputations. Second, E_2 must be well typed with respect to $\diamond$ because we cannot make any assumption about what the next action will be (it may be an action emitted by E_1, or E_1 may suppress all actions until the target has finished executing).

The rules for the disjunctive operators (SE-ParDis and SE-SeqDis1) are identical to their conjunctive counterparts except that they have sum types rather than pair types.

The subsumption rule for computations (SE-Sub) is invariant in regulated sets, covariant in type and effect sets, and contravariant in the type of the next action. It is always OK to consider that a computation has more effects than it actually does. In addition, a computation typed with respect to the possible next actions B' continues to be well typed even if more information about the next action is available.

3.3   Operational Semantics and Safety

We have defined a formal operational semantics and proven the safety of our language using progress and preservation. This result not only guarantees that the ordinary sorts of errors do not occur during evaluation but also rules out various policy conflicts (such as one computation in a parallel conjunction accepting a target action while the other computation suppresses it). The proof is quite long and detailed, but well worth the effort: it helped us catch numerous errors in preliminary versions of our system. Please see our technical report for details [2].

4   Discussion

4.1   Related Work

The SDS-940 system at Berkeley [6] was the first to use code rewriting to enforce security properties. More recently, the advent of safe languages such as Java, Haskell, ML, Modula, and Scheme, which allow untrusted applications to interoperate in the same address space with system services, has led to renewed efforts to design flexible and secure monitoring systems. For example, Evans and Twyman's Naccio system [9] allows security architects to declare *resources*, which are security-relevant interfaces, and to attach *properties*, which are bundles of security state and checking code, to these resources. Erlingsson and Schneider's SASI language [7] and later Poet and Pslang system [8] provide similar power. Grimm and Bershad [12] describe and evaluate a flexible mechanism that separates the access-control mechanism from policy in the SPIN extensible operating system. Finally, the Ariel project [19] allows security experts to write boolean constraints that determine whether or not a method can be invoked.

A shortcoming of all these projects is a lack of formal semantics for the proposed languages and systems. Without a formal semantics, system implementers have no tools for precise reasoning about their systems. They also do not provide a general set of primitives that programmers can use to explicitly construct complex policies from simpler ones.

A slightly different approach to program monitoring is taken by Lee et al. [14, 15] and Sandholm and Schwarzbach [21]. Rather than writing an explicit program to monitor applications as we do, they specify the safety property in which they are interested either in a specialized temporal logic (Lee et al.) or second-order monadic logic (Sandholm and Schwarzbach).

Many monitoring systems may be viewed as a specialized form of aspect-oriented programming. Aspect-oriented languages such as AspectJ [13] allow programmers to specify *pointcuts*, which are collections of program points and *advice*, which is code that is inserted at a specified pointcut. Wand et al. [23] give a denotational semantics for these features using monadic operations. Conflicting advice inserted at the same pointcut is a known problem in aspect-oriented programming. AspectJ solves the problem by specifying a list of rules that determine the order in which advice will be applied. We believe that our language, which allows explicit composition of policies and makes it possible to statically check composed policies for interference, is a more flexible approach to solving this problem.

Theoretical work by Alpern and Schneider [1,22] gives an automaton-theoretic characterization of safety, liveness, and execution monitoring (EM) policies. EM policies are the class of policies enforceable by a general-purpose program monitor that may terminate the target, but may not otherwise modify target behavior. This class of program monitors (called security automata) corresponds precisely to our effect-free monitors, and consequently, as pointed out by Schneider, they are easily composed. We have previously extended Schneider's work by defining a new class of automata [3,4], the *edit automata*, which are able to insert and suppress target actions as well as terminate the target. Edit automata more accurately characterize practical security monitors that modify program behavior. We proved that under certain realistic assumptions such automata are strictly more powerful than security automata.

4.2   Current and Future Work

In order to confirm that our policy calculus is feasible and useful, we have developed a practical implementation of it [2]. Polymer, our language for writing policies, implements most of the policy calculus but uses Java, rather than a lambda calculus, as the core language. Enforcing a policy on a target application involves compiling the Polymer policy into Java bytecode and instrumenting the target to call the policy prior to executing any security-relevant instructions. For simplicity, the target programs we currently consider are Java source programs, but many of the techniques we use can also be extended to handle Java bytecode. We have not yet implemented static checking of effects.

Our immediate concern is to acquire more experience applying our tool to enforcing security policies on realistic applications. We are interested both in testing our tool on untrusted mobile programs as well as using it to make programs and services written by trusted programmers more robust. As an example of the latter application, we intend to follow Qie et al. [20] and use our tool to control resource consumption and to help prevent denial of service in Web servers.

Rather than having an external tool that rewrites Java programs to enforce policies, we are working on internalizing the rewriting process within an extension to the Java language. We hope to develop techniques that allow programmers to dynamically rewrite programs or parts of programs and to update or modify security policies without necessarily bringing down the system. We believe the idea of policies as first-class objects will be crucial in this enterprise.

We plan to implement a mechanism that would allow policy writers to group related methods into "abstract" actions (e.g., constructors for `java.io.FileInputStream`, `java.io.FileWriter`, etc., could be referred to by the abstract action `FileOpenAction(String filename)`). The independence of these abstract actions from the underlying system would allow policies to be ported from one system to another by changing only the definitions of the abstract actions.

We are also investigating additional combinators that could be added to our language. In particular, we are interested in developing fixed-point combinators that extend our sequential operators. These combinators would iteratively combine two policies without restricting their effects or requiring that one supersedes the other. We would also like to make it possible for policy writers to develop their own combinators.

Acknowledgments. The authors would like to thank Dan Wallach for suggesting the Chinese wall policy as a good example of a disjunctive policy. We are also grateful to Dan Grossman for commenting on a draft of this paper.

References

1. Bowen Alpern and Fred Schneider. Recognizing safety and liveness. *Distributed Computing*, 2:117–126, 1987.
2. Lujo Bauer, Jarred Ligatti, and David Walker. A calculus for composing security policies. Technical Report TR-655-02, Princeton University, 2002. Forthcoming.
3. Lujo Bauer, Jarred Ligatti, and David Walker. More enforceable security policies. In *Foundations of Computer Security*, Copenhagen, Denmark, July 2002.
4. Lujo Bauer, Jarred Ligatti, and David Walker. More enforceable security policies. Technical Report TR-649-02, Princeton University, June 2002.
5. David Brewer and Michael Nash. The Chinese wall security policy. In *IEEE Symposium on Security and Privacy*, pages 206–214, Oakland, May 1989.
6. P. Deutsch and C. A. Grant. A flexible measurement tool for software systems. In *Information Processing*, pages 320–326, 1971. Appeared in the proceedings of the IFIP Congress.
7. Úlfar Erlingsson and Fred B. Schneider. SASI enforcement of security policies: A retrospective. In *Proceedings of the New Security Paradigms Workshop*, pages 87–95, Caledon Hills, Canada, September 1999.
8. Úlfar Erlingsson and Fred B. Schneider. IRM enforcement of Java stack inspection. In *IEEE Symposium on Security and Privacy*, pages 246–255, Oakland, California, May 2000.
9. David Evans and Andrew Twyman. Flexible policy-directed code safety. In *IEEE Security and Privacy*, Oakland, CA, May 1999.
10. Andrew D. Gordon and Don Syme. Typing a multi-language intermediate code. In *ACM Symposium on Principles of Programming Languages*, London, UK, January 2001.
11. John Gough. *Compiling for the .NET Common Language Runtime*. Prentice Hall, 2001.

12. Robert Grimm and Brian Bershad. Separating access control policy, enforcement and functionality in extensible systems. *ACM Transactions on Computer Systems*, pages 36–70, February 2001.

13. Gregor Kiczales, Erik Hilsdale, Jim Hugunin, Mik Kersten, Jeffrey Palm, and William Griswold. An overview of AspectJ. In *European Conference on Object-oriented Programming*. Springer-Verlag, 2001.

14. Moonjoo Kim, Mahesh Viswanathan, Hanene Ben-Abdallah, Sampath Kannan, Insup Lee, and Oleg Sokolsky. Formally specified monitoring of temporal properties. In *European Conference on Real-time Systems*, York, UK, June 1999.

15. Insup Lee, Sampath Kannan, Moonjoo Kim, Oleg Sokolsky, and Mahesh Viswanathan. Run-time assurance based on formal specifications. In *International Conference on Parallel and Distributed Processing Techniques and Applications*, Las Vegas, June 1999.

16. Tim Lindholm and Frank Yellin. *The Java Virtual Machine Specification*. Addison-Wesley, 2nd edition, 1999.

17. Erik Meijer and John Gough. A technical overview of the Common Language Infrastructure. `http://research.microsoft.com/~emeijer/Papers/CLR.pdf`.

18. Eugenio Moggi. Notions of computation and monads. *Information and Computation*, 93:55–92, 1991.

19. R. Pandey and B. Hashii. Providing fine-grained access control for Java programs through binary editing. *Concurrency: Practice and Experience*, 12(14):1405–1430, 2000.

20. Xiaohu Qie, Ruoming Pang, and Larry Peterson. Defensive programming: Using an annotation toolkit to build DoS-resistant software. Technical Report TR-658-02, Princeton University, July 2002.

21. Anders Sandholm and Michael Schwartzbach. Distributed safety controllers for web services. In *Fundamental Approaches to Software Engineering*, volume 1382 of *Lecture Notes in Computer Science*, pages 270–284. Springer-Verlag, 1998.

22. Fred B. Schneider. Enforceable security policies. *ACM Transactions on Information and Systems Security*, 3(1):30–50, February 2000.

23. Mitchell Wand, Gregor Kiczales, and Christopher Dutchyn. A semantics for advice and dynamic join points in aspect-oriented programming. In *Workshop on Foundations of Aspect-Oriented Languages*, 2002.

Flexible and Efficient Sandboxing Based on Fine-Grained Protection Domains

Takahiro Shinagawa[1], Kenji Kono[2,3], and Takashi Masuda[2]

[1] Department of Information Science, Graduate School of Science, University of Tokyo
shina@is.s.u-tokyo.ac.jp
[2] Department of Computer Science, University of Electro-Communications
{kono, masuda}@cs.uec.ac.jp
[3] PRESTO, Japan Science and Technology Corporation

Abstract. Sandboxing is one of the most promising technologies for safely executing potentially malicious applications, and it is becoming an indispensable functionality of modern computer systems. Nevertheless, traditional operating systems provide no special support for sandboxing; a sandbox system is either built in the user level, or directly encoded in the kernel level. In the user-level implementation, sandbox systems are implemented by using support for debuggers, and the resulting systems are unacceptably slow. In the kernel-level implementation, users are obliged to use a specific sandbox system. However, users should be able to choose an appropriate sandbox system depending on target applications, because sandbox systems are usually designed for specific classes of applications. This paper presents a generic framework on top of which various sandbox systems can be implemented easily and efficiently. The presented framework has three advantages. First, users can selectively use the appropriate sandbox systems depending on the target applications. Second, the resulting sandbox systems are efficient enough and the performance is comparable to that of kernel-implemented sandbox systems. Finally, a wide range of sandbox systems can be implemented in the user level, thereby facilitating the introduction of new sandboxing systems in the user level. The presented framework is based on the mechanism of fine-grained protection domains that have been previously proposed by the authors.

1 Introduction

Sandboxing is one of the most promising technologies for safely executing applications. A sandbox system enables users to execute untrusted applications without concern, because it allows the users to define a security policy to be enforced on the applications. Even if a malicious one attempts to violate the security policy and to make unauthorized access, the sandbox system detects the access and prevents it. The facilities of sandboxing is indispensable for executing Internet applications in the today's Internet environment. Internet applications, which are applications that process data obtained from the Internet — such as mails, web pages, and electronic documents —, often contain security vulnerabilities to malicious attacks. Such vulnerable applications may be hijacked by crackers if the crackers manipulate the data on the Internet and exploit their vulnerabilities. For example, widely-used Internet applications such as Ghostscript and Adobe Acrobat Reader have pointed out their vulnerabilities to malicious attacks [1,2].

M. Okada et al. (Eds.): ISSS 2002, LNCS 2609, pp. 172–184, 2003.

Many research efforts have been devoted to developing sandbox systems [3,4,5,6,7, 8,9,10,11,12], and some companies are shipping products based on sandbox technology. Many of these sandbox systems use the technique called *system call interception* to monitor the behavior of sandboxed applications. A *reference monitor* is a piece of program code interposed between a sandboxed application and the OS kernel to intercept system calls issued by the sandboxed application. To enforce a security policy, the reference monitor filters out undesired system calls that may violate the given security policy. This technique allows reference monitors to totally control resource access attempts made by sandboxed applications.

A sandbox system is implemented either in the kernel level or in the user level. In kernel-level approaches [3,4,5,6,7], a specific sandbox mechanism is directly encoded in the kernel. These approaches lack *flexibility* because the users are forced to use a specific sandbox mechanism already implemented in the kernel. A sandbox system should allow the users to choose an appropriate sandbox mechanism depending on the target applications because sandbox mechanism are typically designed for a specific class of applications. For example, SubDomain is designed for Internet servers and SBox is for CGI programs. In addition, it is risky to implement a new reference monitor in the kernel, because a trivial flaw in the implementation might expose the entire kernel to the danger of unauthorized access.

In user-level approaches [8,9,10,11,12], a reference monitor is placed in an external process to protect the reference monitor from sandboxed applications. To intercept system calls issued by the sandboxed applications, the reference monitor uses the operating system's (os)'s support for debuggers like ptrace() and /proc file systems. The primary advantage of the user-level approaches is their *flexibility*. Since a reference monitor is implemented in the user level, it is easy to implement various types of sandbox systems and we can choose an appropriate sandbox mechanism that is specific to a certain class of applications. The disadvantage of this approach is that it significantly degrades the performance of sandboxed applications. Whenever a sandboxed application issues a system call, a context switch is made to the reference monitor and the switching incurs terrible runtime overhead.

This paper presents a generic framework for flexible and lightweight sandbox systems. This framework enables various types of sandbox mechanisms to be built on top of the framework. The presented framework exploits *fine-grained protection domains* that have been proposed by the authors [13,14,15]. The framework combines the benefits of both the user-level and kernel-level approaches. In this framework, a reference monitor is implemented in the user level and thus, the flexibility of user-level approaches is retained. To retain the high performance of kernel-level approaches, a reference monitor is placed in the *same* process as the sandboxed application. By doing this, our framework eliminates the overheads involved in context switching. To prevent a sandboxed application from compromising the reference monitor, we use the functionality provided by fine-grained protection domains: a fine-grained protection domain protects a reference monitor from the sandboxed application in the same process, as if the reference monitor were outside the process of the sandboxed application.

The rest of the paper is organized as follows. Section 2 describes the goals of our sandboxing framework. Section 3 discusses the mechanism of fine-grained protection domains and Section 4 describes the implementation of the sandboxing framework. Section 5 shows experimental results obtained measuring the overhead of the sandboxing framework. Section 6 describes related work and Section 7 concludes the paper.

2   Goals of Sandboxing Framework

This section presents the goals of our sandboxing framework and shows approaches to meeting these goals. We have three goals: *flexibility*, *performance*, and *transparency*.

2.1   Flexibility

There are various design choices available in developing sandbox systems, such as passive or active, global or local, mandatory or discretionary, static or dynamic, generic or specific, and transient or persistent [16]. These design choices determine the expressive power of security policies that can be enforced by the resulting sandbox system. Therefore, it is difficult for a *single* sandbox system to enforce various classes of security policies that differ in their expressive power. To make various security policies enforceable, a generic sandboxing framework should be flexible enough to allow sandbox systems of various designs to be implemented on top of it. If a sandboxing framework allows only a specific sandbox design to be implemented, the enforceable security policies are limited, reducing the range of applicability of the sandboxing framework.

The primary goal of our sandboxing framework is flexibility: many types of sandbox systems must be able to be implemented on top of it. To ease the implementation of sandbox systems, our framework allows sandbox systems to be implemented in the user level. User-level sandbox systems are easier to implement, debug, and test than kernel-level systems. Furthermore, our framework enables each application to be sandboxed using different sandbox systems. This allows the users to choose a sandbox system suitable for their needs. Since the expressive power of security policies required for sandboxing depends on the user's demands, this property enhances the flexibility of our sandboxing framework.

2.2   Performance

The second goal of our sandboxing framework is performance. To control resource access attempts made by sandboxed applications, any sandbox system incurs additional overhead to some extent. If the additional overhead is too large, the resulting system is unacceptable for use. Unfortunately, user-level sandbox systems incur large overheads because they require a large number of context switches to intercept system calls issued by a sandboxed application. At least two context switches are required per system call since an external process intercepts the system call. A context switch involves large overhead incurred by scheduling and TLB flushing, therefore, it is difficult to implement lightweight sandbox systems based on the user-level approaches.

To reduce overhead of context switches, our framework places a reference monitor *inside* the sandboxed application's process. By doing this, the overhead involved in the system call interception can be eliminated because no context switch is involved, and the resulting sandbox system is a high-performance system. This approach, of course, poses a new security problem in that a reference monitor itself may be compromised easily because a sandboxed application can tamper with the reference monitor's code or/and data to bypass the reference monitor. To protect a reference monitor from the sandboxed application, we exploit fine-grained protection domains [13,14,15]. Fine-grained protection domains are a kernel-level protection mechanism that establishes *intra*-process protection. Using fine-grained protection domains, we can protect a reference monitor from the sandboxed application, as if the monitor resided in another process. In the next section, we discuss the mechanism of fine-grained protection domains.

2.3 Transparency

The third goal of our sandboxing framework is *transparency*. Transparency here means that an existing application can be sandboxed without having to modify it. As is in other sandbox systems, our framework uses the system call interception technique to accomplish transparency. Since access control is done by intercepting system calls, existing applications do not have to be modified.

3   Fine-Grained Protection Domains

Before describing the implementation of our framework, we briefly summarize the mechanism of fine-grained protection domains. The fine-grained protection domain is a kernel-level extension, currently implemented as an extension to a Linux kernel, and greatly versatile in implementing protection mechanisms [13,14,15]. Here we introduce the functionalities of the mechanism that will be needed to explain the implementation of the sandboxing framework. The details of fine-grained protection domains have been previously reported [13,14,15].

3.1   Intra-process Memory Protection

Traditionally, the notion of the process coincides with that of the protection domain, therefore, *intra*-process memory protection is almost impossible. A fine-grained protection domain is finer than process-level protection domains, and multiple fine-grained protection domains can co-exist inside a single process. Figure 1 illustrates that two fine-grained protection domains, A and B, co-exist inside a process. Each fine-grained protection domain is associated with a code fragment, and determines to which memory pages the associated code can access. In Figure 1, domain A can access the entire memory of the process while domain B can access only memory pages $p1$, $p2$, and $p3$.

Memory protection is set up in the grain of memory pages. For each memory page, different fine-grained protection domains can have different access rights. In Figure 1 memory page $p0$ is accessible from domain A but not accessible from domain B, while memory page $p1$ is accessible from both domain A and domain B.

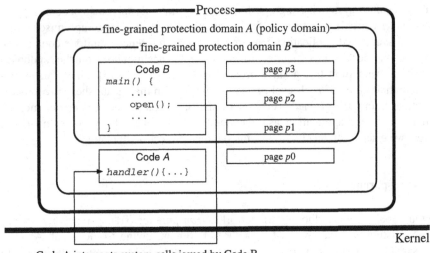

Code A intercepts system calls issued by Code B

Fig. 1. Fine-grained protection domains: two fine-grained protection domains A and B co-exist inside a process. The domain A and B are associated with Codes A and B respectively. Code B can not access Code A and a memory page $p0$. System calls issued by Code B are intercepted by a handler of Code A.

3.2   System Call Interception

For each process, there is exactly one fine-grained protection domain that controls the access rights of all fine-grained protection domains in the same process. This fine-grained protection domain is called a *policy domain* since it determines the policies of memory protection. In Figure 1, domain A is the policy domain. That is, domain A can change the access rights of domains A and B while domain B cannot.

In our implementation of fine-grained protection domains, a policy domain can intercept system calls issued by other fine-grained protection domains. To intercept system calls, a policy domain registers a system call handler *a priori* with the OS kernel. In Figure 1, domain A intercepts system calls issued by domain B. For example, if the code associated with domain B issues an open system call, the OS kernel upcalls the system call handler of domain A, passing the system call number and the system call arguments. Then, the handler examines the arguments. If the policy domain determines that executing the system call does not violate a security policy, the kernel executes it. Otherwise, the kernel returns an error code to domain B.

A policy domain usually has access rights to the entire memory of the process. Therefore, the policy domain can inspect the system call arguments if the arguments contain pointers to the memory of another domain. The policy domain can traverse the pointer structure without any pointer conversions and data copies.

3.3   Implementation Overview

The fine-grained protection domain is implemented as an extension to the Linux kernel. The implementation centers around the *multi-protection* page table, a mechanism that accomplishes the intra-process memory protection. A multi-protection page table is an extension of the traditional page table that enables each memory page to have multiple protection modes at the same time. At any instance in time, one of the multiple protection modes is effective. Since each memory page can have multiple protection modes, each fine-grained protection domain can have its own protection mode for each memory page, thus, memory protection is provided between the fine-grained protection domains. To switch fine-grained protection domains, a special software trap is prepared in which the effective modes of memory protection are switched. By using the memory management unit (MMU) in sophisticated ways, we avoid flushing TLBs and caches that would degrade the performance of switching protection domains.

Our extended kernel can be ported to a wide range of processor architectures. The prototype system is running on Intel IA-32, SPARC, and Alpha processors. To implement the multi-protection page tables efficiently, we used the processor-specific features fully. For the Intel IA-32 family [17], we utilized the segmentation and the ring protection mechanisms. For the SPARC processors (versions 8 and 9) [18], the tagged TLBs and the register windows are used. For the Alpha processors [19], tagged TLBs and PAL code are utilized. Our extensions to the kernel are not large. Only 1,398 lines of code are added to the Linux 2.2.18 in the IA-32 implementation. The details of the implementation can be found in [13,14,15].

4   Implementation of Sandboxing Framework

Our sandboxing framework uses system call interception provided by the facilities of fine-grained protection domains. We prepare two fine-grained protection domains to sandbox an application. One protection domain is assigned to the application itself and the other domain is assigned to a reference monitor. The domain assigned to the reference monitor plays the role of the policy domain. Therefore, the reference monitor can intercept system calls issued by the sandboxed application and set up the memory protection policies. The memory protection policies are as follows. To protect a reference monitor from the sandboxed application, the memory pages of the reference monitor are made *not* accessible from the fine-grained protection domain associated with the sandboxed application. On the other hand, the memory pages of the sandboxed application are made accessible from the fine-grained protection domain associated with the reference monitor. By doing this, the reference monitor can directly access a system call argument even if the argument contains a pointer to the data in the sandboxed application's domain.

In our sandboxing framework, fine-grained protection domains must be created and assigned to a sandboxed application before the application starts executing. We modified a program loader (an ELF loader in the case of Linux) to create and assign fine-grained protection domains. The program loader creates two fine-grained protection domains, loads a reference monitor and a sandboxed application to each domain, and sets up the memory protection policies. Then, the loader jumps to the sandboxed application to start execution.

Our approach makes our sandboxing framework flexible because it allows reference monitors to be implemented in the user level. To implement a reference monitor, the programmer simply prepares system call handlers that determine which system calls are allowed to be executed, based on a given security policy. Therefore, any sandbox systems that use the system call interception technique can be implemented on top of our sandboxing framework. Furthermore, since a reference monitor is associated with each application, the user can choose an appropriate sandbox system based on their needs.

5   Performance Experiments

This section presents the results of performance experiments. We measured the overheads of a sandbox system implemented on top of our sandboxing framework. The experimental results demonstrate that that our sandboxing framework is practical enough to implement lightweight sandbox systems on top of it.

The overheads of sandbox systems are important because sandbox systems would be impractical if their overheads are unacceptably high. To validate our approach, we have implemented a sample sandbox system on top of our framework. We call this sandbox system a *lightweight* sandbox. As a comparison, we also implemented a user-level sandbox system that uses debugging facilities to intercept system calls. We call this sandbox system a *process-based* sandbox since the reference monitor is implemented as an external process. In the experiments, we used a simple security policy designed to protect file systems. The reference monitors intercepted an open() system call, and the pathname passed as an argument is checked to prevent undesired file access. The reference monitor compares the pathname with 10 directory names that contain sensitive files such as /etc/passwd, and denies access to the files under those directory trees.

We conducted micro-benchmark and macro-benchmark tests. In the micro-benchmark tests, the overheads of system call interception are examined. In the macro-benchmark tests, the performances of real applications confined in sandbox systems are measured. We conducted the experiments on a PC having a 1 GHz Pentium III processor, 512 MB of RAM, and a 75 GB hard-disk drive (IBM DTLA-307030). The kernel used was the Linux 2.2.18 that had been extended to support fine-grained protection domains.

5.1   Micro-Benchmark

We measured the performance of system calls issued by a sandboxed application. Using the cycle counter of a Pentium III processor, the time required to complete one system call is measured. The system calls measured were getpid() and open().

The measured performance of getpid() is the minimum overhead of system call interception. In the security policy used in the experiments, the reference monitors do nothing on this system call: they intercept getpid() but no checks are done. The experimental results of getpid() are shown on the left-hand side of Figure 2. In Figure 2, *Lightweight Sandbox* is the sample sandbox system built on our sandboxing framework and *Process-based Sandbox* is the sandbox system that uses an external process for a reference monitor. The lightweight sandbox requires an additional cost of only 523

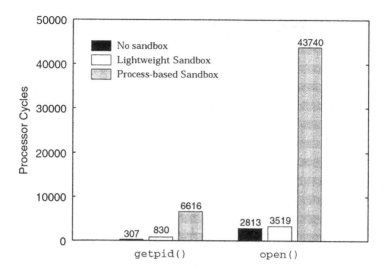

Fig. 2. Performance of system calls in sandbox systems. The lightweight sandbox, our approach, significantly outperforms the traditional process-based sandbox.

processor cycles, while the process-based sandbox adds 6,309 cycles. The lightweight sandbox costs one-twelfth less than the process-based sandbox.

Experimental results of open() are shown on the right-hand side of Figure 2. The results show that the lead is increased. The lightweight sandbox adds 706 cycles, while the process-based sandbox adds 40,927 cycles. The cost of the process-based sandbox is more than 57 times higher than the lightweight sandbox. This is because many interprocess communications are required to check the arguments of system calls. Since the arguments of open() are located in a process different from that of the reference monitor, the reference monitor needs inter-process communications to obtain memory data from the sandboxed application. Due to the limitation of the ptrace() system call, one interprocess communication is required to read four-byte data of the sandboxed process. Therefore, open() system call needs inter-process communications in proportion to the length of the pathname, and this results in large overheads. On the other hand, the lightweight sandbox does not incur any extra costs of inter-process communications, since the reference monitor is located in the same process with that of the sandboxed process. As a result, the advantage of the lightweight sandbox becomes larger.

5.2 Macro-Benchmark

The overhead of the sandbox systems was measured using real applications. Two applications, Ghostscript and Adobe Acrobat Reader, were used in these benchmark tests. Ghostscript is a Postscript document viewer and Acrobat Reader is a PDF document viewer. Each application was sandboxed and processed a lot of documents. For each document, the total execution time is measured. Experiments were performed in three cases for each application: no sandboxes, lightweight sandbox, and process-based sandbox. The overheads were calculated by the following equation.

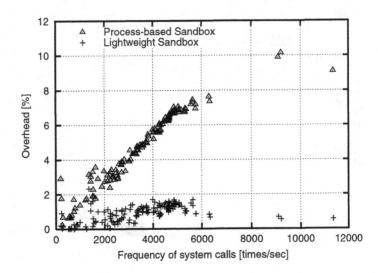

Fig. 3. Overhead of Ghostscript with sandbox mechanisms. The overhead is sorted by the frequency of system calls. The lightweight sandbox (our approach) outperforms the conventional process-based sandbox.

$$overhead = \frac{T_{sandbox} - T_{nosandbox}}{T_{nosandbox}} \qquad (1)$$

$T_{sandbox}$ is the execution time with a sandbox system (the lightweight sandbox or process-based sandbox). $T_{nosandbox}$ is the time without any sandboxes. The calculated overhead is expected to be in proportion to the frequency of system calls, since the overhead is incurred by the cost of system call interception. Therefore, the experimental results were sorted by the frequency of system calls.

In the experiments using Ghostscript, Ghostscript processed 158 Postscript documents, the size of which ranged from 112 bytes to 175 Mbytes. Ghostscript was executed non-interactively and the outputs of Ghostscript were written to /dev/null. The version of Ghostscript used was 5.50.

Figure 3 shows the experimental results obtained for Ghostscript. The lightweight sandbox always outperformed the process-based sandbox. When the frequency of system calls was about 5,000 times per second, the overhead was about 1.5% with the lightweight sandbox, while about 7% with the process-based sandbox. Therefore, the lightweight sandbox was found to be approximately five times as fast as the process-based sandbox.

We performed the same experiments using Acrobat Reader. It processed 172 PDF documents of various sizes ranging from 1.6 Kbytes to 8.1 Mbytes. It converts each PDF document into a Postscript document. Acrobat Reader was executed non-interactively and the outputs were written to /dev/null. The version of Acrobat Reader used was 4.05.

Figure 4 shows the experimental results obtained for Acrobat Reader. With Acrobat Reader, the frequency of system calls tended to be higher than that with Ghostscript: the maximum frequency was about 11,300 times per second, which is ten times higher

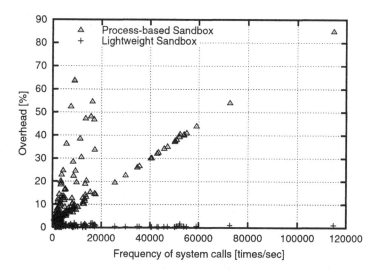

Fig. 4. Overhead of Acrobat Reader with sandbox mechanisms. The overhead is sorted by the frequency of system calls. The lightweight sandbox (our approach) outperforms the conventional process-based sandbox. Note that the scale of x-axis is different from that of the graph of Ghostscript.

than that of Ghostscript. From the trace of system calls, we found that Acrobat Reader issued many _llseek() system calls. As a consequence, the overhead tends to be higher in Acrobat Reader than in Ghostscript. When the frequency of system calls is about 50,000 times per second, the overhead is about 1.6% with the lightweight sandbox, while about 37% with the process-based sandbox. Therefore, the lightweight sandbox is approximately 24 times as fast as the process-based sandbox. In addition, some PDF files incurred higher overheads than expected in comparison to other PDF files. This result was obtained probably because the performance of the process-based sandbox was affected by mysterious behavior of the scheduling, cache misses, and TLB flashes.

In summary, the lightweight sandbox, which is based on our sandboxing framework, outperforms conventional process-based sandboxes. In experiments using real applications, our approach was approximately 5–24 times as fast as traditional process-based approaches.

6   Related Work

A variety of sandboxing techniques have been previously developed. According to the location where reference monitors are interposed, these sandboxes are classified into three approaches: user-level approaches, kernel-level approaches, and application-embedded approaches.

The first approach is to implement reference monitors in the user-level. Several sandbox mechanisms, such as Janus [8], MAPbox [9], SBOX [10], Consh [11], and the system presented in [12] exploit this approach. By using the debugger support of system call tracing, sandboxed applications are monitored by external processes that implement reference monitors, thus performing access control of the sandboxed applications. This approach is advantageous because it is easy to adopt various types of access control mechanisms. On the other hand, this approach incurs substantial overheads because system call interception needs many interprocess communications.

The second approach is to implement reference monitors in the kernel level. Several sandbox systems have a reference monitor directly encoded in the kernel. SubDomain [4] provides a server-specific sandbox mechanism by way of system call interception. TRON [7] allows users to specify capabilities to files and directories, enforced by system call interception. An implementation of Domain and Type Enforcement [6, 20] provides a kind of mandatory access control. The jail() facility of FreeBSD [5] provides simple partitioning of the operating system environment. These kernel-level approaches, in which specific sandbox mechanisms are encoded in the kernel, limit the flexibility to support various security policies to meet the demands of the users.

To overcome the limitations of directly encoding specific sandbox mechanisms in the kernel, some systems employ loadable kernel modules [21,22] to implement a specific sandbox system. LSM (Linux Security Module) [23] provides a general-purpose access control framework for Linux kernels that enables many different access control models to be implemented as loadable kernel modules. These approaches increase the flexibility of supporting various types of security policies. However, embedding reference monitors in the kernel creates significant risks. Implementations of reference monitors must be fully trusted, or the entire system becomes vulnerable. On the contrary, in our sandboxing framework, only the basic mechanism for system call interception is implemented in the kernel and the reference monitors are implemented at the user space. Therefore, implementation flaws in reference monitors do not cause serious system-wide vulnerabilities.

Peterson et al. [16] proposed a generic kernel-level framework for constructing sandboxes. It provides a minimal set of primitives that are designed to implement a wide variety of sandbox mechanisms. Although it provides a flexible sandboxing framework, the expressive power of enforceable security policies are still limited. In addition, it relies on external processes to handle the application-dependent aspects of sandboxing and thus, involves the overheads of interprocess communications.

The third approach is to embed sandboxes in sandboxed applications themselves. Java [24] implements sandboxes at the programming language level. Java ensures type safety at the language level and the Java virtual machine enforces security policies. These language-based approaches restrict the selection of programming languages for programmers. SFI [25] inserts processor instructions to perform memory confinement of sandboxed applications by directly modifying their binary executables. PCC [26] examines the binary code of a sandboxed application and ensures that it obeys predefined security policies. These instruction-level approaches cannot be applied to non-binary programs such as scripts.

Several research efforts are devoted to provide kernel-level protection domains within processes [27,28], which are similar to our fine-grained protection domains. These kernel-level protection domains provide *memory* protection and are designed to support protection among software components or shared libraries. However, they do not address the issues of a generic sandboxing framework.

7   Conclusion

In this paper, we presented a generic and flexible sandboxing framework, on top of which various types of sandbox mechanisms can be implemented. This framework provides a lightweight method of system call interception, allowing user-level reference monitors to efficiently perform access control of sandboxed applications. Lightweight system call interception is accomplished by exploiting the kernel support of intra-process protection domains called fine-grained protection domains, which we have proposed in previous papers [13,14,15]. To apply sandbox systems without modifying existing applications, we developed a program loader that initializes and applies the sandbox mechanisms transparently to sandboxed applications. To demonstrate the feasibility of our approach, we implemented a sample sandbox mechanism on our framework. Our experimental results demonstrate that the overhead of our sandbox mechanism is reasonable. Our sample sandbox incurs only 1.5-1.6% of overheads when sandboxing Ghostscript and Adobe Acrobat Reader.

References

1. SPS Advisory #39: Adobe Acrobat Series PDF File Buffer Overflow, July 2000.
2. CERT Advisory CA-1995-10: Ghostscript Vulnerability, August 1995.
3. Massimo Bernaschi, Emanuele Gabrielli, and Luigi V. Mancini. Remus: A security-enhanced operating system. *ACM Transactions on Information and System Security (TISSEC)*, 5(1):36–61, 2002.
4. Crispin Cowan, Steve Beattie, Greg Kroah-Hartman, Calton Pu, Perry Wagle, and Virgil Gligor. SubDomain: Parsimonious server security. In *Proc. of the 14th Systems Administration Conference*, pages 355–367, December 2000.
5. Poul-Henning Kamp and Robert N. M. Watson. Jails: Confining the omnipotent root. In *Proc. of the2nd International System Administration and Networking Conference (SANE)*, 2000.
6. Lee Badger, Daniel F. Sterne, David L. Sherman, Kenneth M. Walker, and Sheila A. Haghighat. A domain and type enforcement UNIX prototype. In *Proc. of the 5th USENIX UNIX Security Symposium*, June 1995.
7. Andrew Berman, Virgil Bourassa, and Erik Selberg. TRON: Process-specific file protection for the UNIX operating system. In *Proc. of the USENIX Winter 1995 Technical Conference*, pages 165–175, January 1995.
8. Ian Goldberg, David Wagner, Randi Thomas, and Eric A. Brewer. A secure enviroment for untrusted helper applications. In *Proc. of the 6th USENIX Security Symposium*, July 1996.
9. Anurag Acharya and Mandar Raje. MAPbox: Using parameterized behavior classes to confine untrusted applications. In *Proc. of the 9th USENIX Security Symposium*, August 2000.
10. Lincoln D. Stein. SBOX: Put CGI scripts in a box. In *Proc. of the 1999 USENIX Annual Technical Conference*, June 1999.
11. Albert Alexandrov, Paul Kmiec, and Klaus Schauser. Consh: Confined execution environment for internet computations. Available at http://www.cs.ucsb.edu/ berto/papers/99-usenix-consh.ps, 1998.

12. K. Jain and R. Sekar. User-level infrastructure for system call interposition: A platform for intrusion detection and confinement. In *Proc. of the ISOC Network and Distributed Security Symposium (NSDD '00)*, pages 19–34, 2000.

13. Masahiko Takahashi, Kenji Kono, and Takashi Masuda. Efficient kernel support of fine-grained protection domains for mobile code. In *Proc. of the 19th IEEE International Conference on Distributed Computing Systems (ICDCS '99)*, pages 64–73, May 1999.

14. Takahiro Shinagawa, Kenji Kono, and Takashi Masuda. Exploiting segmentation mechanism for protecting against malicious mobile code. Technical Report 00-02, Department of Information Science, Faculty of Science, University of Tokyo, May 2000. An extended version of [15].

15. Takahiro Shinagawa, Kenji Kono, Masahiko Takahashi, and Takashi Masuda. Kernel support of fine-grained protection domains for extention components. *Journal of Information Processing Society of Japan*, 40(6):2596–2606, June 1999. in japanese.

16. David S. Peterson, Matt Bishop, and Raju Pandey. A flexible containment mechanism for executing untrusted code. In *Proc. of the 11th USENIX Security Symposium*, pages 207–225, August 2002.

17. *The Intel Architecture Software Developer's Manual, Volume 3: System Programing Guide*. Intel, 1999. Order Number 243192.

18. Menlo Park and SPARC International. *The SPARC Architecture Manual Version 8*. Prentice Hall, 1992. ISBN 0-13-825001-4.

19. Richard L. Sites and Richard T. Witek. *Alpha AXP Architecture Reference Manual*. Digital Press, 1995. ISBN 1-55558-145-5.

20. Kenneth M. Walker, Daniel F. Sterne, M. Lee Badger, Michael J. Petkac, David L. Shermann, and Karen A. Oostendorp. Confining root programs with domain and type enforcement (DTE). In *Proc. of the 6th USENIX Security Symposium*, July 1996.

21. Timothy Fraser, Lee Badger, and Mark Feldman. Hardening COTS software with generic software wrappers. In *Proc. of the IEEE Symposium on Security and Privacy*, pages 2–16, 1999.

22. Terrence Mitchem, Raymond Lu, and Richard O'Brien. Using kernel hypervisors to secure applications. In *Proc. of the 13th Annual Computer Security Applications Conference (ACSAC '97)*, pages 175–182, December 1997.

23. Chris Wright, Crispin Cowan, James Morris, Stephen Smalley, and Greg Kroah-Hartman. Linux security modules: General security support for the linux kernel. In *Proc. of the 11th USENIX Security Symposium*, August 2002.

24. Java Team, James Gosling, Bill Joy, and Guy Steele. *The Java[tm] Language Specification*. Addison Wesley Longman, 1996. ISBN 0-201-6345-1.

25. Robert Wahbe, Steven Lucco, Thomas E. Anderson, and Susan L. Graham. Efficient software-based fault isolation. In *Proc. of the 14th ACM Symposium on Operating Systems Principles (SOSP '93)*, pages 203–216, December 1993.

26. George C. Necula and Peter Lee. Safe kernel extensions without runtime checking. In *Proc. of the 2nd Symposium on Operating Systems Design and Implementation (OSDI '96)*, pages 229–243, October 1996.

27. Tzi-cker Chiueh, Ganesh Venkitachalam, and Prashant Pradhan. Integrating segmentation and paging protection for safe, efficient and transparent software extensions. In *Proc. of the 17th ACM Symposium on Operating Systems Principles (SOSP '99)*, pages 140–153, December 1999.

28. Arindam Banerji, John Michael Tracey, and David L. Cohn. Protected Shared Libraries – A New Approach to Modularity and Sharing. In *Proc. of the 1997 USENIX Annual Technical Conference*, pages 59–75, October 1997.

Enforcing Java Run-Time Properties Using Bytecode Rewriting

Algis Rudys and Dan S. Wallach

Rice University, Houston, TX 77005, USA
(arudys|dwallach)@cs.rice.edu

Abstract. Bytecode rewriting is a portable way of altering Java's behavior by changing Java classes themselves as they are loaded. This mechanism allows us to modify the semantics of Java while making no changes to the Java virtual machine itself. While this gives us portability and power, there are numerous pitfalls, mostly stemming from the limitations imposed upon Java bytecode by the Java virtual machine. We reflect on our experience building three security systems with bytecode rewriting, presenting observations on where we succeeded and failed, as well as observing areas where future JVMs might present improved interfaces to Java bytecode rewriting systems.

1 Introduction

Bytecode rewriting presents the opportunity to change the execution semantics of Java programs. A wide range of possible applications have been discussed in the literature, ranging from the addition of performance counters, to the support of orthogonal persistence, agent migration, and new security semantics. Perhaps the strongest argument in favor of bytecode rewriting is its portability: changes made exclusively at the bytecode level can be moved with little effort from one Java virtual machine (JVM) to another, so long as the transformed code still complies to the JVM specification [1]. An additional benefit is that code added by bytecode rewriting can still be optimized by the underlying JVM.

JVMs load Java classes from disk or elsewhere through "class loaders," invoked as part of Java's dynamic linking mechanism. Bytecode rewriting is typically implemented either by statically rewriting Java classes to disk, or through dynamically rewriting classes as they are requested by a class loader. This process is illustrated in Figure 1.

In this paper, we describe three systems which we have built that use bytecode rewriting to add security semantics to the JVM. SAFKASI [2] is a bytecode rewriting-based implementation of stack inspection by security-passing style. Soft termination [3] is a system for safely terminating Java codelets.[1] Finally, transactional rollback [4] is a system for undoing the side-effects of a terminated codelet, leaving the system in a consistent state suitable for, among other thing, restarting terminated codelets.

---

[1] The term "codelet" is also used in artificial intelligence, numerical processing, XML tag processing, and PDA software, all with slightly different meanings. When we say "codelet," we refer to a small program meant to be executed in conjunction with or as an internal component of a larger program.

M. Okada et al. (Eds.): ISSS 2002, LNCS 2609, pp. 185–200, 2003.

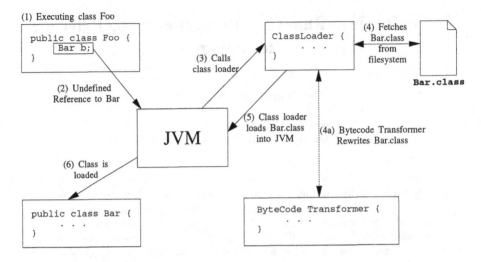

Fig. 1. How a Java bytecode transformation changes the process of loading a class. If an already loaded class, Foo, uses an as yet undefined class Bar (either accesses a static member or creates an instance) (1), the JVM traps the undefined reference to Bar (2), and sends a request for the class loader to load the class (3). The class loader fetches the class file (Bar.class) from the filesystem (4). In standard Java, the input class is then loaded into the JVM (5). In a bytecode rewriting system, the bytecode transformer is first invoked to transform the class (4a). In either case, the class is now loaded in the JVM (6).

Java bytecode rewriting has been applied in far too many other systems to provide a comprehensive list here. We cite related projects in order to discuss the breadth of the use of the technique.

Access Control. By intercepting or wrapping calls to potentially dangerous Java methods, systems by Pandey and Hashii [5], Erlingsson and Schneider [6], and Chander et al. [7] can apply desired security policies to arbitrary codelets without requiring these policies to be built directly into the Java system code, as done with Java's built-in security system.

Resource Management and Accounting. J-Kernel [8] and J-SEAL2 [9] both focus primarily on isolation of codelets. Bytecode rewriting is used to prevent codelets from interfering in each others' operations. JRes [10] focuses more on resource accounting; bytecode rewriting is used to instrument memory allocation and object finalization sites.

Optimization. Cream [11] and BLOAT (Bytecode-Level Optimization and Analysis Tool) [12] are examples of systems which employ Java bytecode rewriting for the purpose of optimization. Cream uses side-effect analysis, and performs a number of standard optimizations, including dead code elimination and loop-invariant code motion. BLOAT uses Static Single Assignment form (SSA) [13] to implement these and several other optimizations.

Profiling. BIT (Bytecode Instrumenting Tool) [14] is a system which allows the user to build Java instrumenting tools. The instrumentation itself is done via bytecode rewriting. Other generic bytecode transformation frameworks, such as JOIE [15] and Soot [16], also have hooks to instrument Java code for profiling.

Other Semantics.   Sakamoto et al. [17] describe a system for thread migration implemented using bytecode rewriting. Marquez et al. [18] describe a persistent system implemented in Java entirely using bytecode transformations at class load time. Notably, Marquez et al. also describe a framework for automatically applying bytecode transformations, although the status of this framework is unclear. Kava [19] is a reflective extension to Java. That is, it allows for run-time modification and dynamic execution of Java classes and methods.

All of these systems could also be implemented with customized JVMs (and many such customized JVMs have been built). Of course, fully custom JVMs can outperform JVMs with semantics "bolted on" via bytecode rewriting because changes can be made to layers of the system that are not exposed to the bytecode, such as how methods are dispatched, or how memory is laid out. The price of building custom JVMs is the loss of portability.

Code rewriting techniques apply equally to other languages. One of the earliest implementations of code rewriting was Informer [20], which, to provide security guarantees, applied transformations to modules written in any language and running in kernel space. In particular, the transformations discussed in this paper could be applied to add similar semantics to other type-safe languages like Lisp and ML as well as such typed intermediate representations as Microsoft's Common Language Infrastructure and typed assembly languages.

A number of issues arise in the course of implementing a bytecode rewriting system. In this paper, we describe our experiences in implementing three such system in Section 2. Section 3 discusses JVM design issues that we encountered when building our systems. Section 4 discusses optimizations we used to improve the performance impact of our systems. Finally, we present our conclusions in Section 5.

2   Bytecode Rewriting Implementations

This paper reflects on lessons learned in the implementation of three security systems built with Java bytecode rewriting. The first, SAFKASI [2], uses bytecode rewriting to transform a program into a style where security context information is passed as an argument to every method invocation. Soft termination [3] is a system for safely terminating Java codelets by trapping backward branches and other conditions that might cause a codelet to loop indefinitely. Transactional rollback [4], intended to be used in conjunction with soft termination, allows the system to undo any side-effects made to the system's state as a result of the codelet's execution, returning the system to a known stable state.

2.1 SAFKASI

SAFKASI [2] (the security architecture formerly known as stack inspection), is an implementation of Java's stack inspection architecture [21] using Java bytecode rewriting. SAFKASI is based on *security-passing style*, a redesign of stack-inspection which provably maintains the security properties of stack-inspection, improves optimizability and asymptotic complexity, and can be reasoned about using standard belief logics.

Stack inspection is a mechanism for performing access control on security-sensitive operations. Each stack frame is annotated with the security context of that stack frame. Stack inspection checks for privilege to perform a sensitive operations by inspecting the call stack of the caller. Starting at the caller and walking down, if it first reaches a frame that does not have permission to perform the operation, it indicates failure. If it first reaches a frame that has permission to perform the operation and has explicitly granted permission, the operation is allowed. Otherwise, the default action is taken as defined by the JVM.

With security-passing style, instead of storing the security context in the stack, the security context is passed as an additional parameter to all methods. This optimizes security checks by avoiding the linear cost of iterating over the call stack.

SAFKASI is implemented by passing an additional parameter to every method in the system. This parameter is the security context. It is modified by the *says* operator, which is used by a class to explicitly grant its permission for some future operation. The stack-inspection check simply checks this context for the appropriate permission.

Performance. SAFKASI was tested using the NaturalBridge BulletTrain Java Compiler, which compiles Java source to native binary code [22]. With CPU-bound benchmarks, SAFKASI-transformed programs executed 15 to 30% slower than equivalent stack inspecting programs.

2.2 Soft Termination

Soft termination [3] is a technique for safely terminating codelets. The basis for soft termination is that the codelet doesn't need to terminate immediately, as long as it is guaranteed to eventually terminate. We implemented soft termination by first adding a termination flag field to each class. We then instrumented each method, preceding all backward branches with termination checks to prevent infinite loops and beginning all methods with termination checks to prevent infinite recursion.

The termination check simply checks the class's termination flag. If set, a Java exception is thrown. The codelet is free to catch the exception, and resume. However, the next time a backward branch or method call is encountered, the exception is thrown anew. Using this mechanism, we can prove that the codelet is guaranteed to terminate in finite time.

Soft termination distinguishes between system code and user code (that is, codelets). System code should not be interrupted, even if the associated codelet has been marked for termination. Codelets are rewritten by the transformer, while system code is not touched. This result can be achieved by performing the transformation in the Java class loader.

Since the system classes and codelets are naturally loaded by different class loaders, the separation becomes natural.

Blocking calls are also addressed in our system. Blocking calls are method calls, most commonly input/output calls, which wait for a response before returning. We wanted to guarantee that a codelet could not use blocking calls to bypass termination. The Thread.interrupt() method allows us to force blocking method calls to return.

To determine which threads to interrupt, we wrap blocking calls with code to let the soft termination system know that a particular thread is entering or leaving a blocking call. This code also uses Java's stack inspection primitives to determine whether the code is blocking on behalf of a codelet or on behalf of the system code. Only threads blocking on a codelet's behalf are interrupted.

Performance. We implemented this system and measured the performance when running on Sun Microsystems Java 2, version 1.2.1 build 4. The worst results, of a simple infinite loop, was 100% overhead. In the real-world applications tested, the overhead was up to 25% for loop-intensive benchmarks, and up to 7% for the less loop-intensive benchmarks.

2.3   Transactional Rollback

Transactional rollback [4] was designed to complement soft termination in a resource management system. Soft termination guarantees that system state is never left inconsistent by a codelet's untimely termination. However, the same guarantee is not made about a codelet's persistent state. Any inconsistencies in this state could destabilize other running codelets as well as complicate restarting a terminated codelet.

We solve this problem by keeping track of all changes made by a codelet, and if the codelet is terminated, the changes are undone. Each codelet is run in the context of a transaction to avoid data conflicts. We implement transactional rollback by first duplicating each method in all classes (including system classes). The duplicate methods take an additional argument, the current transaction.

In the duplicate methods, all field and array accesses (that is, field gets and puts and array loads and stores) are preceded with lock requests by the transaction on the appropriate object. Method calls are also rewritten to pass the transaction parameter along. A number of fields are added to a class to maintain a class's backups and lock state for the class.

If the code is not running in a transaction, the methods called are for the most part exactly the original methods. This allows us to limit the performance impact to code running in a transaction.

Performance. We implemented this system and measured the performance when running on Sun Microsystems Java 2, version 1.3 for Linux. The overhead of the transaction system ranged from 6 to $23\times$. The major component in this overhead was in managing array locks.

3 JVM Design Issues

Bytecode rewriting is inherently different from language run-time system customization. Bytecode rewriting results in classes that are run inside a standard Java virtual machine. These classes treat the JVM as a black box; functionality internal to the JVM cannot be altered. Rewritten classes must be valid bytecode, according to the virtual machine specification [1]. However, because codelets might be malicious, we cannot assume that the code we receive as input was generated by valid Java source, and so cannot necessarily use the Java Language Specification [23] for guidance.

Table 1 summarizes our bytecode rewriting implementations and associated wish list items.

3.1 JVM Internals

The basic distinction of bytecode rewriting as opposed to language run-time system customization is that with bytecode rewriting, operating on JVM internals is not possible.

Class Reloading. Once classes are loaded into the JVM, they can neither be unloaded nor reloaded. Likewise, one cannot control when a class's static initializer will be called or when dead objects' finalizers will be invoked. Java version 1.4 includes a feature in its debugger architecture called *HotSwap*, which allows classes to be reloaded[2]. Existing activation records continue to run with code from the original version of the class. Also, the new class's static initializer is not run again, and new fields added to existing classes will be null or zero. This new feature was not available when we were building our systems, and would have been a welcome addition, despite its limitations.

Memory Management. One of the features on our "wishlist" is the addition of hooks into the JVM's memory system. Had we been able to exploit the garbage collector's safe point traps, our soft termination system could have performed periodic checks with more flexibility and lower overhead than trapping backward branches. Also, by modifying the garbage collector, we might have been able to enforce memory usage policies that are more robust than those used in JRes [10] and J-SEAL2 [9], which assume that whoever allocated a block of memory should be responsible for "paying" for that memory. We implemented exactly such a mechanism to account for memory usage in IBM's RVM [24] by modifying the RVM's garbage collector [25]. New pluggable garbage collection systems for Java, such as GCTk [26], may allow us to implement such features without requiring changes to the underlying JVM. In addition, the Real-time Specification for Java[3] allows programs to create individual memory regions treated differently by the garbage collector and select from which region memory is allocated.

---

[2] See http://java.sun.com/j2se/1.4/docs/guide/jpda/enhancements.html
   for more information.

[3] See http://www.rtj.org/ for more information.

Table 1. This table summarizes the three systems based on bytecode rewriting. It describes the transformations to Java bytecode, JVM-related issues, and items on the JVM wish list inspired by that particular project.

	SAFKASI	Soft Termination	Transactional Rollback
Added Fields	• Security principal	• Termination flag	• Lock state • Class backup
Modified Methods	• Added security context parameter to each method • Added security context parameter to all method invocations • Add Security-passing style security checks • Added stub methods for upcalls	• Added safe point-like termination checks on backward branches and method calls • Wrapped blocking calls to register with soft termination system to allow interrupting	• Duplicated each method • Added transaction parameter to each duplicated method • Added transaction parameter to each method invocation from duplicated methods • Instrumented field and array accesses within methods • Added code in original methods to detect transactional context
Added Classes		• Wrapping subclass for class with blocking native methods	• Added classes for static and instance backups of each existing class
JVM Issues	• Closed world • System classes • Native methods • Bootstrapping	• Synchronization • Blocking calls	• System classes • Native methods • Bootstrapping • Synchronization • Arrays
Wish List Items	• Class file reloading	• Synchronization interface • Garbage collector interface	• Synchronization interface • Access to array implementation

Threads. Thread scheduling is another black box subsystem of the Java virtual machine. No mechanism is provided for either replacing the thread scheduler or fine-tuning how threads are scheduled; the only interface provided is the `Thread.setPriority()`

method. The Real-time Specification for Java does allow for replacing the thread scheduler, but has only recently been finalized.

Native Methods. Native methods, while not strictly part of the JVM, are also treated as black boxes. We cannot control where a native method might go, and how that native method might behave. Native methods might perform arbitrary computations and are not necessarily guaranteed to return in a timely fashion (e.g., I/O routines might block indefinitely while they wait for data to arrive).

Furthermore, we have no control over up-calls from native methods back to the Java classes which we do control. In particular, we have no access to the Java Native Interface (JNI) calls used by native methods to interface with Java. If we could intercept these calls, then we could transform native methods to see a view of the Java classes consistent with what the Java classes themselves see after being transformed. Since that is not an option with current JVMs, we have adopted a number of strategies to cope with native methods, described in Section 3.3.

Note that certain JVMs implemented in Java, such as BulletTrain and IBM's RVM [24], use fewer native methods than JVMs implemented in machine code. The tradeoff is that they have more methods which are not native but are treated specially by the JVM. In our bytecode transformations, these methods need to be treated the same as standard native methods. See Section 3.3 for details on such special methods and how we handled them.

3.2 "Local" Java Semantics

The flexibility of Java bytecode is both its benefit and its curse. A bytecode rewriting system must deal with every feature in the bytecode. We first deal with "local" features, which is to say, aspects of the Java bytecode where an individual class or method can be rewritten without needing any knowledge of how other classes in the JVM might interoperate with it.

Constructors. Constructors have two properties which set them apart from normal methods. First, no operations, whether initialization or otherwise, can be performed until either the super-class constructor or a same-class constructor has been called, although arguments to a super-class constructor may be legally computed. This presented a problem in the soft termination system.

Soft termination is designed to check the value of the termination flag at the beginning of every method, including constructors, but inserting this check into a constructor results in a verifier error. Instead, the best we can do is to check for termination immediately following the call to the super-class constructor. As a result, we may not be able to terminate a loop constructed with constructors that recursively invoke other constructors before calling their super-class constructor.

Transactional rollback requires every object to be locked before it can be modified. Normally, this is accomplished with the addition of a specialized lock instance to every object instance. However, while an object is being constructed, this lock instance will be null. To address this, we needed to add checks *everywhere* an object is accessed to check whether its lock instance is null, slowing down all locking code to handle this special case.

Exceptions. Exceptions (and errors) can introduce implicit or asynchronous control flows into a Java method. Asynchronous exceptions, induced by calls to Thread.stop(), can occur literally anywhere, and at any time. For this reason, among other reasons, Sun has deprecated the method. Implicit exceptions typically occur as a side-effect of a program error, such as a NullPointerException or the various arithmetic errors. Here, the control flow edge from the potentially faulty operation to the construction and throwing of an exception does not appear explicitly in the Java bytecode.

This caused problems for SAFKASI, which needs to pass its security context as a parameter to the exception constructors. The only available choices were to either save the security context in thread-local storage or to give up and pass no context. Using thread-local storage is expensive, requiring a hash table operation on every store, and the exception constructors for Java's implicit exceptions appear to never perform security critical operations. As a result, SAFKASI gives up, allowing these constructors to be invoked with no security context, and letting them start over as if there was no call stack before them.

We also observe that, in Java bytecode, an exception handling block (that is, a try-catch block) is represented as offsets delimiting the try block and the offset for the start of the catch block. The JVM specification requires that the catch block start strictly after the try block ends. That is, an exception-handler cannot handle its own exceptions. However, Sun's JVM does not enforce this restriction.

This can be used by a malicious codelet to evade a soft termination signal. The exception handler acts as a backward-branch; when an exception is thrown in the exception handler, control passes to an earlier point in the text of the program. If this exception always occurs, like the termination signal of soft termination, the result will be an infinite loop. We solved the problem by having the soft termination system detect and reject such exception-handling blocks.

Arrays. Transactional rollback needs to be able to save backup copies of all objects before they are written. For most classes, we can create "backup" fields for every original field in the class. Assigning the backup to refer to the original object is sufficient to preserve the original value of the backup. However, for arrays, this no longer works; there is no place in the array to store a reference to the array's backup. Our solution is to maintain a global hash table that maps arrays to their backups. For each array, the backup array must be the same size as the original. Creating this backup requires copying the whole array. For codelets that make extensive use of arrays, whether large or small, this creates a significant overhead.

Our preferred solution would be for Java to have a mechanism to let us add our own field to all arrays. Java's arrays already track their length; we want one more reference that we can use transparently to the Java application.

Threads. Threads can be thought of as a special case of native methods which make up-calls to Java code (in this case, during thread initialization, the up-call happens to be on a new thread while control returns to the original thread). In both SAFKASI and transactional rollback, we needed state computed in the parent thread to be sent to the child thread. This was performed by modifying java.lang.Thread to have an additional field where the parent thread can store context information in the child thread. This context is consulted when the child's run() method is invoked by the thread run-time system. Since threads are implemented in Java, this modification can be performed as part of the bytecode-rewriting process.

Another important issue with threads is controlling them when they block. Blocking can be caused by synchronization primitives (see below) or by native methods, which might not return right away. Luckily, all of the JVM's methods which might block will respond to calls to Thread.interrupt(), causing the formerly blocked thread to immediately throw an exception and canceling the operation that was previously under-way. We used this mechanism with soft termination to signal blocking threads that we wished to kill.

However, in implementing soft termination, we found that some mechanism was still needed to determine which thread is blocking, and whether it was blocking on behalf of system code (which should not be interrupted) or on behalf of a codelet (which we *want* to interrupt). We chose to wrap blocking methods with code to register the current thread with the soft termination system as blocking before the call, and unregister it afterward. We use Java's stack inspection mechanism to determine the context of the blocking call (system versus codelet). The soft termination system could now interrupt blocking threads as necessary.

Synchronization. The semantics of Java's monitorenter and monitorexit bytecode instructions and synchronized method modifier cannot be changed through bytecode rewriting. When a deadlock occurs in Sun's JDK, the only way to recover is by restarting the JVM. The JDK 1.4 debugging architecture provides a mechanism to address this (a debugger is allowed to forcibly pop activation records from a thread's stack), which might be useful to clean up after deadlock. This can similarly be used to terminate threads that are in a deadlock situation.

Another issue which soft termination had to deal with was the exact semantics of the monitorenter and monitorexit bytecodes, which acquire and release system locks, respectively. If these calls are not properly balanced, it becomes possible to lock a monitor in such a way that terminating the codelet will not cause the monitor to be released. Despite the fact that neither the JVM nor the Java language specifications allow such construction, current JVM bytecode verifiers accept such programs. Our soft termination system did not attempt to deal with this problem.

Verification. We have seen several cases where our own code had to effectively extend the Java bytecode verifier in order to guarantee correctness of our system. We saw these issues with Java's synchronization and exception features. We also saw cases where Java's verifier got in the way of perfectly sound program transformations, particularly with regard to the restrictions on how Java's constructors invoke their super-class constructors.

Ideally, the Java bytecode verifier should be disentangled from the current class loading system to stand on its own. This would simplify the addition of new checks to the verifier, such as checks for undesirable exception and synchronization behavior, and it would make it easier to remove checks that, at least in our context, are unnecessary, such as the super-class constructor checks. Furthermore, a modular Java bytecode verifier would be quite useful to our systems as a mechanism for checking our input *before* we rewrite it, allowing us to make stronger assumptions about the quality of our input and reducing the opportunity for carefully crafted codelets to trick a code rewriting system into mistakenly outputting a rewritten codelet with more privilege than it should have been given.

3.3 "Global" Java Semantics

In many cases, particularly when we consider changes that effect the method signatures advertised by a class, we must consider how our changes interact with other Java classes, with native code, and even with classes that may not have been loaded into the system yet.

"Special" Methods and Classes. Every JVM has certain methods and classes which are special in some way. Sun's JVM, for example, doesn't allow the rewriter to add fields to java.lang.Class or java.lang.Object. The NaturalBridge Java system is even more restrictive, as it is implemented, itself, in Java, and has many "special" Java classes that provide the necessary machinery to implement language internals. Calls to these (privileged) classes are quietly replaced with the (dangerous) primitive operations that they represent. Changes to these classes are simply ignored.

If a global transformation could be applied to *all* Java classes in a consistent way, such as the security-passing style transformation of SAFKASI, then the resulting system would be perfectly self-consistent. However, once special methods and classes are added, everything becomes more difficult. Now, the system must keep a list of special classes and methods and treat calls to them as special cases.

For SAFKASI, this meant that we could not pass our security context as an additional argument to all methods. Instead, we used thread-local storage to temporarily hold the security context, and then called the original, special method. If that method just returned, then everything would continue as normal. If that method were to make a call to another Java method, then it would be using the original Java method signatures, without the additional argument for passing security contexts.

To support this, we were forced to add wrapper methods for every method in the system. These wrappers existed solely to receive calls from special methods, fetch the security context from the thread-local storage, and then invoke the proper target method. Luckily, this wrapper technique proved to be quite general. It also supports native method up-calls and Java reflection (although we never tried to hack Java reflection such that it would see all the classes as if they had never been rewritten). By pairing wrappers, one to convert from security-passing style methods to special methods, and one to convert from regular methods back to security-passing style methods on up-calls from special code, we were able to maintain the illusion that the whole system supported security-passing style calling conventions. We used the same strategy in our transactional rollback system to manage the transactional state, normally passed as an additional argument to all methods.

Inheritance. Java's class inheritance is also a complicating factor in global transformations. When a subclass overrides a special method, as described above, it inherits the "specialness" of the method. For example, `java.lang.Object.hashCode()` is a native method. Any other class can override this, providing a Java (or native) implementation. At an arbitrary call site, where `java.lang.Object.hashCode()` is invoked, there may not be enough information to determine a more specific type for the callee. Thus, the caller must assume the worst case: the callee is special. This requires saving the security context, and then making a call to the special method. Of course, if the concrete type was something other than `java.lang.Object`, and it had, in fact, overridden `hashCode()`, then control would enter a wrapper method which would recover the security context and call back into the world of rewritten code.

Open World Java. Java is an *open world* system. That is, classes can be loaded and the class hierarchy modified at run-time. The only restrictions that Java makes are that, for a class to be loaded, all of its super-classes must already be loaded. Even with this restriction, the open world assumption complicates code analysis. It is no surprise, then, that many systems that change Java's semantics, including SAFKASI, assume a closed world (that once the system starts running, no more classes will be loaded). SAFKASI performs a class hierarchy analysis [27], reading every class in the system into a large data structure that allows a number of queries. SAFKASI uses this to determine if all possible callees of a given call site are "normal" methods. For the `java.lang.Object.hashCode()` example above, SAFKASI would conservatively conclude that the callee might be special, and therefore the security context should be saved. SAFKASI's analysis is fairly simplistic, as it doesn't take advantage of data flow and control flow information to narrow its idea of the type of a given callee. Still, even this simple flow-invariant analysis provided for significant optimizations.

Because Java is actually an open world, every Java class to be inserted into the system can potentially invalidate a judgment made by the optimizer. As a result, the optimizer would need to *back out* the optimizations that now reside in code previously loaded into the system. As we discussed in Section 3.1, such functionality is only now becoming available in the JDK 1.4 debugging architecture, and might make such optimizations possible, even in an open world.

Bootstrapping. Bootstrapping presents a unique problem to bytecode rewriting systems. When the JVM is launched, it normally proceeds through the initialization of its core classes before loading any applications. These core classes are, by necessity, carefully designed to avoid circular dependencies in their static initializers. Circular dependencies can be particularly hazardous in JVMs implemented themselves in Java, where the very first classes to be initialized are all "special" to the system in some way, and are very fragile with respect to changes.

In the implementation of soft termination, we largely did not need to worry about bootstrapping because we only had to transform codelets, not the entire system. For transactional rollback and SAFKASI, we had to transform everything (or as much of everything that was not special, in some fashion or another). In practice, when implementing SAFKASI on the NaturalBridge Java system, we had a large list of "special" classes that we could not touch. Likewise, we had to make sure the bootstrapping process could complete before any of the SAFKASI-specific classes were initialized. Our solution was to pass null in our security context argument and to only allocate a security context, and thus cause the SAFKASI system to be initialized, right before starting a codelet. For transactional rollback, we have the benefit that we support two modes of operation: with and without transactions. As a result, the JVM can initialize itself normally, and we only transition to the transactional world when we are about to start a codelet. Transactional rollback, in practice, proved much simpler to debug.

4   Optimizing Bytecode Rewriting

In the development of our systems, we used extensive profiling to determine where optimization would be necessary and guess at what optimizations might be profitable. For example, if we suspect that, for a large number of call-sites, the callee has a desirable property for optimizing the call-site, then we would instrument the call-sites to count exactly how many callees happen to have the property in question, and at which call-sites. Using this style of analysis, we were able to rapidly focus our attention on the optimizations that might matter for our systems. Of course, running our programs with such profiling slowed them down, but these profiling checks are only actually included during code rewriting when we wish to gather profiling data.

Soft Termination.   The unoptimized design of soft termination required a termination check to be inserted before every call site. For methods with multiple call sites, there would be one termination check added per call site. We measured, through profiling, that on average there was more than one termination check per method invocation. This led us to "push" the termination checks from the call site to the head of the callee, thus reducing the number of termination checks.

Next, we could easily determine which methods, having no backward branches or outward method invocations, are guaranteed to return in a finite time. For these methods, the termination check at the beginning of the method is unnecessary and can be omitted. In some cases, this as much as halved the overhead of soft termination relative to the overhead of the unoptimized soft termination system.

Transactional Rollback.   In our transactional rollback system, we learned a number of seemingly obvious facts through profiling. We observed that, for most lock acquire operations, the transaction acquiring the lock was the same transaction already holding the lock. We also observed that, by far, the most common object to be locked is the this object.

These measurements led us to some simple optimizations with profound effects on system performance. By checking if the lock to be acquired is already held by the current transaction, we generally saved at least one method call, sometimes more. Likewise, by checking if a method contains multiple locking operations on this and consolidating them to a single operation at the head of the method, we were able to remove a significant number of lock operations. These two optimizations alone bought us a 25% speed improvement.

SAFKASI. SAFKASI performed a number of different optimizations aimed at lowering the cost of computing transitions in the security context information for each method invocation. We measured that from 10 to 37% of method invocations were to leaf methods (with no outgoing method calls), leading us to optimizations similar to those described above for soft termination. Likewise, after implementing a global class hierarchy analysis, we were able to determine that we could statically predict the security context information for 10 to 76% of the remaining call-sites. Combining these with a simple one-reference cache of the last security context transition computed at a given call-site, we were able to optimize away virtually all security context transitions, leading us to focus our efforts on other aspects of the system.

We then studied the operations for storing and retrieving context information from thread-local storage. By noting the current method every time one of these operations was performed, and keeping one counter for every method in the system, we quickly realized that most of the context stores were focused on calls to a relatively small number of methods: generally these were methods that were called from all over the system, such as Object.toString() on the result of Hashtable.get(). Further optimization would require implementing control and data flow analysis in order to infer, for example, what the concrete type emerging from the Hashtable might be, rather than just java.lang.Object. Having access to the analysis that is, no doubt, performed within the JVM's internal optimizer may have enabled such optimization.

5   Conclusions

Bytecode rewriting is an extremely powerful mechanism for modifying the behavior of Java by modifying the Java classes directly. It allows for essentially arbitrary changes to Java's semantics. It is portable in that it allows a system based on bytecode rewriting to run on any JVM. There are a number of limitations to bytecode rewriting, as well. These stem from the fact that we cannot directly affect how the JVM processes a given bytecode instruction or set of bytecode instructions, except using a relatively small number of restricted interfaces.

Considering these limitations, bytecode rewriting systems will never be able to match the capabilities and performance of customized JVMs, which have access "under the hood" of the JVM. However, customized run-time systems suffer from a lack of portability. In addition, bytecode rewriting systems benefit from optimization courtesy of the JVM. With appropriate specialized optimizations of the sort discussed above, a system based on bytecode rewriting could be competitive performance- and capability-wise with a system based on language run-time system customization.

Acknowledgement. We would like to thank the anonymous JVM 2002 and ISSS 2002 reviewers for their helpful suggestions. This work is supported by NSF Grant CCR-9985332 and a Texas ATP grant.

References

1. Lindholm, T., Yellin, F.: The Java Virtual Machine Specification. Addison-Wesley, Reading, Massachusetts (1996)
2. Wallach, D.S., Felten, E.W., Appel, A.W.: The security architecture formerly known as stack inspection: A security mechanism for language-based systems. ACM Transactions on Software Engineering and Methodology 9 (2000) 341–378
3. Rudys, A., Wallach, D.S.: Termination in language-based systems. ACM Transactions on Information and System Security 5 (2002) 138–168
4. Rudys, A., Wallach, D.S.: Transactional rollback for language-based systems. In: Proceedings of the 2002 International Conference on Dependable Systems and Networks, Washington, DC (2002)
5. Pandey, R., Hashii, B.: Providing fine-grained access control for Java programs. In Guerraoui, R., ed.: 13th Conference on Object-Oriented Programming (ECOOP'99). Number 1628 in Lecture Notes in Computer Science, Lisbon, Portugal, Springer-Verlag (1999)
6. Erlingsson, U., Schneider, F.B.: IRM enforcement of Java stack inspection. In: Proceedings of the 2000 IEEE Symposium on Security and Privacy, Berkeley, California (2000) 246–255
7. Chander, A., Mitchell, J.C., Shin, I.: Mobile code security by Java bytecode instrumentation. In: 2001 DARPA Information Survivability Conference & Exposition (DISCEX II), Anaheim, CA, USA (2001)
8. Hawblitzel, C., Chang, C.C., Czajkowski, G., Hu, D., von Eicken, T.: Implementing multiple protection domains in Java. In: USENIX Annual Technical Conference, New Orleans, Louisiana, USENIX (1998)
9. Binder, W.: Design and implementation of the J-SEAL2 mobile agent kernel. In: 2001 Symposium on Applications and the Internet, San Diego, CA, USA (2001)
10. Czajkowski, G., von Eicken, T.: JRes: A resource accounting interface for Java. In: Proceedings of the ACM Conference on Object-Oriented Programming, Systems, Languages, and Applications, Vancouver, British Columbia (1998) 21–35
11. Clausen, L.R.: A Java bytecode optimizer using side-effect analysis. Concurrency: Practice and Experience 9 (1997) 1031–1045
12. Nystrom, N.J.: Bytecode level analysis and optimization of Java classes. Master's thesis, Purdue University (1998)
13. Cytron, R., Ferrante, J., Rosen, B.K., Wegman, M.N., Zadeck, F.K.: Efficiently computing static single assignment form and the control dependence graph. ACM Transactions on Programming Languages and Systems 13 (1991) 451–490
14. Lee, H.B., Zorn, B.G.: BIT: A tool for instrumenting java bytecodes. In: USENIX Symposium on Internet Technologies and Systems, Monterey, California, USA (1997)
15. Cohen, G., Chase, J., Kaminsky, D.: Automatic program transformation with JOIE. In: Proceedings of the 1998 Usenix Annual Technical Symposium, New Orleans, Louisiana (1998) 167–178
16. Vallée-Rai, R., Hendren, L., Sundaresan, V., Lam, P., Gagnon, E., Co, P: Soot – a Java bytecode optimization framework. In: Proceedings of CASCON 1999, Mississauga, Ontario, Canada (1999) 125–135
17. Sakamoto, T., Sekiguchi, T., Yonezawa, A.: Bytecode transformation for portable thread migration in Java. In: Proceedings of the Joint Symposium on Agent Systems and Applications / Mobile Agents (ASA/MA). (2000) 16–28

18. Marquez, A., Zigman, J.N., Blackburn, S.M.: A fast portable orthogonally persistent Java. Software: Practice and Experience Special Issue: Persistent Object Systems **30** (2000) 449–479

19. Welch, I., Stroud, R.: Kava – a reflective Java based on bytecode rewriting. In: Lecture Notes in Computer Science 1826. Springer-Verlag (2000)

20. Deutsch, P., Grant, C.A.: A flexible measurement tool for software systems. In: Information Processing 71: Proceedings of the IFIP Congress. Volume 1., Ljubljana, Yugoslavia (1971)

21. Gong, L.: Inside Java 2 Platform Security: Architecture, API Design, and Implementation. Addison-Wesley, Reading, Massachusetts (1999)

22. NaturalBridge, LLC: BulletTrain Java Compiler. (1998) http://www.naturalbridge.-com.

23. Gosling, J., Joy, B., Steele, G.: The Java Language Specification. Addison-Wesley, Reading, Massachusetts (1996)

24. Alpern, B., Attanasio, C.R., Barton, J.J., Burke, M.G., Cheng, P., Choi, J.D., Cocchi, A., Fink, S.J., Grove, D., Hind, M., Hummel, S.F., Lieber, D., Litvinov, V., Mergen, M.F., Ngo, T., Russell, J.R., Sarkar, V., Serrano, M.J., Shepherd, J.C., Smith, S.E., Sreedhar, V.C., Srinivasan, H., Whaley, J.: The Jalapeño virtual machine. IBM System Journal **39** (2000)

25. Price, D., Rudys, A., Wallach, D.S.: Garbage collector memory accounting in language-based systems. Technical Report TR02-407, Department of Computer Science, Rice University, Houston, TX (2002)

26. Blackburn, S.M., Singhai, S., Hertz, M., McKinley, K.S., Moss, J.E.B.: Pretenuring for Java. In: OOPSLA 2001: Conference on Object-Oriented Programming Systems, Languages, and Applications. Volume 36 of ACM SIGPLAN Notices., Tampa Bay, Florida (2001) 342–352

27. Dean, J., Grove, D., Chambers, C.: Optimization of object-oriented programs using static class hierarchy analysis. In: Proceedings of the European Conference on Object-Oriented Programming (ECOOP '95), Århus, Denmark (1995)

AnZenMail: A Secure and Certified E-mail System

Etsuya Shibayama[1], Shigeki Hagihara[1], Naoki Kobayashi[1], Shin-ya Nishizaki[1], Kenjiro Taura[2], and Takuo Watanabe[3,1]

[1] Graduate School of Information Science and Engineering, Tokyo Institute of Technology, 2-12-1 Ookayama, Meguro-ku, Tokyo, Japan
[2] The University of Tokyo, 7-3-1 Hongo, Bunkyo-ku, Tokyo, Japan
[3] The National Institute of Informatics, 2-1-2 Hitotsubashi, Chiyoda-ku, Tokyo, Japan

Abstract. We are developing a secure and certified e-mail system AnZenMail that provides an experimental testbed for our cutting-edge security enhancement technologies. In addition to a provably secure message transfer protocol, we have designed and implemented a server (MTU) and a client (MUA) in order that they could survive recent malicious attacks such as server-cracking and e-mail viruses. The AnZenMail server is implemented in Java, a memory-safe language, and so it is free from stack smashing. Some of its safety properties have been formally verified in Coq mostly at the source code level by manually translating Java methods into Coq functions. The AnZenMail client is designed to provide a support for secure execution of mobile code arriving as e-mail attachments. It has plug-in interfaces for code inspection and execution modules such as static analysis tools, runtime/inline reference monitors, and an anti-virus engine, which are currently being developed by members of our research project.

1 Introduction

The more the Internet is penetrated into our society and tightly connects us, the more malicious attacks as well as accidental faults we undergo in the cyberspace. Recently we have experienced unpleasant incidents, accidents, and even disasters due largely to malicious attacks including:

- worms cracking various servers,
- e-mail and P2P viruses, and
- distributed denial of service (DDoS) attacks.

These attacks produce various symptoms patterns such as backdoor installation, server overload, data removal, and data disclosure. They reveal vulnerabilities of the Internet infrastructure today. There are a variety of causes of the vulnerabilities: some come from human errors; some others are due to the open and extendable natures of the Internet; and yet others are fragile software.

M. Okada et al. (Eds.): ISSS 2002, LNCS 2609, pp. 201–216, 2003.
© Springer-Verlag Berlin Heidelberg 2003

We consider that the most significant threats in modern environments are malicious mobile code, in particular, worms and viruses. Even DDoS attackers often depend on malicious mobile code since they have to exploit thousands of victims before making attacks and thus require mechanized infection techniques. We also consider that software vulnerabilities are the major cause of malicious attacks by mobile code. In most cases their targets are security holes of software systems, though some play on frailties of mankind: it might be difficult to ignore a love letter mail and discard it instantly without opening it.

In response to modern threats, we take the three layered approach, in which we integrate the following three sorts of techniques to protect software infrastructure from malicious attacks.

- static analysis of mobile code and verification of stationary software systems, both based upon rigorous mathematical theories,
- design and implementation of secure programming languages, and
- operating systems and language runtime systems for runtime security enforcement.

This layered approach is being examined in the research project "Research on Implementation Schemes for Secure Software" organized by Akinori Yonezawa and supported by Grant-in-Aid Scientific Research of Priority Area from Japanese Ministry of Education, Culture, Sports, Science, and Technology.

The work presented in this paper is carried out along this line. We are now developing AnZenMail,[1] a secure e-mail system that we consider can tolerate malicious attacks with mobile code. AnZenMail is a real application as well as a platform for our demonstration of technologies. On the one hand, our aim in the former course is to propose a methodology for constructions of secure real world applications, based upon the integration of the three layers. On the other hand, AnZenMail is design to provide an end user interface for security checkers and secure executors, so that we can easily examine our security enhancement technologies.

We have adopted our and related technologies to AnZenMail in the following manner.

- Our message transfer protocol is verified in BAN logic[5].
- Some correctness properties of the AnZenMail server (or mail transfer agent) with respect to the specifications of SMTP (Simple Mail Transfer Protocol)[16] are verified with a proof assistant tool Coq[20] mostly at source code level.
- The AnZenMail system is implemented in a memory-safe language Java, so that the server can escape from stack smashing attacks[2]. For the clearness and ease of verification, the server source code is not written in a flexible object-oriented style but in a rather imperative style.

---

[1] "An-zen" is a Japanese word meaning safe and secure. Pronounce it literally. Note that it is nothing to do with "Zen."

- The AnZenMail client (or mail user agent) is designed to be equipped with pluggable security checkers and secure executors. Currently, we have a simple static verifier for Java byte code and a more sophisticated reference monitoring tool SoftwarePot[14] for Linux/x86 and Solaris/SPARC binaries. We are developing a static analysis tool based upon the notion of resource usage analysis[12] and an inline reference monitor, both of which inspects Java byte code. Also a member of our project is developing an in-depth analysis anti-virus engine for Win32 binaries.

The rest of the paper is organized as follows. First, in Section 2, we summarize previous work that are related to e-mail security. In Section 3, we describe our design principles and approaches for constructing a secure e-mail system. In Sections 4 to 6, we show details of our protocol, server, and client, respectively. In Section 7, we conclude by mentioning the current limit of our approach and future plans.

2   Related Work

Concerning e-mail security, various works have been done, including not only scientific research activities but also standardization of protocols and implementations of working systems. Amongst all, the most investigated topic area in the literature is integrity and secrecy in the context of e-mail. More e-mail specific features such as non-repudiation of submission or acceptance also have been a matter of concern. In contrast, however, our major concern is software security against malicious attacks.

Confidentiality, Integrity, and Authentication

Several secure e-mail specifications have been proposed. For instance, PEM[15], MOSS[7], and S/MIME[19] provide specifications for encryption and signature and support services for confidentiality, integrity, and authentication of data origin. They are compatible with SMTP in the sense that encryptions and decryptions are applied on an end-to-end basis and thus transparent to mail transfer agents (i.e., SMTP servers). Since the AnZenMail server is an enhanced and certified SMTP server, these specifications and AnZenMail can coexist.

SMTP over TLS[11] is an SMTP extension and is not transparent to servers. It relies on a secure transport layer TLS, which protects communication over the Internet from eavesdroppers. With SMTP over TLS, mutual authentications between a client and a server and between a server and a server can be established, if they all have certificates.

AnZenMail employs its own integrity and authentication protocol with which the receiver can authenticate every server on the route along which a mail has been transfered. Later, we will discuss the necessity of "route authentication." For the purpose of e-mail confidentiality, AnZenMail itself does not provide any direct support. Instead, we consider that end-to-end encryption provided, for instance, by S/MIME is sufficient for confidentiality.

Non-repudiation

Non-repudiation properties are often essential in business transactions via e-mail. With digital signature mechanisms supported, for instance, by S/MIME, it is possible for the receiver to authenticate the original sender and thus the latter cannot repudiate the submission. With solely one-way message transmission, however, the receiver can repudiate the reception. For mutual verification, certified mail protocols[8,17] have been proposed, with which the sender can exchange a message for its receipt and the receiver cannot refute the successful delivery. These protocols depend more or less on a trusted third party.

AnZenMail does not directly support certified mails in this sense. The AnZen-Mail server is certified through formal verification, though.

Software Security on the Server Side

In contrast to the related work mentioned so far, which is mostly about protocols and data formats, Qmail is a widely used SMTP server that is considered secure and is relevant to software security[4]. Qmail is designed secure in the following manner.

- The designer follows the principle of least privilege, e.g., only the minimum core is given the root privilege.
- The server consists of mutually untrusted groups and each group has its own protection domain.
- Custom library functions of the language C for the purposes of input and memory allocation are prepared and standard C library functions, which are error prone and can be causes of buffer overruns and memory leaks, are carefully avoided, and so on.

In a more general setting, buffer overrun attacks are one of the most significant threats to software security on the server side. Various solutions have been proposed, including source code auditing, safe libraries (e.g., [3]), non-executable stacks, compiler-supported runtime checks (e.g., [6]), and safe languages. We take the simplest one: just to write a program in a memory-safe language, namely Java.

Similarly to Qmail, we take the security-by-design approach in design of our server. However, we also take a formal verification approach. This we consider is the most significant difference between AnZenMail and Qmail. Since our implementation language is not C but Java, naturally there are some other differences: we can use the standard I/O library without fear of buffer overflows and rely on automatic memory allocation mechanisms; Java provides a support for language-based protection domains; and so on. However, we do not consider that these differences are significant.

Software Security on the Client Side

Today, anti-virus products are certainly protecting client environments from malicious viruses. They mostly depend on scan engines and signature databases.

Therefore, frequent updates of databases are required, even though heuristic scanners are also available. Note that executable e-mail attachments are useful and even required when they are used like active mail[10]. In this case, flexible access control mechanisms (e.g., [13]) are also required. Apparently, however, today's anti-virus products do not support any authorization or access control mechanisms.

The AnZenMail client itself does not support such mechanisms but can be enhanced with external security checkers and secure executors. E-mail attachments are passed to and examined by various sorts of external modules.

3   Goals and Approaches

The following are the major design goals of AnZenMail:

- prevention of message loss,
- prevention of server cracking, and
- secure execution of email attachments.

The first one is about the correctness of application level routing and the other two are about security of software systems. In contrast, however, the following issues are beyond the scope of this paper.

- stable operations of IP routing and DNS, and
- trustworthy public key infrastructure (PKI), operating systems, and language processors

Of course, AnZenMail can tolerate temporary failures of IP routers.

As was mentioned before in Section 1, our approach is three-layered (Fig. 1). These three layers reinforce one another since each layer has both advantages and disadvantages summarized as follows.

Static analysis and verification: Mathematical verification is rigorous but also laborious and expensive. It is a reasonable compromise to precisely verify solely the most critical portions, which should be kept to a minimum in design time. Also, mathematical verification is only correct with respect to the given model. Since we cannot have rigorous proofs of the model's correctness with respect to the real world, we should prepare backup solutions.

Secure programming languages: With memory-safe languages and their robust processors, it is easy to keep applications memory-safe, which is often a minimum common security policy. However, we have to sacrifice expressiveness for security. For instance, dynamic code generation is prohibited in memory-safe languages without any loopholes.

Runtime security enforcement: Operating systems and runtime systems can monitor dynamic behaviors of any programs including self-modifying ones. However, more or less runtime overhead is inevitable.

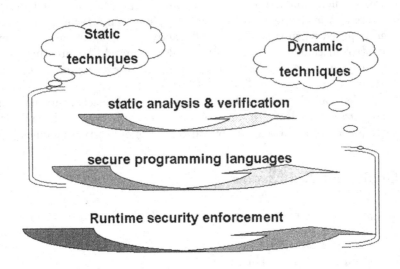

Fig. 1. The three-layered approach

Consequently, the first layer is expressive but its scope is narrow due to its laborious nature. The coverage of the second one is wider but still incomplete. Also it is less expressive than the other two layers. The third one is expressive and has the widest scope, but runtime overhead is inevitably imposed.

In addition to the three-layered approach, we have the following design goals:

- AnZenMail shall be compatible with the Internet mail system deployed so far: otherwise AnZenMail would be just a toy application. Our conclusion is that the server has to accept and handle SMTP sessions properly, even if the initiator is a legacy SMTP server.
- The AnZenMail system shall consist of both server and client applications since they have different characteristics: a server is open to the public by nature and a client can be concealed within a private network; the major threats to servers are worms and those to clients are viruses; a server is running autonomously by itself and a client requires frequent user intervention.
- The design of AnZenMail shall follow empirical wisdom such as the principles of least privilege and minimum trusted base.

4   Protocol Design and Verification

In order to keep compatible with the Internet mail system, we have designed AnZenMail to support SMTP and POP3/IMAP4. However, the plain SMTP lacks important mechanisms for secure communication such as sender authentication: it is easy to forge the sender address in SMTP unless less common extension mechanisms are used. As a compromise between the compatibility and security, we propose a new secure mail protocol on top of SMTP.

4.1 Route Authentication

Our secure mail transfer protocol provides a support for "route authentication," that is, the recipient can authenticate the sender and the servers on the route along which a mail is transfered. However, the sender may not know anything. The protocol guarantees neither message delivery nor non-repudiation of it. Basically, it is a one-way authentication protocol.

In the presence of executable e-mail attachments, we need mechanisms for the recipient to authorize such attachments and enforce the local security policy during their execution. The sender and the receiver are inherently asymmetric in this situation and we consider that, for the purposes, one-way authentications are sufficient.

A route authentication protocol provides a support for traceability. With this protocol, a client or a gateway of an organization may have policies to deny mails without proper authentic signatures. Also, services like the following can be provided.

> Suppose Bob trusts a server S that scans a mail and guarantees its safety with possibly filtering or converting some attachments. He can trust e-mails that are certified by S and are not modified later.

This scenario reveals the fact that route authentication is desirable for servers on the route to cooperate and guarantee the safety of a mail. Note that in an abstract sense there is a similarity between this scenario and the notion of SAFKASI[22] (or stack inspection). A method (in case of SAFKASI) or a server (in our case) gives the privilege or certificate of doing possibly dangerous work to some others.

4.2 Abstract Design

Fig. 2 is abstract descriptions of our secure mail protocol, where:

- A and B are the sender and the receiver, respectively;
- $S_1, \ldots, S_n$ are the servers on the route;
- $T_A, T_{S_1}, \ldots, T_{S_n}$ are timestamps;
- m_0 is the original message and $m_1, \ldots, m_n$ are the updated messages (or the updated portions of messages, in practice) by $S_1, \ldots, S_n$, respectively;
- m_0' is $\{A, B, S_1, T_A, m_0\}_{K_A^{-1}}$, $m_i'(1 \leq i < n)$ is $\{A, B, S_i, S_{i+1}, T_{S_i}, m_i, m_{i-1}'\}_{K_{S_i}^{-1}}$, and m_n' is $\{A, B, S_n, T_{S_n}, m_n, m_{n-1}'\}_{K_{S_n}^{-1}}$, and
- $K_A^{-1}, K_{S_1}^{-1}, \ldots, K_{S_n}^{-1}$ are the private keys of the sender and the servers, respectively.

$$\text{Message 0} \quad A \to S_1: \quad \underbrace{\{A, B, S_1, T_A, m_0\}_{K_A^{-1}}}_{m_0'}$$

$$\vdots$$

$$\text{Message } i \quad S_i \to S_{i+1}: \underbrace{\{A, B, S_i, S_{i+1}, T_{S_i}, m_i, m_{i-1}'\}_{K_{S_i}^{-1}}}_{m_i'}$$

$$\vdots$$

$$\text{Message } n \quad S_n \to B: \quad \underbrace{\{A, B, S_n, T_{S_n}, m_n, m_{n-1}'\}_{K_{S_n}^{-1}}}_{m_n'}$$

Fig. 2. Route authentication protocol

Also, $\{X\}_{K_Y^{-1}}$ denotes a message X signed by Y and, in practice, should be read as $X, \{h(X)\}_{K_Y^{-1}}$ for a secure hash function h.

At first glance, one may consider it exaggerated. For integrity and route authentication, however, the original message, the route, and the signatures and updates by the servers are necessary. Also, a notification of a fatal error and an ordinary message delivery requires the sender and the receiver names, respectively.

Although this protocol might seem too heavy for non-active mails, its overhead is about a few hundred bytes per hop, if the server does not change the message body. It is a little longer than the "Received" field. A concrete example is in Fig. 3.

4.3   Verification in BAN Logic

We have proven authentication properties of our protocol in BAN logic[5], which is also known as a "logic of authentication." As usual, we have expressed the notion of authentication in terms of "beliefs." The following are the proven properties under the assumptions that public keys are properly distributed and that clocks are almost synchronized.

- Upon reception of m_{i-1}', a server $S_i (1 \leq i \leq n)$ believes that A has recently sent m_0 to B.
- Upon reception of m_{i-1}', a server $S_i (1 \leq i \leq n)$ believes that each $S_j (1 \leq j < i)$ has recently sent m_j and m_{j-1}' and that their origin and destination are A and B, respectively.
- Upon reception of m_n', B believes that A submitted m_0 of which destination is B to S_1 at T_A.
- Upon reception of m_n', B believes that $S_j (1 \leq j < n)$ sent m_j and m_{j-1}' to S_{j+1} at T_{S_j} and that their origin and destination are A and B, respectively,
- Upon reception of m_n', B believes that S_n has recently sent m_n and m_{n-1}' of which origin and destination are A and B, respectively.

In summary, the receiver can know and believe the origin and the route of a received mail. In other words, the message transfer route is traceable. However, the receiver may not know anything about lost mails.

4.4   Concrete Design

There can be alternatives to implement our message transfer protocol on top of SMTP:

– implementing it as an SMTP service extension[16];
– encoding it in a header; and
– encoding it in a message body.

The first approach is not transparent to legacy SMTP servers and thus should be excluded. In principle, the other two are transparent to any SMTP servers, but we consider that it is not a good practice for SMTP servers to change message bodies. Therefore, currently we take the second approach. However, we also consider that it might be a reasonable approach to attach authentic signatures to each MIME objects.

Fig. 3 is a concrete example of a signature, where the fm, to, si, di, and ts fields correspond to A, B, S_i, S_{i+1}, T_{S_i}, respectively, in the abstract notation. The message body is abbreviated in this example. In practice, the concrete format includes more information than the abstract one. For instance, the encryption method and hash function (e.g., SHA1withRSA in Fig. 3) should be specified and a single mail often has multiple destinations.

```
X-Anz: fm=etsuya@anzenmail.is.titech.ac.jp,to=etsuya@mail.is.titech.ac.jp
X-Anz-Sig: sn=0,si=anzenmail.is.titech.ac.jp,di=mail.is.titech.ac.jp,ts=1026
378935875,sa=SHA1withRSA,sg=TTRMWBAA6bEJO8I1Tkqj4QNMNyXEFB5eK4uOE4iX
xlzV/uJd80Mn6qsA4f2KtizuRNcnHtXEDlnEGUAu+B2uodLxxra+QfrMsZXZk8cFRf/t
mNiO9SRkOX99Jw/RyB5GGHKhrA5gPdl8xxeQMQ8gKzvXxMa13SA+L5pBvB6oB28=
```

Fig. 3. A concrete example of signature

4.5   Legacy Problems

In the manner described so far, we can establish route authentication, if all the servers support our protocol. However, the presence of legacy SMTP servers on the transfer route breaks this assumption. In such cases, the recipient can only know a partial route.

Another problem is key distribution and safekeeping. Public key infrastructures are not yet ubiquitous and it might be still difficult to assume that each user has its own keys. Also, each user or server must keep its secret key on a local store.

5   A Secure and Certified Mail Server

As we mentioned before, preventions of server cracking and message loss are two major goals on the server side. The first goal can be achieved by satisfying basic security properties such as memory safety and confinement with the Java language semantics and mechanisms. The second goal is more subtle and we depended upon formal verification.

5.1   Architecture

The current version of the AnZenMail server is a plain SMTP server with the route authentication protocol. Roughly speaking, it consists of the following four major modules (Fig. 4):

SMTP receiver: Inbound SMTP requests first arrive at the SMTP receiver, which is responsible for returning replies.

Mail queue: Each arriving mail is once stored in this queue. Physically, it is stored on non-volatile storage so as to avoid mail loss even upon server crashes.

SMTP sender: if the destination of a received mail is not within the domain of this mail server, the SMTP sender transmits this mail to some remote server.

Local deliverer: if the domain of a received mail is within the domain of this mail server, the local deliverer dispatches this mail to the destination mailbox.

5.2   Verification in Coq

The SMTP receiver module is formalized and verified in Coq at source code level. The following are the verified properties.

- The server safely rejects any invalid SMTP session.
- The server accepts and processes any valid SMTP session properly unless a fatal error occurs.
- The server never sends back an acknowledgment until it saves a mail to non-volatile storage.

The first two properties are about conformance to the SMTP specifications and the last one is about server reliability.

Until now, we have not yet formally verified other modules. In order to complete the work we have to formalize other modules and prove several properties including "the conformance of the SMTP sender module to the SMTP specifications" and "the conformance to our route authentication protocol."

Our verification is carried out in the following manner.

- First, the Java source code of the SMTP receiver is manually translated into Coq functions.

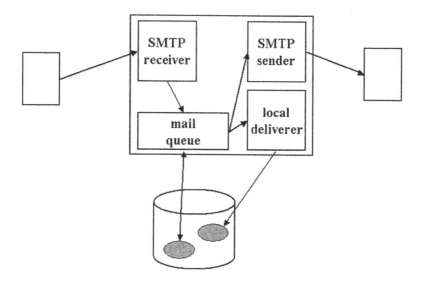

Fig. 4. Server architecture

- Second, the above specifications are described in terms of Coq.
- Finally, the specifications are verified with respect to the Coq functions.

More details of the verification work are reported in a companion paper[1].

This methodology is feasible in our case and we can achieve success by the following reasons.

- The SMTP receiver module is not very large. It is only about 600 lines of code. Note that SMTP itself is a simple protocol.
- Our SMTP server is written in an imperative style. Its code is neither flexible nor extendable but is clear. Also it is almost straightforward to manually translate an imperative Java program into Coq or ML.
- Although we use modern features of Java such as threads and automatic memory management intensively for writing the server, they do not disturb our verification efforts. In our case, fortunately, each thread roughly corresponds to an SMTP session and thus we can assume that multiple threads do not interfere with one another. If they cooperated and had shared resources, the verification would be much more difficult.

If the SMTP receiver were larger, more complicated, or more flexible, we might encounter more severe difficulties.

Though this methodology alone is not always feasible, it may be possible to exploit critical kernels that are small from various server applications. In general, a server application accepts some protocols and thus it certainly has a command loop similar to the one of our server. If this command loop is designed so that the rest of the server does not interfere with it, verification of conformance to the protocols seems within our reach.

Free from stack smashing is not the only advantage of memory-safe languages. Their source code can more likely be translated into Coq or some other formal systems in a straightforward manner, particularly when it is written in a functional or an imperative style. In contrast, in case of the language C, for instance, the possibility of interferences via its flat memory space should be always taken into consideration. This will drastically make inferences difficult.

5.3   Security and Flexibility

Requirements for security and those for flexibility/extendibility often contradict. In our case, the AnZenMail server is designed and verified secure but is not very flexible. Also in the literature[21], a pessimistic programming style is proposed. Substantially, the authors of this article recommended not to use flexible Java language constructs.

In practice, however, both security and flexibility are desirable. In case of AnZenMail, we need an extension mechanism for the server, since as a practical mail server such extensions as mailing list managers are essential.

It is not difficult to implement an external mailing list manager if the server core can trust it:

- the dispatcher module, which is not explicitly illustrated in Fig. 4, passes a mail to the SMTP sender, the local deliverer, or an external module according to its destination; if the destination is a mailing list address, the dispatcher delivers the message to the corresponding external mailing list manager; and
- the external mailing list manager transfers copies of the message to the SMTP sender and/or the local deliverer according to the destinations registered in the mailing list.

For security, however, the server core should not trust external modules and gives them the least privileges necessary for their work. For instance, the external mailing list manager should be allowed to read a configuration file and pass messages to the SMTP sender and local deliverer, but it should not be allowed to access any other files or server resources. In particular, secret keys on the local store and the signer module should be strongly protected. Furthermore, an external module might be limited its resource usage, e.g., the SMTP sender may accept at most some limited number of requests in any time frame from an untrusted module so as to prevent SPAM mails.

Consequently, we consider that the key technologies are verification of stable core modules (e.g., the SMTP receiver) and flexible access control of OS and server resources. We confess that our server lacks flexible access control mechanisms beyond the Java security framework and that we have not yet provided any support tools for sophisticated policy descriptions. As for mechanisms, however, we are now using the AnZenMail client as a proving ground for flexible sandboxing and access control mechanisms. So, the most significant problems we consider are flexible policy descriptions.

6   A Mail Client and Its Security Architecture

In contrast to the AnZenMail server, the AnZenMail client is designed more feature rich. For compatibility and usability, it provides standard features of today's mailers such as a graphical user interface as illustrated in Fig. 5. It also supports standard protocols and formats including SMTP submission, POP3/IMAP4 retrieval, and MIME formats. In Fig. 5, a MIME encoded graphics file is displayed.

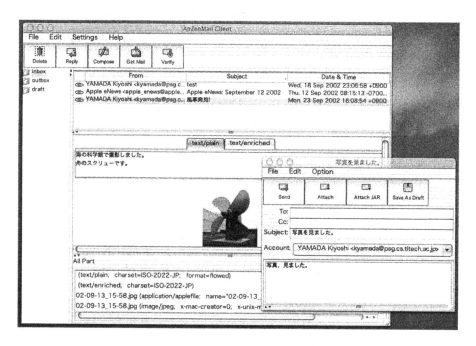

Fig. 5. Appearances of the AnZenMail client

The AnZenMail client is implemented in a fully object-oriented style and depends much on large and complicated Java class libraries such as Java Swing and JavaMail. It is not a target of formal verification now and will not in the foreseeable future. Fortunately, however, a client is less security critical than a server since the IP address of the former does not have to be exposed to the public and thus direct attacks from outside can be naturally prevented. Also, a client does not take any active part in application level routing.

A unique feature of the AnZenMail client is its plug-in interfaces for external security inspectors and secure executors (Fig. 6). According to the MIME type, the client dispatches an e-mail attachment to an appropriate internal or external

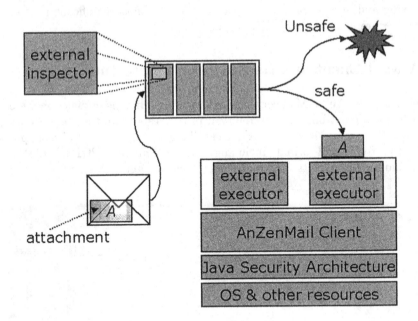

Fig. 6. Security architecture of the AnZenMail client

module(s). For instance, an attachment of type plain/text is sent to the text viewer and one of type application/x-msdownload is sent to an external binary inspector first and if it passes the inspection then to the Windows environment. For a single MIME type, more than one inspector module may be registered.

Our major concern in the client side is secure extension of client functionalities. Note that mailers are often used not only for asynchronous communication but also for personal information management and document exchanges[9]. A mailer is one of the most overloaded applications today and is worth designing extendable.

We have the following external modules, some of which are just being developed.

Java signature checker: A Java archive is checked to see whether or not it has proper signatures.

SoftwarePot: A Linux/x86 or Solaris/SPARC binary is executed within a sandbox, which is constructed by dynamically trapping system calls[14].

Resource usage analysis[12]: Java code with type annotations, in which we can express the order of resource usages, is statically checked to see whether or not the code is consistent with the type annotations.

Anti-virus engine: Win32 binaries are statically checked. This is an in-depth analysis tool and safely simulates the behaviors of the given x86 code and detect malicious one upon its infection points.

These modules in combination more or less cover Java byte code and native code of Win32, Linux/x86, and Solaris/SPARC. However, proper integrations are under investigation. In general, each inspection module provides its own abstractions for policy descriptions and enforcement. For instance, SoftwarePot provides a system call level abstractions and the resource usage analyzer provides type-based ones. Translations among these abstractions are desirable for integration, but we have not yet established them.

7   Conclusion

In this paper, we have described the design, implementation, and verification of our secure mail system AnZenMail. During the course of our development, we have examined the three-layered approach and have learned the following.

- Formal verification of not only protocols but also small portions of programs are feasible, particularly when they are critical. A proof assistance system works fine in our case.
- Verification of larger and more complex software modules like Java Swing is too laborious and beyond our ability. Verification of flexible and extendable software that is constructed in a modern object-oriented style is still a challenge.
- A memory-safe language is usable both for server and client implementations. If you can ignore legacy software written in the language C, it is the simplest solution to avoid buffer overrun attacks.
- The combination of a memory-safe language and an imperative programming style is well suited for verification. A memory-safe language is more tractable than the language C since the former has less unexpected behaviors. An imperative style is more inferable than a modern object-oriented style since the former is simple and naive.
- Security-by-design is certainly a promising approach. However, we need better tools, e.g., design tools for compartmentation.
- As a last resort, runtime monitoring and auditing is useful, particularly when mobile code is inevitable.
- We have various mechanisms for security enforcement, but policy descriptions for them are not necessarily easy and sometime very difficult.

Acknowledgments. We would like to thank Prof. Akinori Yonezawa for his continuous support of AnZenMail and Prof. Kazuhiko Kato and Dr. Yoshihiro Oyama of Tsukuba University for their tremendous efforts in development of SoftwarePot and contributions to AnZenMail. We would also like to thank members of our project for their useful comments in design of AnZenMail.

References

1. Affeldt, R., Kobayashi, N.: Formalization and Verification of a Mail Server in Coq. *Proc. of International Symposium on Software Security*, in this volume, 2003.
2. Aleph One: Smashing the Stack for Fun and Profit, *Phrack*, **49**(7), 1996, http://www.phrack.org/leecharch.php?p=49
3. Baratloo, A., Singh, N., Tsai, T.: Transparent Run-Time Defense Against Stack-Smashing Attacks. *Proc. of USENIX Annual Conference*, 2000.
4. Bernstein, D. J.: The Qmail Security Guarantee.
5. Burrows, M., Abadi, M., Needham, R.: A Logic of Authentication. *Proc. of the Royal Society*, Series A 426, 233–271, 1989.
6. Cowan, C., Pu, C., Maier, D., Walpole, J., Bakke, P., Beattie, S., Grier, A., Wagle, P., Zhang, Q., Hinton, H.: StackGuard: Automatic Adaptive Detection and Prevention of Buffer-Overflow Attacks, *Proc. 7th USENIX Security Conference*, 63–78, 1998.
7. Crocker, S., Freed, N., Galvin, J., Murphy, S.: MIME Object Security Services. RFC 1848, 1995.
8. Deng, R. H., Gong, L., Lazar, A. A., Wang, W.: Practical Protocols for Certified Electronic Mail. *J. of Network and System Management*, **4**(3), 279–297, 1996.
9. Ducheneaut, N., Bellotti, V.: E-mail as Habitat. *Interactions*, ACM, **8**(5), 30–38, 2001.
10. Goldberg, Y., Safran, M., Shapiro, E.: Active Mail - A Framework for Implementing Groupware. *Proc. of the Conf. on Computer Supported Cooperative Work*, 75–83, 1992.
11. Hoffman, P.: SMTP Service Extension for Secure SMTP over TLS. RFC 2487, 1999.
12. Igarashi, A., Kobayashi, N.: Resource Usage Analysis. *Proc. of ACM Symposium on Principles of Programming Languages*, 331–342, 2001.
13. Jaeger, T., Prakash, A., Liedtke, J., Islam, N.: Flexible Control of Downloaded Executable Content. *ACM Trans. on Information and System Security*, **2**(2), 177–228, 1999.
14. Kato, K., Oyama, Y.: SoftwarePot: An Encapsulated Transferable File System for Secure Software Circulation. *Proc. of International Symposium on Software Security*, in this volume, 2003.
15. Kent, S. T.: Internet Privacy Enhanced Mail. *Comm. of the ACM*, **36**(8), 48–60, 1993.
16. Klensin, J. (ed): Simple Mail Transfer Protocol. RFC 2821, 2001.
17. Pfitzmann, B., Schunter, M., Waidner, M.: Provably Secure Certified Mail. *Research Report*, RZ 3207(#93253), IBM, 2000.
18. OpenBSD security. http://www.openbsd.org/security.html
19. Ramsdell, B. (ed): S/MIME Version 3 Message Specification. RFC 2633, 1999.
20. The Coq Development Team: *The Coq Proof Assistant Reference Manual, Version 7.3.* 2002.
21. Viega, J., McGraw, G., Mutdosch, T., Felten, E. W.: Statically Scanning Java Code: Finding Security Vulnerabilities. *IEEE Software*, **17**(5), 68–74, 2000.
22. Wallach, D. S., Appel, A. W., Felten, E. W.: SAFKASI: A Security Mechanism for Language-Based Systems. *ACM Trans. on Software Engineering and Methodology*, **9**(4), 341–378, 2000.

Formalization and Verification of a Mail Server in Coq

Reynald Affeldt[1] and Naoki Kobayashi[2]

[1] Department of Computer Science, University of Tokyo
affeldt@yl.is.s.u-tokyo.ac.jp
[2] Department of Computer Science, Tokyo Institute of Technology
kobayasi@kb.cs.titech.ac.jp

Abstract. This paper reports on the formalization and verification of a mail server (SMTP server) in Coq. The correctness of a mail server is very important: bugs of the mail server may be abused for eavesdropping mail contents, spreading virus, sending spam messages, etc. We have verified a part of a mail server written in Java, by manually translating the Java program into a Coq function as faithfully as possible, and verifying properties of the Coq function. The results of this experiment indicate the feasibility and usefulness of verification of middle-sized system softwares in this style. The verification has been carried out in a few months, and a few bugs in the mail server have been indeed found during the verification process.

1 Introduction

The *AnZenMail* project [13] consists in implementing a secure facility for electronic mail. This is a large system with many subparts and among them the mail server is a central one. In this paper, we report an experiment of formalization and verification of this mail server.

From the security point of view, it is very important to verify that a mail server is correctly implemented because bugs may be responsible for loss of information and flaws may also be abused for eavesdropping mail contents, spreading viruses, sending spam messages, etc.

Concretely, we check by means of a theorem prover (namely Coq [14]) that the implementation of the mail server is correct with respect to Internet standards and reliable. Our approach is to create a model as faithful as possible of the actual mail server by translating the code base written in the Java language into a Coq function and verify the properties of the Coq function.

There are other approaches using a theorem prover such as extraction of an implementation directly from the proofs (in an adequate theorem prover) or direct proofs of the actual code base (without any need for a model). In comparison, our approach is convenient in many respects. First, it does not depend on the implementation language. It is thus possible to use an implementation language with appealing security and efficiency properties such as Java. Second,

M. Okada et al. (Eds.): ISSS 2002, LNCS 2609, pp. 217–233, 2003.

the proof development can be managed in size and time like the source code development; proofs done in parallel with the implementation increase confidence in the code base and it is possible to go back and forth between the specifications and the implementation for adjustments.

We claim that our experiment makes the following contributions:

- it is a large application of theorem proving (large in terms of the size of the original code and proofs),
- it illustrates several techniques to model in a functional interface a reactive system with infinitely many states, and
- it deals exhaustively with system errors.

The rest of this paper is organized as follows. Sect. 2 explains what part of the mail system we formalize. Sect. 3 explains the formalization of the program and its specifications. Sect. 4 presents the results of our verification. Sect. 5 discusses lessons learned from our experiment. Sect. 6 reviews related work. Sect. 7 concludes and lists future work.

2   Mail Server

2.1   A Secure Mail System

The *AnZenMail* project is a subproject of the *secure computing project*, which aims at enhancing the security of computer systems by using three levels of safety assurance mechanisms —formal verification/analysis techniques, compile-time code insertion for dynamic-checking of safety properties, and OS-level protection (see the project home page http://anzen.is.titech.ac.jp/index-e.html for details). The *AnZenMail* system consists of mail servers, which deliver mails, and mail clients, which interact with users and send/receive mails.

The key features of the *AnZenMail* system are as follows:

1. Use of a high-level programming language: both the server code and the client code are written in a safe language (namely Java) to minimize security holes (that are often caused by buffer overflows).
2. Protection against forging or modification of mails: secure protocols based on digital signatures are used to protect the contents of mails and the identity of senders. Correctness of the security protocols are proved in a formal manner.
3. Fault-conscious design of the server code: the server code is carefully designed in such a way that received mails are not lost even if the server crashes.
4. Verification of the server code: the core part of the server code is verified in a formal manner.
5. Safe execution of mail attachments: on the mail client side, safe execution of code received a mail attachment is enforced by static analysis of the code, compile-time code insertion for dynamically checking security properties, and OS-level protection mechanisms.

The present paper is concerned with the fourth feature above. Verification of the server code is also related to the second and third features: the second and third features guarantee certain properties only at algorithm or design level, and give no guarantee that the properties are indeed satisfied by the actual code. By verifying the code, we can check whether the implementation is correct with respect to the algorithm and the design.

2.2   SMTP Model

The overall structure of the mail server is shown in Fig. 1. It consists of two parts: the SMTP receiver, which receives mails from other mail servers and mail clients using the SMTP protocol and stores received mails in a mail queue, and the SMTP sender, which extracts mails from the mail queue and sends them to other mail servers and mail clients using the SMTP protocol.

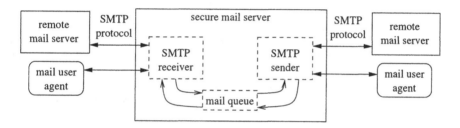

Fig. 1. The structure of the mail server

Fig. 2 illustrates most typical SMTP commands with an automaton. An SMTP protocol session consists of *commands* and some mail contents sent by a mail sender to the SMTP receiver that sends back *replies*. Before a session begins, the SMTP receiver waits for incoming connections. The mail client connects using the HELO command; the server replies with its identity and creates an empty *envelope*. The client sends the MAIL command to set the return path of the envelope with the address of the mail sender. The client then sends one or more RCPT commands to add addresses to the list of recipients of the envelope. The server may reply with error messages to the MAIL and RCPT commands for various reasons (malformed addresses, MAIL and RCPT commands not ordered, etc.) The client eventually sends the DATA command, followed by the mail contents and terminated by a line containing only a period. If the server accepts the data, it delivers the mail contents to recipients and notifies the mail sender if delivery fails. Finally, the client closes the connection with the QUIT command to which the server replies with some greetings. There are a few other commands: the RSET command clears the envelope, the NOOP command just causes the server to reply (it has no effect on the state of the server), etc.

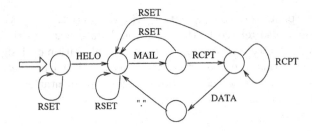

Fig. 2. Abstract state transition

2.3   Target of Formalization and Verification

Our goal is to verify that the implementation of the mail server as a whole satisfies the critical responsibilities highlighted above. Those properties are mainly adequacy of the code with the SMTP protocol and reliability of the implementation, i.e. the fact that accepted mails are eventually delivered.

In this paper, we are concerned with the SMTP receiver part of the mail server. Formalization and verification are therefore restricted to that part of above properties which are relevant to the SMTP receiver. Adequacy with the SMTP protocol amounts to the following properties: the SMTP receiver must handle all correct sessions, reject erroneous commands and send back correct replies. Reliability amounts to the following property: the SMTP receiver must save accepted mail contents in the mail queue for later processing by the SMTP sender.

In the next section, we explain how we formalize the SMTP receiver (hereafter referred to as the mail server) and formulate above properties.

3   Formalization and Verification

The task of formalization can be divided into construction of a model for the execution of the program and specification of the properties to be verified. In the following, we assume some familiarity with the syntax of Java. Other code samples are explained in such a way that no a priori knowledge of Coq is required.

3.1   Model

A model for the execution of the mail server is a program written in the Coq language such that its verification substitutes for the verification of the actual mail server written in Java.

Construction of such a model essentially amounts to conversion of the original program from Java to the Coq language. There are two difficulties. First, Java is an imperative language whereas the Coq language is functional. Second, relevant hardware aspects of the execution environment must be made explicit. For instance, errors due to the network or the host computer may in practice cause the mail server to behave unexpectedly. Therefore, our model must take into account such *system errors* in order for the properties we verify to hold under normal conditions of use. In the following, we first give an overview of code conversion and then explain how we overcome those difficulties.

Code Conversion Overview. We manually convert the original program in such a way that its structure is preserved, i.e. any language construct can easily be associated with its counterpart in the model. Conceptually, this task can be divided into conversion of datatypes and conversion of control structures.

Java datatypes are converted to corresponding Coq types. Java data structures (or object fields) are converted to Coq records or tuples, union or enumeration types are converted to Coq *inductive types* (similar to datatypes in ML-like languages), etc. Those objects belong to the type *Set* of program specifications in Coq. For instance, we represent the global state of the mail server by specifying it as a record:

Record *STATE*: *Set* := *smtp_state{to_client*: *OutputStream*;
    server_name: *String*;
    queue_dir: *File*;
    buf: *Buffer*;
    from_domain: *String*;
    rev_path: *Rfc821_path*;
    fwd_paths: *Rfc821_pathlist*;
    quit: *bool*;
    files: *FileSystem*;
    oracles: *Oracles}*.

The field *to_client* contains replies from the server, the field *rev_path* contains the return path of the envelope, the field *fwd_paths* contains the list of recipients, etc. (Other relevant fields are explained later.) For Coq records to be manipulated as Java data structures, we also provide mutator functions. For instance, the function *enque_reply*, given a *STATE* and an SMTP reply, updates the list of replies sent by the server so far.

Java control structures are converted to corresponding Coq control structures. Java `switch` statements are converted to Coq *Cases* statements, method calls are converted to function calls, Java sequences `a;b` are converted to Coq function calls *(seq a b)* (where the function *seq* is to be defined later), etc. Conversion of control structures is illustrated later in this section.

Monads for Exception Handling. The first difficulty is the conversion of imperative operations in Java to the Coq language. In the case of exception handling, we use monadic style programming [15].

The actual mail server can circumvent some system errors (e.g., network failures) by using Java exceptions. In Coq, we represent all system errors, including *fatal errors* (e.g., host computer failure), by an inductive type:

Inductive *Exception*: *Set* :=
> *IOException*: *Exception*
> | *parse_error_exception*: *Exception*
> | *Smail_implementation_exception*: *Exception*
> | *empty_stream_exception*: *Exception*
> | *system_failure*: *Exception*.

The *IOException* constructor represents network failures, the *system_failure* constructor represents host computer failures, etc.

Using the above definitions for the state of the mail server and for exceptions, we can mimic exception handling by the following monad-like inductive type (bracketed variables are here parameters and the arrow-like notation indicates constructors arguments):

Inductive *Except* [*A*: *Set*]: *Set* :=
> *Succ*: *A* → *STATE* → (*Except A*)
> | *Fail*: *Exception* → *STATE* → (*Except A*).

Definition *Result* : *Set* := (*Except unit*).

Result represents the result of a computation which can be either successful (constructor *Succ*) or a failure (constructor *Fail*).

Test Oracles for Non-deterministic Failures. The second difficulty is the simulation by the model of non-deterministic system errors. For that purpose, we use in Coq a *coinductive type* that represents test oracles in the form of an infinite sequence of booleans:

CoInductive *Set Oracles* := *flip* : *bool* → *Oracles* → *Oracles*.

Test oracles appear as a part of the state of the model (field *oracles* in the record *STATE* above) and are used at any point where a system error may occur. Concretely, the value of the leading test oracle determines whether a system error occurs or not, and whenever a test oracle is used, test oracles are updated (by applying the function *update_coin* to the current *STATE*). For instance, a network failure may occur whenever the mail server sends a reply, hence the following definition of the function that sends replies:

Definition *reply* [*r*:*ReplyMsg*; *st*:*STATE*]: *Result* :=
> (*Cases* (*oracles st*) *of*
>>   (*flip true coin*) ⇒
>>>   (*Succ unit tt* (*update_coin* (*enque_reply st r*) *coin*))
>> | (*flip false coin*) ⇒
>>>   (*Fail unit IOException* (*update_coin st coin*))
> *end*).

Similarly, a host computer failure may occur during the execution of any two successive Java statements. In Coq, we represent the sequence of Java statements by the following function (bracketed variables are here function arguments):

Definition *seq*: *Result* → (*STATE*→*Result*) → *Result* :=
> [*x*: *Result*][*f*: *STATE*→*Result*]

$$
\begin{aligned}
&(Cases\ x\ of \\
&\quad (Succ\ \_\ st) \Rightarrow \\
&\qquad Cases\ (oracles\ st)\ of \\
&\qquad\qquad (flip\ true\ coin) \Rightarrow (f\ (update\_coin\ st\ coin)) \\
&\qquad\qquad |\ (flip\ false\ coin) \Rightarrow (Fail\ unit\ system\_failure\ st) \\
&\qquad end \\
&\quad |\ (Fail\ e\ st) \Rightarrow (Fail\ unit\ e\ st) \\
&end).
\end{aligned}
$$

Example of Code Conversion. Equipped with above objects, we show how we convert a method taken from the original Java program to its Coq counterpart.

The get_helo method (Fig. 3) is essentially a loop that fetches SMTP commands until it receives the HELO command. In case of unexpected commands, it replies with some error message; in case of termination commands, it terminates the SMTP protocol session. Note that the execution of get_helo may also be interrupted by network failures if the socket gets closed or broken.

```
void get_helo() throws IOException {
    while (true) {
        ...
        int cmd = get_cmd();
        String arg = get_arg();
        switch(cmd) {
        case cmd_unknown:
            reply_unknown_cmd(); break;
        case cmd_abort:
            reply_ok_quit(); quit = true; return;
        case cmd_quit:
            reply_ok_quit(); quit = true; return;
        case cmd_rset:
            do_rset();
            reply_ok_rset(); break;
        case cmd_noop:
            reply_ok_noop(); break;
        case cmd_helo:
            if (do_helo(arg)) return;
            else break;
        case cmd_rcpt_to:
            reply_no_mail_from(); break;
        default:
            reply_no_helo(); break;
        }
    }
}
```

Fig. 3. Java get_helo method

The context in which the `get_helo` method is called is the mail server main loop (Fig. 4). Intuitively, upon reception of the HELO command, a loop is entered in which the following MAIL, RCPT and DATA commands are to be processed.

```
void work() throws IOException, Smtpdialog_bug,
                                 Mailqueue_fatal_exception {
    ...
    get_helo();
    int msg_no = 0;
    while (!quit) {
        do_rset();
        if (!get_mail_from()) continue;
        if (!get_rcpt_to()) continue;
        get_data(msg_no++);
    }
    ...
}
```

Fig. 4. Mail system main loop

The first step of code conversion is to convert Java datatypes to Coq types. For instance, SMTP commands represented by the integers `cmd_helo`, `cmd_quit`, etc. in the actual Java code base are converted to the inductive type $SMTP\_cmd$ (Fig. 5).

```
Inductive SMTP_cmd : Set :=
        cmd_helo: String → SMTP_cmd
    |  cmd_mail_from: String → SMTP_cmd
    |  cmd_rcpt_to: String → SMTP_cmd
    |  cmd_data: String → SMTP_cmd
    |  cmd_noop: SMTP_cmd
    |  cmd_rset: SMTP_cmd
    |  cmd_quit: SMTP_cmd
    |  cmd_abort: SMTP_cmd
    |  cmd_unknown: SMTP_cmd.
```

Fig. 5. $SMTP\_cmd$ inductive type

The second step of code conversion is to convert Java control structures to Coq control structures. Let us directly comment on the result of code conversion (Fig. 6). In the resulting get_helo Coq function, we see that Java's `switch` is replaced by Coq's $Cases$, that sequences of statements are replaced by calls to functions seq, $comp$ and seq_b ($comp$ and seq_b are slight variations of seq), and that calls to third-party Java methods are replaced by calls to their respective Coq counterparts (after adequate code conversion). Observe that, as a result of our code conversion, statements that used to appear syntactically after the call to method get_helo in method work now appear inside the function *get_helo*.

```
Fixpoint get_helo [in_stream: InputStream]: STATE → Result :=
    (comp get_cmd
    (comp get_arg
        [st: STATE]
        Cases in_stream of
            nil ⇒ (fail empty_stream_exception st)
        | (cons m in_stream') ⇒
            (Cases m of
                cmd_unknown ⇒
                    (seq (reply_unknown_cmd st) (get_helo in_stream'))
            | cmd_abort ⇒
                    (seq (reply_ok_quit st) succ)
            | cmd_quit ⇒
                    (seq (reply_ok_quit st) succ)
            | cmd_rset ⇒
                    (seq (reply_ok_rset st) (get_helo in_stream'))
            | cmd_noop ⇒
                    (seq (reply_ok_noop st) (get_helo in_stream'))
            | (cmd_helo arg) ⇒
                    (seqb (do_helo arg st)
                        [x:bool]if x then (get_mail_from in_stream')
                                else (get_helo in_stream'))
            | (cmd_rcpt_to b) ⇒
                    (seq (reply_no_mail_from st) (get_helo in_stream'))
            | _ ⇒
                    (seq (reply_no_helo st) (get_helo in_stream'))
            end)
    end))
```

Fig. 6. Coq *get_helo* function

Not all methods are converted as faithfully as our example. Indeed, the method get_helo is specific to the problem at hand and requires careful conversion for the verification to be meaningful. In contrast, methods such as get_cmd and get_arg here are of more general use and can be seen as trusted utility methods. From the viewpoint of our verification, the interesting point about such methods is rather that their execution may cause some errors. As a consequence, *get_cmd* and *get_arg* are simply converted as generators of exceptions in a non-deterministic manner.

Difficulties in Automation. Although the code conversion described here can be applied to many programs, it seems difficult to automate it because it requires human intervention. The latter is for instance necessary to properly model the execution environment and in particular to insert non-determinism at relevant places. In the case of theorem provers such as Coq, human intervention is also required to build a tractable model. As an illustration, the fact that the input stream of SMTP commands is made a parameter of the function *get_helo* is linked to the fact that Coq allows recursive functions to be defined only by structural induction.

3.2 Specification

We have already stated informally the properties we verify in Sect. 2.3. In this section, we formally write those properties in Coq using *inductive predicates* (similar to predicates in logic). Those objects belong to the type *Prop* of logical propositions in Coq. Before, we explain how we formalize the correctness of SMTP protocol sessions and acknowledged and saved mails.

Correct SMTP Protocol Sessions. The relevant Internet standard is the RFC 821[12]. It is a prose description that explains the SMTP protocol, including definitions of correct commands and replies.

By way of example, we show below how correct SMTP protocol sessions are represented in Coq. Let us assume that we are given simple predicates that state the correctness of individual SMTP commands. For instance, *(valid_cmd_helo s)* states that *s* is a correct HELO command. Correct SMTP protocol sessions satisfy the following inductive predicate (not displayed entirely by lack of space):

Inductive *valid_protocol*: *InputStream* → *Prop* :=
      rcv_helo: (*s*: *InputStream*)(*c*: *SMTP_cmd*)
                        (*valid_cmd_helo c*)
                        → (*valid_after_helo s*)
                        →(*valid_protocol* (*cons_stream c s*))
      | *rcv_quit*:
                        (*s*: *InputStream*)(*valid_protocol* (*cons_stream   cmd_quit*
s))
      | *rcv_skip*: (*s*: *InputStream*)(*c*: *SMTP_cmd*)
                        ¬(*valid_cmd_helo c*)
                        → ¬*c*=*cmd_quit* → ¬*c*=*cmd_abort*
                        → (*valid_protocol s*)
                        → (*valid_protocol* (*cons_stream c s*))
      with *valid_after_helo*: *InputStream* → *Prop* :=
            ...

Intuitively, it can be read as follows. There are three cases distinguished by the constructors: (1) an SMTP protocol session that starts with a correct HELO command such that the rest of the session is also correct is itself correct, (2) an SMTP protocol session that starts with a QUIT command is always correct and (3) an SMTP protocol session that starts with any other command such that the rest of the session is also correct is correct.

Similarly, correct replies are represented by an inductive predicate called *correct_reply*.

Messages Stored in the Mail Queue. To specify the reliability property, we need to represent on the one hand mails for which reception is acknowledged by the mail server and on the other hand mails that are indeed saved in the mail queue.

Acknowledged mails are represented by the function *received_mails*.

Saved mails are represented by the following inductive predicate:

Inductive *all_mails_saved_in_file*: (*list Mail*)→*FileSystem*→*FileSystem*→*Prop*:=
  all_saved_none: (*fs1*:*FileSystem*)(*fs2*:*FileSystem*)
      (*eq_fs_except_garbage fs1 fs2*)
      → (*all_mails_saved_in_file* (*nil Mail*) *fs1 fs2*)
  | *all_saved_some*: (*m*:*Mail*)(*mails*: (*list Mail*))
      (*fs1*:*FileSystem*)(*fs2*:*FileSystem*)(*fs3*:*FileSystem*)
      (*mail_saved_in_file m fs1 fs2*) →
      (*all_mails_saved_in_file mails fs2 fs3*) →
      (*all_mails_saved_in_file* (*cons Mail m mails*) *fs1 fs3*).

This requires some explanations. *FileSystem* represents the file system through which the mail queue is actually implemented (the field *files* in the record *STATE* represents the file system in our model). The predicate *eq_fs_except_garbage* is true for file systems whose non-empty files have the same contents and the predicate *mail_saved_in_files* is true if the envelop and the mail contents have been saved in the file system.

Verified Properties. Equipped with above predicates, we can now write the formal specification of the properties we want to verify. They appear as Coq theorems. In the following, parenthesized parameters and the *EX* constructor represent respectively universally and existentially quantified variables. Other logical symbols (→, =, ∧, ∨) have their usual meaning.

- Adequacy with the SMTP protocol:
  - The server handles correct SMTP protocol sessions unless a fatal error occurs:
    Theorem *valid_protocol1*:
      (*s*: *InputStream*)(*st*:*STATE*)
          (*valid_protocol s*) → (*is_succ_or_fatal* (*work s st*)).
  - The server rejects erroneous SMTP protocol sessions:
    Theorem *valid_protocol2*:
          (*s*: *InputStream*)(*st*:*STATE*)(*st'*:*STATE*)
              (*work s st*)=(*succ st'*)→ (*valid_protocol s*).
  - The server sends correct replies:
    Theorem *correct_reply1*:
      (*s*: *InputStream*)(*st*: *STATE*)(*st'*: *STATE*)
          ((*work s st*)=(*succ st'*)∨
          (*work s st*)=(*fail empty_stream_exception st'*))→
          (*correct_reply s* (*to_client st'*)).
  - The server sends correct replies up to failure:

Theorem *correct_reply2*:
$(s: InputStream)(st: STATE)(st': STATE)(exn: Exception)$
$(work\ s\ st)=(fail\ exn\ st') \rightarrow$
$(EX\ s': InputStream —$
$(is\_prefix\ SMTP\_cmd\ s'\ s) \wedge$
$(correct\_reply\ s'\ (to\_client\ st'))).$

- Reliability: Once the server acknowledges reception of a message, the latter is saved in the mail queue and is not lost:

Theorem *reliability*:
$(s: InputStream)(st: STATE)(st': STATE)(exn: Exception)$
$((work\ s\ st)=(succ\ st') \vee (work\ s\ st)=(fail\ exn\ st')) \rightarrow$
$(all\_mails\_saved\_in\_file$
$(received\_mails\ s\ (to\_client\ st'))\ (files\ st)\ (files\ st')).$

4   Verification Results

In this section, we present the results of the verification in Coq of the specification and the model presented above.

The SMTP receiver part of the secure mail system roughly consists of 700 lines of Java, excluding utility code such as parsing which is taken for granted. Our model only accounts for the core part of the SMTP receiver and also roughly consists of 700 lines in the Coq language. We believe that the code and its model grow in size similarly.

The official documentation for the SMTP protocol [12] is 4050 lines long. Our specification only accounts for that part of the documentation describing a simple SMTP receiver and is roughly 500 lines long. Although it is hard to compare prose documentation with formal specifications, we believe that the latter is a concise alternative to the former.

The size of proof scripts are given below (there is a base of common lemmas used throughout the other proofs):

Files	Size (lines)
Lemmas	2324
valid_protocol1	960
valid_protocol2	2842
correct_reply1	5278
correct_reply2	4116
reliability	2071
Total	17591

Although we tried hard to limit the size of proofs, much experience is required to write short proofs in Coq. Sizes we report here should therefore be seen as upper bounds. Yet, it is likely that proof scripts grow quickly with the size of involved inductive predicates.

The model, the specification and the proofs are available at `http://web.yl.is.s.u-tokyo.ac.jp/ affeldt/mail-system.tar.gz`.

The authors (who are not experienced Coq users) have carried out the verification described in this paper in a few months of sparse work. We believe that one person working in optimal conditions may need roughly 150 hours.

Coq 7.1 requires 7.3 minutes (according to Coq's `Time` command) and 157MB of memory (according to Unix's `top` command) to check the proofs (operating system: Solaris 8, architecture: UltraSparc 400MHz)

The main result is that verification has proved to be effective. Indeed, errors were found when building proofs. They appeared as contradictory hypotheses indicating some inconsistency in the state of the mail server. Once the offending operation is identified in the Coq model, the Java code can be immediately corrected accordingly thanks to the program transformation described in the previous section. To be more precise, verification of the mail server allowed us to find the following errors in the Java code base:

- the state of the mail system was not reset upon mail reception and wrongly reset upon reception of the RSET command, and
- a wrong number of reply messages were sent back to the client.

Those errors are only revealed by specific sequences of SMTP commands, that is the reason why they slip through a non-exhaustive testing procedure.

5 Discussion

5.1 Limitations

A first limitation of our approach is that there is a small gap between the implementation and its model. However, alternative approaches also have drawbacks. One can implement the mail server directly in the theorem prover to prove its properties and eventually use an extraction facility to generate a runnable program. Yet, (1) the extracted code may not be directly runnable (because the model contains non-software aspects such as a model of the program environment) and (2) the extracted code is unlikely to be efficient (because handling code optimizations complicates the proof and because extraction facilities are non-optimizing code generators). One can choose a radical approach by formalizing the semantics of an efficient programming language chosen for the implementation as a preliminary step. Yet, (1) it results in a long and intricate development and (2) it may not even be possible since most languages are only described in prose. Another argument in favor of our approach is that it is still possible to defer proof that the model is faithful to the implementation to a later stage of software development.

A second limitation of our approach in general is that it does not deal with threads. However, it is not a major problem here because the processing operated by the SMTP receiver part of the mail server is confined to a single thread.

A last limitation that applies to formal verification in general is that there may be bugs in the specifications we write and in the tools we use (although here we only need to trust the smaller proof checker of Coq).

5.2 Lessons Learned

The main lesson is taught by results in Sect. 4: formal verification of system softwares is feasible (although proofs may become tedious) and useful (since it may uncover errors).

Another lesson is the practical importance of proof modularity because it decreases the size of proofs and facilitates their maintenance. The following two examples illustrate those points.

Reusable lemmas allow for shorter proofs. In the case of the model discussed in Sect. 3.1, when we know that the execution of a sequence of two statements ends up with a success, we may need to show that there is an intermediate successful state. It is possible to unfold objects of the formalization to directly exhibit this state, but it is shorter to use the following lemma:

> Lemma *lem_seq_succ1*:
> $$(v:Result)(g:STATE{\rightarrow}Result)(st:STATE)$$
> $$(seq\ v\ g)=(succ\ st){\rightarrow}$$
> $$(EX\ st1:STATE\ |$$
> $$(EX\ st2:STATE\ |$$
> $$v=(succ\ st1) \wedge (g\ st2)=(succ\ st) \wedge (eqstate\ st1\ st2))).$$

Changes in the actual code base must be reflected in the model; by encapsulating details that are susceptible to change in lemmas, we facilitate maintenance of proofs. For instance, when we know that a call to the *do_helo* function (the Coq counterpart of the Java do_helo method, see Fig. 3 and 6) is successful, we may need to show that the HELO command is well-formed or that addresses of recipients are unchanged. It is possible to unfold objects to exhibit directly those properties but the proof would have to be modified whenever the body of the *do_helo* is changed. In contrast, the proof may not need to be changed if we use the following lemma:

> Lemma *lem_do_helo*:
> $$(s:String)(st:STATE)(b:bool)(st':STATE)$$
> $$(do\_helo\ s\ st)=(Succ\ bool\ b\ st'){\rightarrow}$$
> $$((is\_nullstr\ s)=(negb\ b) \wedge (fwd\_paths\ st)=(fwd\_paths\ st')).$$

Another lesson is the practical importance of support for dealing with redundancies in proofs. Indeed, the proofs made here involve many similar case analyses which are unfortunately difficult to automate with Coq.

A last lesson is that our difficulty to deal with threads emphasizes the importance of proof systems for concurrent programs.

6 Related Work

There are few experiments of verification of existing programs using theorem proving. Most work targets idealized subparts: verification of stripped down algorithms (e.g., [8]), verification of properties of network protocols (e.g., [9]), verification of compilers for languages subsets (e.g., [2]), etc.

Pierce and Vouillon specify a file synchronizer and prove its properties [11] with Coq. The model for file synchronization is a function that takes two possibly inconsistent trees of files as input and outputs a single, 'synchronized' one. In comparison, a mail server is more difficult to model because it is a reactive program dealing with multiple entities communicating by means of messages. Intents are also different: we write our model in order to match the actual code base whereas they do it for the purpose of generating an idealized implementation.

Thttpd is a freely available http daemon that puts an emphasis on security [7]. Black and Windley discuss inference rules of the axiomatic semantics of C with the aim of mechanically verifying a small version (100 lines of C source code) of thttpd [4] with a theorem prover. Verification has been eventually achieved by Black in his Ph.D. thesis [3]. In contrast, we avoid the burden of formalizing such a semantics thanks to a program transformation that allows us to handle a larger program, independently of the implementation language.

Filliâtre [10] studies certification of imperative programs in type theory. One of his achievement is a Coq tactic that generates proof obligations given a program written in some imperative language. The underlying machinery actually makes use of a transformation to an intermediate functional representation using effects and monads. This is reminiscent of the manual transformation we perform here and indicates that it can be automated to a certain extent. However, full automation requires to overcome several difficulties such as non-determinism and general recursion as discussed at the end of section 3.1.

There are several implementation of mail servers. In particular, Dan Bernstein wrote qmail [1] with security and reliability in mind. For instance, qmail's so-called 'straight-paper path' philosophy ensures that accepted mails cannot be lost by design, which corresponds to our reliability property.

Model checking is another well-established approach to verification of system softwares [6]. In the case of a mail server, complex data manipulation is a source of state explosion that makes it not immediate to apply model checking techniques. Of course, it is possible to handle model checking of even infinite state systems by using, for instance, abstraction techniques (e.g., [5]). However, such an approach leads us away from the faithful code transformation we also think is important here. This is the reason that makes us prefer theorem proving to model checking in this paper.

7   Conclusion

In this paper, we report an experiment of verification of the SMTP receiver part of the secure mail system. Such a verification is very important from the viewpoint of security and challenging because of the size of the application. The verification is carried out by the Coq theorem prover. Our approach is to translate manually the actual code base written in Java into a model written in the Coq language. The techniques we use ensure that the verification of the model substitutes for the verification of the actual code base. Then we specify the correctness properties using inductive predicates and prove them mechanically in Coq. Although much effort and care is needed to write proofs, results attest that our approach is feasible and useful in practice, since errors in the actual code base were indeed found during verification.

The verification is in progress. We now have to verify the rest of the mail server (in particular the SMTP sender part, but also some procedures such as parsing whose correctness has been taken for granted). Eventually, we would like to prove formally the correspondence between the Java code and the Coq function, so as to overcome one major limitation of our approach. Concerning applicability to other system softwares, a solution should be devised to handle concurrency. More broadly speaking, the size of proofs in our experiment indicates that our approach to formal verification may become unreasonably tedious. In such situations, a combination of theorem proving and model checking may be worth exploring.

Acknowledgements. The authors are grateful to Kenjiro Taura for providing the source code with detailed explanations and suggestions about verification.

References

1. D. Bernstein and various contributors. The qmail home page. http://www.qmail.org.
2. Y. Bertot. A certified compiler for an imperative language. Technical Report RR-3488, INRIA, Sep. 1998.
3. P. E. Black. *Axiomatic Semantics Verification of a Secure Web Server*. PhD thesis, Department of Computer Science, Brigham Young University, Feb. 1998.
4. P. E. Black and P. J. Windley. Inference rules for programming languages with side effects in expressions. In J. von Wright, J. Grundy, and J. Harrison, editors, *Theorem Proving in Higher Order Logics*, volume 1125 of *Lecture Notes in Computer Science*, pages 51–60. Springer-Verlag, August 1996.
5. E. M. Clarke, O. Grumberg, and D. E. Long. Model checking and abstraction. *ACM Transactions on Programming Languages and Systems*, 16(5):1512–1542, September 1994.
6. E. M. Clarke and J. M. Wing. Formal methods: state of the art and future directions. *ACM Computing Surveys*, 28(4):626–643, 1996.
7. F. B. Cohen. Why is thttpd secure? Available at http://www.all.net/journal/white/whitepaper.html.
8. T. N. Dieter Nazareth. Formal verification of algorithm W: The monomorphic case. In J. von Wright, J. Grundy, and J. Harrison, editors, *Theorem Proving in Higher Order Logics*, volume 1125 of *Lecture Notes in Computer Science*, pages 331–345. Springer-Verlag, Aug. 1996.
9. B. Dutertre and S. Schneider. Using a PVS embedding of CSP to verify authentication protocols. In A. F. Elsa L. Gunter, editor, *Theorem Proving in Higher Order Logics*, volume 1275 of *Lecture Notes in Computer Science*, pages 121–136. Springer-Verlag, Aug. 1997.
10. J.-C. Filliâtre. *Preuve de programmes impératifs en théorie des types*. PhD thesis, Université Paris-Sud, Jul. 1999. Available at http://www.lri.fr/~filliatr/ftp/publis/these.ps.gz.

11. B. C. Pierce and J. Vouillon. Specifying a file synchronizer (full version). Draft, Mar. 2002.

12. J. B. Postel. Rfc 821: Simple mail transfer protocol. Available at http://www.faqs.org/rfcs/rfc821.html, Aug. 1982.

13. E. Shibayama, S. Hagihara, N. Kobayashi, S. Nishizaki, K. Taura, and T. Watanabe. AnZenMail: A secure and certified e-mail system. In M. Okada, B. Pierce, A. Scedrov, H. Tokuda, and A. Yonezawa, editors, *Proceedings of International Symposium on Software Security, Keio University, Tokyo, Japan (Nov. 2002)*, Lecture Notes in Computer Science. Springer-Verlag, Feb. 2003.

14. The Coq Development Team. The Coq proof assistant reference manual. Available at http://coq.inria.fr/doc/main.html, 2002.

15. P. Wadler. Monads for functional programming. In M. Broy, editor, *Marktoberdorf Summer School on Program Design Calculi*, volume 118 of *NATO ASI Series F: Computer and systems sciences*. Springer-Verlag, Aug. 1992. Also in J. Jeuring and E. Meijer, editors, Advanced Functional Programming, Springer Verlag, LNCS 925, 1995. Some errata fixed August 2001.

Design and Implementation of Security System Based on Immune System

Hiroyuki Nishiyama and Fumio Mizoguchi

Information Media Center, Science University of Tokyo.
Noda, Chiba, 278-8510, Japan
{nisiyama, mizo}@ia.noda.tus.ac.jp

Abstract. We design a network security system using an analogy of natural world immunology. We adopt an immune mechanism that distinguishes self or non-self and cooperation among immune cells of the system. This system implements each immune cell as an agent based on our multiagent language, which is an extension of concurrent logic programming languages. These agents can detect and reject intrusion by cooperating with each other.

1 Introduction

Recently, research on security systems for preventing intrusion into a computer via a network has become increasingly important with the spread of the Internet. In this research, we focus on methods for detecting illegal intrusion by analyzing log information collected in packets that flow on a network or the individual computer [2,7,9,12]. However, there are many problems, such as detecting an unknown intrusion, the system load, and system protection after detection. Furthermore, many developed systems already provide security from intrusion, such as firewalls. Protection from internal attack has generally not been considered.

We have therefore conducted research encompassing the immune system of the natural world that protects the body from viruses to address such problems. Forrest et al. incorporated an immune system mechanism that detects the "self" or "non-self" into a network security system [3]. By generating two or more detectors that attack only "non-self," they succeeded in detecting known and strange intrusions and thus protecting files. However, the target of detection was specific log information, as in conventional systems. This differs from the approach of detecting intrusion by combining various information. Hofmeyr et al. designed an artificial immune system (ARTIS) and applied it to a network security system for 50 computers [6]. However, they did not consider cooperation among immunity components, and individual computers detected intrusions.

In our research, we focused on a mechanism for detecting and rejecting the non-self through cooperation among the cells in an immune system. Following this approach, we designed a security system consisting of different kinds of immunity cell agents. These immunity cell agents are generated dynamically by recognizing an access via the network, and individually gather information on a

M. Okada et al. (Eds.): ISSS 2002, LNCS 2609, pp. 234–248, 2003.
© Springer-Verlag Berlin Heidelberg 2003

network or process level in the computer. The agents detect an illegal intruder as non-self by exchanging information with each other. When an immunity agent of an observed network level detects an intruder as non-self, the agent cooperates with other immunity agents of the observed process level. These agents then remove all files and processes executed by the intrusion identified as non-self.

By using our multiagent language MRL [10] to implement this system, we were able to dynamically generate and delete each immunity agent and achieve parallel execution and communication among agents. Using these features, we built an immunity security system that responds dynamically to all internal or external accesses and file operations.

The paper is organized as follows. Section 2 explains the immunity system mechanism. Section 3 introduces some previous research on immunity-based security systems. Section 4 presents an immunity-based security system based on a super-distribution system. Section 5 describes our multiagent immunity-based security system and the mechanisms for detecting and excluding illegal intrusion by cooperation between immune agents. Section 6 describes an implementation example and Sections 7 and 8 present related works and the conclusions.

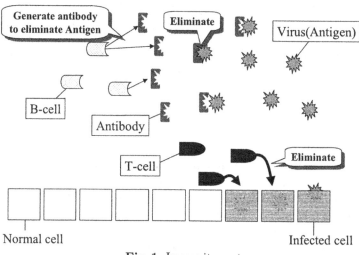

Fig. 1. Immunity system

2   Immunity System

An immunity system distinguishes self and non-self inside the body and eliminates the non-self [11]. In this system, two kinds of cells, "B-cells" and "T-cells," eliminate the non-self objects as shown in the figure 1.

All immunity cells are lymphocyte cells generated from a single atomic cell called a hematopoietic stem cell. The cell of the bone marrow origin is called

"B-cell," and the cell of the Thymus origin is called "T-cell." About two trillion lymphocyte cells constitute man's immunity system, of which 20 to 30% are B-cells and about 70% are T-cells.

2.1   B-Cell

A B-cell generates antibodis that distinguishes the non-self protein called an "antigen," such as a virus, reacts with the antigen, and is eliminated. The B-cell itself does not have the capability to eliminate antigens. However, a B-cell has an antibody molecule like an antenna on the surface of the cell, and the antibody corresponding to the antigen is compounded in large quantities by catching an antigen with the antenna. The B-cell is capable of memorizing the distinguished antigen then generating many antibodies in a short time if an antigen is distinguished again (secondary immunoreaction).

2.2   T-Cell

A T-cell distinguishes a self cell that is deteriorated by the antigen as non-self and eliminates it. A T-cell is generated in the thymus where it is strictly educated to discriminate self and non-self. Specifically, the T-cell is severely tested within the thymus and programmed to die. A few T-cells that only distinguish the self were converted into non-self and do not destroy the self itself, can go away besides thymus. Forrest et al. conducted research on security that focused on the educational function of this thymus. Their research enables detecting strange illegal entry (non-self), without infringing on regular access (self) [3].

2.3   Natural Immunity

In addition to the above-mentioned B-cells and T-cells, the body also contains an immunity cell called natural immunity (Natural killer cell: NK-cell). This immunity cell is not generated after being educated like a T-cell, but exists in "nature" beforehand. In particular, this cell has a function that distinguishes and eliminates a cancer cell. Research conducted by Hanaoka et al. focused on this natural immunity. Detection of non-self is ensured by cooperating with the mechanism of the above-mentioned immunity cell [5].

2.4   Immunity System as a Super-Distribution System

These immunity cells are mutually activated by stimulating each other, and efficiently eliminate cells polluted by invasion of an antigen as well as the antigen itself. For example, if a T-cell detects a cell converted to non-self with the antigen, the T-cell will eliminate that cell and order the B-cell to generate the antibodies for quickly eliminating the antigen. Thus, an immunity system eliminates self cells polluted with the antigen from the outside and also eliminates the antigen itself as non-self. In this mechanism, the immunity cell group, which consists of some two trillion cells, cooperates with each other in super distribution.

As mentioned above, the immune system can distinguish and eliminate efficiently the intruder that entered the inside of the body, because some kinds of immune cells perform own task and cooperate with each other. In the feature of the immune system, a most important point is that not only the system can eliminate intruders in the stage of entering, but also the system can eliminate and restore the infected cell when the intruders entered the body and infected some cells. This means that an immune system is premised on the intruder. This system enables man to survive also in an inferior environment. We paid our attention to the robustness and toughness of such an immune system in network security. Especially the mechanism of cooperation with the immunity cells can distinguish an intruder and an infected cell that are hard to be distinguished by one immunity cell, and after distinguishing, the mechanism can eliminate efficiently intruders and cells. These cooperation mechanisms are effective in the intrusion detection and specification of an intrusion route for the network security.

3   Previous Research on Immunity-Based Security System

Unlike conventional computer security, the immunity model of Forrest et al. [3] does not detect intrusion by matching with previously stored invasion patterns. This model generates a unique pattern of an illegal entry and enables detection of an illegal intrusion. The intrusion pattern randomly generates a candidate pattern consisting of combinations of some actions. Next, an action set of self is matched with this candidate pattern. If one portion of the action set is matched, the candidate will be regarded as a "self" action and will be canceled. Conversely, if not matched, the candidate is used as a detector (illegal intrusion pattern) of "non-self." To detect an intruder, all the generated patterns are checked for matches when action by the user through the network has been recognized. When a pattern is matched, it will be judged to be non-self. The validity was demonstrated using this model to a system call, the packet information on TCP, etc. [1][6][4]. However, a system administrator, i.e., human being, should make a final judgment since a regular user may be included in an action judged to be non-self.

The immunity model developed by Hanaoka et al. [5] corrects and improves the model of Forrest et al. This model introduced the natural immunity of an immunity system into the model of Forrest and eliminated clear non-self before detection by the T-cell. This performs matching to the intrusion pattern used as known in the illegal intrusion detection already studied, and makes it possible to eliminate a clearly illegal intrusion beforehand. Moreover, this model uses evaluation criteria, such as reliability and accuracy, in matching to generate and detect the intrusion pattern. Using this model, the human need only judge situations at the boundary of non-self and self, so it becomes possible to significantly reduce the system administrator's burden. However, intrusion detection on a LAN is not considered. Therefore, it is difficult to specify the intrusion course and files altered by the illegal intrusion.

4   Immunity System Security Based on a Super-Distribution System

The immunity models of Forrest et al. and Hanaoka et al focused only on the T-cell function. In contrast, our research designs a security system for all the computers on a LAN while incorporating functions of both a T-cell and a B-cell.

The human immunity system is a super-distribution system consisting of an immunity cell group and performs intrusion detection and exclusion efficiently because the immunity cells cooperate. Our research emulates such a distributed system and cooperation mechanism to efficiently detect and exclude illegal intrusion.

4.1   Application to Security

When an immunity system concept is applied to computer security, "self" means access and a file created regularly by a regular user. In the non-self, antigens eliminated by B-cells are accesses by illegal intruders and viruses; deteriorated self cells eliminated by the T-cell are files (processes) that are executed irregularly. A cell recognizing access by an illegal intruder will eliminate the process executed by the access. If the cell incorrectly identifies the process performed, the cell will consider that access that executed from the access is an "antigen." Using the feature of secondary immunoreaction, a cell can immediately eliminate a reappearing illegal intruder. In the human immune system, B-cells are generated by bone marrow, and T-cells, by the thymus. Since antigens, such as viruses and bacteria, intrude from all bodily portions, the immune cell is always patrolling inside the body. In contrast, in network security, antigens, such as an illegal intruder or a computer virus, intrude through a single passage called a network cable. Therefore, in order to protect a computer, it is necessary to watch the passage connected with the computer and to watch only the files operated upon or executed by commands flowing through the passage.

4.2   Functions for Immunity System

In order to realize the above immune security system, we must control distribution and cooperation of B-cells and T-cells. For that purpose, we need the following functions.

(1) A function that acts like a B-cell to watch the connection from the exterior.
(2) A function that acts like a T-cell to watch the ongoing process.
(3) A function that dynamically generates and deletes B-cells and T-cells.
(4) A function that exchanges performance information between cells.

Here, when a connection is received from an external computer through a network, the external IP address and external port number of the computer are specified for every connection. Therefore, a B-cell is generated from (3) by receiving every access from other computers. The generated B-cell watches the message received from an accessing computer. Moreover, when the access performs an operation on a file (process), (2) a T-cell is generated for every file (process). Each immune cell will individually collect the information that should be processed. Furthermore, each immune cell exchanges information with every message being received or file being executed, and cooperates in detecting non-self objects. When a non-self object is detected, each immune cell cuts the connection with the illegal intrusion or eliminates the illegal file (process). At this time, T-cells and B-cells can continuously eliminate non-self objects by communicating between themselves. For example, when an illegal intrusion occurs, all file operations that the intruder performed are distinguished as non-self objects. Conversely, when a file is executed without authorization, T-cells and B-cells also continuously distinguish the connection that performed the operation as a non-self object.

In this research, we define the role of each immune cell as either a "B-cell" agent or a "T-cell" agent and design the immune security system using the multiagent concept.

5 Design of Immune Multiagent Security System

In order to realize computer security based on an immune system, we must model distribution and cooperation for processes. In this research, we extend the multiagent language MRL [10] designed based on a parallel-logic programming language and apply it to implementing an immunity-based security system. MRL features synchronization and asynchronous control as well as a stream communication function. MRL can thus realize parallel processing of agents, communicate with each agent, and dynamically generate and delete agents. We performed the following extension so that MRL could be applied to an immune security system.

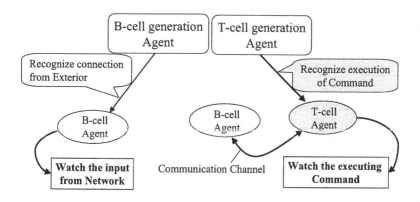

Fig. 2. Generating immune cell agents

- To specify the IP address and port number of a connecting computer, we incorporate a function to collect the information that flows into a computer through a network.
- In order to recognize execution of a new file from the outside, we incorporate a function to watch the file (process) being executed within a computer.

In this way, we define the function of the immune cell described in the previous paragraph as an individual agent and achieve cooperation between immune cells as cooperation between agents.

In addition to the immune cell agents, the following agents are necessary.

- B-cell generation (Bone marrow) agent
  When a connection from outside is recognized, this agent generates a B-cell agent that watches the input.
- T-cell generation (Thymus) agent
  When a new file (process) is detected as being performed from the outside, the thymus agent generates a T-cell agent that watches the file (process).

In order to realize such an immunity cell agent's function, in this research, the network-monitoring tool that monitors the information that flows into a computer via the network, and the process monitoring tool that monitors the processing in a computer are individually developed using the function extended to MRL. By using these tools, each agent is individually generated by execution of a new process or by a new access through the network, and monitors the process or access. In our model, generated cell agent sets are defined as follows.

$$G_B = b\_cell_1, b\_cell_2, ..., b\_cell_m$$

$$G_T = t\_cell_1, t\_cell_2, ..., t\_cell_n$$

Each cell agent model is as follows.

B-cell agent.

$$b\_cell_i(AccessInfo, AccessLog, Rule, Channel)$$

- *AccessInfo* ... Information to monitor accesses, such as an IP address of a partner computer and a port number. This information is received from a network monitoring tool.
- *AccessLog* ... Message information received from the candidate for monitoring.
- *Rule* ... The action rule base for detecting non-self.
- *Channel* ... The communication channel for recognizing self or non-self.

T-cell agent.

$$t\_cell_j(ProcInfo, ProcLog, Rule, Cha, B_{cell}ID)$$

- *ProcInfo* ... Information in the process for monitoring, such as Process ID and parent process ID. This information is received from a process-monitoring tool.
- *ProcLog* ... Information of the performed process
- *Rule* ... The action rule base for detecting non-self.
- *Channel* ... The communication channel for recognizing self or non-self.
- $B_{cell}ID$ ... B-cell agent's ID code connected with itself

Channel is a communication channel currently shared among two or more related immunity-cell agents. When an illegal intrusion from an individual is detected, all the immunity cell agents that monitor behavior of the individual distinguish it as non-self through this communication channel.

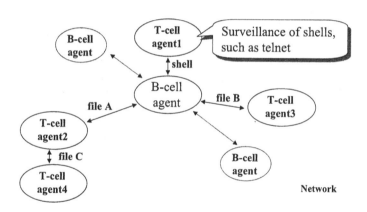

Fig. 3. Connection between immune agents

5.1 Connection between Immune Agents

All T-cell agents will be related to one of the B-cell agents in the generation process. For example, when files A and B are executed from a connecting access watched by a B-cell agent, the T-cell agents (No. 2 and No. 3) that watch each file are generated in Fig. 3. Moreover, when file C is executed during execution of file A, a T-cell is generated to watch file C. The relation of the parent process and child process in the T-cell agent that monitors these processes is realized as shown in Fig. 3. In this figure, the access from a user (user ID : $user\_1$) and its behavior are expressed as the following immunity-cell agent sets.

$$G_{B_{user\_1}} = b\_cell_1, b\_cell_2, b\_cell_3$$

$$G_{T_{user\_1}} = t\_cell_1, t\_cell_2, t\_cell_3, t\_cell_4$$

When two or more users $(user\_1, ..., user_k)$ exist in a LAN, the immunity cell agent group in the LAN is expressed as follows.

$$G_B = G_{B_{user\_1}}, ..., G_{B_{user\_k}}$$

$$G_T = G_{T_{user\_1}}, ..., G_{T_{user\_k}}$$

In each user's B-cell and T-cell agent set, a communication channel *Channel* common at the time of an agent's generation is assigned.

Thus, in this system, all the processes continuously performed by external operation can be monitored as a set of a T-cell agent. Furthermore, when this system was mounted on each computer and an intruder accessed a computer via some other computers, it is also possible to specify the access course by the relation between B-cell agents. Communication between the immunity cells in nature is performed by the signal transfer molecule called "cytokine." This communication of information is not broadcast to all immunity cells, but local communication of information is performed. The transfer is subsequently stimulated, the immunity cells are activated, and the non-self is eliminated. In our research, when a non-self is distinguished, the local message is transmitted and received through communication channel *Channel* among the immunity cell agents of figure 3 in order to eliminate all non-self in a network. The non-self is thus attacked (rejected) by the immunity-cell agent by considering the received message as a stimulus.

5.2   Detecting and Excluding Illegal Intrusion by Cooperation between Agents

Each agent receives information about the watched accesses or files and judges whether a cell is a self or non-self by referring to a rule base. Although this function is the same as that of conventional security systems, it is very difficult to specify an illegal intrusion based only on log information. Therefore, questionable accesses are also designated as detection targets in conventional systems, and final judgment is entrusted to the human administrator to whom the results are reported.

In contrast, when our system distinguishes a questionable access, it cooperates with other agents who are collecting information of a different kind. The truth is thus checked, and it is possible to eliminate illegal intrusion as "non-self" (refer to Fig. 4).

When a T-cell agent is generated in this system, the generating agent establishes a new communication channel with the generated agent. This means that an independent communication channel is established between all the T-cells generated from a B-cell agent. If an agent distinguished as a non-self is found at least once in the hierarchically built immune cell agents, all operations

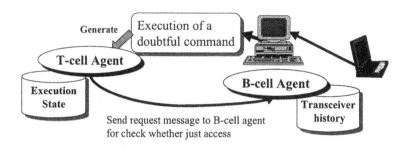

Fig. 4. Detection of non-self through cooperation between immune cell agents

will be distinguished as non-self by broadcasting through the communication channel between connected agents. For example, if a non-self is detected during the surveillance of file C operation in figure 3, execution of files A and B will be distinguished as non-self, and the access from a B-cell agent will be further distinguished as non-self. Thereby, each file execution is interrupted and deleted, and the connection is intercepted. Furthermore, this intrusion method and the method of executing a file are recorded in a non-self judge and are utilized to create rules for a new intrusion pattern.

As mentioned above, our proposed immune security system has the following features.

- Response to a dynamic illegal intrusion is also possible.
  Whenever a new surveillance target is found while preparing the generator for each cell, each cell agent is generated dynamically.
- Efficient rejection of an illegal intrusion is also possible.
  This system can express behavior of an intruder as a connected agent group. All agents in a group can thus recognize the fact by either of the agents detecting illegal intrusion. Thereby, all of the processes that the intruder is performing or has performed are eliminated without affecting other users.
- Cooperative detection of the illegal intrusion is also possible.
  In this system, illegal intruders are detected easily by cooperation between each cell agent. Although conventional systems warn an administrator (human), this system is implemented using other agents. This system can thus detect illegal intrusion by cooperation between agents, without going through a human operator.

By combining these features, we can build security systems that automatically detect and reject intrusions.

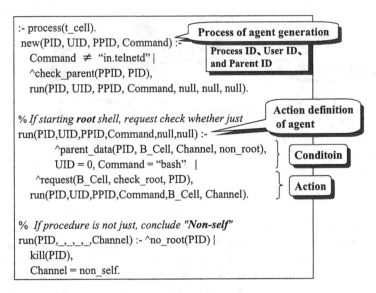

Fig. 5. T-cell agent program

6   Example of Implementation

We mounted the immune security system on a UNIX computer, performed an illegal access to the root directory on the computer, and experimented with the ability of our system to detect and reject the intrusion.

In the experiment, we assume a common user's password has been stolen and that an intruder performs an illegal access to the root directory by overflow hacking.

In the invasion process, a T-cell agent is commissioned to perform surveillance of the process of the root directory (the process ID is 0). This agent requests a check of whether the B-cell agent performed a formal procedure (refer to Fig. 4). The B-cell agent that received the request refers to the transceiver history, and checks whether the formal input for this user acquiring the authority to access the root directory was performed. When the result is negative, the B-cell agent reports the fact to the T-cell agent. The T-cell agent thus concludes that the access is by a non-self and deletes the accessing process. Furthermore, since the processes that the user is performing are expressed by this system as an agent group as in Fig. 3, those processes and connections will be intercepted.

6.1   T-Cell Agent Program

MRL can describe this T-cell agent program as shown in Fig. 5. First, when a T-cell agent is generated (when a **new** predicate is executed), the agent receives information on its own process ID (PID), user ID (UID), parent process ID (PPID) and the command name. This agent then sends a message **check_parent** to the

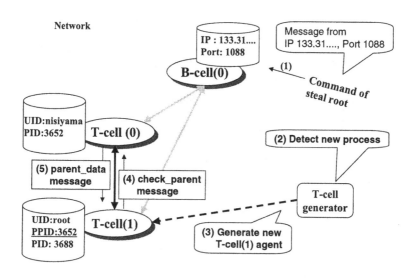

Fig. 6. Flow of detection and elimination (1)

T-cell agent of the parent process. In addition, this agent will have information of the B-cell agent and communication channel for judging whether self or non-self, but in the beginning, this information is `null`.

An agent operation is defined as a `run` predicate. In Fig. 5, the first `run` predicate is executed when the agent receives message `parent_data` from a T-cell agent of the parent process and its own `UID` is 0 (this means that the authority of the watching process is root). Here, the information received from the agent of a parent process is the discernment code (`B_Cell`) of the B-cell agent relevant to starting a parent process, and a communication channel (`Emergent`) for judging whether self or non-self. This channel is shared by all the cell agents in a group. The last `non_root` means that the parent process does not have root authority. When these conditions are satisfied, root authority is possessed although the authority of the parent process is not root. The B-cell agent thus sends a `request` message to (`B_Cell`), and checks whether a regular procedure has been performed.

The second `run` predicate describes the processing when an answer is received from a requesting agent. Here, the `no_root` message, which shows that a regular procedure was not performed, is received. As a result, this predicate forces processing of its PID to terminate `kill` and inputs `non_self` into the communication channel `Emergent` for judging whether self or non-self. In this way, non-self information will spread to all the agents in the same group that share this communication channel.

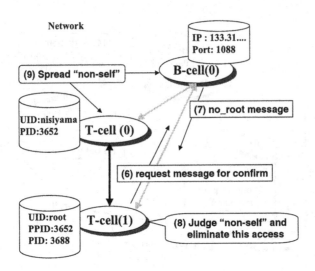

Fig. 7. Flow of detection and elimination (2)

6.2   Execution Result

Using the algorithm of Fig.5, we conducted an experiment to detect and eliminate an illegal intruder who steals root authority. We used "vixie-crontab3.0.1"
which steals root authority by overflow hacking to Redhat Linux as an example
of an illegal intrusion tool. After this tool is executed on account of a general
user who stole authority beforehand, the tool can create a shell of a root by
logging in the special user name.

Fig. 6 and Fig. 7 are flow of detection and elimination of the intruder. It
assumes that a shell (process ID:3652) that $t\_cell(0)$ monitors is performed on
the previously stolen general user account. The intruder logins special user name
"cronexpl" on this shell, and inputs the password ((1) in Fig. 6). (These messages
are recorded by the B-cell agent $(b\_cell(0))$) . The shell of a new root will thus be
started. This system then detects starting of the new process (process ID:3688)
with a process-monitoring tool ((2) in Fig. 6), and generates a new T-cell agent
$(t\_cell(1))$ ((3) in Fig. 6). Generated $t\_cell(1)$ receives the user ID of its own
parent process ((4) and (5) in Fig. 6), and the related B-cell agent's $(b\_cell(0))$
information.

Next, T-cell agent $t\_cell(1)$ recognizes that its own user ID is a root and
its parents' user ID is not a root, and applies the first run predicate of Fig.5.
The $t\_cell(1)$ then requests the check of whether the procedure for acquiring a
root was performed for B-cell agent $b\_cell(0)$ ((6) in Fig. 7). The $b\_cell(0)$ judges
whether a procedure needed from its own message log to obtain a root was
performed, and answers the requesting agent in a message that the procedure
has not been executed ((7) in Fig. 7). The $t\_cell(1)$ that received this answer,

applies the second *run* predicate of Fig.5. Consequently, the $t\_cell(1)$ judges the process as "non-self" and rejects the process ((8) in Fig. 7). Moreover, the judgment of "non-self" is propagated through the shared variable *Channel*. T-cell agent $t\_cell(0)$ that monitors the parent process and related B-cell agent $b\_cell(0)$ are judged as non-self ((9) in Fig. 7), and the shell and access are rejected. Although a specific illegal intrusion tool was used in this experiment, it is possible to eliminate the illegal access to the root authority using only the same methods and the rule of figure 5 in this system.

As mentioned above, this system detects and rejects illegal intrusion by cooperation between immune-cell agents using the recognition mechanism of self or non-self possessed by an immune system.

7   Related Work

Forrest et al. realized a network security system based on an immunity system [6]. However, they did not reference cooperation with immune cells, so each detector in the system performs intrusion detection independently. Moreover, if a human administrator manages the situation after detection based on the number of targets in a computer and the access situation, the burden will become excessive. Our multiagent immune system incorporates a mechanism for sharing information and cooperation between agents, and for automating cooperative detection and exclusion.

Taguchi et al. proposed detecting and tracing an intruder by a mobile agent that can be generated dynamically [12]. However, the log information used as the mark type is single, and the solution after detection is not mentioned. In our proposal, the log information for supervision differs for each kind of immune agent. Agents thus achieve cooperative detection and efficient exclusion by cooperating with each other.

Lane et al. proposed a user distinction method that can discover the similarity of a command sequence by machine learning [7]. We are also conducting research on automatic generation of the rule base of the intruder by machine learning [8]. Our work combines our immune multi-agent system and a learning mechanism in order to detect a strange intrusion.

8   Conclusion

We built a system to detect and reject illegal intrusion using security technology similar to the flexible structure of an immune system. We applied the recognition mechanism of self and non-self objects of an immune system and cooperation among immune cells. We were thus able to realize a security system that automatically detects and eliminates illegal intrusion from inside or outside.

References

1. J. Balthrop, S. Forrest and M. Glickman, Revisiting LISYS: Parameters and Normal Behavior, *Proceedings of the 2002 Congress on Evolutionary Computation* (in press).
2. W. DuMouchel, Computer intrusion detection based on Bay es Factors for comparing command transition probabilities, *National Institut e of Statistical Sciences Technical Report*, 1999.
3. S. Forrest, S. A. Hofmeyr and A. Somayaji, Computer Immunology, *Communications of the ACM*, Vol. 40, No. 10, pp. 88–96, 1997.
4. S. Forrest, A.S. Perelson, L. Allen and R. Cherukuri, Self-Nonself Discrimination in a Computer, *In Proceedings of the 1994 IEEE Symposium on Research in Security and Privacy*, 1994.
5. Yumiko Hanaoka, Goichiro Hanaoka and Hideki Imai, Artificial Immune System: A New Model of Anomaly Detection and Its Methods of Implementation, Computer Security Symposium 2000, pp. 231–236, 2000.
6. S. A. Hofmeyr and S. Forrest, Architecture for an artificial immune system, *Evolutionary Computation*, 7(1), pp. 45–68, 2000.
7. T. Lane and C. E. Brodley, Temporal Sequence Learning and Data Reduction for Anomaly Detection, *ACM Transactions on Information and System Security*, 2(3), pp. 295–331, 1999.
8. Fumio Mizoguchi, Anomaly Detection Using Visualization and Machine Learning, *Proc. of the Ninth IEEE International Workshops on Enabling Technologies: Infrastructure for Collaborative Enterprises (Workshop: Enterprise Security)*, pp. 165–170, 2000.
9. Peter G. Neumann and Phillip A. Porras, Experience with EMERALD to DATE, *Usenix Workshop on Intrusion Detecion*, 1999.
10. H. Nishiyama, H. Ohwada and F. Mizoguchi, A Multiaget Robot Language for Communication and Concurrency Control, *International Conference on Multiagent Systems*, pp. 206–213, 1998.
11. Tomio Tada, Semantics of immunology (in Japanease), Seidosha, 1993.
12. A. Taguchi, et al, The Study and Implementation for Tracing Intruder by Mobile Agent, and Intrusion Detection using Marks, *Proc. of the 1999 Synposium on Cryptography and Information Security*, pp. 627–632, 1999.

Design and Implementation of Access Control System for Smart Office Environment

Wataru Yamazaki and Fumio Mizoguchi

Information Media Center, Tokyo University of Science.
Noda, Chiba, 278-8510, Japan
{yamazaki, mizo}@imc.tus.ac.jp

Abstract. In recent years, electric devices are increasingly being connected to networks. Reflecting this trend, researchers are actively investigating how to control these devices from a network and which combinations of devices provide a user with optimum services. We call the environment produced by such networking a smart office. Such an environment primarily focuses on service or connection methods. However, security in a smart office is important, yet has not been sufficiently discussed. This issues include relations between devices and users, and changing environments and users. In order to solve these problems, we built a security system using role-based access control (RBAC) as the base. RBAC considers cases in which objects and users have a complex relations. In this paper, we present our system that provides not only access control of devices, but also provides access control of services.

1 Introduction

Because of the rapid spread of networks, electrical devices are increasingly being connected to networks. This includes not only PCs, but also appliances such as TVs, refrigerators, and microwave ovens that are being connected to networks in our homes and offices.

Many researchers are actively investigating how to control these devices from a network and which combinations of devices provide a user with optimum services. Such services offer greater comforts to users.

We call the environment produced by such networking a smart office (home). Such an environment primarily focuses on a service or the connection method [1][2]. However, security is also important and has not been sufficiently discussed. Generally, security in a smart office presents the following problems.

Authentication. Services may be accessed by users via an open network, so user authentication is required.

Semi-open environment. Some outside users or guests may share resources in a smart office environment, but not all users are trusted.

Complex relations. Relations between the number of devices and the number of users are complicated. If the number of devices and people using them increase, it will become difficult to accommodate them and securely manage

M. Okada et al. (Eds.): ISSS 2002, LNCS 2609, pp. 249–262, 2003.

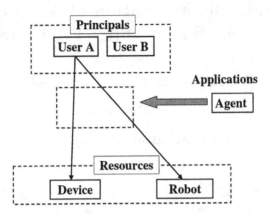

Fig. 1. Agent-based Service

access rights to the devices. This can be seen as a problem of the scalability in access control.

Dynamic execution. The environment and users change often. In an environment containing many physical devices, the number of devices may increase or decrease frequently. Moreover, to control devices, we have to consider about the exclusive control. These problems relate to the dynamic configuration in controlling devices.

Agent-based controlling. Users must access services via agents, but don't control devices directly. Instead, users control agents and their services, and agents control devices. This arises from dynamic collaboration between devices and the necessity of the above dynamic execution.

The last two problems are peculiar to the smart office environment. Figure1 depicts the relation between agents and devices. Controlling a smart office is not so simple as changing a switch, like E-Commerce is not restricted just to the problem of delivering money. Smart office administrators have to consider agent-based applications and agent-based services.

In order to solve the above problems and satisfy the increasing demand, we built a security system using Role-Based Access Control (RBAC) [3][4] as the base. RBAC considers cases in which objects and users have a complicated relation. It is therefore suitable for the security of a smart office. However, the original RBAC is not capable of solving the above dynamic problems. In this paper, we designed a system that not only provides access control of devices but also provides services as a set of these devices. Some research on security in a smart office has already been conducted[5][6][7]. However, the devices to be used are selected statically, and systems are not sufficiently flexible for environmental changes.

In this paper, we propose an access control system that can perform dynamic execution such as exclusion control and static conventional access control like RBAC in a unified way.

The second section presents a brief overview of a smart office environment and its agents in the environment. In the third section, we analyze security issues in a smart office, and suggest security requirements. This is followed by a detailed scheme of the access control system and the agent interactions in the fourth section. In the fifth section, we briefly describe implementation considerations, then present the conclusions and discuss the direction of future work in the final section.

2   Smart Office

In our environment, various devices are connected to the network as shown in Figure2. Each device is connected to a workstation or PC. The devices that cannot use TCP/IP are set up to connect with a gateway. Users can therefore control these devices using TCP/IP protocols. Users normally do not control these devices directly. Instead, an agent provides a user with service and a system controls the devices. Thus, the systems (agents) unify and manage devices and offer services for users, and users access these devices through the agent.

A smart office environment consists of the following elements.

- Devices
  The devices are connected to the network. Users cannot control these devices directly.
- Agents
  Agents manage devices and provide users with services.
- Users
  Users must be distinguished for security.
- User interfaces (UIs)
  User interfaces include PCs, PDAs, Network computers (NCs), and IC cards.

Thus, since devices are controlled by agents and not users, systems can select appropriate devices, based on a user's request. Furthermore, the system is able to provide complex services by cooperation among many devices. The purpose of using agents is to provide services and easily reconfigurable systems based on user requests and profiles.

For example, a print-delivery agent monitors user printer jobs, picks up these papers from the printer and delivers the printed out papers to the user using other agents such as a delivering robot agent, manipulator agent, sensor agents, and camera robots.

In another example, the secretary agent (schedule agent) controls devices such as lights, screens, and blinds for the presentation schedule.

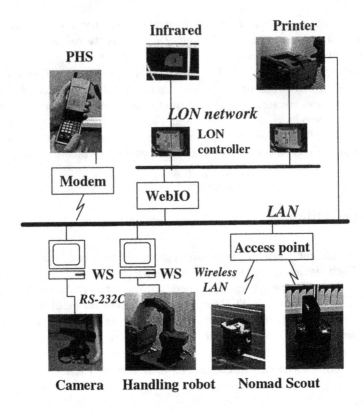

Fig. 2. SmartOffice Environment

2.1 Agent and Its Communication

Agents in a smart office cooperate with each other for achieving a complex task. In order for an agent to cooperate with other agents on a network, the agent needs to communicate to other agents what services are possible.

This communication method is called "Lookup service" in Jini[8] and "Advertisement" in JXTA[9]. In our environment, we call this "Service List." An agent receiving a service request from other agents, the agent will investigate whether the service is on a service list. If the service is on the service list, the agent has the ability to execute the service. To realize implementing cooperative services, other agents are interested only in a "task list" of agents and do not need to know other operational details and values.

A complicated service can be considered as a set of services of each agent and can be divided into simpler services in a layered structure. When our agent in the smart office cannot complete a service itself, it asks another agent to help. The composition of the agent at this time is determined dynamically. The devices used are constituted dynamically each time even when a user tries to repeat

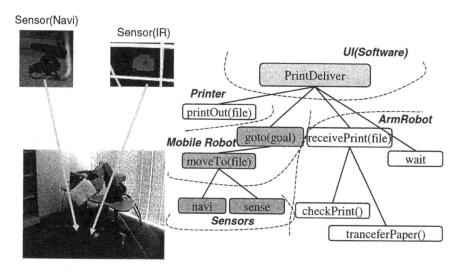

Fig. 3. Cooperation Task

the same task. This enables the system to flexibly cope with changes of the environment and users. Here we will describe the communication between agents in the previously mentioned print delivery service. As shown in Fig. 3, the devices used in the printer delivery system are the user's PC, a printer, a mobile robot, a camera robot that guides the mobile robot, an arm-type robot, various sensors, etc. The boundaries indicated by dotted lines in Figure3 delineate the task each agent performs. As shown in Figure3, the cooperative task has a hierarchical structure. Each agent holds and exhibits a list of services that it can offer. The service currently exhibited can be used by a user or other devices and their agents.

The agent's cooperative services and agent communications dynamically determine redundant services. For example, a system can dynamically determine an optimal robot from many such robots. It is also possible to configure environments composed of an arm-type robot is mounted on a move robot(integrated robot) or composed of separated robots as shown in Fig.3 offer the same service.

3   Analysis of Smart Office Security Requirements

In this section, we analyze the security system for the environment shown in the previous section. The importance of the access control in the security in smart office is first demonstrated by considering the fundamental concepts of authentication and authorization. Next, we will describe access control features for controlling physical devices. We will also illustrate access control for an agent and its services in a smart office environment. In the final part of this section, we present the access control requirements in a smart office environment.

3.1   Authentication and Authorization

There are two problems when controlling devices in a smart office: Who is the controller (authentication) and will he or she control devices appropriately (authorization)? These two points are very important for security in a smart office. Although confidentiality is very important in usual network security systems, it is less important than authentication and authorization in a smart office environment.

Authentication is widely used for network security. ID cards for entrance, fingerprints for computer access permission, PKI[10] and PGP[11] for E-mail clients, and WWW browsers are examples of authentication. By using X.509[12] certificates, we can confirm an entity in the open network. Communication using SSL protocol prevents a malicious entity from posing as another entity, preventing establishment of invalid sessions. Therefore, only valid users can control devices in a smart office environment.

Authorization is very important in a semi-open environment such as our smart office [5]. Existing authorization schemes include Discretionary Access Control (DAC)[13] Mandatory Access Control(MAC)[14], and Role-Based Access Control(RBAC) [3][4]. When access control is implemented through systems such as DAC and MAC, the relation between objects and users is very strict. In a smart office environment, the situation and status for a certain user may change dynamically, and it will be difficult to change access control policy to suit every situation.

RBAC is suitable under such conditions. RBAC prevents control by illegal access and mistakes by classifying a necessary minimum access right according to duty with a layered structure. Furthermore, the system can prevent invalid access caused by administrator error since it also simplifies management.

RBAC can be seen to function as a set of authorizations, and it is suitable for complex relations between users and devices. Therefore, we use RBAC as the base of our smart office access control system.

Two resource granting authority methods can be considered. In the first, the owner of a resource grants authority. In the second, authority can be granted by a centralized function.

3.2   Access Control for Controlling Devices in Smart Office

Here, we consider the access control for controlling devices after authentication and authorization. We assume that the access control in a smart office environment is managed by RBAC as shown in the previous part.

As we described in the previous section, there are many types of devices in a smart office environment. These devices can be classified into two categories according to the usage and intention of the user.

- Sharable Devices (Sensible). Sharable devices usually involve control that ends in a very short time like opening and closing a door, and turning electric lights on and off, and devices that only read information, without controlling (such as sensor systems)

– Exclusive Devices (Controllable). Exclusive devices do not allow simultaneous accesses from two or more users; such devices may control a robot or a camera and include devices controlled with a certain time length.

As mentioned above, all devices are classified, so the Access Control System must not only investigate whether the role has access rights to devices, but must also check if the device allows simultaneous access or not. The device is accessed by roles only when the role has access rights and when the device is controllable. This is the difference between an all-software access control system and an access control system in a smart office environment where many physical devices are used.

We can consider two situations for controlling a light. When we enter our room, we want to keep the switch turned on while we are in the room. In this case, we need exclusive control. In contrast, when we leave the room, we turn off the light but usually do not care if it remains off. In this case, the light may be sharable device.

3.3   Access Control for Services and Agents in a Smart Office

The service that an agent offers can also be classified into two parts: access with exclusive control and access without exclusive control. Therefore, it is necessary to investigate exclusive access and the right to access like a device to determine whether the role can be provided with a certain service. The difference between devices and services is the cooperative services performed by agent communication. Access control in such a situation is divided into two categories.

– Device-Based Access Control.
  In device-based access control, if the role uses hierarchical services, the role must have all access rights for each service. The role can only access devices related to the role even if the service names are the same. In this method, management cost becomes comparatively large but fine controlling according to the role or the profile becomes possible. This system is named in this way since the check of the final right to access is device.
– Service-Based Access Control.
  Service-based access control allows access only to services regardless of the agent performing the service if a role's service is performed. Management cost is very low, but fine management cannot be performed. An access control should consider only investigating whether a role can perform a top-level service and exclusion control of a device.

In the following section, RBAC is extended and defined as the above two access controls, and communication between agents is described in detail.

3.4   Security Requirements for a Smart Office

In this section, we analyze the security requirements in a smart office environment. The results are as follows.

– Only users with access rights can control the device.
  One of the most important security elements in a smart office environment
  is authorization. Persons without such authorization can neither access nor
  control devices.
– Control commands should be authenticated.
  After identifying that a user has the right of access, the system must authenticate the control command.
– The system must be flexible to change and updating.
  In the smart office environment, devices are expected to be added and deleted
  frequently. Therefore, the system needs to be flexible and capable of minimizing changes.
– Each system distributed in the environment must be able to cooperate correctly.
  Each distributed component must function correctly as part of the whole
  system by negotiating safety.

4   Access Control for Smart Office Systems

In this section, we will describe an access control system that fills the requirements presented in the previous section. First, we point out the problems of
basic RBAC in a smart office environment. We will then extend basic RBAC for
such an environment. Next, we will investigate agent communication based on
extended RBAC.

4.1   RBAC and Its Extension

The upper part of the Figure4 illustrates the original RBAC System.

In the original RBAC, a user is mapped by the role, and the role is mapped
with permission. In this method, a new user can be added to the environment
by simply describing the relation between the new user and his role. It is thus
easier to manage the access list than other access control system such as DAC
and MAC. However, the relations between user and role and between role and
permission are static. As shown in the previous section, RBAC is not appropriate
for smart offices where there are many devices of the same kind and therefore
many redundancies.

The bottom of Figure4illustrates our extended RBAC for a smart office environment. A user is mapped by the role in the same way as in the original RBAC
(i.e., this mapping is static). The difference in extended RBAC is that the objects
of roles are services and the services are abstract. The abstract services are not
connected to any agent at that time. This is just like the abstract class and interface in object-oriented programming languages. Abstract services mapped by
the role are static. Abstract services are dynamically bound to concrete services
using agent communication.

In Figure4, the services indicated by dotted lines are abstract services, and
those colored gray are concrete services managed by each agent. In Figure4, solid
lines indicate static mapping, and dotted lines indicate dynamic mapping.

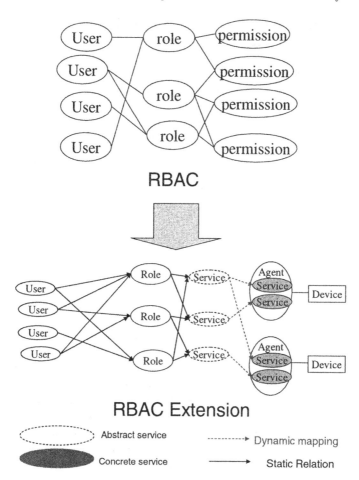

Fig. 4. RBAC for Smart Office

4.2 Agent Communication with Device-Based Access Control

Here, we describe how to add access control to an agent's communication when
the object a role accesses is a device(Device-Based Access Control). Figure 5
illustrates the flow of agent messages in such a situation This method is executed
in the following steps.

[**Step 1**] A user logs on to a system with a user name and password.

[**Step 2**] A user role is obtained.

[**Step 3**] A user requests a service to be performed.

[**Step 4**] The service request is broadcast to all agents. The message contains
at least the network address of the requesting agent, message ID, name of service
and its arguments, and role of the user. If cost is needed for dynamic agent

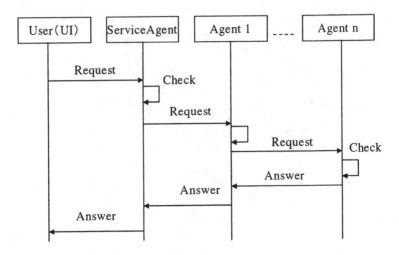

Fig. 5. Sequence Diagram of Agent Communication

selection, the cost for performing a task may also be included. In this case, the cost is initialized to 0.

[**Step 5**] An agent receiving the message checks whether the service is within its capability (i.e., on its service list). If the requested service is on the agent's service list, if the agent can currently provide the service, and if the role can control the device, the process will progress to step 6. Otherwise, it will end.

[**Step 6**] If it does not need another agent's help (service), the agent responds to the message of the requesting agent and indicates that a task can be performed. If a cost is required at this time, the cost for achieving the agent's service will be added to the current cost, and a message containing the new cost will be sent to the original requesting agent. When the agent needs another agents' service, the agent broadcasts the information about the service it needs as in step 5.

[**Step 7**] The agent that required another agent's help waits for a response messages until it times out. If a message does not arrive before it times out, it judges that this service cannot be offered and ends. One message is chosen when there are two or more messages. When the estimated cost is included, the minimum cost is chosen. The agent creates a new response and returns the new message with new cost to the requesting agent. If the requested agent is "user," go to step 8

[**Step 8**] Service is performed.

The method shown here investigates whether the role has the right to accesses all required devices. In this method, the service will be provided only if there are some possible combinations with the role among the composition of the devices for offering certainservice. The cost produced by this method is determined by application. We will not discuss the method that determines the cost here. The system can perform the optimum planning in the range given if a pertinent cost is set up.

4.3 Agent Communication with Service-Based Access Control

In this section, we describe service-based access control in the smart office. Unlike device-based access control in the foregoing paragraph, the object of a role is a service(Service-based Access Control). The method is the same as that of the device-based access control except for this point, so we will describe only the differing points. Steps 5 and 6 are changed. In Step 5, when the addresser of a message is a user (UI) (top level), the agent investigates whether a system can receive the target service with the role. If a system cannot receive the service with a role, the user is informed and the process ends. If the role can receive a service, the process progresses to Step 6. In Step 6, if another agent's help is not needed, the steps are the same as those of the method in 4.2. If help is needed, the role portion of a message will be changed to "System" . The steps will be the same as those of 4.2. For this reason, in Step 5, when the role is "System," we assume that the system has access rights. Steps 5 and 6 after change are as follows (Step 5+ and Step 6+).

[**Step 5+**] The agent that received the message checks whether it is capable of the service, i.e., it investigates whether the service is on its list. The agent also investigates whether it is currently able to provide the service. Next, an agent investigates whether the message is from a user. When the message is from a user, the agent investigates whether its service can be provided considering the user's role. The agent ends if it cannot provide the service. In contrast, if the message is from another agent (or if the role is "System"), the agent goes to step 6+.

[**Step 6+**] If the agent does not need another agent's help (service), the agent answers the requesting agent. If cost is required at this time, the cost for achieving the agent's service will be added to the current cost, and the answering message containing the new cost will be sent to the agent that originated the message. When the agent needs other agents' services, the agent broadcasts information about the service it needs with the role of "System."

5 Implementation Considerations

Our system is implemented in Java language. Information on the service in the case of a message is expressed as an interface (Type) of Java language. Therefore, if two interfaces are the same, users cannot distinguish difference in these implementation between them. The agent's capability is expressed as an object with the interface of service, and is called dynamically at the time of execution. Each message of the system described so far is assumed as correct. Each component is premised on not performing unexpected behavior. Therefore, it is necessary to confirm that each component was manufactured and installed in the appropriate developer and system manger. Moreover, it is necessary to confirm whether each message is altered. When premised on the composition of dynamic apparatus like this research, the size of a message will increase until it offers one service.

We have so far experimentally implemented access control using some public-key crypto systems. First, we developed a Kerberos-based public-key access control system for distributed environments. Kerberos did not have a mechanism for managing key lapse, so we next built a system based on a PKI system. We used an extension of X.509 certificates to implement roles and developed access control systems for our smart office.

There are many advantages of using X.509. It is fairly easy since we can use existing PKI, implementation and management. We can implement temporary tickets because of the X.509 validity. We can also use extensions of X.509 for a role or group.

In addition to using the usual RSA, we built a Java-based SPKI[15] system using the elliptic curve cryptosystem and implemented access control for a smart office. The elliptic curve cryptosystem has been called the strongest public key code per bit. It can realize security of 1024 bits of RSA code with a 160-bit key length so we could use our systems in small devices such as PDAs.

6   Discussions

In this section, we will discuss our system with regard to two-agent communications described in the previous section, exclusive control, and some other issues.

6.1   Method of Access Control

The difference between the two methods shown in section 4 is whether the role object is a service that each device manages or a service that a user can access directly. Each method has its advantages. The advantage of device-based access control is that the devices can be used with a role difference, even when users receive the same service. In device-based access control, the devices that can be changed with the user's role, even when users receive the same service. This means that services can be distinguished by the role based on performance, safety, cost, etc., even if they are functionally equivalent.

Therefore, the role should be managed by considering these differences of device performance. If administrator believe that the apparatus used should not be distinguishable, the method shown in 4.3 is suitable.

6.2   Timing of Exclusive Control

In previous sections, we did not fully discuss the timing of exclusive control. The point is how long the exclusive right should be granted to the role. If those exclusive rights are granted simultaneously with scheduling, an accessed device cannot be used by others during execution of the service. To avoid this problem, the system reschedules activities during execution and sets up the exclusive right to access. In this case, an optimal arrangement for system performance may not be able to be provided during execution. However, we give this system enough redundancy, so there is almost no need to consider the service becoming unavailable.

6.3   Other Problems

Other problems include delegation and the ticket term of validity. Delegation of authorization for multiagent systems using SPIK has been described [5].

The RBAC extension described in this paper provides dynamic communication among agents. We have not considered the delegation of roles in such an environment yet.

The suitable ticket term of validity depends on the kind of application or environment in many cases. We believe an application developer and the office administrator should establish an appropriate policy for the term of validity of a ticket.

7   Conclusion and Future Work

In this paper, we described an RBAC system for a smart office environment. This system supports dynamic agent cooperation. We also proposed two methods for agent communication. These two methods satisfy the requirements for security of a smart office presented in the previous section. The extended RBAC shown in this paper has the following characteristics.

- The system is based on an RBAC system, so it is suitable for complex environments and facilitates easy management.
- In the extended RBAC system, the services related to a role are abstract. The actual services are determined dynamically, so the system ensures redundancy and dynamic characteristics in a smart office environment.
- Agent Communication enables exclusive control in an extended RBAC system.

Our future work will include

- delegating the access role,
- applying the system to mobile agents and P2P systems,
- developing a formal protocol specification, and
- verifying the above protocols.

References

1. F. Mizoguci, H. Nishiyama, H. Ohwada and H. Hiraishi, Smart office robot collaboration based of a multi-agent programming, Artificial Intelligence, Vol.114, 1999.

2. David L. Martin, Dam J. Cheyer and Douglas B., "The Open Agent Architecture: A Framework for Building Distributed Software Systems," Applied Artificial Intelligence, Vol.13, 1999.
3. David F. Ferraiolo, Johon F. Barkley and D. Richard Kuhn A Role Based Access Control Model and Reference Implementation within a Corporatre Internet, ACM Transactions on Information System Security, Vol.1 Number 2, 1999.
4. Ravi Sandhu, David Ferraiolo and Richard Kuhn, The NIST Model for Role-Based Access Control: Towards A Unified Standard, ACM Workshop on Role-Based Access Control 2000.
5. Wu Wen and Fumio Mizoguchi, An Authorization-based Trust Model For Multiagent Systems, To appear, Applied Artificial Intelligence, 2000.
6. Dirk Balfanz, Drew Dean and Mike Spreitzer, A Security Infrastructure for Distributed Java Appication, Proc. of 2000 IEEE System on Security and Privacy, 2000.
7. W. Yamazaki, W. Wen and F.Mizoguchi, Analysys of Security Requirement for Smart Office, The 1999 Symposium on Cryprography and Information Security (Japanese), 1999.
8. http://java.sun.com/jini
9. http://www.jxta.org/
10. Curry, I. Trustedpublic-key infrastructure. Technical Report Entrust Technologies Ltd, 1997.
11. PGP:Pretty good privacy. O'Reily Associates, 1995.
12. Arsenault, A., and S.Turner. Internet x.509 public key infrastructure pkix roadmap, 1999. Technical Report, IETF PKIX Working Group.
13. Bagwill, R. et al. Security in open systems. Technical Report 800-7, National Institute of Standard and Technology, 1994.
14. Bell, D., and L.J. Feigenbaum, and J. Lacy. Decentralized trust management. Technical Report DIMACS, 1996.
15. Ellison C. et al. Spki certificate theory, internet draft, technical Report IETF SPKI Working Group, 1997.
16. Freier, A., P.Kocher, and P.Kaltorn, SSL v3.0 specification. Technical Report http://home.netscape.com/env/ssl3/s-SPEC.HTM, IETF Task Force.

Typing One-to-One and One-to-Many Correspondences in Security Protocols

Andrew D. Gordon[1] and Alan Jeffrey[2]

[1] Microsoft Research
[2] DePaul University

Abstract. Both one-to-one and one-to-many correspondences between events, sometimes known as injective and non-injective agreements, respectively, are widely used to specify correctness properties of cryptographic protocols. In earlier work, we showed how to typecheck one-to-one correspondences for protocols expressed in the spi-calculus. We present a new type and effect system able to verify both one-to-one and one-to-many correspondences.

1 Motivation

A common strategy for specifying a security protocol is to enumerate expected correspondences between actions of the principals running the protocol. For example, if Alice sends a series of instructions to her banker Bob, each acceptance by Bob of an instruction apparently from Alice should correspond to an attempt by Alice to issue the instruction to Bob. Ruling out potential attacks on a protocol reduces to ruling out violations of a set of correspondences.

The idea of specifying authenticity properties as correspondences has appeared in many forms [Gol02], but Woo and Lam [WL93] were early pioneers. Woo and Lam formalise the progress of principals through a protocol via labelled events, divided into two kinds, begin-events and end-events. A correspondence assertion specifies that in any run of the system, each end-event has a distinct, preceding begin-event with the same label. Authenticity properties typically do not rely on liveness, so there is no requirement that every begin-event is subsequently followed by a corresponding end-event. Our previous work on typechecking authenticity properties of security protocols [GJ01b,GJ01a,GJ02,GP02] rests on formulating correspondence assertions by annotating programs with begin- and end-events.

Woo and Lam's assertions are *one-to-one* in the sense there is a distinct begin-event for each end-event. Let a *one-to-many* correspondence be the more liberal condition that there exists a preceding—but not necessarily distinct—begin-event for every end-event. One-to-one correspondences are desirable to rule out replay attacks; if Alice sends a single money transfer instruction to Bob, our specification should prevent Bob being duped into acting on it twice. On the other hand, there are at least two situations when it is appropriate to relax the formal one-to-one requirement.

M. Okada et al. (Eds.): ISSS 2002, LNCS 2609, pp. 263–282, 2003.
© Springer-Verlag Berlin Heidelberg 2003

First, security may not actually depend on one-to-one correspondence. For example, if Alice sends an account balance request, and Bob encrypts his reply, it may be harmless if the attacker replaying the request were to cause Bob to send two balance messages to Alice. Replay protection requires some state to be maintained, which in some applications may be more expensive than simply tolerating replays. For example, messages containing nonces cannot usefully be cached by proxies.

Second, even if security depends on a one-to-one correspondence, it may be acceptable to check only a one-to-many correspondence formally, and then to verify the absence of replays outside the formalism. For example, a protocol based on timestamps may prevent replays by relying on a complex infrastructure for securing and synchronising clocks. It may be expedient to check for a one-to-many correspondence formally, and to argue informally that a standard use of timestamps in fact achieves a one-to-one correspondence. In some protocols, such as those involving freshly generated nonces included in event labels, it may be obvious that no two end-events have the same label. If labels are unique, one-to-one and one-to-many correspondences are equivalent, so it may be preferable simply to verify a one-to-many correspondence.

This paper introduces a type and effect system for verifying both one-to-one and one-to-many correspondences. Hence, we generalize our previous work on type and effect systems [GJ01b,GJ01a] for one-to-one correspondences in the spi-calculus [AG99]. There are many prior systems for verifying one-to-many correspondences; this is the first based on typechecking. It shows that our methodology is not limited to the one-to-one case. The main new construct in our type theory are *ok-types*, types whose inhabitation proves it is ok to perform end-events. Moreover, the technicalities of our operational semantics are simpler than in previous work, allowing a corresponding simplification of our type soundness proofs. Using types to embody security invariants fits cleanly into the development cycle, and is becoming increasingly popular [LY97,LLL+02,SM02]. Still, unlike some other protocol analyses, our method requires human intervention to annotate the protocol with type information, and like other type systems, rejects some well-behaved programs.

We verify that correspondences hold in spite of an attacker able to monitor, modify, and replay messages, and, given suitable keys, to encrypt and decrypt messages [DY83]. Hence, like many other formal techniques, our verifications do not rule out attacks that side-step this attacker model, such as cryptanalyses of the underlying cryptographic algorithms. Unlike some other formal techniques, we have no general model of insider attacks, although some specific situations can be modelled.

We can position our work on the spectrum—ranging from extensional to intensional—of security specifications, as follows. At the extensional end, specifications describe the intended service provided by the protocol, for example, in terms of behavioural equivalence [FG94,AFG98,Aba99,AFG00,FGM00]. At the intensional end, specifications describe the underlying mechanism, in terms of states or events [AB01,WL93,Low97,Ros96,Gol02,Mea96,Pau98,Sch98,GT02].

Correspondences are towards the intensional end of the spectrum; our begin- and end-assertions are intermingled with implementation code. Still, we can informally picture correspondences using message-sequence notations, and there are advantages from making specifications executable.

The rest of the paper is structured as follows. Section 2 gives examples of specifying protocols via correspondences. Section 3 explains how to formulate the problem of checking correspondences within a version of the spi-calculus. Section 4 describes how to typecheck one-to-many correspondences in a spi-calculus, by introducing new ok-types. Section 5 summarises and concludes.

2   Specifying Protocols by Correspondences

The goal of this section is to illustrate one-to-many correspondences via some protocol examples, including a couple of classic protocols from the original paper on the BAN logic [BAN89], and to sketch their encoding within our typed spi-calculus.

Example 1: A Basic One-to-Many Correspondence. Suppose two principals, A and B, share a secret symmetric key K_{AB}. The following protocol protocol uses a timestamp to protect encrypted messages sent from A to B.

Event 1	A begins! $Sending(A, B, M)$
Message 1	$A \to B$: $\{M, T_A\}_{K_{AB}}$
Event 2	B ends $Sending(A, B, M)$

The protocol consists of a single message, Message 1, sent from the initiator A to the responder B. Begin- and end-events mark the progress of the principals through a run of the protocol. Event 1 is a one-to-many begin-event, whose label, $Sending(A, B, M)$ identifies the principals taking part in this run of the protocol, together with the instruction, M, that A wishes to send to B. Event 2 is an end-event by B, whose label matches the earlier begin-event by A. Event 1 occurs immediately before A initiates the protocol. Event 2 occurs only after B is satisfied the protocol run has succeeded, and records the parties B regards as taking part, and the instruction to be acted on.

In general, the assertion induced by begin- and end-events is that each end-event has a corresponding begin-event with the same label. We annotate the begin-event, Event 1, with "!", to indicate that it can match one or more end-events with the same label. This one-to-many correspondence assertion means that every message M accepted by B as coming from A actually came from A, but it does not rule out replays. To specify a one-to-one correspondence, we would omit the "!" to indicate that the begin-event can be matched at most once.

The timestamp serves to narrow the window of opportunity for replay attacks, but it may or may not entirely rule out replays. Typical implementations would reject timestamps older than some limit, for example, five minutes. Stateful servers may also record previously seen timestamps, so as to prevent replays.

Some attention needs to be paid to secure synchronisation of clocks, to prevent, for example, attacks based on fooling a node into issuing requests with future timestamps, for later replay.

Our theory can establish one-to-many correspondences, as specified above, but since it does not deal explicitly with the passage of time, it cannot show that a particular use of timestamps does in fact establish a one-to-one correspondence. We leave this to an informal argument. On the other hand, our earlier papers show how to typecheck the one-to-one correspondences achieved by various kinds of nonce exchanges.

Types for Example 1. We use this basic example to illustrate our use of types and processes to model protocols. Here is the type for the shared key K_{AB}.

$$SharedKey \triangleq \mathsf{Key}(x{:}Msg, t{:}\mathsf{Un}, \mathsf{Ok}(\mathsf{end}\ Sending(A, B, x)))$$

This says K_{AB} is a secret key for encrypting triples (M, T_A, ok), where M has type Msg, T_A has type Un, and ok has type $\mathsf{Ok}(\mathsf{end}\ Sending(A, B, M))$, that is, the type $\mathsf{Ok}(\mathsf{end}\ Sending(A, B, x))$ with the parameter x instantiated to M, the component of the triple labelled x. We leave the type Msg of instructions conveyed by the protocol unspecified. Messages of type Un are public data known to the opponent; we assign timestamps the type Un since they may be published to the opponent. The message ok of type $\mathsf{Ok}(\mathsf{end}\ Sending(A, B, M))$ may be thought of as a certificate testifying that it is justified to perform an end-event labelled $Sending(A, B, M)$.

Ok-types, such as $\mathsf{Ok}(\mathsf{end}\ Sending(A, B, x))$, are one of the main innovations in this paper, compared to our previous type systems for the spi-calculus. The general form is $\mathsf{Ok}(\mathcal{R})$ where $\mathcal{R}$ is a *resource*, a representation of events that may be safely performed. A simple example of a resource is a finite multiset of events, written $\mathsf{end}\ L_1 \mid \cdots \mid \mathsf{end}\ L_n$.

Ok-types are meaningful at compile time—during typechecking—but convey no information at runtime. At compile time, we exploit ok-types to prove that end-events performed in one part of a program are justified by preceding begin-events elsewhere. At runtime, there is exactly one value, written ok, of ok-type. It is the unique inhabitant of every type $\mathsf{Ok}(\mathcal{R})$, and therefore takes no space to represent. We consider $\mathsf{ok} : \mathsf{Ok}(\mathcal{R})$ as simply an annotation, proof that the events in $\mathcal{R}$ are safe to perform. Accordingly, although we formalize Message 1 as an encrypted triple, $\{M, T_A, \mathsf{ok}\}_{K_{AB}}$, as far as runtime behaviour is concerned this is equivalent to the encrypted pair, $\{M, T_A\}_{K_{AB}}$, of our informal description.

Interlude: Resources, Events, and Safety. To describe our process semantics, we suppose that every state of our system includes an imaginary tuplespace, recording those end-events that may be safely performed. It is purely a formal device to record the progress of protocol participants, and cannot be used for actual communication. Accordingly, the opponent cannot read or write the tuplespace. The contents of the tuplespace is a resource, $\mathcal{R}$ (as also found in an ok-type). Here is the full syntax of resources:

Resources:

$\mathcal{R}, \mathcal{S} ::=$	resource: record of allowed end-events
end L	allows one end-event labelled L
$!\mathcal{R}$	allows whatever $\mathcal{R}$ allows, arbitrarily often
$\mathcal{R} \mid \mathcal{S}$	allows whatever R and S allow
$\mathbf{0}$	allows nothing

Syntactically, replication binds tighter than composition; so that $!R \mid R'$ means $(!R) \mid R'$. We identify resources up to an equivalence relation $\mathcal{R} \equiv \mathcal{R}'$, the least congruence relation to satisfy the equations $\mathcal{R} \mid (\mathcal{R}' \mid \mathcal{R}'') \equiv (\mathcal{R} \mid \mathcal{R}') \mid \mathcal{R}''$, $\mathcal{R} \mid \mathcal{R}' \equiv \mathcal{R}' \mid R$, $\mathcal{R} \mid \mathbf{0} \equiv \mathcal{R}$, $!\mathcal{R} \equiv \mathcal{R} \mid !\mathcal{R}$, $!\mathbf{0} \equiv \mathbf{0}$, $!!\mathcal{R} \equiv !\mathcal{R}$, and $!(\mathcal{R} \mid \mathcal{R}') \equiv !\mathcal{R} \mid !\mathcal{R}'$. (Hence, a resource denotes a multiset of end-events, each of which has either finite or infinite multiplicity.) Let $\mathsf{fn}(\mathcal{R})$ be the set of names occurring in any label occurring in $\mathcal{R}$.

We include begin- and end-assertions in the syntax of our spi-calculus to formalize correspondences. These assertions read or write the imaginary tuplespace. A one-to-one begin-assertion begin $L; P$ adds end L to the tuplespace, then runs P. A one-to-many begin-assertion begin$!L; P$ adds the replicated resource $!$end L to the tuplespace, then runs P. An end-assertion end $L; P$ consumes the resource end L from the imaginary tuplespace. The absence of end L, when running end $L; P$, is a deadlock signifying violation of a correspondence assertion. We say a system is *safe* if no reachable state has such a deadlock. Moreover, a system P is *robustly safe* if $P \mid O$ is safe for any process O representing an opponent. We formalize these definitions later; they are similar to those in our previous work, except for the addition of replicated resources and one-to-many begin-assertions, to allow modelling of both one-to-one and one-to-many correspondences.

Processes for Example 1. Returning to our example, the following process represents an attempt by A to send M to B.

$$P_A(M) \stackrel{\triangle}{=} \text{begin } !Sending(A, B, M);$$
$$\text{new}(T_A\text{:Un}); \text{out } net\langle\{M, T_A, \text{ok}\}_{K_{AB}}\rangle$$

The process starts with a one-to-many begin-assertion, that adds the replicated resource $!$end $Sending(A, B, M)$ to the imaginary tuplespace. Since it is replicated, it matches many end-events. The restriction operator $\text{new}(T_A\text{:Un})$ generates a fresh timestamp T_A. The process ends by an output of the encrypted triple $\{M, T_A, \text{ok}\}_{K_{AB}}$ on the public channel net.

We postpone a detailed discussion of intuitions behind the type system to Section 4, but note that the message ok can be assigned $\mathsf{Ok}(\text{end } Sending(A, B, M))$ only due to the presence of $!$end $Sending(A, B, M)$ in the imaginary tuplespace.

Next, process P_B represents B receiving a single message from A.

$$P_B \stackrel{\triangle}{=} \text{inp } net(c\text{:Un}); \text{decrypt } c \text{ is } \{xto\}_{K_{AB}};$$
$$\text{split } xto \text{ is } (x\text{:}Msg, t\text{:Un}, o\text{:Ok}(\text{end } Sending(A, B, x)));$$
$$\text{exercise } o; \text{end } Sending(A, B, x)$$

The process starts with a blocking receive of a message c off the public channel net. It then attempts to decrypt the message with the key K_{AB}, and split the plaintext into its three components x, t, and o. If c is not encrypted with K_{AB} the process will immediately terminate; we assume there is sufficient redundancy in the ciphertext to detect this situation. At runtime, the process exercise o; does nothing; control unconditionally falls through to the end-assertion end $Sending(A, B, x)$ to indicate that B accepts the message x from A. At compile time, the process exercise o; exploits the ok-type assigned to o to show that the following end-assertion cannot deadlock.

Finally, we formalize principal A attempting to send a sequence $M_1, \ldots, M_n$ of messages to B as the process $Sys(M_1, \ldots, M_n)$.

$$Sys(M_1, \ldots, M_n) \triangleq \mathsf{new}(K_{AB}{:}SharedKey); (P_A(M_1) \mid \cdots \mid P_A(M_n) \mid {!}P_B)$$

The process $P_A(M_1) \mid \cdots \mid P_A(M_n)$ is n copies of P_A, one for each of the messages to be sent, running in parallel. The replicated process $!P_B$ is a server run by B that repeatedly runs P_B to try to receive a message from A. The new binder delimits the scope of the key K_{AB} to be the processes representing A and B. The opponent is some process running alongside $Sys(M_1, \ldots, M_n)$ that may send and receive messages on the public net channel. The fact that the opponent O does not know the key K_{AB} is represented by O not being within the scope of the binder for K_{AB}.

This completes our reduction of the one-to-many specification of our protocol to the problem of showing that the process $Sys(M_1, \ldots, M_n)$ is robustly safe. Robust safety follows from the type system of Section 4.

Example 2: The Wide-Mouthed-Frog Protocol. Assume that each of a number of principals A, B, $\ldots$ shares a key K_{AS}, K_{BS}, $\ldots$, with a trusted server S. The Wide-Mouthed-Frog protocol [BAN89] allows one of these principals to create and communicate a key to another, via the server S, using timestamps for replay protection. Here is the protocol and its specification using a one-to-many correspondence.

Event 1	A begins!	$Sending(A, B, K_{AB})$
Message 1	$A \to S$:	$\{msg_1(T_A, B, K_{AB})\}_{K_{AS}}$
Message 2	$S \to B$:	$\{msg_2(T_S, A, K_{AB})\}_{K_{BS}}$
Event 2	B ends	$Sending(A, B, K_{AB})$

Message 1 communicates the new key K_{AB} from A to S, who checks that the timestamp T_A is fresh, and then forwards the key on to B tagged with its own timestamp T_S. The specification says that each time B believes it has received a key K_{AB} from A, by performing Event 2, then in fact A has earlier begun the protocol with B, intending to send K_{AB}, by performing Event 1.

If each principal rejects any message whose timestamp is older than the last message received from the same principal, then the protocol can prevent replays. If so, the specification can be strengthened to a one-to-one correspondence (though this cannot be checked within our type system).

We tag the plaintexts of Messages 1 and 2 to prevent any confusion of the two. This thwarts the "type flaw" attack, reported by Anderson and Needham [AN95], in which an attacker replays Message 2 as Message 1, in order to keep the timestamp fresh.

Types for Example 2. Let variable p range over the principals A, B, ... The longterm key shared between any principal p and the server S has the following type $Princ(p)$, where $SKey$ is the type of session keys, and $Payload$ is the unspecified type of payload data.

$$SKey \triangleq \mathsf{Key}(PayLoad)$$

$$Princ(p) \triangleq \mathsf{Key}(\mathsf{Union}($$
$$msg_1(ta : \mathsf{Un}, b : \mathsf{Un}, kab : SKey, \mathsf{Ok}(\mathsf{end}\ Sending(p, b, kab))),$$
$$msg_2(ts : \mathsf{Un}, a : \mathsf{Un}, kab : SKey, \mathsf{Ok}(\mathsf{end}\ Sending(a, p, kab)))))$$

This says the longterm key for principal p is a secret symmetric key for encrypting two kinds of messages, tagged with msg_1 or msg_2. The first kind are triples (T_A, B, K_{AB}), together with an ok indicating that an end-event labelled $Sending(p, B, K_{AB})$ is safe. Similarly, the second kind are triples (T_S, A, K_{AB}), together with an ok indicating that an end-event labelled $Sending(A, p, K_{AB})$ is safe.

Much as for Example 1, we can encode the protocol behaviour and its specification as a process, but we omit the details.

Example 3: BAN Kerberos. Our final example is a one-to-many specification of an early version of Kerberos [BAN89]. Again, the starting assumption is that there is a set of principals each of which shares a key with an authentication server S. The protocol allows an initiator A to request a fresh session key K_{AB} from S for communication with B, and to have S send the key to both A and B. Here is the protocol and its specification.

Event 1	A begins!	$Init(A, B)$
Message 1	$A \rightarrow S :$	A, B
Event 2	S begins!	$KeyGenInit(A, B, K_{AB})$
Event 3	S begins!	$KeyGenResp(A, B, K_{AB})$
Message 2	$S \rightarrow A :$	$\{msg_{2a}(T_S, L, B, K_{AB}, Tkt)\}_{K_{AS}}$
		where $Tkt = \{msg_{2b}(T_S, L, A, K_{AB})\}_{K_{BS}}$
Event 4	A ends	$KeyGenInit(A, B, K_{AB})$
Message 3	$A \rightarrow B :$	$Tkt, \{msg_3(A, T_A)\}_{K_{AB}}$
Event 5	B ends	$KeyGenResp(A, B, K_{AB})$
Event 6	B ends	$Init(A, B)$
Event 7	B begins!	$Resp(A, B)$
Message 4	$B \rightarrow A :$	$\{msg_4(T_A)\}_{K_{AB}}$
Event 8	A ends	$Resp(A, B)$

Compared to the original presentation, we have added tags to messages, eliminated the decrement of the timestamp in Message 4, and swapped the order of a couple of components of Message 2.

The terms T_A and T_S are timestamps, and L is a lifetime. The specification gives guarantees to the principals performing end-events. At Event 4, A is guaranteed that S generated the session key for use with B, and, symmetrically, at Event 5, B is guaranteed that S generated the session key for use with A. At Event 8, the initiator A is guaranteed that the responder B has run the protocol with A, and, symmetrically, at Event 6, the responder B is guaranteed that the initiator A has run the protocol with B. The server S receives no guarantee that A or B are present or running the protocol.

There are more detailed formal analyses of more recent versions of Kerberos; see the paper [BCJS02], and its bibliography.

Types for Example 3. The longterm key shared between any principal p and the server S has the following type $Princ(p)$, where $SKey(a, b)$ is the type of session keys shared between a and b, and $Payload$ is the unspecified type of payload data.

$$Princ(p) \triangleq \mathsf{Key}(\mathsf{Union}($$
$$msg_{2a}(ta : \mathsf{Un}, l{:}\mathsf{Un}, b{:}\mathsf{Un}, kab{:}SKey(p, b), tkt{:}\mathsf{Un},$$
$$\mathsf{Ok}(\mathsf{end}\ KeyGenInit(p, b, kab))),$$
$$msg_{2b}(ts{:}\mathsf{Un}, l{:}\mathsf{Un}, a{:}\mathsf{Un}, kab{:}SKey(a, p),$$
$$\mathsf{Ok}(\mathsf{end}\ KeyGenResp(a, p, kab)))))$$

$$SKey(a, b) \triangleq \mathsf{Key}(\mathsf{Union}($$
$$msg_3(a'{:}\mathsf{Un}, ta{:}\mathsf{Un}, \mathsf{Ok}(\mathsf{end}\ Init(a, b))),$$
$$msg_4(ta{:}\mathsf{Un}, \mathsf{Ok}(\mathsf{end}\ Resp(a, b, kab)))))$$

As with Example 2, we omit the encoding of protocol behaviour and its specification as an actual process.

3   A State-Based Semantics of Correspondences

The previous section illustrates how to reduce an informal protocol specification to the question of whether a process with embedded begin- and end-assertions is robustly safe. This section formalizes this question by precisely defining a spi-calculus and its operational semantics. The next explains how to check robust safety by typechecking.

Messages. The messages and event labels of our calculus are as follows. The syntax is similar to previous versions of spi, except for the addition of ok.

Messages, Event Labels:

ℓ	message tag
a, b, c, x, y, z	names, variables

$L, M, N ::=$	message
x	name: a key or a channel
$\{M\}_N$	message M encrypted with key N
$\ell(M)$	message tagged with ℓ
(M, N)	message pair
ok	an ok to use some resource

As usual, pairs can represent arbitrary tuples; for example, $(L, (M, N))$ can represent the triple (L, M, N). We use analogous, standard abbreviations at the process and type level, but omit the details. Let $\mathsf{fn}(L)$ be the set of names occurring in L.

Processes. The syntax of processes is as follows. Types, ranged over by T, are defined in Section 4. We write $\mathsf{fn}(P)$ and $\mathsf{fn}(T)$ for the sets of names occurring free in the process P and the type T, respectively.

Processes:

$P, Q, R ::=$	process
out $M\langle N\rangle$	asynchronous output
inp $M(x{:}T); P$	input (scope of x is P)
new$(x{:}T); P$	name generation (scope of x is P)
$!P$	replication
$P \mid Q$	composition
$\mathbf{0}$	inactivity
begin $L; P$	one-to-one begin-assertion
begin $!L; P$	one-to-many begin-assertion
end $L; P$	end-assertion
decrypt L is $\{y{:}T\}_N; P$	decryption (scope of y is P)
case M $(\ell_i(x_i{:}T_i)P_i{}^{i\in 1..n})$	union case, $n \geq 0$ (scope of each x_i is P_i)
split M is $(x{:}T, y{:}U); P$	pair splitting (scope of x is U, P, of y just P)
match M is $(N, y{:}T); P$	pair matching (scope of y is P)
exercise $M; P$	exercise an ok

The first group of constructs forms a typed π-calculus. The middle group consists of the begin- and end-assertions discussed in Section 2. Only one-to-many begin-assertions are new in this paper. The final group is of data manipulation constructs. Only the last, exercise $M; P$, is new, and is described, along with decryption and pair splitting in Section 2. A union case process, case M $(\ell_i(x_i{:}T_i)P_i\{x_i\}^{i\in 1..n})$, behaves as $P_j\{N\}$ if M is the tagged message $\ell_j(N)$ for some $j \in 1..n$, and otherwise is stuck, that is, does nothing. (In general, we use the notation $P\{x\}$ to denote the process P and to note that it may have free occurrences of the variable x. In this context, we write $P\{M\}$ for the outcome of substituting the message M for each of those free occurrences of the variable x in P.) A pair match match M is $(N, y{:}T); P\{y\}$ behaves as $P\{L\}$ if M is the pair (N, L), and otherwise is stuck.

We write $\vec{x}:\vec{T}$ as a shorthand for the list $x_1:T_1, \ldots, x_n:T_n$ of typed variables, when $\vec{x} = x_1, \ldots, x_n$ and $\vec{T} = T_1, \ldots, T_n$. Moreover, we write $\mathsf{new}(\vec{x}:\vec{T}); P$ as shorthand for $\mathsf{new}(x_1:T_1); \cdots \mathsf{new}(x_n:T_n); P$, and also $\mathsf{end}\ L$ for $\mathsf{end}\ L; \mathbf{0}$.

As in many presentations of the π-calculus, we define a *structural equivalence* relation, that identifies processes up to some structural rearrangements. The following table includes equivalence rules, congruence for the basic structural operators (restriction, parallel composition, and replication), monoid laws for composition, Engelfriet's replication laws [Eng96], and the mobility laws for restriction. As usual, the exact choice of rules of structural equivalence is a little arbitrary.

Structural Equivalence of Processes: $P \equiv Q$

$P \equiv P$	(Struct Refl)
$Q \equiv P \Rightarrow P \equiv Q$	(Struct Symm)
$P \equiv Q, Q \equiv R \Rightarrow P \equiv R$	(Struct Trans)
$P \equiv P' \Rightarrow \mathsf{new}(x:T); P \equiv \mathsf{new}(x:T); P'$	(Struct Res)
$P \equiv P' \Rightarrow P \mid R \equiv P' \mid R$	(Struct Par)
$P \equiv P' \Rightarrow\ !P \equiv\ !P'$	(Struct Repl)
$P \mid \mathbf{0} \equiv P$	(Struct Par Zero)
$P \mid Q \equiv Q \mid P$	(Struct Par Comm)
$(P \mid Q) \mid R \equiv P \mid (Q \mid R)$	(Struct Par Assoc)
$!P \equiv P \mid\ !P$	(Struct Repl Unfold)
$!!P \equiv\ !P$	(Struct Repl Repl)
$!(P \mid Q) \equiv\ !P \mid\ !Q$	(Struct Repl Par)
$!\mathbf{0} \equiv \mathbf{0}$	(Struct Repl Zero)
$\mathsf{new}(x:T); (P \mid Q) \equiv P \mid \mathsf{new}(x:T); Q$	(Struct Res Par) (for $x \notin \mathsf{fn}(P)$)
$\mathsf{new}(x_1:T_1); \mathsf{new}(x_2:T_2); P \equiv$	(Struct Res Res)
$\quad \mathsf{new}(x_2:T_2); \mathsf{new}(x_1:T_1); P$	(for $x_1 \neq x_2, x_1 \notin \mathsf{fn}(T_2), x_2 \notin \mathsf{fn}(T_1)$)

States. A computation state takes the form $\mathsf{new}(\vec{x}:\vec{T}); (\mathcal{R} \parallel P)$, where the typed names $\vec{x}$ are freshly generated, the process P represents the running threads of control, and $\mathcal{R}$ is a resource—the imaginary tuplespace—recording which end-events the process may safely perform.

Structural Equivalence of States: $S \equiv S'$

$S \equiv S$	(Struct Refl)
$S' \equiv S \Rightarrow S' \equiv S$	(Struct Symm)
$S \equiv S', S' \equiv S'' \Rightarrow S \equiv S''$	(Struct Trans)
$S \equiv S' \Rightarrow \mathsf{new}(x:T); S \equiv \mathsf{new}(x:T); S'$	(Struct Res)
$\mathcal{R} \equiv \mathcal{R}', P \equiv P' \Rightarrow \mathcal{R} \parallel P \equiv \mathcal{R}' \parallel P'$	(Struct Par)
$x \notin \mathsf{fn}(\mathcal{R}) \Rightarrow \mathsf{new}(x:T); (\mathcal{R} \parallel P) \equiv \mathcal{R} \parallel \mathsf{new}(x:T); P$	(Struct Res State)

State Transitions and Safety. Our operational semantics is a state transition relation, defined by the following rules. The first group are transitions on states of the form $\mathcal{R} \parallel P$, and formalize our intuitive explanations of the various forms of process. The second group includes congruence rules, and the rule (Trans Struct) that allows a state to be re-arranged up to structural equivalence while deriving a transition.

State Transitions: $S \to S'$

$\mathcal{R} \parallel P \mid \text{out } M\langle N\rangle \mid \text{inp } M(y{:}T); Q\{y\} \to$	(Trans I/O)
$\quad \mathcal{R} \parallel Q\{N\}$	
$\mathcal{R} \parallel P \mid \text{begin } L; Q \to$	(Trans Begin)
$\quad \mathcal{R} \mid \text{end } L \parallel P \mid Q$	
$\mathcal{R} \parallel P \mid \text{begin } !L; Q \to$	(Trans Begin!)
$\quad \mathcal{R} \mid !\text{end } L \parallel P \mid Q$	
$\mathcal{R} \mid \text{end } L \parallel P \mid \text{end } L; Q \to$	(Trans End)
$\quad \mathcal{R} \parallel P \mid Q$	
$\mathcal{R} \parallel P \mid \text{decrypt } \{M\}_N \text{ is } \{y{:}T\}_N; Q\{y\} \to$	(Trans Decrypt)
$\quad \mathcal{R} \parallel P \mid Q\{M\}$	
$\mathcal{R} \parallel P \mid \text{case } \ell_j(M) \ (\ell_i(x_i{:}T_i)Q_i\{x_i\}^{\,i\in 1..n}) \to$	(Trans Case)
$\quad \mathcal{R} \parallel P \mid Q_j\{M\} \qquad j \in 1..n$	
$\mathcal{R} \parallel P \mid \text{split } (M, N) \text{ is } (x{:}T, y{:}U); Q\{x, y\} \to$	(Trans Split)
$\quad \mathcal{R} \parallel P \mid Q\{M, N\}$	
$\mathcal{R} \parallel P \mid \text{match } (M, N) \text{ is } (M, y{:}U); Q\{y\} \to$	(Trans Match)
$\quad \mathcal{R} \parallel P \mid Q\{N\}$	
$\mathcal{R} \parallel P \mid \text{exercise ok}; Q \to$	(Trans Exercise)
$\quad \mathcal{R} \parallel P \mid Q$	
$S \to S' \Rightarrow \text{new}(x{:}T); S \to \text{new}(x{:}T); S'$	(Trans Res)
$S \equiv S', S' \to S'', S'' \equiv S''' \Rightarrow S \to S'''$	(Trans Struct)

For example, here is a transition sequence in which a one-to-many begin-assertion is matched by a couple of end-events:

$$0 \parallel \text{begin } !L; \text{end } L; \text{end } L \to !\text{end } L \parallel \text{end } L; \text{end } L$$
$$\equiv !\text{end } L \mid \text{end } L \mid \text{end } L \parallel \text{end } L; \text{end } L$$
$$\to !\text{end } L \mid \text{end } L \parallel \text{end } L \to !\text{end } L \parallel 0$$

On the other hand, a one-to-one begin-assertion matches only one end-event. In the final state $0 \parallel \text{end } L; 0$ of the following sequence, the end-assertion is deadlocked, signifying a violation of a correspondence assertion.

$$0 \parallel \text{begin } L; \text{end } L; \text{end } L \to \text{end } L \parallel \text{end } L; \text{end } L \to 0 \parallel \text{end } L$$

We can now formalize the notions of safety (every end-assertion succeeds) and robust safety (safety in the presence of an arbitrary opponent).

– Let $S \to^* S'$ mean there are $S_1, \ldots, S_n$ with $S \equiv S_1 \to \cdots \to S_n \equiv S'$.

- A state S is *fine* if and only if whenever $S \equiv \text{new}(\vec{x}:\vec{T}); (\mathcal{R} \parallel \text{end } L; P \mid P')$ there is $\mathcal{R}'$ such that $R \equiv \text{end } L \mid \mathcal{R}'$.
- A process P is *safe* if and only if, for all S, if $\mathbf{0} \parallel P \rightarrow^* S$ then S is fine.
- An *untyped process* is one in which every type is Un.
- An *opponent* is an untyped process O containing no begin- or end-assertions, and no exercises.
- A process P is *robustly safe* if and only if $P \mid O$ is safe for all opponents O.

The question now is how to check robust safety by typing.

4   Typing One-to-Many Correspondences

Like our previous systems for typechecking correspondences [GJ01a,GJ02], we assign a resource (a kind of *effect* [GL86]) to each process P: an upper bound on the unmatched end-events performed by P. We prove theorems showing that safety and robust safety follow from assigning a process the $\mathbf{0}$ effect. Unlike our previous systems, we also assign a resource (as well as a type) to each message M: an upper bound on the end-events promised by all the ok terms contained within M.

Types:

$T, U ::=$	type
Un	public data
Key(T)	secret key for T plaintext
Union$(\ell_i(T_i)^{\ i \in 1..n})$	tagged union, $n \geq 0$
$(x{:}T, U)$	dependent pair (scope of x is U)
Ok$(\mathcal{R})$	ok to exercise $\mathcal{R}$

Abbreviation: $(x_1{:}T_1, \ldots, x_n{:}T_n, T_{n+1}) \triangleq (x_1{:}T_1, \ldots, (x_n{:}T_n, T_{n+1}))$

Messages of type Un are public data known to the opponent, including ciphertexts known to but indecipherable by the opponent. Messages of type Key(T) are secret keys for encrypting and decrypting plaintext of type T. Messages of type Union$(\ell_i(T_i)^{\ i \in 1..n})$ take the form $\ell_j(N)$ where ℓ_j is one of the tags $\ell_1, \ldots, \ell_n$, and N is a message of type T_j. Messages of type $(x{:}T, U\{x\})$ are pairs (M, N), where M has type T and N has type $U\{M\}$. (The scope of the bound variable x in $(x{:}T, U)$ is U.) Finally, ok is the unique message of type Ok$(\mathcal{R})$, a pledge that the resource $\mathcal{R}$ is available.

Formation Judgments. Our judgments are defined with respect to an *environment*, E, a list $x_1{:}T_1, \ldots, x_n{:}T_n$ declaring types for those variables in scope. Let $\text{dom}(x_1{:}T_1, \ldots, x_n{:}T_n) = \{x_1, \ldots, x_n\}$. The first three judgments define the correct formation of environments ($E \vdash \diamond$ meaning, roughly, all declarations are distinct) and resources and types ($E \vdash \mathcal{R}$ and $E \vdash T$ meaning, roughly, all free variables are in scope).

Formation Rules:

(Env $\varnothing$)	(Env x)	(Resource Event)	
	$E \vdash T \quad x \notin \mathsf{dom}(E)$	$E \vdash \diamond \quad \mathsf{fn}(L) \subseteq \mathsf{dom}(E)$	
$\varnothing \vdash \diamond$	$E, x{:}T \vdash \diamond$	$E \vdash \mathsf{end}\ L$	

(Resource Repl)	(Resource Par)	(Resource Zero)	(Type Un)
$E \vdash \mathcal{R}$	$E \vdash \mathcal{R} \quad E \vdash \mathcal{S}$	$E \vdash \diamond$	$E \vdash \diamond$
$E \vdash !\mathcal{R}$	$E \vdash \mathcal{R} \mid \mathcal{S}$	$E \vdash \mathbf{0}$	$E \vdash \mathsf{Un}$

(Type Key)	(Type Union)	(Type Pair)	(Type Ok)
$E \vdash T$	$E \vdash A_i \quad \forall i \in 1..n$	$E, x{:}T \vdash U$	$E \vdash \mathcal{R}$
$E \vdash \mathsf{Key}(T)$	$E \vdash \mathsf{Union}(\ell_i(A_i)^{\,i \in 1..n})$	$E \vdash (x{:}T, U)$	$E \vdash \mathsf{Ok}(\mathcal{R})$

Typing Messages. The judgment $E \vdash M : T, \mathcal{R}$ means that, given E, the message M has type T and effect $\mathcal{R}$: it needs the resources $\mathcal{R}$ to justify promises made by the ok messages that may be extracted from M. Recall that an extracted message of type $\mathsf{Ok}(\mathcal{R})$ may subsequently be exercised to justify end-assertions allowed by $\mathcal{R}$.

For example, consider again the type

$$SharedKey \triangleq \mathsf{Key}(x{:}Msg, t{:}\mathsf{Un}, \mathsf{Ok}(\mathsf{end}\ Sending(A, B, x)))$$

of longterm keys from Example 1 in Section 2. Let $E = K_{AB}{:}SharedKey$, $x{:}Msg$, $T_A{:}\mathsf{Un}$ and let message M be the ciphertext $\{x, T_A, \mathsf{ok}\}_{K_{AB}}$. Then we have:

$$E \vdash M : \mathsf{Un}, \mathsf{end}\ Sending(A, B, x)$$

The cipher is well-typed because the triple (x, T_A, ok) has type $(x{:}Msg,\ t{:}\mathsf{Un},\ \mathsf{Ok}(\mathsf{end}\ Sending(A, B, x)))$, and hence can be encrypted with a key of type *SharedKey*. The cipher M has type Un because it may safely be made public. The effect $\mathsf{end}\ Sending(A, B, x)$ arises from the presence of the message $\mathsf{ok} : \mathsf{Ok}(\mathsf{end}\ Sending(A, B, x))$, which may eventually be exercised to justify an end-assertion labelled $Sending(A, B, x)$.

If we have two copies of M, the effect is doubled:

$$E \vdash (M, M) : \mathsf{Un}, \mathsf{end}\ Sending(A, B, x) \mid \mathsf{end}\ Sending(A, B, x)$$

The following table defines message typing. As in earlier work [GJ01a], many constructs have two rules: one for typing data known only to the trusted principals running the protocol, and one for typing Un data known to the opponent. The rules accumulate the effects of components that may be extracted, but ignore the effects of those that cannot. For example, the rules (Msg Encrypt) and (Msg Encrypt Un) assign the effect $\mathcal{R}_1$ of the plaintext M to the ciphertext $\{M\}_N$, since the plaintext may be extracted by decryption, but ignore the effect $\mathcal{R}_2$ of the key N, since there is no primitive to extract it from the ciphertext. Let $\mathcal{R} \leq \mathcal{R}' \triangleq \exists \mathcal{R}''.\mathcal{R} \mid \mathcal{R}'' \equiv \mathcal{R}'$.

Good Messages:

(Msg Subsum)
$$\frac{E \vdash M : T, \mathcal{R} \quad \mathcal{R} \le \mathcal{R}' \quad E \vdash \mathcal{R}'}{E \vdash M : T, \mathcal{R}'}$$

(Msg x)
$$\frac{E \vdash \diamond \quad x \in \mathsf{dom}(E)}{E \vdash x : E(x), \mathbf{0}}$$

(Msg Encrypt)
$$\frac{E \vdash M : T, \mathcal{R}_1 \quad E \vdash N : \mathsf{Key}(T), \mathcal{R}_2}{E \vdash \{M\}_N : \mathsf{Un}, \mathcal{R}_1}$$

(Msg Encrypt Un)
$$\frac{E \vdash M : \mathsf{Un}, \mathcal{R}_1 \quad E \vdash N : \mathsf{Un}, \mathcal{R}_2}{E \vdash \{M\}_N : \mathsf{Un}, \mathcal{R}_1}$$

(Msg Union) (where $T = \mathsf{Union}(\ell_i(T_i)^{i \in 1..n})$)
$$\frac{E \vdash M : T_j, \mathcal{R} \quad j \in 1..n \quad E \vdash T}{E \vdash \ell_j(M) : T, \mathcal{R}}$$

(Msg Union Un)
$$\frac{E \vdash M : \mathsf{Un}, \mathcal{R}}{E \vdash \ell(M) : \mathsf{Un}, \mathcal{R}}$$

(Msg Tuple)
$$\frac{E \vdash M : T, \mathcal{R}_1 \quad E \vdash N : U\{M\}, \mathcal{R}_2 \quad E \vdash (x{:}T, U\{x\})}{E \vdash (M, N) : (x{:}T, U\{x\}), \mathcal{R}_1 \mid \mathcal{R}_2}$$

(Msg Tuple Un)
$$\frac{E \vdash M : \mathsf{Un}, \mathcal{R}_1 \quad E \vdash N : \mathsf{Un}, \mathcal{R}_2}{E \vdash (M, N) : \mathsf{Un}, \mathcal{R}_1 \mid \mathcal{R}_2}$$

(Msg Ok)
$$\frac{E \vdash \mathcal{R}}{E \vdash \mathsf{ok} : \mathsf{Ok}(\mathcal{R}), \mathcal{R}}$$

(Msg Ok Un)
$$\frac{E \vdash \diamond}{E \vdash \mathsf{ok} : \mathsf{Un}, \mathbf{0}}$$

The following lemma asserts that any message originating from the opponent may be assigned the Un type and $\mathbf{0}$ effect.

Lemma 1. *For any M, if* $\mathsf{fn}(M) = \{\vec{x}\}$ *then* $\vec{x}{:}\mathsf{Un} \vdash M : \mathsf{Un}, \mathbf{0}$.

Typing Processes. The judgment $E \vdash P : \mathcal{R}$ means that, given E, the effect $\mathcal{R}$ is an upper bound on the resources required for safe execution of P.

The first group of rules concerns the π-calculus fragment of our calculus. The main intuition is that the effect of a process stems from the composition of the effects of any subprocesses, together with the replicated effects of any extractable messages. The effect of a message must be replicated to account for the possibility that the message may be copied many times. In particular, if an ok is copied, it can be exercised many times. For example, suppose that E is the environment and $M = \{M, T_A, \mathsf{ok}\}_{K_{AB}}$ is the ciphertext from our discussion of the message typing rules above. We have $E \vdash M : \mathsf{Un}, \mathsf{end}\ Sending(A, B, x)$ and so we have:

$$E, net{:}\mathsf{Un} \vdash \mathsf{out}\ net\langle M \rangle : \mathsf{!end}\ Sending(A, B, x)$$

Good Processes: Basics

(Proc Subsum)
$$\frac{E \vdash P : \mathcal{R} \quad \mathcal{R} \le \mathcal{R}' \quad E \vdash \mathcal{R}'}{E \vdash P : \mathcal{R}'}$$

(Proc Output Un)
$$\frac{E \vdash M : \mathsf{Un}, \mathcal{R}_1 \quad E \vdash N : \mathsf{Un}, \mathcal{R}_2}{E \vdash \mathsf{out}\ M\langle N \rangle : \mathsf{!}\mathcal{R}_2}$$

(Proc Input Un)

$$\frac{E \vdash M : \mathsf{Un}, \mathcal{R}_1 \quad E, y{:}\mathsf{Un} \vdash P : \mathcal{R}_2 \quad y \notin \mathsf{fn}(\mathcal{R}_2)}{E \vdash \mathsf{inp}\ M(y{:}\mathsf{Un}); P : \mathcal{R}_2}$$

(Proc Res)(where T is *generative*, that is, either Un or $\mathsf{Key}(T')$ for some T')

$$\frac{E, x{:}T \vdash P : \mathcal{R} \quad x \notin \mathsf{fn}(\mathcal{R})}{E \vdash \mathsf{new}(x{:}T); P : \mathcal{R}}$$

(Proc Par)   (Proc Repeat)   (Proc Zero)

$$\frac{E \vdash P_1 : \mathcal{R}_1 \quad E \vdash P_2 : \mathcal{R}_2}{E \vdash P_1 \mid P_2 : \mathcal{R}_1 \mid \mathcal{R}_2} \qquad \frac{E \vdash P : \mathcal{R}}{E \vdash\ !P\ :\ !\mathcal{R}} \qquad \frac{E \vdash \diamond}{E \vdash \mathbf{0} : \mathbf{0}}$$

The next group of rules concerns begin- and end-assertions. As in our previous work, the effect of a begin-assertion is the effect of its continuation, minus the event, while the effect of an end-assertion is the effect of its continuation, plus the event. What is new here is the use of replication to distinguish one-to-many from one-to-one begin-assertions.

Good Processes: Correspondence Assertions

(Proc Begin)   (Proc Begin!)   (Proc End)

$$\frac{E \vdash P : \mathcal{R} \mid \mathsf{end}\ L}{E \vdash \mathsf{begin}\ L; P : \mathcal{R}} \qquad \frac{E \vdash P : \mathcal{R} \mid\ !\mathsf{end}\ L}{E \vdash \mathsf{begin}\ !L; P : \mathcal{R}} \qquad \frac{\mathsf{fn}(L) \subseteq \mathsf{dom}(E) \quad E \vdash P : \mathcal{R}}{E \vdash \mathsf{end}\ L; P : \mathcal{R} \mid \mathsf{end}\ L}$$

Next, (Proc Exercise) defines that the effect of $\mathsf{exercise}\ M; P$, where M has type $\mathsf{Ok}(\mathcal{R})$, is the effect of P minus $\mathcal{R}$, plus any effect M has itself.

Good Processes: Exercising an Ok

(Proc Exercise)

$$\frac{E \vdash M : \mathsf{Ok}(\mathcal{R}), \mathcal{R}_1 \quad E \vdash P : \mathcal{R} \mid \mathcal{R}_2}{E \vdash \mathsf{exercise}\ M; P : \mathcal{R}_1 \mid \mathcal{R}_2}$$

For instance, looking again at Example 1, we can derive:

$$A, B{:}\mathsf{Un}, x{:}Msg, o{:}\mathsf{Ok}(\mathsf{end}\ Sending(A, B, x)) \vdash \mathsf{exercise}\ o; \mathsf{end}\ Sending(A, B, x) : \mathbf{0}$$

The final group of rules is for typing message manipulation. These rules are much the same as in previous systems [GJ01a,GJ02], except for including the replicated effects of extractable messages.

Good Processes: Message Manipulation

(Proc Decrypt)

$$\frac{E \vdash L : \mathsf{Un}, \mathcal{R}_1 \quad E \vdash N : \mathsf{Key}(T), \mathcal{R}_2 \quad E, y{:}T \vdash P : \mathcal{R}_3 \quad y \notin \mathsf{fn}(\mathcal{R}_3)}{E \vdash \mathsf{decrypt}\ L\ \mathsf{is}\ \{y{:}T\}_N; P :\ !\mathcal{R}_1 \mid \mathcal{R}_3}$$

(Proc Decrypt Un)
$$\frac{E \vdash L : \mathsf{Un}, \mathcal{R}_1 \quad E \vdash N : \mathsf{Un}, \mathcal{R}_2 \quad E, y{:}\mathsf{Un} \vdash P : \mathcal{R}_3 \quad y \notin \mathsf{fn}(\mathcal{R}_3)}{E \vdash \mathsf{decrypt}\ L\ \mathsf{is}\ \{y{:}\mathsf{Un}\}_N; P : !\mathcal{R}_1 \mid \mathcal{R}_3}$$

(Proc Case)
$$\frac{E \vdash M : \mathsf{Union}(\ell_i(T_i)^{\,i \in 1..n}), \mathcal{R}_1 \quad E, x_i{:}T_i \vdash P_i : \mathcal{R}_2 \quad x_i \notin \mathsf{fn}(\mathcal{R}_2) \quad \forall i \in 1..n}{E \vdash \mathsf{case}\ M\ (\ell_i(x_i{:}T_i)P_i^{\,i \in 1..n}) : !\mathcal{R}_1 \mid \mathcal{R}_2}$$

(Proc Case Un)
$$\frac{E \vdash M : \mathsf{Un}, \mathcal{R}_1 \quad E, x_i{:}\mathsf{Un} \vdash P_i : \mathcal{R}_2 \quad x_i \notin \mathsf{fn}(\mathcal{R}_2) \quad \forall i \in 1..n}{E \vdash \mathsf{case}\ M\ (\ell_i(x_i{:}\mathsf{Un})P_i^{\,i \in 1..n}) : !\mathcal{R}_1 \mid \mathcal{R}_2}$$

(Proc Split)
$$\frac{E \vdash M : (x{:}T, U), \mathcal{R}_1 \quad E, x{:}T, y{:}U \vdash P : \mathcal{R} \quad x, y \notin \mathsf{fn}(\mathcal{R})}{E \vdash \mathsf{split}\ M\ \mathsf{is}\ (x{:}T, y{:}U); P : !\mathcal{R}_1 \mid \mathcal{R}}$$

(Proc Split Un)
$$\frac{E \vdash M : \mathsf{Un}, \mathcal{R}_1 \quad E, x{:}\mathsf{Un}, y{:}\mathsf{Un} \vdash P : \mathcal{R} \quad x, y \notin \mathsf{fn}(\mathcal{R})}{E \vdash \mathsf{split}\ M\ \mathsf{is}\ (x{:}\mathsf{Un}, y{:}\mathsf{Un}); P : !\mathcal{R}_1 \mid \mathcal{R}}$$

(Proc Match)
$$\frac{E \vdash M : (x{:}T, U\{x\}), \mathcal{R}_1 \quad E \vdash N : T, \mathcal{R}_2 \quad E, y{:}U\{N\} \vdash P : \mathcal{R} \quad y \notin \mathsf{fn}(\mathcal{R})}{E \vdash \mathsf{match}\ M\ \mathsf{is}\ (N, y{:}U\{N\}); P : !\mathcal{R}_1 \mid \mathcal{R}}$$

(Proc Match Un)
$$\frac{E \vdash M : \mathsf{Un}, \mathcal{R}_1 \quad E \vdash N : \mathsf{Un}, \mathcal{R}_2 \quad E, y{:}\mathsf{Un} \vdash P : \mathcal{R} \quad y \notin \mathsf{fn}(\mathcal{R})}{E \vdash \mathsf{match}\ M\ \mathsf{is}\ (N, y{:}\mathsf{Un}); P : !\mathcal{R}_1 \mid \mathcal{R}}$$

The following asserts that any opponent process may be assigned the **0** effect.

Lemma 2 (Opponent Typability). *For any opponent O, if* $\mathsf{fn}(O) = \{x_1, \ldots, x_n\}$, *then* $x_1{:}\mathsf{Un}, \ldots, x_n{:}\mathsf{Un} \vdash O : \mathbf{0}$.

Proof. Recall that an opponent is an untyped process containing no begin- or end-assertions, and no exercises. The result follows by induction on the size of O, with appeal to Lemma 1, (Proc Output Un), (Proc Input Un), (Proc Res), (Proc Par), (Proc Repeat), (Proc Zero), (Proc Decrypt Un), (Proc Case Un), (Proc Split Un), and (Proc Match Un). □

Runtime Invariant. We say that a state $\mathsf{new}(\vec{x}{:}\vec{T}); (\mathcal{R} \parallel P)$ is *good* if and only if the imaginary resource $\mathcal{R}$ can be assigned to P as an effect. Intuitively, this means the available resource is an upper bound of what is actually needed. Recall that (Proc Subsum) allows us to increase the effect assigned to a process.

Good States:

(State Res)	(State Base)
$E, x{:}T \vdash S \quad T$ generative	$E \vdash P : \mathcal{R}$
$E \vdash \mathsf{new}(x{:}T); S$	$E \vdash \mathcal{R} \parallel P$

The next two propositions assert that being a good state is preserved by the structural equivalence and transition relations.

Proposition 1. *If $E \vdash S$ and $S \equiv S'$ then $E \vdash S'$.*

Proposition 2. *If $E \vdash S$ and $S \to S'$ then $E \vdash S'$.*

We show that good states are fine, that is, contain no deadlocked end-assertions; theorems establishing safety and robust safety then follow easily.

Proposition 3. *If $E \vdash S$ then S is fine.*

Proof. Suppose that $S \equiv \mathsf{new}(\vec{x}{:}\vec{T}); (\mathcal{R} \parallel \mathsf{end}\, L; P \mid P')$. By Proposition 1, $E \vdash \mathsf{new}(\vec{x}{:}\vec{T}); (\mathcal{R} \parallel \mathsf{end}\, L; P \mid P')$. Therefore, $E, \vec{x}{:}\vec{T} \vdash \mathsf{end}\, L; P \mid P' : \mathcal{R}$. It follows there is $\mathcal{R}'$ such that $R \equiv \mathsf{end}\, L \mid \mathcal{R}'$. Hence S is fine. □

Theorem 1 (Safety). *If $E \vdash P : \mathbf{0}$ then P is safe.*

Proof. By (State Base), $E \vdash \mathbf{0} \parallel P$. Consider any S such that $\mathbf{0} \parallel P \to^* S$. By Propositions 1 and 2, $E \vdash S$. By Proposition 3, S is fine. So P is safe. □

Theorem 2 (Robust Safety). *If $x_1{:}\mathsf{Un}, \ldots, x_n{:}\mathsf{Un} \vdash P : \mathbf{0}$, P is robustly safe.*

Proof. Combine Theorem 1 and Lemma 2, and a weakening property of the type system. □

We can apply these theorems to verify the one-to-many correspondences of Examples 1–3 of Section 4, but we omit the details. Given processes annotated with suitable types, we claim that typechecking is decidable, though we currently have no implementation for this type system. On the other hand, we rely on human intervention to discover suitable types, such as the types for principal and session keys.

5   Summary and Conclusion

Our previous work [GJ01b,GJ01a,GJ02] shows how to verify one-to-one correspondence assertions by typechecking process calculus descriptions of protocols. This paper shows how to typecheck one-to-many correspondences. Applications include checking security protocols intended only to offer one-to-many guarantees, but also checking protocols that in fact offer stronger one-to-one guarantees, but via mechanisms, such as timestamps, beyond the scope of our type system.

There is little other work we are aware of on typechecking authenticity properties, but there are several other works on types for cryptographic protocols [Aba99,PS00,AB01,Cer01,Dug02], mostly aimed at establishing secrecy properties. Sometimes, of course, authenticity follows from secrecy [Bla02].

The ok-types introduced here are related to the types in our previous work for typing nonce challenges and responses. Like nonce types, they transfer effects by communication, allowing the type system to verify that an end-assertion in one process is justified by a corresponding begin-assertion in another. Unlike values of nonce types, values of ok-type are copyable, and may transfer an effect many times—hence, they are useful for one-to-many but not one-to-one correspondences.

The states—resources paired with processes—and the state transition relation introduced here allow for a smoother technical development than the labelled transitions and other relations used in our earlier papers. Blanchet [Bla02] formalizes correspondence assertions similarly.

The type system of Section 4 can verify only trivial one-to-one correspondences based on straightline code. In a longer version of this paper, we show how to accommodate the nonce types of an earlier paper [GJ01a] and hence to check protocols with interesting combinations of one-to-one and one-to-many correspondences.

In conclusion, the present paper usefully broadens the class of authenticity properties provable by typechecking. Still, our system continues to lack a general treatment of various issues, such as insider attacks and key compromises. We leave these questions, and the experimental evaluation of this type system, as future work.

Acknowledgements. Stimulating conversations with Ernie Cohen and with Dave Walker helped shape the ideas in this paper. Comments from the anonymous reviewers resulted in improvements to the paper.

References

[AB01]   M. Abadi and B. Blanchet. Secrecy types for asymmetric communication. In *Foundations of Software Science and Computation Structures*, volume 2030 of *Lecture Notes in Computer Science*, pages 25–41. Springer, 2001.

[Aba99]   M. Abadi. Secrecy by typing in security protocols. *Journal of the ACM*, 46(5):749–786, September 1999.

[AFG98]   M. Abadi, C. Fournet, and G. Gonthier. Secure communications implementation of channel abstractions. In *13th IEEE Symposium on Logic in Computer Science (LICS'98)*, pages 105–116, 1998.

[AFG00]   M. Abadi, C. Fournet, and G. Gonthier. Authentication primitives and their compilation. In *27th ACM Symposium on Principles of Programming Languages (POPL'00)*, pages 302–315, 2000.

[AG99]   M. Abadi and A.D. Gordon. A calculus for cryptographic protocols: The spi calculus. *Information and Computation*, 148:1–70, 1999.

[AN95]   R. Anderson and R. Needham. Programming Satan's computer. In J. van
            Leeuwen, editor, *Computer Science Today: Recent Trends and Develop-
            ments*, volume 1000 of *Lecture Notes in Computer Science*, pages 426–440.
            Springer, 1995.

[BAN89]   M. Burrows, M. Abadi, and R.M. Needham. A logic of authentication.
            Proceedings of the Royal Society of London A, 426:233–271, 1989.

[BCJS02]   F. Butler, I. Cervesato, A.D. Jaggard, and A. Scedrov. A formal analysis
            of some properties of Kerberos 5 using MSR. In *15th IEEE Computer
            Security Foundations Workshop*, pages 175–190. IEEE Computer Society
            Press, 2002.

[Bla02]   B. Blanchet. From secrecy to authenticity in security protocols. In *9th
            International Static Analysis Symposium (SAS'02)*, volume 2477 of *Lecture
            Notes in Computer Science*, pages 242–259. Springer, 2002.

[Cer01]   I. Cervesato. Typed MSR: Syntax and examples. In *First International
            Workshop on Mathematical Methods, Models and Architectures for Com-
            puter Network Security*, volume 2052 of *Lecture Notes in Computer Science*,
            pages 159–177. Springer, 2001.

[Dug02]   D. Duggan. Cryptographic types. In *15th IEEE Computer Security Foun-
            dations Workshop*, pages 238–252. IEEE Computer Society Press, 2002.

[DY83]   D. Dolev and A.C. Yao. On the security of public key protocols. *IEEE
            Transactions on Information Theory*, IT–29(2):198–208, 1983.

[Eng96]   J. Engelfriet. A multiset semantics for the pi-calculus with replication.
            Theoretical Computer Science, 153:65–94, 1996.

[FG94]   R. Focardi and R. Gorrieri. A classification of security properties for process
            algebra. *Journal of Computer Security*, 3(1):5–33, 1994.

[FGM00]   R. Focardi, R. Gorrieri, and F. Martinelli. Message authentication through
            non-interference. In *International Conference on Algebraic Methodology
            And Software Technology (AMAST2000)*, volume 1816 of *Lecture Notes in
            Computer Science*, pages 258–272. Springer, 2000.

[GJ01a]   A.D. Gordon and A. Jeffrey. Authenticity by typing for security protocols.
            In *14th IEEE Computer Security Foundations Workshop*, pages 145–159.
            IEEE Computer Society Press, 2001.

[GJ01b]   A.D. Gordon and A. Jeffrey. Typing correspondence assertions for commu-
            nication protocols. In *Mathematical Foundations of Programming Seman-
            tics 17*, volume 45 of *Electronic Notes in Theoretical Computer Science*.
            Elsevier, 2001.

[GJ02]   A.D. Gordon and A. Jeffrey. Types and effects for asymmetric crypto-
            graphic protocols. In *15th IEEE Computer Security Foundations Workshop*,
            pages 77–91. IEEE Computer Society Press, 2002.

[GL86]   D.K. Gifford and J.M. Lucassen. Integrating functional and imperative
            programming. In *ACM Conference on Lisp and Functional Programming*,
            pages 28–38, 1986.

[Gol02]   D. Gollmann. Authentication by correspondence. *IEEE Journal on Selected
            Areas in Communication*, 2002. To appear.

[GP02]   A.D. Gordon and R. Pucella. Validating a web service security abstraction
            by typing. In *ACM Workshop on XML Security*, 2002. To appear.

[GT02]   J.D. Guttman and F.J. Thayer. Authentication tests and the structure of
            bundles. *Theoretical Computer Science*, 283(2):333–380, 2002.

[LLL⁺02]   B.A. LaMacchia, S. Lange, M. Lyons, R. Martin, and K.T. Price. *.NET
            Framework Security*. Addison Wesley Professional, 2002.

[Low97]   G. Lowe. A hierarchy of authentication specifications. In *10th IEEE Computer Security Foundations Workshop*, pages 31–43. IEEE Computer Society Press, 1997.

[LY97]   T. Lindholm and F. Yellin. *The Java^{TM} Virtual Machine Specification*. Addison-Wesley, 1997.

[Mea96]   C. Meadows. The NRL Protocol Analyzer: An overview. *Journal of Logic Programming*, 26(2):113–131, 1996.

[Pau98]   L.C. Paulson. The inductive approach to verifying cryptographic protocols. *Journal of Computer Security*, 6:85–128, 1998.

[PS00]   B. Pierce and E. Sumii. Relating cryptography and polymorphism. Available from the authors, 2000.

[Ros96]   A.W. Roscoe. Intensional specifications of security protocols. In *8th IEEE Computer Security Foundations Workshop*, pages 28–38. IEEE Computer Society Press, 1996.

[Sch98]   S.A. Schneider. Verifying authentication protocols in CSP. *IEEE Transactions on Software Engineering*, 24(9):741–758, 1998.

[SM02]   A. Sabelfeld and A.C. Myers. Language-based information-flow security. *IEEE Journal on Selected Areas in Communication*, 2002. To appear.

[WL93]   T.Y.C. Woo and S.S. Lam. A semantic model for authentication protocols. In *IEEE Computer Society Symposium on Research in Security and Privacy*, pages 178–194, 1993.

Proof-Carrying Code
with Untrusted Proof Rules

George C. Necula[1] and Robert R. Schneck[2],[*]

[1] Department of Electrical Engineering and Computer Sciences
University of California, Berkeley
necula@cs.berkeley.edu
[2] Group in Logic and the Methodology of Science
University of California, Berkeley
schneck@math.berkeley.edu

Abstract. Proof-carrying code (PCC) allows a code producer to associate to a program a machine-checkable proof of its safety. In traditional implementations of PCC the producer negotiates beforehand, and in an unspecified way, with the consumer the permission to prove safety in whatever high-level way it chooses. In practice this has meant that high-level rules for type safety have been hard-wired into the system as part of the trusted code base. This limits the security and flexibility of the PCC system.

In this paper, we exhibit an approach to removing the safety proof rules from the trusted base, with a technique by which the producer can convince the consumer that a given set of high-level safety rules enforce a strong global invariant that entails the trusted low-level memory safety policy.

1 Introduction

Proof-carrying code (PCC) [Nec97] is a technique that shifts the burden of certifying properties of a program or data from the consumer to the producer, with the main goal of keeping the consumer's trusted code base (TCB) as small and trustworthy as possible. However, in the existing implementations of proof-carrying code there seems to exist a tension between the minimality of the TCB and engineering considerations necessary for handling realistic safety policies and large programs.

The system described by Colby et al. [CLN+00] was engineered to scale to large programs (e.g. half a million lines of code) and to realistic safety policies (e.g. a type-safety policy for native machine code compiled from Java [CLN+00]) with a relatively modest investment.

---

[*] This research was supported in part by National Science Foundation Career Grant No. CCR-9875171, ITR Grants No. CCR-0085949, No. CCR-0081588, and No. INT98-15731, and gifts from Microsoft Research; and a National Science Foundation Graduate Research Fellowship. The information presented here does not necessarily reflect the position or the policy of the Government and no official endorsement should be inferred.

M. Okada et al. (Eds.): ISSS 2002, LNCS 2609, pp. 283–298, 2003.

The typical interaction taking place in this PCC system is depicted in Figure 1 as a negotiation between a code producer and a code consumer. Upon being presented with a code fragment, the code consumer uses a verifier to produce a set of verification conditions (VC), whose validity entails the safety of the code. The verifier consists of two components: an instruction decoder that is responsible for interpreting the semantics of individual instructions, and a verification-condition generator (VCGen) that is responsible for handling the control-flow aspects of the code. The validity of the VC must be proved with respect to a set of proof rules that are provided (and trusted) by the code consumer. In the second stage, the code producer constructs a representation of a proof of the VC and presents that to the code consumer, who can now simply run a proof checker to satisfy itself that the VC is provable.

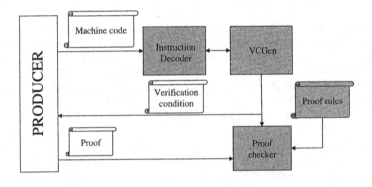

Fig. 1. The structure of a proof-carrying code system showing a dialogue between the code producer (on the left) and the code consumer (comprised of the trusted elements shown shaded).

Thus, in addition to the proof checker, the TCB for this system includes a decoder, a verification-condition generator (VCGen) and a list of proof rules, which together constitute the safety policy. Altogether the TCB requires about 15,000 to 25,000 lines of code, depending on configuration and underlying architecture. It is not inaccurate to describe this infrastructure as simple and small, and therefore easy to trust, at least when one considers possible alternatives such as trusting optimizing compilers.

However, it is reasonable to ask whether it is possible to create a working PCC with a smaller TCB. In particular, we observe that among the many lines of code that one must trust in a PCC implementation, most are independent of the safety policy, and change rarely, which implicitly means that they are tested more extensively and thus are more trustworthy. On the other hand the proof rules of the safety policy change with every safety policy. In our experience these parts are more likely to contain errors. The strategy we adopt in this paper is to use heavy-weight tools such as theorem provers for the purpose of certifying the set of proof rules used in a PCC system, while trusting the implementation of the core system. In future work we will consider mechanisms for moving even components of the VCGen system out of the TCB.

In this paper we introduce a framework in which the proof rules can be formally proven sound (in the sense that they can be used to ensure safety). This increases the security of a PCC system, because it removes the proof rules from the trusted code base, and also increases its flexibility, because code producers would be able to supply their own safety policies without compromising security. One way to view this approach is as an attempt to extend the dialogue between the code producer and the code consumer to the level of the safety-policy rules: the code producer expresses the intention to install a new set of proof rules; the code consumer inspects the rules and replies with a soundness theorem which the code producer must prove. The question then is what is the framework in which the receiver of a set of rules can state and verify a proof of their soundness? And furthermore, what is the reference proof system against which the new rules are being judged?

The supplied framework shows how to take proof rules for a safety policy, and produce a formal theorem to guarantee that, relative to the still-trusted behavior of VCGen, the notion of safety given by the proof rules really does imply memory safety. Note that we do not show how to produce the formal *proof* of this theorem; in particular, although it is necessary to the feasibility of a PCC system that the safety proofs for programs can be generated automatically (e.g. by a certifying compiler), at this point the soundness proofs for safety policies still need to be generated interactively. This is reasonable, as a single safety policy is expected to be used with a large number of individual programs. Also note that our framework ensures only memory safety. Safety policies are often expected to handle more than memory safety: for instance, a type-safety policy may also enforce abstraction, or a safety policy may include other features such as instruction counting. Memory safety can be considered to play the role of a *safety meta-policy*: the system does not accept a new safety policy unless it can at least guarantee memory safety, regardless of what else it promises to do.

In a previous paper [SN02], we first introduced a method to prove a set of safety-policy proof rules sound with respect to a reference policy of memory safety; in that framework we used the specification language of the Coq [Coq02] system to prove the soundness of a set of typing rules for native machine code compiled from Java. This paper introduces a different method to accomplish the same tasks. The new method allows for a more precise description of how the new safety policy is integrated into the PCC system; additionally, we feel that the new method can be extended more easily with plans for removing parts of the VCGen itself from the trusted code base. Although the framework has changed, it seems that much of the formal proof construction done in the older framework can be easily adapted into this new setting.

In order to provide a concrete example for how our framework operates we discuss first an example of a set of safety policy rules. Then, in Section 4, we introduce the method used by the PCC system to enforce safety, and make precise the reference memory-safety policy. In Section 5 we discuss how to incorporate a new custom safety policy, and what is required to show that the custom safety policy is at least as strong as the reference policy; we prove the soundness of the original motivating example in Section 6. Finally we discuss related work and conclude.

The results of this paper (including minor details which have been omitted due to reasons of space or presentation) have been formalized in the Coq [Coq02] system; this development is available on the web at the following URL: http://www.cs.berkeley.edu/~necula/ISSS02 .

2   An Example

Consider a code receiver that sets aside an area of accessible memory for the use of the untrusted code and wishes to ensure that the untrusted code accesses memory only within this area. We are going to refer to addresses that fall in the accessible area as valid addresses.

One producer of untrusted code chooses to use the accessible memory area to store *lists* that use the following representation invariant: (1) the value 1 is a list (the empty list), (2) a valid even address of a memory location containing a list is a list (a non-empty list), and (3) nothing else is a list.[3] We show in Figure 2 one possible fragment of untrusted code that uses this invariant. This code operates on two non-empty lists stored in registers r_a and r_b; it first truncates the list r_a to one element and then sets the second element in the list r_b to point to r_a.

$$
\begin{aligned}
&0 \;\; r_t := 1 \\
&1 \;\; [r_a] := r_t \\
&2 \;\; r_s := [r_b] \\
&3 \;\; \text{branch odd}(r_s), 5 \\
&4 \;\; [r_s] := r_a \\
&5 \;\; \text{halt}
\end{aligned}
$$

Fig. 2. An untrusted code fragment

The notation $[r_1]$ means dereference of address in r_1 and it is a read if appearing on the right-hand side of the assignment or a write otherwise. Notice that if r_a and r_b are aliases then r_s will be equal to 1 and the write at line 4 is skipped.

We can state informally the conditions that the code receiver wants to hold before this code is executed. We state these conditions on the initial values of registers:

– The value of r_a is a valid address (write in line 1 is safe),
– The value of r_b is a valid address (read in line 2 is safe),

---

[3] Such lists are of limited usefulness because there is no data in the list cells. However, they provide a simple but non-trivial example.

 — If $r_a \neq r_b$ and the contents of address r_b is even, then the contents of address r_b is a valid address (write in line 4 is safe)

But as far as the code producer is concerned these conditions are too low-level. Instead, the code producer would prefer to use the following two simple conditions:

 — The value of r_a is a non-empty list
 — The value of r_b is a non-empty list

These conditions, along with a statement of the representation invariant, ensure that our example is memory safe. Not only have we reduced the number of the conditions to be proved but we have also eliminated the need to reason about memory aliasing: as long as all memory writes preserve the representation invariant we can assume that the result of memory reads satisfies the same invariant, without having to consider all of the possible writes that the read depends on. This is arguably one of the secrets that make type checking such a practical method to ensure memory safety.

In traditional implementations of PCC we have taken the view that the producer negotiates beforehand (and in an unspecified way) with the consumer the permission to prove safety at whatever high-level it chooses. In this paper, we show one possible way in which the producer can actually convince the consumer that a given set of high-level safety rules enforce a strong global invariant that entails the low-level memory safety policy.

In the next section we introduce notation necessary for stating the safety conditions formally, first from the low-level perspective of the code consumer and then from the high-level perspective of the code producer.

3   Preliminaries

We work in an underlying logic containing a type val to be used for values and addresses, and a type state of machine states. To keep our approach general we leave the machine state largely unspecified; however for the sake of examples we use a state that consists of various registers of type val together with a pseudo-register r_M of type mem (denoting the state of memory), which comes equipped with functions upd and sel for memory update and select.

A *symbolic expression* is a function of type state $\rightarrow$ val, such that when given some values for the registers we obtain its value. Thus if e is a symbolic expression and ρ a state, then "$e\ \rho$" is the value of e in state ρ. For notational convenience we also write symbolic expressions as expressions involving variable names. For example, we write "$r_1 + r_2$" for the function that given a state yields the sum of the values of registers r_1 and r_2 in that state. Consequently we write "$r_1\ \rho$" for the value of register r_1 in state ρ.

We also use *symbolic predicates* (or simply predicates), which are functions of type state $\rightarrow$ Prop, where Prop is the type of propositions; and we write $A\ \rho$ to say that the predicate A holds in state ρ.

For convenience, we overload the arithmetic operators and the boolean connectives to work on symbolic expressions and predicates. For example, the notation $\exists x. r_1 + r_2 \geq x$ denotes a symbolic predicate whose de-sugared form is $\lambda \rho. \exists x. r_1\, \rho + r_2\, \rho \geq x$. We write $\rho[r_i \mapsto v]$ for the state ρ altered by setting the value of r_i to v. We write $A[r_i \mapsto v]$ to denote the symbolic predicate obtained from A by replacing references to r_i by v, namely $\lambda \rho. (A\, (\rho[r_i \mapsto v]))$. Finally, in order to simplify the handling of assignment, we use $r_i :=_x e$ as shorthand for $r_i = e[r_i \mapsto x]$. With this notation we can say, for example, that after an assignment $r_1 := r_1 + r_1$ the predicate $\exists x. r_1 :=_x r_1 + r_1$ holds, where x is the prior value of r_1.

VCGen works with local invariants, which are a subtype of symbolic predicates (type state $\rightarrow$ Prop). For the purposes of this paper, we assume that all local invariants have the form $(r_{pc} = n) \land A$, where n is a literal of type val denoting the value of the program counter, and A does not depend on the program counter; that is, each local invariant specifies a literal program counter, and (possibly) other facts about the state except the program counter. We use the notation (n, A) to represent this local invariant; we use the type locinv for local invariants.

4   A Formalization of Memory Safety

In this section we are going to describe the precise mechanism that a code consumer can use to enforce memory safety. First, we assume that the logic contains a predicate addr to indicate when a value is a valid address: (addr $\rho\, E$) means that E is a valid address in state ρ. The exact definition of addr depends on the particular machine and safety policy. The dependence on the machine state is useful in the presence of dynamic allocation, where ρ contains the allocation state; as with other symbolic predicates, we often suppress the dependence on ρ for convenience.

The Decoder. The code consumer uses a decoder to interpret individual instructions. In this paper we will define a couple of different decoders. The code consumer specifies a trusted *reference* decoder, and the code producer introduces the untrusted *custom* decoder for its custom safety policy. The result of any decoder for an individual instruction consists of two elements:

- The safety condition, which is a predicate that holds for states in which execution of the instruction meets the safety policy, and
- A set of possible machine states resulting from the execution of the instruction.

For example, the safety condition for memory access instructions specifies that the addresses involved are valid. For all but the branching instructions the decoder returns a single result state.

For convenience we state the decoder as a function of our type locinv of local invariants:

$$\text{decode}_{\text{ref}} : \text{locinv} \rightarrow (\text{state} \rightarrow \text{Prop}) \times (\text{set locinv}).$$

The decoder takes a local invariant (p, A) and produces a pair $(P, \mathcal{D})$; P is a local safety condition, which must hold for a machine state satisfying (p, A) to make safe progress, while $\mathcal{D}$ is a list of local invariants, one of which is guaranteed to hold of the new machine state if safe progress is made.

A possible definition of the decoder for the language used in the example from Figure 2 is shown in the Figure 3. We use r_1, r_2, and r_3 as meta-variables which need not be distinct. Notice that for the assignment instructions the resulting invariants are constructed using strongest postconditions.

Input state (p, A) with $Instr(p) = \ldots$	Local safety condition	Result states
$r_1 := n$	True	$(p+1, r_1 = n \wedge \exists x. A[r_1 \mapsto x])$
$r_1 := r_2 + r_3$	True	$(p+1, \exists x. r_1 :=_x (r_2 + r_3) \wedge A[r_1 \mapsto x])$
$r_1 := [r_2]$	$\lambda \rho.\text{addr } \rho \ (r_2 \ \rho)$	$(p+1, \exists x. r_1 :=_x (\text{sel } r_M \ r_2) \wedge A[r_1 \mapsto x])$
$[r_1] := r_2$	$\lambda \rho.\text{addr } \rho \ (r_1 \ \rho)$	$(p+1, \exists m. r_M = (\text{upd } m \ r_1 \ r_2) \wedge A[r_M \mapsto m])$
branch $Cond, n$	True	$(n, A \wedge Cond), (p+1, A \wedge \neg Cond)$
halt	True	none

Fig. 3. The definition of the reference decoder

The decoder interprets the semantics of an individual instruction. It is the responsibility of the VCGen to reflect in the final verification condition all of the local safe-progress conditions identified by the decoder. It is also the responsibility of VCGen to consider the safety of all of the "next" states specified by the decoder. To do this properly VCGen must recognize loops (possibly helped by some required annotations in the untrusted code that specify loop invariants) and must ensure that the decoder is invoked only once for each loop body.

Details of a possible definition of VCGen can be found in [Nec97,Nec98]. Here by way of example, we show in Figure 4 the sequence of invocations of the decoder that VCGen makes for the untrusted code from Figure 2, where P_0 is the local invariant at the beginning of the code fragment (the precondition of the code fragment). We assume that r_a, r_b, r_s, and r_t are distinct registers. Notice how each of the states mentioned in the column labeled "Result states" is eventually scanned; this is why the instruction at program counter 5 is scanned twice: it is in the result of the instructions at program counters 3 and 4.

To assemble the final verification condition, VCGen states that for each row with a non-trivial safety condition in Figure 4 the local invariant (shown in the column labeled A) implies the local safety condition. By rewriting the equalities generated by the assignments, we find that the resulting verification condition

p	A	Local safety condition	Result states
0	P_0	True	$\{(1, \exists x_t.P_1)\}$ where $P_1 \equiv \mathbf{r}_t = 1 \wedge P_0[\mathbf{r}_t \mapsto x_t]$
1	P_1	addr $\mathbf{r}_a$	$\{(2, \exists x_t \exists x_M.P_2)\}$ where $P_2 \equiv \mathbf{r}_M = (\text{upd } x_M \ \mathbf{r}_a \ 1) \wedge \mathbf{r}_t = 1 \wedge$ $\quad P_0[\mathbf{r}_t \mapsto x_t, \mathbf{r}_M \mapsto x_M]$
2	P_2	addr $\mathbf{r}_b$	$\{(3, \exists x_t \exists x_M \exists x_s.P_3)\}$ where $P_3 \equiv \mathbf{r}_s = (\text{sel } (\text{upd } x_M \ \mathbf{r}_a \ 1) \ \mathbf{r}_b) \wedge$ $\quad \mathbf{r}_M = (\text{upd } x_M \ \mathbf{r}_a \ 1) \wedge \mathbf{r}_t = 1 \wedge$ $\quad P_0[\mathbf{r}_t \mapsto x_t, \mathbf{r}_M \mapsto x_M, \mathbf{r}_s \mapsto x_s]$
3	P_3	True	$\{(4, \exists x_t \exists x_M \exists x_s.P_4), (5, \exists x_t \exists x_M \exists x_s.P_5)\}$ where $P_4 \equiv P_3 \wedge \text{even } (\text{sel } (\text{upd } x_M \ \mathbf{r}_a \ 1) \ \mathbf{r}_b)$ and $P_5 \equiv P_3 \wedge \text{odd } (\text{sel } (\text{upd } x_M \ \mathbf{r}_a \ 1) \ \mathbf{r}_b)$
4	P_4	addr (sel (upd x_M $\mathbf{r}_a$ 1) $\mathbf{r}_b$)	$\{(5, \exists x_t \exists x_M \exists x_s \exists y_M.P_5')\}$ where $P_5' \equiv \mathbf{r}_M = (\text{upd } y_M \ \mathbf{r}_s \ \mathbf{r}_a) \wedge P_4[\mathbf{r}_M \mapsto y_M]$
5	P_5	True	$\{\}$
5	P_5'	True	$\{\}$

Fig. 4. The operation of the reference decoder on the example code.

is essentially:

$$P_0 \Rightarrow \text{addr } \mathbf{r}_a \wedge \text{addr } \mathbf{r}_b \wedge$$
$$\left(\text{even } (\text{sel } (\text{upd } \mathbf{r}_M \ \mathbf{r}_a \ 1) \ \mathbf{r}_b) \Rightarrow \text{addr } (\text{sel } (\text{upd } \mathbf{r}_M \ \mathbf{r}_a \ 1) \ \mathbf{r}_b) \right)$$

If the code producer is willing to prove such safety predicates then we have an effective PCC system. However, one can see that the size of the predicates grows exponentially with the size of the program, and that proving them requires very low-level reasoning about aliasing relationships (which is necessary for reasoning about constructs such as "sel (upd $\mathbf{r}_M$ $\mathbf{r}_a$ 1) $\mathbf{r}_b$"). In the next section we show how a code producer can on one hand construct these proofs at a higher level, and on the other hand convince the code consumer to accept them instead of the low-level proofs.

First, we must state precisely the property that we assume to hold of the reference decoder. Let   represent the state transition relation of the machine, restricted so that only *safe* transitions are allowed; thus for example memory operations will be executed only if they are memory-safe. We assume that the machine is deterministic; if any transition is possible from a state, only one transition is possible. As usual $^+$ indicates a sequence of one or more transitions. The following correctness property is assumed to hold:

Property 1 (Reference Decoder Correctness). Let C be a local invariant. Then

$$\text{decode}_{\text{ref}} \ C = (P, \mathcal{D})$$

where $P : \texttt{state} \rightarrow \texttt{Prop}$ and $\mathcal{D}$ is a set of local invariants, such that

$$\forall \rho : \texttt{state}.(C\ \rho) \wedge (P\ \rho) \Rightarrow \bigvee_{D \in \mathcal{D}} \exists \rho' : \texttt{state}.(\rho^+ \rho') \wedge (D\ \rho').$$

This means that if the local safety condition holds then the machine can make safe progress to a state that satisfies one of the "next" states identified by the decoder.

5   Custom Safety Policies

In the safety policy enforced by the code consumer, memory operations require the provability of particular instances of addr. We shall call this the *reference safety policy*. A code producer may find it easier to prove a stronger property, such as type safety, and prove separately that any program considered safe under this new policy also meets the conditions of the reference policy. For our example with lists, the code producer could add the typing predicates list L (meaning L is a list) and nelist L (meaning L is a non-empty list). For these predicates, the code producer specifies the proof rules shown in Figure 5.

$$\frac{}{\texttt{list } 1} \qquad \frac{\texttt{nelist } L}{\texttt{list } L} \qquad \frac{\texttt{list } L \quad \texttt{even } L}{\texttt{nelist } L}$$

Fig. 5. Proof rules for a type system with lists

These proof rules do not need to be a complete description of the representation invariant. The code producer can choose to publish only those proof rules that it knows are necessary for proving the verification condition. Observe that the proof rules alone provide no instances of the form nelist L. Instead, recall that the *VC* consists of conjuncts that a local invariant implies a local safety condition; so via these implications the local invariants can provide certain nelist assumptions to be used along with the typing rules. For example, we would assume that the code fragment of Figure 2 would be called with the precondition that nelist r_a and nelist r_b.

These rules are not immediately useful for proving the verification conditions that we produced in the previous section. We would very much like to intervene in the process of producing the verification condition in order to produce smaller verification conditions that refer to the newly added predicates. It is apparent from the way in which the verification conditions are created that to accomplish this we must use a different decoder.

The Custom Decoder. The code producer achieves its desired form of the verification condition by changing the instruction decoding rules as shown in Figure 6. There are quite a few differences between this custom decoder and the reference one. The `addr` address validity safety conditions are replaced with stronger conditions, specifically that all memory reads are from non-empty lists and that all memory writes are storing lists to addresses that are non-empty lists. Also, the custom decoder gives only an approximate description of the next state. The value with which a register is initialized is forgotten, unless that value is 1, indicating the empty list. An addition is always safe but since the code producer knows that it never generates code that mixes lists with arithmetic, it chooses to ignore the actual result of the addition. In memory operations the deliberate loss of information is significant in terms of efficiency. For a memory read the decoder does not specify what value was read but only that it must be a list. And for a memory write the new contents of the memory is kept completely abstract. This makes sense because in a subsequent memory read all the decoder cares about is that a read from a non-empty list yields a list value. This last form of abstraction makes sure that terms such as (`sel` (`upd` ...)...) do not arise in the verification condition. Finally, the custom decoder abstracts the state following a conditional except in the case of the parity conditional, which it knows is used to test whether a list is a non-empty list in preparation for a memory operation.

Input state (p, A) with $Instr(p) = \ldots$	Local safety condition	Result states
$r_1 := 1$	True	$(p+1, r_1 = 1 \land \exists x. A[r_1 \mapsto x])$
$r_1 := n$	True	$(p+1, \exists x. A[r_1 \mapsto x])$
$r_1 := r_2 + r_3$	True	$(p+1, \exists x. A[r_1 \mapsto x])$
$r_1 := [r_2]$	nelist r_2	$(p+1, \text{list } r_1 \land \exists x. A[r_1 \mapsto x])$
$[r_1] := r_2$	nelist $r_1 \land$ list r_2	$(p+1, \exists x. A[r_M \mapsto x])$
branch $odd(r_1), n$	True	$(n, A), (p+1, A \land \text{even } r_1)$
branch $Cond, n$	True	$(n, A), (p+1, A)$
halt	True	none

Fig. 6. The definition of the custom decoder

Consider again the program of Figure 2. With the custom decoder the VCGen produces the following verification condition:

$$P_0 \Rightarrow \text{nelist } r_a \land \text{list } 1 \land \text{nelist } r_b \land$$
$$\left(\forall x. \text{list } x \land \text{even } x \Rightarrow \text{nelist } x \land \text{list } r_a\right)$$

Here, nelist $r_a \land$ list 1 arises from the write in line 1; nelist r_b arises from the read in line 2. In the remaining part, the quantified variable x refers to the result of the memory read in line 2; all we know is that, because it is a result of a well-typed memory read, then it is a list. We also have even x as a result of the branch, and finally we must show nelist $x \land$ list r_a for the memory write in line 4.

It is easy to see how this predicate can be proved using the typing rules for lists, provided that the precondition of the code ensures that r_a and r_b

are both non-empty lists. Notice also the similarity between this proof and a typing derivation. This is precisely the situation that the code producer wants to achieve.

The question now is how can the code producer convince the code consumer to use the custom decoder instead of the reference one, and to use the specified typing rules while checking the proof of safety.

6   Checking the Soundness of the Custom Decoder

In this section we describe the steps that the code producer must take to convince the code consumer that the combination of the custom decoder and the custom proof rules is sound with respect to the reference decoder. The overall approach is to prove that there exists a global invariant that is preserved by all instructions whenever their execution is deemed safe by the custom decoder, and furthermore that this global invariant, along with the local safety conditions produced by the custom decoder, implies the local safety conditions of the reference decoder. We use the example of the list safety policy, but will show the general case of the statement of the custom decoder theorem that the code producer must provide to the consumer.

First, observe that the code consumer manipulates the predicates list and nelist (when running the custom decoder) and their associated proof rules (when checking the proof of the VC), without actually having a complete definition of these predicates. The proof of the VC is parametric in the actual definition of the custom predicates, with only the assumption that they satisfy the proof rules. A proof of the VC then applies to *any instantiation of* list *and* nelist *that satisfies the proof rules.*

To formalize this detail, let preds be the type of the tuple of custom predicates used in a particular custom safety policy. (For the example with lists, preds = (val → Prop) × (val → Prop).) The custom proof rules, the custom decoder and the resulting verification condition (i.e., all elements that mention the custom predicates) are parameterized by an actual instantiation ψ : preds for the custom predicates. In all of these elements we attach the subscript ψ to all occurrences of the custom predicates, to denote their particular instantiation under ψ. (For example, list$_\psi$ = fst ψ and nelist$_\psi$ = snd ψ.) In general, we write A_ψ to refer to the predicate A in which all occurrences of custom predicate symbols use the instantiation ψ.

Next, we can write the set of proof rules as a predicate Rules parameterized by an instantiation ψ. In this predicate each of the rules contributes a conjunct. For the example with lists (the rules shown in Figure 5):

$$Rules_\psi = \text{list}_\psi \ 1 \ \wedge$$
$$(\forall L.\text{nelist}_\psi \ L \Rightarrow \text{list}_\psi \ L) \ \wedge$$
$$(\forall L.\text{list}_\psi \ L \wedge \text{even } L \Rightarrow \text{nelist}_\psi \ L)$$

The custom predicates in our example are unary and appear to be independent of the execution state. Yet, their instantiations implicitly refer to the state of the memory since a value can be a non-empty list only in a state in which the memory location it denotes contains a list. In general, the instantiations of the custom predicates depend on the state, and we might need to change the instantiation when the state changes.

The next major element in the proof of soundness of the custom decoder is a generalized form of decoder correctness property that allows for a global invariant:

Property 2 (Generalized Decoder Correctness). Let `preds` be the type of the custom predicates and `Rules : preds → Prop` be the custom proof rules. Let $I : \texttt{preds} \to \texttt{state} \to \texttt{Prop}$, the *global invariant*, be some predicate of states involving the custom predicates. Then we say that a decoder d satisfies the *correctness property with invariant* I if, for any C with $d\,C = (P, \mathcal{D})$, we have

$$\forall \rho : \texttt{state}.\, \forall \psi : \texttt{preds}.\, (\texttt{Rules}_\psi) \wedge (I_\psi\, \rho) \wedge (C_\psi\, \rho) \wedge (P_\psi\, \rho) \Rightarrow$$

$$\exists \rho' : \texttt{state}.\, (\rho^+ \rho') \wedge \bigvee_{E \in \mathcal{D}} \exists \psi' : \texttt{preds}.\, (\texttt{Rules}_{\psi'}) \wedge (I_{\psi'}\, \rho') \wedge (E_{\psi'}\, \rho')$$

This is worth restating: consider a state ρ, and an instantiation ψ of the custom predicates such that ψ obeys the custom proof rules. If ρ satisfies the global invariant, the input local invariant, and the output proof obligation (all instantiated at ψ), then the machine can make safe progress to some new state ρ'. Furthermore, there is a (possibly) new instantiation ψ' of the custom predicates corresponding to the new state, which obeys the custom proof rules, such that ρ' satisfies the global invariant and one of the output local invariants, each instantiated at ψ'.

We use without proof the following fact about the trusted VCGen. VCGen functions correctly—in that the provability of the *VC* implies safety of the program—using any custom predicates, custom proof rules, and custom decoder, as long as there is a global invariant I such that

1. the decoder satisfies the correctness property with invariant I, and
2. there is some instantiation ψ of the custom predicates, obeying the custom proof rules, such that I_ψ holds of the initial state of the machine upon execution of the program.

The second fact depends depends on the particular machine and safety policy, and is typically much less interesting, and so we will not consider this requirement in this paper.

We now consider how to go about proving the correctness of a custom decoder. Since we already have access to the reference decoder, which is known to satisfy the correctness property (with invariant `True`), we can use the reference decoder to prove correctness for the custom decoder. In particular, we have the following lemma that allows us to replace all consideration of the transition relation with consideration instead of the reference decoder.

Lemma 1. *Let* I : preds $\rightarrow$ state $\rightarrow$ Prop. *The following conditions ensure that* decode$_{\text{cus}}$ *satisfies the correctness property with invariant* I: *let* C *be any local invariant (possibly dependent on* preds*) and let* ψ *be any instantiation of* preds *that obeys the custom proof rules* Rules. *Let* decode$_{\text{cus}}$ $C = (P, \mathcal{D}_{\text{cus}})$; *let* decode$_{\text{ref}}$ $(I_\psi \wedge C_\psi \wedge P_\psi) = (Q, \mathcal{D}_{\text{ref}})$. *The conditions are*

1. $\forall \rho.(I_\psi\, \rho) \wedge (P_\psi\, \rho) \Rightarrow (Q\, \rho)$;
2. $\displaystyle\bigwedge_{D \in \mathcal{D}_{\text{ref}}} \forall \rho'.(D\, \rho') \Rightarrow \bigvee_{E \in \mathcal{D}_{\text{cus}}} \exists \psi' : \text{preds}.\, (\text{Rules}_{\psi'}) \wedge (I_{\psi'}\, \rho') \wedge (E_{\psi'}\, \rho')$.

Proof. We are going to show that the custom decoder satisfies the generalized decoder correctness property. Let ρ be any state that satisfies all of I_ψ, C_ψ, and P_ψ. By the first condition, we have that $(Q\, \rho)$, and therefore, by the correctness of the reference decoder, safe progress can be made to a new state ρ' which satisfies one of the local invariants D in $\mathcal{D}_{\text{ref}}$. But then the second condition ensures that there is some local invariant E in $\mathcal{D}_{\text{cus}}$, and a (possibly) new instantiation ψ' that obeys the custom proof rules, such that ρ' satisfies $E_{\psi'}$ as well as $I_{\psi'}$. This suffices to establish the correctness of the custom decoder. □

A decoder can be specified as a table indexed by the instruction kind, as we have seen in previous sections. The code consumer verifies the safety of the custom decoder by applying Lemma 1. Thus, the code producer must supply a global invariant I and a number of proofs, as follows. For each row in the definition of the custom decoder, let P and $\mathcal{D}_{\text{cus}}$ be respectively the local safety condition and the resulting states corresponding to an arbitrary local invariant C. Find the row in the definition of the reference decoder that corresponds to the same instruction kind; let Q and $\mathcal{D}_{\text{ref}}$ be respectively the local safety condition and the resulting states of the reference decoder for the local invariant $(I_\psi \wedge C_\psi \wedge P_\psi)$, where ψ is some instantiation of the custom predicates that obeys the custom proof rules. Observe that since the reference decoder output is parametric in the input local invariant (except the program counter), we can consider Q and each $D \in \mathcal{D}_{\text{ref}}$ to be parameterized by ψ; thus, we write Q_ψ and D_ψ. The following items must be provided:

1. A proof that, for any instantiation ψ such that ψ satisfies the custom proof rules, $I_\psi \wedge P_\psi \Rightarrow Q_\psi$;
2. for each $D \in \mathcal{D}_{\text{ref}}$, and for any instantiation ψ obeying the custom proof rules, a new instantiation ψ' obeying the proof rules together with a proof that $D_\psi \Rightarrow I_{\psi'} \wedge E_{\psi'}$, for some $E \in \mathcal{D}_{\text{cus}}$.

In the absence of any sort of allocation operation, the second condition will often be established with $\psi' = \psi$ as we shall see.

Once the code consumer receives the above elements and checks the included proofs, it knows that all of the conditions required by Lemma 1 are satisfied and thus the combination of the custom proof rules and the custom decoder is safe to use instead of the reference decoder. In the next section we give concrete examples of these elements for the list-based safety policy.

The Soundness of the Example Safety Policy. First we must introduce an appropriate global invariant I with which to prove the correctness of the custom decoder for the `list` safety policy. We will use

$$(I_\psi \; \rho) \overset{def}{=} \forall x.(\mathtt{nelist}_\psi \; x) \Rightarrow \Big((\mathtt{addr} \; \rho \; x) \wedge \big(\mathtt{list}_\psi \; (\mathtt{sel} \; (\mathbf{r}_M \; \rho) \; x)\big)\Big).$$

Thus every non-empty list must be a valid memory address containing a list. For a more complicated safety policy, one can expect some work in determining an invariant which has the correct strength, neither too strong nor too weak, to be preserved. For our example this invariant suffices.

Next we have to provide the necessary proofs for each row in the definition of the custom decoder (shown in Figure 6). We show below only some representative cases.

For an addition, Q is `True`, and thus condition 1 is trivial. For condition 2, there is only one state in $\mathcal{D}_{\mathtt{ref}}$ and also in $\mathcal{D}_{\mathtt{cus}}$, and given an instantiation ψ of the predicates obeying the proof rules, we have to find a new instantiation ψ' obeying the proof rules, such that:

$$(\exists x. \mathbf{r}_1 :=_x (\mathbf{r}_2 + \mathbf{r}_3) \wedge (I_\psi \wedge C_\psi)[\mathbf{r}_1 \mapsto x]) \Rightarrow I_{\psi'} \wedge \exists x. C_{\psi'}[\mathbf{r}_1 \mapsto x]$$

Since the global invariant depends only on the memory, and in particular not on the changed register $\mathbf{r}_1$, we simply choose $\psi' = \psi$ and the required condition follows.

For the case of a memory read we have

$$P_\psi = (\mathtt{nelist}_\psi \; \mathbf{r}_2);$$
$$\mathcal{D}_{\mathtt{cus}} = \{(p+1, (\mathtt{list}_\psi \; \mathbf{r}_1) \wedge \exists x. C_\psi[\mathbf{r}_1 \mapsto x])\};$$
$$Q_\psi = (\mathtt{addr} \; \rho \; \mathbf{r}_2);$$
$$\mathcal{D}_{\mathtt{ref}} = \{(p+1, \exists x. \mathbf{r}_1 :=_x (\mathtt{sel} \; \mathbf{r}_M \; \mathbf{r}_2) \wedge (I_\psi \wedge C_\psi \wedge P_\psi)[\mathbf{r}_1 \mapsto x])\}.$$

Condition 1 ($I_\psi \wedge P_\psi \Rightarrow Q_\psi$) follows from the definition of the global invariant. Condition 2 requires showing that

$$\exists x. \big(\mathbf{r}_1 :=_x (\mathtt{sel} \; \mathbf{r}_M \; \mathbf{r}_2) \wedge (I_\psi \wedge C_\psi \wedge P_\psi)[\mathbf{r}_1 \mapsto x]\big) \Rightarrow$$
$$I_{\psi'} \wedge (\mathtt{list}_{\psi'} \; \mathbf{r}_1) \wedge \exists x. C_{\psi'}[\mathbf{r}_1 \mapsto x].$$

Since a memory read does not change which values denote lists or non-empty lists, we choose $\psi' = \psi$. This mostly follows as for the addition; to show that $(\mathtt{list}_{\psi'} \; \mathbf{r}_1)$, observe that it is equivalent to $(\mathtt{list}_{\psi'} \; (\mathtt{sel} \; \mathbf{r}_M \; \mathbf{r}_2))[\mathbf{r}_1 \mapsto x]$, which follows from $(I_\psi \wedge P_\psi)[\mathbf{r}_1 \mapsto x]$, where x is the value of $\mathbf{r}_1$ prior to the assignment. (The x is only important in the case where $\mathbf{r}_1$ and $\mathbf{r}_2$ are the same register.)

For the case of a memory update, the proof of condition 1 follows in a similar manner. Condition 2 is more interesting, since we must show that the global invariant still holds in the state after the memory update. However, since a memory update does not change which values denote lists or non-empty lists, we can still choose $\psi' = \psi$. In this case we have:

$$P_\psi = (\text{nelist}_\psi \; r_1) \wedge (\text{list}_\psi \; r_2);$$
$$\mathcal{D}_{\text{cus}} = \{(p+1, \exists m.C_\psi[r_M \mapsto m])\};$$
$$Q_\psi = (\text{addr} \; \rho \; r_1);$$
$$\mathcal{D}_{\text{ref}} = \{(p+1, \exists m.r_M = (\text{upd} \; m \; r_1 \; r_2) \wedge (I_\psi \wedge C_\psi \wedge P_\psi)[r_M \mapsto m])\}.$$

The difficult part is to show that, given the fact that $\forall x.(\text{nelist}_\psi \; x) \Rightarrow (\text{list}_\psi \; (\text{sel} \; m \; x))$ for the old memory state m, we still have $\forall x.(\text{nelist}_\psi \; x) \Rightarrow (\text{list}_\psi \; (\text{sel} \; (\text{upd} \; m \; r_1 \; r_2) \; x))$. If $x \neq r_1$ then we use the fact that $(\text{sel} \; m \; x) = (\text{sel} \; (\text{upd} \; m \; r_1 \; r_2) \; x)$; and if $x = r_1$, then $(\text{sel} \; (\text{upd} \; m \; r_1 \; r_2) \; x) = r_2$, and we can use P, which guarantees that $(\text{list}_\psi \; r_2)$.

The remaining rows in the definition of the custom decoder are relatively simple proofs that we omit here. This proof of generalized decoder correctness has been formalized in Coq and is available on the web at the following URL: http://www.cs.berkeley.edu/~necula/ISSS02 . The formal development also includes formalizations of the notions of local invariants and decoders, and the proof of Lemma 1.

Notice that the proofs that the code producer must supply with the custom safety policy are not likely to be produced completely automatically. However, we have found that these proofs can be done with relatively modest effort using a proof assistant such as Coq. Coq has support for the inductive definitions of instantiation predicates and for reasoning with them. Ideally, the code consumer would have a (small, more easily trusted) proof checker that is also able to verify such reasoning.

7   Conclusion and Future Directions

Appel, Felty, and others have introduced *foundational proof-carrying code* (FPCC) [AF00,App01], a variant PCC framework in which the trusted computing base contains only a definition of the semantics of machine instructions and the notion of safety in some foundational logic. The safety theorem is then directly expressible in the logic: simply that when the integers that compose the program are loaded into memory and the machine's program counter is set to the beginning of the program, the machine will never reach a state of attempting an unsafe instruction. Finally, the code is accompanied by a proof of the safety theorem.

It is worth pointing out a difference in our approach to formal type-safety proofs. Appel and Felty in [AF00] advocate a semantic approach: typing judgments are assigned a semantic truth-value relative to the state, such that typing rules are to be proven as lemmas, and the safety of a well-typed machine state follows immediately from the semantic definition of well-typedness. In contrast we have found the syntactic approach (where we work directly with the inductive definitions of derivations of typing judgments) to be successful, and almost certainly conceptually simpler. In this respect, our work bears some similarity to the work of Hamid et al. [HST+02], who also aim to develop a full-fledged FPCC system, but advocate the syntactic approach.

While we think that the FPCC approach is quite a promising research direction it is already apparent that the cost of implementing such a system that operates on large programs is much higher than the cost of implementing a traditional PCC system (such as Touchstone [CLN+00]).

Touchstone and FPCC constitute two extremes in the PCC design spectrum. We propose in this paper one incremental step that will take a traditional PCC system closer to the ideal goal of FPCC. In future work we plan to make more steps in the same direction and more specifically to address the issue of the trusted VCGen. Ideally, we imagine a completely generic PCC system in which the code producer first uploads a custom safety policy consisting of a specialized decoder and VCGen, along with new trusted proof rules. Then, the code producer can upload programs whose proofs can be very short and easy to generate, since the bulk of the safety argument is embodied in the custom safety policy elements.

References

[AF00.]   Andrew W. Appel and Amy P. Felty. A semantic model of types and machine instructions for proof-carrying code. In *POPL '00: The 27th ACM SIGPLAN-SIGACT Symposium on Principles of Programming Languages*, pages 243–253. ACM Press, January 2000.

[App01.]   Andrew W. Appel. Foundational proof-carrying code. In *Proceedings of the 16th Annual IEEE Symposium on Logic in Computer Science*, pages 247–258, June 2001.

[CLN+00.] Christopher Colby, Peter Lee, George C. Necula, Fred Blau, Mark Plesko, and Kenneth Cline. A certifying compiler for Java. *ACM SIGPLAN Notices*, 35(5):95–107, May 2000.

[Coq02.]   Coq Development Team. The Coq proof assistant reference manual, version 7.3. May 2002.

[HST+02.] Nadeem A. Hamid, Zhong Shao, Valery Trifonov, Stefan Monnier, and Zhaozhong Ni. A syntactic approach to foundational proof-carrying code. In *Proceedings of the Seventeenth Annual IEEE Symposium on Logic in Computer Science*, pages 89–100, Copenhagen, Denmark, July 2002.

[Nec97.]   George C. Necula. Proof-carrying code. In *The 24th Annual ACM Symposium on Principles of Programming Languages*, pages 106–119. ACM, January 1997.

[Nec98.]   George C. Necula. *Compiling with Proofs*. PhD thesis, Carnegie Mellon University, September 1998. Also available as CMU-CS-98-154.

[SN02.]   Robert R. Schneck and George C. Necula. A gradual approach to a more trustworthy, yet scalable, proof-carrying code. In *Proceedings of the 18th International Conference on Automated Deduction (CADE-18)*, pages 47–62, Copenhagen, Denmark, July 2002. Springer-Verlag.

Verification of Authentication Protocols Based on the Binding Relation

Masami Hagiya, Ryo Takemura, Koichi Takahashi, and Takamichi Saito

Graduate School of Information Science and Technology,
University of Tokyo
National Institute of Advanced Industrial Science and Technology
Faculty of Science and Technology, Tokyo University of Technology

Abstract. The correctness of an authentication protocol is based on, among others, the relation between nonces and data that is established in the course of execution of the protocol. In this paper, we formulate an inference system that derives the secrecy of nonces and the relation that binds nonces and data. It is easy to show the correctness of a protocol by directly deriving the binding relation using the inference rules. Depending on situations, it is also possible to extend the inference system by simply adding new inference rules. We give some example protocols whose correctness can only be shown using some conditions on nonces that are formulated as additional inference rules.

1 Introduction

There have been proposed a huge number of methods for proving the correctness of an authentication protocol, including BAN logic [2], constructing formal proofs by inductive definitions and mathematical inductions [11,12] under a proof assistant [13], model checking [8,10], formulating inference rules on multiset rewriting [3], the strand space theory [17,18,19,20], its automatic verifier [16, 14], the semi-automatic first-order invariant generator and its verifier [4], and automatic verification by limiting the number of processes [9].

Among the above mentioned methods, the *strand space theory* is widely used to mathematically prove the correctness of an authentication protocol [19]. A *strand* is a thread of execution by a principal or an intruder under the target protocol. More concretely, a strand is a sequence of message sending events and message receiving events of a principal. To prove the correctness of a protocol, we first assume the existence of a strand of the authenticating principal, and then show the existence of the corresponding strand of the authenticated principal. The correspondence between the two strands is known as the *agreement* property of the protocol.

However, using the strand space theory, we often have to prove some fundamental properties of strands before showing the agreement. This makes the strand space theory very cumbersome. Therefore, *authentication tests* were proposed to overcome this situation and simplify inferences under the strand space theory [5]. An authentication test defines a pattern of protocols. Properties of

M. Okada et al. (Eds.): ISSS 2002, LNCS 2609, pp. 299–316, 2003.

such a pattern are prepared as theorems under the strand space theory in advance. Given an actual protocol, we match a part of the protocol with a pattern, and derive the correctness of the protocol from theorems about the pattern.

In general, the correctness of an authentication protocol is based on the relation between nonces and data that is established during execution of the protocol. Such a relation binds nonces and data and guarantees the uniqueness of data with respect to the nonces bound to them. Authentication tests in the strand space theory can also be considered as a method to demonstrate a binding relation between nonces and data.

Therefore, in this paper, we propose a simple method to prove the correctness of an authentication protocol based on the binding relation between nonces and data. We use an inference system that can conclude the secrecy of nonces and the binding relation between nonces and data. Deriving a binding relation by the inference system almost corresponds to an application of an authentication test pattern. But our method can derive a binding relation more directly in the sense that inferences are made at the symbolic level, where the notion of strands is implicit. And the range of verifiable protocols is larger than that of authentication tests. Moreover, we can extend the inference system by simply adding inference rules depending on the situation. We can also automate inferences very easily.

The method deals with two-party protocols with public keys and also with symmetric keys generated by nonces. In the last section, we briefly discuss the possibility of extending the method to three- or multi-party protocols and protocols with time stamps.

Consider a problem that principal A authenticates principal B in such a protocol. A *strand* of a principal is a sequence of nodes each of which describes sending or receiving a message by the principal during execution of the protocol. When we define a protocol, we denote the strand of A and the corresponding strand of B by $S_A(A, B, X_1, \cdots, X_n)$ and $S_B(A, B, X_1, \cdots, X_n)$, respectively. Parameters of a strand other than A and B are represented by $X_1, \cdots, X_n$. They determine the messages sent or received in the strand. They usually include nonces newly generated by A and B during execution of the protocol.

Sending and receiving nodes are alternately arranged in the strands $S_A(A, B, \cdots)$ and $S_B(A, B, \cdots)$. A sending node of one strand corresponds to some receiving node of the other. If the strand $S_A(A, B, \cdots)$ is the initiator of the protocol and the strand $S_B(A, B, \cdots)$ is the responder, they are of the following form.

$$S_A(A, B, X_1, \cdots, X_n) = +t_1, -t_2, +t_3, \cdots$$
$$S_B(A, B, X_1, \cdots, X_n) = -t_1, +t_2, -t_3, \cdots$$

$+t_i$ represents a node sending the message t_i, and $-t_i$ represents a node receiving t_i. Conversely, if the strand $S_A(A, B, \cdots)$ is the responder and the strand $S_B(A, B, \cdots)$ is the initiator, they are of the following form.

$$S_A(A, B, X_1, \cdots, X_n) = -t_1, +t_2, -t_3, \cdots$$
$$S_B(A, B, X_1, \cdots, X_n) = +t_1, -t_2, +t_3, \cdots$$

In this paper, we assume that when a principal sends a message, the principle can construct the message only from atomic symbols. In other words, we only deal with such protocols in this paper.

When we check whether the principal A authenticates the principal B, we assume that the strand of A ends with a message receiving node. That is, the strands are of the following form.

$$S_A(A, B, X_1, \cdots, X_n) = \cdots, -t_k$$
$$S_B(A, B, X_1, \cdots, X_n) = \cdots, +t_k$$

The message t_k is the final one that the principal B sends to the principal A.

In our method, we examine the following two conditions:

- whether the nonce N is kept *secret* from principals other than A and B, and
- whether the parameter X is *bound* to the nonce N.

The sentence "the parameter X is bound to the nonce N" means that the principal A can confirm that the parameter X *corresponds* to the nonce N inside the principal B. In Section 4, we will precisely formalize the concept of *binding*.

We introduce the following three judgements to formalize the above conditions.

$$\vdash N \text{ secret} \qquad \vdash N \text{ binds } X \qquad \vdash N \text{ binds' } X$$

The first judgement means that the nonce N is kept secret from principals other than A and B. The second one means that the parameter X is bound to the nonce N. The third judgement is weaker than the second in the sense that the uniqueness of X is not guaranteed.

Moreover, we introduce the following two judgements for deriving the above judgements.

$$i \vdash N \text{ secret} \qquad i \vdash N \text{ binds } X$$

The first judgement means that the nonce N is kept secret after the exchange of the message t_i (even if an intruder exists between A and B). The second judgement means that the parameter X is bound to the nonce N when B receives the message t_i from A.

The judgement $\vdash N$ **secret** is equivalent to that the judgement $i \vdash N$ **secret** holds for every i ($i \leq k$). (To the contrary, $\vdash N$ **binds** X is not equivalent to that $i \vdash N$ **binds** X holds for every i.)

1.1 Example 1

We describe an example in which the correctness of an authentication protocol is proven by our method. The correctness consists of the secrecy and the authenticity. The secrecy means that the nonce is not leaked out to principals other than A and B, and is represented by the judgement $\vdash N$ **secret**. The authenticity means that for a certain nonce in the strand of the authenticating principal, there exists a corresponding strand of the authenticated principal which shares the nonce and other parameters, and is represented by the judgement of **binds**.

Let us consider the following protocol [15].

$$S_A(A, B, N_A, N_B) = +\{N_A, A\}_{KB}, -\{N_A, N_B\}_{KA}, +\{B\}_{N_B}$$
$$S_B(A, B, N_A, N_B) = -\{N_A, A\}_{KB}, +\{N_A, N_B\}_{KA}, -\{B\}_{N_B}$$

The nonces N_A and N_B are generated by the principals A and B, respectively.

When A authenticates B, the last message is not used, so we consider the following protocol.

$$S_A(A, B, N_A, N_B) = +\{N_A, A\}_{KB}, -\{N_A, N_B\}_{KA}$$
$$S_B(A, B, N_A, N_B) = -\{N_A, A\}_{KB}, +\{N_A, N_B\}_{KA}$$

In this protocol, the principal A is the initiator, who generates nonce N_A and sends the message $t_1 = \{N_A, A\}_{KB}$ to the principal B. This message is encrypted by the public key KB of B. Since principals other than B can never see the contents of the message, when this message is sent by A and is received by B, the following judgement holds.

$$1 \vdash N_A \text{ secret}$$

Since the parameter A is sent together with N_A in an encrypted form in the message t_1,

$$1 \vdash N_A \text{ binds } A$$

holds. This means that A is bound to N_A when the principal B receives the message t_1. And since the message $\{N_A, A\}_{KB}$ is encrypted by the public key of B,

$$1 \vdash N_A \text{ binds } B$$

also holds.

The principal B sends $t_2 = \{N_A, N_B\}_{KA}$ to A in the next step. The principal B correctly recognizes A after B receives t_1, because $1 \vdash N_A$ **binds** A holds. The nonce N_A is still kept secret after the exchange of the message t_2, because t_2 is encrypted by KA. Hence,

$$2 \vdash N_A \text{ secret}$$

holds. Therefore,

$$\vdash N_A \text{ secret}$$

holds because the message t_2 is the last one in the protocol.

The principal A can confirm that the principal B has received the message t_1 because the nonce N_A is included in the received message t_2. Therefore,

$$\vdash N_A \text{ binds } A \quad \text{and} \quad \vdash N_A \text{ binds } B$$

hold from $1 \vdash N_A$ **binds** A and $1 \vdash N_A$ **binds** B, respectively.

The nonces N_A and N_B are encrypted together by KA in the message t_2, so

$$\vdash N_B \text{ binds' } N_A$$

holds. Since N_B is a nonce generated by B, it uniquely determines N_A. Therefore,

$$\vdash N_B \textbf{ binds } N_A$$

is derived, and we have the following judgements, using the transitivity of **binds**.

$$\vdash N_B \textbf{ binds } A \qquad \vdash N_B \textbf{ binds } B$$

As a consequence, the relations that bind A, B and N_A to N_B are established, hence the authenticity holds. (See the theorem in Section 4).

Next, we swap the roles of A and B, and consider the principal B as the initiator and the principal A as the responder in the above example.

$$S_A(A, B, N_A, N_B) = -\{N_B, B\}_{KA}, +\{N_B, N_A\}_{KB}, -\{A\}_{N_A}$$
$$S_B(A, B, N_A, N_B) = +\{N_B, B\}_{KA}, -\{N_B, N_A\}_{KB}, +\{A\}_{N_A}$$

We swap A and B because all the judgements beginning with $\vdash$ are concerned with authentication from A's side. (Later, we introduce judgements beginning with $\vdash_B$, which are concerned with authentication from B's side.)

In this case, we examine $t_2 = \{N_B, N_A\}_{KB}$ first. By similar inferences as above, the following judgements are derived.

$$2 \vdash N_A \textbf{ secret} \qquad 2 \vdash N_A \textbf{ binds } N_B \qquad 2 \vdash N_A \textbf{ binds } B$$

However, note that the judgement $2 \vdash N_A$ **binds** A does not hold because the message $\{N_B, N_A\}_{KB}$ does not include A.

Next, the principal B sends the message $t_3 = \{A\}_{N_A}$ to the principal A. When A receives it, since the nonce N_A is used as the key of t_3, $3 \vdash N_A$ **secret** holds. Therefore, $\vdash N_A$ **secret** holds.

When the principal A receives t_3, the principal A can confirm that the principal B has received t_2, because the nonce N_A is included in t_3 as a key. Therefore,

$$\vdash N_A \textbf{ binds } N_B \qquad \text{and} \qquad \vdash N_A \textbf{ binds } B$$

hold from $2 \vdash N_A$ **binds** N_B and $2 \vdash N_A$ **binds** B, respectively. Moreover, $\vdash N_A$ **binds'** A holds because A is encrypted by N_A in t_3. We then obtain

$$\vdash N_A \textbf{ binds } A$$

from $\vdash N_A$ **binds'** A, $\vdash N_A$ **binds** N_B, and the fact that N_B is generated by B and determines A. Refer to the rule (BD2) in Section 2.8. (The rule is formulated using **guarantees**.)

As a consequence, the authentication is proven because the relations that bind A, B and N_B to N_A are established.

1.2   Outline of the Rest of the Paper

The rest of the paper is organized as follows. In the next section, we define the syntax of messages and explain the inference rules for deriving judgements. We then show some examples of inferences in Section 3, and discuss the soundness of the inference rules in Section 4. In the final section, we give the concluding remarks including the limitation of our method.

2   Inference Rules

In this section, we first define the syntax of messages. We then explain some general inference rules about secrecy and binding. We finally formulate the inference rules about messages from principal A to principal B, and those about messages from B to A.

Below, we assume that the target protocol is given by a sequence $t_1, \cdots, t_k$ of messages exchanged by A and B. The last message t_k is sent from B to A.

The inference rules are fixed once the target protocol is given. In the inference rules, parameters such as A, B and nonces are treated as symbolic names and not as variables. That is, during derivation of judgements by the inference rules, these parameters are are not replaced with some other values. On the other hand, when the protocol is executed, these parameters are instantiated with concrete values.

Note that judgements beginning with $\vdash$ are all intended to show the authentication of B by A, although we introduce judgements beginning with $\vdash_B$ in Section 2.9, which are for showing the authentication of A by B.

2.1   Messages

In this paper, messages between principals are represented by t, t_1, t_2, t', and so on. The syntax of messages is as follows.

$$t ::= A \mid B \mid N \mid c \mid (t,t) \mid \{t\}_K \mid \{t\}_N \mid h(t)$$

A and B represent the names of the principals A and B, respectively. N represents the name of a nonce.

c represents a constant. Especially, the constant that identifies the i-th message of the target protocol is represented by c_i. There may be more than one such constant in the i-th message, but each should occur only once in the message. In the following, one of such constants is denoted by c_i.

(t_1, t_2) represents a pair of messages t_1 and t_2. $\{t\}_K$ represents an encrypted message of t by an asymmetric key K. We consider KA (the public key of A), KB (the public key of B), KA^{-1} (the secret key of A), KB^{-1} (the secret key of B) as asymmetric keys. (We assume that the correspondence between a principal and the public key of the principal is maintained, and the secret key of a principal is never compromised.) $\{t\}_N$ represents an encrypted message of t by a symmetric key generated by N. $h(t)$ represents the result applying a hash function h to t.

2.2   Subterm

We write $s \sqsubseteq t$ to denote that s is a subterm of message t. It means that s occurs as a message in the construction of the message t. Note that N is not a subterm of $\{t\}_N$ unless N is a subterm of t. And we write $s \sqsubseteq_N t$ to denote that s is a subterm of message t that exclusively includes N as a subterm, that is, t does not include N as a subterm outside of s.

2.3   Secrecy

Here, we assume N is a nonce generated by A. When A generates N, it is secret from principals other than A. Therefore,

$$\frac{A \text{ generates } N \text{ when sending } t_i \quad j < i}{j \vdash N \text{ secret}}$$

holds. If the message t_i does not include N as a subterm ($N \not\sqsubseteq t_i$), the secrecy continues to hold.

$$\frac{i - 1 \vdash N \text{ secret} \quad N \not\sqsubseteq t_i}{i \vdash N \text{ secret}}$$

Note that N may occur as a key in t_i.
$\vdash N$ **secret** is equivalent to that $i \vdash N$ **secret** holds for every i ($i \leq k$). This implies the following rules.

$$\frac{k \vdash N \text{ secret}}{\vdash N \text{ secret}}$$

Note that the secrecy of a nonce generated by B cannot be judged from A's side in general. (Remember that all judgements beginning with $\vdash$ are from A's side.)

2.4   Binding

The binding relation $i \vdash N$ **binds** X derived after B receives t_i does not imply the *absolute* binding relation $\vdash N$ **binds** X, unless A receives an appropriate response message from B. This is described by the following rule.

$$\frac{i < i' \quad i \vdash N \text{ binds } X \quad i' \vdash N \text{ guarantees } t' \quad \vdash N \text{ secret}}{\vdash N \text{ binds } X}$$

The judgement $i' \vdash N$ **guarantees** t' means that the nonce N is included in the response message $t_{i'}$ from B to A, and N guarantees the contents of the subterm t' of $t_{i'}$. The above rule means that when $i' \vdash N$ **guarantees** t' holds, the binding relation $i \vdash N$ **binds** X derived before the i'-th step implies the absolute binding relation $\vdash N$ **binds** X. (More precise meaning of the judgements will be given in Section 4. Note that t' is not used in the rule.)

2.5   Decomposition and Construction of Messages

Below, P denotes either the principal A or the principal B. A judgement $i \vdash t_i \downarrow_P t$ means that when the principal P receives the message t_i, P can inspect the subterm t by decomposing t_i. Firstly, we assume that $\downarrow_P$ is a reflective and transitive relation, i.e., the following rules hold.

$$i \vdash t \downarrow_P t \qquad \frac{i \vdash t \downarrow_P t' \quad i \vdash t' \downarrow_P t''}{i \vdash t \downarrow_P t''}$$

The following rules define $\downarrow_P$ according to the structure of messages. Q also denotes either A or B.

$$\frac{i \vdash t \downarrow_P (t_1, t_2)}{i \vdash t \downarrow_P t_j}$$

$$i \vdash \{t\}_{KP} \downarrow_P P \ \wedge \ i \vdash \{t\}_{KP} \downarrow_P t$$
$$i \vdash \{t\}_{KQ^{-1}} \downarrow_P Q \ \wedge \ i \vdash \{t\}_{KQ^{-1}} \downarrow_P t$$
$$\frac{i \vdash P \text{ knows } N}{i \vdash \{t\}_N \downarrow_P N \ \wedge \ i \vdash \{t\}_N \downarrow_P t}$$
$$\frac{i \vdash P \text{ can make } t}{i \vdash h(t) \downarrow_P t}$$

Note that $i \vdash t \downarrow N$ may hold, if N is included in t as a key.

The judgement $i \vdash P$ **knows** N means that a principal P knows N when P decomposes a message t_i. This is defined as follows.

$$\frac{P \text{ generates } N}{i \vdash P \text{ knows } N}$$

$$\frac{j < i \quad j - i \equiv 0 \ (\text{mod } 2) \quad j \vdash t_j \downarrow_P N}{i \vdash P \text{ knows } N}$$

The judgement $i \vdash P$ **can make** t means that a principal P can construct t after receiving t_i.

$$\frac{\forall N. \ \exists t'. \ \{t'\}_N \sqsubseteq t \implies i \vdash P \text{ knows } N}{i \vdash P \text{ can make } t}$$
$$\forall Q. \ \exists t'. \ \{t'\}_{KQ^{-1}} \sqsubseteq t \implies Q = P$$

Of course, when a principal P sends a message t_i, the following condition must hold.

$$i + 1 \vdash P \text{ can make } t_i$$

This is the requirement that when a principal sends a message, the principle can construct the message only from atomic symbols.

2.6   Messages from A to B

If t_i is a message from A to B, the following rules are given. When a message $\{t\}_{KB}$ including a secret nonce N and encrypted by the public key of B is received by B, a parameter X in the message is bound to N.

$$\frac{i \vdash t_i \downarrow_B \{t\}_{KB} \sqsubseteq_N t_i \quad i \vdash t \downarrow_B N \quad i \vdash t \downarrow_B c_i}{i \vdash \{t\}_{KB} \downarrow_B X \quad i - 1 \vdash N \text{ secret}} \quad \text{(ABK)}$$
$$\overline{i \vdash N \text{ binds } X \ \wedge \ i \vdash N \text{ secret}}$$

Simultaneously, the secrecy of N is guaranteed. Here, the constant c_i is used as a tag to prevent replay attacks (i.e., type breaking attacks). (If the message whose form is $\{t\}_{KB}$ is unique in the protocol, c_i is not necessary.) Note that $i \vdash t_i \downarrow_B \{t\}_{KB} \sqsubseteq t_i$ abbreviates $i \vdash t_i \downarrow_B \{t\}_{KB}$ and $\{t\}_{KB} \sqsubseteq t_i$.

Similarly, if a message $\{t\}_N$ encrypted by a secret nonce N includes a parameter X, it is bound to N.

$$\frac{i \vdash t_i \downarrow_B \{t\}_N \sqsubseteq_N t_i \quad i \vdash t \downarrow_B c_i}{i \vdash \{t\}_N \downarrow_B X \quad i - 1 \vdash N \text{ secret}} \quad \text{(ABN)}$$
$$\overline{i \vdash N \text{ binds } X \ \wedge \ i \vdash N \text{ secret}}$$

Simultaneously, the secrecy of N is guaranteed.

2.7   Message from B to A

First, we give rules about the secrecy.

$$\frac{j < i \quad j \vdash N \text{ binds } A \quad i \vdash t_i \downarrow_A \{t\}_{KA} \sqsubseteq_N t_i}{i \vdash t \downarrow_A N \quad i \vdash t \downarrow_A c_i \quad i-1 \vdash N \text{ secret}}{i \vdash N \text{ secret}} \quad \text{(BAKs)}$$

$$\frac{i \vdash t_i \downarrow_A \{t\}_N \sqsubseteq_N t_i \quad i \vdash t \downarrow_A c_i \quad i-1 \vdash N \text{ secret}}{i \vdash N \text{ secret}} \quad \text{(BANs)}$$

For the binding relation, the following rules are given. When a message $\{t\}_{KA}$ including a secret nonce N and encrypted by the public key of A is sent, N guarantees $\{t\}_{KA}$.

$$\frac{i \vdash t_i \downarrow_A \{t\}_{KA} \sqsubseteq_N t_i \quad i \vdash t \downarrow_A N \quad i \vdash t \downarrow_A c_i \quad \vdash N \text{ secret}}{i \vdash N \text{ guarantees } \{t\}_{KA}} \quad \text{(BAK)}$$

(The condition $\{t\}_{KA} \sqsubseteq_N t_i$ could be removed, but it always holds if $\vdash N$ **secret** has been derived.) Similarly, N guarantees a message $\{t\}_N$ which is encrypted by the secret nonce N.

$$\frac{i \vdash t_i \downarrow_A \{t\}_N \sqsubseteq_N t_i \quad i \vdash t \downarrow_A c_i \quad \vdash N \text{ secret}}{i \vdash N \text{ guarantees } \{t\}_N} \quad \text{(BAN)}$$

Finally, if a message t signed by the secret key of B includes N, N guarantees it.

$$\frac{i \vdash t_i \downarrow_A \{t\}_{KB^{-1}} \quad i \vdash t \downarrow_A N \quad i \vdash t \downarrow_A c_i}{i \vdash N \text{ guarantees } \{t\}_{KB^{-1}}} \quad \text{(BAS)}$$

In this case, N need not be secret. (Therefore, N can be a nonce generated by B)

When N' guarantees t, a parameter X included in t is bound to a nonce N in t.

$$\frac{i \vdash N' \text{ guarantees } t \quad i \vdash t \downarrow_A N \quad i \vdash t \downarrow_A X}{\vdash N \text{ binds' } X} \quad \text{(B1)}$$

N may coincide with N'. Note that the conclusion is **binds'**. For deriving **binds** from **binds'**, the rules in the next section are used.

Following is the rule mentioned in Section 2.4.

$$\frac{i < i' \quad i \vdash N \text{ binds } X \quad i' \vdash N \text{ guarantees } t' \quad \vdash N \text{ secret}}{\vdash N \text{ binds } X} \quad \text{(B2)}$$

2.8   Determinacy

The judgement $\vdash N$ **determines** X means that the value of the parameter X is uniquely determined in a strand of B including the nonce N and the parameter X.

If B generates the nonce N, then $\vdash N$ **determines** X holds for any parameter X.

$$\frac{B \text{ generates nonce } N}{\vdash N \text{ determines } X} \quad \text{(D1)}$$

Obviously, N determines itself.

$$\vdash N \textbf{ determines } N \quad \text{(D2)}$$

The judgement is used to derive **binds** from **binds'** as follows.

$$\frac{\vdash N \textbf{ binds' } X \quad \vdash N \textbf{ determines } X}{\vdash N \textbf{ binds } X} \quad \text{(BD1)}$$

The following rule is also useful.

$$\frac{k \vdash N' \textbf{ guarantees } t \quad k \vdash t \downarrow_A N \quad k \vdash t \downarrow_A X}{\vdash N \textbf{ binds } X} \quad \text{(BD2)}$$

The premises in the first row are the same as those of (B1) for the last message. (It guarantees the existence of a complete strand of B including N and X. See Section 4.)

Let us mention some obvious rules on **binds** and **binds'** here. Firstly, **binds'** is symmetric in the following sense.

$$\frac{\vdash N \textbf{ binds' } N'}{\vdash N' \textbf{ binds' } N} \quad \text{(B'sym)}$$

And **binds'** is derived from **binds**.

$$\frac{\vdash N \textbf{ binds } X}{\vdash N \textbf{ binds' } X} \quad \text{(BB')}$$

If $\vdash N$ **binds'** X for some X, then $\vdash N$ **binds'** N.

$$\frac{\vdash N \textbf{ binds' } X}{\vdash N \textbf{ binds' } N} \quad \text{(B'self)}$$

Finally, **binds** is transitive.

$$\frac{k \vdash N' \textbf{ guarantees } t \quad k \vdash t \downarrow_A N}{\vdash N \textbf{ binds } X} \quad \text{(Btrans)}$$

The first row of the premises is similar to that of (BD2).

2.9 Importing the Partner's Inference

We introduce judgements with the mark $\vdash_B$ by swapping A and B in the judgements introduced so far. The protocol for those judgements is shorter than the original by one message, and finishes with the message t_{k-1} sent by A. Inference rules are also obtained by swapping A and B. The original judgements are sometimes represented with the mark $\vdash_A$.

We then introduce the following rule.

$$\frac{\vdash_A N \text{ binds } A \quad \vdash_B N \text{ binds } X \quad \vdash_B N \text{ determines } X \quad k \vdash_A N' \text{ guarantees } t \quad k \vdash_A t \downarrow_A N}{\vdash_A N \text{ binds } X} \quad \text{(I)}$$

This rule is for importing the judgement $\vdash N$ **binds** X from B's side to A's side. The premises in the second row guarantees that there exists a strand of A that includes N and ends with receiving the last message t_k (see Section 4).

3 Examples

In this section, we give several examples. If a message in a protocol can be uniquely identified by its form, we omit the tag c_i.

3.1 Example 2

Let us consider the following protocol.

$$S_A(A, B, N_A, N_B) = +A, -\{N_B\}_{KA}, +\{\{A, N_A\}_{KB}\}_{N_B}, -\{\{c_4\}_{N_A}\}_{N_B}$$
$$S_B(A, B, N_A, N_B) = -A, +\{N_B\}_{KA}, -\{\{A, N_A\}_{KB}\}_{N_B}, +\{\{c_4\}_{N_A}\}_{N_B}$$

N_A and N_B are nonces generated by A and B, respectively.

Authentication of A by B is simple. By (BAN) and (B1), the following judgements hold.

$$\vdash_B N_A \text{ binds' } A \qquad \vdash_B N_A \text{ binds' } B \qquad \vdash_B N_A \text{ binds' } N_B$$

Since A generates the nonce N_A, the following judgements hold by (D1) and (BD1).

$$\vdash_B N_A \text{ binds } A \qquad \vdash_B N_A \text{ binds } B \qquad \vdash_B N_A \text{ binds } N_B$$

Below, we show authentication of B by A. The mark $\vdash$ means $\vdash_A$. Firstly, as in Example 1, the following judgements hold.

$$3 \vdash N_A \text{ binds } A \qquad 3 \vdash N_A \text{ binds } B \qquad 3 \vdash N_A \text{ secret}$$

Moreover, $\vdash N_A$ **secret** holds. Therefore, because of $t_4 = \{\{c_4\}_{N_A}\}_{N_B}$,

$$\vdash N_A \text{ binds } A \quad \text{and} \quad \vdash N_A \text{ binds } B$$

hold.

Now, by instantiating N and N' by N_A and X by N_B in the rule

$$\frac{\vdash_A N \text{ binds } A \quad \vdash_B N \text{ binds } X \quad \vdash_B N \text{ determines } X \quad k \vdash_A N' \text{ guarantees } t \quad k \vdash_A t \downarrow_A N}{\vdash_A N \text{ binds } X} \quad \text{(I)}$$

in Section 2.9, we obtain the following.

$$\frac{\vdash_A N_A \text{ binds } A \quad \vdash_B N_A \text{ binds } N_B \quad \vdash_B N_A \text{ determines } N_B}{\vdash_A N_A \text{ binds } N_B}$$
$$4 \vdash_A N_A \text{ guarantees } \{c_4\}_{N_A} \quad 4 \vdash_A \{c_4\}_{N_A} \downarrow_A N_A$$

The premises are all satisfied, hence $\vdash N_A$ **binds** N_B is derived.

3.2   Example 3

Let us consider the following protocol.

$$S_A(A, B, N_A, N_B) = -\{N_B, B\}_{KA}, +\{N_B, N_A\}_{KB}, -\{N_B, A\}_{KB^{-1}}$$
$$S_B(A, B, N_A, N_B) = +\{N_B, B\}_{KA}, -\{N_B, N_A\}_{KB}, +\{N_B, A\}_{KB^{-1}}$$

N_A and N_B are nonces generated by A and B, respectively.

Authentication of A by B is as in Example 1. Therefore, the following judgements hold by (ABK), (BAK), (B1) and (B2).

$$\vdash_B N_B \text{ binds } A \qquad \vdash_B N_B \text{ binds } B \qquad \vdash_B N_A \text{ binds' } N_B$$

By (D1), (BD1) and the transitivity of **binds**, we have the following.

$$\vdash_B N_A \text{ binds } A \qquad \vdash_B N_A \text{ binds } B \qquad \vdash_B N_A \text{ binds } N_B$$

Therefore, the relations that bind A B and N_B to N_A are established.

Below, we show authentication of B by A. The mark $\vdash$ means $\vdash_A$. We examine $t_2 = \{N_B, N_A\}_{KB}$ as in Example 1. Note that the following judgements hold.

$$2 \vdash N_A \text{ secret} \qquad 2 \vdash N_A \text{ binds } N_B \qquad 2 \vdash N_A \text{ binds } B$$

But $2 \vdash N_A$ **binds** A does not.

Next, we examine $t_3 = \{N_B, A\}_{KB^{-1}}$. Since N_B is signed by the secret key KB^{-1} of B in this message, $\vdash N_B$ **binds'** B holds by (B1). Moreover, since N_B and A are encrypted together, $\vdash N_B$ **binds'** A holds. By (D1) and (BD1), we have $\vdash N_B$ **binds** B and $\vdash N_B$ **binds** A. On the other hand, since t_3 does not include N_A, $\vdash N_A$ **secret** holds.

Now, by instantiating N and N' by N_B and X by N_A in the rule

$$\frac{\vdash_A N \text{ binds } A \quad \vdash_B N \text{ binds } X \quad \vdash_B N \text{ determines } X}{\vdash_A N \text{ binds } X} \quad \text{(I)}$$
$$k \vdash_A N' \text{ guarantees } t \quad k \vdash_A t \downarrow_A N$$

in Section 2.9, we obtain the following.

$$\frac{\vdash_A N_B \text{ binds } A \quad \vdash_B N_B \text{ binds } N_A \quad \vdash_B N_B \text{ determines } N_A}{\vdash_A N_B \text{ binds } N_A}$$
$$3 \vdash_A N_B \text{ guarantees } \{N_B, A\}_{KB^{-1}} \quad 3 \vdash_A \{N_B, A\}_{KB^{-1}} \downarrow_A N_B$$

The premise $\vdash_B N_B$ **determines** N_A means that N_A is uniquely determined from N_B in a strand of A. This does not hold in general. Here, we assume that A remembers the past instances of N_B in the same protocol and checks a replay attack. Then N_A is always determined from N_B uniquely. So, all the premises are satisfied, and $\vdash N_B$ **binds** N_A is derived.

As a consequence, the relations that bind A, B and N_A to N_B are established, hence the authentication is proven.

3.3   Example 4

The Needham-Schroeder protocol before Lowe corrected is as follows.

$$S_A(A, B, N_A, N_B) = +\{N_A, A\}_{KB}, -\{N_A, N_B\}_{KA}, +\{N_B\}_{KB}$$
$$S_B(A, B, N_A, N_B) = -\{N_A, A\}_{KB}, +\{N_A, N_B\}_{KA}, -\{N_B\}_{NB}$$

Let us consider the case B authenticates A, by swapping A and B.

$$S_A(A, B, N_A, N_B) = -\{N_B, B\}_{KA}, +\{N_B, N_A\}_{KB}, -\{N_A\}_{KA}$$
$$S_B(A, B, N_A, N_B) = +\{N_B, B\}_{KA}, -\{N_B, N_A\}_{KB}, +\{N_A\}_{KA}$$

In this case, the secrecy of N_A cannot be shown. The rule (BAKs)

$$\frac{2 < 3 \quad 2 \vdash N_A \text{ binds } A \quad 3 \vdash t_3 \downarrow_A \{t\}_{KA} \sqsubseteq_N t_3}{3 \vdash t \downarrow_A N \quad 3 \vdash t \downarrow_A c_3 \quad 2 \vdash N_A \text{ secret}} \quad \text{(BAKs)}$$
$$\overline{i \vdash N_A \text{ secret}}$$

for $j = 2$ and $i = 3$ cannot be used, because $2 \vdash t_2 \downarrow_B A$ does not hold, so $2 \vdash N_A$ **binds** A does not hold, either.

4   Soundness of Inference Rules

The soundness of the inference rules guarantees the following agreement property between strands, which will be proven by the lemmas in this section.

A strand of B is called complete if it ends with sending the last message t_k. Otherwise, a strand of B is called partial. When we examine the existence of strands of B for the judgement $\vdash N$ **binds** X, we consider possibly partial strands, while we consider complete strands when we examine the uniqueness of X for $\vdash N$ **binds** X. On the other hand, we only consider strands of A that end with receiving t_k.

Theorem (agreement): Consider a protocol in which strands of A are of the form $S_A(A, B, X_1, \cdots, X_n)$ and strands of B are of the form $S_B(A, B, X_1, \cdots, X_n)$. Suppose that the following judgements have been derived.

$$\vdash N \text{ binds } A$$
$$\vdash N \text{ binds } B$$
$$\vdash N \text{ binds } X_1$$
$$\cdots$$
$$\vdash N \text{ binds } X_n$$

N is a nonce that appears in the protocol. Moreover, suppose the following judgements for some N' and t.

$$k \vdash N' \text{ guarantees } t$$
$$k \vdash t \downarrow_A N$$

Then, if there exists a strand s_A of A, there exists a corresponding complete strand of B that shares the values of the parameters with s_A. Moreover, for any complete strand of B that shares the value of N with s_A, it also shares the values of the other parameters.

We represent the values of the parameters A, B and X_j in a strand s by $A(s)$, $B(s)$ and $X_j(s)$, respectively. We sometimes write these values without specifying the strand. For example, we sometimes write N for $N(s)$, when s is obvious.

Lemma (secrecy): Suppose $\vdash N$ **secret** holds and s_A is a strand of A. A principal who knows $N = N(s_A)$ is either the principal A, who is executing the strand s_A, or the principal B, who is executing some strand s_B such that $N = N(s_B)$. When s_A sends a message t_i including N ($N \sqsubseteq t_i$), N is encrypted by KB or N. When s_B sends a message t_i including N ($N \sqsubseteq t_i$), N is encrypted by KA or N.

(Proof) We prove that the lemma by induction on the number of steps in execution of s_A and s_B. That is, assuming that the lemma holds at some point of execution, we prove the lemma still holds after s_A or s_B sends another message.

When s_A sends a message t_i including $N = N(s_A)$ ($N \sqsubseteq t_i$), since $i \vdash N$ **secret** holds, either $i \vdash t_i \downarrow_B \{t\}_{KB} \sqsubseteq_N t_i$ or $i \vdash t_i \downarrow_B \{t\}_N \sqsubseteq_N t_i$ should hold by (ABK) or (ABN). Only the principal B can know N by receiving t_i at the receiving node $-t_i$ of some strand s_B of B such that $N = N(s_B)$.

When s_B sends a message t_i including N ($N \sqsubseteq t_i$), since $i \vdash N$ **secret** holds, either $i \vdash t_i \downarrow_A \{t\}_{KA} \sqsubseteq_N t_i$ or $i \vdash t_i \downarrow_A \{t\}_N \sqsubseteq_N t_i$ should hold by (BAKs) or (BANs). In the latter case, N is included in a term of the form $\{t\}_N$, hence the secrecy still holds.

In the former case, $j < i$ and $j \vdash N$ **binds** A hold. If $j \vdash N$ **binds** A is obtained by (ABK), $j \vdash t_j \downarrow_B \{t'\}_{KB} \sqsubseteq_N t_j$ and $j \vdash \{t'\}_{KB} \downarrow_B A$ should hold. Hence, the strand s_B of B should have received a message including a term of the form $\{t'\}_{KB}$. Since such a message should have been sent at the sending node $+t_j$ of s_A, the equation $A(s_B) = A$ is guaranteed for s_B, which has received t_j. Therefore, when s_B sends t_i, N should be encrypted by KA.

The case $j \vdash N$ **binds** A is obtained by (ABN) is similar.

In any case, when s_B sends a message t_i including N ($N \sqsubseteq t_i$), only A can know N by receiving it at the receiving node $-t_i$ of s_A. (End of proof)

The theorem is derived from the following lemma (binding). We provide three more lemmas.

Lemma (binding): Suppose $\vdash N$ **binds** X holds. If there exists a strand s_A of A, there exists a corresponding (possibly partial) strand s_B of B such that $N(s_B) = N(s_A)$ and $X(s_B) = X(s_A)$. Moreover, for any complete strand s of B such that $N(s) = N(s_A)$, $X(s) = X(s_A)$ holds.

Lemma (binding'): Suppose $\vdash N$ **binds'** X holds. If there exists a strand s_A of A, there exists a corresponding (possibly partial) strand s_B of B such that $N(s_B) = N(s_A)$ and $X(s_B) = X(s_A)$.

Lemma (guarantee): Suppose $i \vdash N$ **guarantees** t holds. If there exists a strand s_A of A, there exists a corresponding (possibly partial) strand s_B of B such that $N(s_B) = N(s_A)$ holds. Moreover, the sending node $+t_i$ of s_B sends t as a subterm of t_i, and the receiving node $-t_i$ of s_A receives it.

Lemma (determinacy): Suppose $\vdash N$ **determines** X holds. For any (possibly partial) strands s and s' of B such that both N and X appear in the messages of s and s', if $N(s) = N(s')$, then $X(s) = X(s')$.

We prove these four lemmas by induction on the number of applications of inference rules.

(BAK)

$$\frac{i \vdash t_i \downarrow_A \{t\}_{KA} \sqsubseteq_N t_i \quad i \vdash t \downarrow_A N \quad i \vdash t \downarrow_A c_i \quad \vdash N \text{ secret}}{i \vdash N \text{ guarantees } \{t\}_{KA}} \quad \text{(BAK)}$$

Let s_A be a strand of A and include $N = N(s_A)$. From the premise $\vdash N$ **secret**, only A and B know N, and if B sends a message including N ($N \sqsubseteq t_j$ for some t_j), the nonce N is encrypted by KA or N. Therefore, if A receives $\{t\}_{KA}$ in s_A, this message should have been sent in t_i by B.

(BAN)

$$\frac{i \vdash t_i \downarrow_A \{t\}_N \sqsubseteq_N t_i \quad i \vdash t \downarrow_A c_i \quad \vdash N \text{ secret}}{i \vdash N \text{ guarantees } \{t\}_N} \quad \text{(BAN)}$$

This case is similar to (BAK).

(BAS)

$$\frac{i \vdash t_i \downarrow_A \{t\}_{KB^{-1}} \quad i \vdash t \downarrow_A N \quad i \vdash t \downarrow_A c_i}{i \vdash N \text{ guarantees } \{t\}_{KB^{-1}}} \quad \text{(BAS)}$$

Let s_A be a strand of A and include $N = N(s_A)$. Only B can construct the message $\{t\}_{KB^{-1}}$. Therefore, if A receives $\{t\}_{KB^{-1}}$ in s_A, there exists a strand s_B of B including N, and the message should have been sent in t_i by s_B.

(B1)

$$\frac{i \vdash N' \text{ guarantees } t \quad i \vdash t \downarrow_A N \quad i \vdash t \downarrow_A X}{\vdash N \text{ binds' } X} \quad \text{(B1)}$$

From the premise $i \vdash N'$ **guarantees** t, if there exists a strand s_A of A, there exists a corresponding strand s_B of B such that $N'(s_B) = N'(s_A)$, a sending node $+t_i$ of s_B sends t, and a receiving node of s_A receives it. Therefore, if $i \vdash t \downarrow_A X$ holds, $N(s_B) = N(s_A)$ and $X(s_B) = X(s_A)$.

(B2)

$$\frac{i < i' \quad i \vdash N \text{ binds } X \quad i' \vdash N \text{ guarantees } t' \quad \vdash N \text{ secret}}{\vdash N \text{ binds } X} \quad \text{(B2)}$$

From the premise $i' \vdash N$ **guarantees** t', if there exists a strand s_A of A, there exists a corresponding strand s_B of B such that $N(s_B) = N(s_A)$.

Next, we consider cases according to how $i \vdash N$ **binds** X is derived. If $i \vdash N$ **binds** X is derived from (ABK), s_A should have sent $\{t\}_{KB}$ at its sending node $+t_i$. Since $\vdash N$ **secret** and N is generated by A, the value of N uniquely determines the value of X in $\{t\}_{KB}$. Therefore, s_B should have received $\{t\}_{KB}$ at its receiving node $-t_i$. So, if $i \vdash \{t\}_{KB} \downarrow_B X$ holds, then $X(s_A) = X(s_B)$. Note that this argument holds for any complete strand s_B of B such that $N(s_B) = N(s_A)$.

The case $i \vdash N$ **binds** X is derived from (ABN) is similar.

(I)

$$\frac{\vdash_A N \text{ binds } A \quad \vdash_B N \text{ binds } X \quad \vdash_B N \text{ determines } X}{\vdash_A N \text{ binds } X} \quad \frac{k \vdash_A N' \text{ guarantees } t \quad k \vdash_A t \downarrow_A N}{} \quad \text{(I)}$$

From the first premise and the premises in the second row, there exists a complete strand s_B of B for a strand s_A of A such that $N(s_B) = N(s_A)$ and $A(s_B) = A$. Then, from the second premise, there exists a strand s of A such that $N(s) = N(s_B)$ and $X(s) = X(s_B)$. The number of nodes in s is fewer than that of s_A, and s may be different from s'_A that is obtained by removing the last node from s_A. But, since $N(s) = N(s_B) = N(s_A) = N(s'_A)$, $X(s) = X(s'_A)$ is derived from the last premise in the first row. Therefore, $X(s_B) = X(s) = X(s'_A) = X(s_A)$ is derived. Note that this argument holds for any complete strand s_B of B such that $N(s_B) = N(s_A)$.

The other rules are easy to handle.

5   Concluding Remarks

In this paper, we gave inference rules that can directly derive binding relations between nonces and data, and showed the authenticity of some protocols using the inference rules. We also introduced the rules on **determines** and the rules for importing the partner's inferences for proving their authenticity.

The rules given in this paper are, of course, not complete. Rather than formulating a complete set of inference rule, we aimed at constructing a system that allows inferences at the symbolic level without explicitly referring to strands. Although this goal was achieved, the resulting system is, unfortunately, unexpectedly complex with a relatively large number of rules.

Another weak point of our system is that the requirement on the secrecy is too rigid. In our system, we derive the authenticity after the secrecy has been proven. In some protocols, the secrecy and the authenticity are mutually involved, so stronger inference rules are necessary.

Recently, authentication tests have been applied to show the correctness of three- or multi-party protocols, including those for e-commerce [6]. Our method in the current form cannot be applied to such protocols, because it is assumed that when a principal sends a message, the principle can construct the message only from atomic symbols. In three- or multi-party protocols, this assumption does not hold in general, because a principal may simply forward a received message to a third principal. In order to deal with such protocols, it is necessary to change some of the judgements. For example, the judgement $\vdash t \downarrow_P X$ should be modified so that P does not inspect the inside of a forwarded message.

It is also interesting to deal with protocols with time stamps. In such a protocol, the judgement **determines** might be strengthened according to the assumption on time stamps.

Rules for importing the partner's inferences might be reminiscent of BAN logic [2], which is a modal logic for inferring the partner's beliefs. In BAN logic, however, there is no direct counterpart corresponding to our binding relation. To the authors' knowledge, BAN logic cannot show the correctness of protocols such as Example 1. It is in general an important challenge to give a semantics to BAN logic based on strands [1].

Acknowledgment. The authors thank the reviewers for valuable comments. In particular, they deeply thank the referees of the Japanese version of this paper, who pointed out errors and suggestions for correction.

This work was partially supported by the Ministry of Education, Culture, Sports, Science and Technology, Grant-in-Aid for Exploratory Research, 14658088, 2002, Grant-in-Aid for Scientific Research on Priority Areas (B), 12133101, 2001, and Grant-in-Aid for Scientific Research on Priority Areas (C), 13224012, 2001.

References

1. Rafael Accorsi, David Basin, Luca Viganò. Towards an Awareness-Based Semantics for Security Protocol Analysis. *Proceedings of the First Workshop on Logical Aspects of Cryptographic Protocol Verification,* 2001, pp. 9–27.
2. Michael Burrows, Martín Abadi and Roger Needham. A Logic of Authentication. *Proceedings of the Royal Society of London,* Vol.426, 1989, pp. 233–271.
3. Iliano Cervesato, Nancy A. Durgin, Patrick D. Lincoln, John C. Mitchell and Andre Scedrov. Relating Strands and Multiset Rewriting for Security Protocol Analysis. *13th IEEE Computer Security Foundation Workshop,* 2000, pp. 35–51.
4. Ernie Cohen. TAPS: A First-Order Verifier for Cryptographic Protocols. *13th IEEE Computer Security Foundation Workshop,* 2000, pp. 144–158.
5. Joshua D. Guttman and F. Javier Thayer Fábrega. Authentication Tests, *Proceedings, 2000 IEEE Symposium on Security and Privacy,* 2000, pp. 96–109.

6. Joshua D. Guttman. Security Protocol Design via Authentication Tests, *15th IEEE Computer Security Foundations Workshop,* 2002, pp. 92–103.

7. Masami Hagiya, Yozo Toda and Yoshiki Fukuba. Implementation and Verification of Authentication Protocols Using Proof Procedures in HOL, *2nd SSR Enterprise Security Workshop,* Information Media Center, Science University of Tokyo, Nov 1999,
   http://nicosia.is.s.u-tokyo.ac.jp/pub/staff/hagiya/ssr99/protveri.ps

8. Gavin Lowe. Breaking and Fixing the Needham-Schroeder Public-Key Protocol using FDR. In T. Margaria and B. Steffen, editors, *Tools and Algorithms for the Construction and analysis of Systems. Second International Workshop, TACAS '96,* Lecture Notes in Computer Science, Vol.1055, 1996, pp. 147–166.

9. J. Millen and V. Shmatikov. Constraint solving for bounded-process cryptographic protocol analysis. *8th ACM Conference on Computer and Communication Security,* pp. 166–175, 2001.

10. John C. Mitchell, Mark Mitchell and Ulrich Stern. Automated Analysis of Cryptographic Protocols Using Murφ. *Proceedings of 1997 IEEE Symposium Security and Privacy,* 1997, pp. 141–151.

11. Lawrence C. Paulson. Proving Properties of Security Protocols by Induction. *10th Computer Security Foundations Workshop,* June 1997.

12. Lawrence C. Paulson. Mechanized Proofs of Security Protocols: Needham-Schroeder with Public Keys. Technical Report 413, Computer Laboratory, University of Cambridge, Jan. 1997.

13. Lawrence C. Paulson. *Isabelle: A Generic Theorem Prover.* Lecture Notes in Computer Science, Vol.828, Springer, 1994.

14. Adrian Perrig and Dawn Song. A First Step on Automatic Protocol Generation of Security Protocols. *Proceedings of Network and Distributed System Security,* February 2000.

15. Takamichi Saito, Masami Hagiya and Fumio Mizoguchi. On Authentication Protocols Using Public-key Cryptography, IPSJ Journal, Information Processing Society of Japan, Vol.42, No.8, pp. 2040–2048 (in Japanese).

16. Dawn Xiaodong Song. Athena: a New Efficient Automatic Checker for Security Protocol Analysis, *Proceedings of the 12th IEEE Computer Security Foundations Workshop,* 1999, pp. 192–202.

17. F. Javier Thayer Fábrega, Jonathan C. Herzog and Joshua D. Guttman. Strand spaces: Why is a Security Protocol Correct? *Proceedings of 1998 IEEE Symposium on Security and Privacy,* 1998, pp. 160–171.

18. F. Javier Thayer Fábrega, Jonathan C. Herzog and Joshua D. Guttman. Honest Ideas on Strand Spaces. *Proceedings of the 11th IEEE Computer Security Foundations Workshop,* 1998, pp. 66–77.

19. F. Javier Thayer Fábrega, Jonathan C. Herzog and Joshua D. Guttman. Strand Spaces: Proving Security Protocols Correct, *Journal of Computer Security,* Vol.7, 1999, pp. 191–230.

20. F. Javier Thayer Fábrega, Jonathan C. Herzog and Joshua D. Guttman. Mixed Strand Spaces. *Proceedings of the 12th IEEE Computer Security Foundations Workshop,* 1999, pp. 72–82.

Hiding Names: Private Authentication in the Applied Pi Calculus

Cédric Fournet[1] and Martín Abadi[2]

[1] Microsoft Research
[2] University of California at Santa Cruz

Abstract. We present the analysis of a protocol for private authentication in the applied pi calculus. We treat authenticity and secrecy properties of the protocol. Although such properties are fairly standard, their formulation in the applied pi calculus makes an original use of process equivalences. In addition, we treat identity-protection properties, which are a delicate concern in several recent protocol designs.

1 Introduction

In recent years, the understanding of basic security properties such as integrity and confidentiality has become both deeper and wider. There has also been substantial progress in the design and verification of protocols that aim to guarantee these properties. On the other hand, fundamental tasks such as secure session establishment remain the subject of active, productive research. Moreover, properties beyond integrity and confidentiality have been studied rather lightly to date. These properties include, for example, protection of identity information and protection against denial-of-service attacks. They may seem secondary but they are sometimes important.

This paper contributes to the ongoing study of security protocols and of their properties. More specifically, this paper presents the analysis of a security protocol in the applied pi calculus [2], a recent variant of the pi calculus. The protocol in question is one for private authentication (the second protocol of [1]). Its analysis is worthwhile for several reasons:

- The protocol is for a standard purpose, namely establishing a session (with associated cryptographic keys), and it is concerned with standard security properties, such as authenticity and secrecy. Therefore, the analysis of the protocol exemplifies concepts and techniques relevant to many other protocols.
- In addition, the protocol is concerned with a privacy property: it aims to guarantee that third parties do not learn the identity of protocol participants. Although this property and similar ones appear prominently in several recent protocol designs, they have hardly been specified and proved precisely to date. Therefore, this paper develops an approach for stating and deriving those properties.

M. Okada et al. (Eds.): ISSS 2002, LNCS 2609, pp. 317–338, 2003.

- The protocol includes some delicate features, and is not a trivial example invented only in order to illustrate formal techniques. On the other hand, the protocol remains fairly simple, so we can give relatively concise treatments of its main properties.

In the applied pi calculus, the constructs of the classic pi calculus can be used to represent concurrent systems that communicate on channels, and function symbols can be used to represent cryptographic operations and other operations on data. Large classes of important attacks can also be expressed in the applied pi calculus, as contexts. These include the typical attacks for which a symbolic, mostly "black-box" view of cryptography suffices (but not for example some lower-level attacks that depend on timing behavior or on probabilities). Thus, in general, the applied pi calculus serves for describing and reasoning about many of the central aspects of security protocols. In particular, it is an appropriate setting for the analysis of the protocol for private authentication. Some of the properties of the protocol can be nicely captured in the form of equivalences between processes. Moreover, some of the properties are sensitive to the equations satisfied by the cryptographic functions upon which the protocol relies. The applied pi calculus is well-suited for expressing those equivalences and those equations.

In a sense, private authentication is about hiding the names (or identities) of protocol participants. The applied pi calculus permits hiding the names that represent private communication channels and secret cryptographic keys (through the restriction construct ν). Despite this superficial coincidence, the name hiding of private authentication and that of the applied pi calculus are rather different. We do not have a direct reduction of one to the other. However, the name hiding of the applied pi calculus is crucial for expressing the protocol under consideration and for deriving the equivalences that express its properties.

The next two sections explain private authentication and the applied pi calculus, respectively. Section 4 shows how to express a protocol for private authentication in the applied pi calculus. Section 5 treats the authenticity and secrecy properties of the protocol; section 6, its privacy properties. (We omit all proofs, because of space constraints.) Section 7 discusses some related work and concludes.

2   Private Authentication

Although we do not aim to provide a general definition of privacy (partly because one might have to be too vague or empty), we focus on the following frequent scenario in which privacy is a central concern: two or more mobile interlocutors wish to communicate securely, protecting their messages and also their identities from third parties. This scenario arises often in mobile telephony and mobile computing [7,14,12,15,6,8]. In these contexts, roaming users may want to conceal their identities from others and even from infrastructure providers and operators. Furthermore, identity protection is a goal of several recent protocols for communication at the IP level [9,5].

More specifically, suppose that a mobile principal A (a user or a computer) wishes to communicate with some other principals, and that A is willing to prove its identity to these principals. Suppose that B is one of them, and that B is willing to communicate with A and to prove its identity to A. After providing these proofs, in the subsequent session, A and B may make sensitive requests from each other and may reveal sensitive data to each other. We study a protocol (from [1]) that enables A and B to establish an authenticated communication channel. By following the protocol, A and B should not have to indicate their identity and presence to any third parties.

In this section, we review the protocol informally. We start by outlining its assumptions, then describe its message flow and (briefly) some of its properties and limitations. Later sections contain a formal development of these points.

2.1   Assumptions

The protocol assumes that messages do not automatically reveal the identity of their senders and receivers—for example, by mentioning them in headers. This assumption entails some difficulties in routing messages. Focusing on a relatively simple but important case, the protocol supposes that all messages are broadcast within some location, such as a physical building or a virtual chat room.

As in most security protocols (following Needham and Schroeder [13]), the communication infrastructure is untrusted. An attacker can interpose itself on all public communication channels, and thus can alter or copy parts of messages, delete messages, replay messages, or emit false material.

The protocol also assumes that each principal A has a public key K_A and a corresponding private key K_A^{-1} (e.g., [11]), and that the association between principals and public keys is known. This association can be implemented with the help of a mostly-off-line certification authority, and it is trivial when one identifies public keys with principal names. Public keys are used for encryption and private keys for the corresponding decryptions. Informally, when K is a public key, we write $\{M\}_K$ for the encryption of M using K. The protocol assumes some properties of the encryption scheme (not all entirely standard). Only a principal that knows the corresponding private key K^{-1} should be able to understand a message encrypted under a public key K. Furthermore, decrypting a message with a private key K^{-1} should succeed only if the message was encrypted under the corresponding public key K, and the success or failure of a decryption should be obvious to the principal who performs it. Finally, someone who sees a message encrypted under a public key K should not be able to tell that it is under K without knowledge of the corresponding private key K^{-1}, even with knowledge of K or other messages under K.

2.2   The Protocol

When a principal A wishes to talk to another principal B, and B is willing to talk to a set of principals S_B, the protocol specifies that A and B proceed as follows:

– A generates a fresh, unpredictable quantity N_A (a "nonce"), and sends out

$$\text{"hello"}, \{\text{"hello"}, N_A, K_A\}_{K_B}$$

– When B receives any message that consists of "hello" and (apparently) a ciphertext, B tries to decrypt the second component using K_B^{-1}. If the decryption succeeds, then B extracts the corresponding nonce N_A and key K_A, checks that $A \in S_B$, generates a nonce N_B, and sends out

$$\text{"ack"}, \{\text{"ack"}, N_A, N_B, K_B\}_{K_A}$$

If the decryption fails, if the plaintext is not of the required form, or if $A \notin S_B$, then B instead sends out a "decoy" message. This message should basically look like B's other message. In particular, it may have the form

$$\text{"ack"}, \{N\}_K$$

where N is a fresh nonce and only B knows K^{-1}, or it may be indistinguishable from a message of this form.

– When A receives a message that consists of "ack" and (apparently) a ciphertext, A tries to decrypt the second component using K_A^{-1}. If the decryption succeeds, then A extracts the corresponding nonces N_A and N_B and key K_B, and checks that it has recently sent N_A under K_B. If the decryption or the checks fail, then A does nothing.

Afterwards, A and B may use N_A and N_B as shared secrets. In particular, A and B may use N_B as a session key, or they may compute session keys by concatenating and hashing the two nonces.

This protocol has some deliberate similarities with several previous ones [13, 10,9]. However, unlike those protocols, it aims to preserve the privacy of the participants, first of all by not publishing their names in cleartext, and also for example through the decoy message. The inclusion of this message prevents an attack where a malicious principal $C \notin S_B$ computes and sends

$$\text{"hello"}, \{\text{"hello"}, N_C, K_A\}_{K_B}$$

and then deduces B's presence and $A \in S_B$ by noticing a response. Moreover, B's response to A when $A \notin S_B$ is a decoy message that any other principal could have sent, so that A cannot confirm B's presence in this case.

2.3   Properties and Limitations

Intuitively, the protocol is supposed to establish the shared secrets N_A and N_B. At the very least, we would expect that A and B, and only them, can derive a session key K from these secrets. We would expect, moreover, that this key be essentially independent of any other data. For example, it should not be possible for an attacker without access to K to compute a ciphertext under K from a record of the protocol messages. In short, K should behave much like a pre-established shared key. The only observable differences between running the protocol and having a pre-established shared key should be that an attacker can disrupt a protocol run, making it fail, and that an attacker can notice that the protocol generates some opaque messages. Our results of section 5 provide a more precise statement of this comparison, in the form of an equivalence.

The protocol is also supposed to assure A and B of each other's identity. However, the two participants have somewhat different states in this respect at the conclusion of a key exchange. The initiator, A, has evidence that it shares the session key K with the principal B that responded. On the other hand, B has evidence that it shares K at most with A, but cannot be certain that A initiated the protocol run. Any other principal C might have contacted B pretending to be A, but then C will not obtain the key. Only after further communication can B be sure of A's participation in the session.

In addition, the protocol is supposed to protect the identity of the participants. This should mean, in particular, that an attacker cannot learn anything when A wishes to communicate with B but not vice versa. It should also mean that an attacker cannot distinguish a run between A and B from a run between two other principals A' and B', under appropriate hypotheses. The hypotheses should say, for example, that B is not the attacker, since B learns A's identity. The hypotheses should also limit what the participants can do besides running the protocol. For example, if A were to broadcast "A knows some nonces!" after every protocol run, then A's identity would clearly not be protected. More generally, the hypotheses need to address possible leaks not caused by the protocol proper. Section 6 develops these hypotheses and gives our privacy results, also relying on equivalences.

3   The Applied Pi Calculus (Overview)

The applied pi calculus is a simple, general extension of the pi calculus with value passing, primitive function symbols, and equations between terms. In [2], we introduce this calculus, develop semantics and proof techniques, and apply those techniques in reasoning about some security protocols. This section gives only a brief overview.

3.1   Syntax and Informal Semantics

A *signature* Σ consists of a finite set of function symbols, such as h and decrypt, each with an integer arity. Given a signature Σ, an infinite set of names, and an infinite set of variables, the set of *terms* is defined by the grammar:

$U, V ::=$	terms
$a, n, \ldots$	name
$x, y, \ldots$	variable
$f(U_1, \ldots, U_l)$	function application

where f ranges over the function symbols of Σ and l matches the arity of f. We use meta-variables u and v to range over both names and variables.

The grammar for *processes* is similar to the one in the pi calculus, except that here messages can contain terms (rather than only names) and that names need not be just channel names:

$P, Q, R ::=$	processes (or plain processes)
$\mathbf{0}$	null process
$P \mid Q$	parallel composition
$!P$	replication
$\nu n.P$	name restriction ("new")
$if\ U = V\ then\ P\ else\ Q$	conditional
$u(x).P$	message input
$\overline{u}\langle V\rangle.P$	message output

The null process $\mathbf{0}$ does nothing; $P \mid Q$ is the parallel composition of P and Q; the replication $!P$ behaves as an infinite number of copies of P running in parallel. The process $\nu n.P$ makes a new name n then behaves as P. The conditional construct $if\ U = V\ then\ P\ else\ Q$ is standard, but we should stress that $U = V$ represents equality, rather than strict syntactic identity. We abbreviate it $if\ U = V\ then\ P$ when Q is $\mathbf{0}$. Finally, the input process $u(x).P$ is ready to input from channel u, then to run P with the actual message replaced for the formal parameter x, while the output process $\overline{u}\langle V\rangle.P$ is ready to output message V on channel u, then to run P. In both of these, we may omit P when it is $\mathbf{0}$.

Further, we extend processes with *active substitutions*:

$A, B, C ::=$	extended processes
P	plain process
$A \mid B$	parallel composition
$\nu n.A$	name restriction
$\nu x.A$	variable restriction
$\{x = V\}$	active substitution

We write $\{x = V\}$ for the substitution that replaces the variable x with the term V. The substitution $\{x = V\}$ typically appears when the term V has been sent to the environment, but the environment may not have the atomic names that appear in V; the variable x is just a way to refer to V in this situation. The substitution $\{x = V\}$ is active in the sense that it "floats" and applies to any process that comes into contact with it. In order to control this contact, we may add a variable restriction: $\nu x.(\{x = V\} \mid P)$ corresponds exactly to $let\ x = V\ in\ P$. Although the substitution $\{x = V\}$ concerns only one variable, we can build bigger substitutions by parallel composition. We always assume that our substitutions are cycle-free. We also assume that, in an extended process, there is at most one substitution for each variable, and there is exactly one when the variable is restricted.

A *frame* is an extended process built up from active substitutions by parallel composition and restriction. Informally, frames represent the static knowledge gathered by the environment after communications with an extended process. We let φ range over frames, and let $\varphi(A)$ be the frame obtained from the extended process A by erasing all plain subprocesses of A. We write $(U = V)\varphi$ when U and V are equal up to φ [2, section 4.2]. An *evaluation context* $C[\_]$ is an extended process with a hole in the place of an extended process. As usual, names and variables have scopes, which are delimited by restrictions and by inputs. When E is any expression, $fv(E)$, $bv(E)$, $fn(E)$, and $bn(E)$ are the sets of free and bound variables and free and bound names of E, respectively.

We rely on a sort system for terms and extended processes [2, section 2]. We always assume that terms and extended processes are well-sorted and that substitutions and context applications preserve sorts.

3.2   Operational Semantics

Given a signature Σ, we equip it with an equational theory (that is, with an equivalence relation on terms with certain closure properties). We write $\Sigma \vdash U = V$ when the equation $U = V$ is in the theory associated with Σ. We usually keep the theory implicit, and abbreviate $\Sigma \vdash U = V$ to $U = V$ when Σ is clear from context or unimportant.

Structural equivalences, written $A \equiv B$, relate extended processes that are equal by any capture-avoiding rearrangements of parallel compositions, restrictions, and active substitutions, and by equational rewriting of any terms in processes. *Reductions*, written $A \rightarrow B$, represent silent steps of computation (in particular, internal message transmissions and branching on conditionals). *Labelled transitions*, written $A \xrightarrow{\alpha} B$, represent interactions with the environment. They consist of message inputs and message outputs, respectively written $A \xrightarrow{a(U)} B$ and $A \xrightarrow{\nu\tilde{u}.\bar{a}\langle U\rangle} B$. An output transition $A \xrightarrow{\nu\tilde{u}.\bar{a}\langle U\rangle} B$ is enabled only if the message U is a very simple term, typically a fresh variable x. Nonetheless, B may contain an active substitution that associates x with any term. An input transitions $A \xrightarrow{a(U)} B$ may use variables defined in A (typically from previous message outputs) to form the message U. Reductions and labelled transitions are closed by structural equivalence, hence by equational rewriting on terms.

3.3   Examples

We further explain the applied pi calculus with examples motivated by the protocol under consideration. We start with formatted messages. We then discuss one-way hash functions and encryption functions.

In our protocol, we use two kinds of formated messages ("hello" and "ack") with two and three variable fields, respectively. Accordingly, we introduce binary and ternary function symbols hello(_, _) and ack(_, _, _) in the signature Σ; these symbols represent the message constructors. In addition, we introduce inverse, unary function symbols hello.0 (_), hello.1 (_), ack.0 (_), ack.1 (_), and ack.2 (_) in order to select particular fields in messages. Finally, we describe the intended behavior of formatted messages with the evident equations:

$$\text{hello.0 (hello}(x_0, x_1)) = x_0$$
$$\text{hello.1 (hello}(x_0, x_1)) = x_1$$
$$\text{ack.0 (ack}(y_0, y_1, y_2)) = y_0$$
$$\text{ack.1 (ack}(y_0, y_1, y_2)) = y_1$$
$$\text{ack.2 (ack}(y_0, y_1, y_2)) = y_2$$

(A first equational theory may consists of these equations, and all equations obtained by reflexivity, symmetry, and transitivity and by substituting terms for the variables $x_0, \ldots, y_2$.)

In order to model the one-way hash computation of a session key out of the nonces N_A and N_B, we introduce a binary function symbol $\mathsf{h}(\_, \_)$ with no equations. The fact that $\mathsf{h}(N_A, N_B) = \mathsf{h}(N_A', N_B')$ only when $N_A = N_A'$ and $N_B = N_B'$ models that h is collision-free. The absence of an inverse for h models the one-wayness of h. In our protocol, these properties are important to guarantee that $\mathsf{h}(N_A, N_B)$ is indeed secret (as long as N_A or N_B is) and, further, that the attacker cannot recover N_A or N_B even if it obtains $\mathsf{h}(N_A, N_B)$.

In order to model symmetric cryptography (that is, shared-key cryptography), we may introduce binary function symbols $\mathsf{encrypt}(\_, \_)$ and $\mathsf{decrypt}(\_, \_)$ for encryption and decryption, respectively, with the equation:

$$\mathsf{decrypt}(\mathsf{encrypt}(x, y), y) = x \tag{1}$$

Here x represents the plaintext and y the key. We often use the notation $\{U\}_V$ instead of $\mathsf{encrypt}(U, V)$. For instance, the (useless) process $\nu K.\bar{c}\langle\{U\}_K\rangle$ sends the term U encrypted under a fresh key K on channel c. It is only slightly harder to model asymmetric (public-key) cryptography, where the keys for encryption and decryption are different. In addition to $\mathsf{encrypt}(\_, \_)$ and $\mathsf{decrypt}(\_, \_)$, we introduce the unary function symbol $\mathsf{pk}(\_)$ for deriving a public key from a private key. Instead of (1), we use the equation:

$$\mathsf{decrypt}(\mathsf{encrypt}(x, \mathsf{pk}(y)), y) = x \tag{2}$$

Since there is no inverse for $\mathsf{pk}(\_)$, the public key $\mathsf{pk}(s)$ can be passed to the environment without giving away the capability to decrypt messages encrypted under $\mathsf{pk}(s)$.

For instance, a principal B with public key K_B can be represented as a process in a context $P_B[\_] \stackrel{\text{def}}{=} \nu s. (\{K_B = \mathsf{pk}(s)\} \mid [\_])$ that binds a decryption key s and exports the associated encryption key as a variable K_B. As this example indicates, we essentially view ν as a generator of unguessable seeds. In some cases, those seeds may be directly used as passwords or keys; in others, some transformations are needed.

3.4   Observational Equivalences

In the analysis of protocols, we frequently argue that two given processes cannot be distinguished by any context, that is, that the processes are observationally equivalent. As in the spi calculus, the context represents an active attacker, and equivalences capture security properties in the presence of the attacker. The applied pi calculus has a useful, general theory of observational equivalence parameterized by Σ and its equational theory [2]. Specifically, the following three relations are defined for any Σ and equational theory:

- *Static equivalence*, written $\approx_s$, relates frames that cannot be distinguished by any term comparison. In the presence of the "new" construct, the relation $\approx_s$ is somewhat delicate and interesting.
  For instance, we have

$$\nu N.\{x = \mathsf{h}(N, K_B)\} \approx_s \nu N.\{x = \mathsf{h}(N, K_C)\}$$

  for any K_B and K_C, since the nonce N guarantees that both terms substituted for x have the same (null) equational properties, but

$$\nu N.\{x = \mathsf{hello}(N, K_B)\} \not\approx_s \nu N.\{x = \mathsf{hello}(N, K_C)\}$$

  as soon as K_B and K_C differ, since the comparison hello.1 $(x) = K_B$ succeeds only with the first frame.
- More generally, *contextual equivalence* relates extended processes that cannot be distinguished by any evaluation context in the applied pi calculus, with any combination of messaging and term comparisons.
- *Labelled bisimilarity*, written $\approx_l$, coincides with contextual equivalence, but it is defined in terms of labelled transitions instead of arbitrary evaluation contexts, and it is the basis for standard, powerful proof techniques.

4   The Protocol in the Applied Pi Calculus

In this section we give a precise model for the protocol described in section 2.2: we first choose an adequate equational theory, then detail our representation of principals and attackers, and finally give processes that express the protocol.

4.1   An Equational Theory

The following grammar of terms indicates the function symbols and notation conventions that we use:

$T, U, V, V_0, \cdots ::=$ terms

$A, B, K, x_1, x_2, \ldots$	variable
$c_1, c_2, init_A, accept_B, connect_A, \ldots$	name (for a channel)
$N, N_A, K_A^{-1}, \ldots$	name (typically for nonces and keys)
$\mathsf{h}(U, V)$	cryptographic hash
$\mathsf{pk}(U)$	public-key derivation
$\{T\}_V$	public-key encryption
$\mathsf{decrypt}(W, U)$	private-key decryption

$\mathsf{hello}(U_0, U_1), \mathsf{ack}(V_0, V_1, V_2)$	constructor for protocol message
$\mathsf{hello.0}\,(U)\,,\ldots,\mathsf{ack.2}\,(V)$	field selector for protocol message
$\emptyset$	empty set
$U.V$	set extension

This grammar includes primitives for constructing sets ($\emptyset$ and .) but not a set membership relation. We write $V \in W$ as an abbreviation for $W.V = W$.

Our equational theory is fairly standard. The equations on terms are:

$$\mathsf{decrypt}(\{x\}_{\mathsf{pk}(z)}, z) = x \qquad \text{private-key decryption}$$

$$\mathsf{hello.j}\,(\mathsf{hello}(x_0, x_1)) = x_j \qquad \text{field selection in ``hello'' message}$$
$$\mathsf{ack.j}\,(\mathsf{ack}(x_0, x_1, x_2)) = x_j \qquad \text{field selection in ``ack'' message}$$

$$(\emptyset.x).x = \emptyset.x \qquad \text{idempotence of set extension}$$
$$(x.y).z = (x.z).y \qquad \text{associativity of set extension}$$

The equational theory implicitly assumes that encryption is "which-key concealing", in the sense that someone who sees a message encrypted under a public key K should not be able to tell that it is under K without knowledge of the corresponding private key K^{-1}. On the other hand, it would be easy to add functions and equations that negate this property, in order to model additional capabilities of an attacker. In particular, for the benefit of the attacker, we could add the function symbols get-key, test-key, or same-key, with respective equations:

$$\mathsf{get\text{-}key}(\{x\}_z) = z$$
$$\mathsf{test\text{-}key}(\{x\}_z, z) = \mathsf{true}$$
$$\mathsf{same\text{-}key}(\{x\}_z, \{y\}_z) = \mathsf{true}$$

These additions would not affect authentication and secrecy properties, but they would compromise privacy properties.

4.2   The Principals

We model arbitrary configurations of principals. Each principal may run any number of sessions, as initiator and responder, and may perform other operations after session establishment or even independently of the protocol. Only some of these principals are trustworthy. We are interested in the security properties that hold for them.

Our model of a principal A has two parts: an implementation of the protocol, written P_A, and a "user process" (or "user protocol"), written U_A. The user process defines any additional behavior, such as when protocol runs are initiated and what happens after each session establishment. It consumes the shared secrets produced during the establishment of sessions and uses these secrets, perhaps to do something useful. According to the user process, each principal may run several sessions of the protocol, possibly playing both the role of initiator and that of responder. Of course, security properties depend on both P_A and U_A. We define P_A below in section 4.4; on the other hand, we treat U_A as a parameter.

We use the following control interface between the (abstract) user process and the (specific) session-establishment protocol. The interface concerns both the roles of session initiator and responder.

init: Principal A sends $\overline{init}_A\langle B\rangle$ to trigger a session-establishment attempt with principal B.

accept: The responder part of the protocol for principal B sends $\overline{accept}_B\langle A, K\rangle$ to notify principal B that it has accepted a session apparently from principal A, with session key K.

connect: The initiator part of the protocol for principal A sends $\overline{connect}_A\langle B, K\rangle$ to notify principal A that its attempt to contact B succeeded, with session key K.

In addition, for each principal B, the set S_B represents all acceptable interlocutors for B. For simplicity, we do not provide an interface for updating this set, so it remains constant. Thus, the interface between the session protocol and the user process for each principal X consists of the communication channels $\mathcal{V}_X \overset{\text{def}}{=} \{init_X, accept_X, connect_X\}$ plus a (constant) set of principals S_X.

Note that the interface provides a key K to the user process, rather than nonces N_A and N_B. We prefer to define K in such a way that N_A and N_B cannot be computed from K (for example, $K = \mathsf{h}(N_A, N_B)$). Our results can thus be independent of how the user process applies K.

As suggested by the informal description of the protocol, we represent the identity of each principal as its public key, using variables A, B, E, X, ... for both identities and public keys (rather than A, B, K_A, and K_B as in section 2.2). For the present purposes, the essence of a principal lies in its ability to decrypt any message encrypted under its public key. Accordingly, we associate a context of the form

$$PK_A\,[\_] \overset{\text{def}}{=} \nu K_A^{-1}.(\{A = \mathsf{pk}(K_A^{-1})\} \mid [\_])$$

with every principal identity A. This context restricts the use of the decryption key K_A^{-1} to the process in the context and it exports the corresponding public key. Whenever we put a process R in this context, our intent is that R never communicates K_A^{-1} to the environment.

By definition of well-formed configurations in the applied pi calculus, a process of the form $C[PK_A\,[R]]$ exports A, only R can access K_A^{-1}, and we cannot apply a context that would redefine A. On the other hand, $C[\_]$ can define any number of other principals. Thus, we obtain a fairly generous and convenient model when we represent an attacker by an arbitrary context.

For example, the process $PK_A\,[\mathbf{0}]$ indicates that A is a principal whose decryption key is never used. This process concisely models an absent principal.

4.3 The Network and the Attacker

In our model of the protocol, network messages are transmitted on the channels named c_1 and c_2. These represent two public communication channels, or a single public channel, perhaps the ether, in which tags serve for differentiating traffic flows.

As explained in section 2, we assume that an attacker can interpose itself on all public communication channels. In our model, an arbitrary environment (an arbitrary evaluation context) represents the attacker. This environment can interact with the configuration of principals using labelled transitions on any free channel name. We obtain an attractively simple representation of broadcast communication: each message is simply made available to the attacker, on a public channel, and the attacker may then decide to transmit the message, again on a public channel, to one or more principals.

In addition, we sometimes model a weaker, passive attacker. An attack step—that is, eavesdropping on a message—amounts to a message interception (formally, with an output label) followed by a re-emission of the same message (with an input label). We write $A \xrightarrow{\nu\tilde{u}.c[\tilde{V}]} A'$ as a shorthand for the sequence of two transitions $A \xrightarrow{\nu\tilde{u}.\bar{c}\langle\tilde{V}\rangle} \xrightarrow{c(\tilde{V})} A'$.

4.4 The Protocol

In this section we give a formal counterpart to the description of message flows of section 2.2.

Messages. We rely on substitutions in order to define the protocol messages and the key derivation, as follows.

$$\sigma_1 \stackrel{\text{def}}{=} \{x_1 = \{\mathsf{hello}(N_A, A)\}_B\}$$
$$\sigma_2 \stackrel{\text{def}}{=} \{x_2 = \{\mathsf{ack}(N_A, N_B, B)\}_A\}$$
$$\sigma_2^{\circ} \stackrel{\text{def}}{=} \{x_2 = N_B\}$$
$$\sigma_K \stackrel{\text{def}}{=} \{K = \mathsf{h}(N_A, N_B)\}$$

Although N_A and N_B are free here, they represent fresh nonces. They will be bound in any process that introduces these substitutions. The substitution σ_2° corresponds to the responder's decoy message, in which here we use a name rather than a ciphertext, for simplicity.

Syntactic Sugar. We sometimes use the following abbreviations.

For testing, we write *if $U_1 = V_1$ and $U_2 = V_2$ then P else Q* for the process *if $U_1 = V_1$ then (if $U_2 = V_2$ then P else Q) else Q*, and rely on other similar abbreviations.

For decryption, we use pattern matching on message contents. Specifically, we write

$$\text{if } x = \{\mathsf{ack}(N_A, \nu N_B, B)\}_A \text{ using } K_A^{-1} \text{ then } P \text{ else } Q$$

for the process

$$\nu N_B. \begin{pmatrix} \{N_B = \mathsf{ack}.1\,(\mathsf{decrypt}(x, K_A^{-1}))\} \mid \\ if \ x = \{\mathsf{ack}(N_A, N_B, B)\}_A \ then \ P \ else \ Q \end{pmatrix}$$

with the assumption that $N_B \notin fv(Q)$, and we use analogous abbreviations with νA and νN_A. Here, we use the identifiers N_A and N_B as variables rather than names, locally.

For filtering duplicate messages, we write

$$!c_1(x \setminus V).if \ x \ fresh \ then \ P \ else \ Q$$

for the process

$$\nu c.\,(\overline{c}\langle V\rangle \mid !c_1(x).c(s).(\overline{c}\langle s.x\rangle \mid if \ x \in s \ then \ Q \ else \ P))$$

where c is a fresh channel name and s is a fresh variable. We use channel c for maintaining a set V of previously received messages; Q is triggered instead of P when one of those messages is received again.

Processes. The following code represents the protocol. It includes definitions of processes both for the initiator role (with A as initiator) and for the responder role (with B as responder).

$$P_A \stackrel{\text{def}}{=} I_A \mid R_A$$

$$I_A \stackrel{\text{def}}{=} !init_A(B).\nu N_A.\,(\overline{c}_1\langle x_1\sigma_1\rangle \mid I_A')$$

$$I_A' \stackrel{\text{def}}{=} c_2(x_2).if \ x_2 = \{\mathsf{ack}(N_A, \nu N_B, B)\}_A \ using \ K_A^{-1} \ then \ \overline{connect}_A\langle B, K\sigma_K\rangle$$

$$R_B \stackrel{\text{def}}{=} !c_1(x_1 \setminus \emptyset).$$
$$if \ x_1 \ fresh \ and \ x_1 = \{\mathsf{hello}(\nu N_A, \nu A)\}_B \ using \ K_B^{-1} \ and \ A \in S_B$$
$$then \ \nu N_B.\,(\overline{c}_2\langle x_2\sigma_2\rangle \mid \overline{accept}_B\langle A, K\sigma_K\rangle) \ else \ \nu N_B.\overline{c}_2\langle x_2\sigma_2^0\rangle$$

Here, I_A shows the initiator receiving an initiation request on channel $init_A$ and sending the first protocol message; I_A' then shows the initiator receiving and checking a response, and passing a session key on channel $connect_A$ if the response is satisfactory. On the other hand, R_B shows the responder receiving a message, processing it, responding, and in some cases passing a session key on channel $accept_B$. Both I_A and R_B are replicated processes. According to R_B, the responder filters duplicate messages. This filtering is not suggested by the informal descriptions of the protocol, but we believe that it is a reasonable refinement, with useful consequences.

As coded, the protocol has little resistance to multiplexing errors. In particular, the initiator fails if the first response that it receives is not the expected one. We could add retries without much difficulty, but this aspect of the protocol is mostly irrelevant in the study of safety properties.

4.5   Configurations of Principals

In our statements of security properties (not in the definition of the protocol itself), we distinguish a particular finite, non-empty set $\mathcal{C}$ of compliant principals

A, B, ... A compliant principal A is one in which the decryption key K_A^{-1} is used exclusively in the session-establishment protocol. The initial configuration of a single compliant principal A with user process U_A is therefore an extended process of the form:

$$Q_A \stackrel{\text{def}}{=} \nu \mathcal{V}_A.(U_A \mid PK_A[P_A])$$

This extended process is parameterized by the set S_A, and (at least) exports the variable A and has free channels c_1 and c_2. In Q_A, by definition, U_A does not have access to K_A^{-1}.

Combining several such extended processes, we obtain a global configuration of the form $\prod_{A \in \mathcal{C}} Q_A$ for any set of compliant principals $\mathcal{C}$. Sometimes, however, we do not need to distinguish the user processes of several compliant principals. We can instead group them in a single expression U, letting $U = \prod_{A \in \mathcal{C}} U_A$. Then, letting $\mathcal{V} = \bigcup_{A \in \mathcal{C}} \mathcal{V}_A$, we consider configurations of the form:

$$P \stackrel{\text{def}}{=} \prod_{A \in \mathcal{C}} PK_A[P_A]$$
$$Q \stackrel{\text{def}}{=} \nu \mathcal{V}.(U \mid P)$$

We assume that the user processes of compliant principals (U_A and U) never communicate control channels ($\mathcal{V}$) in messages. For instance, the process $\bar{c}_1\langle connect_A \rangle$ cannot be the user process of a compliant principal. This assumption can easily be enforced by the sort system.

We use P in section 5 when we establish security properties that do not depend on U, thus effectively regarding U as part of the attacker. We use Q in section 6, with additional restrictions on U, when we study privacy.

5   Authentication and Secrecy Properties

We begin our analysis of the protocol with traditional properties, namely responder authentication and session-key secrecy. Such standard properties are important, and often a prerequisite for privacy properties. Moreover, their formulation in the applied pi calculus illustrates the use of observational equivalence for expressing security properties. In contrast, many other formalisms for similar purposes rely only on properties of traces, rather than on equivalences.

For a given set of compliant principals $\mathcal{C}$, we study runs of the protocol in the presence of an active attacker, by examining transitions $P \xrightarrow{\eta} P'$ from the configuration P defined above to some configuration P', where η is an arbitrary sequence of labels.

In our statements, we let ω and φ abbreviate the series of actions and the equational "net effect" of a successful run of the protocol, and let ω^- and φ^- abbreviate the series of actions and the equational "net effect" of a non-accepted run of the protocol:

$$\stackrel{\omega}{\rightarrow} \stackrel{\text{def}}{=} \stackrel{init_A(B)}{\longrightarrow} \stackrel{\nu x_1.c_1[x_1]}{\longrightarrow}_* \stackrel{\nu x_2.c_2[x_2]}{\longrightarrow} \stackrel{\nu K.\overline{accept}_B\langle A,K\rangle}{\longrightarrow} \stackrel{\overline{connect}_A\langle B,K\rangle}{\longrightarrow}$$

$$\stackrel{\omega^-}{\rightarrow} \stackrel{\text{def}}{=} \stackrel{init_A(B)}{\longrightarrow} \stackrel{\nu x_1.c_1[x_1]}{\longrightarrow}_* \stackrel{\nu x_2.c_2[x_2]}{\longrightarrow}$$

$$\varphi \stackrel{\text{def}}{=} \nu N_A.(\sigma_1 \mid \nu N_B.(\sigma_2 \mid \sigma_K))$$

$$\varphi^- \stackrel{\text{def}}{=} (\nu N_A.\sigma_1) \mid (\nu N_B.\sigma_2^\circ)$$

We have that if $A \in S_B$ then

$$P \stackrel{\omega}{\rightarrow} P_{x1} \mid \varphi$$

else

$$P \stackrel{\omega^-}{\rightarrow} P_{x1} \mid \varphi^-$$

where P_{x1} is P updated so that R_B holds an element x_1 in the set of messages it has received. Thus, P may perform a complete run of the protocol, and this run succeeds if authorized by the responder and fails otherwise. More generally, for any P' such that $P \stackrel{\eta}{\rightarrow} P'$, we have that if $A \in S_B$ then

$$P' \stackrel{\omega}{\rightarrow} P'_{x1} \mid \varphi$$

else

$$P' \stackrel{\omega^-}{\rightarrow} P'_{x1} \mid \varphi^-$$

where P'_{x1} is a corresponding update of P'. These results express the functional correctness of the protocol. They hold independently of whether encryption is which-key concealing.

The following theorem relates the two possible outcomes of an actual run to a "magical" outcome $\varphi^\circ \stackrel{\text{def}}{=} \nu N_1.\{x_1 = N_1\} \mid \nu N_2.\{x_2 = N_2\}$ where the two intercepted messages are trivially independent of the principals A and B and of the established key.

Theorem 1 (Secrecy for complete runs). *Let $A, B \in \mathcal{C}$.*

1. *(Success:) If $P \stackrel{\eta}{\rightarrow} P'$ and $A \in S_B$, then $P' \stackrel{\omega}{\rightarrow}\approx_l P' \mid \varphi^\circ \mid \nu N.\{K = N\}$.*
   (Failure:) If $P \stackrel{\eta}{\rightarrow} P'$ and $A \notin S_B$, then $P' \stackrel{\omega^-}{\rightarrow}\approx_l P' \mid \varphi^\circ$.
2. *Conversely, if $P \stackrel{\omega}{\rightarrow} P''$, then $A \in S_B$ and $P'' \approx_l P \mid \varphi^\circ \mid \nu N.\{K = N\}$.*

The active substitution $\nu N.\{K = N\}$ exports the simplest definition of a fresh secret key, a fresh name, rather than an expression computed from x_1 and x_2. Interestingly, φ° and $\nu N.\{K = N\}$ do not depend on A and B at all, so this theorem implies a first privacy guarantee. The equivalences $\approx_l$ are used for rewriting $P'_{x1} \mid \varphi$ and $P'_{x1} \mid \varphi^-$, by simplifying φ and φ^- and by erasing x_1 from the set of messages that R_B has received, returning to the process P' and hiding that a run has occurred. These equivalences hold only if encryption is which-key-concealing. Otherwise, we obtain only:

$$P'_{x1} \mid \varphi \approx_l P'_{x1} \mid (\nu N_A.\sigma_1) \mid (\nu N_A N_B.\sigma_2) \mid (\nu N.\{K = N\})$$

On the right-hand side, we are left with messages x_1 and x_2 that contain the public keys of A and B. Nonetheless, N_A and N_B are bound around σ_1 and σ_2, so the independence and secrecy of the session key are still guaranteed.

A direct corollary concerns two instances P_A and P_B of the protocol in the initial state. This corollary emphasizes the transitions observed by an environment with no access to the control channels.

$$P_A \mid P_B \mid \overline{init_A}\langle B\rangle \; \xrightarrow{\;\;} \xrightarrow{\nu x_1.c_1[x_1]} \to^* \xrightarrow{\nu x_2.c_2[x_2]} \to \approx_l$$

$$P_A \mid P_B \mid \varphi^\circ \mid \begin{cases} \nu N.\,\big(\overline{accept_B}\langle A, N\rangle \mid \overline{connect_A}\langle B, N\rangle\big) & \text{if } A \in S_B \\ 0 & \text{if } A \notin S_B \end{cases}$$

Intuitively, when we erase control messages, we obtain the same trace and equational effect whether or not $A \in S_B$.

Finally, we also obtain an authentication property:

Theorem 2 (Responder authentication). *Suppose that* $P \xrightarrow{\eta} P'$ *and (1)* η *has no internal communication step on* c_1 *and* c_2; *(2)* P' *has no immediate output on channel* $accept_B$.

If $\overline{connect_A}\langle B, K\rangle$ *occurs in* η, *then* $P \xrightarrow{\omega} \xrightarrow{\eta'} P'$ *for some permutation* $\omega\eta'$ *of* η.

In the statement of the theorem, we rely on α-conversion and assume that the names and variables in processes and labels never clash. With this standard assumption, the commutation of two transition steps (when enabled) can be written simply as the commutation of their labels. Conditions 1 and 2 in the theorem are technically convenient, but not essential. Condition 1 rules out traces where a message is not intercepted by the attacker, and is instead transmitted internally. Any internal communication $A \to A'$ on channel c_i can be decomposed into $A \xrightarrow{\nu x_i.c_i[x_i]} A''$ with $A' \equiv \nu x_i.A''$. Condition 2 rules out traces where the transition $accept_B$ in ω has not occurred and is enabled in P'.

In light of the results above, we can interpret this theorem partly as a correspondence assertion: whenever A receives a connection message after a protocol run, apparently with B, we have that

1. A initiated the session with B;
2. B accepted the session with A;
3. both parties are now sharing a fresh key K, as good as a fresh shared name;
4. intercepted messages x_1 and x_2 are seemingly unrelated to A, B, and K.

6   Privacy Properties

In this section, we focus on privacy properties. For a given set of compliant principals $\mathcal{C}$, we consider the question of whether an attacker can distinguish two user processes U_1 and U_2 when we place these processes in the context $\nu\mathcal{V}.([\_]\|P)$ that provides local access to the session-establishment protocol. Therefore, indistinguishability for user processes depends on the identity-protection features of the protocol, and it is coarser than ordinary observational equivalence $\approx_l$ (that is, indistinguishability in all evaluation contexts).

For instance, if U_1 and U_2 each contain a message $\overline{init}_{A_1}\langle B_1\rangle$ and $\overline{init}_{A_2}\langle B_2\rangle$, and if U_1 and U_2 "behave similarly" once a session is established, then U_1 and U_2 are indistinguishable in this specific sense. On the other hand, we have $\overline{init}_{A_1}\langle B_1\rangle \approx_l \overline{init}_{A_2}\langle B_2\rangle$ only if $A_1 = A_2$ and $B_1 = B_2$.

In order to capture this notion of indistinguishability, we introduce a special labelled transition system and a notion of bisimulation. We obtain a general result in terms of that notion of bisimulation, then derive some privacy properties as corollaries. Thus, for the study of a particular protocol, we develop a special notion of observation of user processes. In contrast, in recent, related work [4,3], we take a standard notion of observation, and develop communication protocols that are secure with respect to it (and which, for instance, rely on "noise" messages in order to hide communication patterns between compliant principals).

We adopt the following notation convention. We write A, B for principals in the set of compliant principals $\mathcal{C}$, and E for a principal not in $\mathcal{C}$.

6.1   A Labelled Transition System

Next we define labelled transitions for user processes with control state. The control state records the sets S_B of acceptable interlocutors and abstractly keeps track of the sessions being negotiated. The labelled transitions reflect only what the environment can observe about these sessions, filtering out identity information.

Formally, a control state ρ consists of two functions, one that maps each principal $B \in \mathcal{C}$ to a set S_B, and the other a finite map from integers to entries t. The entries are of four kinds:

- $A\ B$: a session offer from A to B not yet considered by B.
- $A\ B\ K_i$: a session offer from A to B accepted by B with key K_i (when $A \in S_B$).
- $A\ B -$: a session offer from A to B rejected by B (when $A \notin S_B$).
- $A\ E$: a session offer from A to some non-compliant principal E.

For any ρ and any integer i not in ρ's domain, we let $\rho[i \mapsto t]$ be the control state that extends ρ by mapping i to t. We assume that the keys K_i are all distinct. We let $\mathcal{V}_\rho$ be the union of $\mathcal{V}$ with the keys K_i for all integers i in the domain of ρ.

We pair a process with a control state, with the notation $\rho : U$. We assume that K_i is free in U only if ρ maps i to an entry of the form $A\ B\ K_i$. (In Q, the user process U may have free variables defined by P, such as variables A and B that represent compliant principals, or K_i for a computed key. When we consider transitions of U or $\rho : U$, we treat these variables as names.)

Such a pair $\rho : U$ may have the three sorts of transitions $\rho : U \xrightarrow{\gamma} \rho' : U'$ that we define next: ordinary transitions, blinded transitions, and external transitions.

– Ordinary transitions are essentially those of the process U. For any label α that does not contain control channels or keys K_i, we have:

$$\text{LIFT} \frac{U \xrightarrow{\alpha} U'}{\rho : U \xrightarrow{\alpha} \rho : U'} \quad \text{when} \begin{array}{l} fn(\alpha) \cap \mathcal{V}_\rho = \emptyset \\ bn(\alpha) \cap (\mathcal{C} \cup \mathcal{V}_\rho) = \emptyset \end{array}$$

– The attacker can blindly intercept all messages sent on public channels by the principals in $\mathcal{C}$ and resend any of these messages later. Specifically, the attacker can detect new session attempts, make responders consider session offers (either genuine or fake), and make initiators consider intercepted "ack" messages. We reflect these actions using blinded transitions $\xrightarrow{\overline{init}\,\nu i}$, $\xrightarrow{accept\,i}$, $\xrightarrow{accept_B(A)}$, and $\xrightarrow{connect\,i}$.

$$\text{INIT} \frac{U \xrightarrow{\overline{init}_A\langle B\rangle} U'}{\rho : U \xrightarrow{\overline{init}\,\nu i} \rho[i \mapsto A\,B] : U'}$$

$$\text{ACCEPT} \quad \rho[i \mapsto A\,B] : U \xrightarrow{accept\,i} \begin{cases} \rho[i \mapsto A\,B\,K_i] : U \mid \overline{accept}_B\langle A, K_i\rangle & \text{if } A \in S_B \\ \rho[i \mapsto A\,B-\,] : U & \text{if } A \notin S_B \end{cases}$$

$$\text{ACCEPT-FAKE} \quad \rho : U \xrightarrow{accept_B(A)} \begin{cases} \rho : U \mid \nu N. \overline{accept}_B\langle A, N\rangle & \text{if } A \in S_B \\ \rho : U & \text{if } A \notin S_B \end{cases}$$

$$\text{CONNECT} \quad \begin{array}{l} \rho[i \mapsto A\,B\,K_i] : U \xrightarrow{connect\,i} \rho : \nu K_i.\,(U \mid \overline{connect}_A\langle B, K_i\rangle) \\ \rho[i \mapsto A\,B-\,] : U \xrightarrow{connect\,i} \rho : U \end{array}$$

– In addition, compliant principals may be willing to open sessions with non-compliant ones. These sessions are also mediated by the protocol, even if they are transparent to the attacker who can in principle decrypt all messages in these sessions. We reflect these actions using external transitions $\xrightarrow{\nu i E.\overline{init}_A\langle i,E\rangle}$, $\xrightarrow{accept_B(W,V)}$, and $\xrightarrow{connect_A(i,E,V)}$, where E is a variable and V and W are terms such that $fn(V) \cap \mathcal{V}_\rho = fn(W) \cap \mathcal{V}_\rho = \emptyset$.

$$\text{INIT-E} \frac{U \xrightarrow{\nu E.\overline{init}_A\langle E\rangle} U'}{\rho : U \xrightarrow{\nu E.\overline{init}_A\langle i,E\rangle} \rho[i \mapsto A\,E] : U'} \quad \begin{array}{l} \text{when } (E \neq B)\varphi(U') \\ \text{for all } B \in \mathcal{C} \end{array}$$

$$\text{ACCEPT-E} \quad \rho : U \xrightarrow{accept_B(W,V)} \rho : U \mid \overline{accept}_B\langle W, V\rangle \quad \begin{array}{l} \text{when } (W = A)\varphi(U) \\ \text{for some } A \in S_B \setminus \mathcal{C} \end{array}$$

$$\text{CONNECT-E} \quad \rho[i \mapsto A\,E] : U \xrightarrow{connect_A(i,E,V)} \rho : U \mid \overline{connect}_A\langle E, V\rangle$$

6.2   Private Bisimulation

In order to express hypotheses on the observable properties of user processes, we define an ad hoc notion of bisimulation:

Definition 1. Private bisimilarity $(\approx_C)$ is the largest symmetric relation $\mathcal{R}$ on extended processes with control state such that, whenever $T_1 \ \mathcal{R} \ T_2$ with $T_1 = \rho_1 : U_1$ and $T_2 = \rho_2 : U_2$, we have:

1. $\nu\mathcal{V}_{\rho_1}.U_1 \approx_s \nu\mathcal{V}_{\rho_2}.U_2$,
2. if $T_1 \to T_1'$, then $T_2 \to^* T_2'$ and $T_1' \ \mathcal{R} \ T_2'$ for some T_2',
3. if $T_1 \xrightarrow{\gamma} T_1'$ and $fv(\gamma) \subseteq dom(\nu\mathcal{V}_{\rho_1}.U_1)$ and $bn(\gamma) \cap fn(\nu\mathcal{V}_{\rho_2}.U_2) = \emptyset$, then $T_2 \to^* \xrightarrow{\gamma} \to^* T_2'$ and $T_1' \ \mathcal{R} \ T_2'$ for some T_2'.

This definition is an adaptation of that of weak labelled bisimilarity for the applied pi calculus [2, definition 4]. The three clauses are exactly analogous to those for the applied pi calculus, with different transitions in clause 3.

We also let ε range over initial control states, that is, control states that have no session entries and only define sets S_B for $B \in \mathcal{C}$. We write $P(\varepsilon)$ for the protocol P with these sets S_B. When ε is clear from context, we may write (as usual) P instead of $P(\varepsilon)$.

Our main privacy result states that, if two user processes are privately bisimilar (under our new notion of bisimulation), then the two corresponding configurations are observationally equivalent from the environment's point of view. As we show below, this result provides an effective proof technique for privacy properties.

Lemma 1 (Privacy). If $\varepsilon_1 : U_1 \approx_C \varepsilon_2 : U_2$, then

$$\nu\mathcal{V}.(U_1 \mid P(\varepsilon_1)) \approx_l \nu\mathcal{V}.(U_2 \mid P(\varepsilon_2))$$

The hypothesis $\varepsilon_1 : U_1 \approx_C \varepsilon_2 : U_2$ deals with arbitrary user processes and sets S_B, and is typically not difficult to establish in particular cases. Importantly, its statement does not depend on any detail of the session protocol, only on its control interface. The conclusion $\nu\mathcal{V}.(U_1 \mid P(\varepsilon_1)) \approx_l \nu\mathcal{V}.(U_2 \mid P(\varepsilon_2))$ then says that two composite systems, each with a user process, are indistinguishable.

The converse of Lemma 1 does not quite hold, at least because the definition of labelled transitions is conservative in some respects. (For instance, in that definition, we safely presume that the attacker has a private key associated with any value E that U employs to identify a non-compliant principal.) Thus, user processes that are not privately bisimilar may still be part of undistinguishable systems. Such user processes can easily be excluded with additional hypotheses.

6.3   Applications of the Privacy Lemma

One may formulate and prove many specific privacy properties for the protocol. The various properties may differ, in particular, on which user processes and sets S_B they consider. We give a series of simple examples of such properties. In the examples, the hypotheses can usually be made less demanding, and more specific and complicated. The proofs follow directly from Lemma 1.

We begin with a basic example that concerns the anonymity of failed sessions. Provided that U never inputs on channels $init_X$, if $A \notin S_B$ and $A' \notin S_{B'}$, then replacing $\overline{init_A}\langle B \rangle$ with $\overline{init_{A'}}\langle B' \rangle$ in U does not affect Q (up to observational equivalence).

The next result deals with a single initial session attempt, and states that the session attempt may not compromise any private bisimilarity that would hold after establishing the session.

Theorem 3 (Equivalent sessions). *For $j = 1, 2$, let*

$$U_j \stackrel{def}{=} \overline{init_{A_j}}\langle B_j \rangle \mid connect_{A_j}(B_j, K).V_j$$
$$U'_j \stackrel{def}{=} \nu K. \left(\overline{accept_{B_j}}\langle A_j, K \rangle \mid V_j \right)$$

with $A_j, B_j \in \mathcal{C}$ and $A_j \in S_{B_j}$ in ε_j. If $\varepsilon_1 : U'_1 \approx_{\mathcal{C}} \varepsilon_2 : U'_2$, then $\varepsilon_1 : U_1 \approx_{\mathcal{C}} \varepsilon_2 : U_2$.

For any V_1 and V_2 that do not use the control channels, the private bisimilarity hypothesis holds as soon as $\nu K.V_1 \approx_l \nu K.V_2$. With this additional assumption and Lemma 1, we have a corollary expressed in terms of standard labelled bisimilarity: we obtain that if $\nu K.V_1 \approx_l \nu K.V_2$ then $\nu \mathcal{V}.(U_1 \mid P(\varepsilon_1)) \approx_l \nu \mathcal{V}.(U_2 \mid P(\varepsilon_2))$.

A further privacy property concerns compliant principals that attempt to open sessions with one another but do not perform any action observable by the attacker after establishing a session. (They may for instance use private channels, or public channels with adequate decoys.) We may describe any such configuration of principals in $\mathcal{C}$ by a parallel compositions of $init_A$ messages with $A \in \mathcal{C}$, plus the sets $(S_B)_{B \in \mathcal{C}}$. In this special case, we easily characterize the equivalence of two configurations:

Theorem 4 (Silent sessions). *Let U_1 and U_2 be parallel compositions of messages $\overline{init_A}\langle X \rangle$ with $A \in \mathcal{C}$. If*

1. *U_1 and U_2 contain the same number of messages,*
2. *U_1 and U_2 contain exactly the same messages $\overline{init_A}\langle W \rangle$ for $W \notin \mathcal{C}$, and*
3. *the sets $S_B \setminus \mathcal{C}$ are identical in ε_1 and ε_2,*

then $\nu \mathcal{V}.(U_1 \mid P(\varepsilon_1)) \approx_l \nu \mathcal{V}.(U_2 \mid P(\varepsilon_2))$.

In order to prove the theorem, we may establish $\varepsilon_1 : U_1 \approx_{\mathcal{C}} \varepsilon_2 : U_2$ by enumerating a few blinded and external transitions, then apply Lemma 1. Conversely, these conditions seem clearly necessary: the attacker can count the number of "hello" messages, can decrypt "hello" messages sent to principals outside $\mathcal{C}$ (as long as W is a public key not in $\mathcal{C}$), and can attempt to establish a session with any $B \in \mathcal{C}$.

We can derive other similar privacy results for uniform families of user processes, such as processes that do not use any principal identity after establishing sessions.

Our final result relates a configuration with a present but silent principal to a configuration with an absent principal. (This theorem does not require Lemma 1; it has a simple, direct bisimulation proof.)

Theorem 5 (Absent principal). *Assume that* $|\mathcal{C}| > 1$, *and let* $X \notin \mathcal{C}$ *and* $S_X = \emptyset$. *We have:*

$$Q \mid \nu \mathcal{V}_X.PK_X\,[P_X] \approx_l Q \mid PK_X\,[\mathbf{0}]$$

The process on the left-hand side is structurally equivalent to a configuration Q' with compliant principals $\mathcal{C} \cup \{X\}$; the process on the right-hand side includes an absent principal (a principal X whose decryption key is never used). Hence, one may first use private bisimilarity to show that X is apparently not involved in any session in Q', then apply Theorem 5 to substitute an absent principal for X. (Conversely, if $\mathcal{C} = \{\}$ or $\mathcal{C} = \{A\}$, then the addition of any instance of the protocol is observable.)

7   Conclusions

This paper reports on the analysis of a protocol in the applied pi calculus, covering standard authenticity and secrecy properties and also privacy (identity protection) properties. The formulation of these properties mainly relies on equivalences, which express indistinguishability in an arbitrary context. Our analysis concerns not only the core of the protocol but also its composition with a user process, since this composition may endanger privacy properties. Thus, we examine the protocol under several hypotheses on user processes. We obtain several related results that transfer hypotheses on user processes to security properties of complete systems.

The literature contains many other formal treatments of protocols and of their security properties. We will not attempt to survey that work here, but mention only the two most relevant papers. One of them is our original paper on the applied pi calculus [2], which considers session establishment and some of its properties, and which includes additional references. The other is a recent paper by Shmatikov and Hughes that defines several notions of anonymity and privacy [16], and sketches—in just a few sentences—an analysis of the protocol that is the subject of this paper. Shmatikov and Hughes develop a special formal framework for protocols, communication graphs. Despite some thematic overlap, the applied pi calculus appears to be richer than communication graphs. In particular, communication graphs do not include an account of user processes. While the definitions of anonymity and privacy seem appropriate and useful for communication graphs, it is not yet entirely clear whether and how they would carry over to the applied pi calculus and other settings.

Acknowledgments. We are grateful to Vitaly Shmatikov for helpful discussions, and to the editors for their patience. Part of Martín Abadi's work was done at Microsoft Research, Silicon Valley. Martín Abadi's work was also partly supported by the National Science Foundation under Grants CCR-0204162 and CCR-0208800.

References

[1] Martín Abadi. Private authentication. In *Proceedings of the Workshop on Privacy Enhancing Technologies (PET 2002)*, LNCS. Springer-Verlag, 2002. To appear.

[2] Martín Abadi and Cédric Fournet. Mobile values, new names, and secure communication. In *Proceedings of the 28th ACM Symposium on Principles of Programming Languages (POPL 2001)*, pages 104–115. ACM, January 2001.

[3] Martín Abadi, Cédric Fournet, and Georges Gonthier. Authentication primitives and their compilation. In *Proceedings of the 27th ACM Symposium on Principles of Programming Languages (POPL 2000)*, pages 302–315. ACM, January 2000.

[4] Martín Abadi, Cédric Fournet, and Georges Gonthier. Secure implementation of channel abstractions. *Information and Computation*, 174(1):37–83, April 2002.

[5] William Aiello, Steven M. Bellovin, Matt Blaze, Ran Canetti, John Ionnidis, Angelos D. Keromytis, and Omer Reingold. Efficient, DoS-resistant, secure key exchange for internet protocols. In Vijay Atluri, editor, *Proceedings of the 9th ACM Conference on Computer and Communications Security (CCS 2002)*, pages 48–58. ACM, November 2002.

[6] Giuseppe Ateniese, Amir Herzberg, Hugo Krawczyk, and Gene Tsudik. On traveling incognito. *Computer Networks*, 31(8):871–884, 1999.

[7] Hannes Federrath, Anja Jerichow, and Andreas Pfitzmann. MIXes in mobile communication systems: Location management with privacy. In Ross J. Anderson, editor, *Information hiding: First international workshop*, volume 1174 of *LNCS*, pages 121–135. Springer-Verlag, 1996.

[8] Markus Jakobsson and Susanne Wetzel. Security weaknesses in Bluetooth. In *Topics in Cryptology - CT-RSA 2001, Proceedings of the Cryptographer's Track at RSA Conference 2001*, volume 2020 of *LNCS*, pages 176–191. Springer-Verlag, 2001.

[9] Hugo Krawczyk. SKEME: A versatile secure key exchange mechanism for internet. In *Proceedings of the Internet Society Symposium on Network and Distributed Systems Security*, February 1996. Available at http://bilbo.isu.edu/sndss/sndss96.html.

[10] Butler Lampson, Martín Abadi, Michael Burrows, and Edward Wobber. Authentication in distributed systems: Theory and practice. *ACM Transactions on Computer Systems*, 10(4):265–310, November 1992.

[11] Alfred J. Menezes, Paul C. van Oorschot, and Scott A. Vanstone. *Handbook of Applied Cryptography*. CRC Press, 1996.

[12] Refik Molva, Didier Samfat, and Gene Tsudik. Authentication of mobile users. *IEEE Network*, 8(2):26–35, March/April 1994.

[13] Roger M. Needham and Michael D. Schroeder. Using encryption for authentication in large networks of computers. *Communications of the ACM*, 21(12):993–999, December 1978.

[14] Michael G. Reed, Paul F. Syverson, and David M. Goldschlag. Protocols using anonymous connections: Mobile applications. In B. Christianson, B. Crispo, M. Lomas, and M. Roe, editors, *Security Protocols: 5th International Workshop*, volume 1361 of *LNCS*, pages 13–23. Springer-Verlag, 1997.

[15] Didier Samfat, Refik Molva, and N. Asokan. Untraceability in mobile networks. In *Proceedings of the First Annual International Conference on Mobile Computing and Networking (MobiCom 1995)*, pages 26–36, 1995.

[16] Vitaly Shmatikov and Dominic Hughes. Defining anonymity and privacy (extended abstract). In *Workshop on Issues in the Theory of Security (WITS' 02)*, January 2002.

Environmental Requirements for Authentication Protocols

Ran Canetti[1], Catherine Meadows[2], and Paul Syverson[2]

[1] IBM T.J. Watson Research Center, POB 704
Yorktown Heights, NY 10598
canetti@watson.ibm.com
[2] Naval Research Laboratory
Center for High Assurance Computer Systems
Washington, DC 20375
{meadows, syverson}@itd.nrl.navy.mil

Abstract. Most work on requirements in the area of authentication protocols has concentrated on identifying requirements for the protocol without much consideration of context. Little work has concentrated on assumptions about the environment, for example, the applications that make use of authenticated keys. We will show in this paper how the interaction between a protocol and its environment can have a major effect on a protocol. Specifically we will demonstrate a number of attacks on published and/or widely used protocols that are not feasible against the protocol running in isolation (even with multiple runs) but become feasible in some application environments. We will also discuss the tradeoff between putting constraints on a protocol and putting constraints on the environment in which it operates.

1 Introduction

Much work has been done on ensuring that cryptographic protocols satisfy their security requirements. This work usually assumes a very pessimistic model; it is assumed that the protocol is running in a network controlled by a hostile intruder who can read, alter, and delete messages, and moreover that some legitimate users of the network may themselves be in league with the intruder, who as a result will have access to a certain number of keys and cryptographic algorithms. As might be expected, it is difficult to ensure that a protocol attains its security goals in such an environment, and there are a number of cases in which security flaws have been found in protocols well after they were published or even fielded. However, a number of people have developed formal requirements, that if satisfied, are intended to guarantee that the protocol operates correctly, as well as formal techniques for proving that these requirements hold. Usually, these requirements boil down to requiring that secrets (e.g. cryptographic keys) not be revealed and that, if one side or the other thinks that the protocol completed, then it should not have been interfered with in any "meaningful" way.

M. Okada et al. (Eds.): ISSS 2002, LNCS 2609, pp. 339–355, 2003.

However, most of these formal requirements, as well as the tools for proving them correct, suffer from a limitation. They are generally used to reason about a single set of message flows running in isolation, and usually do not take into account the applications to which the protocol is put, the mechanisms of which the protocol is making use, and any similar protocols with which the protocol may be interacting. But all of these can have a major impact on the security of the protocol.

This paper demonstrates, via some attacks on well-established protocols, the dangers of ignoring the environment (which includes all other protocols that may be running concurrently with the protocol in question) when analyzing the security of authentication and key-exchange protocols. By "environment" we mean the combination of four factors, which we can think of as existing above, below, and on the same level as the protocol, respectively:

1. the intentions and capabilities of an attacker;
2. the applications using the protocol;
3. the functions (e.g. encryption, generation of random numbers, etc.) on which the protocol depends, and;
4. other similar protocol executions with which the current execution may or may not interact.

It is known that, for any cryptographic protocol, it is possible to construct another protocol with which it interacts insecurely [18], given that the two protocols share some secret information. Such general "attack protocols" are not always realistic, but the authors of [18] are able to construct many examples that are, and to develop several design principles that can help to prevent these attacks. The aim of our paper is to extend this approach further by showing that even the strongest requirements on a protocol are not enough to guarantee the security of a protocol interacting with even a "reasonable" environment unless we put restrictions on the environment as well as the protocol. We will do this by presenting as examples protocols that satisfy increasingly strong requirements, each time showing how they could be subverted by seemingly benign aspects of the environment that are exploited by a hostile intruder.

We begin by describing (in Section 2) the notion of a threat environment, which comprises the assumptions made about the capabilities and goals of a possible attacker. We describe two well-known attacks on cryptographic protocols, both of which came about as the result of changing assumptions about the threat environment. We then present the current standard definition of the threat environment, and argue that it is not adequate to prove a protocol's security. In Section 3 we extend our argument by recalling two known attacks. Even though these attacks focus on a protocol run in isolation, they make our point that when analyzing one protocol (or sub-protocol) one must keep in mind the environment in which this protocol is expected to run. The first attack demonstrates that separately analyzing sub-protocols of a given protocol, without making sure that the composition of the two sub-protocols is secure, is dangerous. It also demonstrates our point that the threat environment can vary according to the protocol and its intended application. The second attack concentrates on the danger in several concurrent runs of the same protocol. We discuss requirements on the environment that could have prevented this problem, as well as the protocol requirement known as "matching histories" which requires that principals have identical message histories after a protocol completes. Then, in Section 4 we describe an attack on a protocol satisfying matching histories that demonstrates possible weaknesses that arise from bad interactions between a key exchange protocol and an "application protocol" that uses the key. This also motivates the definition of a stronger requirement, "agreement," which requires that principals not only have identical message histories but agree on who they are talking to. The necessity of protecting secrets, even malformed or immature ones, is discussed in Section 5. In this section we first show how a protocol satisfying agreement can be foiled by an intruder who sends messages that have different meanings to sender and receiver, causing the receiver to respond with an inappropriate message. We then show how a protocol that satisfies the even stronger requirement of extensible-fail-stop, which would outlaw such type of behavior, can be tricked when it interacts with a seemingly harmless challenge-response protocol. We discuss our findings in Section 6 and give some recommendations for environmental requirements, as well as a discussion of open problems.

2 Threat Environments

One of the most obvious features of an environment is the set of assumptions that are made about the capabilities of the intruder who is trying to subvert the protocol. As a matter of fact, many of the attacks that have been found on published protocols are found as a result of changing the threat environment model; a protocol that was designed to be secure against one type of threat may not be secure against another. We give here two examples, discussed by Pancho in [24].

Both of these attacks are on early protocols due to Needham and Schroeder in [23]. These protocols were some of the earliest proposed for distributing keys over a network, so it is not surprising that the threat model was still evolving at the time. In particular, Needham and Schroeder made two assumptions which are not commonly made today. The first was that old session keys would not be vulnerable to compromise, and the second was that principals would only try to communicate securely with other principals that they trusted.

Both of these protocols used an architecture that has become standard among cryptographic protocols today. In this architecture, principals possess long-term, or master, keys which are used to distribute shorter-term, or *session*, keys. The master keys may possibly be distributed by some non-electronic means, while the session keys will be distributed electronically over the network. The rationale behind this is manifold: First, in networks of any size it is infeasible for keys to be generated and assigned so that all principals share a unique key with each other principal. Second, limited use of the master keys makes them less vulnerable to compromise. Third, this limited use makes it possible to restrict more expensive forms of encryption (such as public key) to encryption with the master key and to use cheaper encryption for the session keys, which will encrypt the highest volume of traffic.

The first of these protocols involves two parties who wish to communicate with each other using a key server. Each party shares a pairwise key with the server, and the protocol proceeds as follows:

Message 1 $A \rightarrow S:$ A, B, R_A

A requests a key from the server S to communicate with B. It includes a random nonce R_A so that it can verify the recency of any message it gets from the server. If it receives an encrypted message from the server containing R_A, it will know that the message could only have been generated after the server saw R_A.

Message 2 $S \rightarrow A:$ $\{R_A, B, k_{AB}, \{k_{AB}, A\}_{k_{BS}}\}_{k_{AS}}$

The server creates a key k_{AB}. It encrypts the key together with A's name using the key B shares with S. Then it uses k_{AS}, the key S shares with A, to encrypt R_A, B's name, the new key k_{AB}, and the encrypted message for B.

Message 3 $A \rightarrow B:$ $\{k_{AB}, A\}_{k_{BS}}$

After A receives and decrypts the message from S, it forwards the key to B.

Message 4 $B \rightarrow A:$ $\{R_B\}_{k_{AB}}$

B can verify the the key is from the server and is intended for communication with A, but it still needs to verify that the message is not a replay. It does this by creating its own nonce, encrypting it with k_{AB}, and sending it to A.

Message 5 $A \rightarrow B:$ $\{R_B - 1\}_{k_{AB}}$

A decrypts the nonce, subtracts one, reencrypts it, and sends it to B. When B receives the message and decrypts it, it can verify that it can only have come from someone who knows k_{AB}. Since only A (and the server) is assumed to know k_{AB}, and the server is assumed to be honest, B can assume both that the key is recent and that it is talking to A.

Denning and Sacco found the following attack, based on the assumption that old session keys can be compromised. In this attack, the intruder not only compromises the old session key, but has been able to record the communication by which the old session key was distributed:

Message 3 $I_A \rightarrow B:$ $\{k_{AB}, A\}_{k_{BS}}$

An intruder, pretending to be A, resends an old encrypted message containing an old compromised key for A and B.

Message 4 $B \rightarrow A: \quad \{R_B\}_{k_{AB}}$

B responds according to the rules of the protocol.

Message 5 $I_A \rightarrow B: \quad \{R_B - 1\}_{k_{AB}}$

The intruder intercepts B's message to A. Since it knows the old key, it can decrypt B's message and produce the appropriate response.

The other protocol involves two principals who use public key encryption to set up a session with each other. This protocol has two parts, one in which the principals obtain each other's public keys from a server, and one in which they use the public keys to set up a session with each other. Since the attack does not involve the first part, we present only the second part here:

Message 1 $A \rightarrow B \ : \ \{R_A, A\}_{k_B}$

A sends a nonce R_A, together with A's name to B, encrypted with B's public key. B decrypts to get A's name.

Message 2 $B \rightarrow A \ : \ \{R_A, R_B\}_{k_A}$

B generates a nonce R_B and sends it together with R_A to A, encrypted with k_A. A decrypts the message. If it finds R_A, it assumes that this is a message from B in response to its original message.

Message 3 $A \rightarrow B \ : \ \{R_B\}_{k_B}$

A encrypts R_B with k_B and sends it to B. B decrypts the message. If it finds R_B, it assumes that this is a message from A in response to its original message.

The attack, as presented by Lowe in [20], proceeds as follows. Note that this attack only works if one of the principals attempts to communicate with an untrusted principal first:

Message 1 $A \rightarrow I: \quad \{R_A, A\}_{k_I}$

A initiates communication with I.

Message 1' $I_A \rightarrow B: \quad \{R_A, A\}_{k_B}$

I initiates communication with B, using R_A.

Message 2' $B \to A$: $\{R_A, R_B\}_{k_A}$

B responds to A. A decrypts and finds R_A.

Message 3 $A \to I$: $\{R_B\}_{k_I}$

Thinking that the previous message is a response from I, A responds in kind. I decrypts R_B and can now use it to impersonate A to B.

Message 3' $I_A \to B$: $\{R_B\}_{k_B}$

I completes the protocol with B.

Over the years, the community has come to agree on a standard intruder model which has come to be so widely accepted that it is sometimes assumed that Needham and Schroeder were attempting to design their protocols according to it but failed (see Pancho [24] for a discussion of this). In this model we assume that the network is under the control of a hostile intruder who can read, modify, and delete message traffic, and who may be in league with corrupt principals in the network. We assume that honest principals have no way of telling corrupt principals from other honest principals, and thus may be willing to initiate communication with these dishonest principals. Finally, we assume that old session keys may be compromised, although we usually do not assume that the master key that is used to distribute the session key will be compromised.

This is accepted as the standard intruder model, but is it the last word? We argue that it is not.

First of all, threat models can change. For example, the standard threat model alluded to above takes into account the compromise of old session keys, but does not concern itself with the threat of session keys being compromised while the session is still current. In the next section we will discuss a protocol in which the real-time compromise of session keys is a realistic threat.

Secondly, the model does not take into account other, possibly benign aspects of the environment which may affect the security of the protocol. These include other, similar, protocols that the protocol could be tricked into interacting with, as well as applications that make use of the protocol in ways not anticipated by the designer. We will discuss these aspects of the environment in the remainder of the paper.

3   Protocol Composability and Matching Histories

A first example that illustrates the danger of separately analyzing sub-protocols of a larger protocol is taken from [22] which in turn discusses an attack, first described in [5], on a very early version of SSL. SSL negotiates a key between a client and a server. The early version included an optional client authentication phase, achieved via a digital signature on the key and a nonce provided by the server, in which the client's challenge response was independent of the type of cipher negotiated for the session, and also of whether or not the authentication was being performed for a reconnection of an old session or for a new one. Instead, this information was authenticated by the key that was negotiated between the client and the server. Moreover, this version of SSL allowed the use of cryptographic algorithms of various strength (weak algorithms for export and stronger ones for domestic use), and it was not always clear by inspection of the key whether weak or strong cryptography was being used. This allowed the following attack (note that in this version of SSL, session keys were supplied by the client):

1. A key k is agreed upon for session A using weak cryptography.
2. Key k is broken by the intruder in real time.
3. The client initiates a reconnection of session A.
4. The intruder initiates a new session B, pretending to be the client, using strong cryptography together with the compromised key k.
5. As part of the connection negotiations for session B, the server presents a challenge to the client. The client should return a digital signature of both k and the challenge. The intruder can't do this itself, but it can pass the server's request on to the client, who will take it to be part of the reconnection negotiations for session A, and produce the appropriate response. The intruder passes the response on to the server as part of the session B negotiations, and the protocol completes.
6. If the client would have been given access to special privileges as a result of using strong cryptography, this could lead to the intruder gaining privileges that it should not be able to have by breaking the key k.

This attack involves two environmental features. One involves a confusion of the reconnection protocol with the connection protocol. Thus, it is an example of a failure of composition which would not have been found if the two protocols had been analyzed separately. The second involves the use of strong and weak cryptography. Authentication protocol analysis often assumes that cryptography is "perfect" (i.e., modeled as a black box) and that keys are not broken directly. However, this protocol explicitly distinguishes between strong and weak cryptography, thus explicitly addresses relative invulnerability to key compromise. Although vulnerability of later authentications because of earlier session key compromise has long been recognized as a problem protocols should avoid [12], the use of weak cryptography also raises the possibility of a compromise *during* a session, which can then be used to attack other, concurrent sessions.

The attack is a failure of an authentication requirement called *matching conversations* [4] or *matching histories* [6,13]. We cite the definition from [13]: "in all cases where one party, say Alice, executes the protocol faithfully and accepts the identity of another party: at the time that Alice accepts the other party's identity (before she sends or receives a subsequent message), the other party's record of the partial or full run matches Alice's record." Specifically the (composed) protocol fails to satisfy matching histories because the client's record of the protocol shows a request to use weak crypto via a reconnection, but the server's record shows a request to use strong crypto via a new connection.

Later versions of SSL fixed the above problem by including signed hashes of all messages previously sent in a given protocol round. This prevents an attack on the histories of the runs. Note the subtlety here. If the hashes were authenticated by using the session key, then the protocol would appear to satisfy matching histories. However, an adversary strong enough to break k under weak crypto could then spoof an authentication of k for the client using strong crypto, thus violating matching histories.

A protocol that was designed to meet the matching histories requirement was given in [13]. In this station-to-station (STS) protocol, a publicly known appropriate prime p and primitive element α in $GF(p)$ are fixed for use in Diffie-Hellman key exchange. It is not necessary to understand the underlying mathematics to follow the protocol. All that is necessary is to know the following: A has a public exchange key, R_A, and a private exchange key, x, while B has public exchange key R_B, and private exchange key y. They can form a session key, k_{AB}, because the public-private key pairs are chosen so that $R_A{}^y = R_B{}^x = k_{AB}$. (All arithmetic is *modulo p*.) Parties A and B use a common signature scheme: $s_U[\bullet]$ indicates the signature on the specified argument using the private signature key of party U. $\{\bullet\}_k$ indicates the symmetric encryption of the specified argument under key k. Public key certificates are used to make the public signature keys of A and B available to each other. In a one-time process prior to the exchange between A and B, each party must present to a trusted certificate server, T, her true identity and public key (e.g., ID_A, k_A), have T verify the true identity by some (typically non-cryptographic) means, and then obtain from T her own certificate. The protocol is as follows. (Here the public parameters are a finite group of large prime order, and a generator, α, of this group. All exponentiations are done in the group arithmetic.)

1. A generates a random positive integer x, computes $R_A = \alpha^x$ and sends R_A to a second party, B.
2. Upon receiving R_A, B generates a random positive integer y, computes $R_B = \alpha^y$ and $k_{AB} = (R_A)^y$.
3. B computes the authentication signature $s_B[R_B, R_A]$ and sends to A the encrypted signature $\text{Token}_{BA} = \{s_B[R_B, R_A]\}_{k_{AB}}$ along with R_B and his certificate Cert_B. Here ',' denotes concatenation.
4. A receives these values and from R_B computes $k_{AB} = (R_B)^x$.
5. A verifies the validity of B's certificate by verifying the signature thereon using the public signature-verification key of the trusted authority. If the certificate is valid, A extracts B's public verification key, k_B from Cert_B.
6. A verifies the authentication signature of B by decrypting Token_{BA}, and using k_B to check that the signature on the decrypted token is valid for the known ordered pair R_B, R_A.
7. A computes $s_A[R_A, R_B]$ and sends to B her certificate Cert_A and $\text{Token}_{AB} = \{s_A[R_A, R_B]\}_{k_{AB}}$.
8. A sets k_{AB} to be the shared key with B in this exchange.
9. Analogously, B checks Cert_A. If valid, B extracts A's public verification key k_A and proceeds.

10. Analogously, B verifies the authentication signature of A by decrypting Token$_{AB}$, and checking the signature on it using k_A and knowledge of the expected pair of data R_A, R_B.
11. Analogously, B sets k_{AB} to be the shared key with A in this exchange.

Lowe argued in [21] that this protocol is subject to attack. Specifically:

Message 1 $A \rightarrow C_B : \quad R_A$

     Message 1' $C \rightarrow B : \quad R_A$

     Message 2' $B \rightarrow C : \quad R_B, \{s_B[R_B, R_A]\}_{k_{AB}}$

Message 2 $C_B \rightarrow A : \quad R_B, \{s_B[R_B, R_A]\}_{k_{AB}}$

Message 3 $A \rightarrow C_B : \quad \{s_A[R_A, R_B]\}_{k_{AB}}$

Here, messages 1, 2, and 3 are a protocol run that Alice attempts to run with Bob, but that Charlie attacks. Messages 1' and 2' are a (partial) protocol run that Charlie initiates with Bob. This is an attack according to Lowe because Alice believes (correctly) that she is running the protocol with Bob. But, Bob believes that he is running the protocol with Charlie. Lowe considers this to be an attack "since A ends up holding incorrect beliefs". For reasons such as this, Lowe considers matching histories to be an insufficiently strong requirement. He proposes a requirement he later called *agreement*: whenever an agent A completes a run of the protocol, apparently with B, then B has recently been running the protocol, apparently with A, and the two agents agree upon who initiated the run, and agree upon all data values used in the run; further there is a one-one relationship between the runs of A and the runs of B. (If we take the one-one requirement as implicit in the matching-histories definition, then agreement is just matching histories where the protocol initiator and responder must always be specified in the record of all principals.)

Whether or not the above is correctly called an attack may be argued. The failure of agreement is clear. However, Alice ends up holding incorrect beliefs only if she forms the incorrect belief that Bob believes he has been running the protocol with Alice. There is no specific reason to attribute such a belief to Alice here, since she has received no authenticated information to that effect. Nonetheless, if we consider the protocol in composition with its environment, then an attack may be possible. We consider the effect of composing protocols with different environments in the next section.

4   Application Environments

Until now, our discussion of composition has involved either interleaved runs of a protocol with itself or of different subprotocols of a protocol. But what about other distinct protocols that may be running alongside of the one being considered? This concern may potentially be "brushed aside" by requiring that the protocol in question be the only protocol of its kind (authentication, key-exchange, etc.) to be run in the system. This way, one may not have to consider the potential interactions of different protocols because only one protocol (possibly with subprotocols) is permitted to run in a given context. (An exception to this assumption and analysis of the resulting implications was given in [18].) This may be a reasonable assumption to make in some cases. However, even if we can assume our protocols to be running in isolation we must still contend with the applications that make use of the authenticated keys that were established using the protocol in question.

Consider the following attack, described by Shoup in [25]. It involves the use of an "application protocol" that uses shared keys. Here principals authenticate by encrypting a challenge. To be a bit more vivid, consider an environment in which monitoring devices establish authenticated communications with a server. Perhaps these are used like watch keys to indicate that an actual person is present at the location of the device; someone must physically engage the device in some way for it to operate. The server might send out a nonce challenge, and the monitoring devices would then encrypt the challenge in a return message to prove that a person was present to operate the monitor. Assume that monitors initiate contact with the server. So the application would be something like.

Application Message 1 $B \to A$:   *challenge*

Application Message 2 $A \to B$: $\{challenge\}_{k_{AB}}$

Now, suppose that this application protocol uses STS to establish session keys. Also suppose that monitors are not expected to recognize or test the format of the challenge in any way. This is perhaps reasonable since the challenge should be unpredictable and the authentication gives the monitor credit rather than responsibility [1]. Let us now consider the STS protocol and the putative attack given above. The attacker C has access to R_A and R_B as plaintext. Thus, once the protocol has completed with A, C_B could send to A the challenge $s_c[R_A, R_B]$. To which A would respond with $\{s_c[R_A, R_B]\}_{k_{AB}}$. That is, after the application challenge and response of

Application Message 1 $C_B \to A$: $s_c[R_A, R_B]$

Application Message 2 $A \to C_B$: $\{s_c[R_A, R_B]\}_{k_{AB}}$

the following message may be added to the Lowe attack on STS:

Message 3' $C \to B$: $\{s_c[R_A, R_B]\}_{k_{AB}}$

This way, the above debatable attack by Lowe is turned into a clear attack with more significant consequences. That is, C can now use the resulting message to complete the protocol run begun with B. Consequently, from now on, anytime B issues a challenge, credit for encryption of it with k_{AB} will be given to C rather than to A. Whether or not the Lowe attack indicates an inadequacy of matching histories to capture practical authentication goals, this attack would seem to do so—in the presence of such an application.

One possible solution would be to strengthen the protocol to include the name of the intended recipient of each message within the signature. In fact, this is the revision suggested by Lowe in [21]. STS so strengthened appears to satisfy agreement.

Another possible solution is to restrict the application environment in some way. For example, in the case of the STS protocol, we could require that any protocol that makes use of a key generated by an instance of the STS protocol would need to apply some transformation to it first, such as a hash function. This is indeed what is done in Krawczyk's [19] SKEME protocol, which is based on STS. We consider the implications and limitations of environmental requirements in the next section.

5   Environmental Requirements

The application environment is obviously more difficult to control or specify than the security protocol, so we should justify the need to restrict the environment before we consider how to do so. Are there examples of attacks on protocols that satisfy agreement? One example of such was first given by Davida long ago [11] and later generalized in [17]. Although neither of the papers explicitly notes the connection, the idea relies on a concept similar to blinding in the sense of Chaum [10], who used it effectively in the design of anonymous payment protocols. A public-key encryption is blinded so that the intended recipient gets unrecognizable garbage upon decrypting a message and discards the result as worthless. If the attacker is able to obtain this discarded message, he can then apply the blinding factor to obtain the plaintext.

The attack applies to the RSA cryptosystem, which encrypts a message m by raising it to a public exponent e modulo a public modulus $N = p \cdot q$, where p and q are two primes. Only someone who knows the secret factorization is able to compute d so that $m^{d \cdot e} = m \bmod N$, and so decrypt the message.

The attacker A proceeds by finding an encrypted message, $m^e \bmod N$, that may have previously been sent to a principal B using B's public key e and N. The attacker first computes $x^e \bmod N$ for some x and proceeds as follows:

$$A \rightarrow B: \quad m^e \cdot x^e = (m \cdot x)^e \bmod N$$

B receives the message and decrypts it to obtain $m \cdot x$. Since this looks like garbage to B, he discards it. If the message is discarded in such a way that the attacker A can find it, A can then multiply it by $x^{-1} \bmod N$ to obtain the secret m.

In one sense, this protocol satisfies agreement, since A and B agree on the messages that were sent between the two parties, and on who they were sent to. In another sense, it does not, since A and B disagree on the meaning of the messages sent. Since B "responds" to a nonsense message by putting it in a place where A can find it, this semantic form of disagreement can have serious consequences.

We can prevent problems like this by requiring that people secure their garbage bins—to use the Joye-Quisquater term. If we did this and required protocols to satisfy, not just agreement in Lowe's sense, but also that principals never send anything in response to an improper protocol message, it would seem that we could be free of such questions.

Such an approach was taken in [15] with the introduction of extensible-fail-stop protocols. These effectively require that agreement can be checked on each message as it is received. Active attacks on a message therefore cause any later messages not to be sent. Also, protocols that are extensible-fail-stop can be arbitrarily composed. (Similar concepts were discussed in [16].)

To illustrate, here is a variant on the Needham-Schroeder shared-key protocol presented in Section 2. It has been modified to be extensible-fail-stop.

Message 1 $A \rightarrow S$: $(A, S, T_A, NSSK, R, 1, B),$
$\qquad \{h(A, S, T_A, NSSK, R, 1, B)\}_{k_{AS}}$

Message 2 $S \rightarrow A$: $(S, A, NSSK, R, 2),$
$\qquad \{h(S, A, NSSK, R, 2),$
$\qquad (k_{AB}, B, \{h(S, B, T_s, NSSK, R, 3), (k_{AB}, A)\}_{k_{BS}})\}_{k_{AS}}$

Message 3 $A \rightarrow B$: $(S, B, T_s, NSSK, R, 3),$
$\qquad \{h(S, B, T_s, NSSK, R, 3), (k_{AB}, A)\}_{k_{BS}}$

Message 4 $B \rightarrow A$: $(B, A, NSSK, R, 4),$
$\qquad \{h(B, A, NSSK, R, 4), R_B\}_{k_{AB}}$

Message 5 $A \rightarrow B$: $(A, B, NSSK, R, 5),$
$\qquad \{h(A, B, NSSK, R, 5), R_B\}_{k_{AB}}$

For each message, a hash of the message parameters is encrypted together with message data using a key shared between the sender and receiver. Parameters indicate the sender and receiver, possibly a timestamp, a protocol identifier (we assume for convenience that there is only one version of $NSSK$), a unique and unpredictably generated protocol round identifier, R, a message sequence identifier, and relevant data. Thus in the first message, Alice tells the server that she would like to establish a session key with Bob. The server is assumed to keep a list of previously used round identifiers within the lifetime of the timestamp, T_A and to check that R is not on that list. It should be clear that this protocol is extensible-fail-stop, i.e., that the recipient of each message can completely determine that s/he is receiving the next appropriate message in the protocol. Thus, there is no possibility either of using this protocol as an oracle to generate messages or of inserting a message from another protocol (or from an earlier part of the same protocol) and having it accepted as legitimate. This is therefore about as strong a requirement as one could impose on a protocol itself. Nonetheless, if the application environment is not also restricted in some way, the protocol is subject to attack.

Suppose that an application allows "eager" use of keys before the protocol has been completed. Only if the authentication protocol does not complete within some reasonable timeout is there an alarm or noting of anomaly in the logs. This eagerness might be all the more reasonable if the protocol distributing the keys is extensible-fail-stop and as explicit as this one. In this case, there would seem to be no possibility of mistake about who the session key is for, who the relevant principals are, or the roles they each play (i.e., initiator or responder). But, allowing eager use of keys in an application such as the monitor example described above could be used to attack the protocol.

Specifically, when Alice begins NSSK for a session with Bob, the attacker prevents the third message from arriving. Then, for the application challenge-response he produces:

Application Message 1 $C_B \rightarrow A :\ h(B, A, NSSK, R, 4), R_B$

Application Message 2 $A \rightarrow C_B :\ \{h(B, A, NSSK, R, 4), R_B\}_{k_{AB}}$

The attacker uses the response from Alice for the fourth message in NSSK, and intercepts the final message from Alice to Bob. Alice will now be spoofed into thinking she has completed a handshake with Bob when Bob was never present, with all the potential implications previously discussed.

Note that the original Needham-Schroeder shared-key protocol is just as vulnerable to this attack (and others as well). We have strengthened it to be extensible-fail-stop to show that even such a strong requirement on protocol authentication may not be adequate to preclude failure if the environment is not somehow restricted.

6   Discussion

We have given a set of increasingly stringent definitions of security and shown how they can be subverted by interaction with a carelessly designed environment. The obvious question arises: are there conditions that we can put on an environment so that we can guarantee that it will not subvert the goals of a reasonably well-behaved protocol? Some rules of thumb, in the spirit of Abadi and Needham [2], Anderson and Needham [3], Syverson [26], and Kelsey and Schneier [18]—and expanding on those we presented in [9], are suggested by the examples we have cited.

RoTh 1. Know your threat environment, and the threat environment for which your protocol was designed. If a protocol is being transferred from one threat environment to another, make sure that it is secure in the new environment as well as the old one.

As we saw from our discussion of the Needham-Schroeder protocols threat environments can change, and a protocol which was secure with respect to one set of threats may be insecure with respect to another. And, as we saw from our discussion of the SSL protocol, there is no such thing as a "one-size-fits-all" threat environment. Threats such as the real-time compromise of keys which may be silly under one set of assumptions may be realistic under another set.

RoTh 2. The environment should not use protocol keys or other secrets in unaltered form.

Thus, in the attack on STS above, the session key k_{AB} should not be the same key as the key k used internally in the STS protocol. In fact, the two keys should be "cryptographically independent". For instance, let $k_{sts} = PRF_k(0)$ and $k_{AB} = PRF(1)$, where PRF is a pseudorandom function. Now, use k_{sts} to encrypt the STS messages, and use k_{AB} as the session key. We remark that this technique for guaranteeing the "virginity" of the session key is used in SKEME [19] and in IKE, the Internet Key Exchange protocol (described in [14]). The concept underlying this principle has not only been used in the design of protocols such as IKE and SKEME but also in proving theoretical results about protocol composition [28,27]. It is also similar in spirit to the design principle given in [18] which recommends limiting the scope of keys; indeed, what it does is give a practical means of accomplishing just that. More recent theoretical work along these lines can be found in [8], which proposes a specification for key-exchange protocols, and demonstrates that a key exchanged using a protocol that satisfies the specification can be used within standard shared-key "secure channel" mechanisms, without fear of bad interferences between protocols. Further, [7] provides a general framework for writing specifications for protocols, with an attempt to guarantee that security is maintained in a large set of computational environments.

RoTh 3. A protocol should be designed as much as possible to be resilient against the release of secrets, even potential or obsolete secrets.

We note that the protocol used in the blinding attack failed to satisfy this requirement, as well as the fail-stop version of NSSK, although in the latter case the requirement could have been satisfied with the use of RoTh 2.

RoTh 4. Values established during a protocol run should not be used in applications by a principal before that principal completes his run.

This one might seem obvious, but as we saw above, such eager use might involve a key that has been released at most to valid principals, and so appear harmless. Also, this might be an onerous requirement if applications have tight real-time constraints that would be hard to meet if they must wait for the authentication protocol to finish. In that case, we may want to make use of some of the other Rules of Thumb such as RoTh 2 or RoTh 3 to guarantee security.

RoTh 5. Insist, as much as possible, on only interacting with protocols whose messages contain unique protocol identifiers. More generally, try to make certain that a message intended for use in one protocol, or protocol component, can not be mistaken for a message for use in one protocol, or protocol component.

This use of unique protocol identifiers is recommended in [18] and has also been used in the design of extensible-fail-stop protocols. The general recommendation to avoid confusion of intended message use is similar to the principle in [26] recommending against assuming that a message has only a particular form, even if that form can be checked. We note that, in the attack on the extensible-fail-stop protocol in Section 5, if both protocols involved had followed this principle instead of just one, then the attack would not have been possible. Again, this may be onerous, e.g., if the environment requires the use of off-the-shelf applications that are not extensible-fail-stop. This leads us to

RoTh 6. Any fix to the environment should be made as close to the protocol as possible.

To illustrate what we mean by this, we consider the use of challenge-and-response protocols to illustrate environmental attacks. All of these attacks could have been prevented if each time the principal responded to the challenge it signed, instead of the challenge itself, a hash of the challenge and some text indicating what it believed the challenge was for. Indeed, this was how the weakness in the SSL protocol was ultimately fixed. However, in the case of SSL, the challenge-and-response protocol was directly under the control of the protocol designer, since it was part of the SSL protocol suite. In our other examples this was not necessarily the case. Thus, in the case of the Station-to-Station protocol, it made more sense to require that keys distributed by the protocol be transformed before they were used. This was a feature that could be implemented, for example, by putting a wrapper around the protocol that transformed the keys, a feature that would only have to be added once for every time the protocol was implemented. Thus this was an easier requirement to satisfy than assuring that all challenge-and-response protocols that used keys generated by the protocol were implemented properly.

These observations lead to further questions: Is there a minimal set of requirements that we can put on an environment such that the various types of protocol requirements that we have described will guarantee security? If so, is it unique? If so, what is it? If not, what are the possibilities? Clearly, it is possible for any protocol to generate an environment that will subvert its security goals; the environment that releases all secrets will do the trick. But it seems reasonable to expect, that by using some combination and augmentation of the rules of thumb that we have already described, we should be able to come up with requirements for environments in which the different definitions of protocol security in isolation would also guarantee security in combination with the environment. Moreover, although in this paper we have limited ourselves to attacks involving interactions between protocol messages, we realize that the environment that a protocol depends on includes much more, including sound random or pseudo-random number generation, secure access control for keys, and the behavior and assumptions of users interacting with the system, which could also be brought into play. In summary, we believe that the study of the interaction of a security protocol with its environment, and the interaction of protocol requirements with environmental requirements is a potentially rewarding one of which we have only scratched the surface in this brief study.

Acknowledgements. Portions of this work originally appeared in [9]. This research was partly funded by the Office of Naval Research.

References

1. M. Abadi. Two facets of authentication. In *Proceedings of the 11th IEEE Computer Security Foundations Workshop (CFW11)*, pages 25–32. IEEE Computer Society Press, June 1998.
2. M. Abadi and R. Needham. Prudent engineering practice for cryptographic protocols. *IEEE Transactions on Software Engineering*, 22(1):6–15, January 1996.
3. Ross Anderson and Roger Needham. Robustness principles for public key protocols. In *Proceedings of Crypto 96*, pages 236–247. Springer-Verlag, LNCS 0963, 1996.
4. M. Bellare and P. Rogaway. Entity authentication and key distribution. In *Advances in Cryptology - CRYPTO 93*. Springer-Verlag, 1994.
5. J. Benaloh, B. Lampson, D. Simon, T. Spies, and B. Yee. The private communication technology protocol, October 1995. draft-benaloh-pct-00.txt.
6. R. Bird, I. Gopal, A. Herzberg, P. Janson, S. Kutten, R. Molva, and M. Yung. Systematic design of two-party authentication protocols. In *Advances in Cryptology – Proceedings of CRYPTO 91*. Springer-Verlag, 1991.
7. R. Canetti. A unified framework for analyzing security of protocols, 2000. available at http://eprint.iacr.org/2000/067.
8. R. Canetti and H. Krawczyk. Analysis of key-exchange protocols and their use for building secure channels. In *Proceedings of Eurocrypt 01*. LNCS, May 2001.
9. R. Canetti, C. Meadows, and P. Syverson. Environmental requirements and authentication protocols. In *Symposium on Requirements Engineering for Information Security*, March 2001.
10. D. Chaum. Blind signatures for untraceable payments. In *Advances in Cryptology– Proceedings of Crypto 82*, pages 199–203, 1983.
11. G. Davida. Chosen signature cryptanalysis of the RSA (MIT) public key cryptosystem. Technical Report TR-CS-82-2, Dept. of EECS, University of Wisconsin-Milwaukee, October 1982.
12. D.E.R. Denning and G.M. Sacco. Timestamps in key distribution protocols. *Communications of the ACM*, 24(8):533–536, August 1981.
13. W. Diffie, P. C. van Oorschot, and M. J. Wiener. Authentication and authenticated key exchanges. *Designs, Codes, and Cryptography*, 2:107–125, 1992.
14. N. Doraswamy and D. Harkins. *IPSEC: The New Security Standard for the Internet, Intranets, and Virtual Private Networks*. Prentice Hall, 1999.

15. L. Gong and P. Syverson. Fail-stop protocols: An approach to designing secure protocols. In R. K. Iyer, M. Morganti, W. K. Fuchs, and V. Gligor, editors, *Dependable Computing for Critical Applications 5*, pages 79–100. IEEE Computer Society Press, 1998.

16. N. Heintze and J. D. Tygar. A model for secure protocols and their composition. *IEEE Transactions on Software Engineering*, 22(1):16–30, January 1996.

17. M. Joye and J.-J. Quisquater. On the importance of securing your bins: The garbage-man-in-the-middle attack. In *4th ACM Conference on Computer and Communications Security*, pages 135–141. ACM Press, April 1997.

18. J. Kelsey, B. Schneier, and D. Wagner. Protocol interactions and the chosen protocol attack. In B. Christianson, B. Crispo, M. Lomas, and M. Roe, editors, *Security Protocols 1997*, volume 1361 of *LNCS*, pages 91–104. Springer-Verlag, April 1997.

19. H. Krawczyk. SKEME: A versatile secure key exchange mechanism for Internet. In *Proceedings of the Internet Society Symposium on Network and Distributed System Security (NDSS)*, February 1996.

20. G. Lowe. Breaking and fixing the Needham-Schroeder public-key protocol using FDR. *Software – Concepts and Tools*, 17:93–102, 1996.

21. G. Lowe. Some new attacks upon security protocols. In *Proceedings of the 9th IEEE Computer Security Foundations Workshop (CSFW9)*, pages 162–169. IEEE Computer Society Press, June 1996.

22. C. Meadows. Open issues in formal methods for cryptographic protocol analysis. In *DISCEX 2000: Proceedings of the DARPA Information Survivability Conference and Exposition*, volume I, pages 237–250. IEEE Computer Society Press, January 2000.

23. R. M. Needham and M. D. Schroeder. Using Encryption for Authentication in Large Networks of Computers. *Communications of the ACM*, 21(12):993–999, December 1978.

24. S. Pancho. Paradigm shifts in protocol analysis: Needham and Schroeder again? In *Proceedings of the 1999 New Security Paradigms Workshop*. ACM Computer Society Press, September 1999.

25. V. Shoup. On formal models for secure key exchange (version 4). Available at `http://shoup.net/papers/`, November 1999. Revision of IBM Research Report RZ 3120 (April 1999).

26. P. Syverson Limitations on design principles for public key protocols. In *Proceedings of the 1996 IEEE Symposium on Security and Privacy*, pages 62–72. IEEE Computer Society Press, May 1996.

27. F.J. Thayer Fábrega and J.D. Guttman. Protocol independence through disjoint encryption. In *Proceedings of the 13th IEEE Computer Security Foundations Workshop (CSFW13)*, pages 24–34. IEEE Computer Society Press, June 2000.

28. F.J. Thayer Fábrega, J.C. Herzog, and J.D. Guttman. Mixed strand spaces. In *Proceedings of the 12th IEEE Computer Security Foundations Workshop (CSFW12)*, pages 72–82. IEEE Computer Society Press, June 1999.

A Comparison between Strand Spaces and Multiset Rewriting for Security Protocol Analysis* **

I. Cervesato[1], N. Durgin[2], P. Lincoln[3], J. Mitchell[2], and A. Scedrov[4]

[1] Advanced Engineering and Sciences Division, ITT Industries, Inc.
2560 Huntington Avenue, Alexandria, VA 22303-1410 — USA
iliano@itd.nrl.navy.mil

[2] Computer Science Department, Stanford University
Stanford, CA 94305-9045 — USA
{nad, jcm}@cs.stanford.edu

[3] Computer Science Laboratory, SRI International
333 Ravenswood Avenue, Menlo Park, CA 94025-3493 — USA
lincoln@csl.sri.com

[4] Mathematics Department, University of Pennsylvania
209 South 33rd Street, Philadelphia, PA 19104-6395 — USA
scedrov@cis.upenn.edu

Abstract. Formal analysis of security protocols is largely based on a set of assumptions commonly referred to as the Dolev-Yao model. Two formalisms that state the basic assumptions of this model are related here: strand spaces [FHG98] and multiset rewriting with existential quantification [CDL+99,DLMS99]. Strand spaces provide a simple and economical approach to state-based analysis of completed protocol runs by emphasizing causal interactions among protocol participants. The multiset rewriting formalism provides a very precise way of specifying finite-length protocols, with a bounded initialization phase but allowing unboundedly many instances of each protocol role, such as client, server, initiator, or responder. Although it is fairly intuitive that these two languages should be equivalent in some way, a number of modifications to each system are required to obtain a meaningful equivalence. We extend the strand formalism with a way of incrementally growing bundles in order to emulate an execution of a protocol with parametric strands. We omit the initialization part of the multiset rewriting setting, which formalizes the choice of initial data, such as shared public or private keys, and which has no counterpart in the strand space setting. The correspondence between the modified formalisms directly relates the intruder theory from the multiset rewriting formalism to the penetrator strands. The relationship we illustrate here between multiset rewriting specifications and strand spaces thus suggests refinements to both frameworks, and deepens our understanding of the Dolev-Yao model.

* Partial support for various authors by OSD/ONR CIP/SW URI "Software Quality and Infrastructure Protection for Diffuse Computing" through ONR Grant N00014-01-1-0795, by NRL under contract N00173-00-C-2086, by DoD MURI "Semantic Consistency in Information Exchange" as ONR grant N00014-97-1-0505 and by NSF grants CCR-9509931, CCR-9629754, CCR-9800785, CCR-0098096, and INT98-15731.
** This paper is a revised version of [CDL+00].

M. Okada et al. (Eds.): ISSS 2002, LNCS 2609, pp. 356–383, 2003.

1   Introduction

Security protocols are widely used to protect access to computer systems and to protect transactions over the Internet. Such protocols are difficult to design and analyze for several reasons. Some of the difficulties come from subtleties of cryptographic primitives. Further difficulties arise because security protocols are required to work properly when multiple instances of the protocol are carried out in parallel, where a malicious intruder may combine data from separate sessions in order to confuse honest participants. A variety of methods have been developed for analyzing and reasoning about security protocols. Most current formal approaches use the so-called Dolev-Yao model of adversary capabilities, which appears to be drawn from positions taken in [NS78] and from a simplified model presented in [DY83]. The two basic assumptions of the Dolev-Yao model, perfect (black-box) cryptography and a nondeterministic adversary, provide an idealized setting in which protocol analysis becomes relatively tractable.

One recent setting for stating the basic assumptions of the Dolev-Yao model is given by strand spaces [FHG98,FHG99,Man99]. Strand spaces provide a way of presenting information about causal interactions among protocol participants. Roughly, a strand is a linearly ordered sequence of events that represents the actions of a protocol participant. A strand space is a collection of strands, equipped with a graph structure generated by causal interaction. Strand spaces provide a simple and succinct framework for state-based analysis of completed protocol runs. State space reduction techniques based on the strand space framework are utilized in an efficient automated checker, Athena [Son99].

Protocol transitions may also be naturally expressed as a form of rewriting. This observation may be sharpened to a rigorous, formal definition of the Dolev-Yao model by means of multiset rewriting with existential quantification [CDL$^+$99,DLMS99]. In this framework protocol execution may be carried out symbolically. Existential quantification, as commonly used in formal logic, provides a natural way of choosing new values, such as new keys or nonces. Multiset rewriting provides a very precise way of specifying security protocols and has been incorporated into a high-level specification language for authentication protocols, CAPSL [DM99]. As presented in [CDL$^+$99,DLMS99], a protocol theory consists of three parts: a bounded phase describing protocol initialization that distributes keys or establishes other shared information, a role generation theory that designates possibly multiple roles that each principal may play in a protocol (such as initiator, responder, or server), and a disjoint union of bounded subtheories that each characterize a possible role. The multiset rewriting formalism allows us to formulate one standard intruder theory that describes any adversary for any protocol.

One would expect that strand spaces and multiset rewriting should be equivalent in some way. However, a meaningful equivalence may be obtained only after a number of modifications are made in each setting. To this end, we extend the strand space setting by introducing several dynamic concepts that describe the evolution of parametric strands as an execution of a protocol unfolds. In particular, we present a formalized notion of parametric strands and we describe a way of incrementally growing strand space bundles in order to emulate an execution of a protocol with parametric strands. In addition to contributing to the understanding of the strand space setting, these extensions make possible the comparison with multiset rewriting specifications. In order to obtain a precise equivalence, we also must drop the initialization part of the multiset rewriting formalism, which specifies the choice of initial conditions. In many protocols, the initial conditions specify generation of fresh shared, public, or private keys. The initialization phase generating fresh initial data has no counterpart in the strand space setting. We also anticipate the validation of variable instantiations to the very beginning of the execution of a role. After these modifications, there is a straightforward and direct correspondence between strand spaces and multiset rewriting theories. Moreover, the correspondence directly relates the intruder theories from the multiset rewriting formalism to penetrator strands. We believe that the investigation of the exact nature of the relationship between the two formalisms deepens our understanding of the Dolev-Yao model and can suggest extensions and refinements to these and other specification languages based on strand spaces.

Shortly after publishing the first version of this paper, the authors noticed an error in Lemma 4.1 in [CDL$^+$00]. The corrected version of this lemma is Corollary 1 in the present paper, which rectifies the error and propagates the resulting changes. It also reorganizes the material into a more clear and straightforward presentation.

This paper is organized as follows: the multiset rewriting formalism is discussed in Section 2. In section 3, we discuss strand spaces and present our extensions. The translation from multiset rewriting to strand spaces is presented in Section 4. The translation from strand spaces to multiset rewriting is presented in Section 5.

2   Multiset Rewriting Theories

In Section 2.1 we recall a few multiset rewriting concepts, and, in Section 2.2, we apply them to the specification of cryptoprotocols. We present the multiset rewriting rules implementing the Dolev-Yao intruder in Section 2.3.

2.1   Multiset Rewriting

A *multiset* M is an unordered collection of objects or *elements*, possibly with repetitions. The *empty multiset* does not contain any object and will be written ".". We accumulate the elements of two multisets M and N by taking their *multiset union*, denoted "M, N". The elements we will consider here will be first-order atomic formulas $A(t)$ over some signature.

We will make use of the standard definitions pertaining to the variables of first-order logic. In particular, we write $\mathrm{Var}(A_0, \ldots, A_n)$ for the set of variables occurring in the multiset of atomic formulas $A_0, \ldots, A_n$. We say that a (multiset of) formula(s) is ground if no variable appear in it. Finally, substitutions (generally written θ) are as usual mapping from variables to generic terms. We write $A[\theta]$ for the application of a substitution θ to a formula A, and use a similar notation for multisets of formulas.

In its simplest form, a *multiset rewrite rule* r is a pair of multisets F and G, respectively called the *antecedent* and *consequent* of r. We will consider a slightly more elaborate notion in which F and G are multisets of first-order atomic formulas with variables among x. We emphasize this aspect by writing them as $F(x)$ and $G(x)$.

	Initiator		
r_{A0} :		$\pi_A(A,B) \rightarrow$	$A_0(A,B),\ \pi_A(A,B)$
r_{A1} :		$A_0(A,B) \rightarrow$	$\exists N_A.\ A_1(A,B,N_A),\ \mathsf{N}(\{N_A,A\}_{K_B})$
r_{A2} :	$A_1(A,B,N_A),\ \mathsf{N}(\{N_A,N_B\}_{K_A}) \rightarrow$		$A_2(A,B,N_A,N_B)$
r_{A3} :		$A_2(A,B,N_A,N_B) \rightarrow$	$A_3(A,B,N_A,N_B),\ \mathsf{N}(\{N_B\}_{K_B})$

	Responder		
r_{B0} :		$\pi_B(A,B) \rightarrow$	$B_0(A,B),\ \pi_B(A,B)$
r_{B1} :	$B_0(A,B),\ \mathsf{N}(\{N_A,A\}_{K_B}) \rightarrow$		$B_1(A,B,N_A)$
r_{B2} :		$B_1(A,B,N_A) \rightarrow$	$\exists N_B.\ B_2(A,B,N_A,N_B),\ \mathsf{N}(\{N_A,N_B\}_{K_A})$
r_{B3} :	$B_2(A,B,N_A,N_B),\ \mathsf{N}(\{N_B\}_{K_B}) \rightarrow$		$B_3(A,B,N_A,N_B)$

$$\text{where } \pi_A(A,B) = Pr(A),\ PrvK(A,K_A^{-1}),\ Pr(B),\ PubK(B,K_B)$$
$$\pi_B(B,A) = Pr(B),\ PrvK(B,K_B^{-1}),\ Pr(A),\ PubK(A,K_A)$$

Fig. 1. Multiset Rewriting Specification of the Needham-Schroeder Protocol

Furthermore, we shall be able to mark variables in the consequent so that they are instantiated to *"fresh"* constants, that have not previously been encountered, even if the rule is used repeatedly. A rule assumes then the form

$$r:\ F(x) \rightarrow \exists n.\ G(x,n)$$

where r is a label and $\exists n$ indicates that the variables n are to be instantiated with constants that ought to be fresh. A *multiset rewriting system* $\mathcal{R}$ is a set of rewrite rules.

Rewrite rules allow transforming a multiset into another multiset by making localized changes to the elements that appear in it. Given a multiset of ground facts M, a rule $r:\ F(x) \rightarrow \exists n.\ G(x,n)$ is *applicable* if $M = F(t), M'$, for terms t. Then, *applying r to M* yields the multiset $N = G(t,c), M'$ where the constants c are fresh (in particular, they do not appear in M), x and n have been instantiated with t and c respectively, and the facts $F(t)$ in M have been replaced with $G(t,c)$ to produce N. Here, $\theta = [t/x, c/n]$ is the *instantiating substitution* of rule r with respect to M. We denote the application of a single rule and of zero or more rewrite rules by means of the *one-step* and *multistep transition* judgments:

$$M \xrightarrow{r}_{\mathcal{R}} N \qquad\qquad M \xrightarrow{\mathbf{r}}{}^*_{\mathcal{R}} N$$

respectively. The labels r and $\mathbf{r}$ identify which rule(s) have been applied together with its (their) instantiating substitution(s). Thus, $\mathbf{r}$ acts as a complete trace of the execution.

2.2   Regular Protocol Theories

We model protocols by means of specifically tailored multiset rewriting systems that we call *regular protocol theories*. We present here a simplified version of the model introduced in [CDL$^+$99,DLMS99]. We rely upon the following atomic formulas:

Persistent information: Data such as the identity of principals and their keys often constitute the stage on which the execution of a protocol takes place, and does not change as it unfolds. We will represent and access this *persistent information* through a fixed set of *persistent predicates* that we will indicate using a slanted font (*e.g. KeyP*, as opposed to N).

In [CDL$^+$99,DLMS99], we described the choice of the persistent data by means of a set of multiset rewrite rules of a specific form, that we called the *initialization theory*. We showed that the application of these rules can be confined to an initialization phase that precedes the execution of any other rule. Let Π be the resulting set of ground facts (constraints on the initialization theory prevent Π from containing duplicates [CDL$^+$99,DLMS99]). Strand constructions assume instead that the persistent information is given up-front as a set. We reconcile the two approaches by dropping the explicit initialization phase of [CDL$^+$99,DLMS99] and assuming Π given. We will allow individual rules to query Π (but not to modify it).

Network messages: Network messages are modeled by the predicate N(m), where m is the message being transmitted. Having a distinct network predicate for each message exchanged in a protocol specification, as done in [CDL$^+$99,DLMS99], is equivalent, but would obscure the translation in Section 5. In this paper, messages will consist of the class of terms freely generated from atomic messages (principal names, keys, nonces, etc.) by the operators of concatenation, denoted "$_,_$", and encryption, written "$\{_\}_$".

Role states: We first choose a set of *role identifiers* $\rho_1, \ldots, \rho_n$ for the different roles constituting the protocol. Then, for each role ρ, we have a finite family of *role state predicates* $\{A_{\rho i}(m) \mid i = 0 \ldots l_\rho\}$. They are intended to hold the internal state of a principal in role ρ during the successive steps of the protocol.

This scheme can immediately be generalized to express roles that can take conditional or non-deterministic actions (*e.g.* toss a coin to choose among two messages to send — useful for zero-knowledge proofs for examples — or respond in two different ways depending on the contents of an incoming message — useful for intrusion detection). We simply need to alter our naming convention for role states and rules (below) to take alternatives into account. Indeed, any partial ordering of the role state predicates will implement a *well-founded protocol theory*, as defined in [CDL$^+$99,DLMS99]. This paper will consider only linearly ordered role states, as the layer of technicality required to treat the general case would obscure the comparison with strands.

The additional predicate symbol I is needed to model the intruder's knowledge and its actions. It will be discussed at length in Section 2.3.

We represent each role ρ in a protocol by means of a single *role generation rule* and a finite number of *regular protocol execution rules*. The purpose of the former is to prepare for the execution of an instance of role ρ. It has the form

$$r_{\rho 0} : \ \pi(x) \to A_{\rho 0}(x), \pi(x).$$

where, here and in the rest of the paper, $\pi(x)$ denotes a multiset of persistent atomic formulas that may mention variables among x. Notice how persistent information is preserved. The execution rules describe the messages sent and expected by the principal acting in this role. For $i = 0 \ldots l_\rho - 1$, we have a rule $r_{\rho i + 1}$ of either of the following two forms:

Send: $\mathsf{A}_{\rho i}(x) \qquad\qquad \rightarrow \quad \exists n. \, \mathsf{A}_{\rho i + 1}(x, n), \, \mathsf{N}(m(x, n))$

Receive: $\mathsf{A}_{\rho i}(x), \, \mathsf{N}(m(x, y)) \quad \rightarrow \qquad \mathsf{A}_{\rho i + 1}(x, y)$

where $m(v)$ stands for a message pattern with variables among v. In the first type of rules, we rely on the existential operator $\exists n$ to model the ability of a principal to create nonces when sending a message. Situations where a principal both sends and receives a message, or sends multiple messages, can easily be expressed by these rules.

A protocol is specified as a set $\mathcal{R}$ of these *regular roles*. Every $\mathcal{R}$ constructed in this way is trivially a well-founded protocol theory [CDL+99,DLMS99]. As an example, Figure 1 shows the encoding of the familiar simplified Needham-Schroeder public key protocol in the multiset rewriting notation. For the sake of readability, we omitted the keys in the persistent state predicates.

A *state* is a multiset of ground facts $S = \Pi, A, N, I$, where A is a multiset of role states $\mathsf{A}_{\rho i}(t)$, N is multiset of messages $\mathsf{N}(m)$ currently in transit, and I is a collection of predicates $\mathsf{I}(m)$ summarizing the intruder's knowledge. Notice in particular that the *initial state*, denoted S_0, is just Π, I_0, where I_0 contains the information (*e.g.* keys) initially known to the intruder.

The above *regular* protocol theories upgrade our original definition of (unqualified) protocol theories [CDL+00] with the requirement that all the persistent information used during the execution of a role be accessed in its role generation rule: in [CDL+99,DLMS99], $\pi(z)$ can occur in execution rules as well. While the two definitions are equally acceptable in general, the regularity restriction brings us one step closer to the strand world, where all accessory values are chosen up-front. We discovered however that this is a slippery step as protocol theories cannot be regularized in general without losing transition sequences (see Section 4.1 for additional details on this issue). This is one more restriction that our multiset rewriting formalism shall abide by in order to set up a fair comparison with strand spaces.

2.3   Intruder Theory

The knowledge available at any instant to the intruder consists of the persistent information in Π, of the unused portion of its initial knowledge I_0 (*e.g.* the keys of dishonest principals), and of intercepted or inferred messages. We use the state predicate $\mathsf{I}(\_)$ to contain each piece of information known to the intruder. In particular, we represent the fact that the intruder "knows" m (a message, a key, etc.) as $\mathsf{I}(m)$. The overall knowledge of the intruder at any particular instant is indicated with I. As mentioned above, we write I_0 for the intruder's initial knowledge.

The capabilities of the intruder are modeled by the *standard intruder theory* $\mathcal{I}$ displayed in Figure 2. These rules are taken verbatim from [CDL+99,DLMS99]. $\mathcal{I}$ implements the Dolev-Yao model [DY83,NS78] in our notation. For the sake of readability, we have grayed out the information produced by each rule. Observe that these rules display an overly conservative bookkeeping strategy for the known messages: knowledge is never discarded, but carried along as new messages are inferred.

rec	:	$N(m)$	$\rightarrow$	$I(m)$
dcmp	:	$I(m_1, m_2)$	$\rightarrow$	$I(m_1), I(m_2)$, $I(m_1, m_2)$
decr	:	$I(\{m\}_k), I(k'), KeyP(k, k')$	$\rightarrow$	$I(m)$, $I(\{m\}_k), I(k'), KeyP(k, k')$
snd	:	$I(m)$	$\rightarrow$	$N(m)$, $I(m)$
cmp	:	$I(m_1), I(m_2)$	$\rightarrow$	$I(m_1, m_2)$, $I(m_1), I(m_2)$
encr	:	$I(m), I(k)$	$\rightarrow$	$I(\{m\}_k)$, $I(m), I(k)$
nnc	:	$\cdot$	$\rightarrow$	$\exists n.\ I(n)$
pers	:	$\pi(m)$	$\rightarrow$	$I(m)$, $\pi(m)$

Fig. 2. The Standard Intruder Theory $\mathcal{I}$

rec$'$	:	$N(m)$	$\rightarrow$	$I(m)$
dcmp$'$	:	$I(m_1, m_2)$	$\rightarrow$	$I(m_1), I(m_2)$
decr$'$	:	$I(\{m\}_k), I(k'), KeyP(k, k')$	$\rightarrow$	$I(m), KeyP(k, k')$
snd$'$	:	$I(m)$	$\rightarrow$	$N(m)$
cmp$'$	:	$I(m_1), I(m_2)$	$\rightarrow$	$I(m_1, m_2)$
encr$'$	:	$I(m), I(k)$	$\rightarrow$	$I(\{m\}_k)$
nnc$'$	:	$\cdot$	$\rightarrow$	$\exists n.\ I(n)$
pers$'$	:	$\pi(m)$	$\rightarrow$	$I(m), \pi(m)$
dup	:	$I(m)$	$\rightarrow$	$I(m), I(m)$
del	:	$I(m)$	$\rightarrow$	$\cdot$

Fig. 3. The Modified Intruder Theory $\mathcal{I}'$

The intruder capabilities formalized in the strand model relies on a slightly different strategy for managing captured knowledge: inferring new information has the effect of deleting the data it was constructed from. Moreover, it can discard information. However, explicit duplication is possible. We express this behavior by the set of rules $\mathcal{I}'$ in Figure 3.

Clearly, our original intruder model $\mathcal{I}$ can easily be simulated by a systematic use of the duplication rule of $\mathcal{I}'$. Going in the other direction is slightly trickier as $\mathcal{I}$ never discards any information. The substantial equivalence of these two systems is summarized in the following result.

Property 1. Let $\mathcal{R}$ be an arbitrary protocol theory, and S_1 and S_2 two states.

- For every rule sequence r in $\mathcal{R}, \mathcal{I}$ such that $S_1 \xrightarrow{r}{}^*_{\mathcal{R}, \mathcal{I}} S_2$, there exists a rule sequence r' in $\mathcal{R}, \mathcal{I}'$ such that $S_1 \xrightarrow{r'}{}^*_{\mathcal{R}, \mathcal{I}'} S_2$.
- For every rule sequence r' in $\mathcal{R}, \mathcal{I}'$ such that $S_1 \xrightarrow{r'}{}^*_{\mathcal{R}, \mathcal{I}'} S_2$, there exist a rule sequence r in $\mathcal{R}, \mathcal{I}$ and an intruder state I' such that $S_1 \xrightarrow{r}{}^*_{\mathcal{R}, \mathcal{I}} S_2, I'$.

Proof: The idea underlying the proof of the first statement is that every rule in $\mathcal{I}$ can be emulated by the corresponding rule in $\mathcal{I}'$ preceded by one or more applications of dup. Rule del is never used. The transition sequence r' is derived from r according to this strategy. A formal proof proceeds by induction on r.

The proof of the second half of this property is based on the observation that rule dup can be emulated in $\mathcal{I}$ by applying snd and rec in succession. The additional intruder state I' consists of copies of intermediate information produced by the rules of $\mathcal{I}$ plus whatever data were explicitly discarded by using del. Again, this is formally proved by induction on r'. $\qquad\square$

3   Strand Constructions

We now define strands and related concepts. In order to simplify this task, we first recall some basic definitions from graph theory in Section 3.1. In Section 3.2, we adapt the definitions in [Son99], which is more concise than [FHG98]. In Section 3.3, we extend the strand formalism with a series of new concepts intended to ease the comparison with protocol theories. These extensions are of independent interest and therefore we discuss some of their properties.

3.1   Preliminary Definitions

A *directed graph* G is a pair $(S, \longrightarrow)$ where S is the set of *nodes* of G and $\longrightarrow \subseteq S \times S$ is the set of *edges* of G. We will generally write $\nu_1 \longrightarrow \nu_2$ for $(\nu_1, \nu_2) \in \longrightarrow$. A *directed labeled graph* G_L is a structure $(S, \longrightarrow, L, \Lambda)$ where $(S, \longrightarrow)$ is a directed graph, L is a set of *labels*, and $\Lambda : S \to L$ is a *labeling function* that associates a label to every node. In the sequel, all our graphs will be directed and labeled, but we will generally keep Λ implicit for simplicity. In particular, for $\nu \in S$ and $l \in L$, we will write "$\nu = l$" as an abbreviation of $\Lambda(\nu) = l$. However, for $\nu_1, \nu_2 \in S$, expressions of the form "$\nu_1 = \nu_2$" shall always refer to the nodes themselves, and not to their labels.

A graph $G = (S, \longrightarrow)$ is a *chain* if there is a total ordering $\nu_0, \nu_1, \ldots$ of the elements of S such that $\nu_i \longrightarrow \nu_j$ iff $j = i + 1$. A graph $G = (S, \longrightarrow)$ is a *disjoint union of chains* if $S = \bigcup_{i \in I} S_i$ and $\longrightarrow = \bigcup_{i \in I} \longrightarrow_i$ (for some set I) and $(S_i, \longrightarrow_i)$ are chains for each $i \in I$.

A *bipartite graph* is a structure $G = (S_1, S_2, \longrightarrow)$ such that S_1 and S_2 are disjoint, $(S_1 \cup S_2, \longrightarrow)$ is a graph, and if $\nu_1 \longrightarrow \nu_2$ then $\nu_1 \in S_1$ and $\nu_2 \in S_2$. Observe that all edges go from S_1 to S_2 (i.e. $\longrightarrow \subseteq S_1 \times S_2$). We say that $G = (S_1, S_2, \longrightarrow)$ is

- *functional* if $\longrightarrow$ is a partial function (i.e. if $\nu \longrightarrow \nu'_1$ and $\nu \longrightarrow \nu'_2$ imply $\nu'_1 = \nu'_2$).
- *injective* if $\longrightarrow$ is injective (i.e. if $\nu_1 \longrightarrow \nu'$ and $\nu_2 \longrightarrow \nu'$ imply $\nu_1 = \nu_2$).
- *surjective* if $\longrightarrow$ is surjective onto S_2 (i.e. for each $\nu' \in S_2$ there is $\nu \in S_1$ such that $\nu \longrightarrow \nu'$).

A *bi-graph* G is a structure $(S, \Longrightarrow, \longrightarrow)$ where both $(S, \Longrightarrow)$ and $(S, \longrightarrow)$ are graphs.

In the sequel, we will often rely on the natural adaptation of standard graph-theoretic notions (*e.g.* isomorphism) to labeled graphs and bi-graphs.

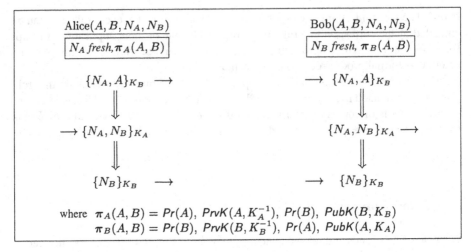

Fig. 4. Parametric Strand Specification of the Needham-Schroeder Protocol

3.2   Strands and Bundles

An *event* is a pair consisting of a message m and an indication of whether it has been sent $(+m)$ or received $(-m)$ [FHG98]. The set of all events will be denoted $\pm\mathcal{M}$.

A *strand* is a finite sequence of events, *i.e.* an element of $(\pm\mathcal{M})^*$. We indicate strands with the letter s, the length of a strand as $|s|$, and its i-th event as s_i (for $i = 1\ldots|s|$). Observe that a strand s can be thought of as a chain graph $(S, \Longrightarrow)$ with labels over $\pm\mathcal{M}$, where $S = \{s_i : i = 1\ldots|s|\}$ and $s_i \Longrightarrow s_j$ iff $j = i + 1$.

Slightly simplifying from [FHG98], a *strand space* is a set of strands with an additional relation $(\longrightarrow)$ on the nodes. The only condition is that if $\nu_1 \longrightarrow \nu_2$, then $\nu_1 = +m$ and $\nu_2 = -m$ (for the same message m). Therefore, $\longrightarrow$ represents the transmission of the message m from the sender ν_1 to the receiver ν_2. Alternatively, a strand space can be viewed as a labeled bi-graph $\sigma = (S, \Longrightarrow, \longrightarrow)$ with labels over $\pm\mathcal{M}$, $\Longrightarrow \subseteq S \times S$, and $\longrightarrow \subseteq S^+ \times S^-$ where S^+ and S^- indicate the set of positively- and negatively-labeled nodes in S respectively, and the constraints discussed above: $(S, \Longrightarrow)$ is a disjoint union of chains, and if $\nu_1 \longrightarrow \nu_2$, then $\nu_1 = +m$ and $\nu_2 = -m$ for some message m.

A *bundle* is a strand space $\sigma = (S, \Longrightarrow, \longrightarrow)$ such that the bipartite graph $(S^+, S^-, \longrightarrow)$ is functional, injective, and surjective, and $(\Longrightarrow \cup \longrightarrow)$ is acyclic. In terms of protocols, the first three constraints imply that a message is sent to at most one recipient at a time, no message is received from more than one sender, and every received message has been sent, respectively. Dangling positive nodes correspond to messages in transit. We should point out that functionality is not required in [FHG98,Son99].

If we think in terms of protocols, a bundle represents a snapshot of the execution of a protocol (therefore a dynamic concept). As we will see, this comprises a current global state (what each principal and the intruder are up to, and the messages in transit), as well as a precise account of how this situation has been reached. Each role is expressed as a strand in the current bundle. The intruder capabilities are themselves modeled as a fixed set of *penetrator strands*, which can be woven in a bundle. We skip the exact definitions [FHG98,Son99] as the construction we propose in the next sections will generalize them.

3.3 Extensions

We now introduce a few new concepts on top of these definitions. Besides contributing to the understanding of this formalism, they will ease the comparison with multiset rewriting specifications.

The notion of role is kept implicit in [FHG98] and rapidly introduced as the concept of *trace-type* in [Son99]. A *role* is nothing but a parametric strand: a strand where the messages may contain variables. An actual strand is obtained by instantiating all the variables in a parametric strand (or an initial segment of one) with persistent information and actual message pieces. For simplicity, we will not define nor consider constructions corresponding to arbitrary well-founded protocol theories (see Section 2 and [CDL+99,DLMS99]).

A *parametric strand* for the role ρ may look as in Figure 5. The freshness of n, *i.e.* the fact that the variables n should be instantiated with "new" constants that have not been used before, is expressed as a side condition. Using the terminology in [FHG98,Son99], the values n are *uniquely originated*. This is a slightly more verbose way of specifying freshness than our use of $\exists$ in the previous section, but it achieves the same effect. What we see as the main difference however is that freshness is presented as a meta-level comment in [FHG98,Son99], while we have it as an operator in our specification calculus. The relationship between variables are expressed in [Son99] using

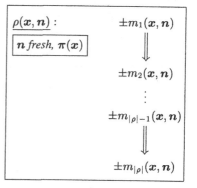

Fig. 5. A Parametric Strand

intuitive notation, *e.g.* k^{-1} for the inverse key of k, or k_A for the key of A. We formalize these relations by equipping ρ with the constraints $\pi(x)$, that, without loss of generality, will be a set of persistent atomic formulas from Section 2, parameterized over x.

As in the case of transition systems, a *protocol* is given as a set of roles. The model of the intruder in the style of Dolev and Yao [DY83,NS78] is also specified as a set of parametric strands $\mathcal{P}(P_0)$ called *penetrator strands*, where P_0 is the intruder's initial knowledge (see Section 3.4 or [Son99] for a definition). As an example, Figure 4 shows how the Needham-Schroeder public key protocol is modeled using parametric strands, where we have used incoming and outgoing arrows instead of the tags $+$ and $-$ for readability.

As usual, a *substitution* is a finite tuple $\theta = (t_1/x_1, \ldots, t_n/x_n)$ of term-variable pairs t_i/x_i. The domain of θ is $\mathrm{dom}(\theta) = (x_1, \ldots, x_n)$, with each x_i distinct. All our substitution will be *ground*, by which we mean that none of the t_i's will contain any variable. We will rely on two types of substitutions: substitutions that replace variables with distinct fresh constants that have not been previously encountered, and substitutions that map variables to previously used ground terms (not necessarily constants). We will use the letters ξ and θ, possibly subscripted, to denote them respectively. Given a parametric message m with variables in $\text{dom}(\theta)$, we denote the application of θ to m as $m[\theta]$. Given substitutions $\theta_1, \ldots, \theta_n$, we write $m[\theta_1 \cdots \theta_n]$ for $(\ldots (m[\theta_1]) \ldots)[\theta_n]$. We extend this notation to nodes, writing $\nu[\theta]$ and to (possibly partially instantiated) parametric strands, with the notation $\rho[\theta]$.

These definitions allow us to specialize the bundles we will be looking at: given a set of parametric strands S, every strand in a bundle σ should be a fully instantiated initial prefix of a protocol (or penetrator) strand. We are interested in initial prefixes since a bundle is a snapshot of the execution of a protocol, and a particular role instance may be halfway through its execution. We then say that σ is a *bundle over* S. We need to generalize strands constructions to admit strand spaces containing partially instantiated parametric strands. We call them *parametric strand spaces*. The bundles we will consider will however always be ground.

We will now give a few definitions needed to emulate the execution of a protocol with parametric strands. No such definitions can be found in the original description of strand constructions [FHG98,Son99], which focuses on analyzing protocol traces, not on specifying how to generate them.

First, observe that the network traffic in a bundle is expressed in terms of events and of the $\longrightarrow$ relation. The edges of $\longrightarrow$ represent past traffic: messages that have been sent and successfully received. The dangling positive nodes correspond to current traffic: messages in transit that have been sent, but not yet received. We will call these nodes the *fringe* of the bundle (or strand space). More formally, given a strand space $\sigma = (S, \Longrightarrow, \longrightarrow)$, its fringe is the set

$$\text{Fr}(\sigma) = \{\nu : \nu \in S, \ \nu = +m, \text{ and } \nexists \nu'. \ \nu \longrightarrow \nu'\}$$

Another component of the execution state of a protocol is a description of the actions that can legally take places in order to continue the execution. First, some technicalities. Let σ be a bundle over a set of parametric strands S, a *completion* of σ is any strand space $\tilde{\sigma}$ that embeds σ as a subgraph, and that extends each incomplete strand in it with the omitted nodes and the relative $\Longrightarrow$-edges. A completion of σ may contain additional strands, possibly only partially instantiated. If s is a strand in σ and $\tilde{s}$ is its extension in $\tilde{\sigma}$, the sequence obtained by removing every event in s from $\tilde{s}$ is itself a (possibly empty) strand. We call it a *residual strand* and indicate it as $\tilde{s} \setminus s$. We then write $\tilde{\sigma} \setminus \sigma$ for the set of all residual strands of $\tilde{\sigma}$ with respect to σ, plus any strands that $\tilde{\sigma}$ may contain in addition to those in σ.

Given these preliminary definitions, a *configuration* over S is a pair of strand spaces $(\sigma, \sigma^\sharp)$ where σ is a bundle over S, and $\sigma^\sharp$ is an extension of σ whose only additional $\longrightarrow$-edges originate in $\text{Fr}(\sigma)$, cover all of $\text{Fr}(\sigma)$, and point to $\sigma^\sharp \setminus \sigma$. Clearly, if $\sigma = (S, \Longrightarrow, \longrightarrow)$ and $\sigma^\sharp = (S^\sharp, \Longrightarrow^\sharp, \longrightarrow^\sharp)$, we have that $S \subseteq S^\sharp$, and $\Longrightarrow \subseteq \Longrightarrow^\sharp$, and finally $\longrightarrow \subseteq \longrightarrow^\sharp$.

A one-step transition is what it takes to go from one bundle to the "next". There are two ways to make progress in the bundle world: extend a strand, or add a new one. Let us analyze them:

- *Extending a strand*: If the configuration at hand embeds a strand that is not fully contained in its bundle part, then we add the first missing node of the latter and the incoming $\Longrightarrow$-edge. If this node is positive, we add an $\longrightarrow$-arrow to a matching negative node. If it is negative, we must make sure that it has an incoming $\longrightarrow$-edge.
- *Creating a strand*: Alternatively, we can select a parametric strand and instantiate first its "fresh" data and then its other parameters. Were we to perform both instantiations at once, there would be no way to run protocols which exchange nonces, such as our example in Figure 4.

We will now formalize this notion. Let $(\sigma_1, \sigma_1^\sharp)$ and $(\sigma_2, \sigma_2^\sharp)$ be configurations over a set of parametric strands S, with $\sigma_i = (S_i, \Longrightarrow_i, \longrightarrow_i)$ and $\sigma_i^\sharp = (S_i^\sharp, \Longrightarrow_i^\sharp, \longrightarrow_i^\sharp)$, for $i = 1, 2$. We say that $(\sigma_2, \sigma_2^\sharp)$ *immediately follows* $(\sigma_1, \sigma_1^\sharp)$ by means of move o, written $(\sigma_1, \sigma_1^\sharp) \stackrel{o}{\longmapsto}_S (\sigma_2, \sigma_2^\sharp)$, if any of the following situations apply. An intuitive sense of what each case formalizes can be gained by looking at the pictorial abstraction to the right of each possibility. Here, ν, ν' and ν'' stand for nodes on fully instantiated strands, while ν_0 will generally be only partially instantiated.

S$_0$: There are nodes $\nu, \nu'' \in S_1^\sharp \setminus S_1$ such that $\nu = +m$, $\nu'' = -m$, no $\longrightarrow$-edge enters ν'', and no $\Longrightarrow$-arrow enters ν. Then,

- $S_2 = S_1 \cup \{\nu\}$,
  $\Longrightarrow_2 = \Longrightarrow_1$,
  $\longrightarrow_2 = \longrightarrow_1$;

- $S_2^\sharp = S_1^\sharp$,
  $\Longrightarrow_2^\sharp = \Longrightarrow_1^\sharp$,
  $\longrightarrow_2^\sharp = \longrightarrow_1^\sharp \cup \{(\nu, \nu'')\}$.

S: There are nodes $\nu, \nu'' \in S_1^\sharp \setminus S_1$ and $\nu' \in S_1$ such that $\nu = +m$, $\nu'' = -m$, no $\longrightarrow$-edge enters ν'', and $\nu' \Longrightarrow_1^\sharp \nu$. Then,

- $S_2 = S_1 \cup \{\nu\}$,
  $\Longrightarrow_2 = \Longrightarrow_1 \cup \{(\nu', \nu)\}$,
  $\longrightarrow_2 = \longrightarrow_1$;

- $S_2^\sharp = S_1^\sharp$,
  $\Longrightarrow_2^\sharp = \Longrightarrow_1^\sharp$,
  $\longrightarrow_2^\sharp = \longrightarrow_1^\sharp \cup \{(\nu, \nu'')\}$.

R$_0$: There are nodes $\nu \in S_1^\sharp \setminus S_1$ and $\nu'' \in S_1$ such that $\nu = -m$, $\nu'' = +m$, $\nu'' \longrightarrow_1^\sharp \nu$, and no $\Longrightarrow$ enters ν. Then,

- $S_2 = S_1 \cup \{\nu\}$,
  $\Longrightarrow_2 = \Longrightarrow_1$,
  $\longrightarrow_2 = \longrightarrow_1 \cup \{(\nu'', \nu)\}$;

- $\sigma_2^\sharp = \sigma_1^\sharp$.

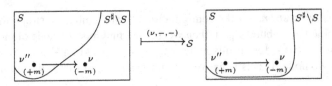

R: There are nodes $\nu \in S_1^{\sharp} \setminus S_1$ and $\nu', \nu'' \in S_1$ such that $\nu = -m$, $\nu'' = +m$, $\nu'' \longrightarrow_1^{\sharp} \nu$, and $\nu' \Longrightarrow_1^{\sharp} \nu$. Then,

- $S_2 = S_1 \cup \{\nu\}$,
  $\Longrightarrow_2 = \Longrightarrow_1 \cup \{(\nu', \nu)\}$,   - $\sigma_2^{\sharp} = \sigma_1^{\sharp}$.
  $\longrightarrow_2 = \longrightarrow_1 \cup \{(\nu'', \nu)\}$;

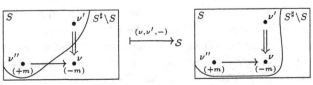

C$_f$: ρ is a parametric strand in S and ξ is a substitution for all its variables marked "fresh" with constants that appear nowhere in $(\sigma_1, \sigma_1^{\sharp})$.

- $\sigma_2 = \sigma_1$;   - $\sigma_2^{\sharp} = \sigma_1^{\sharp} \cup \rho[\xi]$.

where, $\sigma \cup s$ is obtained by taking the union of the nodes and $\Longrightarrow$-edges of σ and s,

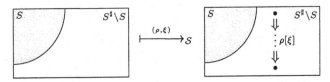

C$_i$: $\rho[\xi]$ is a partially instantiated parametric strand in $\sigma_1^{\sharp}$ and θ is a ground substitution for the remaining variables. In particular, if $\rho[\xi]$ mentions constraints π, then their instantiation should be compatible with the know persistent data, *i.e.* $\pi[\theta] \subseteq \Pi$. Then,

- $\sigma_2 = \sigma_1$;   - $\sigma_2^{\sharp} = \sigma_1^{\sharp} - \rho[\xi] \cup \rho[\xi, \theta]$.

where, $\sigma - s$ is the subgraph of σ obtained by removing all nodes of s and their incident edges.

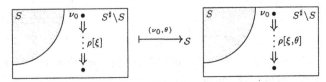

The *move o* that labels the transition arrow $\longmapsto_S$ records the necessary information to reconstruct the transition uniquely. Given a configuration $(\sigma, \sigma^{\sharp})$, a *move* for transitions of type $\mathbf{S_0}$, $\mathbf{S}$, $\mathbf{R_0}$, and $\mathbf{R}$ is a triple $o = (\nu, \bar{\nu}^p, \bar{\nu}^s)$ where ν is a node, $\bar{\nu}^p$ is the parent node ν^p of ν according to the $\Longrightarrow$ relation (or "$-$" if ν is the first node of a chain — cases $\mathbf{S_0}$ and $\mathbf{R_0}$), and $\bar{\nu}^s$ is the recipient ν^s of the message that labels ν along the $\longrightarrow$ relation (if ν is positive, or "$-$" otherwise). For transitions of type $\mathbf{C_f}$ and $\mathbf{C_i}$, moves have the form (ρ, ξ) and (ν_0, θ) respectively, where ρ is the name of the chosen parametric strand, ν_0 is the first node of the partially instantiated strand $\rho[\xi]$, and ξ and θ are the instantiating substitutions.

A *multistep transition* amounts to chaining zero or more one-step transitions. This relation is obtained by taking the reflexive and transitive closure $\longmapsto^o_S$ of $\longmapsto^o_S$, where o is the sequence of the component moves ("$\cdot$" if empty). o is a trace of the computation.

Observe that our definition of transition preserves configurations, *i.e.* if $(\sigma_1, \sigma_1^\#)$ is a configuration and $(\sigma_1, \sigma_1^\#) \longmapsto_S (\sigma_2, \sigma_2^\#)$, then $(\sigma_2, \sigma_2^\#)$ is also a configuration. This property clearly extends to multistep transitions.

Property 2. Let $(\sigma_1, \sigma_1^\#)$ be a configuration. If $(\sigma_1, \sigma_1^\#) \longmapsto^o_S (\sigma_2, \sigma_2^\#)$, then $(\sigma_2, \sigma_2^\#)$ is a configuration.

Proof: By induction on the length of o. $\qquad\qquad\qquad\qquad\qquad\qquad\qquad\qquad\qquad$ $\square$

3.4   Penetrator Strands

We now formalize the intruder model of [FHG98,Son99], which consists of patterns called *penetrator strands*, and of a set of messages P_0 expressing the intruder's initial knowledge. The corresponding parametric strands are shown in Figure 6, which includes a case to handle intruder-generated nonces. This possibility is missing from [FHG98,Son99], but the completion is straightforward. We also distinguished cases $M(m)$ and $M'(m)$, which are identified in [FHG98,Son99]. We refer to the collection of (parametric) penetrator strands in Figure 6 as $\mathcal{P}(P_0)$.

Several observations need to be made. First, the intruder specification underlying penetrator strands follows the Dolev-Yao model [DY83,NS78]. The parametric strands in Figure 6 are indeed closely related to the multiset rewriting intruder model $\mathcal{I}'$ above. A translation can be found in Sections 4.2 and 5.2 below, while a proof-sketch is embedded in the main results in Sections 4.2 and 5.2.

As a final remark, notice that the transition system specification distinguishes between messages transmitted on the network (identified by the predicate symbol N) and messages intercepted and manipulated by the intruder. Indeed, the predicate I implements a private database, a workshop for the fabrication of unauthorized messages, hidden from the honest principals of the system. No such distinction exists in the strand world. Therefore, it may seem that the intruder dismantles and puts together messages in the open, under the eyes of the other principals in the system. This is not the case: the privacy of the intruder is guaranteed by the fact that the $\longrightarrow$ relation is functional (see 3.2). Only the intruder can make use of intermediate results of penetrator manipulations since any other principal observing such messages would make them unavailable to the intruder (and it would not be an intermediate, but a final product of message forgery): since only one $\longrightarrow$-edge can leave a negative node and such an arrow is the only way to communicate (or observe somebody else's) data, the intruder could not access the message in this node for further processing.

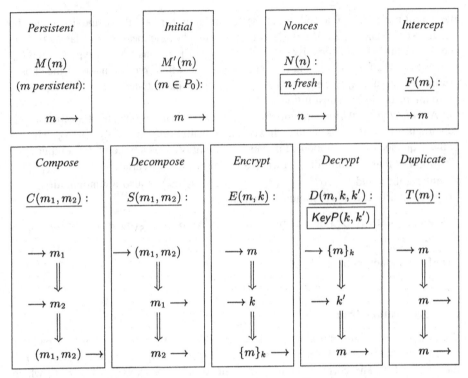

Fig. 6. The Penetrator Strands $\mathcal{P}$

The concepts and extensions we have just introduced set the basis for the translations between the multiset rewriting approach to security protocol specification and strand constructions. We describe the two directions of this translations in Sections 4 and 5, respectively.

4   From Multisets to Strands

The basic idea behind our translation will be to map a set of multiset rewrite rules specifying a role to a parametric strand. In particular, rules will correspond to nodes, and the role state predicates will be replaced by the backbone ($\Longrightarrow$) of the strand. In Section 4.1, we transform a regular protocol theory into an equivalent normal form. This transformation is novel and applies to a more general setting than the multiset rewriting specification of cryptoprotocols. In Section 4.2, we describe the translation proper and prove its correctness.

4.1   Normal Protocol Theories

We present two transformations which demonstrate that, without loss of generality, we can subsequently consider only normalized protocol theories. Their purpose is to restrict protocol theories so that they are closer to the strand model. Note that these transformations are used for mathematical convenience: non-normal, and even non-regular, protocol theories are often more perspicuous than their normalized counterparts.

Role generation rule: We subsume the role generation rule of every role ρ, *i.e.* the rule $r_{\rho 0} : \pi(x) \longrightarrow A_{\rho 0}(x), \pi(x)$, into the first rule of ρ. For each of its two schematic forms:

$$r_{\rho 1} : A_{\rho 0}(x) \longrightarrow \exists n. A_{\rho 1}(x, n), N(m(x, n))$$
$$r_{\rho 1} : A_{\rho 0}(x), N(m(x, y)) \longrightarrow A_{\rho 1}(x, y)$$

we obtain the following rules:

$$\ddot{r}_{\rho 1} : \pi(x) \longrightarrow \exists n. A_{\rho 1}(x, n), N(m(x, n)), \pi(x)$$
$$\ddot{r}_{\rho 1} : \pi(x), N(m(x, y)) \longrightarrow A_{\rho 1}(x, y), \pi(x)$$

respectively. Observe that, by definition of role state predicate, the parameters x include the arguments of the elided $A_{\rho 0}$ (as usual, $m(x)$ does not need to mention each variable in x). This amounts to setting initial values in the first step of a role, rather than prior to any message exchange.

If $\mathcal{R}$ is a regular protocol theory, we will denote the effect of this transformation as $\ddot{\mathcal{R}}$. If S is a state, the transformed state $\ddot{S}$ is obtained by dropping every mention of an initial role state $A_{\rho 0}$ from S. Clearly, $\ddot{S}_0 = S_0$ for any initial state S_0. Similarly, a transition sequence r is mapped to a sequence $\ddot{r}$ from which all the instances of rules for the form $r_{\rho 0}$ have been dropped, and the uses of $r_{\rho 1}$ have been replaced with $\ddot{r}_{\rho 1}$.

The above transformation is sound and complete as witnessed by the following result:

Lemma 1.
Let $\mathcal{R}$ be a regular protocol theory with initial state S_0 and S a state. Then,

1. *If $S_0 \xrightarrow{r}{}^*_{\mathcal{R}} S$, then $S_0 \xrightarrow{\ddot{r}}{}^*_{\ddot{\mathcal{R}}} \ddot{S}$.*
2. *If $S_0 \xrightarrow{\ddot{r}}{}^*_{\ddot{\mathcal{R}}} \ddot{S}$, then $S_0 \xrightarrow{r}{}^*_{\mathcal{R}} S$.*

Proof: In both cases, the proof proceeds by induction on the length of the given transition sequences.   □

Observe that applying this transformation and then "undoing" it as specified in the above lemma is not equivalent to the identical transformation: going in the reverse direction, we group occurrences of $r_{\rho 0}$ and $r_{\rho 1}$ together, and moreover we eliminate every isolated instance of $r_{\rho 0}$.

The original version of this paper [CDL+00] stated this lemma (or more precisely a result akin to the compounded Corollary 1 below) relative to general rather than regular protocol theories. This is incorrect: assume that $S_0 \xrightarrow{r}{}^*_{\mathcal{R}} S_1$ thanks to the initialization rule $r_{\rho 0}$ of some role ρ. Assume also that the first message exchange rule $r_{\rho 1}$ of this role contains a persistent predicate which does not have any instantiation in Π. The normal form of $r_{\rho 0}$ would then contain this constraint, making it inapplicable to any state S_1 would be mapped to. This scenario can clearly not occur when starting from a *regular* protocol theory since, by definition, all the accesses to persistent predicate are confined in the role instantiation rule.

An alternative way to correct the above error is to statically bind persistent information to any point in a protocol description where it is used. A realization of this idea by means of a strong typing infrastructure is at the basis of *MSR* [Cer01], a thorough redesign of the multiset rewriting formalism discussed in this paper. Besides being immune to that kind of errors, *MSR* is altogether a much better specification language as evidenced in [BCJS02].

Nonces: We further transform protocol theories so that all nonces generated by a role are preemptively chosen in the first rule of that role. We accomplish this by adding extra arguments to role state predicates, and pass the nonces generated in the first rule to subsequent uses through fresh variables in these predicates. Since roles are bounded, there are only a small finite number of nonces that need to be generated in an entire role. This transformation intuitively means that a participant should roll all her dice immediately, and look at them as needed later.

More formally, let ρ be the multiset rewriting specification of a role as from the previous transformation, and let $e_{\rho i}$ be the number of existentially quantified variables in rule $r_{\rho i}$, for $i = 1..|\rho|$. We map each role state predicate $\mathsf{A}_{\rho i}(x)$ in ρ to a predicate of the form

$$\bar{\mathsf{A}}_{\rho i}(x, n_{i+1}, \ldots, n_{|\rho|})$$

where, for $j = i + 1..|\rho|$, there are exactly $e_{\rho j}$ elements in n_j, and each of the added arguments is a distinct new variable.

We transform rules by replacing each state predicate $\mathsf{A}_{\rho i}$ with $\bar{\mathsf{A}}_{\rho i}$, and moving existential quantifiers to the first rule of the role. As a result, we are left with the following *normalized rules*:

Role generation rules:
- $\bar{r}_{\rho 1} : \pi(x) \qquad\qquad\qquad \longrightarrow \exists n. \bar{\mathsf{A}}_{\rho 1}(x, n), \quad \mathsf{N}(m(x, n)), \pi(x)$
- $\bar{r}_{\rho 1} : \pi(x), \mathsf{N}(m(x, y)) \longrightarrow \exists n. \bar{\mathsf{A}}_{\rho 1}(x, y, n), \qquad\qquad \pi(x)$

Other rules:
- $\bar{r}_{\rho i+1} : \bar{\mathsf{A}}_{\rho i}(x) \qquad\qquad \longrightarrow \bar{\mathsf{A}}_{\rho i+1}(x), \quad \mathsf{N}(m(x))$
- $\bar{r}_{\rho i+1} : \bar{\mathsf{A}}_{\rho i}(x), \mathsf{N}(m(x, y)) \longrightarrow \bar{\mathsf{A}}_{\rho i+1}(x, y)$

where all the newly introduced variables in rule $\bar{r}_{\rho 1}$ are existentially quantified. Given a role ρ, we denote the normalized specification as $\bar{\rho}$. We write $\bar{\mathcal{R}}$ for the application of this transformation to a protocol theory $\mathcal{R}$.

In order to formally relate a regular protocol theory with its normalized form, we need to assess the effect of normalization on states. Given a ground predicate P in a state S, we construct the open term $\overline{P}$ corresponding to the possible normalizations of P as follows:

$$\begin{cases} \overline{\mathsf{A}_{\rho i}(t)} = \bar{\mathsf{A}}_{\rho i}(t, n_i, \ldots, n_{|\rho|}) & \text{where } n_i, \ldots, n_{|\rho|} \text{ consist of distinct variables} \\ \overline{P} \quad = P & \text{if } P \text{ is not a role state predicate} \end{cases}$$

It is easy to extend this definition to *open states*: if S is a state, we construct the open multiset $\overline{S}$ representing all normalized states it is mapped to. $\overline{S}$ is defined as follows:

$$\overline{S} = \{\overline{P} : P \leftarrow S\}$$

where $\{\ldots\}$ is the multiset equivalent of the usual set notation $\{\ldots\}$, and $x \leftarrow M$ denotes multiplicity-conscious multiset membership. We shall choose different variables for each $\overline{P}$ in $\overline{S}$. Observe that since the initial state S_0 does not contain role state predicates, we have that $\overline{S_0} = S_0$.

The mapping between an open state $\overline{S}$ and states that can be processed by transitions is done by means of substitutions ξ that map each variable in $\overline{S}$ to a distinct constant that does not appear in S. Observe that $\overline{S}[\xi]$ is a (ground) state.

The definition of transition does not change, but we will denote a transition sequence that uses normalized rules as $\overline{r}$ with the usual subscripts. We will shortly see how to normalize a transition sequence r.

Given these various definitions, we are now in a position to prove that normalization preserves transitions. We have the following result.

Lemma 2.
Let $\overset{\approx}{\mathcal{R}}$ be a regular protocol theory that has been subjected to the role generation transformation in the first part of this section, S_0 the initial state, and S a state. Let moreover ξ be an arbitrary substitution from the variables in $\overline{S}$ to distinct unused constants. Then,

1. If $S_0 \overset{r}{\longrightarrow}^*_{\overset{\approx}{\mathcal{R}}} S$, then $S_0 \overset{\overline{r}}{\longrightarrow}^*_{\overset{\approx}{\mathcal{R}}} \overline{S}[\xi]$.

2. If $S_0 \overset{\overline{r}}{\longrightarrow}^*_{\overset{\approx}{\mathcal{R}}} \overline{S}[\xi]$, then $S_0 \overset{r}{\longrightarrow}^*_{\overset{\approx}{\mathcal{R}}} S$.

Proof: In both cases, the proof proceeds by induction on the length of the given transition sequences. We will examine them in turn.   □

In the following we will start from a regular protocol theory $\mathcal{R}$ and apply these two transformations in sequence. For clarity reasons, we will generally write $\overline{\mathcal{R}}$ when $\overset{\approx}{\mathcal{R}}$ would be appropriate. We extend this convention to roles and states.

The following corollary chains the above results together. It also considers protocols augmented with the standard intruder theory $\mathcal{I}$. It must be observed that the above transformations do not have any effect on $\mathcal{I}$.

Corollary 1.
Let $\mathcal{R}$ be a regular protocol theory, S_0 the initial state, and S a state. Let moreover ξ be an arbitrary substitution from the variables in $\overline{S}$ to distinct unused constants. Then,

1. If $S_0 \overset{r}{\longrightarrow}^*_{\mathcal{R},\mathcal{I}} S$, then $S_0 \overset{\overline{r}}{\longrightarrow}^*_{\overline{\mathcal{R}},\mathcal{I}} \overline{S}[\xi]$.

2. If $S_0 \overset{\overline{r}}{\longrightarrow}^*_{\overline{\mathcal{R}},\mathcal{I}} \overline{S}[\xi]$, then $S_0 \overset{r}{\longrightarrow}^*_{\mathcal{R},\mathcal{I}} S$.

Proof: This is a direct consequence of Lemmas 1 and 2 once we observe that the intruder rules never access the role state predicates of a principal. Therefore, the elision of the state predicate A_0 is invisible to the intruder. Similarly, the intruder cannot see nor take advantage of the fact that all existentials in a normal role have been instantiated up-front since they are safely stored in $A_{\rho i}(x, n_i, \ldots, n_{|\rho|})$ until they are made visible in a message.   □

4.2 Translation

We are now in a position to translate protocol representations expressed in the multiset rewriting formalisms into strands. We first show how to map a general protocol theory into a set of parametric strands in Section 4.2, and then relate the intruder theory directly to the penetrators strands in Section 4.2. In Section 4.2, we prove that this translation preserve transitions after discussing how states are handled in Section 4.2.

From Protocol Theories to Parametric Strands. To each normalized role specification $\bar{\rho}$, we associate a parametric strand $\ulcorner \bar{\rho} \urcorner$ of the following form

$$\underline{\rho(x, y, n)} \quad \boxed{n \text{ fresh}, \pi(x)}$$

where n are the existential variables mentioned in the first rule $\bar{r}_{\rho 1}$ of this role, $\pi(x)$ are the persistent predicates accessed in this rule, and y are the other variables appearing in the role (x, y, n appear therefore in its last role state predicate).

Next, we associate a parametric node $\nu_{\bar{r}_{\rho i}}$ with each rule $\bar{r}_{\rho i}$. The embedded message is the message appearing in the antecedent or the consequent of the rule, the distinction being accounted for by the associated action. More precisely, we have the following translation (where we have omitted the argument of the state predicates, the indication of the variables occurring in the message, persistent information, and the existential quantifiers appearing in the role generation rule):

$$\ulcorner \bar{A}_{\rho i} \longrightarrow \bar{A}_{\rho i+1}, N(m) \urcorner \; = \; +m$$
$$\ulcorner \bar{A}_{\rho i}, N(m) \longrightarrow \bar{A}_{\rho i+1} \urcorner \; = \; -m$$

where $\ulcorner \_ \urcorner$ is our translation function.

Finally, we set the backbone of this parametric strand according to the order of the indices of the nodes (and rules):

$$\nu_{\bar{r}_{\rho i}} \Longrightarrow \nu_{\bar{r}_{\rho j}} \qquad \text{iff} \qquad j = i + 1.$$

In this way, we are identifying the role state predicates of the transition system specification with the $\Longrightarrow$-edges constituting the backbone of the corresponding parametric strand. Notice that the well-founded ordering over role state predicates is mapped onto the acyclicity of the $\Longrightarrow$-arrows of the strand constructions.

This completes our translation as far as roles, and therefore protocols, are concerned. Applying it to the Needham-Schroeder protocol yields exactly the parametric strand specification of Figure 4 presented in Section 3. Given a set of roles $\mathcal{R}$ in the transition system notation, we indicate the corresponding set of parametric strands as $\ulcorner \overline{\mathcal{R}} \urcorner$. We will give correctness results at the end of this section after showing how to translate global states.

From Intruder Theory to Penetrator Strands. The introduction of the alternate intruder theory $\mathcal{I}'$ in Section 2.3 enables a trivial mapping to penetrator strands: we simply map every intruder rule to the corresponding penetrator strand, with the exception of rec' and snd', which do not have any correspondent. In symbols:

$$
\begin{array}{rclrcl}
\ulcorner\mathrm{rec}'(m)\urcorner & = & none & \ulcorner\mathrm{snd}'(m)\urcorner & = & none \\
\ulcorner\mathrm{dcmp}'(m_1,m_2)\urcorner & = & S(m_1,m_2) & \ulcorner\mathrm{cmp}'(m_1,m_2)\urcorner & = & C(m_1,m_2) \\
\ulcorner\mathrm{decr}'(m,k)\urcorner & = & D(m,k) & \ulcorner\mathrm{encr}'(m,k)\urcorner & = & E(m,k) \\
\ulcorner\mathrm{nnc}'(n)\urcorner & = & N(n) & \ulcorner\mathrm{pers}'(m)\urcorner & = & M(m) \\
\ulcorner\mathrm{dup}(m)\urcorner & = & T(m) & \ulcorner\mathrm{del}(m)\urcorner & = & F(m)
\end{array}
$$

where we have equipped the intruder rules with arguments in the obvious way. We also need to map the initial intruder knowledge I_0 to a set P_0 of messages initially known to the intruder, to be processed by the penetrator strand M': $\ulcorner I_0 \urcorner = \{m : \mathsf{I}(m) \in I_0\}$. Every access to a message $\mathsf{I}(m)$ in I_0 will be translated to an application of the penetrator strand $M'(m)$.

Relating States and Configurations. In order to show that a transition system specification and its strand translation behave in the same way, we need to relate states and configurations. We do not need to give an exact mapping, since a configuration embeds a bundle expressing the execution up to the current point in fine detail. A state is instead a much simpler construction that does not contain any information about how it has been reached. Therefore, we will consider some properties that a configuration should have to be related to a state.

We say that a state $S = \Pi, A, N(m), I(m')$ is *compatible* with a strand configuration $(\sigma, \sigma^\sharp)$, written $S \sim_\mathcal{R} (\sigma, \sigma^\sharp)$ relative to a protocol theory $\mathcal{R}$, if the following conditions hold:

- $\mathrm{Fr}(\sigma) = m, m'$.
- Let $\bar{A}_{\rho i}(t_\rho, c_\rho)$ in A be the instantiation of the i-th role state predicate of a role $\bar{\rho}$ in $\mathcal{R}$ with terms t_ρ and fresh nonces c_ρ. Then,
  - $\sigma^\sharp$ contains a strand $s^\rho(c_\rho, t_\rho)$, obtained by instantiating the strand $s^\rho = \ulcorner\bar{\rho}\urcorner$ with terms t_ρ and new constants c_ρ.
  - σ contains an initial prefix of $s^\rho(t)$ whose last node has index i.
  Moreover every non-penetrator strand in $(\sigma, \sigma^\sharp)$ is obtained in this way.
- Every instance of a penetrator strand in $(\sigma, \sigma^\sharp)$ is completely contained in σ.

Intuitively, we want the state and the configuration to mention the same nonces, to have the same messages in transit (including the data currently processed by the intruder), to be executing corresponding role instances and have them be stopped at the same point.

Transition to Move Sequences. Given these definitions, we can state the correctness result for our translation of transition systems into strand constructions. We shall start by limiting our attention to normal protocol theories together with the modified intruder theory introduced in Section 2.3.

Lemma 3.

Let $\overline{\mathcal{R}}$ be a normal protocol theory, I_0 some initial intruder knowledge, and $\ulcorner I_0 \urcorner$ its strand translation. If $\Pi, I_0 \overset{r}{\longrightarrow}^*_{\mathcal{I}', \mathcal{R}} S$ is a normal multiset rewriting transition sequence over $\mathcal{I}', \overline{\mathcal{R}}$ from the empty state to state S, then there is a configuration $(\sigma, \sigma^\sharp)$ and a sequence of moves o such that

$$(\cdot, \cdot) \overset{o}{\longmapsto}^*_{\mathcal{P}(\ulcorner I_0 \urcorner), \ulcorner \overline{\mathcal{R}} \urcorner} (\sigma, \sigma^\sharp)$$

is a strand transition sequence from the empty configuration $(\cdot, \cdot)$ to $(\sigma, \sigma^\sharp)$, and $S \sim_{\mathcal{R}}$ $(\sigma, \sigma^\sharp)$, i.e. S is compatible with $(\sigma, \sigma^\sharp)$.

Proof: The proof proceeds by induction on r. The base case is trivial. The inductive step does a case analysis on the last rule applied in r. Intruder rules from $\mathcal{I}'$ are directly emulated by the corresponding penetrator strands, as defined in Section 4.2. The use of protocol rule $r_{\rho i}$ is emulated by a move involving the corresponding node in $\ulcorner \bar{\rho} \urcorner$. For each of these possibilities, we show that the corresponding move in the strand world is possible, and that it preserves the compatibility relation.

We omit formalizing this proof as it relies on exactly the same techniques as the proofs of previous results.   □

We can now extend this result to any regular (not necessarily normal) theory together with the standard intruder model. We have the following theorem:

Theorem 1.

Let $\mathcal{R}$ a regular protocol theory and I_0 be some initial intruder knowledge. For every regular multiset rewriting transition sequence $\Pi, I_0 \overset{r}{\longrightarrow}^*_{\mathcal{I}, \mathcal{R}} S$ there is a configuration $(\sigma, \sigma^\sharp)$ and a sequence of moves o such that

$$(\cdot, \cdot) \overset{o}{\longmapsto}^*_{\mathcal{P}(\ulcorner I_0 \urcorner), \ulcorner \overline{\mathcal{R}} \urcorner} (\sigma, \sigma^\sharp)$$

is a strand transition sequence from the empty configuration $(\cdot, \cdot)$ to $(\sigma, \sigma^\sharp)$, and $S \sim_{\mathcal{R}}$ $(\sigma, \sigma^\sharp)$.

Proof: This is a simple corollary of the above lemma mediated by an application of Lemma 1 to move between regular and normal protocol theories, and Property 1 reconcile using the standard vs. the modified intruder theory.   □

Observe that we cannot further relax the statement of this theorem to consider arbitrary (*i.e.* non-regular) protocol theories as regularization does not preserve transition sequences.

5   From Strands to Multisets

We will now show how to translate a set of parametric strands into a set of transition rules that preserve multistep transitions. Again, there is a slight mismatch between the two formalisms which is addressed in Section 5.1. This technical adjustment of our definition of strands will produce precisely the regular role transition rules we originally defined in Section 2. We describe the translation itself and prove it correct in Section 5.2.

5.1 Decorated Strands

In the previous section, we have observed and taken advantage of the fact that there is a close affinity between the rules in the transition system specification of a role and the nodes in a parametric strand. More precisely, a node together with the outgoing or incoming $\longrightarrow$-edge and an indication of what to do next corresponds to a transition. In transition systems, "what to do next" is specified through the role state predicates $A_{\rho i}$; in strand constructions, by means of the $\Longrightarrow$-edges. Therefore, using the same intuition as in Section 4, we will translate $\Longrightarrow$-edges to state predicates. We need to equip these predicates with the appropriate arguments (while we were able to simply drop them in the inverse translation).

Before describing how to do so, we will address two other minor syntactic discrepancies: the absence of an (explicit) strand equivalent of the role generation rule $\pi(x) \longrightarrow A_{\rho 0}(x), \pi(x)$, and the fact that, in the transition system specification of a role, there is a final state predicate that lingers in the global state no matter what other transitions take place.

Role Generation transition: We add a dummy initial node, say $\top$, to every strand, with no incoming or outgoing $\longrightarrow$-edges, and one outgoing $\Longrightarrow$-edge to the original first node of the strand.

Final state: Dually, we alter the definition of strands to contain a final node, say $\bot$, again without any incoming or outgoing $\longrightarrow$-edge, and with one incoming $\Longrightarrow$-arrow from the original last node of the strand.

This corresponds to redefining strands as strings drawn from the language $\top(\pm\mathcal{M})^*\bot$, rather than just $(\pm\mathcal{M})^*$. Notice that now every (proper) event has both a predecessor and a successor $\Longrightarrow$-edge.

With the addition of these auxiliary nodes, we can label each $\Longrightarrow$-arrow in a strand s with parameters x_s, n_s (n_s marked *fresh*) and a predicate constant A_{si} with progressive indices i. In the case of parametric strands, we equip these labels with arguments drawn from its set of parameters as follows:

Initial arrow: $\top \Longrightarrow \nu$

This is the predicate A_{s0} labeling the $\Longrightarrow$-edge that links the added initial node $\top$ to the first node of the original strand. The arguments of A_{s0} will be x_s.

Successor arrow to a positive node:

$$\ldots \overset{A_{si}(x)}{\Longrightarrow} +m(x, n) \Longrightarrow \ldots$$

Let $A_{si}(x)$ be the label of the incoming $\Longrightarrow$-edge of a positive node $\nu = +m(x, n)$, where m mentions known variables among x and unused nonces n among n_s. Then the outgoing $\Longrightarrow$-arrow of ν will have label $A_{si+1}(x, n)$.

Successor arrow to a negative node:

$$\ldots \overset{A_{si}(x)}{\Longrightarrow} -m(x, y) \Longrightarrow \ldots$$

Let $A_{si}(x)$ be the label of the incoming $\Longrightarrow$-edge of a positive node $\nu = -m(x, y)$, where m mentions known variables among x, and unseen data y. Then, the outgoing $\Longrightarrow$-arrow of n will have label $A_{si+1}(x, y)$.

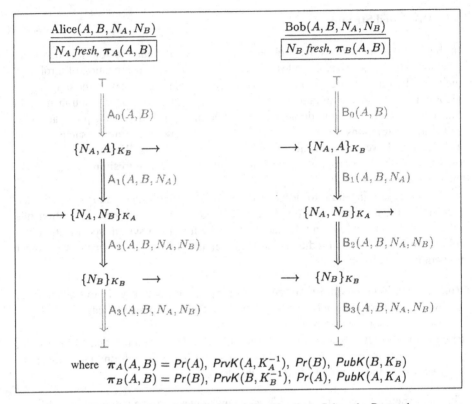

where $\pi_A(A, B) = Pr(A),\ PrvK(A, K_A^{-1}),\ Pr(B),\ PubK(B, K_B)$
$\pi_B(A, B) = Pr(B),\ PrvK(B, K_B^{-1}),\ Pr(A),\ PubK(A, K_A)$

Fig. 7. Extended Strand Specification of the Needham-Schroeder Protocol

Given a parametric strand s, we denote the result of applying these transformations as $\bar{s}$. If $\mathcal{S}$ is a set of parametric strands specifying a protocol, we write $\overline{\mathcal{S}}$ for the transformed set. Applying this transformation to the Needham-Schroeder protocol yields the enhanced strand specification in Figure 7, where the additions have been grayed out.

Since we have changed the syntax of a parametric strand, we need to upgrade its dynamics, originally presented in Section 2. First, an obvious alteration to the instantiation of a parametric strand: we apply the substitution to the labels of the $\Longrightarrow$-edges as well as to the messages embedded in the nodes. We carry on this change to the resulting bundles and configurations: every $\Longrightarrow$-edge between two nodes ν_1 and ν_2 now carries a label $A_{si}(t)$. We indicate this as $\nu_1 \stackrel{A_{si}(t)}{\Longrightarrow} \nu_2$ (or with its vertical equivalent). Notice that we erased this information in the reverse translation. Given a bundle σ and a configuration $(\sigma, \sigma^{\sharp})$ relative to a set of parametric strands $\mathcal{S}$, we write $\bar{\sigma}$ and $(\bar{\sigma}, \bar{\sigma}^{\sharp})$ for the corresponding entities relative to $\overline{\mathcal{S}}$.

The definition of one-step transition, in symbols $(\bar{\sigma}_1, \bar{\sigma}_1^{\sharp}) \stackrel{\circ}{\longmapsto}_{\overline{\mathcal{S}}} (\bar{\sigma}_2, \bar{\sigma}_2^{\sharp})$, changes as follows:

Extension of an existing strand: We proceed exactly as in Section 2, except for the fact that situations $\mathbf{S_0}$ and $\mathbf{R_0}$ in Section 3.3 do not apply.

Installation of a new strand:

We select a parametric strand ρ from $\overline{\mathcal{S}}$, instantiate it with a substitution ξ for its fresh variables and add the resulting strand $\rho[\xi]$ to $\bar{\sigma}_2^\sharp$. This corresponds to upgrading case $\mathbf{C_f}$ in Section 3.3 as outlined in the following figure. We do not formalize this transformation (call it $\mathbf{C_f}'$) it in full detail since it should be obvious how to obtain it.

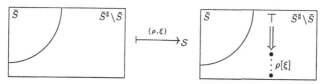

Transition $\mathbf{C_i}$ is consequently upgraded to $\mathbf{C_i}'$ described in the following figure. Notice that we add the first node, $\top$, of $\rho[\xi, \theta]$ to $\bar{\sigma}_2$

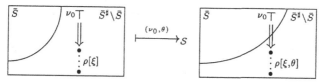

As in the original case, multistep transitions are obtained by taking the reflexive and transitive closure of the above judgment.

This transformation is sound and complete with respect to our original system.

Lemma 4. *Let S be a set of parametric strands, and $(\sigma_1, \sigma_1^\sharp)$ and $(\sigma_2, \sigma_2^\sharp)$ two configurations on it. Then,*

$$(\sigma_1, \sigma_1^\sharp) \overset{o}{\longmapsto}{}^*_S (\sigma_2, \sigma_2^\sharp) \quad \textit{iff} \quad (\bar{\sigma}_1, \bar{\sigma}_1^\sharp) \overset{\bar{o}}{\longmapsto}{}^*_{\overline{S}} (\bar{\sigma}_2, \bar{\sigma}_2^\sharp)$$

where $\bar{o}$ is obtained from o by extending the given transformation to traces.

Proof: In the forward direction, we add the labels as from the definition (they do not constrain the construction in any way); every use of transition $\mathbf{C_f}$ that introduces a new strand is mapped to $\mathbf{C_f}'$, which also installs the node $\top$. In the reverse direction, we simply forget about labels and extra nodes. Formally, both directions require a simple structural induction. $\qquad\qquad\qquad\qquad\qquad\qquad\qquad\qquad\qquad\qquad\qquad\qquad\square$

5.2 Translation

Given the above definitions, we are in a position to propose an transition-preserving translation that maps strand representations of security protocols to the multiset rewriting formalism. We will proceed in stages: in Section 5.2 we concentrate on parametric strands, in Section 5.2 we relate the intruder models, in Section 5.2 we extract a notion of state from a configuration, and finally in Section 5.2 we prove the correctness of our translation.

From Parametric Strands to Roles. We now present a translation of parametric strands to the coordinated sets of transition rules representing a role. Each node is mapped to a rule, the label of its incoming and outgoing $\Longrightarrow$-edge will be the state predicates

$$\left.\begin{array}{c} \top \\ \Big\Downarrow A_{s0}(x) \end{array}\right\} \quad \leadsto \quad \pi(x) \; \longrightarrow \; A_{s0}(x), \pi(x)$$

$$\left.\begin{array}{c} \Big\Downarrow A_{si}(x) \\ m(x,n) \; \longrightarrow \\ \Big\Downarrow A_{si+1}(x,n) \end{array}\right\} \quad \leadsto \quad A_{si}(x) \; \longrightarrow \; \exists n.\, A_{si+1}(x,n), N(m(x,n))$$

$$\left.\begin{array}{c} \Big\Downarrow A_{si}(x) \\ \longrightarrow m(x,y) \\ \Big\Downarrow A_{si+1}(x,y) \end{array}\right\} \quad \leadsto \quad A_{si}(x), N(m(x,y)) \; \longrightarrow \; A_{si+1}(x,y)$$

$$\left.\begin{array}{c} \Big\Downarrow A_{s|s|}(x) \\ \bot \end{array}\right\} \quad \leadsto \quad \textit{(No corresponding rule)}$$

Fig. 8. Transforming Extended Strands to Multiset Rewriting Rules

in the antecedent and consequent, respectively, and the network message will be the message embedded in the node, its polarity dictating on which side of the arrow it should be appear. More formally, we have the translation displayed in Figure 8, where the parameters of the added state predicates are classified as in the above definition.

Given a set of (decorated) parametric strands $\overline{S}$, we write $\ulcorner \overline{S} \urcorner$ for the set of protocol rules resulting from this transformation. Observe that it yields regular rules. Applying this translation to the enhanced parametric strands representing the Needham-Schroeder protocol in Figure 7 produces exactly the original transition system specification given in Figure 1.

From Penetrator Strands to Intruder Theory. The translation of the penetrator strands $\mathcal{P}(P_0)$ in Figure 6 is essentially the inverse of the mapping discussed in Section 4.2. Our target intruder model, in the multiset rewriting world, is $\mathcal{I}'$.

$$\begin{array}{lclcccl}
\ulcorner S(m_1, m_2) \urcorner & = & \mathrm{dcmp}'(m_1, m_2) & \qquad & \ulcorner C(m_1, m_2) \urcorner & = & \mathrm{cmp}'(m_1, m_2) \\
\ulcorner D(m, k) \urcorner & = & \mathrm{decr}'(m, k) & & \ulcorner E(m, k) \urcorner & = & \mathrm{encr}'(m, k) \\
\ulcorner N(n) \urcorner & = & \mathrm{nnc}'(n) & & \ulcorner M(m) \urcorner & = & \mathrm{pers}'(m) \\
\ulcorner T(m) \urcorner & = & \mathrm{dup}(m) & & \ulcorner F(m) \urcorner & = & \mathrm{del}(m) \\
\ulcorner M'(m) \urcorner & = & \textit{(see below)} & & & &
\end{array}$$

where we have again equipped the intruder transition rules with the obvious arguments.

Notice that no penetrator strand is made to correspond to rules rec′ or snd′. When translating transition sequences from the strand world to the transition system setting, we will insert these rules whenever a message sent by a principal's strand is received by a penetrator strand, and vice-versa, respectively. We map P_0 to a multiset I_0 of messages initially known to the intruder in the multiset rewriting framework: $\ulcorner P_0 \urcorner = \wp I(m) : m \in P_0 \wr$. Uses of $M'(m)$ with $m \in P_0$ are translated to accesses to $I(m) \in \ulcorner P_0 \urcorner$, possibly preceded by an application of rule dup if $M'(m)$ is accessed more than once.

From Configurations to States. Before we can show that the translation we just outlined preserves transition sequences, we need to extract a state from a configuration and show that steps between configurations are mapped to steps between the corresponding states.

Let S be a set of parametric strands, $\ulcorner S \urcorner$ its translation as a set of transition rules, and $(\sigma, \sigma^\sharp)$ a configuration over $S, \mathcal{P}(P_0)$ where all penetrator strands have been completed. We define the *state associated with* $(\bar\sigma, \bar\sigma^\sharp)$, written $S_{\overline{S}}(\bar\sigma, \bar\sigma^\sharp)$, as the state Π, A, N, I obtained as follows, where we write $\wp \ldots \wr$ for the multiset equivalent of the usual set notation $\{\ldots\}$:

- $N = \wp \mathsf{N}(m) : \nu \in \mathrm{Fr}(\bar\sigma), \nu$ is not on a penetratorstrand, and ν has label $+m \wr$.
- $I = \wp \mathsf{I}(m) : \nu \in \mathrm{Fr}(\bar\sigma), \nu$ is on a penetrator strand, and ν has label $+m \wr$.
- $A = \wp A_{si}(t) : s_{i-1} \overset{A_{si}(t)}{\Longrightarrow} s_i \in \bar\sigma^\sharp \setminus \bar\sigma$ and $s_{i-1} \in \mathrm{Fr}(\sigma) \wr$.

Intuitively, we collect the messages in transit coming from honest principal's strands in N, the current knowledge of the intruder in I, and the labels of the $\Longrightarrow$-edges at the boundary between $\bar\sigma^\sharp$ and $\bar\sigma$ as the multiset of role state predicates A.

From Move to Transition Sequences. Then, sequences of moves in the strand world and their translation as transition system steps are related as follows:

Theorem 2. *Let P_0 be some initial penetrator knowledge, and $\ulcorner P_0 \urcorner$ its multiset translation as defined in Section 5.2. Let $(\sigma_1, \sigma_1^\sharp)$ and $(\sigma_2, \sigma_2^\sharp)$ be two configurations on the penetrator strands $\mathcal{P}(P_0)$ and a set of parametric strands S such that all penetrator strands have been completed. For every multistep strand transition*

$$(\sigma_1, \sigma_1^\sharp) \overset{o}{\longmapsto}{}^*_{\mathcal{P}(P_0),S} (\sigma_2, \sigma_2^\sharp),$$

and every $I_0' \subseteq \ulcorner P_0 \urcorner$, there exists a regular multiset transition sequence r such that

$$\ulcorner P_0 \urcorner, S_{\overline{S}}(\bar\sigma_1, \bar\sigma_1^\sharp) \overset{r}{\longrightarrow}{}^*_{\mathcal{I}', \ulcorner S \urcorner} S_{\overline{S}}(\bar\sigma_2, \bar\sigma_2^\sharp), I_0'.$$

Proof: The proof of this result proceeds by induction on the structure of o. The only non-obvious aspect is that, as observed in Section 5.2, we need to insert applications of the rule rec′ when processing a message that flows from an honest principal's to a penetrator strands. We add uses of snd′ in the dual case. $\square$

Notice that we do not need to start from the empty configuration.

The mapping from strands to multiset rewriting we have just finished outlining, and the translation from multiset rewriting to strand constructions described in Section 4 are inverse of each other. We leave the proof of this fact to the interested reader.

6   Conclusions and Future Work

We have developed a formal connection between multiset rewriting [CDL+99,DLMS99] and strand constructions [FHG98,Son99]. The formalization of this unsurprising result required a number of unexpected adjustments to both frameworks. In particular, we equipped strands with a dynamic dimension by introducing a notion of transition that allows growing bundles from a set of parametric strands. This enabled us to relate the distinct notions of traces inherent to these formalisms: bundles and multiset rewrite sequences. On the other hand, we omitted the initialization phase of our multiset theories, since this phase has no counterpart in strand spaces.

This work can be applied to strengthen both formalisms. Our results imply that many multiset rewriting concepts and techniques devised over the years are likely to be relevant to the research on strands. The linear logic and rewriting logic foundations of multiset rewriting can thus be brought to bear on strand spaces as well. In addition, clean and intuitively appealing notions from strand spaces can be brought to multiset rewriting. For example, strand space bundles appear to be a better notion of computation trace than rewrite sequences, and therefore analogs could be fruitfully adopted in multiset rewrite systems. This has influenced the redesign of formalism presented here as the *MSR* security protocols specification language [Cer01] and fuels current research in the area. Finally, our work suggests extending strand spaces by embedding an explicit form of initialization, and refining the notion of initialization theories of multiset rewriting.

This paper can also be viewed as another step in a larger program of demonstrating connections between formalisms: the interoperation of logical systems can lead to improvements in the newly connected systems, but also lead to a deeper understanding of the entire problem domain. In this case, we have gained insight into the Dolev-Yao model of cryptoprotocols. Further connections to other formalisms including state-transition systems and linear logic [CDKS00] can improve the situation further. In fact, we are currently investigating properties of the representation of both strand and multiset rewriting constructions as process specification languages such as colored Petri nets and process algebras.

Acknowledgments

We would like to thank Joshua Guttman, Javier Thayer Fábrega, Jonathan Herzog, and Al Maneki for the stimulating discussions about strands. We are also indebted to Sylvan Pinsky for his encouragements to write down our ideas about the relationship between strand construction and our protocol theories. Finally, this work profitted from fruitful discussions with Jon Millen, Cathy Meadows, and Paul Syverson.

References

[BCJS02] Frederic Butler, Iliano Cervesato, Aaron D. Jaggard, and Andre Scedrov. A Formal Analysis of Some Properties of Kerberos 5 Using MSR. In *Fifteenth Computer Security Foundations Workshop — CSFW-15*, pages 175–190, Cape Breton, NS, Canada, June 2002. IEEE Computer Society Press.

[CDKS00] Iliano Cervesato, Nancy Durgin, Max I. Kanovich, and Andre Scedrov. Interpreting Strands in Linear Logic. In H. Veith, N. Heintze, and E. Clark, editors, *2000 Workshop on Formal Methods and Computer Security — FMCS'00*, Chicago, IL, July 2000.

[CDL+99] Iliano Cervesato, Nancy A. Durgin, Patrick D. Lincoln, John C. Mitchell, and Andre Scedrov. A meta-notation for protocol analysis. In P. Syverson, editor, *Proceedings of the 12th IEEE Computer Security Foundations Workshop — CSFW'99*, pages 55–69, Mordano, Italy, June 1999. IEEE Computer Society Press.

[CDL+00] Iliano Cervesato, Nancy A. Durgin, Patrick D. Lincoln, John C. Mitchell, and Andre Scedrov. Relating strands and multiset rewriting for security protocol analysis. In P. Syverson, editor, *13th IEEE Computer Security Foundations Workshop — CSFW'00*, pages 35–51, Cambridge, UK, 3–5 July 2000. IEEE Computer Society Press.

[Cer01] Iliano Cervesato. Typed MSR: Syntax and Examples. In V.I. Gorodetski, V.A. Skormin, and L.J. Popyack, editors, *First International Workshop on Mathematical Methods, Models and Architectures for Computer Networks Security — MMM'01*, pages 159–177, St. Petersburg, Russia, May 2001. Springer-Verlag LNCS 2052.

[DLMS99] Nancy Durgin, Patrick Lincoln, John Mitchell, and Andre Scedrov. Undecidability of bounded security protocols. In N. Heintze and E. Clarke, editors, *Proceedings of the Workshop on Formal Methods and Security Protocols — FMSP*, Trento, Italy, July 1999. Extended version at `ftp://ftp.cis.upenn.edu/pub/papers/scedrov/msr-long.ps`.

[DM99] Grit Denker and Jonathan K. Millen. CAPSL Intermediate Language. In N. Heintze and E. Clarke, editors, *Proceedings of the Workshop on Formal Methods and Security Protocols — FMSP*, Trento, Italy, July 1999.

[DY83] Danny Dolev and Andrew C. Yao. On the security of public-key protocols. *IEEE Transactions on Information Theory*, 2(29):198–208, 1983.

[FHG98] F. Javier Thayer Fábrega, Jonathan C. Herzog, and Joshua D. Guttman. Strand spaces: Why is a security protocol correct? In *Proceedings of the 1998 IEEE Symposium on Security and Privacy*, pages 160–171, Oakland, CA, May 1998. IEEE Computer Society Press.

[FHG99] F. Javier Thayer Fábrega, Jonathan C. Herzog, and Joshua D. Guttman. Mixed strand spaces. In P. Syverson, editor, *Proceedings of the 12th IEEE Computer Security Foundations Workshop — CSFW'99*, pages 72–82, Mordano, Italy, June 1999. IEEE Computer Society Press.

[Man99] A. Maneki. Honest functions and their application to the analysis of cryptographic protocols. In P. Syverson, editor, *Proceedings of the 12th IEEE Computer Security Foundations Workshop — CSFW'99*, pages 83–89, Mordano, Italy, June 1999. IEEE Computer Society Press.

[NS78] R.M. Needham and M.D. Schroeder. Using encryption for authentication in large networks of computers. *Communications of the ACM*, 21(12):993–999, 1978.

[Son99] Dawn Song. Athena: a new efficient automatic checker for security protocol analysis. In *Proceedings of the Twelfth IEEE Computer Security Foundations Workshop*, pages 192–202, Mordano, Italy, June 1999. IEEE Computer Society Press.

Data Access Specification and the Most Powerful Symbolic Attacker in *MSR* *

Iliano Cervesato

Advanced Engineering and Sciences Division, ITT Industries, Inc.
2560 Huntington Avenue, Alexandria, VA 22303 — USA
iliano@itd.nrl.navy.mil

Abstract. Most systems designed for the symbolic verification of security protocols operate under the unproved assumption that an attack can only result from the combination of a fixed number of message transformations, which altogether constitute the capabilities of the so-called Dolev-Yao intruder. In this paper, we show that the Dolev-Yao intruder can indeed emulate the actions of an arbitrary symbolic adversary. In order to do so, we extend MSR, a flexible specification framework for security protocols based on typed multiset rewriting, with a static check called data access specification and aimed at catching specification errors such as a principal trying to use a key that she is not entitled to access.

1 Introduction

Cryptographic protocols are increasingly used to secure transactions over the Internet and protect access to computer systems. Their design and analysis are notoriously complex and error-prone. Sources of difficulty include subtleties in the cryptographic primitives they rely on, and their deployment in distributed environments plagued by powerful and opportunistic attackers. Most systems designed for protocol analysis, *e.g.* [AG99,BAN89,DM99,FHG98,Mea96,GJ02] circumvent the first issue by relying on a symbolic idealization known as the Dolev-Yao model of security [DY83,NS78]: the cryptography is assumed to be flawless, which permits viewing message-forming operations such as encryption as symbolic combinators ultimately applied to atomic abstractions of principal names, keys, nonces, etc, rather than to bit-strings. Systems that adopt the Dolev-Yao idealization achieve relative tractability by empowering their attacker model with a fixed set of basic capabilities, altogether known as the Dolev-Yao intruder. It is a commonly held, but unproved, belief that this model is sufficient to expose any attack that can be mounted by a symbolic adversary, *i.e.* one playing by the rules of the Dolev-Yao abstraction, but otherwise arbitrary.

MSR originated as a simple logic-oriented language aimed at investigating the decidability of protocol analysis within the Dolev-Yao model [CDL⁺99]. It evolved into a precise, powerful, flexible, and still relatively simple framework for the specification of complex cryptographic protocols, possibly structured as a collection of coordinated subprotocols [Cer01a,Cer01b,Cer00]. It uses strongly-typed multiset rewriting rules over

---

* Partially supported by NRL under contract N00173-00-C-2086 and by NSF grant INT98-15731.

M. Okada et al. (Eds.): ISSS 2002, LNCS 2609, pp. 384–416, 2003.

first-order atomic formulas to express protocol actions and relies on a form of existential quantification to symbolically model the generation of nonces and other fresh data. It supports an array of useful static checks that include type-checking [Cer01a]. An earlier version of *MSR* fuels the *CAPSL* authentication protocol verification tool in the form of the underlying *CIL* intermediate language [DM99].

In this paper, we use *MSR* as a formal tool to study the very nature of the Dolev-Yao intruder, and ultimately to show that it subsumes any other attacker that follows the Dolev-Yao abstraction. In order to do so, we endow *MSR* with a novel static check, data access specification (DAS), aimed at enforcing such sensible requirements as, for example, that a principal may access the public key of any other principal, but in general not their private keys. The natural *MSR* specification of the Dolev-Yao intruder is shown not only to satisfy the data access policy, but in doing so to make use of every facet of it. This highlights subtle constraints on the Dolev-Yao intruder model that are typically not exposed by other approaches. Since, differently from most proposals, *MSR* allows specifying an arbitrary attacker using the same syntax as a regular protocol, we can provide an effective construction that shows that our formalization of the Dolev-Yao intruder can emulate the deeds of every adversary that satisfies the typing and data access policies of *MSR*.

The available tools designed to offer automated support to security protocol verification [Bra00,DM99,Low98,Mea96,Pau97,SS98,Son99] provide a limited array of static checks, often just type-checking for simple types. In particular, we are not aware of any proposal that enforces DAS. Moreover, while nearly all approaches rely on some variant of the Dolev-Yao intruder, we could not find a formal proof in the literature that this model indeed implements the most powerful symbolic attacker. Finally, it should be observed that our notion of data access specification is orthogonal to the insightful guidelines of [AN94,Syv97], aimed at constructing protocols that are immune by design to certain classes of attack.

Static checks on dependently typed specifications of security protocols have recently acquired popularity as a verification method for authentication properties [GJ02]. We believe our proposal, which relies on a more traditional use of dependent types for specification rather than verification purposes, is orthogonal to this effort, and could conceivably be integrated with it.

The main contributions of this paper are: 1) the definition of a decidable notion of DAS for *MSR* that is preserved by execution; 2) the formal definition of the concept of a generic symbolic attacker, based on DAS, and the formalization of the Dolev-Yao intruder; 3) a proof highlight that the Dolev-Yao intruder model can emulate an arbitrary attacker that satisfies the data access policy (the full proof can be found in [Cer]). This paper is about the specification of cryptographic protocols, not about protocol analysis.

This paper is structured as follows: in Section 2, we carefully recall the form of an *MSR* specification. Its DAS policy, a major novelty of this paper, and the relative decidability results are the subject of Section 3. In Section 4, we present the execution model of our framework and prove that it preserves access control. In Section 5, we formalize the Dolev-Yao intruder in *MSR* and in Section 6 we prove that it can emulate the actions of an arbitrary attacker. Section 7 hints at directions of future work.

2 MSR

In the past, cryptoprotocols have often been presented as the temporal sequence of messages being transmitted during a "normal" run. Recent proposals champion a view that places the involved parties in the foreground. A protocol is then a collection of independent *roles* that communicate by exchanging messages, without any reference to runs of any kind. A role has an owner, the principal that executes it, and specifies the sequence of messages that he/she will send, possibly in response to receiving messages of some expected form. *MSR* adopts and formalizes this perspective. A role is given as a parameterized collection of multiset rewrite rules that encode the expected message receptions and the corresponding transmission. An illustrative example can be found in Appendix A. Rule firing emulates receiving (and accepting) a message and/or sending a message. The messages in transit, the actions and information available to the roles, and other data constitute the state of execution of a protocol. Rules implement partial transformations between states. Their applicability is constrained by the contents of the current state. Execution is preceded by static type-checking [Cer01a] and DAS validation (see Section 3) which limits the number of run-time checks and allows catching common specification errors early.

2.1 Messages

Messages, or more properly *terms*, are obtained by applying a number of message forming constructs, discussed below, to a variety of *atomic messages*. The atomic messages we will consider in this paper are principal identifiers, keys, nonces, and raw data (*i.e.* information that have no other function in a protocol than to be transmitted):

$$
\textit{Atomic messages: } a ::= \mathsf{A} \ \textit{(Principal)}
$$
$$
| \ \mathsf{k} \ \textit{(Key)}
$$
$$
| \ \mathsf{n} \ \textit{(Nonce)}
$$
$$
| \ \mathsf{m} \ \textit{(Raw datum)}
$$

Although we will limit our discussion to these kinds of atomic messages, it should be noted that others can be accommodated by extending the appropriate definitions [Cer01b]. The *message constructors* we will consider are concatenation, shared-key encryption, and public-key encryption:

$$
\textit{Messages: } t ::= a \quad \textit{(Atomic messages)}
$$
$$
| \ x \quad \textit{(Variables)}
$$
$$
| \ t_1 \, t_2 \quad \textit{(Concatenation)}
$$
$$
| \ \{t\}_k \quad \textit{(Symmetric-key encryption)}
$$
$$
| \ \{\!\{t\}\!\}_k \quad \textit{(Asymmetric-key encryption)}
$$

Observe that we use a different syntax for shared-key and public-key encryption. We could have identified them, as done in many approaches. We choose instead to distinguish them to show the flexibility and precision of our technique. Again, other constructors, for example hash functions and digital signatures [Cer01b], can easily be accommodated by extending the appropriate definitions. Their inclusion would lengthen the discussion without introducing substantially new concepts.

A *parametric message* allows variables wherever terms could appear. We will write A (or B), k, n and m, variously decorated, for atomic constants or variables that are principals, keys, nonces and raw data, respectively. Whenever the object we want to refer to cannot be but a constant, we will use the corresponding seriffed letters: A (or B), k, n and m. Instead, the letters x, y and z will stand for terms that must be variable. Constants and variables constitute the class of *elementary terms*, denoted with the letter e. Finally, we write $[t/x]t'$ for the substitution of a variable x with a term t in another term t' [Cer00].

2.2 Message Predicates and States

States are a fundamental concept in *MSR*: they are the central constituent of the configurations of a protocol execution; they are the objects transformed by rewrite rules to simulate message exchange and information update; finally, together with execution traces, they are the hypothetical scenarios on which protocol analysis is based. A state is a finite collection of atomic first-order formulas called *message predicates i.e.* predicate symbols applied to an ordered sequence of terms:

$$\text{Message tuples } t ::= \cdot \quad \text{(Empty tuple)}$$
$$| \ t, \ t \ \text{(Tuple extension)}$$

Three kinds of predicates can enter a state or a rewrite rule: First, the predicate $N(\_)$ implements the contents of the *public network* in a distributed fashion: for each (ground) message t currently in transit, the state will contain a component of the form $N(t)$. Second, roles rely on a number of *role state predicates*, generally one for each of their rules, of the form $L_l(\_, \ldots, \_)$, where l is a unique identifying label. The arguments of this predicate record the value of known parameters of the execution of the role up to the current point. Third, a principal A can store data in private memory predicates of the form $M_A(\_, \ldots, \_)$ that survives role termination and can be used across the execution of different roles, as long as the principal stays the same. Memory predicates are useful in modeling situations that need to maintain data private across role executions: for example, they allow a principal to remember his Kerberos ticket [Cer01b], or the trusted-third-party of a fair exchange protocol to avoid fraudulent recoveries from aborted transactions. They are also used to encapsulate such entities as local clocks [Cer01b]. Finally, they allow an intruder to accumulate knowledge to be used in mounting attacks, as described in Section 5.

A *state* is a finite collection of ground message predicates, as formalized in the following grammar:

$$\text{States: } S ::= \cdot \qquad \text{(Empty state)}$$
$$| \ S, \ N(t) \quad \text{(Extension with a network predicate)}$$
$$| \ S, \ L_l(t) \quad \text{(Extension with a role state predicate)}$$
$$| \ S, \ M_A(t) \ \text{(Extension with a memory predicate)}$$

We interpret the extension construct "," as a multiset union operator, abstracting in this way from the order of the component predicates of a state.

Protocol rules transform states by removing a number of component predicates, and adding other, usually related, state elements. The antecedent and consequent of a rewrite rule embed therefore parametric substates whose variables are instantiated at application time. However, role state predicates need to be created on the spot in order to avoid interferences between concurrently executing role instances. We achieve this by introducing variables, denoted L, that are instantiated to actual role state predicates during execution.

2.3 Types

Typing is available in *MSR*, as in many languages, as a mechanism for abstracting away aspects of a specification considered too low-level. In the case of a protocol, we are abstracting the method by which a principal distinguishes objects of a different nature and categorizes them: for example field lengths, redundancy, database accesses, trusted subprotocols, etc. *MSR* offers simple yet powerful means to express this abstraction. However, it is ultimately the specifier who is in charge of laying out a sensible set of types for a protocol, and in particular to avoid the danger of over-abstraction.

The typing machinery of *MSR* [Cer01a] is based on the type-theoretic notion of *dependent product types with subsorting* [dG95,HHP93,AC96,Pfe93]. In this paper, we use the following types to classify terms:

$$
\begin{aligned}
\textit{Types: } \tau ::= \ & \text{principal } \textit{(Principals)} \\
& |\ \text{nonce} \quad \textit{(Nonces)} \\
& |\ \text{shK } A\ B\ \textit{(Shared keys)} \\
& |\ \text{pubK } A \quad \textit{(Public keys)} \\
& |\ \text{privK } k \quad \textit{(Private keys)} \\
& |\ \text{msg} \qquad \textit{(Messages)}
\end{aligned}
$$

The types "principal" and "nonce" classify principals and nonces, respectively. The next three productions allow distinguishing between shared keys, public keys and private keys. Dependent types offer a simple and flexible way to express the relations that hold between keys and their owner or other keys. A key "k" shared between principals "A" and "B" will have type "shK A B". Here, the type of the key *depends* on the specific principals "A" and "B". Similarly, a constant "k" is given type "pubK A" to indicate that it is a public key belonging to "A". We use dependent types again to express the relation between a public key and its inverse. Continuing with the last example, the inverse of "k" will have type "privK k".

We use the type msg to classify generic messages. Clearly raw data have type msg. This is however not sufficient since nonces, keys, and principal identifiers are routinely part of messages. We address this issue by imposing a *subsorting* relation between types, formalized by the judgment "$\tau :: \tau'$" (read τ *is a subsort of* τ'). In this paper, the subsorting relation will amount to having each of the types discussed above be a subtype of msg. Its extension can be found in Appendix B.

Again, the above types should be thought of as a reasonable instance of our approach rather than the approach itself. Other schemas can be specified by defining appropriate types and how they relate to each other. For example, digital signatures can be accommodated by introducing dedicated dependent types akin to "pubK A" and "privK k" [Cer01b]. An untyped setting is obtained by ascribing type msg to every entity. On the other hand, other applications may find convenient to define distinct types for long-term keys and have them not be a subsort of msg, prohibiting in this way the transmission of long-term secrets as parts of messages [Cer01a].

We use dependent Cartesian product types, here called *dependent type tuples*, to classify term tuples and consequently predicate symbols. These objects are defined as follows:

$$\text{Type tuples } \tau ::= \cdot \qquad \textit{(Empty tuple)}$$
$$\mid \tau^{(x)} \times \tau \textit{ (Type tuple extension)}$$

The notation $^{(x)}$ on the left of the Cartesian product symbol binds the variable x in the type tuple τ to its right. Dependencies allow capturing fine associations between arguments, such as between a principal and his/her own public key: for example the type tuple "principal$^{(A)} \times$ pubK A" will only classify pairs (A, k) where k is the public key of A. Given a dependent tuple type $\tau^{(x)} \times \tau$, we will drop the label $^{(x)}$ whenever the variable x does not occur (free) in τ. Examples of dependent tuples can be found in Appendix A.

Ground objects are type-checked against a *signature*, defined as a list of type declarations for atomic constants and memory and role state predicate symbols (the network predicate is hardwired in *MSR*):

$$\text{Signatures } \Sigma ::= \cdot \qquad \textit{(Empty signature)}$$
$$\mid \Sigma, a : \tau \quad \textit{(Atomic message declaration)}$$
$$\mid \Sigma, \mathsf{L}_l : \tau \quad \textit{(Local state predicate declaration)}$$
$$\mid \Sigma, \mathsf{M}_- : \tau \textit{ (Memory predicate declaration)}$$

Objects containing variables rely instead on a *typing context*, defined as a signature extended with declarations for variables and role state predicate parameters:

$$\text{Typing context } \Gamma ::= \Sigma \qquad \textit{(Plain signature)}$$
$$\mid \Gamma, x : \tau \textit{ (Variable declaration)}$$
$$\mid \Gamma, L : \tau \textit{ (Role state predicate parameter declaration)}$$

We assume that each object in a signature (or context) is declared exactly once. We promote "," to denote union. This operation is defined only if the resulting sequence does not contain multiple declaration for the same object.

The typing judgments and rules of *MSR* are thoroughly analyzed in [Cer01a] and summarized in Appendix B. In the sequel, we will make use of the typing judgments for terms "$\Sigma \vdash t : \tau$", signatures "$\vdash \Sigma$" and states "$\Sigma \vdash S$". Binary judgments "$\Sigma \vdash X$" will also be used for entities X still to be introduced, in particular rules, protocol theories, and active role sets. Type-checking *MSR* specifications has been proved decidable in [Cer01a].

2.4   Rules

Rules are the basic mechanism that enables the transformation of one state into another, and therefore the simulation of protocol execution: whenever the antecedent matches part of the current state, this portion may be substituted with the consequent (after some processing). Protocol rules are generally parametric so that the same rule can be used in a number of slightly different scenarios (*e.g.* without fixing interlocutors or nonces). Therefore a typical rule mentions variables that are instantiated to actual terms during execution. We introduce them by means of typed universal quantifiers:

$$Rule:\ r ::= lhs \rightarrow rhs\ \textit{(Rule core)}$$
$$|\ \forall x : \tau.\,r \quad \textit{(Parameter closure)}$$

Free variables can occur in the construction of a rule, but well-typed roles themselves have all their variables bound [Cer01a].

The *left-hand side*, or *antecedent*, of a rule is a finite collection of parametric message predicates:

$$Predicate\ sequences:\ lhs ::= \cdot \qquad\qquad \textit{(Empty predicate sequence)}$$
$$|\ lhs,\ \mathsf{N}(t) \quad \textit{(Extension with a network predicate)}$$
$$|\ lhs,\ \mathsf{L}(e) \quad \textit{(Extension with a role state predicate)}$$
$$|\ lhs,\ \mathsf{M}_A(t)\ \textit{(Extension with a memory predicate)}$$

Predicate sequences differ from states mainly by the limited instantiation of role state predicates: in a rule, these objects consist of a role state predicate variable applied to as many elementary terms as dictated by its type (this is enforced by the typing rules in [Cer01a]). Network and memory predicates will in general contain parametric terms, although not necessarily raw variables as arguments. An example involving network and role state predicates is given in Appendix A. In Section 5, we rely on memory predicates to model the intruder's knowledge. Other usages can be found in [Cer01b].

The *right-hand side*, or *consequent*, of a rule consists of a predicate sequence possibly prefixed by a finite string of fresh data declarations such as nonces or, in some applications, short-term keys. We rely on the existential quantification symbol to express data generation.

$$Right\text{-}Hand\ sides:\ rhs ::= lhs \qquad \textit{(Sequence of message predicates)}$$
$$|\ \exists x : \tau.\,rhs\ \textit{(Fresh data generation)}$$

We write $[t/x]rhs$ for the capture-free substitution of a term t for a variable x in the consequent rhs [Cer00]. We adopt a similar notation for rules and predicate sequences.

2.5   Roles and Protocol Theories

Role state predicates record information accessed by a rule. They are also the mechanism by which a rule can enable the execution of another rule in the same role. Relying on a fixed protocol-wide set of role state predicates is dangerous since it could cause unexpected interferences between different instances of a role executing at the same time. Instead, we make role state predicates local to a role by requiring that fresh names be used each time a new instance of a role is executed. As in the case of rule consequents, we achieve this effect by using existential quantifiers.

$$Rule\ collections:\ \rho ::= \cdot \qquad \textit{(Empty role)}$$
$$|\ \exists L : \tau.\,\rho\ \textit{(Role state predicate parameter declaration)}$$
$$|\ r, \rho \qquad \textit{(Extension with a rule)}$$

A *role* is given as the association between a *role owner* A and a collection of rules ρ. Some roles, such as those implementing a server or an intruder, are intrinsically bound to a few specific principals, often just one. We call them *anchored roles* and denote them as ρ^A. Here, the role owner A is an actual principal name, a constant. Other roles can be executed by any principal. These *generic roles* are denoted $\rho^{\forall A}$ where the implicitly typed universal quantification symbol implies that A should be instantiated to a principal before any rule in ρ is executed. We require that the owner of a role ρ be the first argument of all the role state predicates and be the subscript of every memory predicate in ρ. These constraints are formally expressed through the typing and DAS policy of *MSR*.

A *protocol theory*, written $\mathcal{P}$, is a finite collection of roles (see Section 5 and Appendix A for concrete examples):

$$
\begin{array}{llll}
\textit{Protocol theories: } \mathcal{P} ::= & \cdot & & \textit{(Empty protocol theory)} \\
& | & \mathcal{P}, \rho^{\forall A} & \textit{(Extension with a generic role)} \\
& | & \mathcal{P}, \rho^A & \textit{(Extension with an anchored role)}
\end{array}
$$

It should be observed that we do not make any special provision for the intruder. The adversary is expressed as a set of roles in the same way as proper protocols, as described in Section 5 for the standard Dolev-Yao intruder.

2.6   Active Roles

Several instances of a given role, possibly stopped at different rules, can be present at any moment during execution. We record the role instances currently in use, the point at which each is stopped, and the principal who is executing them in an *active role set*. These objects are finite collections of *active roles, i.e.* partially instantiated rule collections, each labeled with a principal name.

$$
\begin{array}{llll}
\textit{Active role sets: } R ::= & \cdot & & \textit{(Empty active role set)} \\
& | & R, \rho^A & \textit{(Extension with an instantiated role)}
\end{array}
$$

The notation ρ^A is reminiscent of anchored roles. Active roles are actually more liberal in that some of the role state predicate symbols as well as their arguments may be instantiated. Intuitively, ρ^A results from instantiating the contents of some role, with A is its elected owner.

3   Data Access Specification

Well-typing does not prevent a rule from looking up and using information its owner should not have access to. For example, the fact that principal A is initiating a session with B shall not allow him/her to access a key that B shares with a server. Similarly, A should not be able to access the memory predicates of any other party. The following role incorporates several violations of this kind:

$$
\left(
\begin{array}{l}
\forall B : \mathsf{principal}.\ k_B : \mathsf{pubK}\ B.\ k'_B : \mathsf{privK}\ k_B.\ k_{BS} : \mathsf{shK}\ B\ S.\ n : \mathsf{nonce}. \\
\mathsf{N}(\{\!\{n\}\!\}_{k_B}) \longrightarrow \mathsf{N}(\{n\}_{k_{BS}}),\ \mathsf{M}_B(n)
\end{array}
\right)^{\forall A}
$$

In this section, we will use the typing declarations of *MSR* to formalize and implement these and other requirements by means of statically checkable *data access specification* (*DAS* for short) judgments. We shall assume that all the expressions we will be analyzing are well-typed. We will start with the presentation of DAS for macroscopic objects such as protocol theories and roles, and only later describe how it is enforced on their components. Therefore, the premises of inference rules will sometimes mention a judgment that has not yet been defined. We mark such occurrences by enclosing them in a gray box and always give abundant explanations. We ask the reader to ignore the boxed text that follows most rules in this section. We will interpret it in Section 6.

3.1   Protocol Theories and Roles

The judgment "$\Sigma \Vdash \mathcal{P}$" expresses the fact that a protocol theory $\mathcal{P}$ realizes correct DAS with respect to a signature Σ. It is implemented by the following three inference rules (in structured operational semantics style), corresponding to the three productions in the syntax of a protocol theory. The right-hand premise of rules has_grole and has_arole invoke the DAS judgment "$\Gamma \Vdash_A \rho$" for rule collections, that will be introduced shortly.

$$\frac{}{\Sigma \Vdash \cdot} \ \text{has\_dot}$$

$$\frac{\Sigma \Vdash \mathcal{P} \quad (\Sigma, A : \text{principal}) \Vdash_A \rho}{\Sigma \Vdash \mathcal{P}, \rho^{\forall A}} \ \text{has\_grole} \qquad \frac{\Sigma \Vdash \mathcal{P} \quad \Sigma \Vdash_A \rho}{\Sigma \Vdash \mathcal{P}, \rho^A} \ \text{has\_arole}$$

The central rule, which applies to generic roles, pushes the declaration for the role owner A in Σ, with the effect of invoking its right-hand premise with a typing context. Rule has_arole deals with anchored roles; since we are working under the assumption that all expressions are well-typed, we do not check that A is has type principal.

Since DAS is about what information the owner of a role is entitled to access, it should come at no surprise that the judgments that operate on rule collections and their components have a principal as a distinguished parameter. We first see this in the rule collection DAS judgment "$\Gamma \Vdash_A \rho$", where A is the owner of ρ: It is implemented by the following syntax-directed rules:

$$\frac{}{\Gamma \Vdash_A \cdot} \ \text{oas\_dot} \ \boxed{\cdot}$$

$$\frac{(\Gamma, L : \tau) \Vdash_A \rho}{\Gamma \Vdash_A \exists L : \tau. \rho} \ \text{oas\_rsp} \ \boxed{\cdot} \qquad \frac{\Gamma \Vdash_A r \quad \Gamma \Vdash_A \rho}{\Gamma \Vdash_A r, \rho} \ \text{oas\_rule} \ \boxed{\cdot}$$

Rule oas_rsp collects the declaration of an existentially quantified role in the context and verifies its body. We rely on implicit α-conversion to rename L in case a parameter with the same name is already declared in Γ. The rightmost inference rule, oas_rule, implements the situation where a collection starts with a rule r. Its left premise validates r itself by means of the DAS judgment for rules, "$\Gamma \Vdash_A r$".

The judgment "$\Gamma \Vdash_A r$" expresses DAS-validity for rules. It is implemented by the following two rules:

$$\frac{\Gamma; \cdot \Vdash_A lhs > \cdot \gg \Delta \quad \Gamma; \Delta \Vdash_A rhs}{\Gamma \Vdash_A lhs \to rhs} \; \text{uas\_core} \; \boxed{\cdot} \qquad \frac{(\Gamma, x : \tau) \Vdash_A r}{\Gamma \Vdash_A \forall x : \tau. r} \; \text{uas\_all} \; \boxed{\cdot}$$

Intuitively, the judgment in the left premise of rule uas_core, "$\Gamma; \cdot \Vdash_A lhs > \cdot \gg \Delta$", collects the data, t say, the rule owner A is given in the left-hand side lhs. This includes network messages and previously gathered information stored in memory or role state predicates. This judgment also produces the knowledge context Δ (defined shortly), which contains information that A can reasonably deduce from t and later use in the right-hand side. Since it contains information about which key belongs to whom, etc., the context Γ plays an important role in deciding what can legitimately enter Δ. This judgment and its realization are the topic of Section 3.2. Informally, the judgment on the right premise of this rule, "$\Gamma; \Delta \Vdash_A rhs$" uses the knowledge Δ produced by analyzing the antecedent to verify that A can construct all the messages mentioned in the right-hand side rhs. This judgment and the inference rules implementing it are the subject of Section 3.3.

We conclude this section by introducing the notion of *knowledge context*, often simply referred to as *knowledge*. These entities collect the information known to the owner of a rule during DAS-validation. Knowledge is deduced by means of simple inferences from data stored in role state or memory predicates, and messages received from the network. The knowledge context of a rule consists of atomic constants or variables only. Active role sets additionally allow ground terms (obtained by instantiating variables).

> *Knowledge contexts:* $\Delta ::= \cdot$ *(Empty knowledge context)*
> $\quad | \; \Delta, a$ *(Extension with atomic knowledge)*
> $\quad | \; \Delta, x$ *(Extension with parametric knowledge)*
> $\quad | \; \Delta, t$ *(Extension with ground terms)*

We will ignore the last production until Section 3.4, where DAS for active roles is discussed. It is convenient to view knowledge contexts as multisets. A knowledge context Δ is said to be *compatible* with a signature Σ if for each term t in Δ, there is a type τ such that $\Sigma \vdash \tau$ and $\Sigma \vdash t : \tau$.

3.2   Accessing Information in the Left-Hand Side

The left-hand side of a rule gathers the information necessary for constructing the messages transmitted or stored in the consequent. The information in the left-hand side of a rule r consists of the arguments of the role state predicates and the data embedded in the messages received from the network or retrieved from memory predicates. We will now take an informal look at each of these sources:

- The arguments $e = (e_1, \ldots, e_n)$ of a role state predicate L represent data passed to a rule from its logical predecessor. The owner of r, call him/her A, knows this information because he/she has put it there. These elementary symbols will generally stand for principal names, keys, or nonces, but variables may also represent complex terms whose inner values A cannot or does not need to access (*e.g.* a message encrypted with a key he/she does not know) [Cer01a]. For example, even if it is clear from the protocol at hand that the variable e_3 can only be substituted with a term of the form $\{y\}_k$, it cannot be used to access y, even if e_7 is precisely k. (This form of delayed message interpretation can easily be realized using memory predicates.)

- The term t in an incoming network message $N(t)$ will generally consist of a number of operators applied to variables (in rare occasions to constants). Some of the associated values are expected to match previously known data (*e.g.* a nonce coming back in response to a challenge), and will be represented by variables listed in a role state predicate. Others will be unknown (*e.g.* a nonce generated by an interlocutor) and shall be bound to previously unused variables. The goal of DAS is to make sure that A has legitimate rights to access this information.

- Finally, A can retrieve previously stored information from a memory predicate $M_A(t)$. As for network messages, each term in t may consist of a series of constructors applied to variables. Again, writing an argument in this way means accessing the subcomponents corresponding to each constant or variable, with the option of using them in the right-hand side. Observe that the fact that A generated $M_A(t)$ does not automatically grant him/her access to the submessages of t. For example, the third argument t_3 may have the form $\{t\}_k$: A is entitled to access t only if he/she is in possession of the private key corresponding to k.

In this section, we will ultimately devise a procedure that certifies that A is entitled to access all the elementary terms mentioned in the antecedent of a rule r. This proceeds in two phases: first we collect the arguments of all the predicates in the left-hand side of r, and then break the composite messages gathered in this way into their elementary components.

The judgment "$\Gamma; \Delta \Vdash_A lhs > t \gg \Delta'$" collects the arguments of the predicates in the left-hand side of a rule. Its meta-variables are interpreted as follows: A is the owner of the rule r whose left-hand side we are analyzing. Γ is the typing context of r. The predicate sequence lhs is the portion of the antecedent of r that has still to be examined. The terms t are the arguments that have been gathered so far and that may need further processing. The *input knowledge* Δ lists collected arguments that are known to be elementary. Finally, the *output knowledge* Δ' stands for the elementary information that will ultimately be extracted from r's left-hand side. It is convenient to interpret this judgment operationally as a partial function that given A, Γ, lhs, t and Δ computes a value for Δ' if the DAS policy is obeyed. We shall interpret t as a multiset. As we start processing the antecedent of a rule in rule uas_core, Δ and t are empty (written "·") as no argument has yet been collected.

Our first rule describes how a role state predicate $L(A, e)$ is processed. Remember that, by definition, L is a parameter, its first argument A is a principal name, and the terms (A, e) must be either constants or variables. Therefore, each object among (A, e) is an elementary piece of information. We can therefore merge (A, e) into the current input knowledge context Δ and use the resulting knowledge context Δ' to analyze the remaining predicates lhs. We have the following rule, which makes use of the merge judgment "$\Delta > e > \Delta'''$", whose simple realization is given in Appendix C.

$$\frac{\Delta > (A,e) > \Delta' \quad \Gamma; \Delta' \Vdash_A lhs > t' \gg \Delta''}{\Gamma; \Delta \Vdash_A (L(A,e), lhs) > t' \gg \Delta''} \; \text{las\_rsp}^{\sharp} \; \boxed{\cdot}$$

We next turn to network and memory predicates in the antecedent of a rule. Since the messages in their arguments may not be elementary, we shall include them in the list of unprocessed arguments t' before examining the remaining predicates lhs. Only memory predicates belonging to A are accepted.

$$\frac{\Gamma; \Delta \Vdash_A lhs > (t, t') \gg \Delta''}{\Gamma; \Delta \Vdash_A (N(t), lhs) > t' \gg \Delta''} \; \text{las\_net} \; \boxed{\text{INT}}$$

$$\frac{\Gamma; \Delta \Vdash_A lhs > (t, t') \gg \Delta'}{\Gamma; \Delta \Vdash_A (M_A(t), lhs) > t' \gg \Delta'} \; \text{las\_mem} \; \boxed{\cdot}$$

Once the arguments of all the predicates on the left-hand side of the rule have been collected, we move to the second phase which ascertains that the uninterpreted terms t satisfy the DAS policy. This is done in the following rule by invoking the judgment "$\Gamma; \Delta \Vdash_A t \gg \Delta'''$", discussed below.

$$\frac{\Gamma; \Delta \Vdash_A t \gg \Delta'}{\Gamma; \Delta \Vdash_A \cdot > t \gg \Delta'} \; \text{las\_dot} \; \boxed{\cdot}$$

The judgment "$\Gamma; \Delta \Vdash_A t \gg \Delta'''$", used in rule las_dot, examines possibly composite terms. The interpretation of its meta-variable is inherited from the argument collection judgment above. Again, this judgment can be seen as a partial function that computes a value for Δ' when given A, Γ, Δ and t. It should be observed that A does have legitimate access to each term in t: we want to verify that this property extends to their subterms.

Our first two rules deal with unchecked elementary messages e. There are two possibilities: either e is known and therefore appears in the current input knowledge, or it must be looked up in the typing context Γ.

$$\frac{\Gamma; (\Delta, e) \Vdash_A t \gg \Delta'}{\Gamma; (\Delta, e) \Vdash_A e, t \gg \Delta'} \; \text{tas\_kn}^{\sharp} \; \boxed{\text{DEL}} \qquad \frac{(\Gamma, e : \tau, \Gamma'); (\Delta, e) \Vdash_A t \gg \Delta'}{(\Gamma, e : \tau, \Gamma'); \Delta \Vdash_A e, t \gg \Delta'} \; \text{tas\_ukn} \; \boxed{\cdot}$$

The rule owner A can access the cleartext t of an encrypted message $\{t\}_k$ (or $\{\!\{t\}\!\}_k$) only if he/she is entitled to access the decryption key corresponding to k. This is ascertained by the left premises of the following rules. The judgment $\Gamma; \Delta \Vdash^{\mathsf{e}}_A k \gg \Delta'$ (resp. $\Gamma; \Delta \Vdash^{\mathsf{a}}_A k \gg \Delta'$) verifies that A can access k (resp. its inverse) and if necessary updates the knowledge context Δ to Δ'. Once the key has been resolved, the cleartext t is put back in the pool of pending messages, which is recursively analyzed in the rightmost premise.

$$\frac{\Gamma; \Delta \Vdash^{\mathsf{e}}_A k \gg \Delta' \quad \Gamma; \Delta' \Vdash_A t, t \gg \Delta''}{\Gamma; \Delta \Vdash_A \{t\}_k, t \gg \Delta''} \; \text{tas\_ske} \; \boxed{\text{SDC}}$$

$$\frac{\Gamma;\Delta \; \Vdash^{p}_{A} \; k \gg \Delta' \quad \Gamma;\Delta' \; \Vdash_{A} \; t, t \gg \Delta''}{\Gamma;\Delta \; \Vdash_{A} \; \{t\}_{k}, t \gg \Delta''} \quad \text{tas\_pke} \; \boxed{\text{PDC}}$$

Concatenated messages can be split unconditionally before recursively analyzing their submessages. Once all possibly composite terms have been reduced to their elementary constituents (and have been shown to respect the DAS policy), we simply return the accumulated input knowledge context as the output knowledge.

$$\frac{\Gamma;\Delta \; \Vdash_{A} \; t_1, t_2, t \gg \Delta'}{\Gamma;\Delta \; \Vdash_{A} \; (t_1 \; t_2), t \gg \Delta'} \quad \text{tas\_cnc} \; \boxed{\text{DCM}} \qquad\qquad \frac{}{\Gamma;\Delta \; \Vdash_{A} \; \cdot \gg \Delta} \quad \text{tas\_dot} \; \boxed{\cdot}$$

We conclude the treatment of the left-hand side of a rule by devising a method to establish when the owner of a rule can decipher (and therefore access) a message encrypted with a key k. Since we assumed in Section 2 to have two kinds of encryption operations (shared-key and public-key), we will present two judgments and the relative rules. It should be noted that richer schemes, *e.g.* including digital signatures or a more refined key taxonomy, would need to define additional judgments and to provide the corresponding DAS rules.

We express the fact that the owner A of a rule can access the cleartext t of a message $\{t\}_k$ encrypted with a shared key k by means of the judgment "$\Gamma;\Delta \; \Vdash^{s}_{A} \; k \gg \Delta'$", where Γ, Δ and Δ' are the typing context, and the input and output knowledge respectively. Again, Δ' is computed from the other entities in this relation. In order for A to decrypt $\{t\}_k$, he/she must have access to k itself since we are in a symmetric-key setting. There are two scenarios to analyze in order to decide this judgment. First, A may know k, for example if it was previously transmitted in the clear. Then, k can be found in the input knowledge context.

$$\frac{}{\Gamma;(\Delta, k) \; \Vdash^{s}_{A} \; k \gg (\Delta, k)} \quad \text{kas\_ss} \; \boxed{\text{DUP}}$$

The second scenario involves a key A does not know (yet) about, but to which he/she has legitimate access. A principal has the right to access a shared key only if this key was intended to communicate with him/her:

$$\frac{}{(\Gamma, k : \text{shK} \; A \; B, \Gamma');\Delta \; \Vdash^{s}_{A} \; k \gg (\Delta, k)} \quad \text{kas\_su1} \; \boxed{\text{IS1}}$$

$$\frac{}{(\Gamma, k : \text{shK} \; B \; A, \Gamma');\Delta \; \Vdash^{s}_{A} \; k \gg (\Delta, k)} \quad \text{kas\_su2} \; \boxed{\text{IS2}}$$

Observe that the relationship between the key owner and the rule owner is encoded in the dependent type that qualifies the key itself. Since k was unknown to A but is being accessed, we include it among the output knowledge of these rules.

The judgment "$\Gamma;\Delta \; \Vdash^{p}_{A} \; k \gg \Delta'$" expresses the similar relation concerning public-key encryption, where the meaning of the meta-variables is as for symmetric keys. In order to decipher a message encrypted with a public key k, we must have access to the corresponding private key, call it k'. As for shared keys, the first place where to look is the current knowledge context. If the private key k' of some principal B has previously been encountered, then we can decipher transmissions encoded with the corresponding public key k.

$$\frac{}{(\Gamma, k : \mathsf{pubK}\, B, \Gamma', k' : \mathsf{privK}\, k, \Gamma''); (\Delta, k')\ \Vvdash^a_A\ k \gg (\Delta, k')} \quad \text{kas\_pus}\ \boxed{\text{DUP}}$$

If A does not know k', then he/she is entitled to access the cleartext of the encrypted message $\{\!|t|\!\}_k$ only if he/she owns k:

$$\frac{}{(\Gamma, k : \mathsf{pubK}\, A, \Gamma', k' : \mathsf{privK}\, k, \Gamma''); \Delta\ \Vvdash^a_A\ k \gg (\Delta, k')} \quad \text{kas\_puu}\ \boxed{\text{IPV, DUP}}$$

3.3   Processing Information in the Right-Hand Side

The right-hand side of a rule is where messages are constructed, either to be emitted over the public network, or stored for future use. However, the first rule of an initiator role will generally have an empty left-hand side, and yet it can send complex messages in its consequent. Therefore, the right-hand side of a rule can also access data on its own, information that is not mentioned in its antecedent. This can happen in two ways: first by generating fresh data (*e.g.* nonces), and second by using information that is "out there" (*e.g.* the name of an interlocutor, or a key shared with him/her). Both alternatives have the potential of violating the DAS policy (*e.g.* when trying to access the private key of a third party).

DAS on the right-hand side rhs of a rule r is expressed by the judgment: "$\Gamma; \Delta \Vdash_A rhs$", where A is the owner of r, Γ is its typing context, and Δ is the knowledge gained by examining its antecedent, it is implemented by rules whose number depends on the intended application of the protocol at hand. Given a consequent of the form "$\exists x : \tau. rhs$". It is tempting to indiscriminately add x to the current knowledge context and proceed with the validation of rhs. This is in general inappropriate since it would allow any principal to construct information that can potentially affect the rest of the system. In most protocols, nobody should be allowed to create new principals. Similarly, only key-distribution protocols should enable a principal to create keys, and typically only short-term keys. On the other hand, principals will generally be allowed to generate nonces and atomic messages (*e.g.* an intruder may want to fake a credit card number). These considerations produce a family of rewrite rules that differ only by the type of the existential declaration they consider. In all cases, we recursively check the body rhs after inserting "$x : \tau$" in the context (for appropriate τ's) and adding x to the current knowledge:

$$\frac{(\Gamma, x : \mathsf{nonce}); (\Delta, x)\ \Vdash_A\ rhs}{\Gamma; \Delta\ \Vdash_A\ \exists x : \mathsf{nonce}.\, rhs}\ \text{ras\_nnc}\ \boxed{\text{GNC}} \qquad \frac{(\Gamma, x : \mathsf{msg}); (\Delta, x)\ \Vdash_A\ rhs}{\Gamma; \Delta\ \Vdash_A\ \exists x : \mathsf{msg}.\, rhs}\ \text{ras\_msg}\ \boxed{\text{GMS}}$$

$$\frac{\Gamma; \Delta\ \leftrightsquigarrow_A\ lhs}{\Gamma; \Delta\ \Vdash_A\ lhs}\ \text{ras\_ps}\ \boxed{\cdot}$$

We must emphasize again that the exact set of rules for data generation depends on the intended functionalities of the protocol. Rule **ras_ps** invokes the predicate sequence validation judgment "$\Gamma; \Delta \nrightarrow_A$ *lhs*", discussed shortly, to verify that the inner core *lhs* of the rule's consequent satisfies DAS.

The premises of rule ras_ps above included the judgment "$\Gamma; \Delta \nrightarrow_A$ *lhs*" which verifies that all the messages in the predicate sequence *lhs* can be constructed in the current rule. It is implemented by the following rules. When *lhs* is not empty, we rely on the term constructions judgments "$\Delta \nrightarrow t$" and "$\Delta \nrightarrow t$" that will be explained shortly.

$$\frac{}{\Gamma; \Delta \nrightarrow_A \cdot} \text{ ras\_dot } \boxed{\text{DEL}(\Delta)} \qquad \frac{\Gamma; \Delta \nrightarrow_A t \quad \Gamma; \Delta \nrightarrow_A lhs}{\Gamma; \Delta \nrightarrow_A \mathsf{N}(t), lhs} \text{ ras\_net } \boxed{\text{DUP}(\Delta), \text{TRN}}$$

$$\frac{\Gamma; \Delta \nrightarrow_A t \quad \Gamma; \Delta \nrightarrow_A lhs}{\Gamma; \Delta \nrightarrow_A \mathsf{M}_A(t), lhs} \text{ ras\_mem } \boxed{\text{DUP}(\Delta)}$$

$$\frac{\Gamma; \Delta \nrightarrow_A (A,e) \quad \Gamma; \Delta \nrightarrow_A lhs}{\Gamma; \Delta \nrightarrow_A \mathsf{L}(A,e), lhs} \text{ ras\_rsp}^{\sharp} \boxed{\text{DUP}(\Delta)}$$

Empty predicate sequences are always valid. Moreover, a principal A is allowed to publish any information he/she can construct on the public network, but he/she shall be able to update only his/her own role state and memory predicates.

The constructibility of a term t in the right-hand side of a rule is expressed by the judgment "$\Gamma; \Delta \nrightarrow_A t$". Elementary information appearing in a rule consequent can come from of two sources: rule cas_kn handles the case where it has been collected in the knowledge context while validating the antecedent and fresh data declarations of a rule. This can also be the first appearance of this information in the rule, in which case we must verify that the role owner is effectively entitled to access it. This achieved in rule cas_ukn through the right-hand side access judgment "$\Gamma \nrightarrow_A e$", discussed below.

$$\frac{}{\Gamma; (\Delta, e) \nrightarrow_A e} \text{ cas\_kn}^{\sharp} \boxed{\text{DEL}(\Delta)} \qquad \frac{\Gamma \nrightarrow_A e}{\Gamma; \Delta \nrightarrow_A e} \text{ cas\_ukn } \boxed{\text{DEL}(\Delta)}$$

The simple rules implementing composite terms can be found in Appendix C, together with the implementation of the judgment "$\Gamma; \Delta \nrightarrow_A t$" that allows constructing message tuples t from the knowledge Δ at hand.

We conclude this section by describing the judgment "$\Gamma \nrightarrow_A e$" that checks that a rule owner A has legitimate access to elementary data e that appear only in the rule consequent. Its implementation depends entirely on the atomic data that can be part of a message and therefore on the types that have been defined to classify them. We will now present inference rules relative to the types defined in Section 2, but it should be clear that different type layouts will require different rules.

Let us start with non-dependent types. We should clearly be able to access any principal name:

$$\frac{}{(\Gamma, e : \text{principal}, \Gamma') \nrightarrow_A e} \text{ eas\_pr } \boxed{\text{IPR}}$$

The remaining simple types are nonce and msg. Were we to have a rule similar to eas_pr for nonces would allow A to access any nonce in the system, including nonces that he/she has not generated. This is clearly undesirable. The only nonces A is entitled to access are the ones he/she has created and the ones he/she has retrieved in received messages or as previously stored data. In all these cases, these nonces are included in some knowledge context. A similar argument applies to elementary objects of type msg: a rule akin to eas_pr would give A access to any message that can be constructed in the system, when invoked with a variable. This is particularly undesirable since msg is a supersort of all our types (see Section 2.3).

Next, we consider keys: A should have free access to all of his/her shared keys, but not to others; similarly, A has legitimate access to his/her private keys, and to the public keys of any principal.

$$\frac{}{(\Gamma, e : \text{shK } A\, B, \Gamma') \looparrowright_A e} \;\text{eas\_s1}\; \boxed{\text{IS1}} \qquad \frac{}{(\Gamma, e : \text{shK } B\, A, \Gamma') \looparrowright_A e} \;\text{eas\_s2}\; \boxed{\text{IS2}}$$

$$\frac{}{(\Gamma, e : \text{privK } k, \Gamma', k : \text{pubK } A, \Gamma'') \looparrowright_A e} \;\text{eas\_pp}\; \boxed{\text{IPV}}$$

$$\frac{}{(\Gamma, e : \text{pubK } B, \Gamma') \looparrowright_A e} \;\text{eas\_p}\; \boxed{\text{IPB}}$$

It should be observed that protocols that make use of a key distribution center should not rely on these rules. These kinds of protocols require a language and type layout that is more elaborate than the one in our running example.

3.4   Active Roles

In Section 2.6 we defined an active role as a role suffix whose free variables have been instantiated to ground terms. They correspond to roles in the midst of execution. Active roles should clearly be subject to the same access constraints as protocol theories. They are handled by allowing ground terms anywhere variables can appear in a role, and by treating them in the same way. Formally, for every of the above rules that look up or store (elementary) information in an active role set, we introduce a variant that performs the same operation on a ground term. The affected rules are marked with the symbol $\sharp$ in the above discussion and in Appendix C. Furthermore, since execution may instantiate a role state predicate parameter L with a constant L_l, we need additional variants of rules las_rsp and ras_rsp.

The judgment "$\Sigma \Vdash R$" expresses the fact that an active role set R satisfies our DAS policy in signature Σ. It is implemented by the following two simple rules:

$$\frac{}{\Sigma \Vdash \cdot} \;\text{aas\_dot}\; \boxed{\cdot} \qquad\qquad \frac{\Sigma \Vdash R \quad \Sigma \Vdash_A \rho}{\Sigma \Vdash R, \rho^A} \;\text{aas\_ext}\; \boxed{\rho^A \;\text{if } A \neq l}$$

3.5   Decidability of DAS

All the judgments presented in this section have decidable implementations. Furthermore, the ones to which we have ascribed a functional behavior implement computable relations. For space reasons, we only give a sketch of the argument underlying this result and a condensed statement relative to protocol theories and active role sets only. A detailed proof of this statement for each of these judgments can be found in [Cer].

Property 1. Given a signature Σ, a protocol theory $\mathcal{P}$ and an active role set R, it is decidable whether the judgments $\Sigma \Vdash \mathcal{P}$ and $\Sigma \Vdash R$ hold.

Proof: All DAS rules are syntax-directed and, with the exception of **uas_core**, **las_rsp** (and variants), **tas_ske** and **tas_pke**, none contains meta-variables in its premises that are not also mentioned in its conclusion. The leftmost premise of each of these rules is a left-hand side judgment J that produces an output knowledge context Δ' (the one meta-variable that does not appear in their conclusion). Thus, we reduce our decidability result to proving that there are only finitely many such Δ' for which J is derivable, assuming all other parameters fixed. A close inspection of the DAS rules reveals a number of pairs of rules (for example **tas_ukn** and **tas_kn**) that may both apply in certain situations, and therefore have J succeed with two output knowledge contexts. In the worst case, the number of output knowledge contexts is exponential (but finite) in the number of symbols appearing in the other parts of J. $\square$

When validating rules, alternative output knowledge contexts are identical up to the duplication of data. On the basis of this observation, we claim that DAS can be implemented with a complexity linear in the number of elementary terms in a rule. This argument extends to active role sets by prioritizing rules that look information up in the current knowledge context (*e.g.* **tas_kn**).

4   Execution Model

Execution is concerned with the use of a protocol theory to move from a situation described by a state S to another situation modeled by a state S'. Referring to the situation that the execution of a protocol has reached by means of a state is an oversimplification. Indeed, execution operates on *configurations* $[S]^R_\Sigma$ consisting of a state S, an active role set R and a signature Σ: R records the roles that can be used in order to continue the execution, at which point they were stopped, and how they were instantiated, while Σ is needed to ensure that variable instantiation is well-typed. No element in a configuration contains free variables. Configurations will be indicated with the letter C.

Given a protocol $\mathcal{P}$, we describe the fact that execution transforms a configuration C into C' in one step by means of the judgment "$\mathcal{P} \rhd C \longrightarrow C'$". The next two rules specify how to extend the current active role set R with a role from $\mathcal{P}$.

$$\frac{}{(\mathcal{P}, \rho^A) \rhd [S]^R_\Sigma \longrightarrow [S]^{R,\rho^A}_\Sigma} \text{ ex\_arole} \qquad \frac{\Sigma \vdash A : \text{principal}}{(\mathcal{P}, \rho^{\forall A}) \rhd [S]^R_\Sigma \longrightarrow [S]^{R,([A/A]\rho)^A}_\Sigma} \text{ ex\_grole}$$

Anchored roles are simply copied to the current active role sets since their syntax meets the requirements for active roles. We instead make a generic role available for execution in rule **ex_grole** by assigning it an owner. The typing judgment in its premise makes sure that A is defined as a principal name.

Once a role has been activated, chances are that it contains role state predicate parameter declarations that require to be instantiated with actual constants before any of the embedded rules can be applied. In rule ex_rsp, L_l shall be a new symbol that appears nowhere in the current configuration (in particular it should not occur in Σ).

$$\frac{}{\mathcal{P} \triangleright [S]_{\Sigma}^{R,(\exists L:\tau.\,\rho)^A} \longrightarrow [S]_{(\Sigma,L_l:\tau)}^{R,([L_l/L]\rho)^A}} \text{ ex\_rsp}$$

$$\frac{\Sigma \vdash t : \tau}{\mathcal{P} \triangleright [S]_{\Sigma}^{R,((\forall x:\tau.\,r),\rho)^A} \longrightarrow [S]_{\Sigma}^{R,(([t/x]r),\rho)^A}} \text{ ex\_all}$$

Rule ex_all instantiates the universal variables that may appear in a rule. The attentive reader may be concerned by the fact that the construction of the instantiating term t is not guided by the contents of the state S. This is a legitimate observation: the rule above provides an idealized model of the execution rather than the basis for the implementation of an actual simulator. An operational model suited for implementation is the subject of current research. It should also be observed that the premise of ex_all describes A's acceptance of t as a term of type τ. How this happens is kept abstract, but it should correspond to some lower level mechanism to adequately express the protocol at hand.

We now consider execution steps resulting from the application of a fully instantiated rule $(lhs \rightarrow rhs)$ from the current active role set R. The antecedent lhs must be ground and therefore it has the structure of a legal state. This rules identifies lhs in the current state and replaces it with a substate lhs' derived from the consequent rhs by instantiating its existential variables with fresh constants of the appropriate type. This latter operation is performed in the premise of this rule by the right-hand side instantiation judgment "$(rhs)_{\Sigma} \gg (lhs')_{\Sigma'}$", whose implementation is given in Appendix C.

$$\frac{(rhs)_{\Sigma} \gg (lhs')_{\Sigma'}}{\mathcal{P} \triangleright [S, lhs]_{\Sigma}^{R,((lhs \rightarrow rhs),\rho)^A} \longrightarrow [S, lhs']_{\Sigma'}^{R,(\rho)^A}} \text{ ex\_core}$$

Security protocols often allow various forms of branching. In a protocol theory, the control structure is mostly realized by the role state predicates appearing in a role. Branching can indeed be modeled by having two rules share the same role state predicate parameter in their left-hand side. Roles, on the other hand, are defined as a linear collection of rules. Therefore, in order to access alternative role continuations, we may need to *skip* a rule, *i.e.* discard it and continue with the rest of the specification.

$$\frac{}{\mathcal{P} \triangleright [S]_{\Sigma}^{R,(r,\rho)^A} \longrightarrow [S]_{\Sigma}^{R,(\rho)^A}} \text{ ex\_skp} \qquad \frac{}{\mathcal{P} \triangleright [S]_{\Sigma}^{R,(\cdot)^A} \longrightarrow [S]_{\Sigma}^{R}} \text{ ex\_dot}$$

Rule ex_dot does some housekeeping by throwing away active roles that have been completely executed.

The judgment "$\mathcal{P} \triangleright C \longrightarrow^* C'''$" allow chaining atomic transitions into multi-step firings. It is defined in Appendix C as the reflexive and transitive closure of the above one-step relation. A parallel version of this judgment has been defined in [Cer00]. Moreover, we have proved in [Cer01a] that well-typing is preserved by execution, *i.e.*

that when starting from well-typed objects firing will always produce well-typed entities (a detailed proof can be found in [Cer]).

A similar result applies to DAS. Indeed, the DAS Preservation Theorem below states that, under reasonable typing assumptions, no execution sequence can take a configuration that satisfies the DAS policy to a situation that violates it. In particular, instantiating variables cannot invalidate DAS.

Theorem 1. (*DAS Preservation*)

Let P be a protocol theory, Σ and Σ' signatures, R and R' active role sets, and S and S' states such that $\vdash \Sigma$, $\Sigma \vdash P$, $\Sigma \vdash R$, $\Sigma \Vdash P$ and $\Sigma \Vdash R$. If

$$P \triangleright [S]_{\Sigma}^{R} \longrightarrow^* [S']_{\Sigma'}^{R'},$$

then the judgments $\Sigma' \Vdash P$ and $\Sigma' \Vdash R'$ are derivable.

Proof: The proof proceeds by induction on a derivation of the given execution judgment. Rules ex_rsp and ex_core rely on a *Weakening Lemma* that allows extending the signature of an DAS judgment without affecting its derivability. Rules ex_grole and ex_all make use of *Substitution Lemma* that states that DAS is preserved under substitution, assuming some simple preconditions are met. □

Because of its passive role, the state S is not required to be well typed for this result to hold, although applications will generally operate on well-typed states. This theorem and the fact that the execution rules do not depend on any DAS judgment makes DAS verification a purely static check.

5   The Dolev-Yao Intruder

The *Dolev-Yao abstraction* [DY83,NS78] assumes that elementary data such as principal names, keys and nonces are atomic symbols rather than the bit-strings implemented in practice. Furthermore, it views the operations needed to assemble messages, *i.e.* concatenation and encryption, as pure constructors in an initial algebra. Therefore, for example, a term of the form $\{t\}_k$ cannot be mistaken for a concatenation $(t_1\ t_2)$, and $\{t\}_k = \{t'\}_{k'}$ if and only if $t = t'$ and $k = k'$. This also means that the Dolev-Yao model abstracts away the details of the cryptographic algorithms in use, reducing in this way encryption and decryption to atomic operations. Indeed, it is often said to adopt a *black box* view on cryptography.

The atomicity and initiality of the Dolev-Yao abstraction limits considerably the attacks that can be mounted against a protocol. In particular, its idealized encryption model makes it immune to any form of crypto-analysis: keys cannot be exhaustively searched, piecewise inferred from observed traffic, or guessed in any other manner. An encrypted message can be deciphered only when in possession of the appropriate key. The symbolic nature of this abstraction allows then to very precisely circumscribe the operations an intruder has at his disposal to attack a protocol. All together, they define what has become to be known as the *Dolev-Yao intruder*. This attacker can do any combination of the following eight operations:

1. Intercept and learn messages.
2. Transmit known messages.
3. Decompose concatenated messages.
4. Concatenate known messages.
5. Decipher encrypted messages if he knows the keys.
6. Encrypt known messages with known keys.
7. Access public information.
8. Generate fresh data.

MSR, like most current systems geared toward specifying security protocol, is an instance of the the Dolev-Yao abstraction. Elementary data are indeed atomic, messages are constructed by applying symbolic operators, and the criterion for identifying terms is plain syntactic equality. We will now give a specification of the Dolev-Yao intruder in *MSR*.

Let I be the elected intruder. We represent the knowledge I has at his disposal to mount an attack in a distributed fashion as a collection of memory predicates of the form $I(t)$ for all known terms t (for conciseness, the subscript "I" of the correct form $I_1(t)$ is kept implicit). Thus, the declarations "I : principal" and "I : principal × msg" constitute the *standard Dolev-Yao intruder signature*, that we denote Σ_{DY}. We express each of the Dolev-Yao intruder's capabilities as one or more one-rule roles anchored at I. We give them a name (written in bold to its left) that will be referred to in Section 6. We also organize rule constituents in columns for legibility. These roles constitute the *standard Dolev-Yao intruder theory* that we denote $\mathcal{P}_{DY}$.

Items (1) and (2) of the description of the Dolev-Yao intruder are specified by rules **INT** and **TRN** below, respectively. The former captures a network message $N(t)$ and stores its contents in the intruder's memory predicate. Observe that the execution semantics of *MSR* implies that $N(t)$ is removed from the current state and therefore this message is not available any more to the principal it was supposed to reach. Rule **TRN** emits a memorized message out in the public network.

$$\textbf{INT:}\ \big(\forall t : \mathsf{msg}.\ \mathsf{N}(t)\ \rightarrow\ I(t)\big)^{\mathsf{I}} \qquad \textbf{TRN:}\ \big(\forall t : \mathsf{msg}.\ I(t)\ \rightarrow\ \mathsf{N}(t)\big)^{\mathsf{I}}$$

From now on, we will only deal with the memory predicate $I(\_)$, which acts as a workshop where I can dismantle intercepted communications and counterfeit messages. Concatenated messages can be taken apart and constructed at will:

$$\textbf{DCM:}\ \left(\forall t_1, t_2 : \mathsf{msg}.\ I(t_1\ t_2)\ \rightarrow\ \begin{matrix} I(t_1) \\ I(t_2) \end{matrix}\right)^{\mathsf{I}}$$

$$\textbf{CMP:}\ \left(\forall t_1, t_2 : \mathsf{msg}.\ \begin{matrix} I(t_1) \\ I(t_2) \end{matrix}\ \rightarrow\ I(t_1\ t_2)\right)^{\mathsf{I}}$$

Items (5) and (6) of the above specification state that I must know the appropriate decryption keys in order to access the contents of an encrypted message. Dually, he must be in possess of the correct key in order to perform an encryption.

$$\textbf{SDC:}\ \left(\begin{matrix} \forall A, B : \mathsf{principal.} \\ \forall k : \mathsf{shK}\ A\ B. \\ \forall t : \mathsf{msg.} \end{matrix}\ \begin{matrix} I(\{t\}_k) \\ I(k) \end{matrix}\ \rightarrow\ I(t)\right)^{\mathsf{I}}$$

$$\text{SEC: } \left(\begin{matrix} \forall A, B : \text{principal.} \\ \forall k : \text{shK } A\ B. \\ \forall t : \text{msg.} \end{matrix} \quad \begin{matrix} I(t) \\ I(k) \end{matrix} \quad \rightarrow \quad I(\{t\}_k) \right)^{\mathsf{I}}$$

$$\text{PDC: } \left(\begin{matrix} \forall A : \text{principal.} \\ \forall k : \text{pubK } A. \\ \forall k' : \text{privK } k. \\ \forall t : \text{msg.} \end{matrix} \quad \begin{matrix} I(\{\!\{t\}\!\}_k) \\ I(k') \end{matrix} \quad \rightarrow \quad I(t) \right)^{\mathsf{I}}$$

$$\text{PEC: } \left(\begin{matrix} \forall A : \text{principal.} \\ \forall k : \text{pubK } A. \\ \forall t : \text{msg.} \end{matrix} \quad \begin{matrix} I(t) \\ I(k) \end{matrix} \quad \rightarrow \quad I(\{\!\{t\}\!\}_k) \right)^{\mathsf{I}}$$

We now tackle the often overlooked item (7) of the Dolev-Yao intruder specification: the ability to access public information. The intruder should clearly be entitled to look up the name and public keys of principals, but any attempted access to more sensitive information such as private keys should be forbidden. Our DAS policy already enforces this kind of requirements. Therefore, we will express the capabilities of the intruder with respect to public information access by means of the strongest rules that satisfy DAS.

$$\text{IPR: } \left(\forall A : \text{principal.} \cdot \quad \rightarrow \quad I(A)\right)^{\mathsf{I}}$$

$$\text{IS1: } \left(\begin{matrix} \forall A : \text{principal.} \\ \forall k : \text{shK } I\ A. \end{matrix} \cdot \rightarrow I(k)\right)^{\mathsf{I}} \quad \text{IS2: } \left(\begin{matrix} \forall A : \text{principal.} \\ \forall k : \text{shK } A\ I. \end{matrix} \cdot \rightarrow I(k)\right)^{\mathsf{I}}$$

$$\text{IPB: } \left(\begin{matrix} \forall A : \text{principal.} \\ \forall k : \text{pubK } A. \end{matrix} \cdot \rightarrow I(k)\right)^{\mathsf{I}} \quad \text{IPV: } \left(\begin{matrix} \forall k : \text{pubK } I. \\ \forall k' : \text{privK } k. \end{matrix} \cdot \rightarrow I(k')\right)^{\mathsf{I}}$$

The last item of the specification of the Dolev-Yao intruder hints at the fact that he should be able to create fresh data. We must again very careful when implementing this requirement: in most scenarios, it is inappropriate for I to generate keys or to create new principals. As for the DAS rules, nonces and atomic messages are however risk-frees.

$$\text{GNC: } \left(\cdot \quad \rightarrow \quad \exists n : \text{nonce. } I(n)\right)^{\mathsf{I}} \quad \text{GMS: } \left(\cdot \quad \rightarrow \quad \exists m : \text{msg. } I(m)\right)^{\mathsf{I}}$$

Observe that the rationale behind these two rules, although reasonable, may conflict with idiosyncrasies of individual protocols. For example, the full version of the Needham-Schroeder public-key authentication protocol presented in [Cer01b] is accurately validated only in the presence of an intruder who can create public keys.

Last, $\mathcal{P}_{DY}$ contains the following two administrative rules that allow the Dolev-Yao intruder to forget information and to duplicate (and therefore reuse) fabricated data, respectively.

$$\text{DEL: } \left(\forall t : \text{msg. } I(t) \quad \rightarrow \quad \cdot\right)^{\mathsf{I}} \quad \text{DUP: } \left(\forall t : \text{msg. } I(t) \quad \rightarrow \quad \begin{matrix} I(t) \\ I(t) \end{matrix}\right)^{\mathsf{I}}$$

It is easy to verify that the above *MSR* formalization of the Dolev-Yao intruder is well-typed and satisfies DAS:

Property 2. The judgments $\vdash \Sigma_{DY}$, $\Sigma_{DY} \vdash \mathcal{P}_{DY}$ and $\Sigma_{DY} \Vdash \mathcal{P}_{DY}$ are derivable.

The validation of the judgment "$\Sigma_{DY} \Vdash \mathcal{P}_{DY}$" makes use of all the DAS rules in Section 3, except the ones dealing with role state predicates.

A few aspects of this encoding deserve to be emphasized: first, this specification lies completely within *MSR* and can therefore be adapted, were the protocol at hand to require it. This differentiates *MSR* from most other formalisms which either rely on a fixed intruder, or express it in a language distinct from regular protocols. Second, typing allows a very precise characterization of what the intruder's capabilities actually are, especially as far as access to public information and fresh data generation are concerned. Third, $\mathcal{P}_{DY}$ can be automatically generated from DAS rules of the given term language [Cer02].

6   The Most Powerful Symbolic Attacker

The Dolev-Yao intruder is by no means the only way to specify a protocol adversary. Indeed, *MSR* allows writing attacker theories of much greater complexity by using multi-rule roles, branching, long predicate sequences, diversified memory predicates, and deep pattern-matching. It is however commonly believed that any attack mounted by such an attacker can be uncovered by using the Dolev-Yao intruder. The assumption that the Dolev-Yao intruder subsumes any other symbolic adversary (*i.e.* that plays by the rules of the Dolev-Yao abstraction) is built into the most successful security protocol verification systems [Bra00,DM99,Low98,Mea96,Pau97,SS98,Son99]. To our knowledge and from discussions with several security experts, it appears that this strongly held belief has never been proved. This is worrisome considering the seldom-acknowledged subtleties that our formalization of the Dolev-Yao intruder has exposed in Section 5. Our precise definition of DAS and the fact that an attacker is specified within *MSR* as any other protocol fragment give us the means to phrase that question and to formally prove that it has a positive answer. We dedicate this section to this task.

Again, let I be the intruder (we will consider situations involving multiple intruders at the end of this section). Assume that we are given a derivation of a generic well-typed and DAS-valid execution judgment $\mathcal{P} \rhd [S]_{\Sigma}^{R} \longrightarrow^{*} [S']_{\Sigma'}^{R'}$. Clearly, $\mathcal{P}$, R and R' can mention arbitrary (active) roles anchored on the intruder. Similarly, S and S' can contain role state and memory predicates belonging to I. We will show that we can construct an encoding $\ulcorner \_ \urcorner$ for the entities appearing in that judgment such that: 1) $\ulcorner \mathcal{P} \urcorner$, $\ulcorner R \urcorner$ and $\ulcorner R' \urcorner$ do not mention any intruder specification besides $\mathcal{P}_{DY}$; 2) $\ulcorner S \urcorner$ and $\ulcorner S' \urcorner$ do not contain any role state predicate for I nor any intruder memory predicate except at most $I(\_)$; and 3) the judgment $\ulcorner \mathcal{P} \urcorner, \mathcal{P}_{DY} \rhd [\ulcorner S \urcorner]_{\ulcorner \Sigma \urcorner}^{\ulcorner R \urcorner} \longrightarrow^{*} [\ulcorner S' \urcorner]_{\ulcorner \Sigma' \urcorner}^{\ulcorner R' \urcorner}$ is derivable.

The encoding $\ulcorner \mathcal{P} \urcorner$ of a protocol theory $\mathcal{P}$ implements the idea that every role anchored on the intruder can be emulated by means of $\mathcal{P}_{DY}$. Therefore, we simply filter out every component of the form $(\rho)^{I}$:

$$\begin{bmatrix} \ulcorner \cdot \urcorner & = & \cdot \\ \ulcorner \mathcal{P}, (\rho)^{\forall A} \urcorner & = & \ulcorner \mathcal{P} \urcorner, (\rho)^{\forall A} \\ \ulcorner \mathcal{P}, (\rho)^{A} \urcorner & = & \begin{cases} \ulcorner \mathcal{P} \urcorner, (\rho)^{A} & \text{if } A \neq I \\ \ulcorner \mathcal{P} \urcorner & \text{otherwise} \end{cases} \end{bmatrix}$$

The Dolev-Yao intruder model does not refer to any role state or memory predicate beside $I(\_)$. Whenever one of these objects appears in a state S, the encoding $\ulcorner S \urcorner$ will account for it by including one instance of the Dolev-Yao intruder memory predicate $I(\_)$ for each of its arguments, as specified by the following definition:

$$
\begin{bmatrix}
\ulcorner \cdot \urcorner & = & \cdot \\
\ulcorner S, N(t) \urcorner & = & \ulcorner S \urcorner, N(t) \\
\ulcorner S, M_A(t) \urcorner & = & \begin{cases} \ulcorner S \urcorner, \ulcorner t \urcorner & \text{if } A = I \\ \ulcorner S \urcorner, M_A(t) & \text{otherwise} \end{cases} \\
\ulcorner S, L_l(A, t) \urcorner & = & \begin{cases} \ulcorner S \urcorner, \ulcorner A, t \urcorner & \text{if } A = I \\ \ulcorner S \urcorner, L_l(A, t) & \text{otherwise} \end{cases}
\end{bmatrix}
\qquad
\text{where}
\quad
\begin{bmatrix}
\ulcorner \cdot \urcorner & = & \cdot \\
\ulcorner t, t \urcorner & = & I(t), \ulcorner t \urcorner
\end{bmatrix}
$$

The encoding of a signature Σ is obtained by including any part of the Dolev-Yao intruder signature Σ_{DY} that may be missing in Σ. More precisely, $\ulcorner \Sigma \urcorner$ is defined as $\Sigma_{DY} \cup (\Sigma \setminus (\Sigma \cap \Sigma_{DY}))$. The target signature Σ' of an execution judgment may contain role state predicate symbol declarations introduced by the execution of a (non Dolev-Yao) attacker role. We shall remove them from the translation, as indicated in the statement of Theorem 2.

While the above entities can be given an encoding based exclusively on their structure, this approach does not work smoothly for active role sets. Attacker rules are problematic: clearly, we want to map their operations to Dolev-Yao intruder roles, but the direct realization of this idea requires a wider context than what offered by a simply-minded recursive definition. For example, upon encountering a term $\{t\}_k$ in an incoming message, we may or may not need to use one of the shared-key roles **IS1** and **IS2** to look up k. Furthermore, it is not clear whether a copy of k is needed in other parts of the rule.

If we only consider entities that satisfy the typing and DAS restrictions, we can circumvent this difficulty by basing the encoding of an active role set R on a derivation $\mathcal{A}$ of the DAS judgment $\Sigma \Vdash R$, for a given signature Σ. Indeed, $\mathcal{A}$ would specify how the key k in the above example is accessed, and indirectly how many times it is needed in the rule it appears in. The translation of each DAS rule is given in Section 3 as a $\boxed{\text{boxed}}$ annotation next to the name of each rule. These annotations are either 1) a non-intruder active role ρ^A, 2) the name of a role in $\mathcal{P}_{DY}$, 3) "·" if no role needs to be mapped to this rule, or finally 4) the abbreviations $\text{DEL}(\Delta)$ and $\text{DUP}(\Delta)$ which stand for as many copies of role **DEL** (resp. **DUP**) as there are elements in the knowledge context Δ appearing in this rule (see [Cer] for a formal definition).

Given a derivation $\mathcal{A}$ of $\Sigma \Vdash R$, we construct $\ulcorner \mathcal{A} \urcorner$ by collecting the active roles corresponding to the annotation of each rule that appears in $\mathcal{A}$. We define $\ulcorner R \urcorner$ as $\ulcorner \mathcal{A} \urcorner$. This definition entails that the encoding of any active role anchored on I consists exclusively of Dolev-Yao roles from $\mathcal{P}_{DY}$.

As an example, consider an active role consisting of the partially instantiated rule $\rho^I = (\forall n_B : \text{nonce}. L(I, B, k_B, n_I), N(\{\!\!\{n_I \; n_B\}\!\!\}_{k_I}) \rightarrow N(\{\!\!\{n_B\}\!\!\}_{k_B}))^I$, taken from the specification of the Needham-Schroeder protocol in Appendix A. This rule is being executed by the intruder. Assuming an appropriate signature Σ, we have the following derivation for ρ^l, where we have reported the non-empty boxed annotations.

$$
\cfrac{
\cfrac{
\cfrac{
\cfrac{
\cfrac{
\cfrac{
\Gamma; \Delta \Vdash^s_A k_l \gg (\Delta, k'_l) \ \boxed{\text{IPV,DUP}}
}{
\cfrac{
\cfrac{
\cfrac{
\cfrac{\Gamma; \Delta', n_B \Vdash_A \cdot \gg (\Delta', n_B)}{\Gamma; \Delta' \Vdash_A n_B \gg \Delta''}{}^{\text{tas\_dot}}
}{\Gamma; \Delta' \Vdash_A n_l, n_B \gg \Delta''}{}^{\text{tas\_ukn}}
}{\Gamma; \Delta' \Vdash_A (n_l\, n_B) \gg \Delta'' \ \boxed{\text{DCM}}}{}^{\text{tas\_kn}}
}{}^{\text{tas\_cnc}}
}{}^{\text{kas\_puu}}
}{\Gamma; \Delta \Vdash_A \{n_l\, n_B\}_{k_l} \gg \Delta'' \ \boxed{\text{PDC}}}{}^{\text{tas\_pke}}
}{\Gamma; \Delta \Vdash_A N(\{n_l\, n_B\}_{k_l}) > \cdot \gg \Delta'' \ \boxed{\text{INT}}}{}^{\text{tas\_net,tas\_dot}}
}{\Gamma; \cdot \Vdash_A L(l, B, k_B, n_l), N(\{n_l\, n_B\}_{k_l}) > \cdot \gg \Delta''}{}^{\text{tas\_rap}}
\qquad
\cfrac{
\cfrac{
\cfrac{
\Gamma; \Delta'' \looparrowright_A n_B \ \boxed{\text{DEL}^6} \qquad \Gamma; \Delta'' \looparrowright_A k_B \ \boxed{\text{DEL}^6}
}{\Gamma; \Delta'' \looparrowright_A \{n_B\}_{k_B} \ \boxed{\text{DUP}^6, \text{PEC}}}{}^{\text{cas\_pke}}
}{\Gamma; \Delta'' \looparrowright_A N(\{n_B\}_{k_B}) \ \boxed{\text{DUP}^6, \text{TRN}, \text{DEL}^6}}{}^{\text{cas\_net}}
}{}^{\text{cas\_kn}}
}{(\Sigma, n_B : nonce) \Vdash_A L(l, B, k_B, n_l), N(\{n_l\, n_B\}_{k_l}) \to N(\{n_B\}_{k_B})}{}^{\text{uas\_core}}
$$

$$
\Sigma \Vdash_A \forall n_B : nonce.\ L(l, B, k_B, n_l), N(\{n_l\, n_B\}_{k_l}) \to N(\{n_B\}_{k_B}) \qquad \text{uas\_ext,uas\_dot,uas\_all}
$$

where $\Gamma = (\Sigma, n_B : nonce)$, $\Delta = (l, B, k_B, n_l)$, $\Delta' = (\Delta, k'_l)$ and $\Delta'' = (\Delta, n_B)$. The translation of ρ^l is the active role given by collecting the boxed Dolev-Yao intruder actions: $\ulcorner \rho^l \urcorner =$ INT,PDC,IPV,DCM,TRN,PEC,DUP[13],DEL[19]. Observe that, the first six rules correspond to the operations needed to dismantle the message $N(\{n_l\, n_B\}_{k_l})$ and construct $N(\{n_B\}_{k_B})$. Most of the duplication and deletion rules elide each other; the remaining six are used to get rid of the knowledge Δ'' since it is not memorized in any way in the consequent of ρ^l.

The family of translations $\ulcorner \_ \urcorner$ for our various objects preserves any entity not pertaining directly to the intruder. In particular, network messages, memory and role state predicates of other principals, and the roles that transform them are unaffected. It is easy to prove that $\ulcorner \_ \urcorner$ preserves typing and DAS [Cer].

Lemma 1. *Let Σ be a signature, $\mathcal{P}$ a protocol theory, S a state, and R an active role set. If $\vdash \Sigma$, $\Sigma \vdash \mathcal{P}$, $\Sigma \vdash S$, $\Sigma \vdash R$, $\Sigma \Vdash \mathcal{P}$ and $\Sigma \Vdash R$ are derivable, then so are $\vdash \ulcorner \Sigma \urcorner$, $\ulcorner \Sigma \urcorner \vdash \ulcorner \mathcal{P} \urcorner$, $\ulcorner \Sigma \urcorner \vdash \ulcorner S \urcorner$, $\ulcorner \Sigma \urcorner \vdash \ulcorner R \urcorner$, $\ulcorner \Sigma \urcorner \Vdash \ulcorner \mathcal{P} \urcorner$ and $\ulcorner \Sigma \urcorner \Vdash \ulcorner R \urcorner$.*

Theorem 2 below states that the Dolev-Yao intruder is the most powerful attacker, in the sense that it can emulate the deeds of any other attacker. A proof of this result relies on a number of lemmas that describe how the translation of derivations for each of the DAS judgments from Section 3 is mapped to an execution sequence. Due to space limitations, we shall refer the interested reader to [Cer] for a presentation of these auxiliary results and of their proofs. We give a flavor of the elegant proof technique underlying our Theorem 2 by displaying the statement of one of these lemmas, which shows how the Dolev-Yao intruder can emulate the access to the information appearing in terms in the left-hand side of a rule. The representation $\ulcorner \Delta \urcorner$ of a knowledge context is defined as for term tuples (see [Cer] for a formal definition). We write "$\mathcal{A} :: J$" to indicate that $\mathcal{A}$ is a derivation of the judgment J.

Lemma 2. *Let Σ be a signature, t a term tuple, and Δ and Δ' knowledge contexts compatible with Σ.*

If $\mathcal{A} :: \Sigma; \Delta \Vdash_{\mathsf{i}} t \gg \Delta'$, then $\cdot \rhd [\ulcorner \Delta \urcorner, \ulcorner t \urcorner]_{\ulcorner \Sigma \urcorner}^{\ulcorner \Delta \urcorner} \longrightarrow^* [\ulcorner \Delta' \urcorner]_{\ulcorner \Sigma \urcorner}$ is derivable.

This result is proved by induction on the structure of the given DAS derivation $\mathcal{A}$ [Cer]. We have the following statement for the main result in this section.

Theorem 2. (*The Dolev-Yao Intruder is the Most Powerful Attacker*)

Let $\mathcal{P}$ be a protocol theory, S and S' two states, R and R' two active role sets, Σ and Σ' signatures such that

$$\vdash \Sigma \quad \Sigma \vdash \mathcal{P}, \quad \Sigma \vdash S, \quad \Sigma \vdash R, \quad \Sigma \Vdash \mathcal{P}, \quad \mathcal{A} :: \Sigma \Vdash R, \quad \mathcal{A}' :: \Sigma, \Sigma' \Vdash R'$$

If $\mathcal{E} :: \mathcal{P} \triangleright [S]_{\Sigma}^{R} \longrightarrow^* [S']_{\Sigma, \Sigma'}^{R'}$, then $(\ulcorner\mathcal{P}\urcorner, \mathcal{P}_{DY}) \triangleright \ulcorner S \urcorner_{\ulcorner\Sigma\urcorner}^{\ulcorner\mathcal{A}\urcorner} \longrightarrow^* \ulcorner S' \urcorner_{\ulcorner\Sigma\urcorner, \Sigma^*}^{\ulcorner\mathcal{A}'\urcorner}$ is derivable.

where Σ^* is a subsignature of Σ' such that $\Sigma' = \Sigma^*, \Sigma_L$ and Σ_L consists only of role state predicate symbol declarations.

Proof: This proof is constructive and proceeds by induction on the structure of $\mathcal{E}$. Due to space constraints, we refer the reader to [Cer] for the technical development and instead give the intuition behind the emulation of the most interesting execution rules.

Our emulation does not interfere with actions that involve non-intruder roles. Installing a role ρ^I anchored on I into the current active role set (rule ex_arole) is emulated by copying as many instances of objects from $\mathcal{P}_{DY}$ as specified by the encoding of ρ^I. Intruder-instantiated generic roles (rule ex_grole) are treated in the same way, which means that our emulation does not allow I to directly execute a generic role. Uses of rule ex_all to instantiate a universal variable in an active intruder rule do not correspond to any action: we have proved that DAS is preserved under substitution [Cer01a] and that this process does not affect the encoding of a DAS derivation [Cer]. Finally, the application of a fully instantiated intruder rule (ex_core) relies on results such as lemma 2 above that specify the behavior of its constituents. □

Since, in models that relies on black-box cryptography, an attack of any kind is ultimately an execution sequence between two configurations, this theorem states that a security protocol has an attack if and only if it has a Dolev-Yao attack. This justifies the design of tools that rely on the Dolev-Yao intruder [Bra00,DM99,Low98,Mea96,Pau97] [SS98,Son99], but it does not mean that considering other specifications of the attacker is pointless. Indeed, precisely because of its generality, a straight adoption of the Dolev-Yao intruder often results in inefficient verification procedures. Overhead can be greatly relieved by relying on general optimizations that cut the search space [Cer00,DMGF00] [MCJ97,SS98] and on per-protocol specializations, for example allowing the intruder to construct only message patterns actually used in the protocol [Mea96,Pau97]. Finally, the environment in which a particular protocol is deployed may be so constraining that a weaker attacker model is sufficient to ensure the desired security goals.

Our result extends to settings that involve multiple intruders $I_1, \ldots I_n$. We process each of these attackers independently as specified above, obtaining n copies of $\mathcal{P}_{DY}$, each anchored on a particular I_i. We then make use of the attack-preservation result in [SMC00] to reduce them to a single attacker I.

7   Conclusions and Future Work

In this paper, we have presented a data access specification system for the security protocol specification framework *MSR* [Cer01a,Cer01b,CDL+99] and used it to show that the Dolev-Yao intruder model embedded in most crypto-protocol verification tools [Bra00,DM99,Low98,Mea96,Pau97,SS98,Son99] is indeed the most powerful attacker. In the near future, we intend to further investigate the relations between DAS and the Dolev-Yao intruder. While it appears that a specification of this attacker can be automatically constructed from the DAS rules [Cer02], it is not yet clear whether a DAS policy can always be derived from an attacker specification. In order to answer this question, we are constructing an extended library of case studies [Cer01a,Cer,Cer01b] that require different DAS assumptions. Another important question that we intend to tackle using *MSR* is whether it is possible to derive sensible DAS rules (and a most powerful intruder model) from the specification of a protocol (including its term language) rather than by imposing them from above [Cer02]. On a more practical side, we want to address the issues of type-reconstruction [Cer01b] and deterministic variable instantiation in order to develop a usable security protocol verification system based on *MSR*.

Acknowledgments

We are grateful to Catherine Meadows, Paul Syverson and Grit Denker for the insightful discussions on the topics presented in this paper. We would also like to thank Frank Pfenning and Andre Scedrov for their interest and encouragement.

References

[AC96]   David Aspinall and Adriana Compagnoni. Subtyping dependent types. In E. Clarke, editor, *Proceedings of the 11th Annual Symposium on Logic in Computer Science*, pages 86–97, New Brunswick, New Jersey, July 1996. IEEE Computer Society Press.

[AG99]   M. Abadi and A. Gordon. A calculus for cryptographic protocols: the spi calculus. *Information and Computation*, 148(1):1–70, 1999.

[AN94]   Martin Abadi and Roger Needham. Prudent engineering practice for cryptographic protocols. Research Report 125, DEC, System Research Center, 1994.

[BAN89]   M. Burrows, M. Abadi, and R. Needham. A logic of authentication. *Proceedings of the Royal Society, Series A*, 426(1871):233–271, 1989.

[Bra00]   Stephen Brackin. Automatically detecting most vulnerabilities in cryptographic protocols. In *Proceedings of the 2000 DARPA Information Survivability Conference and Exposition — DISCEX'00*, volume 1, pages pp. 222–236, Hilton Head, SC, 2000.

[CDL+99]   Iliano Cervesato, Nancy A. Durgin, Patrick D. Lincoln, John C. Mitchell, and Andre Scedrov. A meta-notation for protocol analysis. In P. Syverson, editor, *Proceedings of the 12th IEEE Computer Security Foundations Workshop — CSFW'99*, pages 55–69, Mordano, Italy, June 1999.

[Cer]   Iliano Cervesato. Typed multiset rewriting specifications of security protocols. Unpublished manuscript.

[Cer00]   Iliano Cervesato. Typed multiset rewriting specifications of security protocols. In A. Seda, editor, *Proceedings of the First Irish Conference on the Mathematical Foundations of Computer Science and Information Technology — MFCSIT'00*, Cork, Ireland, 19–21 July 2000. Elsevier ENTCS.

[Cer01a] Iliano Cervesato. A specification language for crypto-protocol based on multiset rewriting, dependent types and subsorting. In G. Delzanno, S. Etalle, and M. Gabrielli, editors, *Workshop on Specification, Analysis and Validation for Emerging Technologies — SAVE'01*, Paphos, Cyprus, 2001.

[Cer01b] Iliano Cervesato. Typed MSR: Syntax and examples. In V. Gorodetski, V. Skormin, and L. Popyack, editors, *Proceedings of the First International Workshop on Mathematical Methods, Models and Architectures for Computer Network Security — MMM'01*, pages 159–177, St. Petersburg, Russia, 2001. Springer-Verlag LNCS 2052.

[Cer02] Iliano Cervesato. The wolf within. In J. Guttman, editor, *Second Workshop on Issues in the Theory of Security — WITS'02*, Portland, OR, 2002.

[dG95] Ph. de Groote, editor. *The Curry-Howard Isomorphism*, volume 8 of *Cahiers du Centre de Logique, Département de Philosophie, Université Catholique de Louvain*. Academia, 1995.

[DM99] Grit Denker and Jonathan K. Millen. CAPSL Intermediate Language. In N. Heintze and E. Clarke, editors, *Proceedings of the Workshop on Formal Methods and Security Protocols — FMSP*, Trento, Italy, July 1999.

[DMGF00] Grit Denker, Jonathan Millen, A. Grau, and J. Filipe. Optimizing protocol rewrite rules of CIL specifications. In *13th IEEE Computer Security Foundations Workshop — CSFW'00*, pages 52–62, Cambrige, UK, July 2000.

[DY83] Danny Dolev and Andrew C. Yao. On the security of public-key protocols. *IEEE Transactions on Information Theory*, 2(29):198–208, 1983.

[FHG98] F. Javier Thayer Fábrega, Jonathan C. Herzog, and Joshua D. Guttman. Strand spaces: Why is a security protocol correct? In *Proceedings of the 1998 IEEE Symposium on Security and Privacy*, pages 160–171, Oakland, CA, May 1998.

[GJ02] Andrew Gordon and Alan Jeffrey. Types and effects for asymmetric cryptographic protocols. In *15th IEEE Computer Security Foundations Workshop — CSFW'02*, pages 77–91, Cape Breton, Canada, 2002.

[HHP93] Robert Harper, Furio Honsell, and Gordon Plotkin. A framework for defining logics. *Journal of the Association for Computing Machinery*, 40(1):143–184, January 1993.

[Low98] Gavin Lowe. Casper: A compiler for the analysis of security protocols. *Journal of Computer Security*, 6:53–84, 1998.

[MCJ97] Will Marrero, Edmund M. Clarke, and Somesh Jha. Model checking for security protocols. In *Proceedings of the 1997 DIMACS Workshop on Design and Formal Verification of Security Protocols*, 1997. A Preliminary version appeared as Technical Report TR-CMU-CS-97-139, Carnegie Mellon University, May 1997.

[Mea96] C. Meadows. The NRL protocol analyzer: an overview. *J. Logic Programming*, 26(2):113–131, 1996.

[NS78] R.M. Needham and M.D. Schroeder. Using encryption for authentication in large networks of computers. *Communications of the ACM*, 21(12):993–999, 1978.

[Pau97] Laurence Paulson. Proving properties of security protocols by induction. In *Proceedings of the 10th Computer Security Foundations Workshop*, pages 70–83, 1997.

[Pfe93] Frank Pfenning. Refinement types for logical frameworks. In Herman Geuvers, editor, *Informal Proceedings of the Workshop on Types for Proofs and Programs*, pages 285–299, Nijmegen, The Netherlands, May 1993.

[SMC00] Paul Syverson, Catherine Meadows, and Iliano Cervesato. Dolev-Yao is no better than Machiavelli. In P. Degano, editor, *First Workshop on Issues in the Theory of Security — WITS'00*, pages 87–92, Geneva, Switzerland, 7-8 July 2000.

[Son99] Dawn Song. Athena: a new efficient automatic checker for security protocol analysis. In *Proceedings of the Twelfth IEEE Computer Security Foundations Workshop*, pages 192–202, Mordano, Italy, June 1999.

[SS98]   Vitaly Shmatikov and Ulrich Stern. Efficient finite-state analysis for large security protocols. In *Proceedings of the 11th Computer Security Foundations Workshop*, pages 106–115, Rockport, MA, 1998.

[Syv97]   Paul F. Syverson. A different look at secure distributed computation. In *Tenth IEEE Computer Security Foundations Workshop — CSFW-10*, pages 109–115, June 1997.

A   Example

In this appendix, we show an actual *MSR* specification by reprinting from [Cer01b] the simple protocol theory that describes the two-party nucleus of the Needham-Schroeder public-key authentication protocol [NS78]. We choose this example for its conciseness and the fact that most reader will be familiar with it. More complex (and interesting) specifications can be found in the same paper and in [Cer01a].

The server-less variant of the Needham-Schroeder public-key protocol [NS78] is a two-party crypto-protocol aimed at authenticating the initiator A to the responder B (but not necessarily vice versa). It is expressed as the expected run on the right in the

1. $A \rightarrow B$: $\{\!|n_A\ A|\!\}_{k_B}$
2. $B \rightarrow A$: $\{\!|n_A\ n_B|\!\}_{k_A}$
3. $A \rightarrow B$: $\{\!|n_B|\!\}_{k_B}$

"usual notation" (where we have used our syntax for messages). In the first line, the initiator A encrypts a message consisting of a nonce n_A and her own identity with the public key k_B of the responder B, and sends it (ideally to B). The second line describes the action that B undertakes upon receiving and interpreting this message: he creates a nonce n_B, combines it with A's nonce n_A, encrypts the outcome with A's public key k_A, and sends the resulting message out. Upon receiving this message in the third line, A accesses n_B and sends it back encrypted with k_B. The run is completed when B receives this message and successfully recognizes n_B.

MSR, like most modern security protocol specification languages, represents roles, *i.e.* the sequence of actions executed by each individual principal. We now express each role in turn in the syntax of *MSR*. For space reasons, we will typeset homogeneous constituents, namely the universal variable declarations and the predicate sequences in the antecedent and consequent, in columns within each rule; we will also rely on some minor abbreviation.

The initiator's actions are represented by the following two-rule role:

$$
\left(
\begin{array}{l}
\exists L : \mathsf{principal} \times \mathsf{principal}^{(B)} \times \mathsf{pubK}\ B \times \mathsf{nonce}. \\[4pt]
\begin{array}{ll}
\forall B : \mathsf{principal}. \\
\forall k_B : \mathsf{pubK}\ B.
\end{array} \quad\cdot\quad \rightarrow \exists n_A : \mathsf{nonce}.\ \begin{array}{l} \mathsf{N}(\{\!|n_A\ A|\!\}_{k_B}) \\ L(A,B,k_B,n_A) \end{array} \\[16pt]
\begin{array}{ll}
\forall \ldots \\
\forall k_A : \mathsf{pubK}\ A. & \mathsf{N}(\{\!|n_A\ n_B|\!\}_{k_A}) \\
\forall k'_A : \mathsf{privK}\ k_A. & L(A,B,k_B,n_A) \quad \rightarrow \qquad \mathsf{N}(\{\!|n_B|\!\}_{k_B}) \\
\forall n_A, n_B : \mathsf{nonce}.
\end{array}
\end{array}
\right)^{\forall A}
$$

Clearly, any principal can engage in this protocol as an initiator (or a responder). Our encoding is therefore structured as a generic role. Let A be its postulated owner. The first rule formalizes line (1) of the "usual notation" description of this protocol from A's point of view. It has an empty antecedent since initiation is unconditional in this protocol fragment. Its right-hand side uses an existential quantifier to mark the nonce n_A as fresh. The consequent contains the transmitted message and the role state predicate $L(A, B, k_B, n_A)$, necessary to enable the second rule of this protocol. The arguments of this predicate record variables used in the second rule.

The second rule encodes lines (2–3) of the "usual notation" description. It is applicable only if the initiator has executed the first rule (enforced by the presence of the role state predicate) and she receives a message of the appropriate form. Its consequent sends the last message of the protocol.

MSR assigns a specific type to each variable appearing in these rules. The equivalent "usual notation" specification relies instead on natural language and conventions to convey this same information, with clear potential for ambiguity. We shall mention that most declarations can be automatically reconstructed [Cer01b]: this simplifies the task of the author of the specification by enabling him or her to concentrate on the message flow rather than on typing details, and of course it limits the size of the specification.

The responder is encoded as the generic role below, whose owner we have mnemonically called B. The first rule of this role collapses the two topmost lines of the "usual notation" specification of this protocol fragment from the receiver's point of view. The second rule captures the reception and successful interpretation of the last message in the protocol by B: this step is often overlooked. This rule has an empty consequent.

$$
\left(
\begin{array}{l}
\exists L : \text{principal} \times \text{nonce}. \\[4pt]
\forall k_B : \text{pubK } B. \\
\forall k'_B : \text{privK } k_B. \\
\forall A : \text{principal.} \quad \mathsf{N}(\{\!|n_A\, A|\!\}_{k_B}) \;\; \rightarrow \;\; \exists n_B : \text{nonce.} \;\; \begin{array}{l} \mathsf{N}(\{\!|n_A\, n_B|\!\}_{k_A}) \\ L(B, n_B) \end{array} \\
\forall n_A : \text{nonce.} \\
\forall k_A : \text{pubK } A \\[6pt]
\forall \ldots \qquad\qquad \mathsf{N}(\{\!|n_B|\!\}_{k_B}) \\
\forall n_B : \text{nonce.} \quad\; L(B, n_B) \qquad \rightarrow \qquad\qquad .
\end{array}
\right)^{\forall B}
$$

Again, most typing information can be reconstructed from the way variables are used.

B   Typing Judgments and Rules

B.1   Typing Judgments

$$
\begin{array}{ll}
\tau :: \tau' & \tau \text{ is a subsort of } \tau' \\[4pt]
\Sigma \vdash t : \tau & \text{Term } t \text{ has type } \tau \text{ in signature } \Sigma \\[4pt]
\Sigma \vdash \tau & \tau \text{ is a valid type in } \Sigma \\[4pt]
\vdash \Sigma & \Sigma \text{ is a valid signatures} \\[4pt]
\vdash_{\mathsf{c}} \Gamma & \Gamma \text{ is a valid typing context} \\[4pt]
\Sigma \vdash t : \tau & \text{Term tuple } t \text{ has type } \tau \text{ in signature } \Sigma \\[4pt]
\Gamma \vdash \tau & \tau \text{ is a valid type tuple in typing context } \Gamma \\[4pt]
\Sigma \vdash P & P \text{ is a valid message predicate in signature } \Sigma \\[4pt]
\Sigma \vdash S & S \text{ is a valid state in signature } \Sigma \\[4pt]
\Gamma \vdash_{\mathsf{c}} rhs & rhs \text{ is a valid rule consequent in typing context } \Gamma \\[4pt]
\Gamma \vdash r & r \text{ is a valid rule in typing context } \Gamma \\[4pt]
\Gamma \vdash \rho & \rho \text{ is a valid rule collection in typing context } \Gamma \\[4pt]
\Sigma \vdash \mathcal{P} & \mathcal{P} \text{ is a valid protocol theory in signature } \Sigma \\[4pt]
\Sigma \vdash R & R \text{ is a valid active role set in signature } \Sigma
\end{array}
$$

B.2   Typing Rules

$$\boxed{\tau :: \tau' \qquad\qquad\qquad \tau \text{ is a subsort of } \tau'}$$

$$\frac{}{\text{principal} :: \text{msg}}\; \text{ss\_pr} \qquad\qquad \frac{}{\text{nonce} :: \text{msg}}\; \text{ss\_nnc}$$

$$\frac{}{\text{shK } A\, B :: \text{msg}}\; \text{ss\_shK} \qquad \frac{}{\text{pubK } A :: \text{msg}}\; \text{ss\_pbK} \qquad \frac{}{\text{privK } k :: \text{msg}}\; \text{ss\_pvK}$$

$$\boxed{\Sigma \vdash t : \tau \qquad \Gamma \vdash t : \tau \qquad\quad \text{Term } t \text{ has type } \tau \text{ in signature } \Sigma \text{ (viz. context } \Gamma)}$$

$$\frac{\Sigma \vdash t_1 : \text{msg} \quad \Sigma \vdash t_2 : \text{msg}}{\Sigma \vdash t_1\, t_2 : \text{msg}}\; \text{mtp\_cnc}$$

$$\frac{\Sigma \vdash t : \text{msg} \quad \Sigma \vdash k : \text{shK } A\, B}{\Sigma \vdash \{t\}_k : \text{msg}}\; \text{mtp\_ske} \qquad \frac{\Sigma \vdash t : \text{msg} \quad \Sigma \vdash k : \text{pubK } A}{\Sigma \vdash \{\!\{t\}\!\}_k : \text{msg}}\; \text{mtp\_pke}$$

$$\frac{\Sigma \vdash t : \tau' \quad \tau' :: \tau}{\Sigma \vdash t : \tau}\; \text{mtp\_ss} \qquad\qquad \frac{}{(\Sigma, a : \tau, \Sigma') \vdash a : \tau}\; \text{mtp\_a}$$

$$\boxed{\Sigma \vdash \tau \qquad \Gamma \vdash \tau \qquad\quad \tau \text{ is a valid type in signature } \Sigma \text{ (viz. context } \Gamma)}$$

$$\frac{}{\Sigma \vdash \text{principal}}\; \text{ttp\_pr} \qquad \frac{}{\Sigma \vdash \text{nonce}}\; \text{ttp\_nnc} \qquad \frac{}{\Sigma \vdash \text{msg}}\; \text{ttp\_msg}$$

$$\frac{\Sigma \vdash A : \text{principal} \quad \Sigma \vdash B : \text{principal}}{\Sigma \vdash \text{shK } A\, B}\; \text{ttp\_shK}$$

$$\frac{\Sigma \vdash A : \text{principal}}{\Sigma \vdash \text{pubK } A}\; \text{ttp\_pbK} \qquad\qquad \frac{\Sigma \vdash k : \text{pubK } A}{\Sigma \vdash \text{privK } k}\; \text{ttp\_pvK}$$

$$\boxed{\vdash \Sigma \qquad\qquad\qquad\qquad \Sigma \text{ is a valid signatures}}$$

$$\frac{}{\vdash \cdot}\; \text{itp\_dot} \qquad\qquad \frac{\Sigma \vdash \tau \quad \vdash \Sigma}{\vdash \Sigma, a : \tau}\; \text{itp\_a}$$

$$\frac{\Sigma \vdash \text{principal}^{(A)} \times \tau \quad \vdash \Sigma}{\vdash \Sigma, \text{L}_l : \text{principal}^{(A)} \times \tau}\; \text{itp\_rsp} \qquad \frac{\Sigma \vdash \text{principal}^{(A)} \times \tau \quad \vdash \Sigma}{\vdash \Sigma, \text{M}_- : \text{principal}^{(A)} \times \tau}\; \text{itp\_mem}$$

$$\boxed{\models^{\underline{c}} \Gamma}$$

$$\frac{\vdash \Sigma}{\models^{\underline{c}} \Sigma}\; \text{ctp\_sig} \qquad \frac{\Gamma \vdash \tau \quad \models^{\underline{c}} \Gamma}{\models^{\underline{c}} \Gamma, x : \tau}\; \text{ctp\_x} \qquad \frac{\Gamma \vdash \text{principal}^{(A)} \times \tau \quad \models^{\underline{c}} \Gamma}{\models^{\underline{c}} \Gamma, L : \text{principal}^{(A)} \times \tau}\; \text{ctp\_rsp}$$

$$\boxed{\Sigma \vdash t : \tau \qquad \Gamma \vdash t : \tau \qquad \textit{Term tuple } t \textit{ has type } \tau \textit{ in signature } \Sigma \textit{ (viz. context } \Gamma)}$$

$$\frac{}{\Sigma \vdash \cdot : \cdot}\;\text{mtp\_dot} \qquad \frac{\Sigma \vdash t : \tau \quad \Sigma \vdash \boldsymbol{t} : [t/x]\tau}{\Sigma \vdash (t, \boldsymbol{t}) : \tau^{(x)} \times \tau}\;\text{mtp\_ext}$$

$$\boxed{\Gamma \vdash \tau \qquad\qquad\qquad \tau \textit{ is a valid type tuple in typing context } \Gamma}$$

$$\frac{}{\Gamma \vdash \cdot}\;\text{ttp\_dot} \qquad \frac{\Gamma \vdash \tau \quad \Gamma, x : \tau \vdash \boldsymbol{\tau}}{\Gamma \vdash \tau^{(x)} \times \boldsymbol{\tau}}\;\text{ttp\_ext}$$

$$\boxed{\Sigma \vdash P \qquad \Gamma \vdash P \qquad P \textit{ is a valid message predicate in signature } \Sigma \textit{ (viz. context } \Gamma)}$$

$$\frac{\Sigma \vdash t : \mathsf{msg}}{\Sigma \vdash \mathsf{N}(t)}\;\text{ptp\_net} \quad \frac{(\Sigma, \mathsf{L}_l : \tau, \Sigma') \vdash t : \tau}{(\Sigma, \mathsf{L}_l : \tau, \Sigma') \vdash \mathsf{L}_l(t)}\;\text{ptp\_rsp} \quad \frac{(\Sigma, \mathsf{M}_\_ : \tau, \Sigma') \vdash (A, t) : \tau}{(\Sigma, \mathsf{M}_\_ : \tau, \Sigma') \vdash \mathsf{M}_A(t)}\;\text{ptp\_mem}$$

$$\boxed{\Sigma \vdash S \qquad \Gamma \vdash lhs\, S \textit{ (viz. lhs) is a valid state (viz. pred. sequence) in sig. } \Sigma \textit{ (viz. context } \Gamma)}$$

$$\frac{}{\Sigma \vdash \cdot}\;\text{stp\_dot} \qquad \frac{\Sigma \vdash S \quad \Sigma \vdash P}{\Sigma \vdash (S, P)}\;\text{stp\_ext}$$

$$\boxed{\Gamma \Vdash rhs \qquad\qquad rhs \textit{ is a valid rule consequent in typing context } \Gamma}$$

$$\frac{\Gamma \vdash \tau \quad (\Gamma, x : \tau) \Vdash rhs}{\Gamma \Vdash \exists x : \tau.\, rhs}\;\text{rtp\_nnc} \qquad \frac{\Gamma \vdash lhs}{\Gamma \Vdash lhs}\;\text{rtp\_seq}$$

$$\boxed{\Gamma \vdash r \qquad\qquad\qquad r \textit{ is a valid rule in typing context } \Gamma}$$

$$\frac{\Gamma \vdash lhs \quad \Gamma \Vdash rhs}{\Gamma \vdash lhs \to rhs}\;\text{utp\_core} \qquad \frac{\Sigma \vdash \tau \quad (\Gamma, x : \tau) \vdash \rho}{\Gamma \vdash \forall x : \tau.\, \rho}\;\text{utp\_all}$$

$$\boxed{\Gamma \vdash \rho \qquad\qquad\qquad \rho \textit{ is a valid rule collection in typing context } \Gamma}$$

$$\frac{}{\Gamma \vdash \cdot}\;\text{otp\_dot} \quad \frac{\Gamma \vdash \tau \quad (\Gamma, L : \tau) \vdash \rho}{\Gamma \vdash \exists L : \tau.\, \rho}\;\text{otp\_rsp} \quad \frac{\Gamma \vdash r \quad \Gamma \vdash \rho}{\Gamma \vdash r, \rho}\;\text{otp\_rule}$$

$$\boxed{\Sigma \vdash \mathcal{P} \qquad\qquad\qquad \mathcal{P} \textit{ is a valid protocol theory in signature } \Sigma}$$

$$\frac{}{\Sigma \vdash \cdot}\;\text{htp\_dot} \qquad \frac{\Sigma \vdash \mathcal{P} \quad (\Sigma, A : \mathsf{principal}) \vdash \rho}{\Sigma \vdash \mathcal{P}, \rho^{\forall A}}\;\text{htp\_grole}$$

$$\frac{(\Sigma, \mathsf{A} : \mathsf{principal}, \Sigma') \vdash \mathcal{P} \quad (\Sigma, \mathsf{A} : \mathsf{principal}, \Sigma') \vdash \rho}{(\Sigma, \mathsf{A} : \mathsf{principal}, \Sigma') \vdash \mathcal{P}, \rho^{\mathsf{A}}}\;\text{htp\_arole}$$

$$\boxed{\Sigma \vdash R} \qquad\qquad R \text{ is a valid active role set in signature } \Sigma$$

$$\frac{}{\Sigma \vdash \cdot}\ \text{atp\_dot} \qquad\qquad \frac{(\Sigma, \mathsf{A} : \text{principal}, \Sigma') \vdash R \quad (\Sigma, \mathsf{A} : \text{principal}, \Sigma') \vdash \rho}{(\Sigma, \mathsf{A} : \text{principal}, \Sigma') \vdash R, \rho^{\mathsf{A}}}\ \text{atp\_ext}$$

C   Other Omitted Rules

C.1   Summary of DAS Judgments

$\Gamma; \Delta \Vdash^{\mathrm{s}}_{A} k \gg \Delta'$	Given knowledge Δ, principal A can decipher a message encrypted with shared key k in context Γ
$\Gamma; \Delta \Vdash^{\mathrm{a}}_{A} k \gg \Delta'$	Given knowledge Δ, principal A can decipher a message encrypted with public key k in context Γ
$\Gamma; \Delta \Vdash_{A} t \gg \Delta'$	Given knowledge Δ and terms t, principal A can know Δ' in context Γ
$\Delta > e > \Delta'$	Merging context knowledge Δ and elementary term tuple e yields Δ'
$\Gamma; \Delta \Vdash_{A} lhs > t \gg \Delta'$	Given knowledge Δ, predicate sequence lhs and terms t, principal A can knows Δ' in context Γ
$\Gamma \leadsto_{A} e$	Principal A can access atomic information e in context Γ
$\Gamma; \Delta \leadsto_{A} t$	Given knowledge Δ, principal A can construct term t
$\Gamma; \Delta \leadsto_{A} t$	Given knowledge Δ, principal A can construct term tuple t
$\Gamma; \Delta \leadsto_{A} lhs$	Predicate sequence lhs is constructible from knowledge Δ for principal A
$\Gamma; \Delta \Vdash_{A} rhs$	Right-hand side rhs implements valid access control for principal A in context Γ given knowledge Δ
$\Gamma \Vdash_{A} r$	Rule r implements valid access control for principal A in context Γ
$\Gamma \Vdash_{A} \rho$	Rule sequence ρ implements valid access control for principal A in context Γ
$\Sigma \Vdash \mathcal{P}$	Protocol theory $\mathcal{P}$ implements valid access control in signature Σ
$\Sigma \Vdash R$	Active role set R implements valid access control in signature Σ

C.2   Omitted Access Control Rules

$$\boxed{\Delta > e > \Delta'} \qquad\qquad \text{Merging context knowledge } \Delta \text{ and term tuple } e \text{ yields } \Delta'$$

$$\frac{}{\Delta > \cdot > \Delta}\ \text{mas\_dot}\ \boxed{\cdot}$$

$$\frac{\Delta > e > \Delta'}{\Delta > e, e > (\Delta', e)}\ \text{mas\_ukn}^{\sharp}\ \boxed{\cdot} \qquad\qquad \frac{\Delta > e > \Delta'}{(\Delta, e) > e, e > (\Delta', e)}\ \text{mas\_kn}^{\sharp}\ \boxed{\text{DEL}}$$

$$\boxed{\Gamma; \Delta \looparrowright_A t \qquad\qquad \textit{Given knowledge } \Delta, \textit{ principal A can construct term } t}$$

$$\cfrac{\Gamma; \Delta \looparrowright_A t_1 \quad \Gamma; \Delta \looparrowright_A t_2}{\Gamma; \Delta \looparrowright_A t_1\, t_2} \; \text{cas\_cnc} \;\boxed{\text{DUP}(\Delta), \text{CMP}}$$

$$\cfrac{\Gamma; \Delta \looparrowright_A t \quad \Gamma; \Delta \looparrowright_A k}{\Gamma; \Delta \looparrowright_A \{t\}_k} \; \text{cas\_ske} \;\boxed{\text{DUP}(\Delta), \text{SEC}}$$

$$\cfrac{\Gamma; \Delta \looparrowright_A t \quad \Gamma; \Delta \looparrowright_A k}{\Gamma; \Delta \looparrowright_A \{\!|t|\!\}_k} \; \text{cas\_pke} \;\boxed{\text{DUP}(\Delta), \text{PEC}}$$

$$\boxed{\Gamma; \Delta \looparrowright_A t \qquad\qquad \textit{Given knowledge } \Delta, \textit{ principal A can construct term tuple } t}$$

$$\cfrac{}{\Gamma; \Delta \looparrowright_A \cdot} \; \text{cas\_dot} \;\boxed{\text{DEL}(\Delta)} \qquad\qquad \cfrac{\Gamma; \Delta \looparrowright_A t \quad \Gamma; \Delta \looparrowright_A t}{\Gamma; \Delta \looparrowright_A (t, t)} \; \text{cas\_ext} \;\boxed{\text{DUP}(\Delta)}$$

C.3   Summary of Execution Judgments

$$\begin{aligned}
(rhs)_\Sigma &\gg (lhs)_{\Sigma'} \qquad && \textit{Right-hand side instantiation} \\
\mathcal{P} \triangleright C &\longrightarrow C' \qquad && \textit{One-step sequential firing} \\
\mathcal{P} \triangleright C &\longrightarrow^* C' \qquad && \textit{Multi-step sequential firing}
\end{aligned}$$

C.4   Omitted Execution Rules

$$\boxed{(rhs)_\Sigma \gg (lhs)_{\Sigma'} \qquad\qquad\qquad \textit{Right-hand side instantiation}}$$

$$\cfrac{}{(lhs)_\Sigma \gg (lhs)_\Sigma} \; \text{ex\_seq} \qquad\qquad \cfrac{([a/x]rhs)_{(\Sigma, a:\tau)} \gg (lhs)_{\Sigma'}}{(\exists x : \tau.\, rhs)_\Sigma \gg (lhs)_{\Sigma'}} \; \text{ex\_nnc}$$

$$\boxed{\mathcal{P} \triangleright C \longrightarrow^* C' \qquad\qquad\qquad \textit{Multi-step sequential firing}}$$

$$\cfrac{}{\mathcal{P} \triangleright C \longrightarrow^* C} \; \text{ex\_it0} \qquad\qquad \cfrac{\mathcal{P} \triangleright C \longrightarrow C' \quad \mathcal{P} \triangleright C' \longrightarrow^* C''}{\mathcal{P} \triangleright C \longrightarrow^* C''} \; \text{ex\_itn}$$

A Logical Verification Method for Security Protocols Based on Linear Logic and BAN Logic

Koji Hasebe and Mitsuhiro Okada*

Department of Philosophy, Keio University
2-15-45, Mita, Minato-ku, Tokyo 108-8345 Japan
{hasebe,mitsu}@abelard.flet.keio.ac.jp

Abstract. A process following a security protocol is represented by a formal proof (of a fragment of linear logic based on the multiset rewriting model), modifying the idea by Cervesato-Durgin-Lincoln-Mitchell-Scedrov [4], while the (modified) BAN logic (which was first introduced by Burrows-Abadi-Needham [2]) is used as an evaluation semantics on security-properties for processes. By this method, we can get rid of the so called "idealization" step in the verification procedure of the BAN framework. In particular, we classify BAN-style belief-inferences into two categories; the inferences which only require some syntactic structure of a process observed by a participant on one hand, and the inferences which require a participant's knowledge on the structure of a protocol and a certain honesty assumption. We call the latter the honesty inferences. We shall show how such honesty inferences are used in the evaluation semantics for the security verification. We also point out that the evaluation inferences on freshness of nonces/keys/messages are classified as in the first category but that some of such inferences lack the information how to evaluate due to the lack of a certain concrete time-constraint setting. We introduce a natural time-constraint setting in our process/protocol descriptions and enrich the expressive power of the freshness evaluation.

1 Introduction

The purpose of this paper is to propose a formal conceptual framework and method for the security protocol study. In particular, we shall give an integration of a protocol reasoning methods based on BAN logic with a transitional framework based on the multiset rewriting model. Up to now the BAN-reasoning framework and the transitional (multiset rewriting) framework have been considered competitors rather than allieds. We shall, however, show that these two can be combined to provide an integrated framework for the

---

* This work was partly supported by Grants-in-Aid for Scientific Research of MEXT, Center of Excellence of MEXT on Humanity Sciences (Keio University), the Japan-US collaborative research program of JSPS-NSF, Oogata-kenkyuu-jyosei grant (Keio University) and Global Security Center grant (Keio University). The first author was also supported by Fellowship for Japanese Junior Scientists from Japan Society for the Promotion of Science.

M. Okada et al. (Eds.): ISSS 2002, LNCS 2609, pp. 417–440, 2003.

security protocol study, where the transitional framework gives the syntactic descriptions of protocols and processes (in terms of linear logical proofs) while the BAN-reasoning framework gives the semantic evaluations for these syntactic descriptions.

We give a formal description language to represent protocols and processes, by slightly modifying the idea of Cervesato-Durgin-Lincoln-Mitchell-Scedrov [4] (also cf. [6]), where the language is considered a fragment of linear logic or, equivalently, an enriched multiset rewriting system. We represent the primitive actions of a process as formal inference rules (equivalently, multiset rewrite rules enriched with some quantifiers) and the initial states as axioms, independently of a specific protocol in question. Then, we identify a process (trace) with a formal (linear logical or rewrite) proof composed of those inference rules and axioms. A *parameterized proof* is obtained from a proof-representation of process by replacing participant names with parameterized names (which we call parameterized variables). A protocol is defined as a composition of many parameterized sub-proof parts (each of which is called a block; see Section 2.1 for the detail). When $P_1, \ldots, P_n$ is the list of participant variables appearing in a protocol Π, Π is also denoted as $\Pi[P_1, \ldots, P_n]$.

In the level of formal proof-representations we introduce the notion of "a process, say π, following a protocol, say Π, with respect to a participant, say A"; π follows Π with respect to A if, under a certain substitution of participant names, say $A, B, \ldots$ into the variables, say $P, Q, \ldots$ of $\Pi[P, Q, \ldots]$, all A's blocks can be embeddable into π. Intuitively speaking, "π follows Π with respect to A" means that π is consistent with Π from the view point of A. This notion allows us to consider a process with intruders' attack which still follows a protocol with respect to all participants other than the intruders. (See Section 2.1 for the formal definitions.)

On the other hand, we use a modified BAN logic-inference rules (initiated by Burrows-Abadi-Needham [2]) as an evaluation semantics for processes. We present the evaluation semantics related to participants' beliefs as a sort of operational semantics based on the syntax of the proof-representations of processes. We show that validity of some BAN-style belief-statements is judged purely operationally to some extent; namely, we determine validity of those basic belief-statements purely by syntactic patterns of a formal proof representing a process. Our use of the belief-statements depends on a position (location) of a proof-representation of a concrete process. In fact, such beliefs correspond to the facts actually occurring in the process. Hence we use the notion *knows*, rather than *believes* in such cases. (See Section 2.2 for the detail.)

At the same time, we investigate what kind of honesty assumptions are required in this evaluation semantics in addition. We shall formalize such belief-inferences, which we call the honesty inferences, that require some honesty assumption of a participant in the sense that the participant knows the structure of the protocol in question and that the participant presumes that the current process follows a specific protocol.

Informally, at an honesty inference you first guess where you are located in the steps of a protocol which you believe to follow, by comparing your knowledge of the structure of the protocol and the history of what you have seen and what you have sent in the past. Then you infer who sent or saw or generated what kind of things (keys, nonces, names, etc.) under the assumption that the other participants follow the protocol honestly. The formalized honesty inferences are represented in a BAN-style inference form. (See Section 3 for the honesty inferences.)

By this method, we can get rid of the so called "idealization" procedure for the security verification in the BAN framework (i.e. the validity for BAN evaluations is automatically derived from the logical structure of a proof-representation of process without any idealization procedure.) The idealization procedure has been often criticized in the literature because of its ambiguous definition (e.g. [1]), while our method clarifies, in our opinion, the BAN-logic framework from a formal point of view. We also get rid of the nested use of the belief-predicate of the original BAN-logic framework, which is a source of complexity of the original BAN-logic theory. Our method simplifies, in our opinion, the BAN-logic theory.

It is known that the expressive power of the notion of freshness in the original BAN-theory is too weak to study security conditions for some protocols (cf. Syverson-Cervesato [16]). In fact, although there is a certain criterion to evaluate (in a participant's knowledge level) freshness in some cases (such as the cases when one receives a nonce/key which you generated in the same session), there are other cases for which the current BAN-framework tells nothing about the criterion for evaluating freshness. In order to supplement the limitation of the BAN-theory we introduce a natural method of time analysis for some protocols with timestamps, by means of a linear logical representation of real time systems proposed in Kanovich-Okada-Scedrov [12]. (See Section 4 on the freshness analysis.)

In this paper, we shall use the following notations: $A, B, C, \ldots$ are used to denote specific participants' names. $A(*), B(*), C(*), \ldots$ are used for participant predicate constants, where $A(s)$ means that "the participant A has information s". $Net(s)$ means that "the message s is currently transmitted through the network". $P(*), Q(*), R(*), \ldots$ are used for participant predicate variables. On the other hand, we shall also use participant names in the term level. $A, B, C, \ldots$ are used to denote participant names and $P, Q, R, \ldots$ are used to denote participant variables in the term level. For readability we often use small letters $a, b, c, \ldots$ and $p, q, r, \ldots$ to denote $A, B, C, \ldots$ and $P, Q, R, \ldots$ in the term level.

Our language is many sorted. We use Name, PublicKey, SecretKey, SharedKey and Nonce as primitive sorts. We also use Key to denote PublicKey or SecretKey or SharedKey. The definition of terms is as follows: The letters $a, b, c, \ldots$ are constants of sort Name and the letters $p, q, r, \ldots$ are variables of sort Name. The capital letters $K, K', \ldots, K_1, K_2, \ldots$ and $N, N', \ldots, N_1, N_2, \ldots$ are constants of sort Key and of sort Nonce, respectively, while the small letters $k, k', \ldots, k_1, k_2, \ldots$ and $n, n', \ldots, n_1, n_2, \ldots$ are variables of the same sorts as above. Any term of Name or Key or Nonce is of sort Message. The letters $x, y, z, \ldots, x', x'', \ldots, x_1, x_2, \ldots$ are used for variables of sort Message. $\{s\}_K$ (the encryption of s with key K) and $\langle s_1, \ldots, s_n \rangle$ (the concatenation of messages $s_1, \ldots, s_n$) are functions of sort Message$\times$Key$\rightarrow$Message and of sort Message$^n \rightarrow$ Message, respectively. The letters $s, u, v, w, \ldots, s_1, s_2, \ldots$ are used to denote terms of the sort Message.

2   A Verification Method for Processes

2.1   The Processes-as-Proofs Interpretation

In this subsection, we give a method for representing a process by a (linear logical) formal proof. In Cervesato-Durgin-Mitchell-Lincoln-Scedrov [4], a specific protocol is represented by a (multiset-rewriting or linear logical) proof, where each primitive action is regarded as a rewrite rule. On the other hand, we use a notion of formal proof to represent not only a specific protocol but also a process independently of a specific protocol. For this purpose, we formalize primitive actions (and initial states, resp.) as inference rules (and axioms, resp.) more generally, independently of a specific protocol. Then we represent a stack of primitive actions as a stack of these inference rules, as a formal logical proof, independently of a specific protocol.

More precisely speaking, our language of representing a process as a proof is a Horn-fragment of first-order linear logic similarly to Cervesato-Durgin-Lincoln-Mitchell-Scedrov [4] (the formal definition is given in Appendix A). We shall use the inference form of one-sided sequents to represent a Horn-clause rule for readability. We shall extend our one-sided sequents to the two-sided sequents in Section 4 later. We represent specific participant's initial states as axioms which mean the abilities of generation of nonces or session keys or the abilities of decryption/encryption, and primitive actions as inference rules; for example, receiving or sending a message from network, encryption or decryption of a key etc. Some examples of A's axioms and of A's inference rules are as below. (See Appendix A for the complete list.)

Nonce generation:

$$\vdash \exists n A(n)$$

public key K:

$$\vdash A(K'), KP(K, K')$$

sending:

$$\frac{\vdash \Gamma, A(s)}{\vdash \Gamma, A(s), Net(s)}$$

receiving:

$$\frac{\vdash \Gamma, Net(s)}{\vdash \Gamma, A(s)}$$

encryption (public key):

$$\frac{\vdash \Gamma, KP(K, K'), A(s)}{\vdash \Gamma, KP(K, K'), A(s), A(\{s\}_K)}$$

decryption (shared key):

$$\frac{\vdash \Gamma, A(K), A(\{s\}_K)}{\vdash \Gamma, A(K), A(\{s\}_K), A(s)}$$

(In the public key axiom, predicate KP means that K and K' are key pair, and K' is secret key of A and K is a public key of A.)

We also assume the linear logical inference rules for $\otimes$, $\exists$, $\forall$ as primitive actions, too. We use "," (comma) for $\otimes$. For the $\exists$-left rule we use not only the usual $\exists$-left but also the natural deduction style $\exists$-elimination rule (to introduce the fresh constant, cf. [4]). The usual $\exists$-left rule with the left-hand side context appears only in Section 4. The resource sensitivity of the linear logical framework is used especially for describing a network state, a participant's state (and a current time state introduced in Section 4). Note that the information s of A is kept "sending" but the information s of Net is erased in "receiving".

Definition 1 A formal proof composed of some axioms for the initial states and some inference rules for the primitive actions is a *proof-representation of a process*. See Appendix A for the full list of axioms and rules. (We use the letters π, ρ in order to denote processes.) We shall identify a proof-representation with a (trace of) *process* in the rest of this paper. When we replace some participant constants, say $A, B, \ldots$ and $a, b, \ldots$, of a proof-representation of a process by variables, say $P, Q, \ldots$ and $p, q, \ldots$, we get a *parameterized proof-representation*. We call a parameterized proof-representation a *parameterized process* in this paper.

If Π is a parameterized proof-representation obtained from a proof-representation π, π is called an *instance* of Π.

We regard a position in a proof as the position of the process represented by this proof. Here $i \leq j$ means that position j is below position i in a thread of proof. We use "end" in order to denote the position of end-sequent of a proof-representation.

In our process-representation framework introduced we can define a specific protocol as a parameterized process. Before we give a formal definition of a (proof-representation of) protocol, we introduce a notion of P's *block* for some participant P. In the following definition of block, A *semi-proof* is a proof whose initial sequents are not necessarily axioms.

Definition 2 A P's *block* is a semi-proof, say Σ, satisfying the following conditions.

1. All initial sequents of Σ are axioms for P or a sequent of the form $\vdash \Gamma, Net(x)$.
2. All inferences of Σ are inference rules for P.
3. Predicate symbol $Net(*)$ doesn't appear in this part except in the initial sequent or end sequent.

We can obtain instantiated A's block by replacing participant variable of the block (say, P and p) by A and a, and we call it simply "A's block".

By means of the notion of block, regarding P's block as P's specific procedure, we define a protocol as a parameterized proof composed of some participants' blocks.

Definition 3 A *protocol*, say Π, is a parameterized process (i.e. a parameterized proof-representation) satisfying the following conditions.

1. Π is composed of some participants' blocks.
2. For each block (say Σ) in Π, all initial sequents of Σ are the axioms of Π or the end sequent of the other block in Π.
3. The end sequent of Σ is the end sequent of Π or the initial sequent of the other block in Π.

For each participant P, P's blocks appear in a protocol Π are called P' s *blocks of Π*.

The letters $\Pi, \Pi_1, \Pi_2, \ldots$ are used to denote protocols. We also use the notation $\Pi[P_1, \ldots, P_n]$ in order to indicate the list of participant variables appearing in Π, and $\Pi[A_1/P_1, \ldots, A_n/P_n]$ in order to indicate an instantiated (proof-representation of) protocol which is obtained by substituting A_i for P_i for each i ($i = 1, \ldots, n$). We use the letters $\sigma, \sigma_1, \sigma_2, \ldots$ to denote substitutions.

Here we show an example of protocol and its blocks.

Example 1 Consider the following informal description of a protocol $\Pi[P, Q]$.

1. $P \rightarrow Q : N$ (N is generated by P.)
2. $Q \rightarrow P : \{N, q\}_K$ (K is shared key with P and Q.)

According to our definitions, we represent this as a parameterized proof-representation in the left-below. This protocol is decomposed into the three blocks as shown in the right-below.

$$
\dfrac{\vdash \exists n P(n) \quad \dfrac{\vdash P(K) \quad \vdash Q(K)}{\vdash P(K), Q(K)}}{\dfrac{\vdash P(N)}{\dfrac{\vdash P(N), P(K), Q(K)}{\vdash Net(N), P(K), Q(K)}}}
$$

$$
\dfrac{\dfrac{\vdash Net(N), P(K), Q(K)}{\dfrac{\vdash Q(N), P(K), Q(K)}{\dfrac{\vdash Q(N), Q(q), P(K), Q(K)}{\dfrac{\vdash Q(\{N, q\}_K), P(K)}{\vdash Net(\{N, q\}_K), P(K)}}}} \quad \dfrac{\vdash \forall p Q(p)}{\vdash Q(q)}}{}
$$

$$
\dfrac{\vdash Net(\{N, q\}_K), P(K)}{\dfrac{\vdash P(\{N, q\}_K), P(K)}{\vdash P(N), P(q)}}
$$

$$
\dfrac{\dfrac{\vdash \exists n P(n) \quad \dfrac{\vdash P(K) \quad \vdash Q(K)}{\vdash P(K), Q(K)}}{\dfrac{\vdash P(N)}{\dfrac{\vdash P(N), P(K), Q(K)}{\dfrac{\vdash Net(N), P(K), Q(K)}{\dfrac{\vdash Q(N), P(K), Q(K)}{\dfrac{\vdash Q(N), Q(q), P(K), Q(K)}{\dfrac{\vdash Q(\{N, q\}_K), P(K)}{\dfrac{\vdash Net(\{N, q\}_K), P(K)}{\dfrac{\vdash P(\{N, q\}_K), P(K)}{\vdash P(N), P(q)}}}}}}}}} \quad \dfrac{\vdash \forall p Q(p)}{\vdash Q(q)}}{}
$$

In other words, we can obtain a protocol by joining the all blocks in the specific order. We call this order as *the order of blocks (of a protocol)*.

In terms of the above definitions, we give a definition of *a process π following a protocol Π with respect to a participant A*.

Definition 4 For a process π and a protocol $\Pi[P, P_1, \ldots, P_n]$ and a substitution $\sigma \equiv (P := A, P_1 := B_1, \ldots, P_n := B_n)$, if π includes all A's blocks of $\Pi[A/P, B_1/P_1, \ldots, B_n/P_n]$ in the order, then π is a process following protocol $\Pi[P, P_1, \ldots, P_n]$ with respect to A and to substitution σ.

Example 2 According to the definition, the following proofs is a process following the protocol $\Pi[P, Q]$ (in the above example) with respect to A (and also with respect to B) and to substitution $\sigma \equiv (P := A, Q := B)$.

$$
\frac{\dfrac{\dfrac{\vdash \exists n A(n)}{\vdash A(N)} \quad \dfrac{\vdash A(K) \quad \vdash B(K)}{\vdash A(K), B(K)}}{\dfrac{\vdash A(N), A(K), B(K)}{\dfrac{\vdash Net(N), A(K), B(K)}{\dfrac{\vdash I(N), A(K), B(K)}{\dfrac{\vdash Net(N), A(K), B(K)}{\dfrac{\vdash B(N), A(K), B(K)}{\dfrac{\vdash B(N), B(b), A(K), B(K)}{\dfrac{\vdash B(\{N, b\}_K), A(K)}{\dfrac{\vdash Net(\{N, b\}_K), A(K)}{\dfrac{\vdash A(\{N, b\}_K), A(K)}{\vdash A(N), A(b)}}}}} \quad \dfrac{\vdash \forall p B(p)}{\vdash B(b)}}}}}}{}}
$$

2.2   The BAN Logic as an Evaluation Semantics about Processes

In this subsection, we introduce an evaluation method about each participant's belief at a position in a process. For this evaluation we use a modified BAN logic or its successors (e.g. Gong-Needham-Yahalom [9], Syverson-van Oorschot [15]), and regard this as some kind of semantics about belief for a process. The formal definition of our evaluation framework is given in Appendix B.

Our evaluation method is different from the original BAN logic framework. The first point is that our method is to evaluate processes, while the original BAN logic is to evaluate protocols. The second point is that we derive belief-statements about each participant's belief from a formal proof representing a process rather than an informal description of a protocol-process. The third point is that we evaluate a belief-statement relative to a position in a process; we use the belief-statement of the form $A \models_i \varphi$ ("A believes φ at position i") rather than $A \models \varphi$. (We omit a position index if we understand which position is intended clearly in the context.)

The features of our evaluation method are listed below:

- We get rid of the "idealization" procedures from the evaluation.
- We get rid of any nested use of the belief predicate (such as $A \models_i B \models_j \varphi$).

In our method, a process is evaluated by the following procedure: First we derive some statements about each participant's belief by the "evaluation criteria" listed below. Next by means of our BAN-style belief-inferences (see Appendix B) we derive new beliefs from these statements.

Before we introduce the evaluation criteria, we introduce some notions for preparation.

Definition 5 (Decomposed subterm) We define a decomposed subterm of a term t as follows:

1. t is a decomposed subterm of t.
2. If t is of the form $\langle s_1, \ldots, s_n \rangle$, and if s is a decomposed subterm of s_i (for some $i \leq n$), then s is a decomposed subterm of t.

Definition 6 (accessible to A) For a sequent $\vdash \Gamma$ and for a participant predicate A, a term s is accessible to A iff there exists a term t such that $A(t)$ appears in Γ and that s is a decomposed subterm of t.

Now we introduce the evaluation criteria.

The Evaluation Criteria

1. **Evaluation criterion for $A \models_i^\pi \overset{K}{\leftrightarrow} B$ and $A \models_i^\pi KP(K, K')$:**
   If the following sequent

   $$\vdash B(K'), KP(K, K')$$

   appears in a proof π as an axiom for some B, then the statements $A \models_i^\pi \overset{K}{\leftrightarrow} B$ and $A \models_i^\pi KP(K, K')$ are evaluated as a valid statements for some A at any position i in the proof π.

2. **Evaluation criterion for $A \models_i^\pi A \overset{K}{\leftrightarrow} B$**
   If the following sequent
   $$\vdash A(K), B(K)$$

   appears in a proof π as an axiom for some A and B, then $A \models_i^\pi A \overset{K}{\leftrightarrow} B$ is evaluated as a valid statement at any position i in the proof π.

3. **Evaluation criterion for $A \models_i^\pi Gen(A, s)$:**
   If the following proof structure

   $$\frac{\vdash \Gamma, \exists x A(x)}{\vdash \Gamma, A(s)} \ \exists\text{-elimination}$$

   appears in a proof π such that the lower sequent has position j for some A, then $A \models_i^\pi Gen(A, s)$ is evaluated as a valid statement at any position $i \geq j$ in the proof π (where the statement $Gen(A, s)$ means that "s is generated by A").

4. **Evaluation criterion for** $A\models^\pi_i \exists y_1 \cdots y_n (A \lhd s)$**:**
   Consider the following proof structure.

$$\frac{\dfrac{\vdash \Gamma_1, Net(s_1)}{\vdash \Gamma_1, A(s_1)} \;\; \text{receiving}}{\vdash \Gamma_2, A(s_2)} \;\; \text{decryption rules and concatenation rules}$$

Here $\vdash \Gamma_2, A(s_2)$ is derived from $\vdash \Gamma_1, A(s_1)$ by only some decryption rules. (We can neglect concatenation rules. See Appendix A.) We assume that the sequent $\vdash \Gamma_2, A(s_2)$ has position j.
If the above proof structure appears in a proof π for some A, then $A\models^\pi_i \exists y_1 \cdots y_n (A \lhd s)$ is evaluated as a valid statement at any position $i \geq j$ in the proof π, where s is obtained from s_1 by replacing each subterm u_l which is not accessible to A in $\vdash \Gamma_2, A(s_2)$ ($l = 1, \ldots, n$) with y_l (cf. see Example 3 below).

Remark. Here by using $\exists y_1 \cdots y_n$ we express that the bound variables $y_1 \cdots y_n$ are messages of which A doesn't know the actual values, because A cannot see the contents of the encrypted messages.

5. **Evaluation criterion for** $A\models^\pi_i \exists y_1 \cdots y_n (B \!\mid\!\sim s)$**:**
   Consider the following proof structure.

$$\frac{\dfrac{\dfrac{\vdash \Gamma_1, Net(s_1)}{\vdash \Gamma_1, A(s_1)} \;\; \text{receiving}}{\vdash \Gamma_2, A(s_2)} \;\; \text{decryption rules and concatenation rules}}{\vdash \Gamma_3, A(s_3)} \;\; \text{decryption with } K$$

Here $\vdash \Gamma_2, A(s_2)$ is derived from $\vdash \Gamma_1, A(s_1)$ by only some decryption rules, and $\vdash \Gamma_3, A(s_3)$ is derived from $\Gamma_2, A(s_2)$ by decryption rule about the key K. The sequent $\vdash \Gamma_3, A(s_3)$ has position j.
If the above proof structure appears in a proof for some A, and if either the statement $A\models^\pi_j A \overset{K}{\leftrightarrow} B$ is valid or $A\models^\pi_j \overset{K'}{\mapsto} B$ and $A\models^\pi_j KP(K', K)$ is valid for some B, then the statement $A\models^\pi_i \exists y_1 \cdots y_n (B \!\mid\!\sim s)$ is evaluated as a valid statement at any position $i \geq j$, where s is obtained from s_3 by replacing each subterm u_l which is not accessible to A in $\vdash \Gamma_3, A(s_3)$ ($l = 1, \ldots, n$) with y_l.

Example 3 We show an example about the criteria 4 and 5. If the following proof structure appears in a proof π;

$$\frac{\dfrac{\dfrac{\vdash \Gamma, Net(\{\{N_1, a\}_{K_2}, N_2\}_{K_3})}{\vdash \Gamma, A(\{\{N_1, a\}_{K_2}, N_2\}_{K_3})} \;\; \text{receiving}}{\vdash \Gamma', A(\langle \{N_1, a\}_{K_2}, N_2\rangle)} \;\; \text{decryption with } K_3}{\vdash \Gamma'', A(\langle\langle N_1, a\rangle, N_2\rangle)} \;\; \text{decryption with } K_2$$

where we assume the positions of lower sequent of receiving rule and the next two sequents are i, $i+1$ and $i+2$, respectively. Then we evaluate $A\models^\pi_{j_1} \exists y(A\triangleleft\{y\}_{K_3})$, $A\models^\pi_{j_2} \exists y(A \triangleleft \{\{y\}_{K_2}, N_2\}_{K_3})$ and $A\models^\pi_{j_3} A \triangleleft \{\{N_1, a\}_{K_2}, N_2\}_{K_3}$ (where $j_1 \geq i$, $j_2 \geq i+1$ and $j_3 \geq i+2$) as a valid statements. Moreover, if $A\models^\pi_{i+1} A \overset{K_3}{\leftrightarrow} B$, then we also evaluate $A\models^\pi_{j_2} \exists y(B\hspace{-0.3em}\sim \langle\{y\}_{K_1}, N_2\rangle)$ as a valid statement, and if $A\models^\pi_{i+2}\overset{K_1}{\leftrightarrow} B$ and $A\models^\pi_{i+2} KP(K_1, K_2)$, then $A\models^\pi_{j_3} B\hspace{-0.3em}\sim \langle N_1, a\rangle$ is evaluated as a valid statement.

6. **Evaluation criterion for** $A\models^\pi_i \exists y_1 \cdots y_n(A\overset{*}{\hspace{-0.3em}\sim} s)$**:**
   Consider the following proof structure.

   $$\frac{\dfrac{\vdash \Gamma_1, A(s_1)}{\vdash \Gamma_2, A(s_2)} \text{ encryption rules and concatenation rules}}{\vdash \Gamma_2, Net(s_2), A(s_2)} \text{ sending}$$

   Here $\vdash \Gamma_2, A(s_2)$ is derived from $\vdash \Gamma_1, A(s_1)$ by only some encryption rules (where we can neglect concatenation rules), and the sequent $\vdash \Gamma_2, Net(s_2), A(s_2)$ has position j.
   If the above proof structure appears in a proof π for some A, then $A|\models^\pi_i \exists y_1 \cdots y_n(A|\overset{*}{\hspace{-0.3em}\sim} s)$ is evaluated as a valid statement at any position $i \geq j$, where s is obtained from s_2 by replacing each subterm u_l which is not accessible to A in $\vdash \Gamma_2, Net(s_2), A(s_2)$ $(l = 1, \ldots, n)$ by y_l.

7. **Evaluation criterion for** $A\models^\pi_i A \ni s$
   If a predicate of the form $A(s)$ appears in a proof π for some A at a position j in π, then $A\models^\pi_i A \ni s$ is evaluated as a valid statement at any position $i \geq j$.

We listed above seven evaluation criteria. By the definition of the criteria, belief-statements derived from the evaluation criteria correspond to the facts actually occurring in the process. Hence, we consider such belief-statements as knowledge rather than belief and we call them *knowledge-statements*. We introduce a notation $A \models^\pi_i \varphi$ which represents "A knows φ at position i in π" and we define if $A \models^\pi_i \varphi$ then $A\models^\pi_i \varphi$ for any A and φ and π. These rules are not enough for belief-inferences. We shall discuss what rules are needed to evaluate such processes and introduce these rules in Section 3.

3   Honesty Inferences and the Use of Belief Histories

3.1   Introduction of Honesty Inferences

In Section 2.2, we introduced some evaluation criteria of participant's belief independently of the participant's knowledge of a protocol (and we treated such the belief as knowledge). However, these criteria are not strong enough for our evaluation semantics. In order to capture stronger belief-inferences, the original BAN logic needed to interpret a protocol (this interpretation is called "idealization") informally. In our framework, instead of such "idealization", we introduce "honesty inferences" into our evaluation framework. These inference rules assume each participant's knowledge about the protocol and his/her belief of the other participants' honesty, (i.e. the other participants faithfully follow the protocol procedure).

First we show an example of an evaluation for a process following a protocol. Here we consider the following protocol $\Pi[P, Q, R]$ which intends to share the key K (created by R) between P and Q, and evaluate a *standard process* following the protocol $\Pi[P, Q, R]$ (which means that the process follows the protocol $\Pi[P, Q, R]$ with respect to A, B and C and substitution $P := A$, $Q := B$ and $R := C$, and does not include any other inferences).

Example 4

(1) An informal description of a protocol $\Pi[P, Q, R]$

1. $P \to R : \{p, q, N_P\}_{K_R}$
2. $R \to Q : \{N_P, p, K\}_{K_Q}, \{N_P\}_K$
3. $Q \to P : \{N_P, q, K\}_{K_P}$
4. $P \to Q : \{N_P, p, K\}_{K_Q}, \{N_P\}_K$

(2) An informal description of a standard process $\pi \equiv \Pi[A/P, B/Q, C/R]$

1. $A \to C : \{a, b, N_A\}_{K_C}$
2. $C \to B : \{N_A, a, K\}_{K_B}, \{N_A\}_K \cdots$ position i
3. $B \to A : \{N_A, b, K\}_{K_A}$
4. $A \to B : \{N_A, a, K\}_{K_B}, \{N_A\}_K \cdots$ position j

(Here we use some abbreviations: in the informal protocol/process-descriptions N_P represents a nonce generated by P with nonce generation rule beforehand, and K_P, K_Q and K_R represent public keys for P, Q, and R, respectively, introduced by suitable axioms for keys beforehand. We also use corresponding abbreviation of some belief-statements: generally $A\models_i B\!\!\mid\!\sim N_C$ is abbreviation of "$A\models_i B\!\!\mid\!\sim N$ and $A\models_i Gen(C, N)$", and $A\models_i B \vartriangleleft \{s\}_{K_C}$ is abbreviation of "$A\models_i B \vartriangleleft \{s\}_K$ and $A\models_i^K C$", and so on.)

In (2) of Example 4 above we consider an evaluation about B's belief at the position where B decrypts the key K_B and K on the line 2 in (2). We call this position as i.

By means of the evaluation criteria of Section 2.2, we can derive the statement $B \models_i^\pi B \vartriangleleft \langle\langle N_A, a, K\rangle, N_A\rangle$. (Namely, B knows that B receives $\langle\langle N_A, a, K\rangle, N_A\rangle$.) However, by means of only the evaluation criteria of Section 2.2 and belief-inferences in Appendix B, B cannot infer who sent this message or who had key K. Generally in a process following a protocol, when a participant receives a message, he/she cannot always know who has sent the message only by the information of the message. However, in the case of Example 4, if B knows the whole structure of the protocol $\Pi[P, Q, R]$ and assumes the other participants' honesty (i.e., A and C follow the protocol $\Pi[P, Q, R]$ with respect to $P := A$, $Q := B$ and $R := C$), and if B knows that B actually follows the protocol (i.e., that B received the message $\langle\langle N_A, a, K\rangle_{K_B}, \{N_A\}_K\rangle$, which is consistent with the process $\pi \equiv \Pi[A/P, B/Q, C/R]$), then B can believe that the message $\langle\langle N_A, a, K\rangle_{K_B}, \{N_A\}_K\rangle$ was sent by C at position i. This is because if A, B and C follow the protocol $\Pi[P, Q, R]$ with respect to $P := A$, $Q := B$ and

$R := C$, then C should send the message $\langle \{N_A, a, K\}_{K_B}, \{N_A\}_K \rangle$, which is actually received by B.

We represent this B's inference as follows.

$$\frac{B \models_i^\pi B \triangleleft \langle \{N_A, a, K\}_{K_B}, \{N_A\}_K \rangle}{B \models_i^{\pi, \Pi} C \overset{*}{\triangleright} \langle \{N_A, a, K\}_{K_B}, \{N_A\}_K \rangle \ [A/P, B/Q, C/R]}$$

In an inference rule of this type, the participant's knowledges of the history of his/her own sending and receiving actions are listed as the upper statements (premises). We call these premises his/her *history*. (Each statement of the history is derived by only the evaluation criteria introduced in Section 2.2.) The lower statement (conclusion) of the above inference rule is B's belief based on his/her knowledge about the whole structure of the protocol $\Pi[P, Q, R]$ and on his/her assumption that the other participants follow the protocol $\Pi[P, Q, R]$ with respect to $P := A$, $Q := B$ and $R := C$ (namely he/she assumes that the process $\pi \equiv \Pi[A/P, B/Q, C/R]$ is realized). We call the part $[A/P, B/Q, C/R]$ an *assignment*. (Generally, for any participant constant A and for any protocol $\Pi[P_1, \ldots, P_n]$ and for any position i of a given process, $A \models_i^{\pi, \Pi} \varphi[B_1/P_1, \ldots, B_n/P_n]$ means that A believes φ at position i in π under the interpretation of P_m by B_m for each $m \leq n$. We call the part $[B_1/P_1, \ldots, B_n/P_n]$ as an assignment. The original notation $A \models_i \varphi$ is interpreted as "$A \models_i \varphi[B_1/P_1, \ldots, B_n/P_n]$ for any $B_1, \ldots, B_n$". However, we shall omit the assignment part $[B_1/P_1, \ldots, B_n/P_n]$ if it is clear from the context.)

Here we point out what is the role of a participant's history. The role of the history is to detect a position in the protocol. For example, in the process (2) of Example 4 above, if B ignores his/her history when B receives the message $\langle \{N_A, a, K\}_{K_B}, \{N_A\}_K \rangle$, then the position cannot be determined and B cannot detect whether A or C sent the message, because B receives the same messages twice in the process. However, if B's history is $B \models_j^\pi B \triangleleft \langle \{N_A, a, K\}_{K_B}, \{N_A\}_K \rangle$, $B \models_j^\pi B \overset{*}{\triangleright} \{N_A, b, K\}_{K_A}$ and $B \models_j^\pi B \triangleleft \langle \{N_A, a, K\}_{K_B}, \{N_A\}_K \rangle$, the current position can be determined as j (where B receives the second $\langle \{N_A, a, K\}_{K_B}, \{N_A\}_K \rangle$) and B can detect that the message is sent from A. This inference is represented as follows.

$$\frac{B \models_j^\pi B \triangleleft \langle \{N_A, a, K\}_{K_B}, \{N_A\}_K \rangle \qquad B \models_j^\pi B \overset{*}{\triangleright} \{N_A, b, K\}_{K_A}}{B \models_j^{\pi, \Pi} A \overset{*}{\triangleright} \{N_A, b, K\}_{K_B} \ [A/P, B/Q, C/R]}$$

We introduce this kind of inference rules as *honesty inferences*. (Formal definition is given in the next subsection.) Using these inferences we evaluate each participant's belief in a process following protocol. Moreover, when we derive some participant's belief about some secrecy properties (a goal of this protocol) however by using some honesty inferences, then the usage of these inferences serves as a detection of the flaw points in a protocol.

3.2 Formal Definition of the Honesty Inferences

Before defining the honesty inferences, we introduce some notions for preparation.

Definition 7 Consider the following P's block.

$$
(\alpha) \begin{cases} \dfrac{\begin{array}{c}\vdash \Gamma, Net(s) \\ \hline \vdash \Gamma', P(s')\end{array}}{\vdash \Gamma'', P(s'')} \text{ lowest decryption rule} \end{cases}
$$

$$
\vdots
$$

$$
(\beta) \begin{cases} \dfrac{\vdash \Delta'', P(u')}{\vdash \Delta', P(u)} \text{ highest encryption rule} \end{cases}
$$

$$
\overline{\vdash \Delta, Net(u)}
$$

The part (α) includes some decryption rules and concatenation rules, and any decryption rule doesn't appear in the lower part of the sequent $\vdash \Gamma'', P(s'')$. The part (β) includes some encryption rules and concatenation rules, and any encryption rule doesn't appear in the upper part of $\vdash \Delta'', P(u')$. Here we call the part (α) as *decryption part of the block* and the part (β) as *encryption part of the block*. (We point out that it is possible that $\vdash \Delta'', P(u')$ appears above $\vdash \Gamma'', P(s'')$.)

If we consider an A's block for any participant constant A, we also define same as above.

From now we give the formal definition of the honesty inferences.

We consider an arbitrary protocol $\Pi[P, Q, R_1, \ldots, R_m]$ and an instance $\Pi[A/P, B/Q, C_1/R_1, \ldots, C_m/R_m]$ for some participant constants A, B and $C_1, \ldots, C_m$. In the following discussion we omit $R_1, \ldots, R_m$ and $C_1, \ldots, C_m$, and we abbreviate $\Pi[A/P, B/Q, C_1/R_1, \ldots, C_m/R_m]$ as $\Pi[A/P, B/Q]$.

Consider the following part of $\Pi[A/P, B/Q]$ (it is called π).

A part of $\Pi[A/P, B/Q]$

$$
\left. \dfrac{\vdash \Gamma, A(s_{n-1})}{\vdash \Gamma, Net(s_{n-1})} \text{ sending} \right\} (\alpha)
$$

$$
\vdots
$$

$$
\boxed{B\text{'s block}} \cdots\cdots (\beta)
$$

$$
\vdots
$$

$$
\dfrac{\vdash \Gamma', Net(s_n)}{\vdash \Gamma', A(s_n)} \text{ receiving}
$$

Assume that π satisfies the following conditions.

1. The part (α) in π is the initial part of a protocol $\Pi[A/P, B/Q]$, which includes A's $n-1$ blocks $(n \geq 1)$.
2. For each A's k-th block $(k = 1, \ldots, n)$, the sequents $\vdash \Gamma_k, Net(s_k)$ and $\vdash \Delta_k, Net(u_k)$ appear in the top and bottom of the block respectively. (If A's first block is a first block of Π, $\vdash \Gamma_1, Net(s_1)$ doesn't appear in the A's first block.)
3. Between A's $n-1$-th block and n-th block, at least one B's block (β).

Honesty Inferences (1)

If the following B's block (β) appears in π,

$$\vdash \Phi, Net(v_1)$$

(decryption part) $\left\{ \dfrac{\vdots}{\vdash \Phi', B(v_1')} \text{ lowest decryption rule} \right.$

$$\vdots$$

(encryption part) $\left\{ \dfrac{\vdash \Psi', B(v_2')}{\vdots} \text{ highest encryption rule} \right.$

$$\vdash \Psi, Net(v_2)$$

then we can use the following inference rules for any position i.

$$\frac{A \models_i^\pi \exists y(A \lhd s_1') \quad A \models_i^\pi \exists y'(A \stackrel{*}{\vdash} u_1') \cdots A \models_i^\pi \exists y(A \lhd s_{n-1}') \quad A \models_i^\pi \exists y'(A \stackrel{*}{\vdash} u_{n-1}') \quad A \models_i^\pi \exists y(A \lhd s_n')}{A \models_i^{\pi,\Pi} \exists nk(B \lhd v_3) \; [A/P, B/Q]}$$

$$\frac{A \models_i^\pi \exists y(A \lhd s_1') \quad A \models_i^\pi \exists y'(A \stackrel{*}{\vdash} u_1') \cdots A \models_i^\pi \exists y(A \lhd s_{n-1}') \quad A \models_i^\pi \exists y'(A \stackrel{*}{\vdash} u_{n-1}') \quad A \models_i^\pi \exists y(A \lhd s_n')}{A \models_i^{\pi,\Pi} \exists nk(B \stackrel{*}{\vdash} v_4) \; [A/P, B/Q]}$$

Here for each s_k' for $k = 1, \ldots, n$ is obtained from s_k by replacing each subterm w_l for $l = 1, \ldots, m$ which is not accessible to A in the decryption part with y_l. Also for each u_k' for $k = 1, \ldots, n-1$ is obtained form u_k by replacing each subterm $w_{l'}'$ for $l' = 1, \ldots, m'$ which is not accessible to A in the encryption part with $y_{l'}'$. v_3 (v_4, resp.) is obtained from v_1 (v_2, resp.) by replacing each constants N and K which are not accessible to A at position i with variables n and k.

Honesty Inference (2)

If the following B's block (β) appears in π,

$$\vdots$$

$$\frac{\vdash \Phi', B(v_1), B(v_2)}{\vdash \Phi', B(\langle v_1, v_2\rangle)} \text{ concatenation}$$

$$\frac{}{\vdash \Phi, B(w)} \text{ encryption rules and concatenation rules}$$

$$\frac{\vdash \Phi, B(w)}{\vdash \Phi, Net(w)} \text{ sending}$$

(where the term w is obtained from $\langle v_1, v_2\rangle$ by some encryption rules and concatenation rules), then we can use the following inference rule at any position i.

$$\frac{A \models_i^\pi \exists y(A \triangleleft s_1') \quad A \models_i^\pi \exists y'(A \stackrel{*}{\sim} u_1') \cdots A \models_i^\pi \exists y(A \triangleleft s_{n-1}') \quad A \models_i^\pi \exists y(A \stackrel{*}{\sim} u_{n-1}') \quad A \models_i^\pi \exists nk(B \stackrel{*}{\sim} v_1) \quad A \models_i^\pi \exists y(A \triangleleft s_n')}{A \models_i^{\pi,\Pi} \exists nk(B \triangleleft \langle v_1, v_2'\rangle) \ [A/P, B/Q]}$$

Here for each s_k' and u_k' ($k = 1, \ldots, n$) is the same as the definition of honesty inference (1). And v_2' is obtained from v_2 by replacing each constants N, K with n and k where each N and K is not accessible to A at position i.

Honesty Inference (3)
   If the following B's block (β) appears in π,

$$\vdots$$

$$\frac{\vdash \Phi', B(u)}{\vdash \Phi', B(\{u\}_K)} \text{ encryption rule}$$

$$\frac{}{\vdash \Phi', B(v)} \text{ encryption rules and concatenation rules}$$

$$\frac{\vdash \Phi', B(v)}{\vdash \Phi, Net(v)} \text{ sending}$$

then we can use the following inference rule at any position i.

$$\frac{A \models_i^\pi \exists y(A \triangleleft s_1') \quad A \models_i^\pi \exists y'(A \stackrel{*}{\sim} u_1') \cdots \quad A \models_i^\pi \exists y(A \triangleleft s_{n-1}') \quad A \models_i^\pi \exists y'(A \stackrel{*}{\sim} u_{n-1}') \quad A \models_i^\pi \exists nk(B \stackrel{*}{\sim} \{u\}_K) \quad A \models_i^\pi \exists y(A \triangleleft s_n')}{A \models_i^{\pi,\Pi} \exists nk(B \triangleleft u) \ [A/P, B/Q]}$$

Here for each s_k' and u_k' ($k = 1, \ldots, n$) is is same as the definition of honesty inference (1) and (2).

Remark on a statement about secrecy. We don't define an inference rule for deriving a statement about secrecy directly (as the original BAN logic did). However, we treat $A|\equiv A \stackrel{s}{\rightleftharpoons} B$ for some A and B and for some s as valid statement if the evaluation criterion 8 below is satisfied at the end position. Before we state the evaluation criterion 8, we introduce a notion s *is preserved to A and B with respect to t* for preparation.

Definition 8 s *is preserved to A and B with respect to t* if the following conditions.

1. If t is of the form $\{s'\}_{K_A}$ or $\{s'\}_{K_B}$ or $\{s'\}_{K_{AB}}$ and if s is decomposed subterm of s', then s is preserved to A and B with respect to t.

2. If t is not subterm of s, then s is preserved A and B with respect to t.

3. If t is of the form $\langle s_1, \ldots, s_n \rangle$ and if s is preserved to A and B with respect to s_i for all i, then s is preserved to A and B with respect to t.

4. If t is of the form $\{s'\}_{K_A}$ or $\{s'\}_{K_B}$ or $\{s'\}_{K_{AB}}$ and if s is preserved to A and B with respect to s', then s is preserved to A and B with respect to t.

8. **Evaluation criterion for** $A \models_{end}^{\pi, \Pi} A \overset{s}{\rightleftharpoons} B$:

If the following conditions are satisfied;

1. $A \models_{end}^{\pi, \Pi} A \ni s$ and $A \models_{end}^{\pi, \Pi} B \ni s$ are valid for a protocol Π and a process $\pi \equiv \Pi[A/P, B/Q]$

2. For each $\vdash \Gamma, Net(t)$, appearing in $\pi \equiv \Pi[A/P, B/Q]$, s is preserved to A and B with respect to t.

then $A \models_{end}^{\pi, \Pi} A \overset{s}{\rightleftharpoons} B$ is evaluated as a valid statement at the end position.

We have shown the criteria for validity of knowledge-statements in Section 2.2 and additional reasoning (honesty inferences) in this section. Using these evaluation frameworks, however, we cannot detect some kind of replay attacks, like an attack on the BAN-Yahalom protocol [2]. According to Syverson-Cervesato[16], these replay attacks cannot be detected in the frameworks based on the original BAN logic because in such frameworks freshness is very weak mechanism only available to distinguish a current run from another. In fact, consider the following belief-inferences based on the original BAN logic.

$$\frac{\dfrac{A \models B \mid\!\sim \langle N, K \rangle \quad \dfrac{A \models \sharp(N)}{A \models \sharp(\langle N, K \rangle)}}{A \models B \mid\!\overset{*}{\sim} \langle N, K \rangle}}{A \models B \ni K}$$

We can observe that these inferences only tell us the need of "freshness of nonce N" to derive $A \models B \ni K$, and tell us nothing as to when this freshness is guaranteed. One may think this problem would be solved with introducing timestamps. However even if we replace the nonce by a timestamp it makes no difference, because one would get exactly the same BAN-inferences as before with a timestamp to rather than a nonce N and it would only tell us the need of $A \models \sharp(t)$, namely the freshness of t, instead of freshness of N.

Therefore we would like to have to make the freshness notion more powerful and more expressive in order to evaluate the validity of $A \models B \ni K$. For this purpose, in the next section, we shall introduce an evaluation criterion for freshness in terms of the real-time notion and its quantitative time-constraints.

4 Improvement of Evaluation Criterion for Freshness

For the purpose of improving freshness mechanism, in Section 4.1 we add the·real-time notion and its quantitative time constraints to our process-representation framework. Our method for the extension is following Kanovich-Okada-Scedrov[12]. In this extended framework, lifetime of a message with times-tamp is defined by upper-bound time-constraint (i.e., lifetime is defined as D-time). Then we can introduce a natural evaluation criterion such that "a message is defined to be fresh within D-time" in the evaluation framework. In Section 4.2, we shall show how to evaluate some participants' knowledge about freshness which depends on lifetime of a message in the extended framework.

4.1 Definition of the Notion of Freshness Using Time-Constraint

We extend the language and inference rules (introduced in Section 2.1) as follows.

Sorts: Time

Terms: Any real number is a term of sort Time. $t, t', \ldots, t_1, t_2, \ldots, H, H_1, H_2, \ldots,$ $D, D_1, D_2, \ldots$ are variables of sort Time. If t_1 and t_2 are terms of sort Time and s is a term of Message, then $u(\langle s, t_1 \rangle, t_2)$ is also a term of Message. (Here u is a function symbol connecting s_1, t_1 and t_2.)

Predicate symbols: $Time(t), L(t)$ where t is a term of sort Time.

Inference rules: we add the *tick axiom* which means the time progression.

Tick:

$$\frac{\Gamma \vdash \Delta, Time(t)}{t < t', \Gamma \vdash \Delta, Time(t')}$$

We set an upper-bound time constraint to a message with timestamp by the next two rules.

Timestamp:

setting rule for A: discarding rule for A:

$$\frac{\Gamma \vdash \Delta, A(s), Time(t)}{\Gamma \vdash \Delta, A(u(\langle s, t \rangle, D), Time(t))} \qquad \frac{\Gamma \vdash \Delta, A(u(\langle s, t \rangle, D)), Time(t')}{t' < t + D, \Gamma \vdash \Delta, A(\langle s, t \rangle), Time(t')}$$

The setting rule means that A adds the timestamp t to message s with time-constraint D. The discarding rule means that A checks freshness of the message s by timestamp t with D, and the time-constraint condition appear in the left-hand side of the lower sequent. Here the term $u(\langle s, t \rangle, D)$ plays a role for the upper-bound timer for lifetime of the message s. (u is a function symbol connecting the terms s, t and D.)

On the other hand, we introduce the following evaluation criterion for freshness into our evaluation semantics.

9. **Evaluation criterion for $A \models_i^\pi \sharp(\langle s, t \rangle)$:**

   If there is a following proof structure in a proof π;

   $$\frac{\Gamma \vdash \Delta, A(u(\langle s, t \rangle, D), Time(t'))}{t' < t + D, \Gamma \vdash \Delta, A(\langle s, t \rangle), Time(t')}$$

   and the left hand side of the lower sequent $t' < t + D$ is valid, then $A \models_i^\pi \sharp(\langle s, t \rangle)$ is evaluated as a valid statement at any position i such that its time is before t'.

We point out that a statement derived by this evaluation criterion is A's knowledge rather than belief (cf. the end of Section 2.2). This criterion means that a message is fresh when the time-constraint condition $t' < t + D$ is satisfied.

4.2   Evaluation of Knowledge about Freshness

In this subsection, we show an evaluation in our extended evaluation framework introduced in the previous subsection. As an example, we introduce here the modified BAN-Yahalom protocol as follows (which is obtained by adding timestamps to the BAN-Yahalom protocol), and show how to evaluate some participant's knowledge about freshness which depends on lifetime of a message.

An Informal Description of the Modified BAN-Yahalom Protocol

    1. $P \to Q : p, N_P$
    2. $Q \to R : q, N_Q, \{p, N_P, t_Q\}_{K_{QR}}$
    3. $R \to P : N_Q, \{q, K_{PQ}, N_P, t_R\}_{K_{PR}}, \{p, N_Q, K_{PQ}, t_R\}_{K_{QR}}$
    4. $P \to Q : \{p, N_Q, K_{PQ}, t_R\}_{K_{QR}}, \{N_Q, t_P\}_{K_{PQ}}$

(Here t_Q, t_R and t_P are timestamps generated by timestamp-setting rules for P (at position 4), Q (at position 2) and R (at position 3), respectively. We set the upper-bound constraints to the freshness of the messages with timestamps t_Q, t_R and t_P as D_1 (for t_Q), D_2 (for t_R checked by P), D_3 (for t_R checked by Q) and D_4 (for t_P), respectively.)

We introduce the lower-bound time constraint to the handling duration of messages by the following two rules (which are modified sending and receiving rules introduced in Section 2.1). These rules mean that it takes more than or equal to H time to handle the message.

sending: **receiving:**

$$\frac{\Gamma \vdash \Delta, A(s), L(t + H), Time(t')}{t + H \le t', \Gamma \vdash \Delta, A(s), Net(s), Time(t')} \qquad \frac{\Gamma \vdash \Delta, Net(s), Time(t)}{\Gamma \vdash \Delta, A(s), L(t + H), Time(t)}$$

For this protocol, we can consider the following two processes: process π_1 is a standard process following this protocol with respect to $P := B$, $Q := A$ and $R := S$, and process π_2 is a process in which A and S follow this protocol and which includes C's attack (due essentially to Syverson[14]). In these processes, the position where S checks freshness of $\langle b, N_1, t_A \rangle$ is indicated as i, and we assume that this checking at position i happens at time t'.

Process π_1 (A standard process following the modified BAN-Yahalom protocol with respect to $P := B$, $Q := A$ and $R := S$)

1. $B \to A : b, N_1$
2. $A \to S : a, N_2, \{b, N_1, t_A\}_{K_1}$ $\cdots\cdots$ position i, time t'
3. $S \to B : N_2, \{a, K, N_1, t_S\}_{K_2}, \{b, N_2, K, t_S\}_{K_1}$
4. $B \to A : \{b, N_2, K, t_S\}_{K_1}, \{N_2, t_B\}_K$

(Here N_1 and N_2 are generated by B and A, respectively. K_1 and K_2 are shared keys for A with S and B with S, respectively, and K is session key generated by S for B with A. t_A, t_S and t_B are timestamps generated by timestamp-setting rules for A, S and B respectively.)

Process π_2 (An attacked process on the BAN-Yahalom protocol)

1. $\quad A \to C(B) : a, N_1$
  I. $\quad C(B) \to A : b, N_1$
  II. $\quad A \to C(S) : a, N_2, \{b, N_1, t_A\}_{K_1}$
  ii. $C(A) \to S : a, N_1, \{b, N_1, t_A\}_{K_1}$ $\cdots\cdots$ position i, time t'
  iii. $S \to C(B) : N_1, \{a, K, N_1, t_S\}_{K_2}, \{b, K, N_1, t_S\}_{K_1}$
3. $\quad C(S) \to A : N_3, \{b, K, N_1, t_S\}_{K_1}, \{a, K, N_1, t_S\}_{K_2}$
4. $\quad A \to C(B) : \{a, K, N_1, t_S\}_{K_2}, \{N_1, t_A\}_K$

(Here N_1, N_2 and N_3 are generated by A, A and C, respectively. K_1, K_2 and K are same as process π_1. t_A and t_S are timestamps generated by timestamp-setting rules for A and S, respectively.)

As for process π_1 we can observe that if and only if the time t' satisfies the following condition

$$t_A + H \leq t' < t_A + D_1 \cdots\cdots (1)$$

$S \models_i^{\pi_1} \sharp(\langle b, N_1, t_A \rangle)$ is valid, and $S \models_i^{\pi_1} A |\overset{*}{\sim} \langle b, N_1, t_A \rangle$ and $S \models_i^{\pi_1} A \ni N_1$ are also valid (cf. a typical BAN-proof of $A \models B |\overset{*}{\sim} s$ and $A \models B \ni s$ can be seen in Section 3.2). This is because process-representation of the position i is as follows and the time-constraint condition $t' < t_A + D_1$ is valid, hence the condition of the evaluation criterion 9 is satisfied.

$$\vdots$$

$$\frac{\Gamma \vdash \Delta, S(u(\langle b, N_1, t_A\rangle, D_1)), Time(t')}{t' < t_A + D_1, \Gamma \vdash \Delta, S(\langle b, N_1, t_A\rangle), Time(t')} \quad \text{timestamp}$$

$$\vdots$$

As for process π_2, we can observe that if and only if the time t' satisfies the following condition

$$t_A + 2H \leq t' < t_A + D_1 \cdots\cdots (2)$$

$S \models_i^{\pi_2} \sharp(\langle b, N_1, t_A\rangle)$, $S \models_i^{\pi_2} A \overset{*}{\mid\sim} \langle b, N_1, t_A\rangle$ and $S \models_i^{\pi_2} A \ni N_1$ are valid.

Thus, if the negation of the condition (2)

$$t' < t_A + 2H \quad \text{or} \quad t_A + D_1 \leq t' \cdots\cdots (2')$$

is satisfied, then we cannot derive the statements $S \models_i^{\pi_2} \sharp(\langle b, N_1, t_A\rangle)$ nor $S \models_i^{\pi_2} A \overset{*}{\mid\sim} \langle b, N_1, t_A\rangle$ nor $S \models_i^{\pi_2} A \ni N_1$.

Therefore from the above results (1) and (2'), as long as t' satisfies the following condition

$$t_A + H < t' < \min\{t_A + D_1, t_A + 2H\}$$

$S \models_i \sharp(\langle b, N_1, t_A\rangle)$, $S \models_i A \overset{*}{\mid\sim} \langle b, N_1, t_A\rangle$ and $S \models_i A \ni N_1$ are valid in the standard process (which follows the BAN-Yahalom protocol with respect to $P := B$, $Q := A$ and $R := S$), however these are not valid in the attacked process π_2.

We also consider A's knowledge on freshness in the standard process which follows the BAN-Yahalom protocol with respect to $P := A$, $Q := B$ and $R := S$ (say π_1') as well as in the attacked process π_2. We assume that A checks the freshness of $\langle b, t_S, K, N_1\rangle$ at time t' in π_1' and π_2. In this setting by the same reason of the above example, as long as t' satisfies the following condition

$$t_S + H < t' < \min\{t_S + D_2, t_S + 2H\}$$

$A \models \sharp(\langle b, t_S, K, N_1\rangle)$ is valid in π_1', however not valid in the attacked process π_2.

5   Concluding Remark and Further Works

In this paper we have given a framework of proof-representation of process/protocol and defined some notions about security protocol study (e.g., "a process following a protocol") in this framework. Moreover, we have given an evaluation framework about each participant's knowledge/belief of proof-representation of a process. Especially, we introduce the distinction of belief and knowledge. Based on these frameworks, we have made an evaluation mechanism of freshness more powerful and expressive than the original BAN logic by means of the method of Kanovich-Okada-Scedrov [12]. These frameworks which we have given as a whole are the integration of protocol reasoning methods based on BAN logic within the multiset rewriting model. Up to now the BAN-reasoning framework and the transitional (multiset rewriting) framework have been considered competitors rather than allieds. We have shown, however, that these two can be combined to provide an integrated framework for the security protocol study.

One of further works of this paper is to investigate meaningful sufficient conditions for "if $A \models \varphi$ then actually φ". (We point out that in our evaluation framework "if $A \models \varphi$ then actually φ" in general.) This is essential for further applications of our framework to the security verification.

Acknowledgement. We would like to thank our US collaborative research teams under the NSF-JSPS joint project. Our research in this paper was carried out based on discussion with and suggestion from our US partner team members; in particular, our proof-representation framework was based on discussion with I.Cervesato-N.A.Durgin-P.Lincoln-J.Mitchell-A.Scedrov's group at the occasions of three US-Japan meetings (in March 2000, Oct. 2001 and Nov. 2002), and on their former work, as well as discussion with/suggestion from M.Abadi. Our framework of time analysis is based on collaborative research with M.Kanovich-A.Scedrov's group. We would like to express our thanks to those US researchers for discussions and suggestions on this paper. We would also like to express our thanks to the anonymous referees for their comments.

References

1. C. Boyd and W. Mao. On a Limitation of BAN Logic. LNCS Vol. 765, Eurocrypt '93, edited by T. Helleseth, pp. 240–247, 1993.
2. M. Burrows, M. Abadi and R. Needham. A Logic of Authentication. *Technical Report 39*, Digital System Research Center, 1989.
3. F. Butler, I. Cervesato, A. Jaggard, and A. Scedrov. A formal analysis of some properties of Kerberos 5 using MSR. In: *S. Schneider, ed., 15-th IEEE Computer Security Foundations Workshop*, Cape Breton, Nova Scotia, Canada, June, 2002, IEEE Computer Society Press, 2002, pp. 175–190.
4. I. Cervesato, N.A. Durgin, P.D. Lincoln, J.C. Mitchell and A. Scedrov. A meta-notation for protocol analysis. *12th IEEE Computer Security Foundations Workshop*, 1999.
5. J. Clark and J. Jacob. A Survey of Authentication Protocol Literature: Version 1.0 (web draft).
6. N.A. Durgin, P.D. Lincoln, J.C. Mitchell and A. Scedrov. Undecidability of bounded security protocol. *The 1999 Federated Logic Conference (FLoC '99)*, 11 pages, 1999.
7. N. Durgin, J. Mitchell, and D. Pavlovic. A Compositional Logic for Protocol Correctness. In: *S. Schneider, ed., 14-th IEEE Computer Security Foundations Workshop*, Cape Breton, Nova Scotia, Canada, June, 2001, IEEE Computer Society Press, 2001.
8. J.-Y. Girard. Linear Logic. *Theoretical Computer Science*, Vol. 50, pp. 1–102, 1987.
9. L. Gong, R. Needham and R. Yahalom. Reasoning About Belief in Cryptographic Protocols. *Proceedings 1990 IEEE Symposium on Research in Security and Privacy*, pp. 234–248, 1990.

10. G. Lowe. An Attack on the Needham-Schroeder Public Key Authentication Protocol. *Information Processing Letters*, 56 (3), pp. 131–136, 1995.
11. R. Needham and M. Schroeder. Using encryption for authentication in large networks of computers. *Communications of the ACM* pp. 993–999, 1978.
12. M. Kanovich, M. Okada and A. Scedrov. Specifying Real-Time Finite-State Systems in Linear Logic. *Proc. International Workshop on Time-Sensitive Constraint Programming* and *Electronic Notes of Theoretical Computer Science 16*, No. 1, 14 pages, 1998.
13. M. Okada and K. Hasebe Logical Verifications for Security Protocols Based on Linear Logic. (in Japanese) *Technical report of IEICE*, 102(91), pp. 49–54, 2002.
14. P. Syverson. A taxonomy of replay attacks. *Proceedings of the Computer Security Foundations Workshop (CSFW7)*, pp. 187–191, 1994.
15. P. Syverson and P. C. van Oorschot. A unified cryptographic protocol logic. *NRL Publications*, 5540–227, Naval Research Lab, 1996.
16. P. Syverson and I. Cervesato. The Logic of Authentication Protocols. *Lecture Notes in Computer Science*, Vol. 2171, pp. 63–136, 2001.

Appendix

A   The Logical System for Representing Processes-as-Proofs Interpretation

The Language

Sorts and **Terms**: See Section 1 for the definition of sorts and terms.

Predicates: $A(*), B(*), \ldots$ are used for participant predicate constant. $P(*)$, $Q(*), \ldots$ are used for participant predicate variables. ($*$ is any term of Message.) $KP(*_1, *_2), Net(*)$. ($*$ is any term of Message and $*_1, *_2$ are terms of sorts PublicKey and SecretKey respectively.)

Formulas: The logical connectives of our language are only $\otimes$ of the linear logic and the first-order quantifiers ($\forall$ and $\exists$).

Axioms and Inference Rules

Logical Inference Rules ($\otimes$ Introduction Rule):

$$\frac{\vdash \Gamma, \varphi \quad \vdash \Delta, \psi}{\vdash \Gamma, \Delta, \varphi \otimes \psi}$$

for any formula φ and ψ.

We define axioms and inference rules about each participant A as follows:

Axioms for A:
nonce generation:

$\vdash \exists n \, A(n)$ (n is bound variable with the sort Nonce.)

name generation:
  $\vdash \forall p \, A(p)$ (p is bound variable with the sort Name.)

key generation:
  $\vdash \forall k \, A(k)$ (k is bound variable with the sort Key.)

public keys:
  $\vdash A(K'), KP(K, K')$

shared keys:
  $\vdash A(K), B(K)$

Special Inference Rules for A:

- $\exists$–elimination rule and $\forall$–elimination rule (See Section 2.1 for a remark on $\exists$–elimination rule). We also use the usual left- and right- $\exists$–introduction rules in Section 4.
- Concatenation rules for A

$$\frac{\vdash \Gamma, A(\langle s_1, \ldots, s_n \rangle)}{\vdash \Gamma, A(s_1), \ldots, A(s_n)} \qquad \frac{\vdash \Gamma, \overset{\bullet}{A}(s_1), \ldots, A(s_n)}{\vdash \Gamma, A(\langle s_1, \ldots, s_n \rangle)}$$

sending: **receiving:**

$$\frac{\vdash \Gamma, A(s)}{\vdash \Gamma, A(s), Net(s)} \qquad \frac{\vdash \Gamma, Net(s)}{\vdash \Gamma, A(s)}$$

encryption (shared key):   **decryption (shared key):**

$$\frac{\vdash \Gamma, A(K), A(s)}{\vdash \Gamma, A(K), A(s), A(\{s\}_K)} \qquad \frac{\vdash \Gamma, A(K), A(\{s\}_K)}{\vdash \Gamma, A(K), A(\{s\}_K), A(s)}$$

(for any K:SharedKey)   (for any K:SharedKey)

encryption (public key):   **decryption (public key):**

$$\frac{\vdash \Gamma, KP(K, K'), A(s)}{\vdash \Gamma, KP(K, K'), A(s), A(\{s\}_K)} \qquad \frac{\vdash \Gamma, KP(K, K'), A(K'), A(\{s\}_K)}{\vdash \Gamma, KP(K, K'), A(K'), A(\{s\}_K)), A(s)}$$

(for any K:PublicKey and for   (for any K:PublicKey and for
any K':SecretKey)   any K':SecretKey)

encryption (secret key):   **decryption (secret key):**

$$\frac{\vdash \Gamma, A(K), A(s)}{\vdash \Gamma, A(K), A(s), A(\{s\}_K)} \qquad \frac{\vdash \Gamma, KP(K, K'), A(\{s\}_{K'})}{\vdash \Gamma, KP(K, K'), A(\{s\}_{K'}), A(s)}$$

(for any K: SecretKey)   (for any K:PublicKey and for
    any K':SecretKey)

B   The Modified BAN Logic for Evaluation of Belief

Notations: The letters $A, B, C, \ldots$ are used to denote specific participants ($P, Q, R, \ldots$ are used to denote parameterized participants). As for the term level objects, we use the same symbols as syntactic level.

Statements: Atomic statements are as follows: $P \overset{K}{\leftrightarrow} Q$ (K is a shared key for P and Q), $\overset{K}{\mapsto} P$ (P has K as a public key), $P \overset{s}{\rightleftharpoons} Q$ (s is a shared secret with P and Q), $P \triangleleft s$ (P has received s), $P \ni s$ (P has s), $P \hspace{-2pt}\mid\hspace{-4pt}\sim s$ (P said s), $P \hspace{-2pt}\mid\hspace{-4pt}\overset{*}{\sim} s$ (Q says s), $\sharp(s)$ (s is fresh), $Gen(P, s)$ (s is generated by P). When φ is atomic statement, then $P \models_i \varphi$ and $P \models \varphi$ are statements.

Inference Rules for Evaluation:

Freshness:

$$\frac{A \models_i \sharp(s) \quad A \models_i B \hspace{-2pt}\mid\hspace{-4pt}\sim s}{A \models_i B \hspace{-2pt}\mid\hspace{-4pt}\overset{*}{\sim} s} \qquad \frac{A \models_i \sharp(s)}{A \models_i \sharp(\langle s, u \rangle)} \qquad \frac{A \models_i \sharp(u)}{A \models_i \sharp(\langle s, u \rangle)} \qquad \frac{A \models_i Gen(A, N)}{A \models_i \sharp(N)}$$

Possession:

$$\frac{A \models_i B \hspace{-2pt}\mid\hspace{-4pt}\overset{*}{\sim} s}{A \models_i B \ni s} \qquad \frac{A \models_i B \triangleleft s}{A \models_i B \ni s}$$

Concatenation:

$$\frac{A \models_i B \ni \langle s_1, s_2, \ldots, s_n \rangle}{A \models_i B \ni s_k} \qquad \frac{A \models_i B \triangleleft \langle s_1, s_2, \ldots, s_n \rangle}{A \models_i B \triangleleft s_k} \qquad \frac{A \models_i B \hspace{-2pt}\mid\hspace{-4pt}\overset{*}{\sim} \langle s_1, s_2, \ldots, s_n \rangle}{A \models_i B \hspace{-2pt}\mid\hspace{-4pt}\overset{*}{\sim} s_k}$$

Decryption:

$$\frac{A \models_i B \triangleleft \{s\}_K \quad A \models_i \overset{K}{\mapsto} B}{A \models_i B \triangleleft s} \qquad \frac{A \models_i B \triangleleft \{s\}_K \quad A \models_i B \ni s}{A \models_i B \triangleleft s}$$

$$\frac{A \models_i B \triangleleft \{s\}'_K \quad A \models_i B \ni K \quad A \models_i KP(K, K')}{A \models_i B \triangleleft s}$$

Formal Analysis of the *i*KP Electronic Payment Protocols

Kazuhiro Ogata[1] and Kokichi Futatsugi[2]

[1] NEC Software Hokuriku, Ltd.
ogatak@acm.org
[2] Japan Advanced Institute of Science and Technology (JAIST)
kokichi@jaist.ac.jp

Abstract. *i*KP (*i*-Key-Protocol, $i = 1, 2, 3$) is a family of payment protocols and one of the ancestors of SET. We have analyzed *i*KP on the property that if an acquirer authorizes a payment, then both the buyer and seller concerned always agree on it. We have found that even 2KP/3KP do not possess the property and then proposed a possible modification of 2KP/3KP. We have verified that the modified 2KP/3KP possess the property. We mainly describe the verification in this paper.

1 Introduction

*i*KP (*i*-Key-Protocol, $i = 1, 2, 3$)[1,2] is a family of payment protocols and has affected the design of SET[3]. We have analyzed *i*KP on the property that if an acquirer authorizes a payment, then both the buyer and seller concerned always agree on it. The property is called *agreement property* in this paper. As the designers of *i*KP point out, 1KP does not have the property. We have found, however, that there exists a counter example to 2KP/3KP concerning the property and then proposed a possible modification of 2KP/3KP[4]. We have verified that the modified 2KP/3KP possess the property. In this paper, we mainly describe the verification that the modified 3KP possesses the property.

The verification has been done with CafeOBJ[5,6]. CafeOBJ is an algebraic specification language. The CafeOBJ system, an implementation of CafeOBJ, can be used as an interactive proof-checker or verifier on several levels[7]. We have used it as proof score executor. The verification process is roughly as follows. First the modified 2KP/3KP have been abstracted to ease the verification, which are called AM2KP/AM3KP. Next each of AM2KP/AM3KP has been modeled as an observational transition system (OTS)[8], which is described in CafeOBJ. Then proof scores to show that AM2KP/AM3KP possess agreement property have been written in CafeOBJ and have got executed by the CafeOBJ system.

The rest of the paper is organized as follows. Section 2 mentions CafeOBJ and OTSs. Section 3 describes *i*KP. Section 4 defines agreement property. The counter example and the modified *i*KP are shown in Sect. 5. Section 6 describes a way of modeling AM3KP. Section 7 describes the verification. Section 8 discusses another version of *i*KP, related work and our future work. Finally we conclude the paper in Sect. 9.

M. Okada et al. (Eds.): ISSS 2002, LNCS 2609, pp. 441–460, 2003.

2   Preliminaries

2.1   CafeOBJ in a Nutshell

CafeOBJ[5,6] can be used to specify abstract machines as well as abstract data types. A visible sort denotes an abstract data type, while a hidden sort the state space of an abstract machine. There are two kinds of operations to hidden sorts: action and observation operations. An action operation can change a state of an abstract machine. Only observation operations can be used to observe the inside of an abstract machine. An action operation is basically specified with equations by describing how the value of each observation operation changes. Declarations of observation and action operations start with bop or bops, and those of other operations with op or ops. Declarations of equations start with eq, and those of conditional ones with ceq. The CafeOBJ system rewrites a given term by regarding equations as left-to-right rewrite rules.

2.2   Observational Transition Systems

We assume that there exists a universal state space called Υ. A system is modeled by observing only quantities that are relevant to the system and how to change the quantities by state transition from the outside of each state of Υ. An OTS[8] can be used to model a system in this way. An OTS $S = \langle \mathcal{O}, \mathcal{I}, \mathcal{T} \rangle$ consists of:

- $\mathcal{O}$: A set of observations. Each $o \in \mathcal{O}$ is a function $o : \Upsilon \to D$, where D is a data type and may be different for each observation. The value returned by an observation (in a state) is called the value of it (in the state). Given an OTS S and two states $v_1, v_2 \in \Upsilon$, the equality between two states, denoted by $v_1 =_S v_2$, w.r.t. S is defined as $v_1 =_S v_2$ iff $\forall o \in \mathcal{O}.o(v_1) = o(v_2)$, where '=' in $o(v_1) = o(v_2)$ is supposed to be well defined.
- $\mathcal{I}$: The initial condition. This condition specifies the initial value of each observation that defines initial states of the OTS.
- $\mathcal{T}$: A set of conditional transition rules. Each $\tau \in \mathcal{T}$ is a function $\tau : \Upsilon/=_S \to \Upsilon/=_S$ on equivalent classes of Υ w.r.t. $=_S$. Let $\tau(v)$ be the representative element of $\tau([v])$ for each $v \in \Upsilon$ and it is called *the successor state* of v w.r.t. τ. The condition c_τ for a transition rule $\tau \in \mathcal{T}$, which is a predicate of states, is called *the effective condition*. Given a state $v \in \Upsilon$, c_τ is true in v, namely τ is *effective* in v, iff $v \neq_S \tau(v)$.

An OTS is described in CafeOBJ[8]. Observations are denoted by CafeOBJ observation operations, and transition rules by CafeOBJ action operations.

An execution of an OTS S is an infinite sequence $v_0, v_1, \ldots$ of states satisfying:

- *Initiation*: For each $o \in \mathcal{O}$, $o(v_0)$ satisfies $\mathcal{I}$.
- *Consecution*: For each $i \in \{0, 1, \ldots\}$, $v_{i+1} =_S \tau(v_i)$ for some $\tau \in \mathcal{T}$.

A state is called *reachable* w.r.t. S iff it appears in an execution of S.

All properties considered in this paper are safety properties. *Safety properties* are defined as follows: a predicate $p : \Upsilon \to \{\text{true}, \text{false}\}$ is a safety property w.r.t.

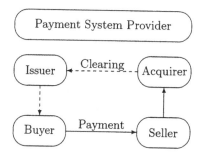

Fig. 1. Generic model of a payment system

$\mathcal{S}$ iff $p(v)$ holds for every reachable $v \in \varUpsilon$ w.r.t. $\mathcal{S}$. We prove that an OTS $\mathcal{S}$ has a safety property p mainly by induction on the number of transition rules applied (executed) as follows:

- Base case: For any state $v \in \varUpsilon$ in which each observation $o \in \mathcal{O}$ satisfies $\mathcal{I}$, we show that $p(v)$ holds.
- Inductive step: Given any (reachable) state $v \in \varUpsilon$ w.r.t. $\mathcal{S}$ such that $p(v)$ holds, we show that, for any transition rule $\tau \in \mathcal{T}$, $p(\tau(v))$ also holds.

3   The *i*KP Electronic Payment Protocols

All *i*KP protocols are based on the existing credit-card payment system. The parties in the payment system are shown in Fig. 1. The *i*KP protocols deal with the payment transaction only (namely the solid lines in Fig. 1) and therefore involve only three parties called B (Buyer), S (Seller) and A (Acquirer). Note that A is not the acquirer in the financial sense, but a gateway to the existing credit card clearing/authorization network.

The payment system is operated by a payment system provider who maintains a fixed business relationship with a number of banks. Banks act as credit card (account) issuers to buyers, and/or as acquirers of payment records from merchants (sellers). It is assumed that each buyer receives his/her credit card from an issuer, and is somehow assigned (or selects) an optional PIN. In 1KP/2KP, payments are authorized only by means of the credit card number and the optional PIN (both suitably encrypted), while, in 3KP, a digital signature is used, in addition to the above. A seller signs up with the payment system provider and with a specific bank, called an acquirer, to accept deposits. Clearing between acquirers and issuers is done using the existing financial networks.

All *i*KP protocols are based on public key cryptography, and each acquirer A has a private key K_A that enables signing and decryption. In this paper, for brevity, we assume that its public counterpart K_A^{-1} that enables signature verification and encryption is securely conveyed to every buyer and seller participating the protocols. Each seller S in 2KP/3KP and each buyer B in 3KP has a private/public key-pair (K_S, K_S^{-1}) and (K_B, K_B^{-1}). We also assume that each

Initiate:	$B \longrightarrow S$: $\mathrm{SALT}_B, \mathrm{ID}_B$
Invoice:	$S \longrightarrow B$: Clear, $[_{2,3}\mathrm{Sig}_S]$
Payment:	$B \longrightarrow S$: EncSlip, $[_3\mathrm{Sig}_B]$
Auth-Request:	$S \longrightarrow A$: Clear, $\mathcal{H}_k(\mathrm{SALT}_B, \mathrm{DESC})$, EncSlip, $[_{2,3}\mathrm{Sig}_S, [_3\mathrm{Sig}_B]]$
Auth-Response:	$A \longrightarrow S$: RCODE, Sig_A
Confirm:	$S \longrightarrow B$: RCODE, $\mathrm{Sig}_A, [_{2,3}\mathrm{V}|\mathrm{VC}]$

Fig. 2. The iKP protocols

seller's public key is securely conveyed to every acquirer and buyer in 2KP/3KP, and that each buyer's public key to every acquirer and seller in 3KP.

Cryptographic primitives used in the protocols are as follows:

- $\mathcal{H}(\cdot)$: A one-way hash function.
- $\mathcal{H}_k(K, \cdot)$: A keyed one-way hash function; the first argument K is the key.
- $\mathcal{E}_X(\cdot)$: Public-key encryption with K_X^{-1}.
- $\mathcal{S}_X(\cdot)$: Signature computed with K_X.

Figure 2 shows the three iKP protocols. Parts enclosed by $[_{2,3}...]$ and $[_3...]$ are ignored for 1KP and 1KP/2KP respectively. The main difference between 1, 2 and 3KP is the increasing use of digital signatures as more of the parties involved possess a private/public key-pair.

Quantities occurring in the protocols are as follows:

- SALT_B : Random number generated by B. Used to salt DESC.
- PRICE : Amount and currency.
- DATE : S's time stamp used for coarse-grained payment replay protection.
- NONCE_S : S's nonce used for more fine-grained payment replay protection.
- ID_S : S's ID.
- TID_S : Transaction ID.
- DESC : Description of purchase/goods, delivery address, etc.
- BAN : B's Account Number such as credit card number.
- EXP : Expiration date associated with BAN.
- R_B : Random number chosen by B to form ID_B.
- ID_B : A B's pseudo-ID computed as $\mathrm{ID}_B = \mathcal{H}_k(\mathrm{R}_B, \mathrm{BAN})$.
- RCODE : Response from the credit card authorization system.
- PIN : B's PIN (Personal Identification Number).
- V and VC: Random numbers generated by S in 2KP/3KP for use as proofs that S has accepted payment and has not accepted payment respectively.

Composite fields used in the protocols are as follows:

- Common : $\mathrm{PRICE}, \mathrm{ID}_S, \mathrm{TID}_S, \mathrm{DATE}, \mathrm{NONCE}_S, \mathrm{ID}_B, \mathcal{H}_k(\mathrm{SALT}_B, \mathrm{DESC})$, $[_{2,3}\mathcal{H}(\mathrm{V}), \mathcal{H}(\mathrm{VC})]$
- Clear : $\mathrm{ID}_S, \mathrm{TID}_S, \mathrm{DATE}, \mathrm{NONCE}_S, \mathcal{H}(\mathrm{Common}), [_{2,3}\mathcal{H}(\mathrm{V}), \mathcal{H}(\mathrm{VC})]$
- SLIP : $\mathrm{PRICE}, \mathcal{H}(\mathrm{Common}), \mathrm{BAN}, \mathrm{R}_B, [\mathrm{PIN}], \mathrm{EXP}$
- EncSlip : $\mathcal{E}_A(\mathrm{SLIP})$

- $\text{Sig}_A : \mathcal{S}_A(\text{RCODE}, \mathcal{H}(\text{Common}))$
- $\text{Sig}_S : \mathcal{S}_S(\mathcal{H}(\text{Common}))$
- $\text{Sig}_B : \mathcal{S}_B(\text{EncSlip}, \mathcal{H}(\text{Common})))$

We are about to describe how the iKP protocols work. Before each protocol starts, each party has the information as follows:

- $B : \text{DESC}, \text{PRICE}, \text{BAN}, \text{EXP}, \text{K}_A^{-1}, [\text{PIN}], [_{2,3}\text{K}_S^{-1}], [_3\text{K}_B]$
- $S : \text{DESC}, \text{PRICE}, \text{K}_A^{-1}, [_{2,3}\text{K}_S], [_3\text{K}_B^{-1}]$
- $A : \text{K}_A, [_{2,3}\text{K}_S^{-1}], [_3\text{K}_B^{-1}]$

Each buyer B has an account number BAN and associated EXP, both known to the payment system. B may also have a secret PIN that is also known (possibly under a one-way function image) to the payment system.

Initiate: B forms ID_B by generating R_B and computing $\mathcal{H}_k(\text{R}_B, \text{BAN})$, and generates SALT_B to salt the hash of DESC. B sends Initiate to S.

Invoice: S retrieves SALT_B and ID_B from Initiate, obtains DATE and generates NONCE_S. The combination of DATE and NONCE_S is used later by A to uniquely identify this payment. S then chooses TID_S and computes $\mathcal{H}_k(\text{SALT}_B, \text{DESC})$. In 2KP/3KP, S also generates V and VC, and then computes $\mathcal{H}(\text{V})$ and $\mathcal{H}(\text{VC})$. S forms Common and computes $\mathcal{H}(\text{Common})$. In 2KP/3KP, S also computes Sig_S. Finally S sends Invoice to B.

Payment: B retrieves Clear from Invoice and validates DATE within a predefined time skew. B computes $\mathcal{H}_k(\text{SALT}_B, \text{DESC})$ and $\mathcal{H}(\text{Common})$, and checks the latter matches the corresponding value in Clear. In 2KP/3KP, B also validates the signature retrieved from Invoice using K_S^{-1}. Next B forms SLIP and encrypts it using K_A^{-1}. In 3KP, B also computes Sig_B. Finally B sends Payment to S.

Auth-Request: In 3KP, S validates the signature retrieved from Payment using K_B^{-1}. S forwards EncSlip (and also Sig_B in 3KP) along with Clear and $\mathcal{H}_k(\text{SALT}_B, \text{DESC})$ (and also Sig_S in 2KP/3KP) as Auth-Request to A.

Auth-Response: A extracts Clear, EncSlip and $\mathcal{H}_k(\text{SALT}_B, \text{DESC})$ (and also Sig_S in 2KP/3KP and Sig_B in 3KP) from Auth-Request. A then does the following:

1. Extracts ID_S, TID_S, DATE, NONCE_S and the value h_1 presumably corresponding to $\mathcal{H}(\text{Common})$ from Clear. In 2KP/3KP, also extracts $\mathcal{H}(\text{V})$ and $\mathcal{H}(\text{VC})$. A checks for replays, namely makes sure that there is no previously processed request with the same quadruple (ID_S, TID_S, DATE, NONCE_S).
2. Decrypts EncSlip. If decryption fails, A assumes that EncSlip has been altered and the transaction is therefore invalid. Otherwise, A obtains SLIP and, from it, extracts PRICE, h_2 (corresponding to $\mathcal{H}(\text{Common})$), BAN, EXP, R_B and optionally PIN.
3. Checks that h_1 and h_2 match.

Initiate:	IB	$\longrightarrow S$	: $\mathrm{SALT}_{IB}, \mathrm{ID}_{IB}$
Invoice:	S	$\longrightarrow IB$	: $\mathrm{Clear}, \mathrm{Sig}_S$
Auth-Request:	$IS(S)$	$\longrightarrow A$	: $\mathrm{Clear}, \mathcal{H}_k(\mathrm{SALT}_{IB}, \mathrm{DESC}), \mathrm{EncSlip}, \mathrm{Sig}_S, [_3\mathrm{Sig}_{IB}]$
Auth-Response:	A	$\longrightarrow S$	: $\mathrm{RCODE}, \mathrm{Sig}_A$

IB and IS stand for the intruder acting as a buyer and a seller respectively. $IS(S)$ means that IS fakes a message seemingly sent by S and sends it.

Fig. 3. Counter examples

4. Rebuilds Common, computes $\mathcal{H}(\mathrm{Common})$ and checks that it matches h_1.
5. In 2KP/3KP, validates Sig_S using K_S^{-1}.
6. In 3KP, validates Sig_B using K_B^{-1}.
7. Uses the credit card authorization system to obtain on-line authorization of this payment. This entails forwarding BAN, EXP, etc. as dictated by the authorization system. Upon receipt of RCODE from the authorization system, A computes a signature on RCODE and $\mathcal{H}(\mathrm{Common})$.

Finally A sends Auth-Response to S.

Confirm: S extracts RCODE and Sig_A from Auth-Response. S then validates Sig_A using K_A^{-1} and forwards both RCODE and Sig_A as Confirm to B. In 2KP/3KP, either V or VC is also included in Confirm depending on RCODE.

4   Agreement Property

The property, called *agreement property*[4], discussed in this paper is as follows:

> *If an acquirer authorizes a payment, then both the buyer and seller concerned always agree on it.*

In iKP, that an acquirer authorizes a payment implies that the acquirer receives the valid Auth-Request corresponding to the payment. Moreover that the · buyer and seller concerned agree on the payment (namely the valid Auth-Request) can be stated as they have actually sent the Initiate and Payment, and the Invoice and Auth-Request corresponding to the valid Auth-Request, respectively. Therefore agreement property can be restated as follows:

> *If an acquirer receives valid Auth-Request stating that a buyer pays a seller some amount, no matter who has sent the valid Auth-Request, then the buyer has always sent the Initiate and Payment corresponding to the valid Auth-Request to the seller and the seller has always sent the Invoice and Auth-Request corresponding to the valid Auth-Request to the buyer and the acquirer respectively.*

Initiate: $B \longrightarrow S$: $\text{SALT}_B, \text{ID}_B$
Invoice: $S \longrightarrow B$: Clear, $[_{2,3}\text{Sig}_S]$
Payment: $B \longrightarrow S$: EncSlip, $[_3\text{Sig}_B]$
Auth-Request: $S \longrightarrow A$: Clear, $\mathcal{H}_k(\text{SALT}_B, \text{DESC})$, EncSlip, $[_{2,3}\text{Sig2}_S, [_3\text{Sig}_B]]$
Auth-Response: $A \longrightarrow S$: RCODE, Sig_A
Confirm: $S \longrightarrow B$: RCODE, $\text{Sig}_A, [_{2,3}\text{V}|\text{VC}]$

Fig. 4. The modified iKP protocols

5 Modification of the iKP Protocols

We found an counter example showing that 2KP/3KP does not possess the property[4]. The counter example is shown in Fig. 3. We assume that there exists an intruder that can also act as a legitimate principal in the protocols. The intruder can eavesdrop any message flowing in the network and, from it, glean any quantity except those cryptographically processed (namely it is assumed that the cryptosystem used cannot be broken). Based on the gleaned information, the intruder fakes messages to attack and/or confuse the payment system.

We have proposed a possible modification of iKP to have 2KP/3KP possess the property[4]. The reason why the counter example can occur is that IB receives Invoice and gains all the quantities to generate valid Auth-Request. If S newly computes another signature when it sends Auth-Request, not reusing Sig_S used for sending Invoice, then the counter example cannot occur. Therefore the modification is computing a different signature for sending Auth-Request than that used for sending Invoice.

Figure 4 shows the modified iKP protocols. Sig2_S is newly introduced, which is defined as follows:

- Sig2_S : $\mathcal{S}_S(\mathcal{H}(\text{Common}), \text{EncSlip})$

It is used for sending Auth-Request instead of Sig_S.

Although the basic idea used for the modification can be found in the sixth message flow of NetBill[9] and the **AuthReq** message flow of SET[3], both message flows are more elaborate than the modified Auth-Request message flow because the essential parts of both messages are encrypted using the key that is only available to the merchant and the NetBill server (or the Payment Gateway).

6 Modeling the Modified 3KP Protocol

6.1 Abstraction

The modified 3KP is simplified to ease the verification that the protocol possesses agreement property. The simplification abstracts away quantities and messages that are supposed not to affect the property. The simplified protocol is called the AM3KP protocol, which is shown in Fig. 5. Composite fields used in the protocol are as follows:

Initiate:	$B \longrightarrow S$: ID_B
Invoice:	$S \longrightarrow B$: $\mathrm{Clear}, \mathrm{Sig}_S$
Payment:	$B \longrightarrow S$: $\mathrm{EncSlip}, \mathrm{Sig}_B$
Auth-Request:	$S \longrightarrow A$: $\mathrm{Clear}, \mathrm{EncSlip}, \mathrm{Sig2}_S, \mathrm{Sig}_B$
Auth-Response:	$A \longrightarrow S$: $\mathrm{RCODE}, \mathrm{Sig}_A$

Fig. 5. The AM3KP protocol

- Common : S, B, ID_B
- SLIP : $\mathcal{H}(\mathrm{Common}), \mathrm{BAN}, \mathrm{R}_B$
- Sig_A : $\mathcal{S}_A(\mathrm{RCODE}, \mathcal{H}(\mathrm{Common}))$
- $\mathrm{Sig2}_S$: $\mathcal{S}_S(\mathcal{H}(\mathrm{Common}), \mathrm{EncSlip})$
- Clear : $\mathcal{H}(\mathrm{Common})$
- EncSlip : $\mathcal{E}_A(\mathrm{SLIP})$
- Sig_S : $\mathcal{S}_S(\mathcal{H}(\mathrm{Common}))$
- Sig_B : $\mathcal{S}_B(\mathrm{EncSlip}, \mathcal{H}(\mathrm{Common}))$

SALT_B, DESC, PRICE, $\mathcal{H}(\mathrm{V})$, $\mathcal{H}(\mathrm{VC})$ and Confirm message flow are hidden. TID_S, DATE and NONCE_S are basically hidden. Since they are also used so that S can remember which buyer S is dealing with, however, they are replaced with the buyer's ID. In AM3KP, principals' names are used as their IDs. BAN, PIN and EXP are used so that A can check that the credit card is valid. In AM3KP, only BAN is used and the remaining two are hidden.

We have to show that there exists a relation between AM3KP and the modified 3KP such as a simulation relation between I/O automata[10] in order to conclude that the modified 3KP possesses agreement property if we prove that AM3KP does. We believe that there exists such a relation because the simplification only abstracts away quantities and messages that are supposed not to affect the property.

6.2   Modeling Strategy

We suppose that there exists one and only legitimate (trustable) acquirer. We also suppose that there not only exist multiple trustable buyers and sellers but also multiple malicious (untrustable) buyers and sellers. Trustable principals exactly follow the protocol, while malicious principals may do something against the protocol as well, namely intercepting and/or faking messages so as to attack the protocol. Generally speaking, we cannot predict what exactly those malicious principals do and how many there are. Therefore, instead of describing each of the malicious principals, their combination and cooperation is modeled as the most general intruder à la Dolev and Yao[11]. The intruder can do the following:

- Eavesdrop any message flowing in the network.
- Glean any quantity from the message; however the intruder can decrypt a cipher text only if he/she knows the key to decrypt, and cannot compute preimages of a hash value if he/she does not know the preimages.
- Fake and send messages based on the gleaned information; however the intruder can sign something only if he/she knows the key to sign.

Accordingly we can regard the network as part of the intruder or the storage that the intruder can use.

6.3   Formalization of Messages

There are five kinds of messages that are Initiate, Invoice, Payment, Auth-Request and Auth-Response. Data constructors for those messages are im, vm, pm, qm and sm. im stands for Initiate message, vm for Invoice message, pm for Payment message, qm for Auth-Request message and sm for Auth-Response message. The data constructors are declared as follows:

```
op im : Buyer    Buyer    Seller   Hban                      -> Msg
op vm : Seller   Seller   Buyer    Clear Sigs                -> Msg
op pm : Buyer    Buyer    Seller   Eslp  Sigb                -> Msg
op qm : Seller   Seller   Acquirer Clear Eslp Sigs2 Sigb -> Msg
op sm : Acquirer Acquirer Seller   Rcode Siga                -> Msg
```

Buyer, Seller, Acquirer, Hban, Clear, Eslp, Sigs, Sigs2, Sigb, Siga, Rcode and Msg are visible sorts denoting B, S, A, ID_B, Clear, EncSlip, Sig_S, $Sig2_S$, Sig_B, Sig_A, RCODE and messages respectively.

The first, second and third arguments of each constructor mean the actual generator or sender, the source and the destination of the corresponding message. The first argument is meta-information that is only available to the outside observer and that cannot be forged by the intruder, while the remaining arguments may be forged by the intruder. Therefore, suppose that there exists a message in the network. It is true that the message originates at the principal denoted by the first argument. If the principal is trustable, we can also deduce that the second argument equals the first one. On the other hand, if the principal is the intruder, the second argument may differ from the first one, which means that the intruder has faked the message.

6.4   Formalization of the Network

The network is modeled as a bag (multiset) of messages. Any message that has been sent or put once into the network is supposed to be never deleted from the network because the intruder can replay the message repeatedly. Consequently, the emptiness of the network means that no messages have sent.

The intruder obtains 10 kinds of quantities from the network. The 10 kinds of quantities are $\mathcal{H}(\text{Common})$, ID_B, BAN, R_B, EncSlip, RCODE, Sig_A, Sig_S, $Sig2_S$ and Sig_B. The collections of the quantities are denoted by CafeOBJ operators hcoms, hbans, bans, rands, eslps, rcodes, sigas, sigss, sigs2s and sigbs respectively. Those are declared as follows:

```
op hcoms  : Network -> ColHcoms    op hbans  : Network -> ColHbans
op bans   : Network -> ColBans     op rands  : Network -> ColRands
op eslps  : Network -> ColEslps    op rcodes : Network -> ColRcodes
op sigas  : Network -> ColSigas    op sigss  : Network -> ColSigss
op sigs2s : Network -> ColSigs2s   op sigbs  : Network -> ColSigbs
```

Network is a visible sort for the network. Col$X$s (X = Hcom, Hban, Ban, Rand, Eslp, Rcode, Siga, Sigs, Sigs2, Sigb) are visible sorts for collections of the quantities, where each X is the visible sort of each quantity.

The quantities gleaned by the intruder are defined with equations. If there exists an Invoice or Auth-Request message in the network, the $\mathcal{H}(\text{Common})$ appearing in clear in the message is available to the intruder; if there exists a

Payment or Auth-Request message in the network and the key used to decrypt the EncSlip in the message is available to the intruder, the $\mathcal{H}$(Common) in the EncSlip is available to the intruder. Hence hcoms is defined as follows:

```
eq  HC \in hcoms(void)   = false .
ceq HC \in hcoms(M,NW)   = true     if vm?(M) and HC = hcom(clear(M)) .
ceq HC \in hcoms(M,NW)   = true
    if pm?(M) and pk(ia) = pk(eslip(M)) and HC = hcom(slip(eslip(M))) .
ceq HC \in hcoms(M,NW)   = true     if qm?(M) and HC = hcom(clear(M)) .
ceq HC \in hcoms(M,NW)   = true
    if qm?(M) and pk(ia) = pk(eslip(M)) and HC = hcom(slip(eslip(M))) .
ceq HC \in hcoms(M,NW)   = HC \in hcoms(NW)
    if not(vm?(M) and HC = hcom(clear(M))) and
       not(pm?(M) and pk(ia) = pk(eslip(M)) and HC = hcom(slip(eslip(M)))) and
       not(qm?(M) and HC = hcom(clear(M))) and
       not(qm?(M) and pk(ia) = pk(eslip(M)) and HC = hcom(slip(eslip(M)))) .
```

vm?, pm? and qm? are predicates checking if a given message is Invoice, Payment and Auth-Request respectively. ia and pk(ia) denote the intruder acting as an acquirer and his/her public key. clear and eslip return the Clear and EncSlip of a given message respectively, if the message includes them. hcom returns the $\mathcal{H}$(Common) of Clear and SLIP. pk and slip return the key used for making EncSlip and the palin text of EncSlip. void denotes the empty bag and \in is the membership predicate of bags. HC, M and NW are CafeOBJ variables for Hcoms, Msg and Network respectively.

6.5   Formalization of Trustable Principals

Before modeling the behavior of trustable principals, we describe the values observable from the outside of the protocol. We suppose that the network and a perfect random number generator are observable. The observable values are denoted by CafeOBJ observation operators nw and rand, respectively, which are declared as follows:

```
bop nw   : Protocol -> Network
bop rand : Protocol -> Rand
```

The behavior of trustable principals is modeled by five kinds of transition rules that correspond to sending the five kinds of messages. The five kinds of transition rules are denoted by CafeOBJ action operators sdim, sdvm, sdpm, sdqm and sdsm. sdim stands for send Initiate message, sdvm for send Invoice message, sdpm for send Payment message, sdqm for send Auth-Request message and sdsm for send Auth-Response message. The operators are declared as follows:

```
bop sdim : Protocol Buyer  Seller         -> Protocol
bop sdvm : Protocol Seller Msg            -> Protocol
bop sdpm : Protocol Buyer  Rand Msg Msg   -> Protocol
bop sdqm : Protocol Seller Hban Msg Msg   -> Protocol
bop sdsm : Protocol Msg                   -> Protocol
```

Protocol is a hidden sort denoting the state space.

Given a buyer and a seller, sdim corresponds to that the buyer sends Initiate to the seller. The effective condition is always true.

Given a seller and a message, sdvm corresponds to that the seller sends Invoice to a buyer if there exists the message in the network and the message is Initiate which source and destination (namely the second and third arguments) are the buyer and the seller respectively. The effective condition means that the seller receives Initiate from the buyer, although the buyer may not be the actual sender (namely that the first argument may be the intruder).

Given a buyer, a random number and two messages $m1, m2$, sdpm corresponds to that the buyer sends Payment to a seller if the following hold: there exist the two messages in the network, $m1$ is Initiate sent by the buyer to the seller, $m2$ is Invoice seemingly sent by the seller to the buyer in response to $m1$, and the random number is used to compute ID_B in $m1$. The first argument of $m1$ is the buyer, while the first argument of $m2$ may be the intruder.

Given a seller, ID_B and two messages $m1, m2$, sdqm corresponds to that the seller sends Auth-Request to the legitimate acquirer if the following hold: there exist the two messages in the network, $m1$ is Invoice sent by the seller to a buyer corresponding to ID_B, and $m2$ is Payment seemingly sent by the buyer to the seller in response to $m1$.

Given a message, sdsm corresponds to that the legitimate acquirer sends Auth-Response to a seller if the message is valid Auth-Request seemingly sent by the seller to the acquirer.

The CafeOBJ action operators are defined with equations by describing how the observable values change if the corresponding transition rules are executed. For example, sdqm is defined as follows:

```
op c-sdqm : Protocol Seller Hban Msg Msg -> Bool {strat: (0 1 2 3 4 5 0)}
eq  c-sdqm(P,S,HN,M1,M2)
    = M1 \in nw(P) and vm?(M1) and M2 \in nw(P) and pm?(M2) and
      S = vc(M1) and S = vs(M1) and vd(M1) = ps(M2) and S = pd(M2) and
      hcom(clear(M1)) = h(com(S,ps(M2),HN)) and
      sigs(M1) = sig(sk(S),hcom(clear(M1))) and
      sigb(M2) = sig(sk(ps(M2)),eslip(M2),hcom(clear(M1))) .
ceq nw(sdqm(P,S,HN,M1,M2))
    = qm(S,S,la,clear(M1),eslip(M2),sig(sk(S),h(com(S,ps(M2),HN)),eslip(M2)),sigb(M2))
      , nw(P) if c-sdqm(P,S,HN,M1,M2) .
eq  rand(sdqm(P,S,HN,M1,M2)) = rand(P) .
ceq sdqm(P,S,HN,M1,M2)      = P if not c-sdqm(P,S,HN,M1,M2) .
```

P, S, HN, M1 and M2 are CafeOBJ variables for the intended sorts. c-sdqm denotes effective conditions of transition rules corresponding to sdqm. The first two lines of the right-hand side of the equation defining c-sdqm mean that there exists Invoice (denoted by M1) sent by a seller (denoted by S) to a buyer identified by his/her pseudo-ID (denoted by HN) in the network and there exists Payment (denoted by M2) seemingly sent by the buyer to the seller in the network. The remaining three lines mean that the Payment is sent in response to the Invoice. If a transition rule corresponding to sdqm is executed in a state in which the effective condition is true, Auth-Request, which is sent by the seller to the legitimate acquirer, is put into the network in the successor state denoted by sdqm(P,S,HN,M1,M2), which is described by the second equation. If the effective condition is false, nothing changes, which is described by the last equation.

More specific comments on the above CafeOBJ code is as follows. The comma ',' between the term denoting the message and the term nw(P) denoting the network is the data constructor of bags. vc, vs and vd return the first, second and third arguments of Invoice, and ps and pd return the second and third arguments

of Payment. com and h are data constructors for Common and $\mathcal{H}$(Common).
sigs, sigb and eslip return Sig_S, Sig_B and EncSlip in a given message, respectively, if the message includes them. sk and sig are data constructors for
private keys and digital signatures. The first argument of sig is a private key.
Bool is a visible sort denoting truth values. c-sdqm is given the local strategy
(0 1 2 3 4 5 0) to control rewriting a term which top operator is c-sdqm.

6.6   Formalization of the Intruder

Part of the intruder has been modeled as the network. We have defined what
information the intruder can glean from the network. We next describe what
messages the intruder fakes based on the gleaned information in this subsection.

The transition rules corresponding to the intruder's faking messages are divided into five classes, each of which fakes each type of messages. The effective
condition of these transition rules are that the intruder can take advantage of
the necessary information to fake messages.

We suppose that the intruder can fake any message if the message can be
made from the quantities gleaned by the intruder. However we do not have
the intruder fake meaningless messages because such messages do not attack
the protocol. For example, Invoice messages such as Clear, Sig_B are not faked,
although construction of such messages is rejected by the CafeOBJ parser.

Transition rules faking messages are denoted by CafeOBJ action operators.
In this paper, we show the CafeOBJ action operators corresponding to transition
rules faking Payment messages, which are declared as follows:

```
bop fkpm1 : Protocol Buyer  Seller Eslp Sigb      -> Protocol
bop fkpm2 : Protocol Seller Ban    Rand Hcom Sigb -> Protocol
bop fkpm3 : Protocol Seller Ban    Rand Sigb      -> Protocol
bop fkpm4 : Protocol Buyer  Seller Eslp Hcom      -> Protocol
bop fkpm5 : Protocol Buyer  Seller Eslp Hban      -> Protocol
bop fkpm6 : Protocol Seller Eslp   Ban  Rand      -> Protocol
bop fkpm7 : Protocol Seller Ban    Rand Hcom      -> Protocol
bop fkpm8 : Protocol Seller Ban    Rand           -> Protocol
```

fkpm stands for fake Payment message.

For example, given a seller, a BAN, a random number, $\mathcal{H}$(Common) and Sig_B,
fkpm2 corresponds to that the intruder fakes Payment from those quantities if
they are available to the intruder. fkpm2 is defined with equations as follows:

```
op  c-fkpm2 : Protocol Seller Ban Rand Hcom Sigb -> Bool {strat: (0 1 2 3 4 5 6 0)}
eq  c-fkpm2(P,S,N,R,HC,GB) = N \in bans(nw(P)) and R \in rands(nw(P)) and
                             HC \in hcoms(nw(P)) and GB \in sigbs(nw(P)) .
ceq nw(fkpm2(P,S,N,R,HC,GB)) = pm(ib,b(N),S,enc(pk(la),slp(HC,N,R)),GB) , nw(P)
    if c-fkpm2(P,S,N,R,HC,GB) .
eq  rand(fkpm2(P,S,N,R,HC,GB)) = rand(P) .
ceq fkpm2(P,S,N,R,HC,GB)       = P if not c-fkpm2(P,S,N,R,HC,GB) .
```

P, S, N, R, HC and GB are CafeOBJ variables for the intended sorts. c-fkpm2
denotes effective conditions of transition rules corresponding to fkpm2.

The CafeOBJ specification has 27 modules, and is approximately of 850
lines. The main module in which the OTS modeling AM3KP is described is
approximately of 300 lines.

7   Verification

7.1   Formalization of Property to Verify

According to the way of modeling the protocol, the receipt of a valid Auth-Request by the legitimate acquirer implies the existence of the valid Auth-Request in the network, and the existence of a message in the network implies that the transmission of the message by the principal denoted by the first argument of the message. Consequently agreement property can be restated as follows: *if there exists valid* Auth-Request *stating that a buyer pays a seller, although the first argument of the valid* Auth-Request *may be the intruder, then there exist the* Initiate *and* Payment *that corresponds to the valid* Auth-Request, *which first and second arguments are the buyer and which third arguments are the seller, and there exist the* Invoice *and* Auth-Request *that corresponds to the valid* Auth-Request, *which first and second arguments are the seller and which third arguments are the buyer and the acquirer respectively.* This is described in CafeOBJ as follows:

Claim 0. *For any reachable* p : Protocol, *any* s1 s2 : Seller, *any* b1 : Buyer, *any* r1 : Rand,

```
not(s1 = is and b1 = ib)
and
qm(s2,s1,la,cl(h(com(s1,b1,h(r1,ban(b1))))),
          enc(pk(la),slp(h(com(s1,b1,h(r1,ban(b1)))),ban(b1),r1)),
          sig(sk(s1),h(com(s1,b1,h(r1,ban(b1))))),
            enc(pk(la),slp(h(com(s1,b1,h(r1,ban(b1)))),ban(b1),r1))),
          sig(sk(b1),enc(pk(la),slp(h(com(s1,b1,h(r1,ban(b1)))),ban(b1),r1)),
            h(com(s1,b1,h(r1,ban(b1)))))))) \in nw(p)
implies
im(b1,b1,s1,h(r1,ban(b1))) \in nw(p)
and
vm(s1,s1,b1,cl(h(com(s1,b1,h(r1,ban(b1))))),
          sig(sk(s1),h(com(s1,b1,h(r1,ban(b1)))))))) \in nw(p)
and
pm(b1,b1,s1,enc(pk(la),slp(h(com(s1,b1,h(r1,ban(b1)))),ban(b1),r1)),
          sig(sk(b1),enc(pk(la),slp(h(com(s1,b1,h(r1,ban(b1)))),ban(b1),r1)),
            h(com(s1,b1,h(r1,ban(b1)))))))) \in nw(p)
and
qm(s1,s1,la,cl(h(com(s1,b1,h(r1,ban(b1))))),
          enc(pk(la),slp(h(com(s1,b1,h(r1,ban(b1)))),ban(b1),r1)),
          sig(sk(s1),h(com(s1,b1,h(r1,ban(b1))))),
            enc(pk(la),slp(h(com(s1,b1,h(r1,ban(b1)))),ban(b1),r1))),
          sig(sk(b1),enc(pk(la),slp(h(com(s1,b1,h(r1,ban(b1)))),ban(b1),r1)),
            h(com(s1,b1,h(r1,ban(b1)))))))) \in nw(p)
```

is and ib denote the intruder acting as a seller and a buyer. If the protocol is performed by la, is and ib, namely the legitimate acquirer and the intruder, then it is clear that this setting breaks the property because the intruder fake any Auth-Request stating that ib pays any amount to is. That is why the first conjunct of the premise of the property is added.

7.2   Verification Outline

To prove Claim 0, we need 17 more claims as lemmas. Five of the claims (including Claim 0) have been proved by case analysis only, and the remaining by induction described in Sect. 2.2. In any case, we write proof scores in CafeOBJ. We outline how to write proof scores if we prove a claim by induction.

Suppose that we prove that the protocol possesses a property denoted by $PROP(P, X)$ where P is a state of the protocol and X is any other parameters. We first write a module, PRED, in which the property is declared and a constant x denoting arbitrary value corresponding to X is declared. The operator prop denoting the property and the equation defining it are also declared as follows:

```
op prop : Protocol SortX -> Bool
eq prop(P,X) = PROP(P,X) .
```

Let init denote any initial state of the protocol. To show that the property holds in any initial state, the following proof score is written:

```
open PRED
  red prop(init,x) .
close
```

CafeOBJ command red reduces a given term by regarding declared equations as left-to-right rewrite rules.

We next write a module, ISTEP, in which the predicate to prove in each inductive step is declared and two constants p and p' are declared, denoting any (reachable) state in which the property holds and the successor state after executing a transition rule in p. The predicate to prove in each inductive step and the equation defining it are also declared as follows:

```
op istep : SortX -> Bool
eq istep(X) = prop(p,X) implies prop(p',X) .
```

In each inductive step, we usually split the state space into multiple sub-spaces, namely doing case analysis, and in each case we write a proof score that looks like the following:

```
open ISTEP
  Declare constants denoting arbitrary objects.
  Declare equations denoting the case or assumption.
  Declare equations denoting facts (e.g. from lemmas) if necessary.
  eq p' = action(p,...) .
  red istep(x) .
close
```

In the proof score, we declare constants denoting arbitrary objects that are used in action and equations denoting the case. We also declare equations denoting facts (e.g. from lemmas) if necessary. The equation which left-hand side is p' specifies that p' is the successor state. If istep(x) is reduced to true, part of the inductive step corresponding to the case succeeds. Otherwise, we may have to split the case again, may need lemmas, or the property may not be proved.

7.3   Verification of Claims

In this paper, we describe part of the proof for Claim 8, in which Claim 2 is required as lemma. The claims are as follows:

Claim 2. *For any reachable* p : Protocol, *any* n1 : Ban,

```
n1 \in bans(nw(p)) implies n1 = ban(ib)
```

Claim 8. *For any reachable* p : Protocol, *any* b1 : Buyer, *any* r1 : Rand,

```
not(b1 = ib)
and
enc(pk(la),slp(h(com(is,b1,h(r1,ban(b1))))),ban(b1),r1)) \in eslps(nw(p))
implies
vm(is,is,b1,cl(h(com(is,b1,h(r1,ban(b1))))),
          sig(sk(is),h(com(is,b1,h(r1,ban(b1)))))) \in nw(p)
```

Claim 2 states that the only BAN available to the intruder is his/hers. Claim 8 states that if EncSlip created by a different buyer from the intruder for sending Payment to seller is (the intruder) is available to the intruder, there exists Invoice, generated by the intruder, including $\mathcal{H}$(Common) appearing in the EncSlip, which means that if a different buyer from the intruder sends Payment to the intruder as a seller, then the intruder has always sent the corresponding Invoice to the buyer.

Proof (of Claim 8). We first write a module in which the property to prove is declared. In the module called PRED8, two constants (b1, r1) denoting any intended sorts are declared. Operator p8 denoting the property and the equation defining it are declared as follows:

```
op p8 : Protocol Buyer Rand -> Bool
eq p8(P,B1,R1)
   = not(B1 = ib)
     and
     enc(pk(la),slp(h(com(is,B1,h(R1,ban(B1))))),ban(B1),R1)) \in eslps(nw(P))
     implies
     vm(is,is,B1,cl(h(com(is,B1,h(R1,ban(B1))))),
               sig(sk(is),h(com(is,B1,h(R1,ban(B1)))))) \in nw(P) .
```

where P, B1 and R1 are CafeOBJ variables.

Base Case: In any initial state init, to show that the predicate holds, the following proof score is described and executed by the CafeOBJ system:

```
open PRED8
  red p8(init,b1,r1) .
close
```

Inductive Step: The predicate to prove in each inductive step is defined in module ISTEP8, in which two constants (p, p') are declared. The predicate and the equation defining it are declared as follows:

```
op istep8 : Buyer Rand -> Bool
eq istep8(B1,R1) = p8(p,B1,R1) implies p8(p',B1,R1) .
```

All we have to do is to show istep8(b1,r1) for every transition rule. In this paper, we describe proof scores showing that any transition rule denoted by fkpm2 preserves property p8. The state space is split into three cases basically according to the effective condition and a new message added into the network as follows:

1	c-fkpm2(n10,r10,hc10,sb10)	b1 = ib
2		not(b1 = ib)
3	not c-fkpm2(n10,r10,hc10,sb10)	

Each case is denoted by the predicate obtained by connecting ones appearing in the row with conjunction. For example, case 2 means any state satisfying c-fkpm2(n10,r10,hc10,sb10) and not(b1 = ib).

In this paper, we show the proof score for case 2 as follows:

```
open ISTEP8
-- arbitrary objects
    op s10 : -> Seller .  op n10 : -> Ban .  op r10 : -> Rand .
    op hc10 : -> Hcom .   op sb10 : -> Sigb .
-- assumptions c-fkpm2(n10,r10,hc10,sb10)
    -- eq n10 \in bans(nw(p)) = true .
    eq ban(ib) \in bans(nw(p)) = true .   eq r10 \in rands(nw(p)) = true .
    eq hc10 \in hcoms(nw(p)) = true .      eq sb10 \in sigbs(nw(p)) = true .
    --
    eq (b1 = ib) = false .
-- facts
    eq n10 = ban(ib) . -- from Claim 2 (n10 \in bans(nw(p)))
-- successor state
    eq p' = fkpm2(p,s10,n10,r10,hc10,sb10) .
-- check if the property is also true in p'.
    red istep8(b1,r1) .
close
```

A comment starts with '--' and terminates at the end of the line.

The size of all the proof scores is approximately of 22,000 lines. It took about 4 minutes to have the CafeOBJ system load the CafeOBJ specification and execute all the proof scores on a laptop with 850MHz Pentium III processor and 512MB memory.

The verification that AM2KP possesses agreement property is very similar to that for AM3KP. Basically by deleting parts related to Sig_B from the CafeOBJ specification and proof scores for AM3KP, we can get the proof for AM2KP.

8   Discussion

8.1   Another Version of iKP

Another version of iKP is proposed in [12] that is probably the earliest paper on iKP and the counter example shown in this paper cannot occur in 2KP/3KP of the version[1]. A seller initiates a protocol run in the version proposed in [12], while a buyer does in the one proposed in [1,2]. In the version proposed in [12], a seller first sends Invoice to a buyer, who replies with Payment including $\mathcal{E}_A$(SLIP) to the seller, and the seller then sends Auth-Request including the seller's digital signature of $\mathcal{E}_A$(SLIP) and a hash value to an acquirer. Since Invoice does not include the seller's digital signature, the buyer does not have enough information to fake valid Auth-Request just after he/she receives Invoice, and the seller does not have enough data to generate valid Auth-Request unless he/she receives Payment. That is why the counter example cannot occur in 2KP/3KP of the version proposed in [12]. Although we have not verified 2KP/3KP of the version concerning agreement property, they most likely possess it.

---

[1] We are grateful to Professor Doug Tygar for pointing this out.

8.2   Related Work

Kailar[13] proposes a logic, called Kailar's accountability logic, to analyze security protocols such as electronic commerce protocols that require accountability. The central construct of the logic is A CanProv x, which means that principal A can convince anyone in an intended audience sharing a set of assumptions that x holds without revealing any secrets other than x. Four protocols are analyzed with the logic. Some of their weakness concerning accountability are found in the course of the analyses and the modifications are proposed.

Clarke, et al.[14] propose a logic for specifying security properties of electronic commerce protocols. The central construct in the logic is s **Knows** m, which means that principal s knows message m. They demonstrates how to specify security requirements of 1KP proposed in [1] in the logic.

Heintze, et al.[15] analyze NetBill and a digital cash protocol with the FDR model checker concerning money atomicity and goods atomicity. Money atomicity means that money should neither be created nor destroyed by electronic commerce protocols, and goods atomicity that a merchant should receive payment iff the consumer receives the goods. For each of the protocols, a finite model consisting one consumer, one merchant and one bank is made and one protocol run is considered. FDR is used to check if the models satisfy money atomicity and goods atomicity. As the results of the analyses, NetBill satisfies both properties, while the digital cash protocol does neither property.

Lu, et al.[16] analyzes a system consisting of two cardholders, one merchant and one payment gateway that perform payment transactions according to SET with FDR. One protocol run is considered. One of the cardholders has a legitimate credit card, and the other does not. Both cardholders may try to pay less than the amount agreed on previously with the merchant. The merchant may try to overcharge a cardholder. The payment gateway is trustable. Five properties are checked to the system with FDR.

Paulson's inductive method[17] is used to analyze TLS (Transport Layer Security), Cardholder Registration phase of SET and the SET purhcase protocols (the simplified and combined Payment Authorization with Purchase Request). Inductive method models a system in which an arbitrary number of principals including the intruder take part in a protocol by inductively defining traces generated by a set of rules that correspond to the possible actions of the principals including the intruder. Security properties can be stated as predicates over the traces. You can inductively prove that a certain property holds of all possible traces for a certain protocol. The proof can be supported by the the theorem prover Isabelle/HOL. All the expected security goals of TLS are proved such that session resumption is secure even if previous session keys from that session have been compromised[18]. On Cardholder Registration phase of SET, it is verified that if a trusted CA keeps track of the registered keys, the protocol is robust enough to guarantee that two different agents will never get the same key certified by the same CA; however, different agents may collude and register the same key with different CAs[19]. On the SET purhcase protocols, it is verified that the protocols possess several desirable properties including one corresponding to agreement property[20]. Besides, it is found that the Cardholder and Payment Gateway cannot agree on the latter's identity, giving rise to potential vulnerabilities. A possible modification is proposed.

Bolignano[21] proposes a way of expressing and verifying properties of electronic commerce protocols such as SET. Bolignano claims that some properties relevant to those protocols cannot be directly expressed by simple invariants and should rely on the history of each protocol run such as a property that principal A can be sure as the time when he/she receives message M that this message really originates from principal B and has not been tempered with. Hence such a property is expressed by a pair of a regular language or a finite automaton L and a filtering function $ff_x(y)$ where x is used to parameterize the function and y ranges in the domain of actions corresponding to transmission and receipt of messages. L is used to observe that any finite protocol run follows the property, and $ff_x(y)$ selects actions relevant to the property from the protocol run. A property expressed by L and $ff_x(y)$ is satisfied iff for any finite trace t and for any x, $ff_x(y) \in L$. The proof can be reduced to one for a simple invariant property, which is supported by the proof assistant Coq.

Meadows, et al.[22] propose a way of expressing properties relevant to payment protocols such as SET and of describing the properties in the temporal language NPATRL developed for the NRL Protocol Analyzer. A payment transaction is modeled as a vector of quantities used in the transaction, and projection functions on vectors are used to give each party's view of the transaction at each point of the protocol. Projection functions are used to define a vector agreement relation that means that two principals agree on some quantities used in a payment transaction. With these constructs, several SET payment protocol requirements are formally described in NPATRL. NPATRL is used to define correctness simply in terms of what events must precede others.

8.3   Comparison

Our approach is similar to Paulson's inductive method supported by Isabelle/HOL. Paulson's inductive method automates verification process more than our approach because the basic functionality for verification in Isabelle/HOL is resolution using higher-order unification, while that in CafeOBJ is rewriting. On the other hand, proof scores are written in a more clear and explicit way in our approach. For example, if we prove that transition rules corresponding to a CafeOBJ action operator preserves a property, we describe how to split the state space explicitly in proof scores, by which we can confirm that the state space is entirely covered, and write a proof score for each case, which convinces us that the transition rules surely preserve the property for that case. Besides, to understand such proof scores, all that is needed is a way of reasoning used in everyday life, namely equational reasoning. This is why proof scores in our approach are easier to read and understand, especially to those who are not necessarily experts in theorem proving. Generally a specification language such as CafeOBJ is more expressive than a programming language such as ML.

Actually we can define various kinds of data structures such as bags. Therefore we can write specifications easier to read and understand in our approach.

The difference between our approach and the model-checking approach or the modal logic approach is the same as that between Paulson's inductive method and those approaches. Thanks to our way of modeling messages and the network, we can describe what events must precede others by simple invariants. It is not necessary to introduce other constructs such as finite automata and filtering functions, which tends to make verification complicated.

8.4 Future Work

In this case study, 2KP/3KP have been analyzed on one property only, although a dozen of properties have been verified as lemmas. On the other hand, Bolignano and Meadows' group try to identify what properties are relevant to payment protocols and formulate them. We should do the same thing in order to prove (modified) 2KP/3KP secure on condition that the cryptosystem used is secure.

For that end, moreover, since accountability is important to payment protocols as Kailar claims, we should formalize accountability in our approach and analyze it. Although *i*KP does not possess goods atomicity because it deals with payment transactions only, atomicity such as goods atomicity is also important to electronic commerce protocols. For example, NetBill[9] is designed to possess goods atomicity, and Heintze, et al. have checked that NetBill actually does with FDR. We should also formalize atomicity in our approach and analyze it in order to deal with various kinds of electronic commerce protocols.

9   Conclusion

We have shown that even 2KP/3KP do not possess agreement property and a possible modification of *i*KP. We have described the verification that the modified 3KP possesses the property. To the best of our knowledge, we are the first to analyze 2KP/3KP formally, although 1KP has been analyzed by Clarke, et al.[14]. Besides, the analysis and proof are done by writing proof scores in algebraic specification languages. The techniques have been developed for more than 15 years in OBJ/CafeOBJ[6,7]. This paper has shown that the techniques can be applied to analyze/verify security protocols.

Acknowledgment. We wish to thank Professor Doug Tygar and the anonymous referees for the numerous useful comments on earlier versions of this paper.

References

1. Bellare, M., Garay, J.A., Hauser, R., Herzberg, A., Krawczyk, H., Steiner, M., Tsudik, G., Waidner, M.: *i*KP – a family of secure electronic payment protocols. In: First USENIX Workshop on Electronic Commerce (1995) 89–106 (http://www.usenix.org/publications/library/proceedings/ec95).

2. Bellare, M., Garay, J.A., Hauser, R., Herzberg, A., Krawczyk, H., Steiner, M., Tsudik, G., Herreweghen, E.V., Waidner, M.: Design, implementation and deployment of the iKP secure electronic payment system. IEEE Journal of Selected Areas in Communications 18 (2000) 611–627

3. MasterCard/Visa: SET secure electronic transactions protocol. Book One: Business Specifications, Book Two: Technical Specification, Book Three: Formal Protocol Definition (http://www.setco.org/set_specifications.html) (1997)

4. Ogata, K., Futatsugi, K.: Flaw and modification of the iKP electronic payment protocols. Inf. Process. Lett. (to appear)

5. CafeOBJ: CafeOBJ web page. http://www.ldl.jaist.ac.jp/cafeobj/ (2001)

6. Diaconescu, R., Futatsugi, K.: CafeOBJ report. AMAST Series in Computing, 6. World Scientific, Singapore (1998)

7. Futatsugi, K., Ogata, K.: Rewriting can verify distributed real-time systems. In: Int'l Symposium on Rewriting, Proof, and Computation. (2001) 60–79

8. Ogata, K., Futatsugi, K.: Rewriting-based verification of authentication protocols. In: WRLA '02. Volume 71 of ENTCS., Elsevier Science Publishers (2002)

9. Cox, B., Tygar, J.D., Sirbu, M.: NetBill security and transaction protocol. In: First USENIX Workshop on Electronic Commerce. (1995) 77–88

10. Lynch, N.A.: Distributed algorithms. Morgan-Kaufmann (1996)

11. Dolev, D., Yao, A.C.: On the security of public key protocols. IEEE Trans. Inform. Theory IT-29 (1983) 198–208

12. Bellare, M., Garay, J.A., Hauser, R., Herzberg, A., Krawczyk, H., Steiner, M., Tsudik, G., Waidner, M.: iKP – a family of secure electronic payment protocols (WORKING DRAFT). http://citeseer.nj.nec.com/bellare95ikp.html (1995)

13. Kailar, R.: Accountability in electronic commerce protocols. IEEE Trans. Softw. Eng. 22 (1996) 313–328

14. Clarke, E., Jha, S., Marrero, W.: A machine checkable logic of knowledge for specifying security properties of electronic commerce protocols. In: Workshop on Formal Methods and Security Protocols. (1998)

15. Heintze, N., Tygar, J., Wing, J., Wong, H.C.: Model checking electronic commerce protocols. In: Second USENIX Workshop on Electronic Commerce. (1996) 147–164

16. Lu, S., Smolka, S.A.: Model checking the Secure Electronic Transaction (SET) protocol. In: MASCOTS '99. (1999) 358–365

17. Paulson, L.C.: The inductive approach to verifying cryptographic protocols. J. Comput. Security 6 (1998) 85–128

18. Paulson, L.C.: Inductive analysis of the internet protocol TLS. ACM Trans. Infom. and Sys. Sec. 2 (1999) 332–351

19. Bella, G., Massacci, F., Paulson, L.C., Tramontano, P.: Formal verification of Cardholder Registration in SET. In: ESORICS 2000. LNCS 1709, Springer (1997) 159–174

20. Bella, G., Massacci, F., Paulson, L.C.: Verifying the SET purchase protocols. http://citeseer.nj.nec.com/503068.html (2001)

21. Bolignano, D.: Towards the formal verification of electronic commerce,. In: 10th IEEE CSFW. (1997) 133–146

22. Meadows, C., Syverson, P.: A formal specification of requirements for payment transactions in the SET protocol. In: FC '98. LNCS 1465, Springer (1998) 122–140

CafeOBJ as a Tool for Behavioral System Verification

Akira Mori[1] and Kokichi Futatsugi[2]

[1] Japan National Institute of Advanced Industrial Science and Technology
amori@carc.aist.go.jp
[2] Japan Advanced Institute of Science and Technology
kokichi@jaist.ac.jp

Abstract. We report on a machine supported method for verifying safety properties of dynamic systems based on the first-order description of underlying state transition systems. By capturing a set of states by a state predicate, we can verify safety properties of infinite-state systems using predicate calculus in the set-theoretic iterative calculation of least fixpoints.

1 Introduction

In this paper, we propose using behavioral specification based on hidden algebra [1] as uniform description of abstract state machines and report on a tool we are developing for model checking such specification by means of predicate calculus. The system attempts to calculate iteratively the set of hazardous states from which unsafe states may be reached. The procedure is based on a standard backward model checking algorithm (e.g.,[2]). The iteration may not converge in finite steps, but if it does, the safety can be checked by showing that the initial state does not belong to such hazardous states. We use **state predicates** to represent (possibly infinite) sets of states sharing the same properties (called **predicate abstraction**) and **predicate transformation** along transitions with appropriate parameters to obtain a symbolic representation of the set of previous states. To cope with subsumption checking between state predicates required for convergence checking of iteration, a resolution/paramodulation based theorem prover called **PigNose** has been built on top of the CafeOBJ algebraic specification language system [3]. We take examples of mutual exclusion, incremental garbage collection, and an authentication protocol to demonstrate achieved degrees of automation.

2 Behavioral Specification

In this section, we illustrate by way of an example the concepts of behavioral specification using signatures of hidden algebra [1,3]. Two types of sort symbols are used in hidden algebra to distinguish dynamic state elements from static data elements and the behavior of the system is defined in terms of behavioral

M. Okada et al. (Eds.): ISSS 2002, LNCS 2609, pp. 461–470, 2003.

operations that have exactly one state sort in the sources. A behavioral operation that ranges in a state sort (called a **method**) is interpreted as a state transition function that changes the state of the system, and the one that ranges in a data sort (called an **attribute**) is interpreted as an observation function that returns an observable value of the system. A CafeOBJ behavioral specification of a simple bank account is shown below.

Example 1. Behavioral Specification of Bank Account

```
mod* ACCOUNT {
protecting(INT)                                 -- data type
*[ Account ]*                                    -- state sort
op new-account : -> Account                      -- new account
bop balance : Account -> Int                     -- attribute
bop deposit : Int Account -> Account   -- method
bop withdraw : Int Account -> Account  -- method
var A : Account     vars N : Int
ax balance(new-account) = 0 .
ax 0 <= N -> balance(deposit(N,A)) = balance(A) + N .
ax ~(0 <= N) -> balance(deposit(N,A)) = balance(A) .
ax N <= balance(A) -> balance(withdraw(N,A)) = balance(A) - N .
ax ~(N <= balance(A)) -> balance(withdraw(N,A)) = balance(A) .
}
```

The meaning should be self-explanatory. Behaviors of a bank account are defined in terms of observable changes on attributes (e.g., balance). Now one may check that balance(A) ≥ 0 for any reachable state A of ACCOUNT by proving the following formulas:

- balance(new-account) ≥ 0.
- $\forall[A : Account, N : Int]$ balance(A) $\geq 0 \Rightarrow$ balance(deposit(N, A)) ≥ 0.
- $\forall[A : Account, N : Int]$ balance(A) $\geq 0 \Rightarrow$ balance(withdraw(N, A)) ≥ 0.

We will see such behavioral verification (called invariant checking) is a prototype of safety model checking in the next section.

3 Model Checking Behavioral Specification

We will use **state predicates** to represent (possibly infinite) sets of states in reasoning about infinite-state systems. A state predicate P over a state sort h is a formula constructed by behavioral operations and data types with no free variable other than a designated variable X of sort h. The variable X is called a **base variable** of P and may be specified by writing P as $P(X : h)$.

A state predicate may be viewed as intensional description of a subset. For example, the safety predicate $P(X : Account) \triangleq$ balance(X) ≥ 0 for ACCOUNT represents the set of Account states whose balances are non-negative. Then the syntactic restrictions of hidden algebra make it possible to calculate a set of previous states by replacing the base variable of the predicate with a linear expression composed of a method operation with appropriate existentially quantified variables (predicate transformation). For example,

$Q(X) \triangleq \exists[N : \text{Int}] \neg P(\text{withdraw}(N, X))$ represents a set of states whose next states via `withdraw` operation may see a negative balance. By taking disjunction on all possible transitions (i.e., methods), we can obtain the set of previous states of $P(X : h)$ as $\text{pre}(P(X : h)) \triangleq \bigvee_{\sigma:wh' \to h} (\exists V : w) P(\sigma(V, X' : h'))_h$, where $V : w$ denotes a sequence of variable-sort bindings $V_1 : w_1, \ldots, V_n : w_n$ for a string of sort symbols $w = w_1 \ldots w_n$. To be precise, $\text{pre}(P(X : h))$ is a family (disjunction) of state predicates in many-sorted case, however, for the sake of simplicity, we assume for the rest of the paper that the target system has only one state sort modeling its states, in which case $\text{pre}(P(X : h))$ is again a state predicate over h.

As a matter of well-known fact (e.g., [2]), showing that a state predicate P is safe starting from the initial state I is equivalent to showing that $I \notin \text{pre}^*(\neg P)$ where $\text{pre}^*(P) \triangleq \mu Z. P \vee \text{pre}(Z)$ is the least fixpoint of pre including P and represents the set of all states from which a state satisfying P may be reached. If we can check subsumption between two state predicates, the least fixpoint may be calculated by a simple iteration. For this purpose, we have developed a theorem prover called **PigNose** on top of the CafeOBJ system to prove corresponding implication formulas in many-sorted first-order predicate logic with equality.

The model checking procedure implementing above ideas is shown in Figure 1. It maintains an indexed family F^i ($i \geq 0$) of sets of state predicates and a natural number N. Let $F(X : h)$ be the disjunction of all state predicates in F^i ($i \geq 0$) and note again that we only consider the case with only one state sort.

Model checking procedure MC(I,P)
(I: initial state, P: safety predicate)

1. $F^0 = \{\neg P(X : h)\}$; $F^i = \phi$ ($i > 0$) ; $N = 1$
2. for each formula $Q \in F^{N-1}$
   for each method $\sigma : wh \to h$, let
   $G(X : h)$ be $(\exists V : w) Q(\sigma(V, X : h))$ and do
   a) if $(\forall X : h) G(X) \Rightarrow F(X)$ is provable then skip
   b) if $G(I)$ is provable then exit with <u>failure</u>
   c) if $\neg G(I)$ is provable then add G to F^N and skip
   d) exit with <u>unknown</u>
3. if $F^N = \phi$ then exit with <u>success</u>
4. $N = N + 1$; go to Step 2

Fig. 1. Model Checking Procedure **MC(I,P)**

The PigNose theorem prover is invoked when checking provability of the implication formulas. Since first-order theorem proving is not decidable in general, the task must be terminated when exceeding the predefined limit on computational resources such as the number of generated clauses and the time spent, in which case the result is reported as "unprovable".

By taking the duals of implication formulas, one will understand that the invariant checking in Section 2 is indeed safety model checking which terminates in the first iteration.

4   Model Checking Bakery Algorithm

We first take an example of the 2-process Bakery Algorithm to show how infinite-state systems are model checked. See the pseudo code in Figure 2. Two customers C1 and C2 are in the bakery shop, in which a customer gets a ticket (T1, and T2) and proceeds to enter the critical section according to the ticket numbers.

Proving mutual exclusion of the algorithm is not trivial not only because the ticket numbers are unbounded, but also the fixpoint is not obtained in one step unlike the proof of the ACCOUNT invariant in Section 2. Due to space limit, we shall omit the specification code and only illustrate how mutual exclusion is established in the analysis diagram in Figure 3, where crossed boxes represent contradictory (i.e., empty) states, dotted arrows correspond to subsumption relation, north-east arrows to the first customer's transitions, north-west ones to the second customer's, and boxes to the states represented by the state predicate shown inside, where s1 stands for the status of the first customer (either of non-CS, wait, or CS), t1 for the ticket number of the first customer, and so on. PigNose reaches the fixpoint in the 4th iteration after pruning 23 out of 31 subgoals by means of theorem proving. In a standard setting of the theorem prover, the total execution time is about a couple of minutes while in an optimized setting for demonstration purpose, it takes about 20 seconds, both on a PentiumIII 866MHz machine.

5   Verifying Incremental Garbage Collection

Our next example is incremental garbage collection, that is, the on-the-fly algorithm invented by Dijkstra and others [4]. We will explain how safety properties involving inductive data structures such as pointers are verified without going into implementation details of the algorithm.

The algorithm is based on a traditional mark-sweep collector with tricolor marking (black, gray and white), however, the garbage collection is incremental

```
T1, T2: Integer := 0;
task body C1 is                      task body C2 is
begin loop                           begin loop
a1:Non_Critical_Section_1;           a2:Non_Critical_Section_2;
b1:loop exit when T2 = 0 or T1 <= T2; b2:loop exit when T1 = 0 or T2 < T1;
   end loop;                            end loop;
c1:Critical_Section_1;               c2:Critical_Section_2;
d1:T1 := 0;                          d2:T2 := 0;
end loop;                            end loop;
end C1;                              end C2;
```

Fig. 2. Bakery Algorithm

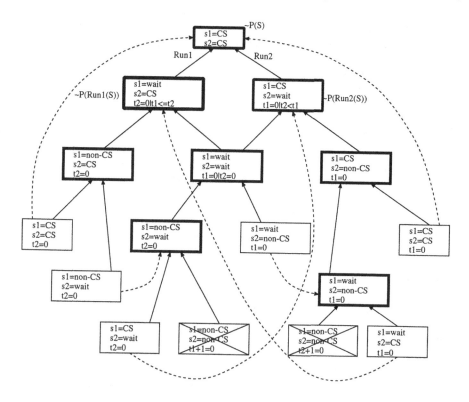

Fig. 3. Results: Model Checking Bakery Algorithm

in the sense that the collector does not need to freeze the system to start cell marking. The system is modeled by asynchronous execution of a **mutator** that corresponds to an application program modifying pointers, and a **collector** collecting garbage. A cell is called **garbage** when it cannot be reached from designated root cells by traversing pointers; otherwise called **accessible**. For expository purpose, we assume that each cell has only one pointer and has one of the following colors: white, gray, black, or free, where the color **free** is used to represent the cells on the **free list** to which the cells considered as garbage by the collector are linked.

While the mutator executes one of the following operations

- update(i,j)
  - if cell j is accessible, then redirect cell i's pointer to cell j, and if cell j is white, then paint it gray.
  - otherwise skip.
- new(i): redirect i's pointer to a free cell that is then painted gray.
- null(i): ground (or nullify) i's pointer.

the collector goes around four states **shade**, **mark**, **append**, and **unmark** in this order, and performs the following operations depending on the state it is in:

1. **shade** paint all root cells gray.
2. **mark** pick a gray cell and paint it black, if it points to a white cell, paint that cell gray.
3. **append** pick a white cell and free it (paint it free).
4. **unmark** pick a black or gray cell and paint it white.

Note that for steps 2, 3 and 4, the collector skips to the next state if there is no such cell. The repeat-until behaviors are implicitly assumed.

The behavioral specification of the algorithm has three data sorts corresponding to cell indices, collector states, and cell colors as shown in Figure 4. The signature declaration, variable declaration and the initial state (init) specification are also shown in Figure 4.

```
mod* INDEX {                    mod* GC {
[ Cx ]                          protecting(INDEX + STATUS + COLOR)
op root : Cx -> Bool            *[ Gc ]*
op nil : -> Cx                  bop ptr : Cx Gc -> Cx          -- cell pointer
}                               bop color : Cx Gc -> Color     -- cell color
                                bop stat : Gc -> Status        -- Gc status
mod! STATUS {                   bop R : Cx Gc -> Bool          -- accessibility
[ Status ]                      bop update : Cx Cx Gc -> Gc    -- cell assignment
ops shade mark : -> Status      bop new : Cx Gc -> Gc          -- new cell
ops append unmark : -> Status   bop null : Cx Gc -> Gc         -- nullify
}                               bop collect : Gc -> Gc         -- garbage collection
                                op init : -> Gc               -- initial state
mod! COLOR {                    -- variable declaration
[ Color ]                       vars I J K : Cx  var S : Status  var G : Gc
ops free white : -> Color       -- initial state
ops gray black : -> Color       ax R(I,init) -> ~(color(I,init) = free) .
}                               ax stat(init) = shade .
```

Fig. 4. Signature for the on-the-fly algorithm

Due to space limit, we only present part of the axioms. Figure 5 shows the axioms for the **update** behavior and Figure 6 contains the axioms for the **collector** behavior in the **mark** state. The problem is to show that "only garbage is collected" or "no accessible cells are ever collected" for the algorithm. Formally, we need to show that the state predicate

```
ax stat(update(I,J,G)) = stat(G) .
ax ~(R(J,G)) -> update(I,J,G) = G .
ax ~(K = I) -> ptr(K,update(I,J,G)) = ptr(K,G) .
ax ~(K = J) -> color(K,update(I,J,G)) = color(K,G) .
ax R(J,G) -> ptr(I,update(I,J,G)) = J .
ax R(J,G) & (color(J,G) = free | color(J,G) = white) ->
   color(J,update(I,J,G)) = gray .
ax R(J,G) & ~(color(J,G) = white) & ~(color(J,G) = free) ->
   color(J,update(I,J,G)) = color(J,G) .
```

Fig. 5. Mutator's update behavior

```
ax stat(G) = mark & (\A[I:Cx] ~(color(I,G) = gray)) ->
        stat(collect(G)) = append &
        color(I,collect(G)) = color(I,G) .
ax stat(G) = mark & (\E[I:Cx] color(I,G) = gray) ->
   stat(collect(G)) = mark &
   (\E[K:Cx] color(K,G) = gray &
            color(K,collect(G)) = black &
   (color(ptr(K,G),G) = white | color(ptr(K,G),G) = free ->
            color(ptr(K,G),collect(G)) = gray) &
   (~(color(ptr(K,G),G) = white) & ~(color(ptr(K,G),G) = free) ->
            color(ptr(K,G),collect(G)) = color(ptr(K,G),G)) &
   (\A[J:Cx] ~(J = K) & ~(J = ptr(K,G) & color(J,G) = white) ->
            color(J,collect(G)) = color(J,G))) .
```

Fig. 6. Collector's behavior in mark state

```
P(G:Gc) ::= \A[I:Cx] R(I,G) -> ~(color(I,G) = free) .
```
is safe for the algorithm. In fact, the task is too complex for model checking and the following lemmas are needed.

- \A[I:Cx,G:Gc] ~(stat(G) = unmark) & color(I,G) = black ->
  ~(color(ptr(I,G),G) = white) & ~(color(ptr(I,G),G) = free) .
- \A[I:Cx,G:Gc] stat(G) = mark & root(I) ->
  (color(I,G) = black | color(I,G) = gray) .
- \A[I:Cx,G:Gc] stat(G) = append & root(I) ->
  color(I,G) = black .
- \A[I:Cx,G:Gc] R(I,G) ->
  (stat(G) = append -> (color(I,G) = black | color(I,G) = gray)) .

The PigNose theorem prover easily proves that all but the last one is invariant. The last one involves accessibility predicate R and requires explicit induction. This is what we call a **inductive safety predicate**, for which induction can only be applied after both the base case and the induction step are shown to be safe. To be precise, we need to show the following two state predicates

```
\A[I:Cx] root(I) ->
  (stat(G) = append -> (color(I,G) = black | color(I,G) = gray)) .

\A[I:Cx] (stat(G) = append -> (color(I,G) = black | color(I,G) = gray)) ->
  (stat(G) = append -> (color(ptr(I,G),G) = black | color(ptr(I,G),G) = gray)) .
```

are safe before concluding the state predicate

```
\A[I:Cx R(I,G) -> (stat(G) = append -> (color(I,G) = black | color(I,G) = gray)) .
```

is also safe by way of induction. It turns out that both the base case and the induction step are indeed invariant and the proof of the last lemma is completed. It is an easy task to show that the predicate P is invariant assuming lemmas. The overall verification involves invariant checking for six state predicates, each of which takes less than 20 seconds on PigNose except the first lemma above which takes about 90 seconds on the same PentiumIII 866MHz machine.

$$\frac{m \in \mathbf{closure}(M, S)}{\langle M, S \rangle \to \langle M \cup \{m\}, S \rangle}(\text{spy})$$

$$\frac{n_A \in \mathbf{nonce}(M, S)}{\langle M, S \rangle \to \langle M \cup \{m_0(A, n_A)_{\mathbf{pb}(B)}\}, S \cup \{A : s_0(B, n_A)\} \rangle}(\text{initiate})$$

$$\frac{m_0(A, n_A)_{\mathbf{pb}(B)} \in M \quad n_B \in \mathbf{nonce}(M, S)}{\langle M, S \rangle \to \langle M \cup \{m_1(A, n_A, n_B)_{\mathbf{pb}(A)}\}, S \cup \{B : s_1(A, n_A, n_B)\} \rangle}(\text{respond})$$

$$\frac{A : s_0(B, n_A) \in S \quad m_1(B, n_A, n_B)_{\mathbf{pb}(A)} \in M}{\langle M, S \rangle \to \langle M \cup \{m_2(n_B)_{\mathbf{pb}(B)}\}, S \cup \{A : s_2(B, n_A, n_B)\} \rangle}(\text{confirm})$$

$$\frac{B : s_1(A, n_A, n_B) \in S \quad m_2(n_B)_{\mathbf{pb}(B)} \in M}{\langle M, S \rangle \to \langle M, S \cup \{B : s_3(A, n_A, n_B)\} \rangle}(\text{reconfirm})$$

Fig. 7. NSLPK protocol

We believe that the way the induction is used in this example is rather new. It was also vital for maintaining the abstraction level and keeping the verification task manageable. Attempts at formally verifying garbage collection algorithms tend to fall into the pitfall of over-specification, being forced to describe implementation details of pointers, by means of arrays for instance, and accessibility checking over that concrete data structures. In fact, we are not aware of any other work that has mechanized formal verification of Dijkstra's on-the-fly algorithm.

6 Verifying Authentication Protocol

Finally, we show how properties about authentication protocols are verified by an example of Needham-Schroeder-Lowe public key (NSLPK) protocol [5]. We follow the formulation by Takahashi and others [6] with slight modification.

The system state is modeled as a pair $\langle M, S \rangle$ of a set M of messages transmitted over the network and a set S of pairs $p : s$ where p is a principal and s is its state. The behavior of the protocol is then formulated as transitions $\langle M; S \rangle \to \langle M', S' \rangle$ between states following the inference rules defined in Figure 7, where $\mathbf{closure}(M, S)$ denotes a set of messages that intruders can compose based on the knowledge they have, $\mathbf{nonce}(M, S)$ denotes a set of nonces that have not been used in the system, and $\mathbf{pb}(A)$ denotes a public key of principal A. A message is either of the forms $m_0(A, n_A)$, $m_1(B, n_A, n_B)$ and $m_2(n_B)$ where A and B are principals and n_A and n_B are nonces, and a key subscripted message represents an encrypted messaged by the key. A principal state is either of the forms $s_0(B, n_A)$, $s_1(A, n_A, n_B)$, $s_2(B, n_A, n_B)$ and $s_3(A, n_A, n_B)$. For example, the second one represents the state in which the principal B has responded with nonce n_B to the communication request by principal A with nonce n_A.

As the protocol is already modeled as a state transition system, it is a straightforward task to have behavioral specification of the protocol. Figure 8

```
mod* DATA {                          mod* MPOOL {
[ Nonce Agent ]                      protecting(MESSAGE)
op spy : Agent -> Bool               *[ Mp ]*
}                                    bop sent? : Msg Mp -> Bool
mod* MESSAGE {                       bop used? : Nonce Mp -> Bool
protecting(DATA)                     bop exposed? : Nonce Mp -> Bool
[ Msg ]                              op send : Msg Mp -> Mp
op m0 : Agent Nonce Agent -> Msg     op m-init : -> Mp
op m1 : Agent Nonce Nonce Agent -> Msg   }
op m2 : Agent Nonce -> Msg
}
```

Fig. 8. Signature for NSLPK messages

```
mod* NSLPK {
  protecting(MPOOL + SPOOL)
  *[ Protocol ]*
  op nslpk : Mp Sp -> Protocol
  bop contact  : Agent Agent Nonce Protocol -> Protocol
  bop respond  : Agent Agent Nonce Nonce Protocol -> Protocol
  bop confirm  : Agent Agent Nonce Nonce Protocol -> Protocol
  bop reconfirm : Agent Agent Nonce Nonce Protocol -> Protocol
  bop spy1  : Agent Agent Nonce Protocol -> Protocol
  bop spy2  : Agent Agent Nonce Nonce Protocol -> Protocol
  bop spy3  : Agent Nonce Protocol -> Protocol
  bop In? : Stat Protocol -> Bool
  op init : -> Protocol
}
```

Fig. 9. Signature for NSLPK protocol

contains signatures related to message specification. The module MESSAGE defines data constructors for encrypted messages with first argument representing the owner of the public key, i.e., a term m0(B,NA,A) is equivalent to $m_0(A, n_A)_{\mathbf{pb}(B)}$ in the description of the protocol above. The module MPOOL defines the set of messages with an axiom

```
vars S S' : Msg    var P : Mp
ax sent?(S,send(S',P)) -> (S = S' | sent?(S,P)) .
```

where predicate sent? returns true when the message has been sent by send operation. Similar modules STATUS and SPOOL are defined for the set of states with in? and put having the same roles as sent? and send, respectively.

Figure 9 contains the signature of the NSLPK protocol which has a non-behavioral operation nslpk that defines a procotols state as a pair of the message set and the state set. The transition rules corresponding to the rules in Figure 7 are defined in a straightforward manner. For example, the respond rule is specified as follows.

```
vars NA NB : Nonce  vars A B  : Agent  var I : Mp  var J : Sp
ax ~(used?(NB,I)) & sent?(m0(B,NA,A),I) ->
   respond(B,A,NA,NB,nslpk(I,J)) =
         nslpk(send(m1(A,NA,NB,B),I),put(s1(B,NA,NB,A),J)) .
```

```
ax used?(NB,I) | ~(sent?(m0(B,NA,A),I)) ->
    respond(B,A,NA,NB,nslpk(I,J)) = nslpk(I,J) .
```

We can now check if the non-injective agreement property is safe by defining a state predicate below.

```
P(R:Protocol) ::= \A[A:Agent]\A[B:Agent]\A[NA:Nonce]\A[NB:Nonce]
            In?(s3(B,NA,NB,A),R) -> In?(s2(A,NA,NB,B),R) .
```

where In? is defined by ax In?(X,nslpk(I,J)) = in?(X,J) .

The verification takes the same course as the Bakery example in Section 4, following the safety model checking procedure in Section 3 step by step manually this time. In fact, the way the state space is explored is very much similar to the way by **Athena** [7], with much less efficiency. More than 40 state predicates are explored, most of which are trivial and take less than 20 seconds but some of which take as much as 5 minutes. In addition to the fact that Athena is enriched with a domain specific logic and an efficient inference mechanism, the relative low efficiency comes from the fact that behavioral model checking has to be performed in a sequential way. We are currently working on a 32 CPU cluster for parallelization.

7   Concluding Remarks

We have proposed a technique to verify safety properties of dynamic systems by combining model checking with theorem proving. Although the task of writing complete specification and organizing exhaustive verification is painful, the method is capable of verifying infinite-state systems and is practical in many cases with the help of an automated theorem prover. Our goal is to offer a generic and integrated environment for analyzing and verifying various security related issues. We have gained positive experiences with the examples presented in the paper, which we hope are shared with the reader.

References

1. Goguen, J., Malcolm, G.: A Hidden Agenda. *Theoretical Computer Science*, **245(1)** (2000) 55–101
2. Cousot, P., Cousot, R.: Refining Model Checking by Abstract Interpretation. *Automated Software Engineering Journal*, **6(1)** (1999) 69–95
3. Diaconescu, R., Futatsugi, K.: CafeOBJ *Report*. World Scientific (1998)
4. Dijkstra, E. W., Lamport, L., Martin, A. J., Scholten, C. S., Steffens, E. F. M.: On-the-Fly Garbage Collection: An Exercise in Cooperation. *Communications of the ACM*, **21(11)** (1978) 966–975
5. Lowe, G.: Breaking and fixing the Needham-Schroeder public-key protocol using FDR. *Lecture Notes in Computer Science*, **1055** (1996) 147–166
6. Takahashi, K., Toda, Y., Hagiya, M.: Nonce Analysis and Strand Space Model, *Japan Society for Software Science and Technology* (2000)
7. Song, D., Berezin, S., Perrig, A.: Athena, a Novel Approach to Efficient Automatic Security Protocol Analysis. *Journal of Computer Security*, **9(1,2)** (2001) 47–74

Author Index

Lecture Notes in Computer Science

For information about Vols. 1–2505

please contact your bookseller or Springer-Verlag